HISTORICAL DICTIONARIES OF
INTERNATIONAL ORGANIZATIONS SERIES
Jon Woronoff, Series Editor

1. *European Community*, by Desmond Dinan. 1993
2. *International Monetary Fund*, by Norman K. Humphreys. 1993 *Out of print. See No. 17*
3. *International Organizations in Sub-Saharan Africa*, by Mark W. DeLancey and Terry M. Mays. 1994. *Out of print. See No. 21*
4. *European Organizations*, by Derek W. Urwin. 1994
5. *International Tribunals*, by Boleslaw Adam Boczek. 1994
6. *International Food Agencies: FAO, WFP, WFC, IFAD*, by Ross B. Talbot. 1994
7. *Refugee and Disaster Relief Organizations*, by Robert F. Gorman. 1994. *Out of print. See No. 18*
8. *United Nations*, by A. LeRoy Bennett. 1995
9. *Multinational Peacekeeping*, by Terry Mays. 1996. *Out of Print. See No. 22.*
10. *Aid and Development Organizations*, by Guy Arnold. 1996
11. *World Bank*, by Anne C. M. Salda. 1997
12. *Human Rights and Humanitarian Organizations*, by Robert F. Gorman and Edward S. Mihalkanin. 1997
13. *United Nations Educational, Scientific, and Cultural Organization (UNESCO)*, by Seth Spaulding and Lin Lin. 1997
14. *Inter-American Organizations*, by Larman C. Wilson and David W. Dent. 1997
15. *World Health Organization*, by Kelley Lee. 1998
16. *International Organizations*, by Michael G. Schechter. 1998
17. *International Monetary Fund: Second Edition*, by Norman K. Humphreys. 1999
18. *Refugee and Disaster Relief Organizations: Second Edition*, by Robert F. Gorman. 2000
19. *Arab and Islamic Organizations*, by Frank A. Clements. 2001
20. *International Organizations in Asia and the Pacific*, by Derek McDougall. 2002
21. *International Organizations in Sub-Saharan Africa: Second Edition*, by Terry M. Mays and Mark W. DeLancey. 2002
22. *Multinational Peacekeeping: Second Edition*, by Terry M. Mays. 2004
23. *League of Nations*, by Anique H. M. van Ginneken. 2006
24. *European Union*, by Joaquín Roy and Aimee Kanner. 2006
25. *United Nations: New Edition*, by Jacques Fomerand. 2007

Historical Dictionary of the United Nations

New Edition

Jacques Fomerand

Historical Dictionaries of
International Organizations, No. 25

The Scarecrow Press, Inc.
Lanham, Maryland • Toronto • Plymouth, UK
2007

SCARECROW PRESS, INC.

Published in the United States of America
by Scarecrow Press, Inc.
A wholly owned subsidiary of
The Rowman & Littlefield Publishing Group, Inc.
4501 Forbes Boulevard, Suite 200, Lanham, Maryland 20706
www.scarecrowpress.com

Estover Road
Plymouth PL6 7PY
United Kingdom

British Library Cataloguing in Publication Information Available

Library of Congress Cataloging-in-Publication Data

Fomerand, Jacques.
    Historical dictionary of the United Nations / Jacques Fomerand. — New ed.
        p. cm. — (Historical dictionaries of international organizations ; 25)
    Rev. ed. of: Historical dictionary of the United Nations / by A. LeRoy Bennett.
c1995.
    Includes bibliographical references.
    ISBN-13: 978-0-8108-5494-9 (hardcover : alk. paper)
    ISBN-10: 0-8108-5494-5 (hardcover : alk. paper)
    1. United Nations—History—Dictionaries. I. Bennett, A. LeRoy (Alvin LeRoy),
1914– Historical dictionary of the United Nations. II. Title.

JZ4984.5.B395 2007
341.2303—dc22

2006028406

©™ The paper used in this publication meets the minimum requirements of
American National Standard for Information Sciences—Permanence of Paper
for Printed Library Materials, ANSI/NISO Z39.48-1992.
Manufactured in the United States of America.

To Marianthi and Maman, Papa, Ross, and Thierry

Contents

Editor's Foreword   *Jon Woronoff*   ix

Acknowledgments   xi

Acronyms and Abbreviations   xiii

Chronology   xxiii

Introduction   liii

THE DICTIONARY   1

Appendixes

A   Charter of the United Nations   407

B   Universal Declaration of Human Rights Adopted by
     the General Assembly on 19 December 1948   441

C   Membership of the United Nations   449

D   Assessed Contributions to the UN Regular Budget of
     the 15 Largest Assessed Contributors for 2003–2004   453

E   Nomenclature of the United Nations System   455

F   Timelines   457

Bibliography   471

About the Author   571

Editor's Foreword

Looking back, it is amazing just how much has been achieved since 1945 by the United Nations, an untried international organization in a world that was much more dangerous and complicated than the authors of its charter ever thought. Over the past six decades, it has been laboring to achieve almost unachievable goals laid down idealistically at its origin or imposed along the way. These include such vital tasks as maintaining peace and security while bringing erstwhile colonies to statehood (and membership). It has also had to contribute to economic prosperity through development aid and technical advice. It has been called on to look after refugees and increasingly guarantee human rights. Then there was the need to contribute to health, education, and environmental protection, to say nothing of promoting gender equality and human rights. Judging by the incredible number of conferences it has held and conventions it has adopted and, more palpably, the development projects it has launched and peacekeeping operations it has managed, you would think that it would be generally appreciated. Probably it is by most. But there are as always complaints and presently particularly strident—and in some ways justified—calls for "reform."

So this is a particularly good time to take another look at the past with a view to seeing what can be done in the future. Such an exercise is greatly facilitated by this new edition of *Historical Dictionary of the United Nations*. Its chronology traces the amazingly busy progression of the organization. The introduction balances its achievements against its failures and focuses on the need for reform. The dictionary section then examines the UN in greater detail, with literally hundreds of entries on its basic organs, subsidiary bodies, related specialized and other agencies, and nongovernmental actors as well as outstanding figures in its history. Other entries describe the many fields it deals with and the major activities in each. To facilitate reading this book, and anything else on the United Nations, there is a well nigh indispensable list of acronyms. Finally, the substantial bibliography directs readers to essential sources of information including both internal documentation and external assessments.

It is increasingly difficult for any outsider to follow the numerous bodies and activities of the United Nations, and it is doubtlessly helpful that the author of this new edition is an insider of sorts. Jacques Fomerand joined the United Nations Secretariat in 1977 where he followed economic, social, and coordination issues for some 15 years. Then he moved to the United Nations University, where he served as director of its North American office. Dr. Fomerand is now more of an outsider, teaching at the Department of Government at John Jay College of the City University of New York and elsewhere. During this whole period, he has written countless internal reports and also various scholarly works. This was good preparation for authoring this basic reference work, although it is even broader than anything he took on before. And it certainly benefits from this unique combination of insider-outsider by someone who has access to the information and also knows how to deliver it.

Jon Woronoff
Series Editor

Acknowledgments

I have had the good fortune to receive the assistance of many in the preparation of this book. I owe a special debt to the students who worked with me, notably Ayca Ariyoruk, David Berman, Vanessa Bermann, Lance Blank, Ala Buhisi, Brendan Monahan, and Roopa Rangaswmi. I am particularly grateful to my graduate assistant Anne Murat for her tireless and outstanding research assistance.

Special thanks to the staff of the Dag Hammarskjöld Library at the United Nations, especially Maria Montagna who guided me with great patience in the use of the library's labyrinthine collection.

Last but not least, I would like to thank my editor at Scarecrow, Jon Woronoff, whose lucid and constructive comments greatly improved the original manuscript and helped me avoid numerous causes of embarrassment.

Needless to say that all remaining sins of omission or commission remain mine.

Acronyms and Abbreviations

ABM	Antiballistic Missile Treaty
ACABQ	Advisory Committee on Administrative and Budgetary Questions
ACC	Administrative Committee on Coordination
ACUNS	Academic Council on the United Nations System
ADB	Asian Development Bank
AEC	Atomic Energy Commission
AfDB	African Development Bank
AI	Amnesty International
AIDS	Acquired Immune Deficiency Syndrome
ANWFZ	African Nuclear Weapons Free Zone Treaty
AOSIS	Alliance of Small Island States
APMs	Antipersonnel Mines
AU	African Union
BCUN	Business Council for the United Nations
BWC	Biological Weapons Convention
BWIs	Bretton Woods Institutions
CARE	Care International
CAT	Committee against Torture
CBD	Convention on Biological Diversity
CCCW	Convention on Certain Conventional Weapons
CCD	Conference of the Committee on Disarmament
CD	Conference on Disarmament
CDP	Committee for Development Policy
CEB	Chief Executives Board
CEDAW	Convention on the Elimination of All Forms of Discrimination against Women
CENRD	Committee on Energy and Natural Resources for Development

CERD	Committee for the Elimination of Racial Discrimination
CESCR	Committee on Economic, Social, and Cultural Rights
CESR	Center for Economic and Social Rights
CFE	Treaty on Conventional Armed Forces in Europe
CIEC	Conference on International Economic Cooperation
CIS	Commonwealth of Independent States
CITES	Convention on International Trade in Endangered Species of Wild Fauna and Flora
CIVPOL	Civilian Police
CONGO	Conference on NGOs in Consultative Status
CPC	Committee for Programme and Coordination
CRC	Committee on the Rights of the Child
CSD	Commission for Sustainable Development
CSOP	Commission to Study the Organization of Peace
CSW	Commission on the Status of Women
CTBT	Comprehensive Nuclear Test Ban Treaty
CWC	Chemical Weapons Convention
CTC	Counterterrorism Committee
DC	Disarmament Commission
DDA	Department for Disarmament Affairs
DESA	Department of Economic and Social Affairs
DOMREP	Mission of the Representative of the Secretary-General in the Dominican Republic
DPA	Department of Political Affairs
DPI	Department of Public Information
DPKO	Department of Peacekeeping Operations
DRC	Democratic Republic of the Congo
EAD	Electoral Assistance Division
ECA	Economic Commission for Africa
ECDC	Economic Cooperation among Developing Countries
ECE	Economic Commission for Europe
ECHA	Executive Committee on Humanitarian Affairs
ECLAC	Economic Commission for Latin America and the Caribbean
ECOSOC	Economic and Social Council
ECOWAS	Economic Community of West African States
ENDC	Eighteen-Nation Committee on Disarmament

ENMOD	Convention on the Prohibition of Military or Any Other Hostile Use of Environmental Modification Techniques
EPTA	Expanded Programme of Technical Assistance
ESCAP	Economic and Social Commission for Asia and the Pacific
ESCWA	Economic and Social Commission for Western Asia
EU	European Union
FAO	Food and Agriculture Organization
FDI	Foreign Direct Investment
G-8	Group of Eight
G-24	Group of Twenty-Four
G-77	Group of Seventy-Seven
GA	General Assembly
GATT	General Agreement on Tariffs and Trade
GCD	General and Comprehensive Disarmament
GCIM	Global Commission on International Migration
GEF	Global Environmental Facility
GEMS	Global Environmental Monitoring System
GNP	Gross National Product
GPF	Global Policy Forum
GSP	General System of Preferences
Habitat	United Nations Conference on Human Settlements
HDI	Human Development Index
HDR	Human Development Report
HIPC	Heavily Indebted Poor Country Initiative
HIV	Human Immuno-Deficiency Virus
HLCM	High-Level Committee on Management
HLCP	High-Level Committee on Programs
HLP	High-Level Panel on Threats, Challenges, and Change
HRC	Human Rights Committee
HRW	Human Rights Watch
IACB	Interagency Consultative Board
IAEA	International Atomic Energy Agency
IBRD	International Bank for Reconstruction and Development
ICAO	International Civil Aviation Organization
ICBL	International Campaign to Ban Landmines

ICC	International Chamber of Commerce
ICC	International Criminal Court
ICCPR	International Covenant on Civil and Political Rights
ICESCR	International Covenant on Economic, Social, and Cultural Rights
ICIDI	Independent Commission on International Development Issues
ICJ	International Commission of Jurists
ICJ	International Court of Justice
ICPD	International Conference on Population and Development
ICRC	International Committee of the Red Cross
ICSU	International Council for Science
ICTR	International Criminal Tribunal for Rwanda
ICTY	International Criminal Tribunal for the Former Yugoslavia
IDA	International Development Association
IDB	Inter-American Development Bank
IDPs	Internally Displaced Persons
IDS	International Development Strategy
IEA	International Energy Agency
IFAD	International Fund for Agricultural Development
IFC	International Finance Corporation
IGP	Institute for Global Policy
ILC	International Law Commission
ILO	International Labour Organization
IMCO	Intergovernmental Marine Consultative Organization
IMF	International Monetary Fund
IMO	International Maritime Organization
INSTRAW	International Research and Training Institute for the Advancement of Women
IOC	Intergovernmental Oceanographic Commission
IOM	International Organization for Migration
IPA	International Peace Academy
IPC	Integrated Programme for Commodities
IPRs	Intellectual Property Rights
IRO	International Refugee Organization
ISA	International Sea-Bed Authority

IT	Information Technology
ITC	International Trade Centre
ITO	International Trade Organization
ITU	International Telecommunications Union
JIU	Joint Inspection Unit
LCNP	Lawyers Committee on Nuclear Policy
LDCs	Least Developed Countries
MDBs	Multilateral Development Banks
MDGs	Millennium Development Goals
MICAH	International Civilian Mission Support in Haiti
MICIVIH	International Civilian Mission in Haiti
MIGA	Multilateral Investment Guarantee Agency
MINUCI	United Nations Mission in Cote d'Ivoire
MINUGUA	United Nations Verification Mission in Guatemala
MINURCA	United Nations Mission in the Central African Republic
MINURSO	United Nations Mission for the Referendum in Western Sahara
MINUSTAH	United Nations Stabilization Mission in Haiti
MIPONUH	United Nations Civilian Police Mission in Haiti
MNCs	Multinational Corporations
MONUA	United Nations Observer Mission in Angola
MONUC	United Nations Organization Mission in the Democratic Republic of the Congo
MSF	Médecins Sans Frontières
NAM	Nonaligned Movement
NATO	North Atlantic Treaty Organization
NEPAD	New Partnership for Africa's Development
NGLS	Nongovernmental Liaison Service
NGOs	Nongovernmental Organizations
NIEO	New International Economic Order
NPT	Nonproliferation Treaty
NWFZs	Nuclear Weapons Free Zones
NWICO	New World Information and Communication Order
OAPEC	Organization of Arab Petroleum Exporting Countries
OAS	Organization of American States
OAU	Organization of African Unity
OCHA	Office for the Coordination of Humanitarian Affairs

ODA	Official Development Assistance
OECD	Organization for Economic Cooperation and Development
OFFP	Oil for Food Program
OHCHR	Office of the United Nations High Commissioner for Human Rights
OIC	Organization of the Islamic Conference
OIOS	Office of Internal Oversight Services
OLA	Office of Legal Affairs
ONUB	United Nations Operation in Burundi
ONUC	United Nations Operation in the Congo
ONUCA	United Nations Observer Group in Central America
ONUSAL	United Nations Observer Mission in El Salvador
ONUVEH	United Nations Observer Group for the Verification of Elections in Haiti
ONUVEN	United Nations Observer Group for the Verification of Elections in Nicaragua
OPCW	Organization for the Prohibition of Chemical Weapons
OPEC	Organization of Petroleum Exporting Countries
ORCI	Office for Research and Collection of Information
OSCE	Organization for Security and Cooperation in Europe
PCA	Permanent Court of Arbitration
PCIJ	Permanent Court of International Justice
PTBT	Partial Test Ban Treaty
RDBs	Regional Development Banks
SC	Security Council
SEANWFZ	Southeast Asia Nuclear Weapons Free Zone Treaty
SG	Secretary-General
SID	Society for International Development
SIDS	Small Island Developing States
SRSG	Special Representative of the Secretary General
SUNFED	Special United Nations Fund for Economic Development
TI	Transparency International
TNCs	Transnational Corporations
TRCs	Truth and Reconciliation Commissions
TRIPs	Trade Related Aspects of Intellectual Property Rights
TWN	Third World Network

UDHR	Universal Declaration of Human Rights
UNAIDS	Joint United Nations Programme on HIV/AIDS
UNAMA	United Nations Assistance Mission in Afghanistan
UNAMET	United Nations Mission in East Timor
UNAMIC	United Nations Advance Mission in Cambodia
UNAMIR	United Nations Assistance Mission in Rwanda
UNAMSIL	United Nations Mission in Sierra Leone
UNASOG	United Nations Aouzou Strip Observer Group
UNA-USA	United Nations Association of the United States of America
UNAVEM	United Nations Angola Verification Mission
UNCCD	United Nations Convention to Combat Desertification
UNCDF	United Nations Capital Development Fund
UNCED	United Nations Conference on Environment and Development
UNCHS	United Nations Centre on Human Settlements
UNCIP	United Nations Commission for India and Pakistan
UNCITRAL	United Nations Commission on International Trade Law
UNCOPUOS	United Nations Committee on the Peaceful Uses of Outer Space
UNCRO	United Nations Confidence Restoration Operation
UNCTAD	United Nations Conference on Trade and Development
UNDAF	UNDP Assistance Framework
UNDCP	United Nations Drug Control Program
UNDG	United Nations Development Group
UNDOF	United Nations Disengagement Observer Force
UNDP	United Nations Development Program
UNDRO	United Nations Disaster Relief Organization
UNEF	United Nations Emergency Force
UNEP	United Nations Environment Programme
UNESCO	United Nations Educational, Scientific, and Cultural Organization
UNFCCC	United Nations Framework Convention on Climate Change
UNFF	United Nations Forum on Forests
UNFICYP	United Nations Peacekeeping Force in Cyprus

UNFIP	United Nations Fund for International Partnerships
UNFPA	United Nations Population Fund
UNGOMAP	United Nations Good Offices Mission in Afghanistan and Pakistan
UN-Habitat	United Nations Centre on Human Settlements
UNHCHR	United Nations High Commissioner for Human Rights
UNHCR	United Nations High Commissioner for Refugees
UNICEF	United Nations Children's Fund
UNICs	United Nations Information Centers
UNICRI	United Nations Interregional Crime and Justice Research Institute
UNIDIR	United Nations Institute for Disarmament Research
UNIDO	United Nations Industrial Development Organization
UNıFEM	United Nations Development Fund for Women
UNIFIL	United Nations Interim Force in Lebanon
UNIIMOG	United Nations Iran-Iraq Military Observer Group
UNIKOM	United Nations Iraq-Kuwait Observation Mission
UNIPOM	United Nations India-Pakistan Observation Mission
UNITA	National Union for the Total Independence of Angola
UNITAR	United Nations Institute for Training and Research
UNKRA	United Nations Korean Reconstruction Agency
UNMEE	United Nations Mission in Ethiopia and Eritrea
UNMIBH	United Nations Mission in Bosnia and Herzegovina
UNMIH	United Nations Mission in Haiti
UNMIK	United Nations Mission in Kosovo (also United Nations Interim Administration Mission in Kosovo)
UNMIL	United Nations Mission in Liberia
UNMIS	United Nations Mission in the Sudan
UNMISET	United Nations Mission of Support in East Timor
UNMIT	United Nations Integrated Mission in Timor-Leste
UNMOGIP	United Nations Military Observer Group in India and Pakistan
UNMOP	United Nations Mission of Observers in Prevlaka
UNMOT	United Nations Mission of Observers in Tajikistan
UNMOVIC	United Nations Monitoring, Verification, and Inspection Commission
UN-NADAF	United Nations New Agenda for the Development of Africa
UNOB	United Nations Operation in Burundi

UNOCI	United Nations Operation in Cote d'Ivoire
UNODC	United Nations Office on Drugs and Crime
UNOGIL	United Nations Observation Group in Lebanon
UNOMB	United Nations Observer Mission in Bougainville
UNOMIG	United Nations Observer Mission in Georgia
UNOMIL	United Nations Observer Mission in Liberia
UNOMOZ	United Nations Operation in Mozambique
UNOMSA	United Nations Observer Mission in South Africa
UNOMSIL	United Nations Observer Mission in Sierra Leone
UNOMUR	United Nations Observer Mission in Uganda-Rwanda
UNOPS	United Nations Office for Project Services
UNOSOM	United Nations Operation in Somalia
UN-PAARD	United Nations Programme of Action for African Economic Recovery and Development
UNPFIP	United Nations Permanent Forum for Indigenous Peoples
UNPREDEP	United Nations Preventive Deployment Force
UNPROFOR	United Nations Protection Force
UNPSG	United Nations Civilian Police Support Group
UNRISD	United Nations Research Institute for Social Development
UNRRA	United Nations Relief and Rehabilitation Administration
UNRWA	United Nations Relief and Works Agency for Palestine Refugees in the Near East
UNSCOB	United Nations Special Committee on the Balkans
UNSCOM	United Nations Special Commission
UNSF	United Nations Security Force in West New Guinea
UNSF	United Nations Special Fund
UNSMIH	United Nations Support Mission in Haiti
UNTAC	United Nations Transitional Authority in Cambodia
UNTAES	United Nations Transitional Administration for Eastern Slavonia, Baranja, and Western Sirmium
UNTAET	United Nations Transitional Administration in East Timor
UNTAG	United Nations Transition Assistance Group
UNTEA	United Nations Temporary Executive Authority
UNTMIH	United Nations Transition Mission in Haiti
UNTSO	United Nations Truce Supervision Organization

UNU	United Nations University
UNV	United Nations Volunteers
UNWTO	United Nations World Tourism Organization
UNYOM	United Nations Yemen Observation Mission
UP	University for Peace
UPU	Universal Postal Union
WB	World Bank or International Bank for Reconstruction and Development (IBRD)
WCC	World Council of Churches
WFP	World Food Programme
WFM	World Federalist Movement
WFUNA	World Federation of United Nations Associations
WHO	World Health Organization
WIPO	World Intellectual Property Organization
WMDs	Weapons of Mass Destruction
WMO	World Maritime Organization
WMO	World Meteorological Organization
WMU	World Maritime University
WRI	World Resources Institute
WSSD	World Summit on Sustainable Development
WTO	World Trade Organization

Chronology

1864   Creation of the International Telegraphic Union. Renamed in 1934, International Telecommunications Union (ITU). In October 1947, ITU becomes a specialized agency of the United Nations.

1873   World Meteorological Organization (WMO) begins operation as a nongovernmental organization (NGO).

1874   Establishment of the General Postal Union renamed Universal Postal Union (UPU) in 1878. Becomes a United Nations specialized agency in 1948.

1883   World Intellectual Property Organization (WIPO) begins operation under various names.

1919   Paris Peace Conference approves Covenant of the League of Nations and creation of the International Labour Organization (ILO).

1920   20 January: League of Nations begins operations.

1941   14 August: President Franklin Delano Roosevelt and Prime Minister Winston Churchill issue Atlantic Charter.

1942   1 January: Declaration by United Nations signed by 26 allied nations stating their war and peace aims.

1943   18 May–3 June: United Nations Conference on Food and Agriculture (Hot Springs, Virginia) sets up a committee to draw up constitution of a Food and Agricultural Organization (FAO). **30 October:** Declaration of Four Nations on General Security ("Moscow Declaration") pledging the establishment of a "general international organization." **9 November:** Agreement signed in Washington by representatives of 44 nations creating the United Nations Relief and Rehabilitation Administration (UNRRA), the first of the United Nations agencies to come into being.

1944   20 April–12 May: Twenty-sixth session of the International Labour Conference. **1–22 July:** United Nations Monetary and Financial Conference (Bretton Woods, New Hampshire) lays down plans for the creation of the International Bank for Reconstruction and Development (IBRD) and the International Monetary Fund (IMF). **21 August–2 October:** Dumbarton Oaks Conversations on World Organization mainly concerned with the security provisions of the United Nations Charter. **1 November–7 December:** International Civil Aviation Conference convenes in Chicago paving the way to the creation of the International Civil Aviation Organization (ICAO).

1945   4–11 February: Yalta Conference attended by Winston Churchill, Franklin D. Roosevelt, and Joseph Stalin reaches agreement on voting formula in the Security Council. **21 February–8 March:** Inter-American Conference on Problems of War and Peace held in Mexico. **25 April–26 June:** United Nations Conference on International Organization in San Francisco. **August 15:** International Civil Aviation Organization (ICAO) comes into being. **16 October:** Quebec conference of 44 nations creates Food and Agriculture Organization. **24 October:** Charter enters into force. That day is celebrated as United Nations Day. **1–16 November:** International conference draws up constitution of the United Nations Educational, Scientific, and Cultural Organization (UNESCO). **16 December:** USSR, U.S., and UK foreign ministers agree to the creation of a United Nations Commission on Atomic Energy.

1946   10 January: General Assembly opens its first session. **17 January:** Security Council holds its first meeting in London. **24 January:** General Assembly adopts its first resolution that establishes Atomic Energy Commission (AEC). **19–30 January:** Security Council considers the withdrawal of Soviet forces from Northern Iran. **23 January–18 February:** First session of the Economic and Social Council (ECOSOC). **1 February:** Trygve Lie elected secretary-general. **1–6 February:** Security Council considers the Greek question. **4 February:** First meeting of the Military Staff Committee. **6 February:** Judges of the International Court of Justice (ICJ) elected. **13 February:** General Assembly adopts Convention on the Privileges and Immunities of the United Nations. **14 February:** General Assembly establishes interim United Nations headquarters in New York City. **16 February:** Soviet Union casts first veto in the Security Council. **16 February:** Commission for Human Rights and Commission for Narcotic Drugs established by the Economic and Social Council (ECOSOC). **3 April:** First meeting of the International Court of Justice. **18 April:** League of Nations is dissolved and turns over its assets to the United Nations. **14 June:** United States submits Baruch Plan to Atomic Energy Commission. **21 June:** ECOSOC establishes Commission for Social Development and Commission on the Status of Women. **21 June:** Economic and Social Council adopts "consultative status" for nongovernmental organizations. **19 June–22 July:** Constitution of the World Health Organization (WHO) established. **21 September:** General Assembly creates the Administrative Committee on Coordination. **1 October:** International Military Tribunal at Nuremberg renders its judgment. **3 October:** ECOSOC sets up Commission on Population (renamed in 1994 Commission on Population and Development). **19 November–10 December:** First session of UNESCO's General Conference in Paris. **7 December:** General Assembly adopts UN emblem. **11 December:** International Children's Emergency Fund (UNICEF) established by the General Assembly. **14 December:** General Assembly constitutes the Trusteeship Council after approving Trusteeship Agreements for eight territories. General Assembly recommends that Southwest Africa be placed under International Trusteeship System. General Assembly approves New York City as the permanent headquarters of the United Nations and adopts budgets of $19 million and $27 million for 1946 and 1947, respectively. General Assembly approves specialized agency agreements with the International Labour Organization (ILO); the Food and Agriculture Organization (FAO); the United Nations Educational, Scientific, and Cultural organization (UNESCO); and the International Civil Aviation Organization (ICAO). **15 December:** General Assembly approves constitution of the International Refugee Organization (IRO).

1947   27 January–10 February: First session of the Commission for Human Rights. **10–24 February:** First session of the Commission on the Status of Women. **28 March:** Creation of the Economic Commission for Europe (ECE) and of the Economic Commission for Asia and the Far East (ECAFE) (later renamed Economic and Social Commission for Asia and the Pacific [ESCAP]), the first of five regional commissions to be set up by the Economic and Social Council (ECOSOC). **28 April–15 May:** First special session of the General Assembly on Palestine requested by the United Kingdom. **29 May:** Security Council calls for a cessation of hostilities in Palestine and authorizes the creation of the United Nations Truce Supervision Organization (UNTSO) to monitor the truce. **24 July–8 August:** First session of the Commission on Narcotic Drugs. **20 October:** General Assembly adopts the United Nations Flag. **30 October:** Birth of the General Agreement on Tariffs and Trade (GATT) signed by 23 countries in Geneva. **21 November:** General Assembly creates the International Law Commission. **29 November:** General Assembly endorses plan to partition Palestine and creates the state of Israel.

1948   16 February: Economic and Social Council (ECOSOC) sets up Statistical Commission. **25 February:** Establishment of the Economic Commission for Latin America (ECLA) by ECOSOC. Renamed the Economic Commission for Latin America and the Caribbean (ECLAC) in 1984 to include Caribbean countries. **16 April–14 May:** Second special session of the General Assembly on Palestine at the request of the Security Council. **21 April:** Security Council establishes United Nations Commission for India and Pakistan. **29 May:** Establishment of the first United Nations observer mission in Palestine—the United Nations Truce Supervision Organization (UNTSO). **10 July:** World Health Organization (WHO) becomes a specialized agency of the United Nations. **17 September:** United Nations Special Representative to Palestine assassinated. **4 December:** Assembly approves a special technical assistance appropriation for "advisory welfare services," the forerunner of the UN technical assistance programs. **8 December:** General Assembly creates United Nations Relief and Works Agency for Palestine Refugees (UNRWA). **9 December:** General Assembly adopts Convention on the Prevention and Punishment of the Crime of Genocide. **10 December:** Universal Declaration on Human Rights approved by the General Assembly.

1949   7 January: A United Nations envoy, Ralph Bunche, secures a cease-fire between Israel and Arab states. **9 April:** International Court of Justice (ICJ) hands down its first decision against Albania in Corfu Channel Case. **16 November:** Acting on a recommendation of the Economic and Social Council (ECOSOC), the General Assembly sets up Expanded Programme of Technical Assistance (EPTA). **2 December:** General Assembly adopts Convention for the Suppression of the Traffic in Persons and of the Exploitation of the Prostitution of Others. **8 De-**

cember: General Assembly creates United Nations Relief and Works Agency for Palestine Refugees in the Near East (UNRWA).

1950   27 June: Acting in the absence of the Soviet Union, the Security Council calls on member states to repel the North Korean military attack on South Korea. **3 November:** General Assembly adopts Uniting for Peace Resolution providing for the convening of emergency sessions of the General Assembly when the Security Council is deadlocked by a veto. **14 December:** Assembly adopts the statute of the office of the United Nations High Commissioner for Refugees (UNHCHR).

1951   12 January: Genocide Convention enters into force. **1 February:** People's Republic of China condemned as an aggressor in Korea by the General Assembly. **28 March:** United Nations reaches agreement with the United States allowing the Organization to use its own stamps. **28 July:** A United Nations conference adopts the Convention Relating to the Status of Refugees and Stateless Persons. **20 December:** World Meteorological Organization (WMO) becomes a specialized agency.

1952   11 January: General Assembly replaces Atomic Energy Commission with the Disarmament Commission. **27 February:** Formal inauguration of the United Nations headquarters building in New York. **Fall:** General Assembly places the question of apartheid in South Africa on its agenda and will consider it until 1993. **10 November:** Secretary-General Trygve Lie submits his resignation. **20 December:** General Assembly approves Convention on the Political Rights of Women.

1953   7 April: Dag Hammarskjöld unanimously elected secretary-general. **27 July:** Korean war armistice signed at Panmunjun ending three years of fighting. **6 October:** United Nations Children's Fund (UNICEF) becomes a permanent agency. **8 December:** U.S. President Dwight D. Eisenhower delivers "Atoms for Peace" statement in General Assembly.

1954   22 April: Convention on the status of refugees enters into force. **31 August–10 September:** First UN-sponsored population conference of scientific experts in Rome. **4 December:** General Assembly approves the Statute of the International Atomic Energy Agency (IAEA).

1955   1 July: "Open Skies" proposal made by U.S. President Eisenhower. **8–20 August:** International Conference on the Peaceful Uses of

Atomic Energy. **22 August–3 September:** First United Nations Congress on the prevention of crime and the treatment of offenders. **3 November:** General Assembly approves the charter of the International Finance Corporation (IFC) as an affiliate of the World Bank. **December:** East West "package deal" enabling 16 states to enter the UN after a ten-year deadlock. **10 December:** High Commissioner for Refugees accepts Nobel Peace Prize awarded to United Nations High Commissioner of Refugees (UNHCR) in 1954 for its work in Europe.

1956   13 October: Security Council endorses principles for the settlement of the Suez crisis. **28 October:** Security Council takes up the Hungarian crisis. **30 October:** France and the United Kingdom veto resolution of the Security Council calling on them to refrain from the use of force in the Suez crisis. **1–10 November:** General Assembly convenes in emergency special session to consider the Suez Canal crisis. **4–10 November:** Second emergency special session of the General Assembly on Hungary. **5 November:** General Assembly creates United Nations Emergency Force (UNEF), the first UN peacekeeping operation.

1957   24 January: Security Council calls for plebiscite in Kashmir. **20 February:** General Assembly approves Convention on the Nationality of Married Women. **29 July:** Statute of the International Atomic Energy Agency (IAEA) enters into force. **14 December:** Special United Nations Fund for Economic Development set up by General Assembly.

1958   29 April: Economic Commission for Africa (ECA) created by the Economic and Social Council (ECOSOC). **11 June:** Security Council establishes United Nations Observer Group in Lebanon (UNOGIL). **8–21 August:** General Assembly convenes emergency special session on the crisis in Lebanon and Jordan. **14 October:** General Assembly creates United Nations Special Fund to concentrate on preinvestment projects. **9 December:** UNOGIL ceases operations.

1959   1 January: Special United Nations Fund for Economic Development comes into being. **8–21 August:** Third emergency special session of the General Assembly on Lebanon and Jordan. **20 November:** General Assembly adopts Declaration of the Rights of the Child, stating that children are entitled to protection, education, health care, shelter, and good nutrition. **1 December:** Antarctic Treaty signed by 12 nations.

13 December: General Assembly sets up Committee on the Peaceful Uses of Outer Space (COPUOS).

1960   17 March–26 April: Second Law of the Sea Conference. **13 July:** Secretary-General Hammarskjöld invoking Article 99 of the charter brings the Congo crisis to the attention of the Security Council. **14 July:** United Nations Operation in the Congo (ONUC) involving 20,000 peacekeeping personnel established by the Security Council. **8–19 August:** Second UN Congress on the Prevention of Crime and Treatment of Offenders, London. **17–19 September:** Fourth emergency special session of the General Assembly on the Congo question triggered by Soviet vetoes in the Security Council. **22 September:** Soviet premier Nikita Khrushchev proposes replacing the post of secretary-general with a three-person committee. **September–October:** Seventeen new states join the United Nations. **8 November:** International Development Association (IDA), an affiliate of the World Bank, begins operations. **14 December:** General Assembly adopts Declaration on the Granting of Independence to Colonial Countries and Peoples, a sweeping anticolonial statement.

1961   21 February: Security Council authorizes the use of force in order to prevent civil war in the Congo. **21–25 August:** Third special session of the General Assembly on Tunisia at the request of 38 member states. **21–31 August:** UN conference on new sources of energy. **18 September:** Secretary-General Dag Hammarskjöld dies in an aircraft crash while on mission in the Congo. **3 November:** U Thant named acting secretary-general. Will stay in office until 31 December, 1971. **24 November:** General Assembly endorses declaration prohibiting the use of nuclear and thermonuclear weapons. **19 December:** World Food Programme (WFP) established initially on an experimental basis and as a joint program of the United Nations and the Food and Agriculture Organization (FAO).

1962   1 May: United Nations Temporary Executive Agency Authority transfers administrative control over West New Guinea to Indonesia. **20 July:** International Court of Justice (ICJ) issues advisory opinion that peacekeeping costs are "expenses of the organization" to be paid from the UN regular budget. **2 August:** Economic and Social Council (ECOSOC) sets up Committee on Housing, Building, and Planning transformed in 1978 into Commission on Human Settlements. **23–25 October:** Security Council debates Cuban Missile Crisis. **14 December:**

Adoption by the General Assembly of a resolution proclaiming the right of permanent sovereignty of states over their natural resources.

1963   14 May–27 June: Fourth special session of the General Assembly on the financial crisis of the United Nations arising from the Congo peacekeeping operation. **11 June:** Security Council authorizes the creation of the United Nations Yemen Observation Mission (UNYOM). **7 August:** Security Council calls for voluntary arms embargo against South Africa. **20 November:** General Assembly adopts Declaration on the Elimination of All Forms of Racial Discrimination.

1964   4 March: Security Council dispatches peacekeeping force in Cyprus. **23 March–16 June:** United Nations Conference on Trade and Development (UNCTAD) meets in Geneva. **30 June:** United Nations Operation in the Congo terminated. **1–23 December:** "No vote" session of the General Assembly in order to avoid invocation of charter's Article 19 suspending the vote of financially delinquent states. **30 December:** United Nations Conference on Trade and Development established by the General Assembly as permanent institution.

1965   9–18 August: Third United Nations Congress on the Prevention of Crime and Treatment of Offenders, Stockholm. **20 August–10 September:** Second UN sponsored conference on population in Belgrade. **31 August:** UN Charter amended enlarging membership of Security Council and Economic and Social Council. **20 November:** For the first time, Security Council imposes sanctions against Rhodesia (now Zimbabwe). **22 November:** Assembly merges the Expanded Programme of Technical Assistance (EPTA) and the United Nations Special Fund into the United Nations Development Program (UNDP). **10 December:** United Nations Children's Fund (UNICEF) awarded Nobel Peace Prize "for the promotion of brotherhood among nations." **20 December:** General Assembly approves Declaration on the Rights of the Child. Assembly extends the World Food Programme (WFP) "on continuing basis for as long as multilateral food aid is found feasible and desirable." **21 December:** Assembly adopts Convention on the Elimination of All Forms of Racial Discrimination. General Assembly approves Declaration on Principles of International Law Concerning Friendly Relations and Cooperation among States in Accordance with the Charter of the United Nations.

1966   27 October: General Assembly strips South Africa of its mandate to govern Southwest Africa. **16 December:** General Assembly approves the International Covenant on Civil and Political Rights (ICCPR) and the International Covenant on Economic, Social, and Cultural Rights (ICESCR). Mandatory sanctions imposed against Rhodesia. **17 December:** Assembly calls for an expanded program of action in the field of population. General Assembly creates the United Nations Commission on International Trade Law (UNCITRAL). **19 December:** General Assembly adopts Outer Space Treaty.

1967 21 April–13 June: Fifth special session of the General Assembly devoted to Southwest Africa (Namibia). **18 May:** At the request of Egypt, Secretary-General U Thant withdraws United Nations Emergency Force (UNEF) from Suez Canal zone. **17 June–18 September:** Fifth emergency special session of the General Assembly on the Middle East at the request of the USSR. **7 November:** General Assembly adopts Declaration on the Elimination of Discrimination against Women. **22 November:** Following the Six Days' War, the Security Council adopts Resolution 242 (1967) as a basis for achieving peace in the Middle East.

1968 1 February–29 March: Second Conference on Trade and Development in New Delhi, India. **22 April–13 May:** International Conference on Human Rights (Tehran, Iran). **27 May:** Security Council imposes comprehensive mandatory economic sanctions against Rhodesia. **12 June:** General Assembly approves nonproliferation of nuclear weapons treaty. **1 July:** Treaty on the Nonproliferation of Nuclear Weapons (NPT) opens for signature.

1969 4 January: UN Convention on Elimination of all Forms of Racial Discrimination becomes effective. **9 April–22 May:** United Nations Conference on the Law of Treaties adopts International Convention on the Law of Treaties. **10 December:** Nobel Peace Prize awarded to International Labour Organization. **11 December:** Assembly adopts Declaration on Social Progress and Development.

1970 17–26 August: Fourth United Nations Congress on the Prevention of Crime and the Treatment of Offenders. **24 October:** General Assembly adopts Declaration on Principles of International Law Concerning Friendly Relations and Cooperation among States in Accordance with the Charter of the United Nations. Assembly adopts international development strategy (IDS) for the second United Nations development decade. **7 December:** Assembly creates United Nations Volunteers (UNV) to operate in ways similar to the American Peace Corps. **17**

December: General Assembly approves declaration setting forth principles to govern the sea-bed and ocean floor beyond the limits of national jurisdiction.

1971   21 July: International Court of Justice (ICJ) issues advisory opinion declaring South Africa's control of Namibia illegal. **25 October:** General Assembly expels Chinese Nationalist representatives and seats representatives of the People's Republic of China. **14 December:** General Assembly sets up United Nations Disaster Relief Organization (UNDRO). **16 December:** Assembly adopts the Biological Weapons Convention (BWC). **20 December:** General Assembly recommends further enlargement of the Economic and Social Council (ECOSOC) from 27 to 54 members.

1972   1 January: Kurt Waldheim begins his first term as secretary-general. **13 April–21 May:** Third United Nations Conference on Trade and Development in Santiago, Chile. **5–16 June:** United Nations Conference on the Human Environment (Stockholm). **2 November:** General Assembly designates 1973–1982 as decade for Action to Combat Racism and Racial Discrimination. **1 December:** Assembly establishes United Nations University. **15 December:** General Assembly sets up United Nations Environment Programme (UNEP). **18 December:** Assembly places the United Nations Fund for Population Activities under its authority.

1973   3 March: Convention on International Trade in Endangered Species of Wild Fauna and Flora (CITES) signed by 80 nations. **9 August:** The Economic and Social Council (ECOSOC) establishes the Economic Commission for Western Asia as the successor to the United Nations Economic and Social Office in Beirut (UNESOB). Renamed Economic and Social Commission for Western Asia in 1985. **22 October:** Second United Nations Emergency Force (UNEF II) authorized by the Security Council. **16 November:** Law of the Sea Conference begins work on comprehensive treaty covering all legal aspects of ocean access and uses. **30 November:** General Assembly adopts the International Convention on the Suppression and Punishment of the Crime of Apartheid.

1974   9 April–2 May: Sixth special session of the General Assembly on raw materials and development convened at the request of Algeria adopts a Declaration and Programme of Action on the Establishment of a New International Economic Order. **3 May:** Security Council authorizes United Nations Disengagement Observer Force (UNDOF). **16 May:** Economic and Social Council (ECOSOC) sets up the voluntary fund for the International Women's Year, forerunner of the present United Nations Development Fund for Women. **19–30 August:** World Population Conference (Bucharest), third in a series. **5–16 November:** World Food Conference (Rome) sponsored by the Food and Agriculture Organization (FAO). **12 November:** Assembly endorses convention on the registration of objects launched into outer space. **13 November:** General Assembly recognizes the Palestine Liberation Organization as "the sole representative of the Palestinian people." **12 December:** General Assembly adopts Charter of Economic Rights and Duties of States. **14 December:** Assembly adopts resolution defining aggression. **17 December:** Assembly creates the World Food Council. General Assembly approves agreement establishing the World Intellectual Property Organization (WIPO) as a specialized agency.

1975 17–28 March: First meeting of the Commission on Transnational Corporations. **26 March:** Convention on the prohibition of bacteriological weapons enters into force. **19–30 May:** International Civil Service Commission meets for the first time. **19 June–2 July:** World Conference of the International Women's Year (Mexico City), first in a series. **1–12 September:** Fifth United Nations Congress on the Prevention of Crime and the Treatment of Offenders, Geneva. **1–16 September:** Seventh special session of the General Assembly devoted to development and international economic cooperation. **10 November:** General Assembly passes resolution equating Zionism with racism. **9 December:** Adoption by the Assembly of the Declaration on the Protection of All Persons from Being Subjected to Torture and Other Cruel, Inhuman, or Degrading Treatment or Punishment. General Assembly endorses Declaration on the rights of disabled persons.

1976 3 January: International Covenant on Economic, Social, and Cultural Rights (ICESCR) enters into force. **5–31 May:** Fourth United Nations Conference on Trade and Development in Nairobi, Kenya. **31 May–11 June:** United Nations Conference on Human Settlements formulates strategies to mitigate the negative effects of rapid urbanization (Vancouver). **4–17 June:** Tripartite World Conference on Employment, Income Distribution, and Social Progress and the International Division of Labor (Geneva). **13–22 September:** Conference on Economic

Cooperation Among Developing Countries (Mexico City). **10 December:** General Assembly refers the Convention on the Prohibition of Military or Any Other Hostile Use of Environmental Modification Techniques to member states for consideration, signature, and ratification.

1977 **14–25 March:** United Nations Water Conference (Mar del Plata, Argentina). **22–26 August:** World Conference against Apartheid (Lagos, Nigeria). **29 August–9 September:** United Nations Conference on Desertification (Nairobi). **4 November:** Security Council adopts mandatory arms embargo against South Africa. **15 December:** Assembly approves designation of International Fund for Agricultural Development (IFAD) as a specialized agency.

1978 **19 March:** Security Council calls upon Israel to cease its military action against Southern Lebanon and establishes the United Nations Interim Force in Lebanon (UNIFIL). **20–21 April:** Eighth special session of the General Assembly on the financing of the UNIFIL. **24 April–3 May:** Ninth special session of the General Assembly on Namibia. **23 May–1 July:** Tenth special session of the General Assembly on disarmament. **14–26 August:** World Conference to Combat Racism and Racial Discrimination. **30 August–12 September:** Conference on Technical Co-operation among Developing Countries (Buenos Aires). **6–12 September:** International conference on primary health care (Alma-Ata, USSR) sponsored by the World Health Organization (WHO) and United Nations Children's Fund (UNICEF). **9–13 October:** Disarmament Commission meets for the first time.

1979 **7 May–3 June:** Fifth United Nations Conference on Trade and Development (Manila, Philippines). **12–20 July:** World Conference on Agrarian Reform and Rural Development (Rome) organized by the Food and Agriculture Organization (FAO). **20–31 August:** United Nations Conference on Science and Technology (Vienna). **4 November:** Iranian militants seize the U.S. embassy in Tehran, Iran. **11 December:** Assembly adopts Declaration calling for international cooperation for disarmament. **17 December:** Assembly approves international convention against the taking of hostages. **18 December:** General Assembly endorses Convention on the Elimination of All Forms of Discrimination against Women. Moon treaty opens for signature. **21 December:** Sanctions against Southern Rhodesia lifted. **27 December:** Soviet Union invades Afghanistan.

1980 **10–14 January:** Sixth emergency special session of the General Assembly on Afghanistan deplores the Soviet military intervention and calls for the immediate and unconditional withdrawal of foreign troops from Afghanistan. **8 May:** World Health Organization (WHO) declares smallpox eradicated. **24 May:** International Court of Justice (ICJ) rules in favor of the United States and against Iran in the Iran hostage crisis. **14–30 July:** World Conference of the United Nations Decade for Women (Copenhagen). **25 August–5 September:** Sixth United Nations Congress on the Prevention of Crime and Treatment of Offenders (Caracas, Venezuela). **12 December:** General Assembly sets up system of yearly standardized reporting of military expenditures through the secretary-general.

1981 **22–29 July:** Seventh emergency special session of the General Assembly on Palestine (reconvened on 20–28 April 1982, 25–26 June 1982, 16–19 August 1982, 24 September 1982). **10–21 August:** UN Conference on New and Renewable Sources of Energy (Nairobi, Kenya). **25 August–15 September:** Eleventh special session on International Economic Cooperation. **1–14 September:** First United Nations Conference on the Least Developed Countries (Paris). **3–14 September:** Eighth emergency special session of the General Assembly on Namibia. **14 October:** United Nations High Commissioner for Refugees (UNHCR) wins Nobel Prize for its assistance to Asian refugees. **3 December:** Assembly approves resolution proclaiming the 1980s as the second disarmament decade. Assembly adopts declaration on the inadmissibility of intervention and interference in the internal affairs of states. **5 December:** Assembly launches international strategy for the third United Nations development decade. **December 14:** General Assembly proclaims right to development as a fundamental human right.

1982 **1 January:** Javier Perez de Cuellar takes office as secretary-general. **29 January–5 February:** Ninth emergency special session of the General Assembly on the Israeli-occupied Arab territories. **April 16:** Establishment of the Committee on the Elimination of Discrimination against Women (CEDAW). **7 June–10 July:** Twelfth special session of the General Assembly on disarmament. **26 July–6 August:** World Assembly on Aging in Vienna recommends employment and income security, health and nutrition, housing, education, and social welfare strategies to meet the needs of older persons. **October 28:** General Assembly adopts World Charter for Nature. **25 November:** General Assembly approves Declaration on the Elimination of All Forms of Intolerance and of Discrimination Based on Religion or Belief. **3 December:** Assembly endorses Declaration on the Participation of Women in Promoting International Peace and Security. **10 December:** After nine years of negotiations, United Nations Convention on the Law of the Sea opens for signature. **13 December:** General Assembly approves creation of United Nations Institute for Disarmament Research (UNIDIR) as an autonomous research institution within the United Nations.

1983 **6 June–2 July:** Sixth United Nations Conference on Trade and Development in Belgrade. **1–12 August:** Second World Conference to Combat Racism and Racial Discrimination (Geneva). **11 August:** International Research and Training Institute for the Advancement of Women begins operation in Santo Domingo, Dominican Republic. **1 November:** Convention on the Conservation of Migratory Species of Wild Animals enters into force. **29 December:** United States notifies the United Nations Educational, Scientific, and Cultural Organization (UNESCO) of its intent to withdraw from the organization.

1984 **6 April:** United States withdraws from the compulsory jurisdiction of the International Court of Justice (ICJ) in Central America cases. **11 June:** Moon agreement enters into force. **6–14 August:** Fourth United Nations sponsored International Conference on Population (Mexico City). **3 December:** General Assembly adopts declaration on the critical economic situation of Africa. **10 December:** General Assembly adopts Convention against Torture and Other Cruel, Inhuman, or Degrading Treatment or Punishment. **11 December:** First World Survey on the Role of Women in Development published. **14 December:** Voluntary Fund for the United Nations Decade for Women becomes United Nations Development Fund for Women within the United Nations Development Program.

1985 **26 February:** Secretary-general appoints a coordinator for the improvement of the status of women within the secretariat. **22 March:** Vienna Convention for the Protection of the Ozone Layer signed by 20 countries. **28 May:** Economic and Social Council (ECOSOC) establishes Committee on Economic, Social, and Cultural Rights (CESCR) to monitor implementation of the International Covenant on Economic,

Social, and Cultural Rights (ICESCR). **15–26 July:** Third United Nations World Conference on Women in Nairobi, Kenya, marks the end of the United Nations Decade for Women. **26 August–September:** Seventh United Nations Congress on the Prevention of Crime and Treatment of Offenders (Milan). **17 December:** Assembly converts United Nations Industrial Development Organization (UNIDO) into specialized agency. **18 December:** Assembly sets up a "Group of Eighteen" (G-18) countries to recommend administrative and financial reforms.

1986   **27 May–1 June:** Thirteenth special session of the General Assembly on the Critical Economic Situation in Africa. **27 June:** International Court of Justice (ICJ) rules against United States' mining of Nicaragua's ports as violation of customary international law. **August 18:** Group of Eighteen (G-18) submits 71 recommendations to the secretary-general on reform of the United Nations. **17–20 September:** Fourteenth special session of the General Assembly on Namibia. **10 October:** Secretary-General Javier Perez de Cuellar wins second term in office. **4 December:** General Assembly approves Declaration on the Right to Development.

1987   **May 14:** Security Council condemns the use of chemical weapons by Iraq and Iran as violation of the 1925 Geneva Protocol. **26 June:** Convention against torture enters into force. **9 July–3 August:** Seventh United Nations Conference on Trade and Development in Geneva. **7 August:** Heads of five Central American countries sign Guatemala Agreement for the establishment of peace in the region. **19 August:** Bro Harlem Brundland submits the Report of the World Commission on Environment and Development coining the novel concept of "sustainable development" to the General Assembly. **16 September:** Signing of treaty on the protection of the ozone layer. **24 August–11 September:** International Conference on the Relationship Between Disarmament and Development (New York). **18 November:** United Nations General Assembly adopts Declaration on the Enhancement of the Effectiveness of the Principle of Refraining from the Threat or Use of Force in International Relations.

1988   **April:** Multilateral Investment Guarantee Agency (MIGA) begins operations as a subsidiary body of the World Bank. **31 May–25 June:** Fifteenth special session of the General Assembly on disarmament unable to reach a consensus. **30 July:** Common Fund for Commodities providing capital to finance buffer stocks of commodities in price stabilization plan enters into force. **2–5 August:** United States, Angola, Cuba, and South Africa reach agreement on the withdrawal of South Africa from Namibia. **20 August:** UN-sponsored cease-fire in the Iran-Iraq war enters into effect. **22 September:** Vienna Convention for the Protection of the Ozone Layer enters into force. **29 September:** United Nations peacekeeping operations awarded Nobel Peace Prize. **25 November–20 December:** UN-sponsored conference adopts Convention against the Illicit Traffic in Narcotic Drugs and Psychotropic Substances, which enters into force in 1990. **5 December:** Assembly approves declaration on the peaceful settlement of disputes. **22 December:** Security Council launches first United Nations Angola Verification Mission (UNAVEM I).

1989   1 January: Montreal Protocol on Substances that Deplete the Ozone Layer enters into force. **16 February:** Security Council establishes United Nations Transition Assistance Group (UNTAG) to help Namibia transition to independence. **20–22 March:** UN conference endorses Basel Convention on the Control of Transboundary Movements of Hazardous Wastes and their Disposal. **27 July:** Security Council sets up United Nations Observer Mission for the Verification of Elections in Nicaragua (ONUVEN). **20 November:** General Assembly adopts Convention on the Rights of the Child. **12–14 December:** Sixteenth special session of the General Assembly on Apartheid. **15 December:** Assembly adopts protocol to the International Covenant on Civil and Political Rights (ICCPR) banning death penalty.

1990   20–23 February: Seventeenth special session of the General Assembly on drug abuse problems. **5–9 March:** World Conference on Education for All (Jomtien, Thailand) sponsored by United Nations Educational, Scientific, and Cultural Organization (UNESCO). **23–27 April:** Eighteenth special session of the General Assembly on international economic cooperation ends in stalemate. **1 May:** Assembly adopts declaration on international economic cooperation and the revitalization of economic growth and development in developing countries. **2 August:** Iraq invades Kuwait. **6 August–29 November:** Security Council considers Iraq's invasion of Kuwait and authorizes the use of "all necessary means" to ensure compliance with its resolutions with a 15 January 1991 deadline. **27 August–7 September:** Eighth United Nations Congress on the Prevention of Crime and Treatment of Offenders in Havana, Cuba. **2 September:** Convention on the Rights of the Child comes into force. **3–14 September:** Second United Nations Conference on the Least Developed Countries (Paris). **29–30 September:** World Summit for Children (New York). **10 October:** General Assembly asks the secretary-general to support Haiti's request for UN assistance in the organization and observation of its first democratic elections. **4 December:** General Assembly proclaims the 1990s as third disarmament decade. **18 December:** Adoption by the General Assembly of the International Convention on the Protection of the Rights of All Migrant Workers and Members of Their Families. **21 December:** Assembly approves International Development Strategy for the Fourth United Nations Development Decade.

1991   **3 April:** With a cease-fire in place in the Iraq Kuwait war, the Security Council decides to maintain its full trade embargo and imposes unprecedented additional measures on Iraq including international border delimitations, inspection and verification of the dismantlement of its weapons of mass destruction, and war damage reparations. **9 April:** United Nations Iraq-Kuwait Observation Mission (UNIKOM) established by the Security Council to monitor the Iraq-Kuwait border. **29 April:** Security Council authorizes United Nations Mission for the Referendum in Western Sahara (MINURSO). **20 May:** Security Council establishes the United Nations Observer Mission in El Salvador (ONUSAL) to monitor cease-fire and human rights situation. **30 May:** With cease-fire achieved in Angola war, Security Council sets up second United Nations Angola Verification Mission (UNAVEM II). **9 June:** United Nations Special Commission established by Security Council to monitor and verify Iraq's compliance with ban of its weapons of mass destruction commences first chemical weapons inspection mission in Iraq. **25 September:** Security Council imposes general and complete embargo on all deliveries of weapons and military equipment to Yugoslavia. **27 September:** Foreign ministers of the five permanent members of the Security Council issue statement recognizing the central role of the United Nations in the maintenance of peace and security and pledging support for preventive diplomacy and increased peacekeeping efforts. **16 October:** Security Council establishes United Nations Advance Mission in Cambodia (UNMIC). **6 December:** General Assembly institutes a Register of Conventional Arms, to include data on international arms transfers as well as information provided by member states on military holdings, procurement through national production, and relevant policies. **16 December:** General

Assembly revokes 1975 "Zionism is Racism" resolution. **18 December:** General Assembly adopts United Nations New Agenda for the Development of Africa in the 1990s. **31 December:** Good offices of the secretary-general bring civil war in El Salvador to an end.

1992   1 January: Boutros Boutros-Ghali takes office as secretary-general. **31 January:** First ever meeting of the Security Council at the level of heads of state requests the secretary-general to submit proposals to strengthen the peacemaking and peacekeeping functions of the UN. **23 January:** Security Council imposes arms embargo on Somalia. **6 February:** Commission on Crime Prevention and Criminal Justice established as a functional commission of the Economic and Social Council (ECOSOC) to replace the Committee on Crime Prevention and Control. **8–25 February:** Eighth United Nations Conference on Trade and Development. **21 February:** Security Council sets up the United Nations Protection Force (UNPROFOR) to ensure security in Yugoslavia pending a final settlement. **28 February:** Security Council authorizes 22,000-strong United Nations Transitional Authority in Cambodia (UNTAC) to assist in the transition toward new government. **24 April:** Security Council establishes United Nations Operation in Somalia (UNOSOM I) to obtain a cease-fire and provide humanitarian assistance. **30 April:** ECOSOC merges its Intergovernmental Committee on Science and Technology for Development and the Advisory Committee on Science and Technology for Development into a Commission on Science and Technology for Development. **5 May:** Basel Convention on Hazardous Wastes enters into force. **30 May:** Security Council demands that the parties to the conflict in Bosnia and Herzegovina allow the unimpeded delivery of humanitarian supplies. **3–14 June:** United Nations Conference on Environment and Development (UNCED) in Rio de Janeiro. **4 June:** United Nations Framework Convention on Climate Change (UNFCCC) opens for signature. **5 June:** Convention on Biological Diversity opens for signature. **17 June:** Secretary-general issues "An Agenda for Peace." **20 October:** Security Council authorizes the deployment of military observers in the Prevlaka Peninsula. **16 November:** Security Council condemns "ethnic cleansing" in Bosnia and Herzegovina. **19 November:** Security Council imposes arms embargo on Liberia. **30 November:** General Assembly adopts Chemical Weapons Convention (CWC). **16 December:** Security Council establishes the United Nations Operation in Mozambique (UNOMOZ).

1993 **12 February:** Economic and Social Council's (ECOSOC) Commission on Sustainable Development comes into existence. **22 February:** Security Council establishes International Criminal Tribunal for the Former Yugoslavia (ICTY). **26 March:** Security Council authorizes United Nations Operation in Somalia (UNOSOM II) under Chapter VII to restore peace and security and assist in the rebuilding of Somalia's government and economy. **14–25 June:** World Conference on Human Rights in Vienna reaffirms the universality of human rights and calls for the creation of a High Commissioner for Human Rights. **16 June:** Security Council imposes an arms and oil embargo on Haiti and freezes its foreign assets. The embargo is suspended on 27 August and reimposed on 18 October. **24 August:** Security Council establishes the United Nations Observer Mission in Georgia (UNOMIG). **15 September:** Security Council imposes arms embargo along with petroleum sanctions against the National Union for the Total Independence of Angola (UNITA). **23 September:** United Nations Mission in Haiti (UNMIH) set up by the Security Council to oversee the implementation of the provisions of the Governors Island Agreement of 3 July 1993. **5 October:** Security Council sets up the United Nations Assistance Mission in Rwanda (UNAMIR). **13 October:** Security Council reimposes economic and oil embargo against Haiti and demands the removal of illegal military government. **20 December:** General Assembly proclaims the International Decade of the World's Indigenous People and launches Third Decade to Combat Racism and Racial Discrimination. General Assembly creates Office of the High Commissioner for Human Rights (UNHCHR).

1994 **25 April–6 May:** Global Conference on the Sustainable Development of Small Island Developing States (Bridgetown, Barbados). **26–29 April:** Elections held in South Africa monitored by the United Nations Observer Mission in South Africa (UNOMSA). **May:** World Conference on Natural Disaster Reduction outlines strategies for disaster prevention, mitigation, preparedness, and relief (Yokohama, Japan). **6 May:** Security Council expands the embargo imposed on Haiti to include all commodities and products with the exception of medical supplies and foodstuffs. The secretary-general produces "An Agenda for Development." **17 May:** Security Council votes arms embargo on Rwanda. **25 May:** Security Council lifts its arms embargo and other restrictions against South Africa. **23 June:** South Africa returns to the General Assembly. **5–15 September:** International Conference on

Population and Development (ICPD, Cairo, Egypt) focuses on population issues in relation to economic growth and development. **29 September:** All sanctions imposed on Haiti are lifted following the return to Haiti of President Jean-Bertrand Aristide. **27–29 October:** Mozambique's first multiparty elections held, monitored by international observers. **8 November:** International Criminal Tribunal for Rwanda (ICTR) established by the Security Council. **16 November:** Convention on the Law of the Sea enters into force. **9 December:** General Assembly adopts Declaration on Measures to Eliminate International Terrorism. Assembly launches International Decade for the World's Indigenous Peoples.

1995 Worldwide, year-long celebrations marking the fiftieth anniversary of the United Nations. **1 January:** World Trade Organization (WTO) formed superseding General Agreement on Tariffs and Trade. **8 February:** Security Council authorizes United Nations Angola Verification Mission (UNAVEM III). **6–12 March:** World Summit for Social Development (Copenhagen, Denmark) concerned with eradication of poverty, expansion of productive employment, reduction of unemployment, and social integration. **31 March:** Security Council sets up United Nations Preventive Deployment Force (UNPREDEP). **14 April:** Security Council authorizes Iraq to sell up to $1 billion of oil every 90 days and use the proceeds for humanitarian supplies to the country. The "Oil for Food" program becomes operational in the spring of 1997. **28 April–5 May:** Ninth UN Congress on the Prevention of Crime and Treatment of Offenders (Cairo, Egypt). **4–15 September:** Fourth World Conference on Women: Action for Equality, Development and Peace primarily addresses women's issues related to poverty and human rights (Beijing). **24 October:** Assembly adopts declaration marking the fiftieth anniversary of the United Nations. **22 November:** Sanctions against Yugoslavia indefinitely suspended. **4 December:** Agreement for the Implementation of the Provisions of the United Nations Convention on the Law of the Sea Relating to the Conservation and Management of Straddling Fish Stocks and Highly Migratory Fish Stocks opens for signature. **11 December:** General Assembly establishes a preparatory committee to draft the statute of an International Criminal Court (ICC). **21 December:** Security Council approves the formation of the United Nations Mission in Bosnia and Herzegovina (UNMIBIH).

1996 **1 February:** Establishment of the United Nations Mission of Observers in Prevlaka (UNMOP) by the Security Council to monitor the demilitarization of the Prevlaka Peninsula. **27 April–11 May:** Ninth United Nations Conference on Trade and Development (Midrand, South Africa) gives new market-oriented mandate for United Nations Conference on Trade and Development (UNCTAD). **10 May:** Security Council imposes sanctions on Sudan for not complying with its request to extradite three suspects wanted in connection with an attempted assassination of the president of Egypt. **3–14 June:** Second United Nations Conference on Human Settlements (Habitat II) in Istanbul, Turkey, underscores the linkages between human settlements, environmental conditions, and lack of access to land and secure tenure. **28 June:** Security Council sets up the United Nations Support Mission in Haiti (UNSMIH). **10 September:** General Assembly adopts Comprehensive Nuclear Test Ban Treaty (CTBT). **1 October:** Security Council terminates sanctions against Yugoslavia. **13–17 November:** World Food Summit focuses on food security with particular attention to food production and population growth, environmental impact, nutrition, international trade, and lessons learned from the green revolution (Rome). **16 December:** General Assembly adopts Model Law on Electronic Commerce. **17 December:** Assembly approves declaration supplementing the 1994 Declaration on Measures to Eliminate International Terrorism. Assembly decides to hold diplomatic conference of plenipotentiaries in 1998 to finalize and adopt convention on the establishment of an International Criminal Court (ICC). **26 December:** Convention to Combat Desertification enters into force.

1997   1 January: Kofi Annan becomes seventh secretary-general. **20 January:** Security Council authorizes the deployment of military observers in the United Nations Verification Mission in Guatemala (MINUGUA) to monitor a cease-fire in the civil war. **3 April:** Security Council adopts resolution setting detailed conditions for a formal cease-fire in the Iraq-Kuwait war including a demilitarized zone to be monitored by a United Nations Iraq-Kuwait Observation Mission (UNIKOM). **24–27 April:** Tenth emergency special session of the General Assembly on occupied East Jerusalem and the rest of the occupied Palestinian territories (reconvened on 15 July 1997; 13 November 1997; 17 March 1998; 5, 8, and 9 February 1999; 18 and 20 October 2000; 20 December 2001; 7 May 2002; 5 August 2002). **29 April:** Convention on the prohibition of chemical weapons enters into force. **20 June:** General Assembly adopts Agenda for Development. **23–27 June:** Nineteenth special session of the General Assembly reviews progress made five years after the Earth Summit in Rio. **30 June:** Security Council establishes the United Nations Observer Mission in Angola (MONUA). **16 July:** Secretary-general issues *Renewing the United Nations: A Program for Reform*. **25 July:** Economic and Social Council (ECOSOC) establishes Intergovernmental Forum on Forests. **30 July:** Establishment of the United Nations Transition Mission in Haiti (UNTMIH) for a single four-month period. **28 August:** Security Council imposes mandatory travel sanctions on senior National Union for the Total Independence of Angola (UNITA) officials. **8 October:** Security Council imposes oil and arms embargo as well as restrictions on the travel of Sierra Leone military junta. **28 November:** Security Council establishes the United Nations Civilian Police Mission in Haiti (MIPONUH). **3 December:** Convention on the Prohibition of the Use, Stockpiling, Production, and Transfer of Antipersonnel Mines and on Their Destruction opens for signature. **11 December:** Parties to the United Nations Framework Convention on Climate Change adopt Kyoto Protocol. **15 December:** General Assembly adopts International Convention for the Suppression of Terrorist Bombings.

1998   **19 January:** Security Council establishes United Nations Transitional Authority in Eastern Slavonia, Baranja, and Western Sirmium. **27 March:** Security Council authorizes United Nations Mission in the Central African Republic (MINURCA). **31 March:** For the purpose of fostering peace and stability in Kosovo, Security Council imposes arms embargo on Yugoslavia. **5 June:** Security Council lifts oil embargo on Sierra Leone but imposes arms embargo and selective travel ban on nongovernmental forces. **8–10 June:** Twentieth special session of the General Assembly on world drug problems. **15 June–28 July:** United Nations Conference on the establishment of an International Criminal Court (ICC). **13 July:** First peacekeeping operation in Sierra Leone set up by the Security Council. **12 and 24 June:** Security Council prohibits the import from Angola of all diamonds not controlled through certificates of origins issued by the government of Angola and imposes financial sanctions on the National Union for the Total Independence of Angola (UNITA). **22–24 June:** Five-year review conference of the World Conference on Human Rights in Ottawa. **29 June:** Security Council holds open debate on the impact of armed conflict on children. **28 July:** Negotiating parties adopt the statute of a permanent ICC. Economic and Social Council (ECOSOC) merges its committees on natural resources and energy into a single expert body, the Committee on Energy and Natural Resources for Development. **26 October:** Assembly adopts resolution on Elimination of Coercive Economic Measures as a Means of Political and Economic Compulsion. **31 October:** Security Council endorses agreement reached by Afghanistan, Pakistan, the Soviet Union, and the United States, which includes the creation of the United Nations Good Offices Mission in Afghanistan and Pakistan (UNGOMAP) to observe the withdrawal of Soviet troops from Afghanistan.

1999 **31 January:** Secretary-general proposes Global Compact at World Economic Forum in Davos. **28 February:** Security Council terminates mandate of United Nations Preventive Deployment Force in the Former Yugoslav Republic of Macedonia (UNPREDEP). **3 June–2 July:** Twenty-first special session of the General Assembly on population and development assesses the implementation of the plan of action adopted at the 1995 Cairo conference. **10 June:** Security Council establishes the United Nations Interim Administration Mission in Kosovo (UNMIK). **11 June:** Security Council sets up the United Nations Mission in East Timor (UNAMET), first in a series of three successive missions. **30 June–2 July:** Special session of the General Assembly to review the implementation of the International Conference on Population and Development Plan of Action. **25 August:** Security Council expresses "grave concern at the harmful and widespread impact of armed conflict on children and the long-term consequences this has for durable peace, security and development." **17 September:** Security Council "strongly condemns" the deliberate targeting of civilian populations in armed conflicts. **27–28 September:** Twenty-second special session of the General Assembly reviews the problems of small-island developing states. **6 October:** General Assembly adopts protocol to the Convention on the Elimination of All Forms of Discrimination against Women empowering the Committee on the Elimination of Discrimination against Women (CEDAW) to entertain individual complaints and to initiate investigations about alleged violations of women's rights. **15 October:** Security Council adopts sweeping sanctions against Taliban regime in Afghanistan. **22 October:** Security Council dissolves United Nations Observer Mission in Sierra Leone (UNOMSIL) and establishes the United Nations Mission in Sierra Leone (UNAMSIL). **25 October:** United Nations Transitional Administration in East Timor (UNTAET), second peacekeeping operation authorized by the Security Council. **9**

December: General Assembly adopts International Convention for the Suppression of the Financing of Terrorism. **17 December:** Security Council sets up United Nations Monitoring, Verification, and Inspection Commission (UNMOVIC) superseding United Nations Special Commission.

2000   10 January: Month-long meeting of the Security Council devoted to Africa's problems. **12–19 February:** Tenth United Nations Conference on Trade and Development in Bangkok, Thailand. **24 February:** United Nations Organization Mission in the Democratic Republic of the Congo (MONUC) authorized by the Security Council. **9 March:** President of the Security Council issues statement recognizing the humanitarian dimension of international peace and security. **10–17 April:** Tenth United Nations Congress on the Prevention of Crime and Treatment of Offenders, Vienna. **16 May:** General Assembly adopts protocols to the Convention of the Child on the Involvement of Children in Armed Conflicts and on the Sale of Children, Child Prostitution, and Child Pornography. **17 May:** Security Council imposes arms embargo against Eritrea and Ethiopia. **25 May:** Assembly endorses protocol to the Convention on the Rights of the Child banning the use of children in armed conflicts. **5–9 June:** Twenty-third special session of the General Assembly reviews progress made on gender issues since1995 Beijing conference. **26–30 June:** Twenty-fourth special session of the General Assembly takes stock of progress made in the implementation of the outcome of the Copenhagen conference on social development. **5 July:** Security Council imposes a ban on the import of rough diamonds from Sierra Leone not controlled by the government of Sierra Leone through a certificate of origins regime. **17 July:** Security Council adopts resolution recognizing that HIV-AIDS may have an impact on the maintenance of international peace and security. **26 July:** Security Council holds day-long open debate on children and armed conflicts, the second since 1998. **28 July:** Permanent Forum on Indigenous Issues established as a subsidiary body of the Economic and Social Council (ECOSOC). **31 July:** Establishment of the United Nations Mission in Ethiopia and Eritrea (UNMEE) by the Security Council. **31 July–1 August:** Security Council holds exploratory public meeting involving governments, nongovernmental organizations (NGOs), and the diamond industry on the links between the trade in illicit Sierra Leone diamonds and the arms trade. **23 August:** Brahimi report recommends major improvements in planning and implementation of UN peacekeeping operations. **6–8 September:** Millennium Assembly draws 152 heads of states and governments and adopts resolution reaffirming the central role of the United Nations in world affairs. **31 October:** Security Council discusses women's issues and adopts resolution recognizing the role of women in the maintenance of peace and security and calling for gender mainstreaming in UN peacekeeping operations. **15 November:** General Assembly approves United Nations Convention against Transnational Organized Crime together with protocols banning the smuggling of migrants, the trafficking of women and children, and the illicit manufacturing and trafficking of firearms. **December 1:** Assembly adopts resolution on "conflict diamonds." **December 17:** General Assembly approves the International Civilian Mission Support in Haiti (MICAH). **19 December:** Security Council broadens sanctions against Afghanistan and demands extradition of Osama bin Laden.

2001   31 January: Security Council devotes day-long meeting to strengthening cooperation with troop-contributing countries in peacekeeping operations. **5 February:** Security Council holds meeting on all aspects of peace building. **7 March:** Security Council lifts its 1992 arms embargo on Liberia but votes new sanctions including a ban on import of rough diamonds from the country and measures to prevent the travel of senior Liberian government officials. **14–20 May:** Third United Nations Conference on the Least Developed Countries meets in Brussels. **31 May:** General Assembly adopts Protocol against Illicit Manufacturing of and Trafficking in Firearms. **6–8 June:** Twenty-fifth special session of the General Assembly assesses progress made since Habitat II. **25–27 June:** Twenty-sixth special session of the General Assembly on HIV/AIDS approves Declaration of Commitments on HIV/AIDS. **29 June:** Kofi Annan appointed for a second term of office. **9–20 July:** United Nations Conference on the illicit trade in small arms and light weapons in New York. **10 September:** Security Council lifts all remaining sanctions adopted against Yugoslavia in regard to the Kosovo crisis. **11 September:** United Nations postpones opening of the 56th session of the Assembly following terrorist attacks on New York City. **28 September:** Security Council invoking Chapter VII of the charter adopts resolution requiring states to prevent the financing of terrorist groups and setting up a Counterterrorism Committee (CTC). Council lifts sanctions targeted at Sudan. **31 September–7 August:** World Conference against Racism, Racial Discrimination, Xenophobia, and Related Intolerance (Durban, South Africa). **12 October:** United Nations and Secretary-General Kofi Annan awarded Nobel Peace Prize. **9**

November: General Assembly approves Global Agenda for Dialogue among Civilizations. **12 November:** Security Council adopts declaration on global efforts to combat terrorism. **17–20 December:** Second World Congress against the Commercial Sexual Exploitation of Children takes place in Yokohama sponsored by Japan, United Nations Children's Fund (UNICEF), and several nongovernmental organizations (NGOs).

2002   12 February: Optional Protocol to the Convention on the Rights of the Child on the involvement of children in armed conflicts enters into force. **18–22 March:** International Conference on Financing for Development (Monterrey, Mexico). **28 March:** Security Council establishes the United Nations Assistance Mission in Afghanistan (UNAMA). **8–12 April:** Second World Assembly on Aging (Madrid, Spain). **3 May:** Security Council approves methods to strengthen sanctions regime against Somalia. **8–10 May:** Twenty-seventh special session of the United Nations General Assembly on Children convened to review progress made since the 1990 World Summit for Children. **10 May:** "A World Fit for Children" declaration adopted by special session of the General Assembly. **11 May:** Rome treaty establishing the International Criminal Court (ICC) enters into force. **13–24 May:** First session of the Permanent Forum on Indigenous Peoples. **17 May:** United Nations Mission of Support in East Timor (UNMISET) set up by the Security Council. **26 August–4 September:** World Summit on Sustainable Development convenes in Johannesburg, South Africa. **16 September:** General Assembly adopts Declaration on the New Partnership for Africa's Development.

2003   11 March: Inauguration of the International War Crime Tribunal in The Hague. **18 March:** UN and Cambodia reach draft agreement for prosecuting Khmer Rouge. **20 March:** United States and United Kingdom launch attack on Iraq. **13 May:** Security Council establishes the United Nations Mission in Cote d'Ivoire (MINUCI). **22 May:** Security Council terminates all sanctions against Iraq. **1 July:** International Convention on the Protection of the Rights of All Migrant Workers and Members of Their Families enters into force. **3 July:** General Assembly adopts resolution recognizing the important role of civil society in the prevention of armed conflict. **10 July:** Economic and Social Council (ECOSOC) adopts draft agreement with the World Tourism Organization (WTO) granting it the status of specialized agency. **1 August:** Security Council authorizes the establishment of a multinational force in

Liberia. **28–29 August:** International conference on the special issues faced by landlocked and transit countries adopts Almaty Program of Action (Kazakhstan). **11 September:** Cartagena Protocol on biosafety establishing rules for the safe transfer and use of genetically modified organisms enters into force. **29 September:** Convention against Transnational Organized Crime enters into force. **31 October:** General Assembly adopts Convention against Corruption. **19 November:** Security Council debates and recognizes importance of mine action in peacekeeping operations.

2004 **19 January:** President of the Security Council issues statement calling for national, regional, and international measures to combat the illicit trade of small arms. **27 February:** United Nations Operation in Cote d'Ivoire (UNOCI) set up by Security Council. **30 January:** Security Council strengthens sanctions regime against Taliban and al-Qaida organization. **30 March:** Security Council extends the mandate of United Nations Mission in Sierra Leone (UNAMSIL) for another six months. **15 April:** Security Council holds open debate on the role of business in conflict prevention, peacekeeping, and postconflict peace building. **18–25 April:** Eleventh UN Congress on crime in Bangkok. **21 April:** Secretary-general announces formation of an independent panel to conduct an inquiry into allegations of impropriety in the administration and management of the Iraq Oil for Food program. **22 April:** Security Council condemns the recruitment of child soldiers and calls upon the secretary-general to create a monitoring mechanism to provide timely, objective, and reliable information on the recruitment and use of child soldiers in violation of applicable international law. **28 April:** Security Council adopts resolution requiring states to refrain from any support to nonstate actors attempting to develop or acquire weapons of mass destruction. **30 April:** United Nations Stabilization Mission in Haiti (MINUSTAH) set up by Security Council acting under Chapter VII. **17 May:** Security Council reviews UN peacekeeping operations and calls on UN members for more political and financial engagement. **21 May:** Security Council establishes United Nations Operation in Burundi (UNOB). **1 June:** United Nations Stabilization Mission in Haiti (MINUSTAH) formally launched. **3 June:** Special Court for Sierra Leone begins trial of three militia leaders accused of unlawful killing, physical violence, mental suffering, terrorizing civilians, and using child soldiers during Sierra Leone civil war. **4 June:** Advisory Committee on Administrative and Budgetary Questions (ACABQ) approves $2.8 billion for peacekeeping missions for 2004–2005 amid warnings that the organization is facing unprecedented demand for peacekeeping support. **8 June:** Security Council unanimously adopts comprehensive resolution on Iraq, endorsing the formation of an interim government and defining the role of the United Nations in the political transition. **13–18 June:** Eleventh United Nations Conference on Trade and Development in Sao Paulo, Brazil. **16 June:** International Labour Organization (ILO) approves plans for the drafting of an international convention extending fair labor standards to the world's 86 million migrant workers. **22 June:** Security Council holds a day-long open debate on the role of civil society in postconflict peace building. **24 June:** Chief prosecutor of the International Criminal Court (ICC) initiates investigation of its first case, alleged war crimes in the Democratic Republic of the Congo (DRC). **1 October:** Security Council broadens mandate of United Nations Organization Mission in the Democratic Republic of the Congo (MONUC). **6 October:** After day-long debate, Security Council issues statement stressing that "climate of impunity" must end in postconflict nations and that peace and reconciliation processes entail the restoration of justice and the rule of law and must be inclusive and gender sensitive. **8 October:** Condemning terrorism as one of the most serious threats to peace and security, the Security Council unanimously calls on countries to prosecute or extradite anyone supporting terrorist acts or participating in the planning of such schemes. **15 November:** Security Council imposes arms embargo on Cote d'Ivoire and a travel ban on persons that it designates. **29 November–3 December:** First review of the 1998 mine ban treaty.

2005   10–14 January: International Meeting to Review the Implementation of the Programme of Action for the Sustainable Development of Small Island Developing States (Mauritius). **18–22 January 2005:** World Conference in Disaster Reduction (Kobe, Hyogo, Japan). **1 February:** Panel constituted to investigate charges of genocide in Darfur concludes that rebel forces in this province of Sudan are responsible for possible war crimes and recommends that the Security Council refer the case to the International Criminal Court (ICC). **16 February:** With Russian ratification, Kyoto Protocol to 1992 Convention on Climate Change becomes effective. **17 February:** Security Council adopts declaration acknowledging that small-arms trafficking may threaten international peace and security. **28 February:** United Nations global treaty seeking to curb production, consumption, and smuggling of tobacco enters into force. **24 March:** Security Council determines that the situation in the Sudan constitutes a threat to international peace and establishes United Nations Mission in the Sudan (UNMIS). **29 March:** Security Council adopts a U.S.-sponsored resolution imposing sanctions on individuals suspected of having committed atrocities or broken cease-fire agreements in the Sudanese province of Darfur. In a subsequent resolution, the Council refers the Darfur situation to the prosecutor of the International Criminal Court. **7 April:** Security Council sets up independent probe into Lebanese ex-premier's murder. **13 April:** General Assembly adopts International Convention for the Suppression of Acts of Nuclear Terrorism. **2–19 May:** UN peacekeeping mission in Timor-Leste comes to an end. **2–27 May:** Seventh (and inconclusive) review conference of the nuclear nonproliferation treaty in New York. **26 May:** Security Council discusses possible improvements in post-conflict peace building. **2 June:** High-level General Assembly meeting on HIV/AIDS. **21 June:** Security Council debates ways and means to strengthen the protection of civilians in armed conflicts. **23–24 June:** General Assembly holds informal "hearings" with civil society organizations and private sector. **27–28 June:** Second High-Level Dialogue on Financing for development. **26 July:** Security Council sets up mechanism to monitor the illegal recruitment and use of children in armed conflicts. **14 September:** At a meeting at the level of heads of state and government, Security Council adopts declaration affirming its resolve to strengthen the effectiveness of the United Nations in conflict prevention. **14–16 September:** High-Level Plenary meeting of the General Assembly on the Millennium Development Goals and UN reform. **5 October:** Global Commission on International Migration presents its report on global policy issues in the field of international migration to UN secretary-general. **17 October:** Security Council expresses its determination to intensify cooperation between United Nations and regional organizations in the prevention and management of international conflicts. **27 October:** Oil for Food probe issues final report. **16–18 November:** World Summit on the Information Society (Tunis, Tunisia). **28 November–9 December:** Eleventh Conference of the Parties to the United Nations Convention on Climate Change meets in Montreal, Canada, and adopts resolutions seeking to strengthen global efforts against climate change. **14 December:** Convention against Corruption enters into force. **24 December:** General Assembly adopts $3.8 billion biennial budget averting financial crisis. **Late December:** General Assembly and Security Council announce the creation of a Peace-Building Commission.

2006 7 January: World Food Programme (WFP) halts food assistance to North Korea at request of its government. **4 February:** International Atomic Energy Agency (IAEA) Board votes to refer Iran to Security Council over its nuclear activities. **17 February:** United Nations human rights investigators urge United States to close Guantanamo detention center. **7–10 March:** International Conference on Agrarian and Rural Development held in Porto Alegre, Brazil. **10 March:** New United Nations fund, the Central Emergency Response Fund, set up in secretariat to finance early UN response to humanitarian disasters. **12 March:** Former Yugoslav president, Slovodan Milosevic, found dead in his cell in The Hague. **15 March:** UN General Assembly overwhelmingly endorses creation of Human Rights Council. **16–22 March:** Fourth World Water Forum (Mexico City, Mexico). **17 March:** Congolese leader suspected of war crimes and conscription and recruitment of child soldiers placed in custody of International Criminal Court (ICC). **22 March:** Economic and Social Council (ECOSOC) formally abolishes Commission for Human Rights. **27 March:** Three-day-long UN-backed conference on early warning systems for natural disasters opens in Bonn, Germany. **27 March:** Human Rights Commission ends its last meeting after adopting resolution transferring its work to Human Rights Council, scheduled to first meet on 19 May. **21 August:** Security Council assigns new tasks to United Nations Interim Force in Lebanon (UNIFIL). **25 August:** Security Council sets up United Nations Integrated Mission in Timor-Leste (UNMIT). **13 October:** Acting on the recommendation of the Security Council, the General Assembly appoints Foreign Minister Ban Ki-moon of the Republic of Korea as the next secretary-general to succeed Kofi Annan, effective 1 January 2007.

Introduction

Born out of the horrors and ashes of World War II, the creation of the United Nations in 1945 aroused the universal hope that the new system of collective security enshrined in the world organization would prevent the recurrence of the catastrophic events of the first half of the 20th century and build a pathway toward greater justice and prosperity. Some 60 years later, this optimism appears to have waned. The United Nations has been marginalized since the outbreak of the current Persian Gulf War. The fracas over the "Oil for Food Program" has tarnished its public image and reputation. Renewed calls for "reforming" the organization seem to yield only modest and imperfect improvements in its mode of operation. And the long-awaited 2005 Summit convened to celebrate the 60th anniversary of the organization and instill it with a renewed sense of mission and commitment around shared values and goals, only produced a blurred and uncertain strategic vision of what the international community expects from it.

Looking back over the past tribulations of the United Nations, one can indeed find sobering instances of inconsistencies, benign neglect, and outright cases of failures to act: the paralysis of the Security Council stymied by an abusive use of the "veto" throughout the Cold War; the intractable issues of Palestine, Kashmir, Cyprus, and western Sahara; the ignominious hands-off posture in the 1975–1978 and 1994 genocides in Cambodia and Rwanda; the abrupt withdrawal from Somalia in 1993; the massacre of thousands in Srebrenica, after the council had declared the town a "safe area" in 1995. On the other hand, the history of the United Nations does include a number of remarkable successes: its work in support of self-determination and decolonization; the dismantlement of apartheid; the invention of peacekeeping; its promotion and protection of universal human rights; the control or eradication of infectious diseases, the humanitarian relief it provides to millions displaced by man-made or natural catastrophes.

The record is indeed mixed, but hardly perplexing if it is understood from the outset that the United Nations is not a world government but an intergovernmental organization comprising states—each claiming to be sovereign and exerting plenary and exclusive control over persons and things within its borders—that allows them a forum to enjoy equal status with other states regardless of size and power. But too often it is forgotten that the United Nations was neither designed nor intended to acquire the supranational capacity to effectuate commands over its member states. It is primarily an arena where sovereign national governments clash and seek to reconcile their differences, and its capacity to act is shaped and, by and large, determined, by the constraints and possibilities posed by its members' willingness to cooperate and compromise and the evolving international environment.

In brief, the United Nations is rarely more than the sum of its parts, and it mirrors the divisions as well as the hopes and convictions of the world's governments. From this vantage point, the road taken by the international community through the United Nations toward making the world a safer and better place can hardly be presumed to be a "superhighway." Rather, it has been, remains, and will remain, short of a revolutionary change in the state-based nature of the international society, a long, winding, and bumpy country road requiring constant maintenance and upgrading. This metaphor encapsulates much of the story of the United Nations in the past 60 years. For in typically incremental, ad hoc, disjointed, and slow-paced manner, much has been accomplished through or under the aegis of the organization. Far more, in fact, as shall be seen, than was anticipated or expected from it in 1945. Originally conceived as a standing conference machinery and a big-power instrument devoted primarily to the maintenance of peace and security, the United Nations has quietly and without preestablished blueprint evolved into a peacekeeper, a nation and state builder, a standard- and norm-setting mechanism, and a provider of services. This essay spells out some of the political factors that have nurtured the UN's remarkable growth and development in its six decades of existence, highlights the equally noteworthy limitations and imperfections of this process, and underlines the continuing efforts of the organization to address emerging new global issues and problems.

THE ORIGINAL DESIGN:
DUMBARTON OAKS AND SAN FRANCISCO

In a formal but very real and often overlooked sense, the United Nations is a treaty-based organization. It is an institution established by agreement of its affiliated members to fulfill common objectives agreed to and set forth in the United Nations Charter. This document, which became effective on 24 October 1945, when a sufficient number of ratifications of the treaty had been obtained, spells out in its opening article these "common objectives": to maintain international peace and security; to develop friendly relations among nations based on the respect for the principle of equal rights and self-determination of peoples; to achieve international cooperation in solving problems of an economic, social, cultural, or humanitarian character; and to encourage respect for human rights and for fundamental freedoms for all without distinction as to race, sex, language, or religion. From this vantage point, the United Nations was expected to act as "a center for harmonizing the actions of nations in the attainment of these common goals."

This broad and vague language was a negotiated compromise text that incorporated competing definitions of the functions of a global international organization. It was worked out by the representatives of 50 allied countries during the United Nations Conference on International Organization, held in San Francisco from April through June 1945, on the basis of proposals tendered by China, the USSR, the United Kingdom, and the United States in meetings held a year earlier in 1944 in Dumbarton Oaks. By and large, though, the foundations, principles and machinery of the new world organization grew out of American thinking and blueprints guided by the "lessons" of the recent past, notably the "failures" of the League of Nations in averting World War II, the traumatic experience of the Great Depression, the rise of nondemocratic regimes, and the explosion of economic nationalisms that followed. Hence the American belief that wartime great-power cooperation in the postwar period through a variety of multilateral instruments for conflict prevention was necessary to avoid future wars. A stable and enduring world political order accordingly rested on U.S. membership and robust leadership in a "general security organization" with a wide array of powers to maintain international peace and security and promote sound socioeconomic growth, an open world economy, and the spread of democratic government.

These ideas provided the backbone of the "Tentative Proposals for a General International Organization," which the United States submitted in August 1944 to the Dumbarton Oaks "Conversations." The primary purpose of the organization would be to maintain international peace and security and, in a derivative manner and cautious language, "to foster through international cooperation the creation of conditions of stability and well being necessary for peaceful and friendly relations among nations which are essential to the maintenance of security and peace." The organization would be made up of four "principal organs": a General Assembly, an Executive Council, an International Court of Justice (ICJ), and a General Secretariat.

In the economic and social fields, the assembly could "initiate studies and make recommendations for the promotion of international cooperation, the development and revision of rules of international law and the promotion of the observance of basic human rights." Chapter IX on "Arrangements for International Economic and Social Cooperation" elaborated, stating that "with a view to the creation of stability and well being which are necessary for peaceful and friendly relations among nations, the general international organization should facilitate and promote solutions of international economic and social problems, including educational and cultural problems." These functions would be carried out by the General Assembly and, under its authority, by an Economic and Social Council (ECOSOC). The membership of the council was restricted to 18 member states elected by the General Assembly. Weighted voting schemes had been dropped in favor of an egalitarian one-state-one-vote system on the grounds that it was necessary to counterbalance the nondemocratic nature of the peace and security system. The proposals also envisaged that the council could set up an economic commission, a social commission, "and such other commissions as may be required" consisting of experts. The council could only make recommendations in economic and social problems, "including those beyond the scope of the specialized agencies with a view to promoting the fullest and most effective use of the world's economic resources, to achieving high and stable levels of employment, and in general in advancing the well being of all peoples."

At Dumbarton Oaks, a broad commonality of views was soon reached between the United States, Great Britain, and China. The main business of the meeting was in fact to secure the support of the Soviet

Union, which initially took the position that economic and social activities should be parceled out to separate and distinct organizations outside of the United Nations. American insistence on factoring respect for human rights into the broad principles of the organization also elicited Soviet objections. The matters were settled in a series of compromises, and when the meeting closed on 7 October, the American blueprint defining the parameters of the political, economic, and social work of the United Nations had been accepted.

The charter that emerged from San Francisco the following year did not fundamentally alter the framework of the Dumbarton Oaks agreement. In fact, San Francisco encapsulated a broad (though grudging) acquiescence to two key American notions: that the big powers had a quasi-exclusive responsibility in the maintenance of peace and security and that, in regard to economic and social questions, the General Assembly had only a power of discussion and recommendation.

For the small countries, which so far had had little to say in the negotiations for a new world organization, San Francisco offered an opportunity to air their dissatisfaction and press their views. They had little influence on the charter arrangements in regard to peace and security. The dominance of the major powers was overwhelming. They were somewhat more successful in economic and social matters, but only marginally so. In their interventions, all small countries articulated their expectation of "achieving high living standards and expanded rights through the new world organization." They invoked profusely a wide panoply of normative principles: equity, justice, nonintervention, self-determination, and basic human rights. They forcefully underlined the "indivisibility of peace" and called for the creation of "equitable foundations" in international economic relations.

To a certain extent, the pressures of developing countries, combined with those of medium-sized powers, did lead to a number of marginal changes in the charter that noticeably strengthened the role of the United Nations in the economic and social fields: the ECOSOC became one of the principal organs of the United Nations, and its powers and functions were enlarged. Culture, education, and health entered into the charter. More important, "development," crept into Article 55 of the charter. A fragile consensus was also achieved over a host of issues related to "self-determination," which provoked intense debates fueled by the unwillingness of imperial European powers to relinquish their rule over Asian and African territories and the resolve of the handful of "backward countries" present in San Francisco bent on winning acceptance of the illegitimacy of colonialism.

The political dynamics between colonial powers, the ambivalent Wilsonian zeal of the United States, and the forcefulness of anticolonial forces, notably the Soviet Union, in addition to the vigorous efforts of such countries as Egypt, Syria, Iraq, and India at San Francisco, produced the Declaration Regarding Non-Self-Governing Territories contained in Chapter XI of the charter and the trusteeship system spelled out in Chapters XII and XIII. Through the declaration, colonial powers did acknowledge a "sacred trust" to promote the well-being and self-government of their dependencies and agreed to submit data "of a technical nature relating to [their] economic, social and educational conditions" From their perspective, such agreement did not mean acceptance of the goal of independence. But the declaration embodied, if not an obligation, at least a moral commitment to a limited UN right of oversight and supervision. The objective of the trusteeship system, which replaced the weaker mandate system of the League of Nations, was self-determination possibly leading to independence. The system applied to those mandates of the League that were scheduled for independence and to territories "detached from enemy states as a result of the Second World War."

The provisions of the charter on human rights were equally clouded with uncertainty. In many respects, the charter's emphasis on human rights was a sharp break from diplomatic tradition. Neither international law nor the practice of states had made significant room for the international protection of individuals. The rare exceptions to this prevailing norm were the treaties concluded at the end of World War I requiring the new states and defeated countries to protect the linguistic, educational, and cultural rights of their ethnic minorities. The League Covenant also had called upon the "advanced nations" serving as "Mandatories on behalf of the League" to "secure [the] just treatment of the native inhabitants" of their dependent territories. In reaction to the massive atrocities committed in the course of World War II, the charter does pay considerable attention to human rights. The Preamble; Article 1 (Purposes and Principles); Article 13, concerned with responsibilities of the General Assembly; Articles 55 and 56, dealing with the objectives of economic and social cooperation; Article 62 on the functions and powers of the ECOSOC; Article 58, setting up a commission to promote human rights; and Article 76, spelling out the objectives of the trusteeship system, all refer to human rights. But none of these provisions place any specific legal obligations on UN member states in regard to the protection of their nationals. Nor do they grant any enforcement right to the organization. The definition of individual rights and the protection that they should be given were in effect left to the sovereign authority of UN member states.

A number of conclusions emerge from the foregoing. Smaller and developing countries participating in the San Francisco Conference were perhaps more inclined than larger powers to assign broader functions and responsibilities to the new organization, especially the General Assembly, notably in regard to human rights and development. But none of them, including the United States, saw the United Nations as a supranational entity or a "world government" endowed with regulatory and legislative policy-making powers. The norm of sovereignty prevailed then as it still does today. As a voluntary association of sovereign states and a center for the harmonization of their national policies, the United Nations was only empowered to function as a "catalyst," a "facilitator," a "conveyor." It was, in the words of an American diplomat present at San Francisco, "a town meeting of the world where public opinion is focused as an effective force."

The norm of sovereignty meant not only that all nations represented in the United Nations were equal, irrespective of differences in power — hence the one-state-one-vote rule in the assembly and its subsidiary organs — but also that the organization, with the exception, as shall be seen below, of situations involving the Security Council acting under Chapter VII of the charter, could not under any circumstances deal with subjects considered to be the exclusive province of governments. The charter thus confines the ECOSOC to the subordinate status of an "auxiliary executive agency" of the General Assembly. The assembly itself — like the Council — can only adopt nonbinding recommendations. Articles 10–17 of the charter merely empower the assembly to "discuss," to "consider," "to initiate studies and make recommendations" and to "receive and consider annual and special reports." It is essentially a debating chamber, a forum for discussion and the exchange of ideas. Furthermore, Article 2.7 of the charter — the so-called domestic jurisdiction clause — rules out any possible transgression by plainly stating that "nothing contained in the present Charter shall authorize the United Nations to intervene in matters which are essentially within the domestic jurisdiction of any state."

Second, for the charter's intellectual architects, the main raison d'être of the United Nations was the maintenance of peace and security. In this regard, the charter enjoins the UN member states to "refrain in their international relations from the threat or use of force" (Article 2.4) and states may use force only defensively in cases of "armed attacks" (Article 51). This prohibition of the use of force goes along with another normative injunction to settle interstate disputes by peaceful means. Article 2, paragraph 3 of the charter thus stipulates that "All Members shall settle their international disputes by peaceful means in such a manner that international peace and security, and justice, are not endangered." The procedures for settlement of disputes are listed in Article 33, paragraph 1 of the charter: "The parties to any disputes, the continuance of which is likely to endanger the maintenance of international peace and security, shall, first of all, seek a solution by negotiation, enquiry, mediation, conciliation, arbitration, judicial settlement, resort to regional agencies or arrangements, or other peaceful means of their choice." Both the Security Council and the General Assembly may make recommendation on the resolution of a dispute submitted to either one of them by any one of the parties, any member of the United Nations, or the secretary-general. The assembly may not, however, intervene as long as the Security Council is seized of the question and, in any case, neither body can impose a settlement.

Mindful of the "mistakes" of the founders of the League of Nations, which had been paralyzed by the overlapping competing functions of its executive and legislative organs, the drafters of the United Nations Charter provided for a body small in size endowed with the "primary" responsibility to facilitate prompt and effective action. Both the General Assembly (under Article 10) and the Security Council (under Article 33) can recommend solutions to disputes likely to endanger peace and security. But only the council can "determine the existence of any threat to the peace, breach of the peace, or act of aggression" and make recommendations or decisions as to measures to be taken to maintain or restore international peace and security (Article 39). Under Articles 41 and 42 of the charter, the Security Council may decide what related measures are needed to implement its decisions. The charter states that the council may order the complete or partial interruption of economic relations with states violating international law. And if these states do not comply, the council may use air, sea, or land forces as necessary to maintain or restore peace and security. In effect, the United Nations Security Council possesses a legal monopoly of the use of force, which it could use, under the terms of Article 47, with the assistance of a Military Staff Committee consisting of the Chiefs of Staff of the permanent members of the Security Council on all questions relating to the employment and command of forces placed at its disposal, the regulation of armaments, and possible disarmament.

To further enhance the effectiveness of the council, the charter devises a system of decision making circumventing the rule of unanimity that had paralyzed the League of Nations security arrangements. A majority of votes—originally 7 out of 11 and now, since the enlargement of the council in 1966, 9 out of 15—suffice to trigger Security Council action. Such a majority vote, however, must include the concurring votes of the permanent members of the Security Council. Widely decried at San Francisco by the smaller powers, the "veto" provision of Article 27 of the charter (the word does not appear, however) has ever since been a source of ongoing controversy. "Dictatorship of the powerful within a democracy"? Pragmatic acknowledgement of the special role of larger powers in the maintenance of peace and security? Stark reminder of the futility of efforts to draw them into an armed conflict against their will? . . . The debate still rages today, shaping the discourse and negotiations over the enlargement of the council to reflect the new distribution of political and economic power in the world.

Third and final observation: the experience of the 1920s and 1930s had demonstrated that peace rested on sound economic, trade, and social relations; educational advancement; and the observance of human rights. As Article 55 of the charter puts it, it is "with a view to the creation of conditions of stability and well being which are necessary for peaceful and friendly relations among nations," that the United Nations "shall promote higher standards of living, full employment and conditions of economic and social progress and development, solutions of international economic, social, health and related problems and universal respect for and observance of human rights."

The prudential language of the charter needs to be noted, as, again, it could lend itself to diametrically conflicting interpretations. Does the charter impose upon states an obligation to act on this pledge? Alternatively, has each state simply acquiesced to cooperate through the United Nations in promoting respect for human rights and conditions of economic and social progress? Is each state, in accordance with the domestic jurisdiction clause, implicitly authorized to defer decision as to how and to what extent this pledge should be implemented and acted upon until it deems it politically expedient and appropriate? As shall be seen later, these questions were answered (and still are) through the political process in the United Nations.

For the time being, it suffices to note that other strata of conflict lay below the lofty language of Article 55. For the United States, the reconstruction of Europe, the restoration of a viable and expanding international economy, stable currencies, and freer trade were priority areas for action. In contrast, Latin American and other developing countries were focused on creating the domestic and international basis of their "industrialization" and showed little enthusiasm for the virtues assigned to the market by American "liberal-interventionists." Still another bone of contention was the central role that American policy makers gave to the International Bank for Reconstruction and Development (IBRD or World Bank) and the International Monetary Fund (IMF) rather than to the United Nations in the field of economic and social cooperation. In fact both the bank and the fund had come into existence at U.S. prodding at the July 1944 Bretton Woods Conference *prior to the United Nations*. The World Bank was designed to assist in the reconstruction and development of territories of its members and promote or supplement private foreign investment. The complementary role of the IMF was to promote exchange stability, maintain orderly exchange arrangements among members, and assist in the establishment of a multilateral system of payments in respect of current transactions between members and in the elimination of foreign exchange restrictions hampering the growth of world trade.

The IBRD and the IMF were thus expected to contribute to the promotion and maintenance of high levels of employment and real income and to the development of the productive resources of all members as primary objectives of economic policy. The Bretton Woods Conference also invited its participants to discuss ways and means to "reduce obstacles to international trade and in other ways promote mutually advantageous international commercial relations." Even before the creation of the United Nations, the United States thus envisaged the establishment of a trade organization in support of the activities of the financial institutions created at Bretton Woods that would deal with restrictions on trade by governments or cartels and monopolies, cyclical fluctuations in production and employment, and adjustments in the production and trade of primary commodities.

In stark contrast with the United Nations, the IBRD and the IMF were endowed with vast "discretionary" and "regulatory" functions. But the institutions that had emerged from Bretton Woods were plainly and visibly "an Anglo-Saxon creation with the United States very much the senior partner." Neither the bank nor the fund could realistically embark on policies colliding with American views and interests. In both institutions, the allocation of voting power was proportional to their members' financial contribution, thus giving the United States one-third of the voting power, in effect a virtual veto. The question of the scope of the United Nations' authority over the Bretton Woods institutions was basically left untouched at San Francisco, as developing countries unsuccessfully sought to bring them under the aegis of the General Assembly. Likewise, the issue of the role of the United Nations in the "coordination" of the specialized agencies that had sprung up since 1943 with the creation of the Food and Agriculture Organization (FAO) and the establishment five months later of the United Nations Relief and Rehabilitation Administration (UNRRA) to assist liberated peoples in Europe and Asia remained unresolved. In April 1944, the International Labour Organization (ILO) met for the first time since the outbreak of the war in an effort to revitalize itself. Similar international bodies were planned or envisaged throughout that period including the International Civil Aviation Organization (ICAO), the World Health Organization (WHO), and the International Refugee Organization (IRO), not to mention the revamping of the antiquated International Telecommunications Union (ITU). The long-term implications of this proliferation of functional agencies for the role to be assigned to the United Nations were not immediately self-evident although it was then already clear that the United Nations would have no exclusive jurisdiction over economic and social affairs.

In spite of obvious organizational defects and considerable ambiguity in its objectives, the system of collective security that had emerged from World War II had logic, coherence, and purpose. The system rested on a set of institutions, each designed for specific purposes, all complementing each other: the United Nations' primary purpose would be to deter aggression. Economic questions would come under the purview of the Bretton Woods institutions and other "specialized agencies," with the United Nations cast in the peripheral role of standard setter and "town meeting of the world." An International Trade Organization (ITO) in the making would soon complement this edifice. Under no circumstances could the UN "system" operate in opposition to the United States, the country that had played a central role in its creation. How could a UN responsive to the needs of the entire international community not inevitably clash with the United States and be able to function without its support? The tensions generated by these questions loomed large and cast a long shadow over the deliberations of the San Francisco proceedings. In the euphoria provoked by the end of five years of carnage and destruction, they receded into the background. But they never disappeared altogether. In recent years, they have resurfaced with unprecedented acuity.

THE COLD WAR AND CONFLICT SETTLEMENT

The drafters of the United Nations Charter had theorized that the unity of the war coalition was a sine qua non condition for the successful operation of the United Nations. The outbreak of the Cold War quickly rent asunder their assumption. In fact, the charter system of conflict prevention never worked as intended. The ideological and political split between the United States and the USSR turned the relatively benign "town meetings of the world" into engines of war in the arsenal of the superpowers as well as arenas where confrontation became the rule and winning points on the scoreboard of world public opinion the ultimate objective. Rather than an instrument of international cooperation, the United Nations thus turned into an arena where issues were brought up less for the purpose of resolving them than to mobilize numerical majorities condemning either one of the superpowers' "utter disregard and contempt for human dignity."

The politicization of public parliamentary diplomacy in the polarized setting of the Cold War meant in practice subordinating international cooperation to the strategic imperatives of the superpowers. Intent on using the United Nations to pursue the goal of a more equitable distribution of power and wealth, developing countries throughout this process remained in a minority position and had not yet coalesced into a tangible international force. Yet their argument that, as the majority of the countries of the world containing the majority of the world population, they should determine the kind of world in which they wished to live, had resonance with the two superpowers, who were ever concerned to find allies in their global struggle. The pressures of developing countries for a fair deal, combined with the U.S. fear that failure to address the socioeconomic conditions of developing countries might lead them to fall prey to "the false prophets of communism," thus had two unintended but momentous consequences: first, the system of dispute settlement and collective security laid down in the charter was drastically altered and, second, the role of the United Nations in economic and social affairs expanded considerably way beyond what had been originally envisaged.

The historical record of the United Nations in the peaceful settlement of disputes appears relatively unimpressive. According to a study conducted in the mid-1980s and covering the years 1945–1984, the United Nations contributed to the settlement of only less than half of the disputes brought before it. No similar study exists for the period since 1984, but prima facie, it does not seem that the UN performance improved markedly. During the Cold War, the organization was least effective in resolving conflicts between opposing Cold War coalitions, more effective in promoting settlement between an aligned and nonaligned state, and quite effective in dealing with decolonization disputes. Soviet and American interests rarely converged, and their lack of consensus accounts for the spotty record of the United Nations. Other factors include the defiance of the disputants in reaction to Security Council recommendations.

Throughout this process, the role of the General Assembly expanded considerably, beginning, as shall be seen, in the 1950s with the Korean question, followed in 1956 by the Suez crisis, which it helped defuse, and its involvement in the Congo crisis in 1960. Other security issues have crowded the agenda of the assembly: the Middle East, southern Africa, Cambodia, Grenada, Central America, the Falklands, Afghanistan, and Bosnia. As a large public forum, the proceedings of the General Assembly, however, have been used more with a view to legitimizing the position of one side at the expense of another than promoting a peaceful settlement of international disputes. Occasionally, the General Assembly did play a third-party role, extending beyond its legitimizing role, as was the case in the Suez and Congo crises. The assembly has also had recourse to the appointment of UN mediators, as it did in the early stages of the Arab-Israeli dispute. Mediation now is more likely to be undertaken by the secretary-general.

Indeed, one of the most extraordinary developments arising from the Cold War has been the emergence, against all expectations, in 1945, of the secretary-general of the United Nations as a significant political actor in his own right. All of them have made it a practice to exert independent political initiatives by relying in particular on the seemingly innocuous provision in Article 98, which authorizes the secretary-general to "perform such other functions as are entrusted to him." All incumbents have considered themselves spokesmen for the world community. Acting, in the words of Trygve Lie, "as a force for peace," they have defended their rights to speak out on the whole range of issues facing the international community, from human rights to economic development to the environment to UN reform. They have taken positions in support of UN purposes and policies. The large number of United Nations officials crisscrossing the world on behalf of the secretary-general, studying contending positions and seeking to devise compromises acceptable to parties in conflict, is a revealing indicator of the expansion and influence of the office in multilateral diplomacy. But this exercise in leadership carries with it enormous political risks and, ultimately, hinges on the political support the secretary-general gets from the membership of the organization and especially from its most powerful constituent members. When this support evaporates, so does his influence: Lie resigned in ignominy, pilloried by both the United States and the USSR. U Thant's criticisms of the United States involvement in Vietnam in the 1960s and efforts to mediate the conflict triggered first displeasure and then benign neglect. Boutros Boutros-Ghali's unabashed criticism of the Security Council's relative indifference to the plight of the African continent put him on a collision course with the United States. Kofi Annan's public statement portraying the American decision to invade Iraq in 2003 as contradictory to international law severely undermined his capacity for leadership.

Collective Security or Unilateralism?

During the Cold War, the required cooperation of the five permanent powers evaporated. The Soviet Union viewed the organization as being run and controlled by the Western powers and made extensive use of its veto power to protect its perceived national interests. In the early years of the United Nations, the United States could forgo the use of the veto, as it was able to enlist "mechanical majorities" in support of its policy goals. As the membership of the world organization changed and became more restive, these "automatic majorities" disappeared and American support for the organization became more qualified and diffident.

In any event, the collective security system laid down in the charter was superseded by time-honored balance-of-power strategies implemented by and large outside of the United Nations. From 1946 to 1990, only twice—Korea in 1950 and the Falklands in 1986—did the Security Council determine there had been "breaches to the peace." Likewise, the council adopted binding nonmilitary sanctions only twice, an economic blockade against Southern Rhodesia following the seizure of power by a white minority regime (1966–1979) and an arms embargo imposed on South Africa in 1977 for its apartheid policies.

None of the international conflicts that occurred until the end of the Cold War triggered the use of Chapter VII. During the 1962 Cuban Missile Crisis, the United States justified its unilateral "quarantine" action primarily on the basis of the authority of the Organization of American States. The Vietnam War was kept outside of the United Nations altogether. All attempts by the council to impose sanctions in the Arab-Israeli conflict were thwarted by vetoes. The Security Council was unable to reach a consensus on sanctions during the 1979–1980 Teheran hostage crisis. Throughout its military intervention in Afghanistan from 1979 to 1989, the Soviet Union stymied all council attempts (and the General Assembly's as well) to bring the conflict to an end.

Doubts have in fact been expressed about whether Korea constitutes a bona fide collective security response as envisaged by the charter. The council did respond swiftly to the June 1950 invasion of South Korea by North Korea. But only the temporary absence of the Soviet Union enabled the council to pass a resolution recommending to member states to "furnish such assistance to the Republic of Korea as may be necessary to repel the armed attack and to restore international peace." To mobilize the council and the United Nations against one of its permanent members was consistent neither with the letter nor the spirit of the charter. In addition, the entire operation rested on individual and voluntary commitments. The forces dispatched to Korea were authorized and placed by the council under a "unified command" and a United Nations flag. But by and large, it was a U.S. operation under U.S. control. Only 22 members of the United Nations (out of 60 at the time) offered military forces, as the United States contributed more than half of the ground forces, 85 percent of naval forces, and 95 percent of the air force involved.

Likewise, the council's actions following its condemnation of the August 1990 Iraqi invasion of Kuwait as a breach of the peace and international security have raised similar troubling questions. As Iraq did not comply with its demand for an immediate and unconditional withdrawal of Iraqi troops, the council passed further resolutions imposing an arms and trade embargo and authorizing an armed blockade. Acting under Chapter VII of the charter, the council finally authorized member states to use all necessary means to uphold its previous resolutions. Under the leadership of the United States, the coalition forces launched military attacks in January 1991 and hostilities ceased on 28 February with the ousting of Iraqi troops from Kuwait.

One question is whether the council may delegate its military power by authorizing unnamed states to use force at their own discretion without retaining at least some degree of control. Some have seen in this a "rebirth" of the United Nations collective security system. Others have accused the United States of trying to keep the council under its tutelage. Equally troublesome is the fact that the resort to force took place without a prior formal determination by the council that those economic sanctions had failed, thus justifying the use of force. Finally, as had been the case in Korea, the bulk of the military power came from the United States. In any case, both the Korean and Iraqi "collective actions" make it plain that no major UN enforcement action is possible without an adequate consensus among the permanent members of the Security Council.

More to the point, it is doubtful that the UN can launch a collective security action without the willingness of the United States to provide the necessary military power. Its national interests must be engaged and must coincide with those of others to form a "coalition of the willing."

In addition and contrary to the letter and spirit of a bona fide system of collective security, granting discretionary powers to the United States appears to be a sine qua non condition for maintaining American involvement in the resolution of the crisis.

Under such circumstances, the United Nations collective security system has acquired few unconditional advocates. The second Gulf War was an even more blatant challenge that rekindled the profound uneasiness of most members of the United Nations. Launched on 20 March 2003 by the United States and the United Kingdom with the support of a "coalition of the willing," the invasion of Iraq came to an end three weeks later with the complete military and political collapse of the Iraqi regime. Because the invasion was undertaken without the explicit approval of the Security Council, many observers have labeled it as a violation of the charter and a breach of one of its cardinal principles: the nonuse of force. The officially stated justifications for the invasion have in fact varied over time, ranging from Iraq's noncompliance with the sanctions regime imposed on it in 1991, purported links with terrorist organizations, and human rights violations under the Saddam Hussein regime. Ultimately, the Iraq war was justified as an effort to remove banned weapons from Iraq within the broader framework of a war on international terrorism embedded in a doctrine of "preemption" justifying the use of force against an imminent threat.

The political debate over the legality of the war is unlikely to come to any conclusion soon. But, in the meantime, it is clear that the emergence of terrorism as a global security issue after the 11 September attacks on U.S. soil, has recast the collective security provisions of the charter in a new framework while at the same time enhancing feelings of unease about the United States, which has taken the lead in this process.

Less than 24 hours after 11 September, the Security Council adopted a "declaration" asserting that acts of international terrorism constituted one of the most serious threats to international peace and security in the 21st century and underlining the obligation of states to deny financial and other forms of support and safe haven to terrorists and to all those who support them. Following a pattern established in previous resolutions targeted at the Taliban regime in Afghanistan, which it has accused of harboring terrorism, the council subsequently adopted yet another resolution on 28 September, imposing drastic binding obligations on all states. All members of the United Nations are now required to deny all forms of support for terrorist groups; to share information with other governments on any groups planning or practicing terrorism; to cooperate with other governments in the investigation, detection, arrest, and prosecution of people involved in terrorist acts; to criminalize active and passive assistance for terrorism in domestic laws; and to become party as soon as possible to relevant UN conventions and protocols dealing with terrorism.

A Counterterrorism Committee (CTC) composed of all members of the Security Council monitors the implementation of that resolution and assesses compliance on the basis of state reports describing measures taken by governments in such areas as financial law, customs, immigration, extradition, and illegal arms legislation and practices. If not satisfied with the pace of effective counterterrorism legislation and effective police, intelligence, customs, immigration, and border controls measures, the CTC may ask further questions and dispatch field missions. In 2004, the council further tightened the screws of this new collective security regime by deciding, again under Chapter VII, that all states must adopt appropriate legislation and effective enforcement measures to prevent nonstate actors from developing, acquiring, possessing, transporting, transferring, and using nuclear, chemical, or biological weapons and their means of delivery.

Like piracy and slavery in international law, terrorism has become a nonderogable offense and states have in effect become internationally accountable for its prevention and punishment. For many, the old charter-based boundaries between national and international affairs have become blurred as the United Nations Security Council has established itself as an international rule maker and overseer of national legislators. At the same time, the concept of security, which had been traditionally defined as the protection of the territorial integrity, stability, and vital interest of states, has been broadened so as to include nonmilitary threats that lead to violent conflicts and affect the security of individuals, communities, and states.

THE PEACEKEEPING ALTERNATIVE

The Cold War effectively stymied any effective peacemaking by the United Nations. Early on, negotiations stumbled on the size and composition of the force to be made available to the United Nations and no "standing army" for possible police action as contemplated under Article 43 ever materialized. The Military Staff Committee could only agree to hold further meetings. In the absence of the Soviet Union, the Security Council was able to initiate the Korean police action in August 1950 but was paralyzed by Soviet vetoes upon its return to the council. Acting on a U.S. proposal, the General Assembly adopted the Uniting for Peace Resolution (UFP), which empowers it to take action when the council is blocked by a veto of any of its permanent members. The legality of the UFP resolution has ever since been a continuing matter of dispute among legal scholars and practitioners, as it lays down a strategy that had never been contemplated by the charter's framers: authorizing the assembly to initiate measures to restore peace, including through the use of armed force. UFP in effect was a major rewriting of the charter and was the basis for the creation of the first major UN "peacekeeping" operation to resolve the 1956 Suez Canal crisis. Stalemated by French and British vetoes, the assembly invoked UFP to deploy troops serving as a buffer between Egypt and its French, British, and Israeli adversaries. UFP was again used to overcome Soviet opposition to the UN operation in the Congo in 1960–1964. It has rarely been used since, as the Security Council, especially after the end of the Cold War, has reasserted its exclusive role in the maintenance of peace and security.

In any event, UFP gave further impetus to the involvement of the UN in peacekeeping, a set of activities that started modestly with the establishment of the 1948 UN Truce Supervision Organization to monitor cease-fires, supervise armistice agreements, and attempt to prevent escalation of the conflict in the Middle East. Since 1948, the United Nations has mounted 60 peacekeeping operations involving an estimated 1 million soldiers, police officers, and civilians from some 130 countries, who served under the UN flag. The cumulative total of UN peacekeeping expenditures (from 1948 to June 2005) exceeds $36 billion. The scale of UN peacekeeping operations has varied widely over the years. With the launching of major operations in the former Yugoslavia and Somalia, annual peacekeeping operations peaked at some U.S. $3.6 billion with almost 80,000 peacekeepers deployed in the field. By 1998, the number of peacekeepers had dropped to between 12,000 and 15,000, with expenses of less than $1 billion. With the large-scale operations authorized by the council in Sierra Leone, Congo, East Timor, and Kosovo, costs began to rise again reaching $2.6 billion in 2000 and $3 billion in 2001. The dispatching of UN peacekeepers to Cote d'Ivoire, Haiti, and Sudan brought the total number of operations in 2005 to 17 at a budgeted cost of about $4.47 billion and involving 82,000 military, police, and civilian personnel and troops.

Throughout the Cold War, UN peacekeeping operations, under the control of the secretary-general and the force commander under the authority of the United Nations, involved the fielding of unarmed or lightly armed observers placed between warring states to monitor compliance with cease-fire agreements. They were a temporary measure designed to allow the peacemaking process to unfold. Acting as a buffer in an interstate conflict, peacekeepers were thus expected to be strictly neutral in the conflict and to use their weapons only in self-defense. Furthermore, their presence was grounded on the consent of the states concerned. Already in the early years of the United Nations, unarmed and impartial observers were used to monitor cease-fire lines. This was done by the council in 1948 in the Middle East with the establishment of the United Nations Truce Supervision Organization (UNTSO). Later that same year, a similar observer operation—United Nations Military Observer Group in India and Pakistan (UNMOGIP)—was launched to observe the cease-fire line between Pakistan and India in Kashmir. Both these operations continue to this day. In November 1956, the first United Nations Emergency Force (UNEF) was established in order to secure and supervise the cessation of hostilities in the region of the Suez Canal. Other instances of such "first-generation" peacekeeping operations include the United Nations Operation in the Congo (ONUC)—at least in its first phase—and the United Nations Peacekeeping Force in Cyprus (UFICYP).

The peacekeeping doctrine that prevailed until the demise of the Cold War, called for a UN military presence that would make possible, in line with Article 33 of the charter, the negotiation of a permanent settlement by diplomatic means. Since then, the Security Council, acting under Chapter VII, has established larger and increasingly complex peacekeeping missions that are often an integral part of comprehensive peace agreements between protagonists in intrastate civil conflicts. Thus, peacekeeping has moved beyond its traditional role as a monitor to cease-fires and a buffer force between two states. It is now understood as "a way to help countries torn by conflict create the conditions for sustainable peace." UN peacekeepers—soldiers and military officers, civilian police officers, and civilian personnel—monitor and observe peace processes that emerge in postconflict situations. They also help ex-combatants implement their peace agreements, which encompass confidence-building measures, power-sharing arrangements, electoral support, strengthening the rule of law, and economic and social development. So-called "second-" and "third-generation" peacekeeping operations now include tasks like the disarming of militias and former combatants and their reintegration in society, the supervision of elections and the constitution of political institutions, the training of police officers and creation of judicial bodies, the nurturing of civil society organizations, supporting economic reconstruction, the facilitation of humanitarian aid programs, the resettling of refugees and internally displaced persons (IDPs), and the promotion and protection of human rights. Peacekeeping has virtually become a synonym for a blurred mix of nation and state building and development.

The United Nations Force in the Congo (1960–1964) was a distant precursor to future post–Cold War operations. Its original task was to restore law and order and to supervise the withdrawal of Belgian forces. As the internal situation continued to deteriorate, ONUC was authorized to use force to prevent civil war and to remove mercenaries that had supported the secession of one of the countries provinces. The 1989 United Nations Transition Assistance Group (UNTAG) was the first instance of a large-scale multidimensional operation where the military element supported the work of other components concerned with border surveillance; monitoring the reduction and removal of South African military presence; organizing the return of Namibian exiles; supervising voters' registration; and preparing, observing, and certifying the results of national elections. Similar political tasks in addition to the collecting of small arms from irregular forces were given to United Nations peacekeeping missions in Central America in the context of domestic peace settlements. Even more ambitious objectives were assigned to the United Nations in Somalia and the former Yugoslavia. Since 1999 in the Democratic Republic of the Congo (DRC)—a country with little infrastructure and national cohesion—nearly 17,000 UN peacekeepers have stopped a war involving six nations and are attempting to shore up a transitional government in an effort to bring about a durable political settlement. Large scale operations have also been mounted in Haiti, Sierra Leone, Liberia, Cote d'Ivoire, and Sudan.

So-called "transitional administrations" undoubtedly represent the most complex operations undertaken by the United Nations. An early precedent of such undertakings may be found in the executive and legislative functions that the United Nations exerted in West Papua before the population voted for reintegration in Indonesia in 1962–1963. The dilution of the principle of sovereignty, a convergence of great-power interests with humanitarian concerns, had facilitated their establishment in the Cold War period. After easing Namibia's transition to independence, the UN in 1992–1993 engaged in a major effort to restore peace in Cambodia with a complex mandate touching on the protection of human rights, the preparation of elections, civil administration, civilian police, and the repatriation of refugees. The 1995 United Nations Mission in Bosnia-Herzegovina (UNMIBH) had policing functions that were handed over to the European Union in 2002. From 1996 to 1998, the United Nations Transitional Administration in Eastern Slavonia, Baranja, and Western Sirmium (UNTAES), which was responsible for policing, wielded executive power and organized elections. In East Timor (Timor-Leste since the country became independent) and now in Kosovo, the United Nations has exerted quasi-governmental sovereign powers.

Another innovation brought about by UN peacekeeping has been the new role played by regional organizations. While granting to the Security Council a primary responsibility for international peace and security, the charter does encourage regional organizations to take the initiative in settling local disputes, but it also tersely stipulates that "no enforcement action shall be taken under regional arrangements or by regional agencies without the authorization of the Security Council" (Articles 52–53). In practice, the split between East and West during the Cold War led to a reversal of roles. The Security Council never performed its collective security functions. Instead, its members set up and had recourse to an elaborate system of regional collective defense arrangements. Thus came into existence the Pact of Rio de Janeiro (1947), the North Atlantic Treaty Organization (NATO) (1949), the Australia, New Zealand, United States Security Treaty (ANZUS) (1951), the Southeast Asia Treaty Organization (SEATO) (1954), the Central Treaty Organization (CENTO) (1955), and the Warsaw Pact. Much of this regional alliance system has disintegrated with the end of the Cold War. A notable exception is NATO, which acquired a new life by providing the military component of such UN peacekeeping operations as the United Nations Protection Force (UNPROFOR). Other regional organizations have since followed the example set by NATO. The council has thus authorized regional organizations to implement a number of peacekeeping operations or enforcement functions.

The first UN operation relying on a regional peacekeeping force was in Liberia in 1993 when that force was deployed by the Economic Community of West African States (ECOWAS). Subsequent instances of the involvement of regional organizations in UN peacekeeping may be found in the United Nations Operation in Georgia (UNMIG), where the United Nations was assisted by a peacekeeping force of the Commonwealth of Independent States (CIS). UNMIBH in Bosnia and Herzegovina and United Nations Mission in Kosovo (UNMIK) in Kosovo have cooperated not only with NATO but also the European Union (EU) and the Organization for Security and Cooperation in Europe (OSCE). In Afghanistan, the NATO-led International Security Assistance Force works closely with the United Nations Assistance Mission in Afghanistan (UNAMA). More recently, regional organizations have stepped in to bridge critical gaps in the deployment of military forces in the field, acting as a rapid response force. In October 2003, in Liberia and more recently in Cote d'Ivoire, ECOWAS forces paved the way for the deployment of United Nations troops. Similar arrangements were made with the African Union peacekeeping mission in Burundi.

The extraordinary expansion of the role of the United Nations in "peacekeeping" since the end of the Cold War poses perplexing fundamental questions about the nature of the organization and its changing functions. In the first place, what have they resolved? Some argue that in El Salvador, Namibia, Cambodia, East Timor, and Mozambique, the United Nations provided ways to achieve self-sustaining peace. Although beset with problems, the operations in Afghanistan and Kosovo are nevertheless attempting to manage their challenges. Others point to a much longer list of failures or unfinished work. Once terminated in November 1993 with the adoption of a constitution, the mission in Cambodia was followed by a resurgence of internal fighting and left behind major reconstruction and rehabilitation tasks undone. In Somalia, the UN was unable to bring about national reconciliation among competing factions and it is still blamed for the deaths of U.S. soldiers who were neither peacekeepers nor under UN command. The original peacekeeping mandate of UNPROFOR was supplemented with elements of enforcement. But the imposition of an arms embargo by the council between 1991 and 1995 supplemented by further sanctions on the Federal Republic of Yugoslavia, without commensurate levels of troops, failed to prevent ethnic cleansing, cease-fire violations, hostage taking, the shelling of civilian targets, and violations of human rights and humanitarian laws. The war came to an end only after a stronger mobilization of political will by the United States, which resulted in November 1995 in the peace agreement of Dayton and the dispatch of a NATO-led implementation force (FOR) to enforce it. In Haiti, undersupported missions have failed to solve the long-standing problems of a failed predatory state.

These failures—especially the 1994 genocide in Rwanda and the 1995 massacre in Srebrenica (Bosnia and Herzegovina)—led to a period of retrenchment and self-examination in UN peacekeeping, which prompted the secretary-general to order an internal evaluation of UN operations in 2000. In the wake of this review, incremental improvements have been introduced. The Department of Peacekeeping Operations within the secretariat has increased its headquarters staff to support field missions. A "best practices unit" has been set up to analyze lessons learned from field experience and advise missions on gender issues; peacekeeper conduct; and the planning of disarmament, demobilization, and reintegration programs. A prefinancing mechanism has been set up to ensure that funds would be available for new missions start-ups. The department logistics base in Brindisi (Italy) has received funding to acquire strategic deployment stocks. Stand-by arrangements have been improved through the development of a roster of states in a position to make available to the United Nations specialized military and civilian personnel and material and equipment.

These measures may marginally improve the capacity of the United Nations to more speedily launch new operations. But they provide no answer to more fundamental unresolved financial, logistical, and ultimately political questions. Financial issues have plagued UN peacekeeping since the 1960s when political disputes flared up over the legality of the General Assembly involvement in the setting up and running of the first United Nations Emergency Force (UNEF) and the United Nations Force in the Congo. Decisions by the Security Council and the General Assembly and a 1962 advisory opinion of the International Court of Justice have confirmed that peacekeeping costs should be considered "expenses of the organization" to be borne by all members. Many countries have nevertheless continued to pay their peace-keeping assessments late or only partially. The UN peacekeeping has thus been repeatedly jolted by recurring financial shortfalls compounded by the unilateral decision of the United States—the main contributor to the UN—to limit its payments to the peacekeeping budget of the organization and to withhold parts of its assessed contributions to the regular budget.

The time lag elapsing between the authorization of a peacekeeping operation by the Security Council and the actual deployment of the force in the field has also been a source of baffling problems. The charter does stipulate that to assist in the maintenance of peace and security all member states of the UN should make available to the council necessary armed forces and facilities. In this connection, one priority of UN peacekeeping officials has been the creation of a "strategic reserve" of civilian police, military battalions, and support staff—from 3,000 to 6,000 troops—prepared to deploy immediately and lay the groundwork for a full UN force. The units would be deployed as soon as the Security Council approves a mission until the arrival of the full contingent. The idea has been around for years but has foundered over lack of support from member states, which cite financial and budgetary constraints and loathe anything approximating the notion of a "UN standing army." A related but perhaps more disquieting development is that despite the large number of contributors, the greatest burden continues to be borne by a core group of developing countries like Pakistan, Bangladesh, Nigeria, Ghana, India, Ethiopia, South Africa, Uruguay, Jordan, and Kenya. Only 10 percent of the troops and civilian police deployed in UN peacekeeping missions come from the European Union and 1 percent from the United States. Advanced nations have thus emerged as the bankrollers of UN peacekeeping (when they pay their dues!) while peace enforcement itself has been left to the relatively untrained, underequipped, and unprepared soldiers of developing countries. This little-noticed but real "division of labor" along North-South lines raises troubling ethical issues. In practical terms, it means, in effect, that the United Nations lacks the intelligence, communications, and logistics-specialized support units that give a modern army its edge in conflict prevention and resolution.

One final symptom of the malaise pervading current UN peacekeeping practice needs to be mentioned here. A typical ongoing operation relates to internal rather than interstate conflicts, with which the charter is concerned. Many of these recent operations have been taken by the council "acting under Chapter VII." This imprimatur may make it possible to launch an operation without the prior consent of parties, but to have any chance of success, transitional arrangements must be based on consensual nation and institution building. Sustainable peace building in conflict-prone societies takes time. Developing capacity for security maintenance, democratic governance, and the rule of law requires a full and genuine involvement of local institutions and leadership. These elements are rarely present when the United Nations is thrown into an internal conflict.

In addition, peacekeeping operations must be linked to longer-term plans for achieving this sort of stability. Unfortunately, the political consensus that led to the authorization and deployment of a UN peacekeeping operation does not always extend into the longer term. All too often, the organization of elections to redress a democratic deficit becomes a substitute to the sustained financial effort that is needed to build effective and legitimate government and state institutions and to eliminate the root socioeconomic causes of internal conflicts. In this regard, the postconflict experience in Nicaragua, El Salvador, and Guatemala heralded by many as early "successes" of the United Nations in postconflict peace building offer little comfort. In all these countries, the relative success of democratic political reforms appears to be eroded by the effects of internationally sponsored economic adjustment policies that have further aggravated conditions of the socioeconomic inequalities that caused the wars to begin with.

Unless these disparities are addressed and reduced, democratic consolidation will remain uncertain and the threat of renewed violence will persist. The Peace-Building Commission set up at the end of 2005 by the General Assembly and the Security Council as part of UN reform is precisely designed to deal with some of these problems. The new body—a subsidiary organ of the assembly and the council—will advise and propose integrated strategies for postconflict recovery in countries emerging from conflict.

THE ELUSIVE SEARCH FOR DISARMAMENT

In an anarchical international society where self-help prevails, national defense and security is the main raison d'être of states. Preserving and enhancing political and military power becomes of the essence. These sobering realities have severely constrained the United Nations and cast it almost exclusively into the role of effecter of great power agreement in disarmament questions.

In many respects, UN disarmament efforts have essentially been an extension—in fact virtually a repeat—of the prewar League of Nations experience. Evolving conceptions of international security and growing concerns over "new" types of security threats, have recently contributed to a redefinition of the terms of disarmament negotiations but yielded few if any tangible achievements.

In the 1920s, negotiations by the major powers focused mainly on the limitations of their armed forces. Initial successes, notably in regard to naval armaments, quickly gave way, however, to stalemate in the wake of the rise of military dictatorships in Europe and Asia. All throughout this process, the main actors involved were the major powers themselves, the League of Nations' role being limited to that of a framework for negotiations and collective legitimizer of the notion that the reduction of armaments was an essential component of the maintenance of international peace and security.

Mindful of these precedents, the drafters of the charter did not list disarmament among the purposes and the principles of the United Nations. They merely granted the General Assembly the authority to "consider general principles . . . governing disarmament" (Article 11) and empowered the Security Council, with the assistance of a Military Staff Committee, to formulate "a system for the regulation of armaments . . . with the least diversion for armaments of the world's human and economic resources" (Article 26). The Military Staff Committee was also called upon to advise the Security Council on "the regulation of armaments, and possible disarmament" (Article 47). Whatever this elusive language may have meant, the American use of nuclear weapons hardly four months after the signing of the charter and the outbreak of the Cold War made these charter provisions by and large obsolete. Cold War tensions refocused attention on nuclear disarmament and produced an enduring political process overshadowed by the superpowers that relegated nonnuclear powers and the United Nations to a peripheral role.

One of the first decisions of the General Assembly was to establish the Atomic Energy Commission (AEC) in 1946, and at the opening meeting of the commission, the United States proposed to bring nuclear weapons under the supervision and control of a United Nations mechanism that would have supranational decision-making authority and where none of its members would enjoy a veto. Insofar as the United States could at the time easily muster a majority of votes in support of its policies, the USSR perceived the so-called Baruch Plan as a poorly veiled attempt by the United States to preserve its monopoly over nuclear weapons and rejected it promptly. The alternative that it submitted—a moratorium on atomic weapons development accompanied by complete nuclear disarmament—was equally unacceptable to the United States, which saw it as a ploy to constrain U.S. defense efforts and to allow the USSR to pursue its development of nuclear weapons.

Stumbling on the unmovable blocks of mutually unacceptable demands for either "verifiable inspections" (by the United States) or "general and complete disarmament" (by the USSR), meaningful negotiations became impossible and institutional tinkering prevailed for over two decades. In 1952, the AEC and the United Nations Commission on Conventional Armaments were merged into a United Nations Disarmament Commission. The commission's subcommittee on disarmament, which comprised the United States, USSR, United Kingdom, France, and Canada, became the main setting for disarmament discussions.

At the insistence of the growing number of "nonaligned" Third World states entering the United Nations, this body was enlarged in 1959 to include Bulgaria, Czechoslovakia, Poland, and Romania from the Warsaw Pact and Italy from the NATO pact, thus becoming the Ten-Nation Disarmament Committee, which in turn was further enlarged in 1961 to be known as the Eighteen-Nation Disarmament Committee (ENDC). After the adoption of the Nonproliferation Treaty (NPT) in 1968, the General Assembly again expanded the membership of the ENDC to 30 members and named it the Conference of the Committee on Disarmament (CCD). In 1979 it was rechristened the Conference on Disarmament (CD) and by 1983, it had grown to 38 members. In June 1996 it was expanded to a membership of 61 (the CD has a current membership of 66 countries). Concurrently, since 1978, the General Assembly has held three special sessions on disarmament. In addition, a committee of the General Assembly annually debates disarmament issues and, since the reforms introduced by Secretary-General Boutros-Ghali within the United Nations Secretariat in the early 1990s, a full-fledged department provides ongoing support to the work of intergovernmental disarmament bodies.

The Conference on Disarmament is billed as the "world's multilateral treaty negotiating body," and its terms of reference are broad since they encompass no less than 10 subjects (the so-called "Decalogue"), including nuclear weapons, weapons of mass destruction, conventional weapons, the reduction of military budgets and armed forces, disarmament and development, confidence-building measures, and general and complete disarmament under effective international control. Negotiations within the CD involve several groupings, the Western Group, the Nonaligned Movement (NAM), the Group of Eastern European States, the P5 (the five permanent members of the Security Council, the five declared nuclear weapons states), with China often declaring itself the Group of One. Decisions are reached by "consensus." This apparent "democratization" and multilateralization of disarmament negotiations has not, however, erased the weight of the nuclear powers in the multilateral negotiations.

Thus, the Cuban Missile Crisis led the United States and the USSR to agree to the 1963 Partial Test Ban Treaty (PTBT) and the creation of a communications hotline between Washington and Moscow. Likewise, in 1972 the two countries independently reached agreement on an Antiballistic Missile Treaty (ABMT). The 1959 Antarctic Treaty, the first agreement to ban nuclear weapons on a regional basis, was sponsored by nuclear states. Similar treaties banning nuclear weapons in most of the world's regions have since been concluded in subsequent years, mainly at the prodding of the United Nations. But the intractable conflicts between Israel and Arab states in the Middle East and between India and Pakistan have stymied efforts to reach similar "nuclear free zone" treaties in these regions.

The 1968 NPT was the product of extensive multilateral negotiations, but these were based on a joint draft originally submitted to the Eighteen Nations Committee by the United States and the USSR. In fact, the NPT has little if anything to do with disarmament, except perhaps, as its critics argue, that it aims at disarming potential acquirers of nuclear weapons while placing no obligation to disarm on those already in possession of them. The NPT treaty provided for five-year-review conferences as well as for a conference 25 years after its entry into force to determine whether it should be indefinitely extended. The conference was held at United Nations headquarters in 1995 and, after protracted discussions, agreed to extend indefinitely the treaty (now rechristened the Comprehensive Nuclear Test Ban Treaty [CTBT]).

Nuclear weapons have unquestionably been the main focus of attention in the United Nations, but the organization has also dealt with other categories of weapons, notably weapons of mass destruction, in relation to which the United Nations has sought to obtain a mix of measures entailing arms reductions or their complete elimination in combination with verification procedures. Thus, in 1972, the General Assembly endorsed a convention prohibiting the development and possession of biological weapons. Under the convention, the secretary-general has the authority to investigate the alleged use of biological weapons. Likewise, in 1992 the assembly adopted a convention banning chemical weapons and creating an international body—the Organization for the Prohibition of Chemical Weapons—empowered to conduct surprise inspections. At the same time, the assembly has promoted what is called, in the vernacular of disarmament specialists, "confidence building measures." In 1980, the General Assembly launched a system of yearly reporting of military expenditures. Ever since a 1991 enabling resolution of the assembly, the secretary-general maintains at United Nations headquarters in New York a universal Register of Conventional Arms with data on international arms transfers and member states' military holdings and procurement.

With the end of the Cold War and the proliferation of internal conflicts, conventional weapons such as landmines and small arms have received increasing attention. The United Nations had been involved in efforts to ban landmines since the 1970s, but the grinding pace of negotiations within the CD eventually prompted several states—Canada and Belgium, in particular—to build a political consensus for a new legal instrument outside the structure of the UN. In fact, the 1997 convention on the prohibition of antipersonnel mines was the outcome of a broad-based process involving a network of states and nonstate actors such as Médecins Sans Frontières, the International Committee of the Red Cross (ICRC), and the International Campaign to Ban Landmines (ICBL). In that process, the United Nations was at best a junior policy partner.

More recently, small arms and light weapons have also moved center stage as it is increasingly recognized that their proliferation and availability destabilize regions, prolong conflicts, undermine peace initiatives, exacerbate human rights abuses, and hamper development. However, efforts to regulate the movement of small arms through international treaties or other legal instruments have so far stalled. In 2001, the UN convened a Conference on the Illicit Trade in Small Arms and Lights Weapons in All Its Aspects. The conference resulted in a "consensus" program of action calling for national, regional, and global measures for the destruction of confiscated or seized weapons and for strengthening the capacity of states to identify and trace illicit arms and light weapons trafficking. But even within this limited framework, no agreement could be reached to include in the program provisions that would have encouraged states to establish or maintain regulations on the ownership of small arms and light weapons or their transfer to non-state actors. It may be noted that a protocol to the 2000 United Nations Convention against Transnational Organized Crime would obligate governments to adopt legislative measures criminalizing the illicit manufacturing and trafficking of firearms. The protocol has not yet received the required number of ratifications to become effective.

Overall, the postwar role of the United Nations has been restricted to that of an advocate of multilateral solutions to disarmament issues. The organization has also usefully served as a multilateral arena for the development of legal normative standards. But unilateralism and bilateralism have prevailed, with a small group of powerful states shaping and determining the outcome of international negotiations while nonstate actors and lesser powers remained on the sidelines flouting multilateral channels. The structural defects of the nonproliferation nuclear regime underline the tensions and dilemmas that severely constrain the United Nations. The NPT rested on a bargain between nuclear and nonnuclear states. The latter accepted the obligation to subject their peaceful nuclear programs to safeguards and inspections by the International Atomic Energy Agency (IAEA). In exchange, the former agreed not to transfer nuclear weapons to any nonnuclear weapons states or to assist them in manufacturing and acquiring such weapons. More importantly, this understanding enjoined nuclear powers to end their arms race at "an early date." This pledge has remained unfulfilled, thus generating, heightening, and perpetuating walls of distrust against which international responses to threats—"new" and otherwise—have foundered. World military expenditures keep rising, amounting now to some $750 billion every year and representing 2.5 percent of the world's gross domestic product. The legal trade in armaments is worth $50 billion annually and vast stocks of small arms and light weapons fall into illicit channels that sustain guerilla armies, networks of terrorists, and drug traffickers.

THE "OTHER" UNITED NATIONS: DEVELOPMENT AND GLOBAL CONFERENCES

No less than 5 of the United Nations Charter's 18 chapters deal with peace and security issues, underlining the priority given to them by its drafters. In contrast, only one article, Article 55, assigns to the United Nations the task of promoting "higher standards of living," "full employment," and "conditions of economic and social progress." In spite of this thin constitutional basis, the United Nations' economic and social activities did expand rapidly throughout the organization's first three decades of existence. Beginning with the creation of the United Nations Children's Fund (UNICEF) in 1946, numerous programs and agencies thus came into existence, such as the United Nations Development Program (UNDP), the World Food Programme (WFP) and the United Nations Conference on Trade and Development (UNCTAD). This pattern of institutional growth slowly came to an end in the 1970s as the political focus moved to "streamlining," "rationalizing," and "consolidating" an organization that, in the eyes of its main stakeholders, had grown out of control. In the past 20 years, only a handful of new institutions have come into existence: the Global Environmental Facility (GEF), the Commission for Sustainable Development (CSD), the Permanent Forum for Indigenous Peoples, and the Forum on Forests.

In any event and against all expectations, some 60-odd years after its establishment, development has become one of the fundamental tasks of the United Nations. Thirty percent of the United Nations' regular budget is channeled into development activities (three times as much as its peace and security budget if peacekeeping operations, which are funded separately, are excluded). More than one-third of the posts of the secretariat are earmarked for international and regional cooperation for development, human rights, and humanitarian affairs.

The current work of the United Nations development system draws from and vastly expands the modest activities of the League of Nations, which had primarily been concerned with health, slavery, drug trafficking, and labor issues. Like its predecessor organization, but on a much larger scale, the United Nations compiles and standardizes statistical data. *The Statistical Yearbook*, the *Demographic Yearbook*, and the *International Trade Statistics Yearbook* are all examples of this outstanding and by and large uncontroversial work. The United Nations also produces numerous policy-oriented studies and reports, covering a wide range of economic and social issues of global concern: national accounts, tax and accounting, finance and investment, natural resources, agriculture, industry, employment and labor markets, the environment, human settlement, transnational corporations, transportation, refugees and displaced persons, public health, social statistics, gender issues, and children. These studies are used for monitoring and early warning purposes and provide guidance to the deliberations of intergovernmental bodies. Some of them have made important contributions to international discussions on the international economy. The annual *World Economic Survey*, which began publication in the immediate postwar years was for a long time the only publication providing an overview of the global economy. The *Human Development Report* (HDR) of the United Nations Development Program (UNDP), launched in 1990, has redefined the concept of development and provided alternative policy recommendations that changed prevailing economic orthodoxies.

Closely related are the activities carried out primarily by the United Nations specialized agencies. There are currently 16 agencies such as the United Nations Education, Scientific, and Cultural Organization (UNESCO), the World Health Organization (WHO), the International Labour Organization (ILO), the Food and Agricultural Organization (FAO), the United Nations Industrial Development Organization (UNIDO), the World Meteorological Organization (WMO), and the International Fund for Agricultural Development (IFAD). Their primary function is to develop international rules governing international commercial, telecommunications, and transportation through the standardization of technologies and procedures, international laws governing commercial transactions, and intellectual property rights to cite only a few instances. This "soft infrastructure" of the United Nations has steadily expanded and become an indispensable underpinning of the functioning of the global economy.

These multifaceted tasks are carried out under the authority of the General Assembly. The so-called funds (i.e., the United Nations Development Program [UNDP], the United Nations Children's Fund [UNICEF], the United Nations Fund for Population Activities [UNFPA], and the World Food Programme [WFP]) and programs (the United Nations Conference on Trade and Development [UNCTAD], the

United Nations Environment Programme [UNEP], the United Nations Center for Human Settlements [Habitat], and the United Nations High Commissioner for Refugees [UNHCR]) report to the General Assembly. Other entities concerned with research and training and enjoying a significant degree of autonomy, such as the United Nations University (UNU) and the United Nations Institute for Disarmament Research (UNIDIR) likewise report to the assembly.

Under the authority of the General Assembly, the ECOSOC acts as a forum for the discussion of economic and social issues. The council is responsible for the coordination of all UN economic, social, and humanitarian activities. It also oversees the governance of the UN's operational activities and approves the work of its "functional commissions" (social development, human rights, narcotic drugs, crime prevention and criminal justice, women, population, statistics and sustainable development) and of five regional commissions (in Latin America and the Caribbean, Europe, Asia and the Pacific, Africa, and Western Asia). Formally, the specialized agencies report to ECOSOC. In practice, they are largely autonomous, as they have their own separate constitutions, governing bodies, and budgets. The Bretton Woods institutions, namely the World Bank (WB), the IMF and their affiliates; the International Development Association (IDA); and the International Finance Corporation (IFC) for all intents and purposes operate independently. The World Trade Organization (WTO) is not a United Nations organization but maintains functional ties with ECOSOC.

Two major factors account for the vast expansion of UN development activities. One, the political dynamics of East-West conflict gave considerable leverage to developing countries as both the United States and the Soviet Union wooed international public opinion and sought to win their support. The 1948 Expanded Programme of Technical Assistance, which propelled the United Nations in the field of technical assistance, was an offshoot of an American initiative primarily designed to "encourage the development of democratic institutions and respect for human rights in a world menaced by totalitarianism." The establishment of the International Finance Corporation in 1956 to promote private investment in developing countries, the International Development Association in 1960 to make soft loans to developing countries, and the UN Special Fund in 1957, to undertake preinvestment feasibility studies all arose from United States-led proposals designed to placate the Soviet-supported southern drive for a capital development fund controlled by the United Nations.

Second, the accelerating process of decolonization in the late 1950s and early 1960s led to the mass entry of Third World countries into the United Nations. Using their voting power, developing countries relentlessly pressed for a "New Deal," thus radically transforming the policy agenda and priorities of the United Nations. The creation of the United Nations Conference on Trade and Development in 1964 with the sweeping mandate to "provide by means of international cooperation, appropriate solutions to the problems of world trade in the interests of all peoples, and particularly to the urgent trade and development problems of the developing countries," was an important turning point in this process. Ten years later, developing countries again overrode U.S. and European opposition by mobilizing a numerical majority in the assembly inviting the international community to embrace a New International Economic Order (NIEO) and a Charter of Economic Rights and Duties of States, two "affirmative action" resolutions designed to facilitate their integration in the world economy.

These, however, were Pyrrhic victories. Repeated majority votes never overcame the deep-seated resistance of industrial countries. With the demise of the Cold War, Southern countries also lost a key resource for power and influence, but it should be understood that ever since the Dumbarton Oaks and San Francisco conferences, North and South have been feuding with one another over the meaning of development, ways and means to achieve "conditions of economic and social progress," and the United Nations' role therein. Industrial countries, and the United States in particular, never assigned more than limited functions to the United Nations. From their perspective, the United Nations remained a voluntary association of sovereign states with no supranational binding legislative functions. At best, it was a "center for the harmonization of national policies," a "catalyst," a "facilitator." The governance of cooperation for economic and social development and the management of the world economy properly belonged to the Bretton Woods institutions and other non-UN institutions such as the Group of Eight and the Organization for Economic Cooperation and Development (OECD).

Conversely, the main concern of developing countries was the elimination of the structural problems—internal and international—that hampered their drive toward modernization, industrialization, or, in today's parlance, "sustainable development." Development could not be left to the vagaries of international financial, monetary, and commercial markets and the state had an essential role to play in the definition of the international development agenda. International regulatory mechanisms and agencies should be established to ensure that markets operated in a manner consistent with and supportive of national development efforts. Against this background, the United Nations undoubtedly stood for a compact among sovereign and equal states but, from a Southern perspective, the General Assembly was the keystone of the governance architecture of the world economy and development cooperation and should enjoy authoritative decision-making powers, especially over the Bretton Woods institutions.

In this polarized setting, long-lasting agreement has proved elusive. Parliamentary victories by one side have been matched by the determined efforts of the other to undo the accords reached on paper. Over time, the result has been a seesaw process of legitimization and delegitimization of competing and, by and large, mutually exclusive development concepts and policy practices.

In the mid-1970s, the United States led the counterattack against the "tyranny of the majority" through the selective withholding of its assessed contributions. Within a few years' time, the Third World coalition was tamed. Crushed by the weight of its debt crisis, the Third World collapsed as an organized political force. Its main institutions — the Group of Seventy-Seven and the NAM — sank into internal squabbling and recriminations. At the same time, the demise of the Soviet Union discredited the prevailing Keynesian model of development and the notion of state interventionism in national and international markets.

Today, the United Nations' advocacy of "statist theories" is a memory of the past. Its administrative, budgetary, and institutional growth has come to a standstill. Governments in the South have, under duress, restructured their public sector, opened their economies, and shifted to macroeconomic stabilization policies. A new development paradigm has taken hold of the UN agenda. Now the UN bills itself as the keystone of "coalitions of change" as it seeks new "partnerships" and "new structures of cooperation" with nongovernmental organizations (NGOs) and private business organizations in support of a development process deemed to be governed primarily by market forces. The North-South split no longer occupies center stage, but it continues to simmer below the seeming tranquility of UN proceedings. This has been particularly true in regard to the global conferences sponsored by the UN since the early 1990s.

Global conferences are a long-standing practice of multilateral diplomacy but their number and frequency immeasurably expanded with the establishment of the UN. Designed to address specific global development issues, UN global conferences have dealt with virtually all developmental issues: international trade, money and finance, employment, energy, water, technical cooperation among developing countries, health, agrarian reform, science and technology, desertification, aging, gender, human rights, population, food, human settlement.

Cast against the background of the widening social and economic inequalities between North and South arising from the unrelenting pace of globalization, UN global conferences have provided the setting for continuing polarized debates on the long standing issues of money, finance, debt, and trade that continue to pit North against South. They have also revealed new fault lines on relatively novel issues like intellectual property rights and trade, the "digital divide" in information technology, and the exploitation of the global commons. UN global conferences have thus predictably elicited diametrically opposed assessments. Western governments increasingly view them as lavish and inefficient talk shows, while Southern countries see them as useful agenda-building opportunities. Although "conference fatigue" prevails nowadays, on balance, UN global conferences have nevertheless served useful purposes.

In a globalizing, shrinking, and interdependent world, they have provided the setting for the production and exchange of information. As incubators of ideas, they have occasionally contributed to paradigmatic changes in development thinking and to the formation of an international consensus over global issues. The importance now given to gender equality, the notion that development is a holistic process to be tackled in an integrated manner, and the concept of sustainability are ideas that germinated, crystallized, and won acceptance in UN global conferences. The informal transnational "networks of concern" linked to one another through the Internet that have emerged in the wake of UN global conferences have played a major role in this process. Last but by no means least, global conferences have provided new space for the involvement of civil society in multilateral diplomacy, either through the inclusion of NGOs in national delegations or their participation in parallel side events and forums. To a certain extent, UN global conferences have thus legitimized a role for civil society in the formation of national and international policies.

Capacity Development

One of the most prominent and concrete manifestations of the United Nations' work in development is the technical assistance activities that it carries out in developing countries. Flows of resources allocated to such "operational activities" amounted to more than $2 billion in 1979 and reached $6 billion in 1992. The total value of contributions received by the United Nations system for development cooperation activities exceeded $10 billion in 2003 spread over 150 recipient countries. For the period between 1993 and 2003, expenditures of the United Nations' system for operational activities sourced from grants and concessional loans totaled about $68 billion.

Once again, the drafters of the United Nations Charter certainly never foresaw let alone planned such large-scale activities. The involvement of the UN in technical cooperation goes back to a first mission authorized in a little-noted 1947 resolution of the ECOSOC, and in 1948, the assembly budgeted a modest sum of $288,000 for technical assistance. Great-power Cold War rivalries again fed the growth of the system until it gained a momentum of its own with the ascendancy of the concept of "human security." In 1949 the assembly endorsed an American proposal to create "an expanded program of technical assistance for economic development for under-developed countries" through the United Nations and its specialized agencies. The operational activities of the UN were further expanded with the establishment in 1958 of a Special Fund "to provide systematic and sustained assistance in fields essential to the integrated technical, economic and social development of the less developed countries." The two institutions were merged in 1965 into a single agency, the United Nations Development Program (UNDP), in order to resolve problems of coordination and eliminate the scrambling for technical-assistance funds among implementing UN agencies in the field and at headquarters.

The meaning of *technical assistance* has considerably changed over time. Initially, the term meant the provision of expert advice and training, the pooling of particular "know-how" developed in individual countries, and the application of that know-how to the problems of underdeveloped countries. With the establishment of the Special Fund, technical assistance also began to encompass preinvestment activities. These services were undertaken at the request of governments and were entirely funded by voluntary contributions. More encompassing conceptions of development have since led to a redefinition of the purposes and modalities of technical assistance, which was rechristened "capacity building" in the early 1990s. In essence, capacity building is human resource development and institution building with particular reference to the public sector, it being understood that UN operational activities should lead to a pattern of "locally owned" and sustainable development. The growing involvement of private enterprise and civil society organizations in the development process has further broadened the idea of organizational engineering beyond the formal functions of public sector organizations. UN parlance has now embraced the notion of "capacity development" to draw attention to the need to design UN assistance in such a way as to strengthen "capacities in the society as a whole." UNDP capacity development work thus focuses on poverty eradication, gender, the environment, and good governance in postconflict rehabilitation and reconstruction situations. Typical UNDP projects seek to strengthen political institutions and local civil society organizations, reconstruct public services, and organize consultative forums for community-based organizations.

The planning, programming, and implementation of these multifaceted operational activities have raised thorny questions of coordination that have never been satisfactorily resolved. In theory, the coordination of UN operational activities at the country level is the responsibility of a "resident coordinator" who is also the UNDP representative. In this capacity and in consultation with the recipient government, donor countries, and UN agencies concerned, one of the main tasks of the UN resident coordinator, on behalf of the United Nations, is to assess a country's development needs, help identify operational projects, and facilitate their elaboration and implementation. In many emergency situations, the UNDP representative also acts as humanitarian coordinator for the UN system.

The system has built-in structural and functional weaknesses. UN agencies are reluctant to yield to the authority of a single UN official and frequently initiate and develop projects directly with governmental authorities. In this competitive environment, UNDP officials are caught in conflicting roles as defenders of their own agency and representatives of the UN system. In humanitarian emergencies, NGOs pursue their own agenda and priorities oblivious of the need to act in tandem with other actors. At the intergovernmental level, the bilateral interests of donor countries clash with those of recipient countries, thus contributing to a political stalemate that stymies meaningful reform. By and large, a genuine culture of cooperation among UN entities is still missing. Joint programming remains more an aspiration than a reality. At the same time, projects running on separate tracks tend to proliferate, drawing strength less on objective development needs than on the influence of ad hoc coalitions of political forces and the absence of effective oversight political mechanisms. Under these circumstances, UNDP has been most successful in its capacity development work in situations where aid donors, international financial institutions, and UN agencies opted to remain on the sidelines and were inclined to defer to UNDP expertise and networks. In many ways, this is consistent with the catalytic preinvestment function originally assigned to UNDP. In more competitive conditions, the success of UNDP as a coordinating agency ultimately depends on the diplomatic and professional skills of the resident coordinator.

Disaster Relief and Humanitarianism

Another instance of the UN presence in the field and equally ignored by the charter is the UN's role in the provision and coordination of worldwide disaster relief. The scope and range of UN humanitarian activities has truly become impressive in its own right. Since 1991, the organization has raised close to $30 billion in voluntary contributions, and each year it assists scores of countries affected by natural and human-made disasters. The global reach of the UN humanitarian enterprise can be further highlighted by its response to the catastrophic 26 December 2004 tsunami disaster, which killed more than 200,000 people, injured half a million others, and left up to 5 million people in need of basic services in a dozen countries. Within six weeks after the disaster, the United Nations had raised $775 million for reconstruction efforts while coordinating the distribution of food to 1.2 million and supplying clean drinking water to 500,000 individuals.

As is the case for its other activities, the involvement of the United Nations in humanitarian relief has been gradual and began modestly with the creation of the International Refugee Organization and UNICEF to address the mass social disruptions, famine, and resulting refugee flows brought about by World War II. As postwar reconstruction efforts in Europe wound up, the growing presence of developing countries in the United Nations progressively led to a refocusing of the relief work of the United Nations on countries of the Southern Hemisphere. A succession of natural disasters in the 1960s and early 1970s focused attention on the need to achieve greater coordination among UN agencies, member states, and the Red Cross in the provision of humanitarian assistance and, for that purpose, in 1972, the General Assembly created the United Nations Disaster Relief Organization (UNDRO). In 1991, the assembly strengthened the humanitarian mandate of the organization by setting up the Department of Humanitarian Affairs, the precursor of today's Office for the Coordination of Humanitarian Affairs (OCHA), the agency at the forefront of the UN's humanitarian relief efforts.

While remarkable, the institutional growth of the UN humanitarian system has been fraught with political tensions that pitted advocates of a greater UN role against those who adhered to a strict interpretation of the norm of sovereignty and wished to limit the activities of the organization. These contradictory pushes and pulls still shape and constrain the humanitarian capacity of the United Nations, especially in the typical post–Cold War internal conflicts that it has been drawn into. But as has happened time and again in the past, geo-political factors prevailed and provided the immediate impetus for the most dramatic changes to the UN humanitarian assistance regime. With the end of the Cold War, the UN has been given a newfound authority to intervene in crisis situations. The 1991 resolution of the Security Council calling for the creation of safe havens for Kurdish refugees stranded in the highlands of the Iraqi-Turk border established the radical precedent that military force could sanction humanitarian relief operations without the recipient country's consent. Subsequent UN interventions in Bosnia (1991), Somalia (1992), and Haiti (1993–1994) further highlighted the inclination of member states to allow the UN to intervene in civil wars for the sake of humanitarian causes. The defenders of the norm of sovereignty were perhaps even more baffled by the 1999 NATO intervention in Kosovo, which was initiated without UN sanction.

Developing countries have been particularly apprehensive about these trends. For them, the absence of agreed-upon criteria to trigger a humanitarian intervention under UN auspices has led to suspicions that man-made or natural disasters can be used as pretexts for intrusions in their internal affairs. Donor states' talk of sovereignty as a "responsibility" rather than a state right, their emphasis on "effectiveness," "quality," and "accountability" and the glaring fact that the same Western governments provide the bulk of humanitarian funding give further credence to the widespread belief that the humanitarian enterprise is primarily a Western undertaking designed to promote its political, economic, and cultural agenda. Still another concern of developing countries is that humanitarian aid is doled out haphazardly. Global levels of funding fluctuate widely from one year to the next compounding difficulties arising from unmet financial requirements or late funding. In addition, all too often, humanitarian aid is targeted to a few high-profile cases favored by donor countries, thus leading to the emergence of "forgotten tragedies" involving countries—primarily African—with no perceived strategic value.

Deep-seated North-South cleavages thus cast a long shadow over the political legitimacy, governance, and priorities of humanitarianism through the United Nations. The changing nature of humanitarianism since the demise of the Cold War has undoubtedly exacerbated that debate. The increasing number of interventions in the post–Cold War years, described by some as "humanitarian" operations, by others as smokescreens for the pursuit of strategic, political, and military objectives, has exacerbated the political debate and called in question the age-old humanitarian principles of independence, impartiality, and neutrality. In both Afghanistan and Iraq, these sacrosanct notions have crumbled under the weight of the realities of a Manichean struggle against global terrorism. UN access to populations in need has been subordinated to the exigencies of the military and security situation. And in the final analysis, the political tiptoeing of UN agencies did not forestall the perception that their presence was an act of partisanship, as evidenced by the 2003 lethal attacks on the Red Cross and United Nations in Baghdad.

The embedding of humanitarianism in UN peacekeeping operations since the 1990s also poses new conceptual challenges without clear-cut political and operational solutions. The rationale behind this trend is the recognition that poverty and more specifically "horizontal inequalities" are major causes of humanitarian crises and that their prevention must rest on development policies linking long-term economic, social, and political measures to short-term relief. To cast the humanitarian effort within a broader developmental picture, however, blurs the traditional distinction between development and humanitarian aid. It also strips the notion of humanitarianism of its functional specificity. Internal crises have indeed become "complex," so much so as to prompt practitioners to bemoan that it is now difficult "to distinguish the ambulance from the combatants soup truck, the military from the civilians, humanitarian from development assistance, serious from frivolous undertakings, cluster bombs from food drops, solidarity from neutrality."

Humanitarian assistance and development may very well dovetail one another. But then a question arises. Has the international community the willingness to supplement its humanitarian efforts with longer-term reconstruction measures that will strengthen the capacity of war-torn countries to forestall possible future societal breakdowns? Neither the "pick and choose" pattern that appears to prevail in the humanitarian landscape nor the fact that, at least until recently, the overall increase in humanitarian aid has taken place largely at the expense of development funding, offer grounds for optimism. The UN humanitarian enterprise has aptly been compared to a poorly patched up assembly line. Yet, however imperfect the system may be, the "anarchy of altruism" and the normative appeals of the United Nations have kept the world's attention on many humanitarian tragedies that governments might have otherwise preferred to let go unnoticed. That system, perfectible in terms of its funding, staffing, and institutional capacity, meets one litmus test that justifies its continuing existence: it does save lives.

Human Rights

As pointed out earlier, the drafters of the United Nations Charter considered the denial of human rights if not a root cause of many international conflicts, at least a major trigger of their outbreak. For that reason, they empowered the organization to serve as an instrument of international cooperation for "promoting and encouraging respect for human rights and for fundamental freedoms for all without distinction as to race, sex, language, or religion." It is doubtful, however, that they ever entertained the idea of allowing the United Nations to cross the "domestic jurisdiction" line and enable it to scrutinize, censure, condemn, and legislate the manner in which states treat their citizens. Yet, against all expectations, and again as a result of the pushes and pulls of the political process, over the years, the United Nations has clearly broadened its mandate from the sheer "promotion" of human rights to practices far more intrusive of the norm of sovereignty than had been expected.

The process started innocuously with the establishment of the Commission for Human Rights by ECOSOC in 1946. In its early years, the commission focused primarily on the elaboration of human rights standards. Thus, in December 1948, it completed and adopted the Universal Declaration of Human Rights, which urged member states to promote human, civil, economic, and social rights "as a common standard of achievement for all peoples and all nations." Technically speaking, the declaration is only a recommendation of the assembly. As such, it is not a legally binding document. In the following years, the commission then endeavored to turn the declaration's broad normative injunctions into treaty obligations. This work came to fruition in 1966 when, as part of a grand bargain between East and West, the commission approved two covenants on civil and political rights and economic, social, and cultural rights respectively. These covenants took effect ten years later. Together with the Universal Declaration, they constitute what is commonly known in the international human rights community as the International Bill of Human Rights.

Other conventions regarding particular aspects (torture, racial discrimination, women, children, and migrant workers rights) have since emerged from the work of the commission. They all constitute the core legal instruments of United Nations human rights system. The implementation of each of these conventions is monitored by committees of independent experts—the so-called "treaty bodies"—who review measures taken by state parties to give effect to their obligations and may recommend remedial policy measures. A particularly striking innovation is that a number of these treaty bodies set forth procedures for bringing complaints of violations of human rights before them through individual "communications," state-to-state complaints, or inquiries.

Outside the treaty body system, there are other procedures for complaints, which first arose from the demands of developing countries in the mid-1960s to set up tighter mechanisms of international accountability for human rights violations in European colonies and the racist regimes of southern Africa. These demands resulted in the creation in 1970 of mechanisms enabling the commission to investigate complaints that "appear to reveal a consistent pattern of gross and reliably attested violations of human rights," the so-called "1503 procedure," so named after the number of the resolution of the ECOSOC establishing it. Spurred by continuing human rights abuses and violations by military regimes in Latin America in the 1980s, the commission expanded the scope of its human rights instruments with the creation of "special procedures," a technique entailing the appointment of United Nations officials to examine allegations of human rights violations in specific country situations or broad categories of human rights. Variously known as "special rapporteurs," "special representatives," or "independent experts," these experts may receive information provided by individuals and civil society organizations, carry out fact-finding country visits, receive complaints about human rights violations, intervene with governments on victims' behalf, and recommend remedial programs and policies. The human rights practices of such countries as Afghanistan, Iran, the former Yugoslavia, Myanmar, Cambodia, Equatorial Guinea, Somalia, Sudan, Congo, Burundi, Haiti, and Rwanda have thus come under international scrutiny. A host of issues has also been brought to the attention of the international community including police brutality, enforced disappearances, extra-judicial summary executions, violence against women, persecution of ethnic minorities, the role of nonstate actors in human rights violations, the predicament of internally displaced persons and children in armed conflicts, the links between extreme poverty and respect for the right to education, the rights of migrants, the right to adequate housing, the right to food, and the impact of structural adjustment policies and foreign debt on the enjoyment of individual rights.

The Office of the High Commissioner for Human Rights, a post created by the General Assembly in 1993 and long sought after by civil society organizations and a number of key states, crowns this remarkable institutional edifice. The High Commissioner is "the principal United Nations official responsible for United Nations human rights activities" and acts "under the direction and authority of the secretary-general." Broadly speaking, its mandate is to promote and protect the enjoyment and full realization of all civil, political, economic, social, and cultural human rights established by the Charter of the United Nations and international human rights instruments. This includes the prevention of human rights violations, securing respect for human rights, and encouraging international cooperation for human rights. Since its creation, the office has quietly developed activities at the country level through stand-alone offices established on the basis of agreements with the government concerned, technical cooperation projects, regional offices located in the Regional Economic Commissions, and human rights advisers posted in UN peacekeeping missions authorized by the United Nations Security Council or the General Assembly.

The present United Nations human rights system, with its extensive body of international human rights standards and wide range of mechanisms, represents a remarkable achievement of the past 60 years that stands in stark contrast with the general indifference that met violations of human rights in the interwar period. The procedures developed over time through the United Nations have unquestionably increased general awareness of human rights issues. They have mobilized civil society organizations and focused public opinion on violations at least in a few countries and on a few types of pervasive and reprehensible types of violations such as torture and enforced disappearances. All UN peacekeeping operations now have a human rights "component," a pragmatic acknowledgment that the denial of human rights is an early sign and manifestation of brewing peace and security troubles.

During the 1990s, international criminal justice mechanisms were created to hold perpetrators of war crimes and crimes against humanity accountable. Prodded by a number of governments and citizens groups, the Security Council established in 1993 and 1994 respectively, two ad hoc international criminal tribunals to try perpetrators of grievous violations of international humanitarian law in the civil wars in the former Yugoslavia and Rwanda. Special tribunals have also been set up to deal with crimes committed in Sierra Leone and Cambodia. These special tribunals, which have limited jurisdictions and will be disbanded when they complete their work, gave impetus to the formation of the International Criminal Court (ICC), a permanent international court charged with prosecuting war crimes, crimes against humanity, and genocide, which began operations in 2002.

In spite of these major innovations, the burgeoning field of human rights remains constrained by serious structural weaknesses and is clouded by political controversies. The existence, validity, and content of human rights continue to be the subjects of divisive debate. The view that human rights are "inalienable" and belong to all humans simply because they are "human" is by no means universally shared. Some states invoke the notion of "cultural relativism," arguing, for example, that "equality" among men and women in or out of wedlock is a notion alien to their cultures. Others go a step further taking the position that international human rights are a form of cultural imperialism dictated by powerful countries on weaker ones. Which rights should be viewed as fundamental human rights: Civil and political rights? Economic, social, and cultural rights? Or, alternatively or concurrently, the rights of groups of individuals sharing some common characteristics, be it poverty and lack of development, food insecurity, or access to health services? Should all human rights be considered equal and "indivisible," or is there a hierarchy among them? What kind of obligations does the enjoyment of human rights place on national governments and the international community? Have national governments a "responsibility to protect" their citizens? And, if they fail to do so, has the international community a "duty" to intervene?

Human rights issues indeed pose troubling and unresolved political questions. In a state-based international society, the lack of a political consensus among states over these unresolved issues constitutes the root cause of the United Nation's mixed record in the promotion and protection of international human rights. Willy-nilly, the UN human rights machinery and operation still remains state-driven and controlled. Many member states of the United Nations with questionable if not appalling human rights records have escaped and continue to escape serious international scrutiny. The reporting procedures called for under the treaty bodies' conventions are often circumvented or altogether ignored and flaunted by state parties. The 1503 procedure involves stringent criteria of admissibility and deals only with situations—not particular violations—of gross and systematic violations. The resources made available to the United Nations for human rights activities are ridiculously small. To implement its immense mandate, the Office of the High Commissioner for Human Rights receives only 3 percent ($30 million) from the UN regular budget, which it must supplement by repeated appeals for voluntary contributions. The developing international criminal justice system has been hampered by a lack of resources, the insistence of the Security Council that the ad hoc tribunals complete their tasks by a set date and the reluctance of states where the crimes occurred to cooperate in the arrest and prosecution of key suspects. The hostility of the United States poses a major challenge to the effectiveness and existence of the ICC itself.

Not surprisingly, caught in the middle of these political cross currents, the functioning of the Commission for Human Rights—in spite of its major accomplishments—has been the target of widespread and rising criticism. For widely disparate but ironically converging political reasons, the Commission has been accused of "politicization," "double standards," low credibility, and lack of professionalism. Its resolutions have not infrequently been watered down to the point of uselessness for the sake of achieving an elusive consensus among states as different in their human rights record and policies as the United States, China, Pakistan, and India. The Commission has also been berated for including in its membership states that are viewed by others as human rights abusers. In the spring of 2005, the assembly established a Human Rights Council replacing the commission. The hope is that the new council will act with "universality, impartiality, objectivity, and non-selectivity," and that its work will enhance human rights protection under the aegis of the United Nations.

Will the council have the capacity to hold all member states to their human rights obligations fairly and equally, without selectivity or double standards? Will its practice lead to a more "effective" international human rights regime? On all such questions, the jury is still out because the fact of the matter remains that adherence to and compliance by governments with international human rights standards ultimately rest on their consent. The norm of sovereignty still prevails over the norm of accountability and the UN may have a major forum for the development of international human rights standards and norms but it has not been allowed to venture into the areas of implementation and enforcement beyond naming and shaming. Sixty years ago, human rights were almost universally viewed as the exclusive preserve of the state. This is no longer true, especially when the unrelenting involvement of NGOs is factored into the political equation. But moving beyond the stage of a declaratory regime and the making of international conventions remains a hotly contested objective.

THE QUESTION OF "REFORM"

As should now be obvious, the United Nations has shown a remarkable capacity for change and adaptation in responding to major changes in the structure and operation of its international environment. In fact, it is no exaggeration to state that from its very inception the United Nations can be said to have been in a state of "permanent revolution." To speak of UN "reform" is therefore at best a misnomer, at worst a very misleading call for action.

Once or twice each decade, roughly every eight years—1953–1956, 1964–1966, 1974–1977, 1985–1986, and 1992–1997—member states embark on a feverish search for "reforms" that, cumulatively, either cancel each other out or add up to little more than modest incremental changes. For instance, in 1975–1977, pressured by developing countries, the UN undertook a major overhaul of its economic and social sectors. Throughout the next decade, developed countries counterattacked and, in the name of "efficiency" and "effectiveness," dismantled most of the gains previously achieved by Southern countries. Prodded by Northern countries, Secretary-General Boutros Boutros-Ghali made further structural and functional changes within the secretariat, streamlining its security and developmental institutions. Most of his own proposals in the fields of peace and security, development, and democratization, however, fell on deaf ears. His successor, Kofi Annan, has in turn initiated no less than three rounds of further reforms. His latest proposals not only sought to introduce additional administrative improvements in the operation of the secretariat but also proposed a common definition of terrorism and criteria for legitimate collective interventions for humanitarian purposes. This ambitious reform agenda has only yielded incremental changes.

The limited scope of change achieved through this steady stream of formal reform efforts is attributable to the conflicting views among member states of the role and priority tasks that they assign the United Nations. There is, in effect, very little clarity, let alone consensus, about what reform means in practical and operational terms among member states, and the fact that everyone uses the same language while assigning different meanings to seemingly identical concepts tends to further obscure and muddle the nature of the political debate.

The North-South split, which has in so many ways and for so long shaped the activities of the organization, has proved to be a defining source of durable divisions and unending power struggles. Southern countries wish to have a more "democratic" United Nations playing a greater role in world affairs. They want to see greater normative and operational authority granted to the General Assembly, especially in the fields of international trade, finance, and monetary- and other development-related matters, which, for them, should be the paramount priorities of the organization. Strengthening the United Nations, however, does not extend to empowering the organization to intervene in countries that do not protect their citizens from egregious violations of human rights. On these issues, the norms of state sovereignty and nonintervention remain paramount and rule out the notion that national governments should be accountable to the international community in cases of massive violations of human rights.

Northern countries and the United States in particular would like to have more power vested in the Security Council, which they control through their veto power, rather than in the General Assembly, where they can be outvoted by a majority of its members. The priorities they assign to the United Nations clash with those of developing nations. These include waging war against terrorism and emerging nonstate threats and dealing with "trans-sovereign" issues such as transnational crime and corruption (narcotic trafficking, trafficking in persons, small arms, money laundering), HIV/AIDS, preventing the proliferation of weapons of mass destruction, providing humanitarian assistance, and promoting respect for universal civil and political rights. For most Northern countries, the UN should adopt policies encouraging the development of market economies, promote privatization, and cease to advocate any "redistributive" Keynesian developmental policies as championed by Southern countries.

Looming large over all discussions on UN reform are the perennial questions related to the membership of the Security Council. Everyone agrees that the council is an outmoded vestige of a now defunct world order. But there is considerable discord as to exactly what kind of reform is necessary to bring it in line with the power realities of the 21st century. Should more states—rising powers like India, Nigeria, Japan, Germany—be granted permanent membership with a veto power? Should the move be accompanied by the abolition of the U.K. and

French seats, with the European Union as a bloc taking over? Should the permanent members of the council be stripped of their veto power? For close to two decades these questions have been debated without tangible progress.

Finally, there is the recurring practical organizational and institutional issue of "coordination." As noted earlier, the drafters of the charter were aware of the linkages between peace and security, human rights and development. Their institutional prescriptions though were baffling because they parceled out sectoral functions to separate and distinct agencies that were virtually sovereign in their own respective areas of competence. In effect, they constructed a decentralized system of fragmented institutions that often stood in the way of an integrated approach to multisectoral issues. From its very inception, the United Nations has thus had to come to grips with the thorny issues of "coordination" in order to avoid overlap and redundancies in its work. In recent years, changes in conceptual thinking about the nature of global threats and development have further heightened the need for more effective coordination. The developing norm of human security is still contested in some quarters but it does underline the need to think in a holistic manner and to develop and implement integrated and comprehensive policies bringing together the work of separate agencies under a common roof and toward a common objective. There is no dearth of blueprints of structures and institutions deemed to enable the United Nations to respond to traditional and nontraditional threats to security in a correspondingly "integrated" and "holistic" approach. Since the mid-1980s, for example, proposals have been made to create a "Security Economic Council." But none of these proposals has found sufficient political support.

Outside of the United Nations, there are far more radical proposals emanating from civil organizations. Most of them aim at making the United Nations truly "democratic" in line with the opening words of the Charter "We the Peoples . . ." These plans would make population the basis for representation at the United Nations, abolish the veto in the Security Council, and grant legislative, taxing powers to the United Nations over governments and their citizens. Such ideas have been around for a long time and can be traced back to the years of the League of Nations. They remain thought-provoking but politically unfeasible speculations.

Should one then conclude that "plus ça change . . . plus c'est la même chose"? Such cynicism may not be altogether warranted. Behind the brouhaha and hubris of the formal process of "reform" and the public posturing of member states, there are unmistakable signs that not all roads to reform need to take the official path of intergovernmental processes and decisions, let alone a charter amendment. The Charter of the United Nations itself has proved to be sufficiently elastic and malleable to allow for remarkable changes in the functions of the organization within an admittedly unchanged set of institutions. These functional changes have come about through the praxis of institutions in an incremental and disjointed manner. As pointed out, UN peacekeeping operations started without much fanfare and have over time evolved into a major activity of the organization. The work of the United Nations in development, humanitarian assistance, and capacity building has grown out of a similar process of informal accretions.

Viewed from this vantage point, the United Nations has shown a remarkable degree of responsiveness and adaptability to the changing needs of its constituencies. And there are many signs that this model of change is still unfolding through the political process. The Security Council unquestionably remains a profoundly undemocratic institution. There may be legitimate grounds for calling into question the notion that increasing its membership for the sake of making it more "representative" will necessarily make it more "effective" in dealing with security threats. In the meantime, the council has developed unheralded informal consultative arrangements allowing representatives of nonmembers of the council and civil society organizations to be heard by the council on issues placed on its agenda. At the 1992 summit meeting of the Security Council, it was recognized that "nonmilitary sources of instability in the economic, social, humanitarian, and ecological fields have become threats to the peace and security." Since then, it has not been uncommon for the council to devote several sessions to thematic discussions of crosscutting issues that it needs to take account of in its consideration of individual country cases. In reviewing such questions as HIV/AIDS, terrorism, small arms trafficking, the rule of law in postconflict national reconciliation processes, women and peace and security, children in armed conflicts, the protection of civilians in armed conflicts, and postconflict peace building as they relate to the maintenance of international peace and security, the council has increasingly recognized that conflict settlement has broad multifaceted implications that need to be translated into a "coherent and integrated mix of peace-building and peacekeeping activities, including political, civilian, humanitarian, and development activities."

The modestly expanding institutionalization of civil society organizations in the work of United Nations intergovernmental bodies further illustrates the need to look at informal rather than formal processes of change. The presence of NGOs in international debates and proceedings has become ubiquitous, as evidenced by their involvement in United Nations global conferences. Their number has grown exponentially worldwide. Cross-border networks and coalitions of civil society organizations have spearheaded efforts to stop the trade in natural resources that perpetuate internal conflicts, campaigned in support of debt alleviation measures for the poorest among developing countries, and pressured governments to protect human rights standards. NGOs have also become privileged actors in humanitarian crises and postcrisis peace-building situations, and governments increasingly outsource their financial assistance through them. (The total value of the financial flows channeled through NGOs is believed to exceed $1.5 trillion.)

In recognition of and in response to these developments, repeated efforts have been made to broaden the limited consultative arrangements of the charter beyond those provided for the ECOSOC. Proposals to further institutionalize NGOs participation in UN governmental processes have elicited little more than polite expressions of interest and quietly fallen into oblivion. By and large, as an organization of states, the United Nations has been and remains inhospitable to NGOs. Some governments question their accountability and representativeness. Others suspect them to be front organizations controlled by powerful Western nations.

Be that as it may, in spite of these obstacles, NGOs have made major strides in their formal interaction with United Nations bodies. Forty-one NGOs enjoyed consultative status in ECOSOC in 1948. Currently, ECOSOC has some 2,000 accredited NGOs. Specialized programs like UNICEF also have formal ties with NGOs. The Joint United Nations Programme on HIV/AIDS (UNAIDS), which coordinates the work of the UN in the field of HIV/AIDS has NGO representatives in its governance structures. The specialized agencies, UNESCO, FAO, and WHO, for instance, have consultative status arrangements for NGOs similar to

ECOSOC. More importantly, nonofficial, behind-the-scenes interactions have sprung up and become common currency throughout the system and in the field. Numerous United Nations intergovernmental organs like the Commission for Human Rights and the Commission on Sustainable Development and treaty bodies routinely consider alternate reports of NGOs. As indicated earlier, NGO experts can brief the Security Council in informal meetings outside of Council chambers. Numerous NGOs work closely with UN humanitarian missions and development projects. They also commonly participate in UN country-level planning processes. Clandestinity seems to be the most effective modality of UN "reform."

CONCLUSION

The accomplishments of the United Nations in the past 60 years are impressive in their own terms. Progress in human development during the 20th century has been dramatic and the UN and its agencies have certainly helped the world become a more hospitable and livable place for millions. The organization has established itself as a major provider of humanitarian relief or technical assistance. It is also a major producer of information, data, and analyses that have mobilized governmental attention and brought into focus emerging issues such as development and the protection of the environment. In striking contrast with the decades that preceded the outbreak of World War II, an unprecedented body of international law has been developed through or under the aegis of the United Nations on a wide ranging set of issues related to peace and security, development, and the environment. Since the historic adoption by the United Nations General Assembly in 1948 of the Universal Declaration of Human Rights, more than 80 treaties have been hatched through the United Nations to protect and promote specific classes of human rights about refugees, children, women, migrant workers, and indigenous peoples. In the decades of the 1950s and 1960s, the UN was a prime mover of decolonization, a process that led to the independence of more than 80 countries and profoundly altered the agenda and functioning of the organization. Since then, the United Nations has helped strengthen the democratic process in many of these countries through election monitoring and reporting.

At the same time, daunting challenges still confront the international community. "Freedom from fear," that is, international peace and security, remains an elusive goal in many parts of the world. The Security Council can hardly be said to have ever functioned as originally planned. The ultimate impact of UN peacekeeping activities remains a matter of controversy. Most governments find it necessary (or expedient) to ratify human rights covenants and conventions, but human rights are violated daily. The world economy is split between haves and have-nots. Poverty and deprivation remain the lot of much of the developing world, and inequality between North and South nations as well as within nations has significantly increased over the past decade.

At the same time, the world has changed profoundly since 1945. Power relationships have evolved from rigid bipolarity to a state of unipolarity overshadowed by the power of the United States. The unilateral use of American military in Iraq is by no means the first political turbulence experienced by the United Nations. But while the 2003 Iraq War under international law is the subject of sharply polarized debates, perhaps more importantly, it has rekindled fears about a further weakening of United States support for the United Nations and heightened the profound political malaise that has pervaded the organization since its inception concerning the political and financial weight of the United States within the organization. Today, more than ever, the United Nations cannot function without U.S. support and there are concerns that the influence of the array of internal forces that supported the postwar multilateral structure has been eroded and is being replaced by influential groups that are ideologically opposed to imposing any international constraints on U.S. foreign policy. But an organization reflecting the "collective will" of 191 nations cannot simply be viewed as the instrument of a single country or of a group of the most powerful nations. It must embody a genuine collective will in the absence of which it will lose its legitimacy and credibility. The search for such a political balance remains as difficult as it was 60 years ago.

New problems confronting the international community, unheard of, let alone anticipated in 1945, have surfaced in the closing years of the 20th century. International peace and security is now less threatened by conquering and aggressive states than "failed states." The parameters of state sovereignty are being redefined by globalization and transboundary phenomena, notably transnational networks of nonstate actors involved in narcotic drugs trafficking, money laundering, and terrorism which are swelled by an expanding underground global economy. The spread of literacy and information technologies have given impetus to the emergence of self-confident and forceful civil society organizations whose role can no longer be discounted. To meet the interrelated modern-day needs of development, security, and human rights and emerging new threats may conceivably require, as the secretary-general recently put it, a reinterpretation, if not a redrawing of the United Nations mission and founding charter. But as long as state sovereignty still provides the ordering basis of the international political system and the foundations of the United Nations, it would be illusory to believe that the United Nations can or, for that matter, should automatically reinterpret its mandate in a "rational-comprehensive" manner. Its capacity for change and adaptation will remain incremental, limited, and imperfect, fed as it is by the realities of an unequal and changing distribution of political power.

The recurring battles over United Nations finances, marked by an intensity inversely correlated to the amounts involved—the United Nations and all its agencies and funds spend about $10–12 billion each year, about less than $2 for each of the world's inhabitants, a patently minuscule sum compared to most government budgets or the world's military spending—are a terse reminder of the tutelage that all states and most particularly the most powerful among them wish to maintain over it. Proposals to restructure UN funding and seek alternative financing sources have floundered on the bedrock of the opposition of the most important contributors, who prefer to maintain an uneasy status quo to losing or eroding their financial leverage.

The multilateral framework set up 60 years ago unquestionably faces new and unprecedented challenges that cannot and should not be underestimated. The political constraints the United Nations faces are equally taxing. They rule out millennialist dreams of a "new world order" that are bound to lead to self-fulfilling "disillusionment." But they certainly leave room for progress toward a better world. However flawed, imperfect, and incomplete this progress may be, it does not follow that the United Nations is a worthless debating society that the world could do away with easily. Bearing in mind both what has been achieved and the inescapable need for international cooperation to meet the problems that humanity faces in an increasingly interdependent and interconnected world, the international community has no choice but to continue reforming, adapting, and equipping the United Nations with structures and resources better suited and commensurate to its evolving tasks, as was recently done with the creation of a Peace-Building Commission, a Human Rights Council, and a modestly funded emergency fund to enable UN agencies to jump-start relief operations. Such innovations will be decried by dreamers of "new world orders" as sheer tinkering and by violators of human rights as intolerable intrusions in the sovereignty of states. Such contrasted views are, if anything, useful reminders that politics is the art of the possible and that if the world were to cast away the United Nations, it would have, willy-nilly, to reinvent it. As Dag Hammarskjöld, the second secretary-general, was fond of saying, "the UN was not created to take humanity to heaven but to save it from hell." His insight has lost none of its relevance.

The Dictionary

– A –

ABKHAZIA. *See* GEORGIA CONFLICT.

ACADEMIC COUNCIL ON THE UNITED NATIONS SYSTEM (ACUNS). International professional organization of scholars and practitioners concerned with the United Nations created in 1987 to build new institutional ties between academe and the United Nations and to bring fresh research perspectives on the work and activities of the United Nations. ACUNS has some 900 members worldwide and has been granted consultative status in the **Economic and Social Council (ECOSOC)**. *See also* NONGOVERNMENTAL ORGANIZATIONS (NGOs).

ACHESON, DEAN (1893–1971). U.S. diplomat and lawyer. During World War II, Dean Acheson served as assistant secretary in the Department of State and was involved in the drafting of the United Nations **Charter**. First undersecretary of state in 1945 and then secretary of state in 1949, he was one of the architects of the doctrine of **containment** and of the Marshall Plan, which provided large-scale assistance to European war-torn countries for their reconstruction. *See also* COLD WAR; UNITED NATIONS CONFERENCE ON INTERNATIONAL ORGANIZATION.

ACID RAIN. Broad term used to describe precipitations of rain and snow polluted by sulfur dioxide and nitrogen oxides, which come largely from the burning of coal and gasoline. Prevailing winds may blow these compounds sometimes over hundreds of miles across national borders. Acid rain causes acidification of lakes, streams, and

1

rivers; damages forests; accelerates the decay of building materials; and may have hazardous health consequences. Regions affected include Scandinavia and Central Europe and parts of Asia. *See also* AIR POLLUTION; COMMISSION ON SUSTAINABLE DEVELOPMENT (UNITED NATIONS) (CSD); ECONOMIC COMMISSION FOR EUROPE (ECE); ENVIRONMENT.

ACQUIRED IMMUNE DEFICIENCY SYNDROME (AIDS). *See* HIV/AIDS.

AD HOC GROUP OF EXPERTS ON INTERNATIONAL COOPERATION IN TAX MATTERS. Expert body reporting to the **Economic and Social Council (ECOSOC)**. Originally created in 1967 to facilitate the conclusion of tax treaties between developed and developing countries, its mandate was expanded to study the implementation of tax agreements and examine the question of tax evasion. One of its main achievements is the elaboration of a United Nations model convention for the avoidance of double taxation between developed and developing countries. *See also* FUNCTIONALISM.

ADJUDICATION. *See* JUDICIAL SETTLEMENT.

ADMINISTRATIVE COMMITTEE ON COORDINATION (ACC). Set up by the **Economic and Social Council (ECOSOC)** in 1946 originally to supervise the implementation of the agreements between the United Nations and the **specialized agencies** (at the time three). This interagency body evolved into an instrument to facilitate programmatic and managerial collaboration between the organizations of the UN system. The committee was chaired by the **secretary-general** and met twice a year. It brought together the heads of the UN funds and programs as well as the specialized agencies, the **World Trade Organization (WTO)** and the **Bretton Woods institutions**. The ACC's work was carried out through a sprawling machinery of subsidiary bodies concerned with administrative, program, and operational questions. In October 2000, the ACC was replaced by a **Chief Executive Board (CEB)** as part of the **reform** efforts of the secretary-general. *See also* COORDINATION; DEPUTY SECRETARY-GENERAL.

ADMISSION TO THE UNITED NATIONS. *See* MEMBERSHIP (UNITED NATIONS).

ADVISORY COMMITTEE ON ADMINISTRATIVE AND BUD-GETARY QUESTIONS (ACABQ). Group of experts nominated by their governments and elected by the **General Assembly** which reviews the initial **budget** proposals of the **secretary-general**. Its advice is only consultative but carries considerable weight in shaping the final contents of the UN budget. *See also* COMMITTEE FOR PROGRAMME AND COORDINATION (CPC); UNITED NATIONS BOARD OF AUDITORS.

ADVISORY OPINION. The **International Court of Justice (ICJ)** may render consultative and nonbinding opinions on international legal issues at the request of the principal organs of the United Nations (UN) and the **specialized agencies**. The court has issued advisory opinions on questions related to UN **membership**, reparations for injuries suffered in the service of the UN, the territorial status of **Southwest Africa** and the **Western Sahara**, the **peacekeeping** expenses of the UN, the applicability of the **United Nations headquarters** Agreement, and the legality of the use and threat to use nuclear weapons. *See also* BUDGET (UNITED NATIONS); FINANCIAL CRISES OF THE UNITED NATIONS.

AFGHANISTAN QUESTION. For three decades following the overthrow of the monarchy in 1973, Afghanistan was crippled by political and civil violence among ethnic-based factions. Bloody coups by Communist groups in 1978 and 1979 triggered Islamic insurgencies and a Soviet military intervention in December 1979 to bolster the fledging control of the central government. Fighting by Soviet and Afghan government troops against mujahideen guerrillas backed by Pakistan and the United States continued for 10 years. Following the withdrawal of Soviet troops in 1989, the mujahideen coalition seized power in early 1992. Its control over the country proved short-lived as the Taliban, a Pakistan-backed group of Islamist fundamentalists launched military operations from the Pakistani border and finally captured the capital, Kabul, in 1996.

The Taliban's rule, however, met opposition from ethnic minorities in the northern part of the country. Its strict Islamic stance and the restrictions that it imposed on the population led to continuing unrest and international isolation. Suspicions that the Taliban were harboring al-Qaeda terrorists responsible for the bombing of the United States embassies in Kenya and Tanzania prompted the Security Council to impose economic sanctions on Afghanistan in 1998. The terrorist attacks of 11 September 2001, in turn, triggered a US-led armed intervention under United Nations auspices that removed the Taliban from power.

The new government, mainly composed of northern ethnic groups, faces major challenges. It is perceived as ethnically unrepresentative in the southern part of the country. Its authority backed up by a 5,000-strong International Security Assistance Force (ISAF) under American command does not extend much beyond the capital where rival warlords thrive on a lucrative illegal trade in gems and opium. The civil war has created one of the worst **refugee** crises (one in four Afghans has been a refugee). The country suffers from enormous **poverty**, a crumbling infrastructure, and widespread **landmines**. International aid aimed at social welfare and reconstruction has been slow in coming and plagued by competition among bilateral and multilateral donors.

In an arena of conflict involving major global and regional powers, the political role of the United Nations has been useful but modest. Throughout the Cold War and beginning with a **special emergency session** held in 1980, the **General Assembly** issued repeated unheeded calls for the withdrawal of Soviet troops. But since 1981, a personal representative of the secretary-general quietly endeavored to seek a diplomatic solution and kept the negotiations alive until a fundamental change in Soviet policy came about. This instance of **quiet diplomacy** involving Pakistan and Afghanistan eventually paved the way to the 1988 Geneva accords committing the Soviets to withdraw from Afghanistan and the creation of the **United Nations Good Offices Mission in Afghanistan and Pakistan (UNGOMAP)**. At the same time, the United Nations provided much-needed humanitarian assistance including repatriation programs for refugees, health services, rehabilitation of water supplies, and basic education projects. This work, which was frequently interrupted by sporadic acts of violence, continues today under the umbrella of the **United Nations Assistance Mission in Afghanistan (UNAMA)**, a **peacekeeping** operation with a relatively strong mandate and centralized control structure but with no authority over member-state aid agencies or the international financial institutions. *See also* CORDOVEZ, DIEGO (1935–).

AFRICAN DEVELOPMENT BANK (AfDB). Located in Abidjan, Cote d'Ivoire, the AfDB was established by the **Organization of African Unity (OAU)** in 1963 at the prodding and with the assistance of the **Economic Commission for Africa (ECA)**. Initially, only independent African states could become members of the bank. Since 1982, membership has been opened to nonregional countries as well. Currently, the AfDB has 53 regional member countries and 24 nonregional members, primarily industrialized countries, which provide the bulk of its capital. The bank's principal functions are to make loans (repayable over 25 to 30 years) and equity investments for the economic and social advancement of regional member countries, to provide them with technical assistance for the preparation and execution of development projects and programs, and to promote investment of public and private capital for development purposes. Its modest initial capital of U.S. $250 million has grown to over U.S. $30 billion. *See* also AFRICAN ECONOMIC CONDITIONS; MULTILATERAL DEVELOPMENT BANKS (MDBs); SINGER, HANS (1910–2005).

AFRICAN ECONOMIC CONDITIONS. Since gaining independence from European colonial powers in the 1960s, nearly all African countries have been caught in a spiral of increasing political, social, and economic turmoil. The excessive fragmentation of the continent in terms of political and economic units, continuing high rates of **population** growth, inadequate human resources, and weak institutional capacities in support of **development** from within are among the adverse internal factors that have stymied the actions taken by African countries and the international community for the continent's economic and social recovery. Structural handicaps include the heavy dependence of African economies on a few primary export **commodities** and an unfavorable international environment. Most particularly, deteriorating terms of trade, the burden of debt servicing, and stagnating flows of external resources have compounded the problems facing African leaders. Civil war, recurring environmental crises, and the **HIV/AIDS** pandemic have also taken a heavy human and material toll leading to widespread **poverty** and deprivation.

The **General Assembly** held special sessions in 1986 and 1991 resulting in the adoption of declarations calling for special measures to be taken by African countries and the international community. Neither these exhortations nor the various blueprints promulgated by the assembly have had much practical visible effects. Poverty retains its grip on the region. Several of the continent's wars have abated in recent years, but peace is usually partial and brittle. However, welcome political and socioeconomic changes have come in two of Africa's largest countries: South Africa and Nigeria. *See also* LAGOS PLAN OF ACTION (1980); NEW PARTNERSHIP FOR AFRICA'S DEVELOPMENT (NEPAD); UNITED NATIONS NEW AGENDA FOR THE DEVELOPMENT OF AFRICA (UN-NADAF); UNITED NATIONS PROGRAMME OF ACTION FOR AFRICAN ECONOMIC RECOVERY AND DEVELOPMENT (UN-PAARD, 1986–1990).

AFRICAN UNION (AU). Successor organization to the **Organization of African Unity (OAU)** set up in 2000, the African Union has broadly similar functions to the OAU. Its constitutive charter places greater emphasis on the promotion of democracy and the protection of **human rights**. The AU has mounted a **peacekeeping** operation in **Burundi** and tried to mediate several regional conflicts like the Darfur conflict in **Sudan**. The AU is currently considering setting up a permanent peacekeeping force, which would enable it to intervene more effectively and speedily in conflict areas. *See also* UNITED NATIONS MISSION IN THE SUDAN (UNMIS, 24 March 2005–present); UNITED NATIONS OPERATION IN BURUNDI (ONUB).

AGENDA 21. Voluminous compendium of desirable national and international policies for the sustainable management of all sectors of the **environment**. Agenda 21 emerged from the 1992 **United Nations Conference on Environment and Development (UNCED)** but makes no provision for mandatory rules. Its implementation rests on voluntary follow-up processes focused on the **Commission on Sustainable Development (CSD)**. *See also* RURAL DEVELOPMENT; UNITED NATIONS CONVENTION TO COMBAT DESERTIFICATION (UNCDD, 1996).

AGENDA FOR DEMOCRATIZATION. Aborted effort of **Secretary-General Boutros Boutros-Ghali** to map out a strategy for strengthening the spread of democracy worldwide. Clashing views among member states—essentially along North-South lines—about the very concept of democracy and the weight of internal and external factors in sustaining transitions to democracy stymied a project that the secretary-general considered a complement to his earlier **Agenda for Peace** and **Agenda for Development**. Instead, a compromise was found in setting up a system of annual reporting by the secretary-general to the **General Assembly** on United Nations efforts to assist governments in the promotion and consolidation of "new" and "restored" democracies combined with periodic conferences sponsored by interested governments.

AGENDA FOR DEVELOPMENT. Lengthy document prepared by **Secretary-General Boutros Boutros-Ghali** in part to counter developing countries' charges that **peacekeeping** had been given priority over developmental issues in the post–Cold War years. Asserting that **development** is a right, the secretary-general underlined that peace and development—in the broad sense of sustainable economic growth, social justice, democracy, and the protection of **human rights**—are inextricably linked. Written at a time when concepts of development were changing and political interest in development in developed countries seemed to be waning, an Agenda for Development was meant to stimulate discussion and rekindle international efforts in support for development. Unlike the **Agenda for Peace**, which was more specific in its prescriptions, it does not appear to have had a significant impact. *See also* AGENDA FOR DEMOCRATIZATION.

AGENDA FOR PEACE. Meeting in 1992 in the euphoric atmosphere created by the demise of the **Cold War**, the **Security Council** requested the **secretary-general** to prepare recommendations for strengthening the capacity of the United Nations for **preventive diplomacy**, **peacemaking**, and **peacekeeping**. **Boutros Boutros-Ghali**'s proposals contained in a document called *Agenda for Peace* included the establishment of an **early warning** system, the **preventive deployment** of UN forces where conflict appeared imminent, and the establishment of peace enforcement units to be made available to the United Nations on short notice. These recommendations generated considerable interest among scholars and structured the ensuing debate among practitioners. But they far exceeded the expectations of member states and their willingness to act upon them was further tempered by the peacekeeping failures experienced in **Somalia** and **Rwanda** in particular. In a 1995 *Supplement to An Agenda for Peace*, the secretary-general pragmatically acknowledged the reticence of member states and called for caution in launching new peacekeeping initiatives. The **General Assembly** has continued to discuss some of the themes of *An Agenda for Peace* with particular attention to **prevention** and peacemaking, **postconflict peacebuilding** coordination, and the use of **sanctions**. *See also* AGENDA FOR DEMOCRATIZATION; AGENDA FOR DEVELOPMENT; BRAHIMI REPORT.

AGGRESSION. The first article of the United Nations **Charter** states that one of the main purposes of the organization is to suppress acts of aggression. Article 2.4 of the charter also enjoins the members of the United Nations to refrain from the threat or **use of force** in their international relations.

In 1974, the **General Assembly** defined aggression as "the use of armed force by a state against the sovereignty, territorial integrity, or political independence of another state." But in the same resolution and over the objections of numerous Northern countries, the assembly posited that acts carried out in the context of a people's exercise of their right of **self-determination** or of a struggle against colonial domination, foreign occupation, or racist regimes did not constitute acts of aggression.

The charter recognizes that a state may have recourse to the **use of force** in **self-defense** (Article 51) and force may be used in the context of collective measures of security adopted by the **Security Council** (Article 42). Yet, there is still no universally accepted precise and codified definition of the notion of aggression. *See also* COLLECTIVE SECURITY; HIGH-LEVEL PANEL ON THREATS, CHALLENGES, AND CHANGE (HLP); INTERNATIONAL CRIMINAL COURT (ICC); PEACEKEEPING; PREEMPTION; PREVENTIVE OR ENFORCEMENT ACTION; REGIONAL ARRANGEMENTS; SANCTIONS; TERRORISM.

AGING. The combined effects of increases in life expectancy and declines in fertility rates have led to a worldwide demographic transition that will result in the old and the young representing an equal share of the world's population by the mid-21st century. Developed countries face challenges resulting from the relationship between aging and unemployment and the sustainability of their pension systems. Developing countries face the dual challenge of development and population aging.

The United Nations organized two major conferences on these emerging issues in 1982 and 1992 respectively. *See also* SECOND WORLD ASSEMBLY ON AGING (2002); SOCIAL INTEGRATION; WORLD ASSEMBLY ON AGING (1982).

AGRARIAN REFORM. Redistribution of privately or publicly owned land to landless small farmers intended to promote the economic and social development of rural populations. In the wake of the agrarian reform measures implemented in Japan and Eastern European countries in the postwar years, the subject was a major focus of political interest in various United Nations forums throughout the 1950s, especially in the **Economic and Social Council (ECOSOC)** and the **Food and Agriculture Organization (FAO)**, which adopted numerous resolutions and programs recognizing the importance of agrarian reform in **developing countries**.

Interest in agrarian reform faded out thereafter but was rekindled by a World Conference on Agrarian Reform and Rural Development organized by the FAO in 1979. **Agenda 21**, adopted by the 1992 **United Nations Conference on Environment and Development (UNCED)**, stresses that agrarian reform is an important tool to achieve sustainable agriculture and **rural development**. FAO sponsored yet another conference on agrarian reform and rural development in 2006 in Porto Alegre (Brazil). *See also* AGRICULTURAL DEVELOPMENT; FOOD SECURITY; HUNGER; RURAL DEVELOPMENT.

AGRICULTURAL DEVELOPMENT. Agriculture has been and remains the largest economic sector in **developing countries**, especially among the least developed. In this context, **rural development**, that is, improvements in the living standards of small farmers and a reduction of urban-rural imbalances in incomes and economic opportunities, has been a long-standing objective of development strategies. Agricultural progress, however, has not been forthcoming. Over time, agricultural productivity has failed to expand adequately, despite a "green revolution" in India and some other countries. In the 1990s the growth of per capita output declined, jeopardizing domestic food, security, and export earnings. Minimal growth of production, in combination with extreme fluctuations of output are persistent problems in developing countries, thus contributing to the perpetuation of **poverty** and raising food insecurity. Furthermore, the expected increase of population in developing countries will increase the pressures on governments to provide for food and other agricultural commodities.

Domestic and international factors constrain rural development. Domestic issues include low productivity, inadequate production and market structures, limited educational and skills base, low life expectancy, lack of basic infrastructure, and inefficient institutional and policy frameworks. At the international level, developing countries also have to cope with increasing external competition, resulting in part from market liberalization.

Because of the price fluctuations of primary **commodities** that are the main export base of numerous developing countries, those nations are highly vulnerable to global changes in demand, and consequently to deteriorating **terms of trade**. Agricultural subsidies in developed nations render the export of agricultural products from developing nations virtually impossible. Moreover, the inability to compete on world markets often translates to domestic markets as well, causing increases of food imports and corresponding decreases of valuable foreign exchange.

The role of the United Nations and specialized agencies such as the **United Nations Conference on Trade and Development (UNCTAD)**, the **Food and Agriculture Organization (FAO)**, and **International Fund for Agricultural Development (IFAD)** has been to draw attention to these negative trends and to promote the integration of developing countries in the global economy through a comprehensive set of measures targeting both domestic and international issues. *See also* AGRARIAN REFORM; FOOD SECURITY; HUNGER; LEAST DEVELOPED COUNTRIES (LDCs); WORLD FOOD SUMMIT (13–17 November 1996).

AHMED, RAFEEUDDIN (1932–). Pakistani diplomat who held posts in Beijing, Cairo, Ottawa, and New York (as his country's representative in the economic and social committee of the **General Assembly**) prior to joining the United Nations in 1970. He began his long career at the United Nations as secretary of the **Economic and Social Council (ECOSOC)** and subsequently served as chef de cabinet of **Secretary-General Kurt Waldheim**, undersecretary-general for International Economic and Social Affairs while also acting as **special representative** of the secretary-general for Humanitarian Affairs in South-East Asia, executive secretary of the **Economic and Social Commission for Asia and the Pacific (ESCAP)**, and associate administrator of the **United Nations Development Program (UNDP)**. A consummate diplomat, he played a discreet but important role in the settlement of a number of international disputes, notably in **Afghanistan** and **Timor-Leste**.

AIR POLLUTION. Introduction of gaseous, liquid, or solid contaminants in the atmosphere such as carbon dioxide and sulfur emissions resulting in deleterious effects on human health, living resources, ecosystems, and material property. Industrialization and the increasing use of vehicles with internal combustion engines have been the main causes of air pollution. **Agenda 21** adopted at the 1992 **United Nations Conference on Environment and Development (UNCED)**, outlines a set of desirable actions by industrialized and developing countries for the protection of the atmosphere. An important contribution of the United Nations in this field is the 1979 Convention on Long Range Transboundary Air Pollution. Negotiated under the aegis of the **Economic Commission for Europe (ECE)**, this convention now has 49 signatories and has been extended by eight protocols, identifying specific measures to be taken by the parties. *See also* ACID RAIN; COMMISSION ON SUSTAINABLE DEVELOPMENT (UNITED NATIONS) (CSD); ENVIRONMENT; GLOBAL WARMING.

AIR TRANSPORT. The rapid development of the airplane and growing network of passenger and freight carriers in the wake of World War II has drawn increasing attention to the need for effective strategies in dealing with both political and technical obstacles relating to air transport. Since its creation in 1947, the **International Civil Aviation Organization (ICAO)**, a **specialized agency** of the United Nations, has endeavored to develop uniform standards and rules for the orderly growth of international civil aviation. *See also* FUNCTIONALISM.

ALGERIAN QUESTION. Placed on its agenda by developing countries in spite of strenuous objections by France, the **General Assembly** considered the Algerian armed struggle for independence from 1955 through 1961. Initially, it urged a peaceful and negotiated settlement, later asserting the right of the Algerian people to **self-determination** and subsequently calling for the independence of Algeria. The French decision to grant independence to Algeria in 1962 may not have been an outcome of the actions of the General Assembly, but its debates were indicative of the growing political influence of **developing countries** in the United Nations. *See also* DECOLONIZATION; TUNISIAN QUESTION.

ALLIANCE OF SMALL ISLAND STATES (AOSIS). Coalition of small-island and low-lying coastal countries sharing similar development challenges and concerns about the **environment**, especially their vulnerability to the potentially disastrous effects of global **climate change**. The specificity of the development needs of these countries was recognized at the 1992 **United Nations Conference on Environment and Development (UNCED)**. The group itself grew out of the 1994 **United Nations Conference on the Sustainable Development of Small Island Developing Countries** and has a membership of 43 states and observers representing 5 percent of the world's population. The group has no formal constitution, no secretariat, and no regular budget. It functions as a lobby and negotiating instrument for small-island developing states within the United Nations system. *See also* GROUPS AND GROUPINGS; INTERNATIONAL MEETING TO REVIEW THE IMPLEMENTATION OF THE PROGRAMME OF ACTION FOR THE SUSTAINABLE DEVELOPMENT OF SMALL ISLAND DEVELOPING STATES (PORT-LOUIS, MAURITIUS, 10–14 January 2005).

ALMA-ATA HEALTH DECLARATION (1978). Document emerging from a conference sponsored by the **World Health Organization**

(WHO) on primary **health** care held in Alma-Ata (USSR) in 1978. The declaration reaffirmed that health was a state of complete physical, mental, and social well-being and not merely the absence of disease or infirmity and that achieving this objective hinged on growth and **development**. As a fundamental **human right**, the attainment of the highest possible level of health entailed greater reliance on primary health care policies based on practical, scientifically sound, and socially acceptable methods and technologies made universally accessible to individuals and families. Such policies required **education** concerning prevailing health problems and the methods of preventing and controlling them; the promotion of food supply and proper nutrition; an adequate supply of safe water and basic sanitation; maternal and child health care, including family planning; immunization against major infectious diseases; the prevention of locally endemic diseases; and the provision of essential drugs. Their implementation should rest not only on formally trained physicians but also on nurses, midwives, auxiliaries, and community workers. *See also* BASIC HUMAN NEEDS.

AMENDMENT (UNITED NATIONS CHARTER). Amendments to the **United Nations Charter** can be effected through two different procedures. Under Article 109 of the charter, an amendment comes into force when adopted by a vote of two-thirds of the **General Assembly** and after ratification by two-thirds of the **members** of the United Nations including all the permanent members of the **Security Council**.

Amendments to the charter may also be proposed by a two-thirds vote of a General Conference called by both the Security Council and the General Assembly. Amendments under this procedure take effect when ratified by two-thirds of the members of the United Nations including the permanent members of the Security Council (Article 109). As required by Article 109, the question of convening a General Conference was placed on the agenda of the 10th session of the assembly. But there was (and still is) no support for holding such a conference.

Four articles of the charter have been amended in accordance with the first procedure. In 1965, the membership of the council was increased from 11 to 15 and the number of affirmative votes needed for a decision increased from 7 to 9, including the concurring votes of the permanent members of the council for all matters of substance rather than procedure (Article 27). The same year, the size of the **Economic and Social Council (ECOSOC)** was enlarged from 18 to 27. The membership of the ECOSOC was further enlarged to 54 in 1973 (Article 61). In 1968, the number of votes required in the Security Council to convene a General Conference to review the charter was increased from 7 to 9 (Article 109). *See also* REFORM, UNITED NATIONS; SPECIAL COMMITTEE ON THE CHARTER OF THE UNITED NATIONS AND ON THE STRENGTHENING OF THE ROLE OF THE ORGANIZATION.

AMERASINGHE, HAMILTON SHIRLEY (1913–1980). Sri Lankan diplomat who presided over a number of United Nations bodies, including the **General Assembly** 1976–1977. He is best remembered for his skillful chairmanship of the United Nations Conference on the **Law of the Sea**, which he assumed from 1973 to his death.

AMNESTY INTERNATIONAL (AI). Influential London-based voluntary worldwide **nongovernmental organization (NGO)** created in 1961 to promote respect for **human rights**. With its 2 million members and supporters in 150 countries and a budget in excess of £25 million, AI undertakes grassroots campaigns and carries out research focused on the prevention and redress of human rights violations.

AI initially focused its research work and campaigns on political prisoners, the abolition of the death penalty, torture, extrajudicial executions, and "disappearances." Its reports and international campaigns exposing political oppression and the widespread commission of atrocities in Chile and Argentina in the 1970s contributed in no minor way to the return of law and democracy in these countries.

In 1991, AI expanded its mandate to encompass all the rights in the **Universal Declaration of Human Rights** and started to work on such human rights abuses committed by **nonstate actors** and armed political groups as hostage-taking, unlawful killings, and abuses against civilians and noncombatants in armed conflicts. AI has targeted governments complicit in or failing to take effective action against human rights abuses and, in that context, actively campaigned for the creation of a permanent **International Criminal Court (ICC)**. AI enjoys consultative status with the **Economic and Social Council (ECOSOC)**, the **United Nations Educational, Scientific, and Cultural Organiza-**

tion **(UNESCO)**, and a number of regional organizations such as the Inter-American Commission on Human Rights. AI also works closely with the United Nations **Commission for Human Rights**. Its extensive contributions to human rights protection have received worldwide recognition and AI was awarded the **Nobel Peace Prize** in 1977. *See also* CIVIL SOCIETY; NONSTATE ACTORS.

ANGOLA CONFLICT (1975–2002). Typical instance of a long and bitter civil war rooted in ethnic struggles and prolonged by strategic **Cold War** calculations and the illicit international trafficking of **natural resources**. By the time of independence in 1975, political rivalries between two major nationalist groups (the Popular Movement for the Liberation of Angola [MPLA] and the National Union for the Total Independence of Angola [UNITA]) had degenerated into a vicious civil war. With the military assistance of Cuba, the leftist MPLA emerged as the victor of the national liberation struggle and took power. The MPLA was aided by the Soviet Union and Cuba while UNITA was backed by neighboring South Africa and the United States. The civil war thus became an extension of the East-West conflict and dragged on until the end of the Cold War.

Negotiations by South Africa, Angola, Cuba, and the United States led to the withdrawal of Cuban forces from Angola and of South African troops from **Southwest Africa** (Namibia), which had been used as a military support base against the MPLA in Angola. The withdrawal of Cuban troops was verified by the **United Nations Angola Verification Mission (UNAVEM I)** from 1988 to 1991. Namibia became independent in 1990 under United Nations supervision.

In a subsequent round of negotiations, the MPLA and UNITA reached agreement on a cease-fire, the formation of a unified national army, and the holding of multiparty presidential elections. A second United Nations **peacekeeping** operation (**United Nations Angola Verification Mission II**) was brought in to monitor the peace agreement and commenced operation in 1991. Presidential elections were held in 1992 resulting in the victory of the MPLA candidate. The outcome was contested by the UNITA candidate, and civil war resumed. At the time, UNITA occupied more than half of Angola's territory including remote areas rich in diamonds, which it used to finance its armed struggle against the MPLA.

A new peace accord allowed the **Security Council** to authorize a third peacekeeping operation (**United Nations Angola Verification Mission III**) which, in 1997, totaled 5,560 military personnel, police, and observers with the mandate to separate the combatants. UNAVEM III was subsequently transformed into the **United Nations Observer Mission in Angola (MONUA)**. The failure of UNITA to adhere to these new peace terms and the resumption of hostilities in 1998 prompted the council to allow the termination of MONUA in 1999 and to impose **sanctions** targeted at UNITA.

The death of the UNITA leader in 2002 has brought to an end the civil war. But after almost three decades of war, the country faces overwhelming economic, social, and humanitarian challenges. At the height of the conflict more than 4 million persons—over one-third of the population of 12 million—were internally displaced. Despite impressive rates of return, continued reports of **human rights** violations against returnees perpetrated by national authorities underline the precariousness of the political situation. *See also* ANSTEE, JOAN (1926–); INTERNALLY DISPLACED PERSONS (IDPs); SOUTHWEST AFRICA; UNITED NATIONS TRANSITION ASSISTANCE GROUP (UNTAG, February 1989–April 1999).

ANNAN, KOFI (1938–). Seventh **secretary-general** of the United Nations, he began his first term of office on 1 January 1997 and was elected to a second term beginning on 1 January 2002. Annan is the first secretary-general to have risen from the ranks of the United Nations staff. He served in the **World Health Organization (WHO)**, the **Economic Commission for Africa (ECA)**, the **United Nations Emergency Force (UNEF II)** and the Office of the **United Nations High Commissioner for Refugees (UNHCR)**. At United Nations headquarters in New York, he headed the Departments of Human Resources Management, Program Planning, Budget and Finance, and Peacekeeping Operations. A "consummate insider" bolstered by a moral authority that he fostered by candidly acknowledging his responsibility in the **Bosnian** and **Rwandan** tragedies when he was in charge of the **Department of Peacekeeping Operations (DPKO)**, Annan has throughout his tenure endeavored to steer the organization between a restless, diffident, and ineffectual Third World majority and the hegemonic influence of the United States.

Annan's first major initiative was to present a comprehensive blue-print for **reform** of the United Nations in 1997. Most of his propos-als were endorsed by the **General Assembly** and led to the enactment of a broad range of measures including a reallocation of resources from low- to high-priority areas; a reduction of administrative costs with savings used for **development** activities; the organization of the UN's work program into four core areas—peace and security, devel-opment, economic and social affairs, and humanitarian affairs—with **human rights** as a crosscutting issue; the appointment of a **deputy secretary-general** to oversee the day-to-day work of the UN and co-ordinate UN reform efforts; the establishment of a cabinet comprised of UN senior managers to speed decision making and enhance coor-dination; and a major reform of personnel aimed at improving man-agement of staff. Further reform efforts were continued in 2002 fo-cused on administrative issues and the process of resource allocation in the preparation of the UN **budget**.

Annan has used his good offices in numerous political situations. In 1998, he attempted to secure Iraq's compliance with **Security Council** resolutions and, more successfully, to promote the transition to civilian rule in Nigeria. In 1999, he helped forge an international response to vi-olence in **East Timor** and launched his **Global Compact** in an effort to ease the strained relations between the United Nations and the private sector and to mobilize it in the fight against **poverty**.

His April 2000 "Millennium Report" formed the basis for the **Mil-lennium Declaration** adopted by the summit meeting of the assem-bly nine months later, which set out ambitious development goals for the international community. Kofi Annan has also made a special ef-fort to encourage the international community to devote more sus-tained attention to the disastrous economic and political situation of Africa and to **HIV/AIDS**.

The outbreak of the second Persian Gulf War in 2003 which he portrayed as illegal under **international law** and the improprieties which came to light in the management of the **Oil for Food Program** have considerably weakened his capacity for political leadership. In 2001, Kofi Annan was awarded the Nobel Peace Prize. In 2007 he was succeeded by **Ban Ki-Moon**. *See also* HIGH-LEVEL PANEL ON THREATS, CHALLENGES, AND CHANGE (HLP); MIIL-LENNIUM DEVELOPMENT GOALS (MDGs).

ANSTEE, JOAN (1926–). British national who served the United Nations for over four decades. She spent most of her career in the field working for the **United Nations Development Program (UNDP).** In 1987, she rose to the rank of undersecretary-general when she became director general of the United Nations in Vienna, head of the Centre for Social Development and Humanitarian Affairs, and coordinator of all UN narcotic drug control programs. From 1992 to 1993, she was the secretary-general's special representative to Angola and head of the **United Nations Angola Verification Mission (UNAVEM II).**

ANTARCTIC TREATY. Signed in 1959 and in force as of 1961, the purpose of this multilateral treaty is to ensure "in the interests of all mankind that Antarctica shall continue forever to be used exclusively for peaceful purposes and shall not become the scene or object of international discord." The treaty thus prohibits military activity, nuclear explosions, and the disposal of radioactive waste in the Antarctic continent and holds all its parties' territorial claims in abeyance. At the same time, it seeks to promote scientific research and the exchange of data among its parties.

   Prodded by **developing countries**, the **General Assembly** has adopted several resolutions affirming that Antarctica should continue forever to be used exclusively for peaceful purposes and that it should not become the object of international disputes. Developing countries have also pressed—but in vain—for recognition of the principle of universal participation in the management of the continent's **natural resources**. *See also* ARMS CONTROL; COMMON HERITAGE OF MANKIND; DISARMAMENT.

ANTIPERSONNEL MINES (APMs). Landmines were originally developed for military use, to protect strategic areas or to restrict the movement of enemy forces. As such, they were first used on a large scale during World War II and, since then, in many other conflicts, including the **Korean War**, the Vietnam War, and the first **Persian Gulf War**. Cheap to make and buy, landmines have been deliberately used in recent internal conflicts to target civilian populations and control their movements. Their presence poses a major threat, often making it impossible for **refugees** and **internally displaced people** to return to their homes. While the actual figures are uncertain, a 2003 estimate suggests that an average number of 15,000 to 20,000 people are being killed or injured by landmines every year worldwide. Landmine casualties are reported in more than 60 countries worldwide.

Stigmatized by a wide array of **nongovernmental organizations (NGOs)**, like the **International Campaign to Ban Landmines (ICBL)**, the use of landmines is now regulated by the 1997 **Convention on the Prohibition of the Use, Stockpiling, Production, and Transfer of Antipersonnel Mines and on Their Destruction**. *See also* POSTCONFLICT PEACE BUILDING.

AOUZOU STRIP. *See* UNITED NATIONS AOUZOU STRIP OBSERVER GROUP (UNASOG, April–June 1994).

APARTHEID. Term coined in the 1930s and referring to legislation enacted in the 1950s in South Africa which restricted the political and civil rights of the nonwhite population, prohibited most social contacts between the races, enforced the segregation of public facilities, and created race-specific job categories. The issue initially came to the **General Assembly** in 1946 at the initiative of India, which complained about South Africa's treatment of its Indian minority. The Indian complaint merged in the 1950s with the broader issue of South African **racial discrimination** policies encapsulated in the government's policy of apartheid, which it claimed was within its **domestic jurisdiction** and therefore of no concern to the United Nations.

Pressure on South Africa increased over time as the membership of the United Nations expanded to include a growing number of developing nations. In 1962, the General Assembly created a Special Committee against Apartheid to gather information and monitor developments about apartheid. Subsequently, the assembly urged members to cut their economic and political ties with South Africa, began to advocate "armed struggle" in South Africa and, in 1973, endorsed an International Convention on the Suppression and Punishment of the Crime of Apartheid.

From 1960 on, the **Security Council** was also involved in the dispute. In 1963, the Council called for a voluntary embargo on the sale of arms to South Africa, which it made mandatory in 1977. In 1985, the council took the stronger measure to recommend nonmandatory economic **sanctions** against South Africa.

Whether such international diplomatic pressures and economic sanctions played a determinant role in persuading the South African government to dismantle apartheid remains a matter of controversy, as the increasingly anti-South African policies of the United States, the United Kingdom, and Western European countries also impacted on the situation. In any event, a national referendum held in 1992 endorsed the repeal of apartheid legislation and paved the way to new constitutional arrangements and the creation of a democratic and multiracial society. *See also* CREDENTIALS COMMITTEE OF THE GENERAL ASSEMBLY; HUMAN RIGHTS; SOUTHWEST AFRICA.

ARAB LEAGUE. Informal name of the League of Arab States, a multipurpose regional organization founded in 1945 by Egypt, Iraq, Saudi Arabia, Syria, Transjordan (Jordan, since 1950), and Yemen and headquartered in Cairo. Fifteen other countries and the Palestine Liberation Organization later joined. The purpose of the League is to serve as a forum for member states to promote their cooperation in political, economic, cultural, and social matters. Internal dissensions have hampered the effectiveness of the organization as a means of regional integration and as an instrument for the peaceful settlement of intraregional disputes.

ARAB-ISRAELI CONFLICT. A perennial subject of acrimonious and, by and large inconclusive, discussions and debates in virtually all United Nations forums since 1947 when Great Britain relinquished its **League of Nations mandate** over Palestine and placed the issue on the agenda of the **General Assembly**.

Throughout the past half century, the problem in its various aspects—relief and settlement of **refugees, human rights** violations, Israel's withdrawal from conquered territories, the creation of an independent Palestinian state, acts of **terrorism**, and full-scale war—has repeatedly mobilized the **Security Council** and the General Assembly and spilled over in the deliberations of the **specialized agencies**' governing bodies.

The roots of the conflict may be traced back to the influx of Jewish immigrants in Palestine after World War I and the failures of Arabs and Jews to reach agreement on how—and whether—to divide

Palestine. The assembly's 1948 plan to partition Palestine into two separate states forming an economic union with Jerusalem as their capital was thwarted by Arab opposition and the first military conflict, which came to an end through the efforts of a UN mediator appointed by the General Assembly and a truce commission authorized by the Security Council.

The **United Nations Truce Supervision Organization (UNTSO)** created in 1948 to report on cease-fire and armistice violations was only the first in a series of **peacekeeping** operations launched by the United Nations in the region. The most important ones were the **United Nations Emergency Force (UNEF) I and II** set up after the 1957 and 1973 wars. In a 1967 resolution, the Security Council defined the broad parameters of a settlement of the conflict. But whatever diplomatic headway has been made in the conflict has since originated from outside the United Nations. In part, the marginalization of the organization is a consequence of a 1975 resolution of the General Assembly (rescinded in 1991) equating Zionism to racism, which changed the public perception of the United Nations as a relatively even-handed mediator to that of a partisan of the Arab cause. *See also* BUNCHE, RALPH (1904–1971); BERNADOTTE, COUNT FOLKE (1895–1948); UNITED NATIONS DISENGAGEMENT OBSERVER FORCE (UNDOF, 1974–); UNITED NATIONS INTERIM FORCE IN LEBANON (UNIFIL, 19 March 1978–present); UNITED NATIONS RELIEF AND WORKS AGENCY (UNRWA).

ARBITRATION. Procedure whereby the parties to a dispute agree to refer their difference to a judge (or panel of judges), an ad hoc arbitral body, or in the framework of an existing mechanism of their choice, for its final and binding disposition. Members of the United Nations are required to seek a solution to their disputes by arbitration, among other procedures laid down in Article 33 of the **charter**. The **Security Council** may also recommend appropriate procedures or methods of adjustment to the disputants including a recourse to the **International Court of Justice (ICJ)**.

Arbitration is a common practice in trade, investment, and business matters and has been institutionalized in the **World Trade Organization (WTO)**. It is more rarely used to settle political disputes. A notable exception was the establishment of a U.S.-Iran Claims

Tribunal, which handled claims arising from Iran's seizure in 1979 of the United States embassy in Tehran. *See also* CONCILIATION; ENQUIRY; IRAN HOSTAGE CRISIS (4 November 1979–20 January 1981); JUDICIAL SETTLEMENT; MEDIATION; PEACEFUL SETTLEMENT OF DISPUTES; PERMANENT COURT OF ARBITRATION (PCA); UNITED NATIONS COMMISSION ON INTERNATIONAL TRADE LAW (UNCITRAL).

ARBOUR, LOUISE (1947–). Canadian magistrate who was chief prosecutor of the **International Criminal Tribunal for the Former Yugoslavia (ICTY)** and the **International Criminal Tribunal for Rwanda (ICTR)** from 1996 to 1999. From 1999 to 2004, she served on the Supreme Court of Canada. In 2004, she became **United Nations High Commissioner for Human Rights (UNHCHR)**. *See also* AYALA-LASSO, JOSE (1932–); DE MELLO, SERGIO VIERA (1948–2003); OGATA, SADAKO (1927–); ROBINSON, MARY (1944–); WAR CRIMES TRIBUNALS.

ARIAS, OSCAR (1941–). President of Costa Rica from 1986 to 1990. He assumed an active role in the search for a settlement of the conflicts in Central America and drew up the peace plan that was used as a basis for their resolution in 1989. For his personal efforts, he was awarded the **Nobel Peace Prize** in 1987. *See also* CENTRAL AMERICA CONFLICTS; EL SALVADOR CONFLICT (1972–1992); GUATEMALA CONFLICT (1960–1995); NICARAGUA QUESTION.

ARMS CONTROL. In contrast to **disarmament**, which aims at the reduction or elimination of weapons, arms control agreements are designed to limit the growth of armaments or to restrict their testing, production, deployment, and use. The 1963 **Partial Test Ban Treaty**, the 1967 **Outer Space Treaty**, the 1971 **Seabed Demilitarization Treaty**, the 1972 **Biological Weapons Convention**, the 1977 **Environmental Modification Convention**, and the 1991 **Register of Conventional Arms and Standardized Reporting of Military Expenditures** are instances of arms control multilateral agreements. *See also* CONFERENCE ON DISARMAMENT (CD); INTERNATIONAL ATOMIC ENERGY AGENCY (IAEA); NUCLEAR WEAPONS FREE ZONES (NWFZs).

ASIAN DEVELOPMENT BANK (ADB). Established at the prodding of Japan and the United Nations **Economic and Social Commission for Asia and the Pacific (ESCAP),** this **regional development bank** commenced lending operations in 1968. The ADB makes loans and equity investment for the economic and social advancement of its Asian region members. Its total authorized capital stock is valued at some U.S. $45 billion. *See also* AFRICAN DEVELOPMENT BANK (AfDB); INTER-AMERICAN DEVELOPMENT BANK (IDB); MULTILATERAL DEVELOPMENT BANKS (MDBs).

ASYLUM. The granting of **refugee** status to an alien who is in danger of persecution or death for racial, religious, political, or other reasons in his/her own country. Increasing numbers of asylum seekers in recent decades from Eastern Europe and **developing countries** have prompted resistance on the part of receiving Northern countries because they are suspected of seeking better employment opportunities and higher standards of living rather than fleeing persecution. Asylum seekers are protected by international **human rights** instruments such as the **International Covenant on Civil and Political Rights** and the **International Covenant on Economic, Social, and Cultural Rights**. Their flows, which appear to have ebbed in recent years, are monitored by the **United Nations High Commissioner for Human Rights (UNHCHR).** *See also* MIGRATION (INTERNATIONAL).

ATLANTIC CHARTER. Joint statement of common "purposes and principles" to govern the postwar world order issued following a meeting between U.S. president **Franklin Delano Roosevelt** and **Winston Churchill**, the British prime minister, off the coast of Newfoundland in the summer of 1941. The charter inferentially recognized the need for some form of permanent international organization, as it asserts that the disarmament of aggressor nations was essential "pending the establishment of a wider and permanent system of general security." *See also* DECLARATION BY UNITED NATIONS (1942); MOSCOW DECLARATION ON GENERAL SECURITY (1943); YALTA CONFERENCE (1945).

ATOMIC ENERGY. Early American proposals to bring atomic energy under some degree of United Nations oversight foundered upon

Soviet opposition. Whether they constituted bona fide proposals for serious negotiations remains debatable. In any case, atomic energy always was a matter far too close to the security interests of the big powers, and the role of the United Nations has remained residual, limited essentially to the promotion of scientific and technical cooperation and the establishment of standards for nuclear safety and environmental protection. *See also* BARUCH, BERNARD (1870–1965); DISARMAMENT; INTERNATIONAL ATOMIC ENERGY AGENCY (IAEA).

ATOMIC ENERGY COMMISSION (AEC). Subsidiary body of the **General Assembly** established in 1946 to make proposals for the elimination of atomic weapons, the verification of **disarmament** measures, and the exchange of scientific information. Composed of all the members of the Security Council and Canada, the AEC was soon deadlocked by the diametrically opposed views of the United States and the USSR. In 1952, it was merged with another commission dealing with conventional armaments into a single **Disarmament Commission**. *See also* BARUCH, BERNARD (1870–1965); CONFERENCE ON DISARMAMENT (CD).

"ATOMS FOR PEACE." Proposal made in 1953 by U.S. president **Dwight D. Eisenhower** in a statement to the United Nations **General Assembly** offering a blueprint of international cooperation for the peaceful uses of atomic energy through a new institutional entity within the United Nations. The idea eventually led to the establishment of the **International Atomic Energy Agency (IAEA)**.

AYALA-LASSO, JOSE (1932–). Ecuadorian career diplomat and first **United Nations High Commissioner for Human Rights (UNHCHR)**. Appointed in 1994 by the **secretary-general** of the United Nations with the unanimous approval of the **General Assembly**, he resigned from his post in 1997 following his designation as minister of foreign affairs of Ecuador.

– B –

BACTERIOLOGICAL WEAPONS. Use of disease-causing microorganisms (i.e., bacteria and viruses) in a weapon system. Biological warfare is by no means new, as historians refer to instances of it extending as far back as the sixth century BC. The use of bacteriological or biological weapons was banned in international law by the 1925 **Geneva Protocol**, the scope of which was in turn broadened by the 1972 **Convention on the Prohibition of the Development, Production, and Stockpiling of Bacteriological (Biological) and Toxin Weapons and on Their Destruction**.

BAN, KI-MOON (1944–). South Korean career diplomat who succeeded Kofi Annan as **secretary-general** of the United Nations on 1 January 2007. He entered the Foreign Service in 1970 and subsequently served in various capacities in his capital, New York, and Washington. While serving as ambassador to Austria, Ban was elected as chairman of the preparatory Commission for the **Comprehensive Nuclear Test Ban Treaty** Organization in 1999. He was "chef de cabinet" to the South Korean President of the United Nations **General Assembly** in 2001 and became South Korea's foreign minister in 2004.

BARUCH, BERNARD (1870–1965). American financier and government adviser on national defense and armament industry matters. As the U.S. representative to the United Nations **Atomic Energy Commission**, he presented a plan for the international control of **atomic energy** that bears his name, which was rejected by the Soviet Union. *See also* DISARMAMENT.

BASEL CONVENTION ON THE CONTROL OF TRANS-BOUNDARY MOVEMENTS OF HAZARDOUS WASTES AND THEIR DISPOSAL (1989). The basic purpose of this treaty, concluded under the auspices of the **United Nations Environment Programme (UNEP)**, is to reduce the movement of hazardous wastes between states, and in particular to prevent the dumping of wastes from developed to developing countries. It requires state parties to adopt national legislation in order to minimize the toxicity of the wastes they produce and to ensure that their management is environmentally sound. The treaty entered into force in 1992. *See also* COMMISSION ON SUSTAINABLE DEVELOPMENT (UNITED NATIONS) (CSD); ENVIRONMENT.

BASIC HUMAN NEEDS. An approach to **development** focused on **employment** creation as a means to achieve the satisfaction of essential food, **shelter**, and **health** requisites. This shift in development thinking was triggered in the mid-1970s by the persistence of high levels of **poverty**, growing unemployment, and deepening inequalities in income distribution in spite of two decades of unprecedentedly high economic growth rates. The **International Labour Organization (ILO)** played a key role in this process. The idea was subsequently embraced by the United Nations, the **Organization for Economic Cooperation and Development (OECD)**, and the **World Bank** until the return of neoclassical laissez-faire policies in the 1990s. Aspects of the basic-needs approach have resurfaced in some of the recommendations contained in the **Millennium Declaration.** *See also* ALMA-ATA HEALTH DECLARATION (1978); EDUCATION; WASHINGTON CONSENSUS; WORLD EMPLOYMENT CONFERENCE (1976).

BERNADOTTE, COUNT FOLKE (1895–1948). Swedish diplomat and Red Cross official remembered for his humanitarian efforts during World War II. In May 1948, he was asked by the United Nations **Security Council** to act as a mediator in the **Arab-Israeli conflict**. Less than four months later he was assassinated in the Israeli-held sector of Jerusalem. His attempts to bring about a military truce between Israel and its Arab neighbors were brought to fruition by **Ralph Bunche**, his American aide, who succeeded him in his functions.

BERTINI, CATHERINE (1950–). American public official who served in the United States Departments of Agriculture and Health and Human Services. For 10 years (1992–2002), she was executive director of the **World Food Programme (WFP)**. She modernized the administration of the WFP and was widely praised for her efforts to assist millions of victims of wars and natural disasters, notably in Afghanistan, **North Korea**, Bosnia, **Kosovo**, and the Horn of Africa. After leaving WFP, she briefly served as undersecretary-general for management in the United Nations **secretariat.** *See also* HUMANITARIAN AGENCIES; HUMANITARIAN ASSISTANCE.

BERTRAND, MAURICE (1922–). French national who served for many years in the **Joint Inspection Unit**. In that capacity, he produced several influential reports that contributed to the professionalization of UN **personnel** recruitment methods. The sweeping **reforms** he advocated in his latest evaluation study, issued on the eve of his retirement from service in 1985, provoked considerable controversy and went largely unheeded.

BIOLOGICAL DIVERSITY. While biologists and ecologists assign different meanings to this term, the most commonly accepted definition may be found in the United Nations **Convention on Biological Diversity (CBD)**, which characterizes it as "the variability among living organisms from all sources, including, inter alia, terrestrial, marine, and other aquatic ecosystems and the ecological complexes of which they are part: this includes diversity within species, between species, and of ecosystems."

Biodiversity is the result of 3.5 billion years of evolution, and estimates of global diversity vary from 2 million to 100 million species. New species are regularly discovered, especially in tropical forests. Brazil is believed to represent one-fifth of the world's biodiversity and India some 8 percent of recorded species.

Biodiversity is essential to human development and sustenance because it constitutes a reservoir of economic resources. Biodiversity provides food (crops, livestocks, forestry, and fish) and medicine (promising anticancer drugs come from tropical rainforest plants). It is a source of energy (biomass and oil); fibers for clothing; building materials for shelter; and industrial products like lubricants, perfumes, dyes, paper, rubber, latexes, and resins. It also provides incentive for tourism.

Pressures arising from a growing human **population** and unbridled economic activities have led to an observable pattern of erosion of biodiversity in the past century. There is still considerable dispute about the extent and scope of current extinction, but the conservation, management, and protection of biological diversity has become an increasingly major global concern, often adding another layer of contentious issues between Northern and Southern countries.

A 1972 United Nations Educational, Scientific, and Cultural Organization (UNESCO) convention posited the controversial principle that biological resources, such as plants, were a **common heritage of mankind**. The 1992 United Nations **Convention on Biological**

Diversity enjoins countries to conserve biodiversity and share the benefits resulting from the use of biodiversity while giving them sovereign national rights over biological resources. The spirit of this normative regime implies that the collection of natural products (bioprospecting, mainly by firms from industrial countries) must rest on the prior consent of the source country (mainly developing countries) in exchange for a fair distribution of the benefits. The latter point has turned into a hotly contested **North-South** issue as it relates directly to the continuing relevance and acceptation of legal rules of patenting.

Another political dimension of the question of patenting concerns the rights of indigenous populations to exert ownership over their traditional biodiverse environment, which is increasingly threatened by outside forces beyond the control of national governments or, at times, supported by them. *See also* CARTAGENA PROTOCOL ON BIOSAFETY (2003); UNITED NATIONS PERMANENT FORUM FOR INDIGENOUS PEOPLES (UNPFIP); WORLD INTELLECTUAL PROPERTY ORGANIZATION (WIPO).

BIOLOGICAL WEAPONS CONVENTION (BWC, 1972). *See* CONVENTION ON THE PROHIBITION OF THE DEVELOPMENT, PRODUCTION, AND STOCKPILING OF BACTERIOLOGICAL (BIOLOGICAL) AND TOXIN WEAPONS AND ON THEIR DESTRUCTION (1972).

BLANCHARD, FRANCIS (1916–). French international civil servant who began his career in 1947 when he joined the **International Refugee Organization (IRO)**. Blanchard joined the **International Labour Organization (ILO)** in 1951 and rapidly rose to senior positions. In 1973, he was elected director general and, in that capacity, skillfully steered the expansion of ILO **technical assistance** programs and the extension of its **human rights** work in the midst of **Cold War** tensions. Blanchard retired from the ILO in 1989 after 38 years of service.

BLIX, HANS (1928–). Swedish official who was foreign minister of Sweden in 1978. From 1981 to 1997, he became the director-general of the **International Atomic Energy Agency (IAEA)** and, in that capacity, played a key role in the implementation of the disarmament measures imposed by the **Security Council** on Iraq in the wake of the second **Persian Gulf War**. From 2000 to the outbreak of the second Gulf War, Hans Blix headed the **United Nations Monitoring, Verification, and Inspection Commission (UNMOVIC)**. While being critical of the Iraqi regime for not fully cooperating with UNMOVIC, Blix also publicly contradicted American claims that Iraq was in possession of **weapons of mass destruction**.

BOSNIA-HERZEGOVINA. *See* BOSNIAN CONFLICT (1992–1995).

BOSNIAN CONFLICT (1992–1995). An ethnic tangle of Muslims, Serbs, and Croats, Bosnia-Herzegovina proclaimed its independence from Yugoslavia in 1992. War broke out as the Serbian and Croat minorities with the help of regular military forces of Serbia and Croatia sought to carve out territorial enclaves for their own communities. Undeterred by an ineffectual United Nations **peacekeeping** presence, the conflict was marked by ruthless campaigns of **ethnic cleansing** and massacres, primarily targeted at Muslims. By mid-1992, rebel Bosnian Serbs had conquered two-thirds of Bosnia.

United States–sponsored peace talks in 1995 brought the conflict to an end with the creation of a Muslim-Croat federation and a Serb entity within the larger federation of Bosnia. The fragile agreement is policed by forces of the **North Atlantic Treaty Organization (NATO)**. Several individuals indicted for war crimes, **crimes against humanity**, and genocide, are being tried by the **International Criminal Tribunal for the Former Yugoslavia (ICTY)** in the Hague. A key defendant in the trial, former Serbian president Slobodan Milesovic, died of a heart attack hours away from possible conviction of some of these charges. *See also* CONVENTION ON THE PREVENTION AND PUNISHMENT OF THE CRIME OF GENOCIDE; UNITED NATIONS PROTECTION FORCE (UNPROFOR, 1992–1995).

BOUTROS-GHALI, BOUTROS (1922–). Egyptian lawyer, scholar, politician, statesman, and sixth **secretary-general** of the United Nations from 1992 to 1996. At the time of his appointment, Boutros-Ghali had been Egypt's deputy prime minister for foreign affairs since 1991 and had served as minister of state for foreign affairs from

1977 until 1991. Over four decades, he participated in numerous international meetings dealing with **international law**, **human rights**, economic and social **development**, **decolonization**, and issues related to the **Nonaligned Movement (NAM)**. As minister of state for foreign affairs, he played an important role in the negotiation of the 1979 peace accords between Israel and Egypt.

During his tenure, he sought, with limited success, to strengthen the UN's peacekeeping functions as the financially strapped organization was faced with crises in **Somalia**, **Rwanda**, **Angola**, and the former Yugoslavia. He oversaw the drafting of an **Agenda for Peace**, an **Agenda for Development**, and an **Agenda for Democracy** in a systematic effort to sharpen the objectives of the United Nations. During his term, **apartheid** came to an end in South Africa with the UN-supervised election of Nelson Mandela in 1994.

Boutros-Ghali's term of office as secretary-general was nevertheless marked by considerable controversy. In response to criticism about UN bureaucratic wastefulness and ineffectiveness, he initiated a process of streamlining and reorganization of the **secretariat**. He also agreed to the creation of a virtually independent **Office of Internal Oversight Services (OIOS)** with the mandate to conduct broad investigations to eliminate fraud, waste, and abuse.

But his views of a stronger and invigorated United Nations brought him early on into direct conflict with the United States where, in 1994, off-year elections gave Republicans a majority in both houses of the U.S. Congress. His advocacy of the need to identify "at risk" states and act early to avoid their collapse and his proposal to place military forces at the disposal of the United Nations for rapid action in crisis situations fell on deaf ears. They also created the image of an incumbent bent on gaining power at the expense of state sovereignty. In addition and notwithstanding the fact that both failures were primarily due to the lack of United States support, he was criticized for Somalia's debacle and the subsequent UN incapacity to act during the Rwandan **genocide**. Continuing policy disagreements with the United States made him the target of acerbic remarks by senior U.S. senators and in the course of the 1996 presidential campaign as well. His bid for a second term was blocked by the United States in the **Security Council**. From 1997 to 2002, Boutros-Ghali was secretary-general of La Francophonie, an organization of French-speaking nations.

BRAHIMI REPORT. Investigation conducted in 2002 by a panel of experts ordered by the **secretary-general** in the wake of UN **peace-keeping** failures in the 1990s. Headed by Ambassador **Lakhdar Brahimi** of Algeria, the panel made a critical assessment of past UN peacekeeping efforts with particular emphasis on the management and financial capacity of the organization to support a growing number of operations of an increasingly complex nature. Its recommendations focus on measures designed to enhance the capacity of the **Department of Peacekeeping Operations (DPKO)** in the planning, rapid deployment, and management of civilian, military, and multidimensional peace operations. At the same time, the report underlines the critical importance of the political support and will of member states without which the performance of the United Nations in peacekeeping will not improve.

BRAHIMI, LAKHDAR (1934–). Algerian diplomat who served as ambassador to the **Arab League** and the United Kingdom. He was foreign minister from 1991 to 1993. He has subsequently taken on several delicate assignments for the United Nations first as **special representative** of the secretary-general for **Haiti** (1994–1996), South Africa (1993–1994), and **Afghanistan** (1997–1999), and then as head of the **United Nations Assistance Mission in Afghanistan (UNAMA)** (2001–2004). He played a key role in brokering an agreement between Iraqi leaders and the United States on the formation of the transitional government that took power at the end of June 2004.

Between his Afghanistan assignments, Ambassador Brahimi chaired an independent panel established by the **secretary-general** to review United Nations peacekeeping operations. The group's report, known as the "**Brahimi Report**," was the basis for significant operational and organizational changes in the management of UN peacekeeping. *See also* REFORM, UNITED NATIONS.

BRAIN DRAIN. Refers to the emigration of highly trained, educated, and qualified people searching for better **employment** and financial opportunities abroad. The brain drain has mainly originated from **developing countries**. Because of its adverse consequences on the capacity of developing countries to embark on sustained **development**, the matter has been repeatedly addressed by various United Nations organs, notably the **Economic and Social Council (ECOSOC)** and the **General Assembly**. *See also* MIGRATION (INTERNATIONAL).

BRANDT COMMISSION. *See* INDEPENDENT COMMISSION ON INTERNATIONAL DEVELOPMENT ISSUES (ICIDI).

BRETTON WOODS CONFERENCE AND AGREEMENT (1944). Common terminology used to refer to the United Nations Monetary and Financial Conference held in 1944 from 1–22 July that led to the creation of the **International Monetary Fund (IMF)** and the **International Bank for Reconstruction and Development (IBRD)**. The IMF and the IBRD are often called the **Bretton Woods institutions (BWIs)**.

BRETTON WOODS INSTITUTIONS (BWIs). *See* BRETTON WOODS CONFERENCE AND AGREEMENT (1944); INTERNATIONAL BANK FOR RECONSTRUCTION AND DEVELOPMENT (IBRD); INTERNATIONAL MONETARY FUND (IMF).

BRICKER AMENDMENT. Proposal to amend the United States constitution in the early 1950s that sought to limit the treaty-making powers of the president. The move, which was prompted by fears in the American Senate that United Nations **human rights** treaties might override U.S. civil laws and **sovereignty**, eventually failed. But it contributed to the emergence of a durable and still persistent pattern of senatorial ambivalence and reluctance to ratify United Nations human rights instruments.

BRUNDTLAND, GRO HARLEM (1939–). Leading political figure in Norway. Dr Brundtland entered the Norwegian government in 1974 as environment minister and subsequently served three terms as Norwegian premier, ending in 1995. Widely respected for her commitment to improving public health on a global scale, she headed the **World Health Organization (WHO)** from 1998 to 2003. Starting in 1983, Dr Brundtland chaired the **World Commission on Environment and Development**, which developed the broad political concept of "**sustainable development**" in its report "Our Common Future" thus paving the way toward the first **Earth Summit** in Rio de Janeiro in 1992. *See also* DEVELOPMENT.

BRUNDTLAND COMMISSION. *See* WORLD COMMISSION ON ENVIRONMENT AND DEVELOPMENT.

BUDGET (UNITED NATIONS). Worldwide expenditures channeled through the UN system amount to roughly U.S. $10–12 billion a year, representing only 0.0005 percent of the world's gross domestic product and an expenditure of $1.90 per human being. These operations are funded through three separate budget categories: the regular budget, which is financed by a mandatory assessment from member states; the **peacekeeping** budget, which is also financed by assessment but is separate from the regular budget; and, finally, voluntary contributions, which finance most of the United Nations' humanitarian and **development** activities.

The regular budget of the United Nations covers the costs of the organization's recurrent activities, including staff salaries and retirement, travel, buildings and equipment, conferences, servicing of meetings, and other administrative costs. The **secretary-general** prepares two-year-program regular-budget estimates, which are reviewed by the **Advisory Committee on Administrative and Budgetary Questions (ACABQ)** and the **Committee for Programme and Coordination (CPC)** prior to their adoption by the **General Assembly**.

Regular-budget expenses are apportioned among member states by the assembly on the basis of a **scale of assessment** determined by their capacity to pay. In 1946, the UN regular budget amounted to U.S. $21.5 million. The 2004–2005 budget adopted by the assembly slightly exceeded U.S. $3 billion. In real terms the UN regular budget has grown only 10 times between 1946 and 1992 and shown no growth since. The UN budget process has been plagued by nonpayment or late payment of dues, and selective withholding by member states, especially the United States. These problems arise in part from the fact that a handful of rich countries pay over 70 percent of the total budget and can be outvoted by overwhelming majorities of mostly developing states that have the voting power to determine how much and for what purposes the money should be spent, while contributing less than 30 percent of the budget.

With the exception of two operations authorized by the **General Assembly**, the costs of peacekeeping operations mandated by the **Security Council** are covered by a separate and distinct budget. The peacekeeping scale of assessment is roughly similar to the scale of assessment used for the UN regular budget with provisions made for the permanent members of the Security Council to carry a proportionately higher responsibility in their financing. The peacekeeping budget of the United Nations has widely fluctuated over the years reflecting the ever changing scale and scope of peacekeeping operations. The cost of peacekeeping operations surged in the early 1990s hitting a $3.5 billion peak in 1994, plummeted precipitously thereafter, and rebounded in the past few years. The latest peacekeeping budget adopted by the General Assembly for the period mid-2006 to mid-2007 amounts to $4.75 billion.

The humanitarian relief and economic and social development work of the United Nations, undertaken by such entities as the **United Nations Development Programme (UNDP)**, the **United Nations Children's Fund (UNICEF)**, the **World Food Programme (WFP)**, and **the United Nations Population Fund (UNFPA)**, is funded by voluntary contributions. Their level has also widely fluctuated over the years and currently reaches some $4.5 billion.

The **specialized agencies** have their separate and distinct finances. As is the case for the United Nations, their funding falls into two broad categories: a regular biennial budget composed of assessed mandatory contributions from member states and adopted by their respective governing bodies, and voluntary contributions covering their field and technical assistance operations. The large specialized agencies such as the **Food and Agriculture Organization (FAO)** and the **United Nations Educational, Scientific, and Cultural Organization (UNESCO)** have biennial budgets exceeding half a billion U.S. dollars. *See also* COMMITTEE ON CONTRIBUTIONS; FINANCING OF THE UNITED NATIONS.

BUNCHE, RALPH J. (1904–1971). American scholar, civil rights leader, and diplomat who joined the United Nations in 1947, where he first dealt with trusteeship questions. In 1949, Bunche successfully mediated a truce in the **Arab-Israeli conflict**, for which he was awarded the **Nobel Peace Prize**. In subsequent years, in addition to his continuing work in the Middle East, Bunche organized and directed United Nations **peacekeeping** operations in the 1956 Suez crisis and the 1960 Congo crisis. *See also* BERNADOTTE, COUNT

FOLKE (1895–1948); TRUSTEESHIP SYSTEM; UNITED NATIONS EMERGENCY FORCE (UNEF I; November 1956–June 1967); UNITED NATIONS OPERATION IN THE CONGO (ONUC; July 1960–June 1964); URQUHART, SIR BRIAN (1919–).

BURUNDI. Little attention has been given to this civil war that broke out in October 1993 following the assassination by a group of Tutsi army officers. Since then, some 300,000 Burundians—mostly civilians—have perished in intense ethnic violence, which began when varying groups drawn from the country's large Hutu majority rose up against the Tutsi-led government. The government of Burundi signed a cease-fire agreement in December 2002 with three of the four Hutu rebel groups. The government signed another accord in October 2003, agreeing yet again to end the civil war. The accord was followed by the deployment of the African Mission in Burundi (AMIB) the first peacekeeping operations mounted by the **African Union (AU)** to oversee the implementation of the peace accords.

As peace prospects improved in early 2004, the United Nations **secretary-general** recommended in March 2004 that the **Security Council** establish a UN peacekeeping mission in Burundi to replace and expand the existing African Force. The proposal of the secretary-general was endorsed by the council and, on 21 May 2004, the Council established the **United Nations Operation in Burundi (ONUB)**. After elections held in 2005, the mission is expected to support the **peace-building** process in the country.

BUSH, GEORGE W. (1946–). Forty-third president of the United States. He captured the presidency in 2000 after a contentious election and won a second term in 2004. His foreign policy has been markedly different from his predecessors. He rejected a series of international agreements, notably the **Kyoto Protocol** treaty on global warming, the **Comprehensive Test Ban Treaty (CTBT)**, and the treaty establishing the **International Criminal Court (ICC)**. Arguing that the September 11 attacks had made the doctrine of **containment** irrelevant, he articulated a new national security strategy of **preemption**, which holds that the United States must have recourse to the use of force in order to prevent enemies from striking first. This doctrine is viewed by many scholars and diplomats as a challenge to the United Nations **Charter** provisions on the **use of force** and a rejection of multilateral approaches to global security. *See also* HIGH-LEVEL PANEL ON THREATS, CHALLENGES, AND CHANGE (HLP); PERSIAN GULF WAR, SECOND (March–April 2003).

BUSINESS AND THE UNITED NATIONS. On the whole, business organizations initially welcomed the creation of the United Nations. But the Keynesian interventionist and regulatory policies advocated by the organization for promoting growth in **developing countries**, beginning in the 1950s onward, quickly soured its relations with the international business community. These relations reached their nadir in the 1970s as policy discussions focused on the right of developing countries to exert their full **sovereignty over their natural resources** (a claim that included a right of nationalization without compensation) and the formulation of mandatory **codes of conduct** establishing binding norms of conduct on investment and corporate profit. These demands, articulated in the 1974 developing countries' manifesto of a **"New International Economic Order (NIEO),"** faced the determined and eventually successful resistance of developed countries.

With the resurgence of interest in market-oriented solutions to **development** issues that coincided with the end of the **Cold War**, political attention has shifted toward the search for incentives to prompt business adherence to norms of corporate responsibility. The global reach of **multinational corporations (MNCs)** has, in particular, come under renewed scrutiny in the context of the civil wars in **Angola**, **Sierra Leone**, **Liberia**, and the **Democratic Republic of the Congo**. These brutal armed conflicts have usually been induced, fueled, funded, and prolonged by intransigent warlords, renegade militias, and rebel groups that depend on the illegal sale of commodities (e.g., diamonds, timber, oil) in exchange for weapons, fuel, and assorted war matériel including **antipersonnel landmines**. Bringing under control the networks of international business, brokers, and other intermediaries that have emerged in African regional countries, Eastern Europe, Russia, the Balkans and the Middle East has proved to be a major challenge.

The **Security Council** has adopted increasingly fine-tuned **sanctions** designed to curb these illicit activities. Another approach undertaken under the aegis of the **Commission for Human Rights** has been to formulate norms defining the responsibilities of MNCs in the protection of human rights in situations of armed conflict. **Secretary-General Kofi Annan**'s initiative in 1999 to launch a "**Global Compact**" may be viewed as an integral part of this effort. *See also* CRIME PREVENTION; INTERNATIONAL CHAMBER OF COMMERCE (ICC); UNITED NATIONS CONVENTION AGAINST CORRUPTION (2003); UNITED NATIONS CONVENTION AGAINST TRANSNATIONAL ORGANIZED CRIME (2003).

BUSINESS COUNCIL FOR THE UNITED NATIONS (BCUN). Network of U.S. business executives seeking to develop UN/private sector partnerships. The BCUN played an important role in mobilizing U.S. business participation in the 2002 Monterrey **International Conference on Financing for Development**. It also organizes conferences and working groups bringing together UN agencies together with banks, investment banks, ratings agencies. and other corporations with a view to mobilizing private sector capital for **development** and the achievement of the **Millennium Development Goals**. In 1999, the BCUN merged with the **United Nations Association of the United States of America (UNA-USA)**.

– C –

CAMBODIA CONFLICT (1954–2003). After obtaining its independence from France in 1954, Cambodia embraced a foreign policy of neutrality. The country, however, was soon drawn into the escalating war in Vietnam by ethnic Khmer refugees fleeing persecution in neighboring South Vietnam, Vietnamese Communists seeking safe havens, U.S. military incursions, and extensive American bombing of its border areas with Vietnam. Civil war broke out in 1967 culminating, in 1975, with the ousting of the U.S.-supported military regime by Communist insurgents known as Khmer Rouge. Pogroms, and ethnic cleansing targeted the Chinese, Muslim, and Vietnamese minorities accompanied by the forcible and brutal deportation of the urban civilian population into agricultural labor camps. Executions, starvation, overwork, disease, and denial of medical care took the lives of some 1.7 million people between 1975 and 1979. The Khmer Rouge regime was toppled by invading Vietnamese forces in 1979 and, for some 10 years, Cambodia suffered diplomatic isolation.

International negotiations initiated in 1988 under the aegis of the United Nations brought together all Cambodian internal political forces and the great powers that supported them (China, the USSR, and the United States). Agreement among them was reached in 1991 in Paris, setting up the **United Nations Transitional Authority in Cambodia (UNTAC)** to run the country pending the outcome of national elections. Elections were held in 1993 under the supervision of UNTAC. They have since brought precarious political stability to a country that also faces massive reconstruction tasks.

After several years of negotiations, the United Nations and the Cambodian government reached an agreement in 2003 to set up a mixed international-national criminal tribunal to try the surviving Khmer Rouge leaders on charges of genocide and **crimes against humanity**. *See also* CREDENTIALS COMMITTEE OF THE GENERAL ASSEMBLY; TRANSITIONAL ADMINISTRATION; WAR CRIMES TRIBUNALS.

CAPACITY DEVELOPMENT. Redefinition of the old concept of **technical assistance** that has gained currency in the late 1990s as a result of changing conceptions of the notion of **development**. Capacity development has come to mean not only the transfer and acquisition of know-how skills but also the sustainable creation, utilization, and retention of the ability of individuals, organizations, and societies to perform functions and solve problems in order to reduce poverty, enhance self-reliance, improve people's lives, and transform society. The most innovative implications of capacity development are the emphases placed on the value of individual participation in the elaboration and implementation of projects and the sustainable development of social capital. *See also* CAPACITY STUDY OF THE UNITED NATIONS DEVELOPMENT SYSTEM (1970).

CAPACITY STUDY OF THE UNITED NATIONS DEVELOPMENT SYSTEM (1970). Overall review of the United Nations' operational activities carried out at the request of the **United Nations**

Development Program (UNDP) by a team of analysts under the direction of **Sir Robert Jackson**. The study was forthright in its criticisms of the UN capacity to handle the resources made available for **technical assistance** purposes, singling out the absence of an effective system for the control of the resources entrusted to it, the diffusion of responsibility throughout the system, and the general reluctance of the **specialized agencies** to contract outside the system. As the report put it bluntly, "the UN development system has tried to wage a war on want for many years with very little organized 'brain' to guide it. Its absence may well be the greatest constraint of all on capacity. Without it, the future evolution of the UN development system could easily repeat the history of the dinosaur."

The report called for a complete restructuring of UN development operations with considerably increased power for the UNDP backed up by organizational, managerial, and administrative changes. Though well justified, the recommendations of the capacity study only brought incremental improvements in the coordination of United Nations field activities. *See also* CAPACITY DEVELOPMENT; COORDINATION, UNITED NATIONS SYSTEM; RESIDENT REPRESENTATIVES; TECHNICAL ASSISTANCE; REFORM, UNITED NATIONS.

CAPE VERDE. *See* PORTUGUESE COLONIES.

CARDOSO, FERNANDO HENRIQUE (1931–). Brazilian scholar turned politician who was an early exponent of the "**dependencia**" theory of North-South relations. Elected president of Brazil from 1995 to 2002, he is credited with turning around the Brazilian economy, reforming state institutions, and promoting dialogue and collaboration with civil society. President Cardoso served as special advisor to the **secretary-general** and, in that capacity, chaired a panel of eminent persons who took stock of UN-civil society relations and made recommendations on improving them. *See also* NONGOVERNMENTAL ORGANIZATIONS (NGOs), PANEL OF EMINENT PERSONS ON UNITED NATIONS–CIVIL SOCIETY RELATIONS.

CARE INTERNATIONAL (CARE). Independent humanitarian **nongovernmental organization (NGO)** primarily involved in **poverty**

eradication issues. CARE has programs in over 70 countries and its work has an impact on an estimated 45 million of the world's poorest people. Its projects focus on emergency **food** and shelter to survivors of **natural disasters**, wars, and conflicts. They also have a longer-term development dimension, as they are concerned with the delivery of primary **health** care, the promotion of sustainable **agriculture**, and support for savings and loan projects. *See also* DISASTER RELIEF; HUMANITARIAN AGENCIES; HUMANITARIAN ASSISTANCE.

CARITAS INTERNATIONALIS. Confederation of Catholic relief, development, and social services organizations focusing on **poverty** alleviation. Its first national constituent units were created at the turn of the century in Germany, Switzerland, and the United States. Concerned with poverty and discrimination issues, this **nongovernmental organization (NGO)** has focused its advocacy work on Palestine; the humanitarian cost of sanctions; and debt, finance, and trade questions. It also provides relief and helps raise funds for major natural and man-made emergencies. *See also* DISASTER RELIEF; HUMANITARIAN AGENCIES; HUMANITARIAN ASSISTANCE.

CARLSSON, INGVAR (1934–). Swedish politician and prime minister 1986–1991 and 1994–1996 who played an active role in support of nuclear **disarmament.** He cochaired the **Commission on Global Governance** and was one of the authors of a study requested by the **secretary-general** on the role of the United Nations in the **Rwandan** genocide.

CARNEGIE ENDOWMENT FOR INTERNATIONAL PEACE. Private, nonprofit organization dedicated to advancing cooperation between nations and promoting active international engagement by the United States. Founded in 1910 with a gift from Andrew Carnegie, an American industrialist with an interest in world peace, the Carnegie Endowment for Peace initially focused its research work on the development of international law and the settlement of disputes, the study of the causes of war, and the promotion of international understanding and cooperation. Its current research and networking among governments, businesses, international organizations, and **civil society** concentrate on the economic, political, and technological forces driving global change, especially democracy and the rule of law, nuclear nonproliferation, trade equity and development, and the U.S. role in international affairs. *See also* NONGOVERNMENTAL ORGANIZATIONS (NGOs).

CARTAGENA PROTOCOL ON BIOSAFETY (2003). Powerful tools for the improvement of human welfare and conditions or threats to human health and **biological diversity**. The debate over the practical applications of biotechnology is still unfolding. Adopted in January 2000 by the parties to the 1992 **Convention on Biological Diversity (CBD)**, this protocol seeks to protect biological diversity from the potential risks posed by genetically modified organisms (GMOs) resulting from modern biotechnology by establishing rules for the safe transfer, handling, and use of GMOs. If a party approves for domestic use and marketing living modified organisms intended for direct use as food, feed, or processing, and these are exported, this party must communicate its decision and details to importing countries and make this information available through a worldwide information clearinghouse. *See also* INTELLECTUAL PROPERTY RIGHTS (IPRs); TRADE-RELATED ASPECTS OF INTELLECTUAL PROPERTY RIGHTS (TRIPs).

CARTER, JIMMY (1924–). Thirty-ninth president of the United States. Once derided as a weak president, Carter is remembered for having brokered the Camp David peace accords between Israel and Egypt and his efforts to integrate human rights in U.S. foreign policy. Since his retirement from politics, he has been an active international mediator and promoter of democracy and **human rights**, for which he was awarded the **Nobel Peace Prize**. *See also* ARAB-ISRAELI CONFLICT; IRAN HOSTAGE CRISIS (4 November 1979–20 January 1981).

CASSIN, RENE (1887–1976). Prominent French jurist and internationalist. One of the world's leading **human rights** advocates, he was an active and influential member of the United Nations **Commission for Human Rights** from its creation in 1946. He chaired the commission from 1955 to 1957. He was one of the principal architects of the 1948 **Universal Declaration of Human Rights**. For this contribution, Cassin received the **Nobel Peace Prize** in 1968.

CAUCUSING GROUPS. *See* GROUPS.

CENTER FOR ECONOMIC AND SOCIAL RIGHTS (CESR). Leading **nongovernmental organization (NGO)** created in 1993 seeking to promote social justice and universal **human rights** through advocacy and field research in **developing countries** integrating **human security**, social equality and political freedom concerns. CESR's main concern is to refocus basic human needs for **health**, housing, **education**, **food security**, **employment**, and a safe **environment** into enforceable human rights.

CENTRAL AMERICA CONFLICTS. Throughout the 1980s, several states of Central America were embroiled in civil wars pitting governments against leftist insurgencies that found safe havens in neighboring countries, thus precipitating border problems involving Costa Rica, **El Salvador**, **Guatemala**, Honduras, and **Nicaragua**. The root causes of these conflicts may be traced back to long-standing and deep internal social and economic inequalities. They were compounded by the support provided by the United States and the Soviet Union to the warring parties. Peacemaking efforts supported by the United Nations began in 1983. The lessening of Cold War tensions and the mediating interventions of President **Oscar Arias** of Costa Rica resulted in a 1989 collective agreement that called for an end to hostilities, the suspension of outside military aid to irregular forces and insurrectional movements, the nonuse of the territory of one state to attack other states, disarmament and weapons control measures, as well as longer-term measures such as the setting up of national reconciliation procedures and the organization of free elections. The accords also made provision for international monitoring and verification of these commitments.

Five peacekeeping missions were undertaken by the United Nations for this purpose: the **United Nations Observer Group in Central America (ONUCA)**, the **United Nations Observer Mission to Verify the Electoral Process in Nicaragua (ONUVEN)**, the **United Nations Observer Mission in El Salvador (ONUSAL)**, and the **United Nations Verification Mission in Guatemala (MINUGUA)**.

CHARTER OF ECONOMIC RIGHTS AND DUTIES OF STATES (1974). An important component of the demands articulated by the **developing countries** throughout the 1970s for far-reaching changes in the world economy. The charter, adopted by the **General Assembly** over the objections of developed countries, contained two basic and controversial provisions. It set the principle of states' full and **permanent sovereignty over their natural resources** and economic activities, a principle that included the right to nationalize foreign property without compensation. It also proclaimed the right of primary product producers to associate in producers' cartels and a corresponding duty of other countries to refrain from efforts to break these cartels. *See also* COMMODITIES; DECLARATION ON THE ESTABLISHMENT OF A NEW INTERNATIONAL ECONOMIC ORDER (NIEO).

CHARTER OF THE UNITED NATIONS. Founding document of the United Nations. The charter was signed at San Francisco on 26 June 1945 by its 50 original members (later joined by Poland). It entered into force on 24 October 1945 (a day observed each year as United Nations Day), after being ratified by China, France, the USSR, the United Kingdom, the United States, and a majority of the other signatories.

The charter evolved from a series of wartime Allied conferences, notably the 1941 **Atlantic Charter**, the 1942 **Declaration by United Nations**, and the 1944 **Dumbarton Oaks Conference**. It was finalized at the 1945 **United Nations Conference on International Organization** in San Francisco.

The charter lays out in a more detailed and comprehensive manner than the Covenant of the **League of Nations** the general framework for its activities, the purposes of the organization, membership, structure, as well as arrangements for the maintenance of peace and security and international economic and social cooperation. The charter is based on the principles that states are equal, have sovereignty over their own affairs, enjoy territorial independence, and must fulfill international obligations (as a treaty, all signatories are bound by international law to comply with the provisions of the charter). *See also* AMENDMENT (UNITED NATIONS CHARTER); ECONOMIC AND SOCIAL COUNCIL (ECOSOC); GENERAL ASSEMBLY;

INTERNATIONAL COURT OF JUSTICE (ICJ); PRINCIPLES OF THE UNITED NATIONS; REFORM, UNITED NATIONS; REVIEW OF THE UNITED NATIONS CHARTER; SECRETARIAT (UNITED NATIONS); SECRETARY-GENERAL; SECURITY COUNCIL; TRUSTEESHIP COUNCIL.

CHECHNYA CONFLICT. Conflict over the region now known as Chechnya in the Caucasus has raged intermittently since the mid-18th century between the Czarist and the Soviet government and local irredentist Muslim populations. The region experienced an uneasy calm during the 1970s and 1980s, but with the disintegration of the USSR, Chechnya again made moves toward independence. As in the past, the situation has evolved into a guerilla war between the Russian army and militant separatists. The conflict, viewed by some as "an ugly mixture of secessionism and criminality," has been marked by widespread destruction, gross **human rights** abuses, and atrocities by both sides, as the United Nations remains on the sidelines because of Russian insistence on portraying the issue as an internal matter, an argument that gained further political credence after the 11 September terrorist attacks on the United States. *See also* DOMESTIC JURISDICTION; PRINCIPLES OF THE UNITED NATIONS.

CHEMICAL WEAPONS. Gaseous, liquid, or solid substances used in military operations to kill, injure, or incapacitate people. Chemical weapons were first used in modern warfare during World War I, killing around 92,000 and causing a total of 1.3 million casualties. Chemical weapons were not used in the course of World War II, but there are numerous accounts of the use of chemical warfare agents during the 1980s in Laos, Cambodia, **Afghanistan**, Iran, and Iraq. Initially signed by 38 nations and now by over 130 nations, the 1925 **Geneva Protocol** prohibits the use in war of asphyxiating, poisonous, or other gases, and of bacteriological methods of warfare. The protocol does not prohibit the manufacture and threat of use of chemical weapons and makes no provision for the punishment of countries that use chemical weapons. It was supplemented in 1997 by a convention prohibiting the development, production, stockpiling, and use of chemical weapons. That convention also calls for their destruction. *See also* CAMBODIA CONFLICT (1954–2003); CON-

VENTION ON THE PROHIBITION OF THE DEVELOPMENT, PRODUCTION, STOCKPILING, AND USE OF CHEMICAL WEAPONS AND ON THEIR DESTRUCTION (1997); IRAN-IRAQ WAR (1980–1988); WEAPONS OF MASS DESTRUCTION (WMDs).

CHEMICAL WEAPONS CONVENTION (CWC, 1997). *See* CONVENTION ON THE PROHIBITION OF THE DEVELOPMENT, PRODUCTION, STOCKPILING, AND USE OF CHEMICAL WEAPONS AND ON THEIR DESTRUCTION (1997).

CHIEF EXECUTIVES BOARD (CEB). Successor body of the **Administrative Committee on Coordination (ACC)** set up in 2000 as part of an effort to simplify the structure of the United Nation interagency machinery. Like the ACC, it is chaired by the **secretary-general** and comprises the heads of the UN **specialized agencies**, programs and funds including the **International Bank for Reconstruction and Development (IBRD)**, the **International Monetary Fund (IMF)**, and the **World Trade Organization (WTO)**. The CEB carries out its work through a High-Level Committee on Programs and a High-Level Committee on Management composed of senior representatives and authorized to take decisions on behalf of the heads of their organizations. Its current activities focus on the implementation of the **Millennium Development Goals** and **African Economic Conditions**. *See also* COORDINATION, UNITED NATIONS SYSTEM.

CHILDERS, ERSKINE (1929–1996). Irish broadcaster and journalist who served the United Nations for over two decades, notably in the **United Nations Development Programme (UNDP)**. Following his retirement from UN service in 1989, and until assuming the post of secretary-general of the **World Federation of United Nations Associations (WFUNA)** a few months before his death, he lectured and wrote extensively on UN matters. A staunch internationalist, Childers advocated the vision of a more democratic and representative organization, which has so far proved to be impolitic. But his proposals for improvements in the internal management of the United Nations that appeared in publications coauthored with **Sir Brian Urquhart**, have inspired many of the efforts of the **secretary-general** in the 1990s.

See also REFORM, UNITED NATIONS; WORLD FEDERALIST MOVEMENT (WFM).

CHILDREN. In spite of considerable progress achieved in the past few decades, by any measurable yardstick, children remain unquestionably among the most vulnerable groups in society. Children suffer violence in their families, schools, the work place, and correctional facilities. The continued prevalence of **poverty**, armed conflicts, and the **HIV/AIDS** pandemic pose continuing threats to their well-being and rights. Today, an estimated 600 million children still live in extreme poverty. Some 150 million children are malnourished, over 10 million die every year, often from problems that could easily be dealt with, 100 million are not in school. An estimated 246 million children are trapped in exploitative labor conditions and 1.2 million children are trafficked each year for sex or labor. Millions have either died or been displaced from their homes in wars in the 1990s.

The efforts of the United Nations targeted at child survival go back to the 1940s and 1950s when the **United Nations Children's Fund (UNICEF)** provided food and basic health interventions to children in war-torn countries. While refocusing its work on children in subsequent years within a developmental perspective, the organization has served as an arena for the development of international norms and standards for the protection of children. First and foremost among them is the **Convention on the Rights of the Child**, which was adopted by the **General Assembly** in 1989. This landmark legal instrument defines and aims to protect the rights of children in times of peace as well as situations of internal armed conflicts. Two optional protocols endorsed by the Assembly in 2000 complement the convention by banning the involvement of children in armed conflicts and prohibiting the sale of children, child prostitution, and child pornography. The new child soldiers protocol represents a significant advance over previous international standards, which allowed children as young as 15 to be recruited and trained for armed combat. The **International Labour Organization (ILO)** has also provided the setting for the elaboration of international legal instruments protecting children's rights. Of particular importance is a 2000 Convention on the Worst Forms of Child Labor, which requires states to abolish such practices as child slavery, trafficking, debt bondage, and forced labor.

In 2002, the General Assembly held a special session devoted exclusively to children and was the first to include them as official delegates to review progress since the 1990 **World Summit for Children**. *See also* CHILDREN IN ARMED CONFLICTS; COMMITTEE ON THE RIGHTS OF THE CHILD (CRC); SAVE THE CHILDREN.

CHILDREN IN ARMED CONFLICTS. The impact of armed conflicts on **children** has received increasing attention in the United Nations agenda. It is estimated that 300,000 children are currently participating in fighting in more than 35 countries. Some 25 million have been uprooted from their homes. Over the last decade, 2 million children have been killed, 6 million wounded or permanently disabled, and 12 million made homeless in some 50 countries affected by armed conflicts. The magnitude of the phenomenon has prompted repeated calls for the protection of the rights of children and for regulations governing the trafficking in small arms which fuel these conflicts. The **Security Council** has passed several resolutions on the subject. In the early 1990s, the **secretary-general**, at the request of the **Committee on the Rights of the Child (CRC)**, commissioned a study published in 1996 that called for an end to "the cynical exploitation of children as soldiers." Since 1997, a special representative of the secretary-general for Children in Armed Conflicts has led international efforts to improve the situation of children in war situations and to promote the application of international legal humanitarian standards for the protection of war-affected children.

International humanitarian law provides broad protection for children. In the event of armed conflict, either international or noninternational, children benefit from the general protection provided for civilians not taking part in hostilities. Noncombatant civilians are guaranteed humane treatment and covered by the legal provisions on the conduct of hostilities. Given the particular vulnerability of children, the **Geneva Conventions** of 1949 and their 1977 Additional Protocols lay down a series of rules according them special protection. The 1989 **Convention on the Rights of the Child** also set limits on children's participation in hostilities, and an Optional Protocol to the Convention banning the use of under-18s in armed conflict came into force in 2002.

The atrocities committed by and against child soldiers in various African countries have led to the outlawing of the use of child soldiers. Lobbying by **Amnesty International (AI)**, **Human Rights Watch (HRW)**, and other **nongovernmental organizations (NGOs)** has helped criminalize the recruitment of those under 18. One key addition to international law has resulted from this late 1990s focus on child soldiers. The Rome treaty creating the **International Criminal Court (ICC)** establishes that anyone responsible for recruiting a child soldier under 15 can be prosecuted for war crimes. *See also* LIBERIA CONFLICT (1980–2003); OTUNNU, OLARA (1950–); SIERRA LEONE CONFLICT (1991–2002); UNITED NATIONS CONFERENCE ON THE ILLICIT TRADE IN SMALL ARMS AND LIGHT WEAPONS (NEW YORK, 9–20 July 2001).

CHILDREN'S FUND. *See* UNITED NATIONS CHILDREN'S FUND (UNICEF).

CHINA REPRESENTATION IN THE UNITED NATIONS (1949–1971). The Republic of China (ROC) was one of the founding members of the United Nations and a permanent member of the **Security Council** from its inception. When, in 1949, the Communist Party seized power and proclaimed the creation of the People's Republic of China (PRC), it also claimed to be the sole representative of China in the United Nations, while the ROC government withdrew to the Chinese island of Taiwan and made an identical claim. Throughout the 1950s and 1960s, the **General Assembly** debated each year resolutions seeking to transfer China's seat at the United Nations from the ROC to the PRC.

The admission of newly independent developing nations in the 1960s eroded the United States–led resistance to these moves. With the influx of new countries sympathetic to the PRC, a majority in the General Assembly passed a resolution in 1971 recognizing the PRC as the sole legitimate government of China and representative at the United Nations. China's **membership** in the United Nations was never questioned. The political and legal issue that the General Assembly was called upon to settle was to determine which of the two contending governments' claim to represent China in the organization was legitimate. *See also* CREDENTIALS COMMITTEE OF THE GENERAL ASSEMBLY; EXPULSION FROM THE UNITED NATIONS.

CHURCHILL, WINSTON (1874–1965). British politician and wartime leader, Churchill entered Parliament in 1901, served as first lord of the admiralty 1911–1915 and 1939–1940 and then as prime minister 1940–1945 and 1951–1955. Churchill participated with **Franklin D. Roosevelt** and Stalin in a series of meetings that led to the creation of the United Nations. He initially advocated a scheme of regional security councils for Europe, the Western Hemisphere, and Asia comprised of one or two great powers and a number of smaller states but he eventually shifted to **Cordell Hull**'s concept of an overall world organization. *See also* ATLANTIC CHARTER; MOSCOW DECLARATION ON GENERAL SECURITY (1943).

CIVIL AVIATION. *See* INTERNATIONAL CIVIL AVIATION ORGANIZATION (ICAO).

CIVIL SOCIETY. United Nations documents define civil society as organizations, institutions, movements, and networks that are autonomous from the state (hence the term "**nongovernmental organizations**" **[NGOs]**), are not intergovernmental and do not emanate from the private business sector. They are in principle nonprofit entities and act locally, nationally, and internationally in defense and promotion of social, economic, and cultural interests.

This definition is not universally accepted. But it is generally agreed that civil society is a concept rooted in the European cultural context and that the role of NGOs in international relations, while still clouded in controversies about their legitimacy, transparency, modes of financing, and involvement in humanitarian issues, has increased considerably as a result of **globalization**.

Issue-specific across-borders coalitions of groups have become an important source of information in pre- and postconflict situations. Their actions also act as catalysts for governmental accountability and transparency. The participation of civil society organizations in intergovernmental UN deliberative processes has considerably expanded, notably in the context of UN **global conferences**, but, by and large, remains ad hoc and fraught with inconsistencies. *See also* INTERNATIONAL CAMPAIGN TO BAN LANDMINES (ICBL); JUBILEE RESEARCH; NONSTATE ACTORS; PANEL OF EMINENT PERSONS ON UNITED NATIONS–CIVIL SOCIETY RELATIONS.

CLIMATE CHANGE. Increasing concentrations of "greenhouse gases" trapping heat in Earth's atmosphere (the so-called **global warming** effect) are feared to be increasing the planet's temperature such that it will rise by as much as two to five degrees over the next hundred years with climatic changes that could lead to **desertification**, the melting of the polar icecaps, the rise of ocean levels, and the swamping of low-lying lands.

Throughout the 1980s, climate change was the subject of scientific conferences sponsored by the **World Meteorological Organization (WMO)**, the **United Nations Environment Programme (UNEP)**, and **nongovernmental organizations (NGOs)** such as the **International Council for Science (ISCU)**. The appearance of the so-called Antarctic ozone hole in the upper atmosphere prompted agreement on the **Montreal Protocol on Substances That Deplete the Ozone Layer** in 1987. At the request of the **General Assembly**, an intergovernmental negotiating group involving numerous scientists, experts, and scientific NGOs was set up in 1990 to negotiate an international climate change convention in time for signature at the 1992 **United Nations Conference on Environment and Development** in Rio de Janeiro.

Greater industrial and agricultural production; greater use of oil, coal, and natural gas; and deforestation are known to cause dramatic increases in the emissions of greenhouse gases. Nevertheless, much remains unknown in the area of climate change and lack of conclusive scientific evidence and differences over the potential effects of greenhouse gases have left the **United Nations Framework Convention on Climate Change (UNFCCC)** with many unresolved issues. *See also* ACID RAIN; ALLIANCE OF SMALL ISLAND STATES (AOSIS); COMMISSION ON SUSTAINABLE DEVELOPMENT (UNITED NATIONS) (CSD); DESERTIFICATION; ENVIRONMENT; INTERNATIONAL MEETING TO REVIEW THE IMPLEMENTATION OF THE PROGRAMME OF ACTION FOR THE SUSTAINABLE DEVELOPMENT OF SMALL ISLAND DEVELOPING STATES (PORT-LOUIS, MAURITIUS, 10–14 January 2005); KYOTO PROTOCOL.

CLINTON, WILLIAM J. (1946–). Forty-second president of the United States. Under the Clinton administration, support for worldwide **human rights**, democracy, the **environment**, and **trade** liberalization became priority concerns of American foreign policy. Washington-led diplomatic efforts resulted in the restoration of civilian rule in **Haiti**, brought an uncertain end to the **Bosnian conflict**, resulted in the ousting of Yugoslavia from **Kosovo**, and paved the way to **Timor-Leste** independence. These relative accomplishments stand in contrast with the failure to address the humanitarian and political issues in **Somalia** and to prevent the 1994 genocide in **Rwanda**. Several trade liberalization organizations came into existence under the Clinton administration and U.S. prodding contributed to the establishment of the **World Trade Organization (WTO)**, the successor organization to the **General Agreement on Tariffs and Trade (GATT)**.

CODES OF CONDUCT. While corporate codes of conduct are individual company statements defining their own ethical standards, corporate codes of conduct for **transnational corporations (TNCs)** are externally generated and imposed on them. Such codes of conduct address a variety of TNCs' practices including their labor policies (terms and condition of **employment**), environmental standards (compliance with national emissions standards), and **health** and safety issues related to individual products.

Codes of conduct for TNCs were the subject of acrimonious and divisive discussions in United Nations forums throughout the 1970s and 1980s, the controversy pitting Northern against Southern countries, which took diametrically opposed views focused on whether such codes had legally binding regulatory effects on TNCs. The **Global Compact** launched by the **secretary-general** in 1999 was an effort to bridge these divergent positions.

The question of strengthening or developing a body of rights and duties under international law to which multinational corporations are bound has been rekindled by the proliferation of internal conflicts in the post–**Cold War** period. Several of these conflicts, notably in **Angola**, the **Democratic Republic of the Congo**, **Liberia**, and **Sierra Leone**, have been sustained and prolonged by combatants in control of local **natural resources** with access to international commodity, finance, and insurance markets. *See also* BUSINESS AND THE UNITED NATIONS; SCIENCE AND TECHNOLOGY FOR DEVELOPMENT; SHIPPING.

CODEX ALIMENTARIUS COMMISSION. Joint program set up by the **Food and Agricultural Organization (FAO)** and the **World Health Organization (WHO)** to protect the health of consumers and ensure fair practices in food trade by initiating and publicizing international food standards and by promoting the coordination of all work on food standards undertaken by international organizations. *See also* FUNCTIONALISM.

COLD WAR. Generic term referring to the ideological conflict and hostile relations between the USSR and the United States and their respective allies. Their confrontation lasted roughly from 1946 to 1991 and shaped many United Nations activities. Throughout this period, the Cold War led to a redefinition of the role originally assigned to the United Nations in the field of peace and security as the organization moved away from **collective security** to **peacekeeping**. The East-West rivalry also provided **developing countries** with considerable political leverage in their attempt to enlarge the **development** agenda of the United Nations. *See also* AGENDA FOR PEACE; CONTAINMENT.

COLLECTIVE SECURITY. Arrangement whereby each state in the system accepts that the security of one is the concern of all and agrees to join in a collective response to **aggression**. Collective security first took form in the **League of Nations**. The system of collective security laid down in the **Charter of the United Nations** enjoins states to refrain from the **use** or threat **of force** except in cases of self-defense (Articles 2.4 and 51). The charter also provides for a two-step procedure (placed under the authority of the **Security Council**) that includes mechanisms for the **peaceful settlement of disputes** and responses to threats to the peace and acts of aggression. Other systems of collective security exist at the regional level. *See also* HIGH-LEVEL PANEL ON THREATS, CHALLENGES, AND CHANGE (HLP); INTERNATIONAL CRIMINAL COURT (ICC); PEACE-KEEPING; PREEMPTION; REGIONAL ARRANGEMENTS; SANCTIONS; SELF-DEFENSE, RIGHT OF; TERRORISM.

COLLECTIVE SELF-DEFENSE. *See* SELF-DEFENSE, RIGHT OF.

COMMISSION FOR SOCIAL DEVELOPMENT (UNITED NATIONS). One of the functional commissions of the **Economic and Social Council (ECOSOC)** established in 1946. Its task is to advise the council on policies to promote social progress with particular attention to the formulation of social objectives and UN program priorities and research in areas related to social and economic **development**. The commission played a key role in the preparation of the 1995 **World Summit for Social Development** and is mandated to monitor its implementation.

COMMISSION ON CRIME PREVENTION AND CRIMINAL JUSTICE (UNITED NATIONS). Functional commission of the **Economic and Social Council (ECOSOC)** set up in 1992 to replace a preexisting Committee on Crime Prevention and Control. Its broad mandate is to provide policy guidance to the United Nations in the field of **crime prevention** and criminal justice and to prepare quinquennial United Nations congresses on these subjects. *See also* BUSINESS AND THE UNITED NATIONS; UNITED NATIONS CONVENTION AGAINST CORRUPTION (2003); UNITED NATIONS CONVENTION AGAINST THE ILLICIT TRAFFIC IN NARCOTIC DRUGS AND PSYCHOTROPIC SUBSTANCES (1988); UNITED NATIONS CONVENTION AGAINST TRANSNATIONAL ORGANIZED CRIME (2003); UNITED NATIONS CRIME CONGRESSES; UNITED NATIONS INTERREGIONAL CRIME AND JUSTICE RESEARCH INSTITUTE (UNICRI); UNITED NATIONS OFFICE ON DRUGS AND CRIME (UNODC).

COMMISSION ON GLOBAL GOVERNANCE. Group of eminent political leaders led by **Ingvar Carlsson**, the former prime minister of Sweden, **Shridath Ramphal**, the former secretary-general of the **Commonwealth**, and **Jan Pronk**, the former minister for Development Cooperation of the Netherlands, which was constituted to prepare a study on the opportunities for global governance. "*Our Global Neighborhood*," the report of the commission, released in 1998, made several specific proposals to expand the authority of the United Nations, including the creation of a standing UN army, the creation of an Economic Security Council, an end to the veto power of the permanent members of the Security Council, and the establishment of a new parliamentary body of "civil society" representatives. *See also* INDEPENDENT COMMISSIONS; REFORM, UNITED NATIONS.

COMMISSION FOR HUMAN RIGHTS (UNITED NATIONS). A subsidiary body of the **Economic and Social Council (ECOSOC)** established by the council in 1946 to promote **human rights**. The commission is composed of 54 states, meets once a year, and has the authority to create subsidiary organs. In 1947, it set up an advisory expert body, the Subcommission on Prevention of Discrimination and Protection of Minorities, renamed in 1999 the **United Nations Subcommission on the Promotion and Protection of Human Rights**.

The commission's main mandate is to carry out studies, make recommendations, and prepare drafts of human rights conventions. It originated the 1948 **Universal Declaration of Human Rights (UDHR)** and the two 1966 **International Covenants on Civil and Political Rights** and **on Economic, Social, and Cultural Rights**.

In the late 1960s, ECOSOC broadened the mandate of the commission to the protection of human rights. The commission may thus address violations of human rights through a process of public discussion that may lead to resolutions condemning the practices of a state. It may also appoint special rapporteurs to review major crosscutting issues where there is a need to strengthen human rights instruments, for example: involuntary disappearances; arbitrary detention; the right to development, education, food, and adequate housing; human rights and extreme poverty; structural adjustment policies and foreign debt; the rights of migrant workers; and indigenous peoples. Finally, the commission may consider and review communications submitted by **nongovernmental organizations (NGOs)** and individuals to the **United Nations High Commissioner for Human Rights (UNHCHR)**. This procedure is confidential but may become public if violations of human rights by a state persist and are serious. The commission has in recent years come under increasing criticism from various quarters. After protracted negotiations, it was dissolved in 2006 and replaced by a **Human Rights Council**. *See also* REFORM, UNITED NATIONS.

COMMISSION ON HUMAN SETTLEMENTS (UNITED NATIONS). Established by the **General Assembly** in 1977, a year after the **United Nations Conference on Human Settlements** in Vancouver (Habitat I), this intergovernmental body deals with problems stemming from massive urban growth, especially among cities of the developing world. The commission meets once every two years and formulates United Nations policies in regard to **shelter** and social services and the management of the urban environment and infrastructure. In 2002, the agency's mandate was strengthened and its status elevated to that of a fully fledged "program" of the UN system similar to the United Nations Children's Fund, or the United Nations Development Program. The work of the commission has been refocused on strategy clusters for achieving the urban development and shelter goals and targets of the **Millennium Declaration**. *See also* UNITED NATIONS CENTRE ON HUMAN SETTLEMENTS (UNCHS or HABITAT); UNITED NATIONS CONFERENCE ON HUMAN SETTLEMENTS (HABITAT II, ISTANBUL, 1996); URBANIZATION.

COMMISSION ON INTERNATIONAL DEVELOPMENT (PEARSON COMMISSION). Precursor of the **independent commissions** set up subsequently in the 1970s, 1980s, and 1990s. Constituted by the then president of the **World Bank**, Robert S. McNamara, to investigate the effectiveness of the bank's development assistance and make recommendations for its future policies, the commission was headed by the former Canadian prime minister **Lester Pearson** and issued its report "Partners in Development" in 1969. Many of the report's proposals were reiterated in the recommendations of the **Independent Commission on International Development Issues** (the Brandt Commission). *See also* REFORM, UNITED NATIONS.

COMMISSION ON NARCOTIC DRUGS (UNITED NATIONS). One of the functional commissions of the **Economic and Social Council (ECOSOC)** created in 1946. The commission advises the council on matters pertaining to the control of **narcotic drugs** and psychotropic substances, analyzes the world drug situation, develops proposals to strengthen the international drug control system to combat the world drug problem, and prepares and monitors the implementation of draft international conventions. Three such conventions have thus been adopted: the 1961 Convention on Narcotic Drugs; the

1971 Convention on Psychotropic Substances; and the 1988 **Convention against the Illicit Traffic in Narcotic Drugs and Psychotropic Substances**. In 1998, the **General Assembly** held a special session devoted to the world drug problem and strengthened the mandate of the commission in its role as a global forum for international cooperation to combat the international drug problem. *See also* CRIME PREVENTION; UNITED NATIONS CONVENTION AGAINST TRANSNATIONAL ORGANIZED CRIME (2003); UNITED NATIONS CRIME CONGRESSES.

COMMISSION ON POPULATION AND DEVELOPMENT (UNITED NATIONS). One of the oldest and most respected functional commissions of the **Economic and Social Council (ECOSOC)** set up by the council in 1946. Originally composed of individual experts, the commission was turned into an intergovernmental body in 1995. Its mandate is to advise the council on population issues and trends and their integration into development strategies and to monitor and assess the implementation of decisions and recommendations emanating from UN **global conferences** devoted to population. *See also* INTERNATIONAL CONFERENCE ON POPULATION (BUCHAREST, 1974); INTERNATIONAL CONFERENCE ON POPULATION (MEXICO, 1984); INTERNATIONAL CONFERENCE ON POPULATION AND DEVELOPMENT (ICPD, CAIRO, 1994); POPULATION PROGRAMS OF THE UNITED NATIONS.

COMMISSION ON SCIENCE AND TECHNOLOGY FOR DEVELOPMENT (UNITED NATIONS) (CSTD). Established in 1992 by the **Economic and Social Council (ECOSOC)**, this functional commission of the council superseded the Intergovernmental Committee on Science and Technology for Development created by the **General Assembly** set up following the 1979 Vienna **United Nations Conference on Science and Technology**. The main role of the commission is to promote international cooperation in the field of science and technology in support of **developing countries** and to identify new scientific and technological developments that may affect adversely their efforts. *See also* SCIENCE AND TECHNOLOGY FOR DEVELOPMENT.

COMMISSION ON SUSTAINABLE DEVELOPMENT (UNITED NATIONS) (CSD). Established in 1992 as a functional commission of the **Economic and Social Council (ECOSOC)**, the mandate of the commission is to assess and review the implementation of the recommendations contained in the final documents of the 1992 **United Nations Conference on Environment and Development (UNCED)** including **Agenda 21**, the Rio Declaration on Environment and Development and the Non-Legally Binding Authoritative Statement of Principles for a Global Consensus on the Management, Conservation and Sustainable Development of All Types of Forests. The CSD also provides a forum for dialogue and the formation of partnerships between governments and the major groups involved in **sustainable development**, notably **women**, **youth**, **indigenous peoples**, **nongovernmental organizations** (NGOs), local authorities, workers and trade unions, **business** and industry, the scientific community, and farmers. The commission is composed of 53 members elected by ECOSOC and meets annually for a period of two to three weeks. *See also* WORLD COMMISSION ON ENVIRONMENT AND DEVELOPMENT.

COMMISSION ON THE STATUS OF WOMEN (UNITED NATIONS) (CSW). A functional commission of the **Economic and Social Council (ECOSOC)** that began work in 1946. Its mandate has been modified several times, but its basic function remains to promote **women**'s political, economic, civil, social, and educational rights and to make recommendations thereon to the council. The CSW served as an incubator of the **Convention on the Elimination of All Forms of Discrimination against Women**. In recent years, the main focus of its work has been to act as the preparatory body for the 1995 Fourth World Conference on Women in Beijing and to monitor the implementation of its outcome document, the so-called Beijing Platform for Action. *See also* GENDER; GLOBAL CONFERENCES (UNITED NATIONS).

COMMISSION TO STUDY THE ORGANIZATION OF PEACE (CSOP). American internationalist think tank set up at the outset of World War II to facilitate the creation of an international organization at the end of the war. Comprised of prominent university professors, lawyers, business executives, and experts in international organization, the CSOP had close connections with highly placed officials in the U.S. Government, particularly **Cordell Hull**, the head of the Department of State, and **President Franklin D. Roosevelt**. The commission still exists and its members have backgrounds broadly similar to those of its original members. It is currently headed by Louis B. Sohn, an eminent academic and advocate of **world government**.

COMMITTEE AGAINST TORTURE (CAT). A body of experts established in accordance with the provisions of the **Convention against Torture and Other Cruel, Inhuman, or Degrading Treatment or Punishment** adopted by the **General Assembly** in 1984, to monitor the implementation of the convention. The committee reviews mandatory country reports, conducts confidential inquiries, and examines complaints submitted by individuals. It may also undertake on-site visits of detention centers. The CAT reports annually to the General Assembly. *See also* HUMAN RIGHTS; TREATY BODIES.

COMMITTEE FOR DEVELOPMENT POLICY (CDP). High-level advisory body established by the **Economic and Social Council (ECOSOC)** in 1966 as the Committee for Development Planning and renamed Committee for Development Policy in 1998. The basic function of the CDP is to assess emerging **development** issues and propose policy recommendations to the **secretary-general**. The committee consists of 24 experts from the fields of economic and social development and environmental protection appointed in their personal capacity upon the nomination of the secretary-general. *See also* LEAST DEVELOPED COUNTRIES (LDCs).

COMMITTEE FOR PROGRAMME AND COORDINATION (CPC). Subsidiary organ of the **Economic and Social Council (ECOSOC)** and the **General Assembly** established in 1962 to review United Nations programs in terms of their priority and budgetary implications. *See also* ADVISORY COMMITTEE ON ADMINISTRATIVE AND BUDGETARY QUESTIONS (ACABQ); BUDGET (UNITED NATIONS).

COMMITTEE FOR THE ELIMINATION OF RACIAL DISCRIMINATION (CERD). A body of independent experts established pursuant to the provisions of the 1965 **International Convention on the Elimination of All Forms of Racial Discrimination** to monitor the implementation of the convention. The first body created by the United Nations to review the application of a **human rights** treaty, the procedures of the CERD set a model for those of subsequently created treaty-based monitoring committees. These include a review by the committee of recurrent country reports on the measures adopted by state parties leading to nonbinding recommendations. The CERD may offer its **good offices** in situations involving complaints by a state party against another for its failure to implement the convention. The committee may review communications by individuals or groups of persons claiming to be victims of a violation of the convention by their state. *See also* TREATY BODIES.

COMMITTEE OF TWENTY-FOUR. Established by the **General Assembly** to monitor the implementation of its 1960 **Declaration on the Granting of Independence to Colonial Countries and Peoples**, this committee in effect took over and widely expanded the functions of the preexisting Committee on Information from Non-Self-Governing Territories, which reviewed information transmitted by administering authorities in accordance with the charter's **Declaration on Non-Self-Governing Territories**. Tightly controlled by developing countries, the Committee of Twenty-Four (so named because of the number of countries sitting in it) assumed the power to hear petitions, send missions, and make recommendations to administering authorities. A powerful agent in the **decolonization** process, its functions are now limited to a review of residual colonial cases such as Bermuda, the British Virgin Islands, the Cayman Islands, New Caledonia, St. Helena, the U.S. Virgin Islands, and Pitcairn.

COMMITTEE ON CONFERENCES. Subsidiary body of the **General Assembly** established in 1974 to recommend to the assembly the draft calendar of conferences and meetings and the most effective utilization of conference services resources.

COMMITTEE ON CONTRIBUTIONS. A special committee given the task of recommending to the **General Assembly** periodic revisions of the **scale of assessment** to be used in apportioning the assessed contributions of member states to the United Nations **budget**.

COMMITTEE ON ECONOMIC, SOCIAL, AND CULTURAL RIGHTS (CESCR). A committee of experts established by the **Economic and Social Council (ECOSOC)** under the terms of the 1966 **International Covenant on Economic, Social, and Cultural Rights (ICESCR)** to monitor the implementation of the covenant. The committee reviews periodic reports of the states parties to the covenant. In turn, it submits its views and comments to ECOSOC. *See also* HUMAN RIGHTS; TREATY BODIES; UNIVERSAL DECLARATION OF HUMAN RIGHTS (UDHR, 1948).

COMMITTEE ON ENERGY AND NATURAL RESOURCES FOR DEVELOPMENT (CENRD). Expert body of the **Economic and Social Council (ECOSOC)** created in 1998 out of the merger of two committees of the council concerned with natural resources and new and renewable sources of **energy** respectively. The committee deals primarily with energy, water, and minerals questions. *See also* NATURAL RESOURCES.

COMMITTEE ON NONGOVERNMENTAL ORGANIZATIONS. Article 71 of the United Nations **Charter** enables **nongovernmental organizations (NGOs)** to participate in the deliberations of the **Economic and Social Council (ECOSOC)** and its various subsidiary bodies through attendance at these meetings, oral interventions, and written statements. The main function of the Committee on Nongovernmental Organizations, a subsidiary body of ECOSOC, is to consider and make recommendations to the council on the applications of nongovernmental organizations for such "consultative status" with the council. *See also* CIVIL SOCIETY; PANEL OF EMINENT PERSONS ON UNITED NATIONS–CIVIL SOCIETY RELATIONS; REFORM, UNITED NATIONS.

COMMITTEE ON THE ELIMINATION OF DISCRIMINATION AGAINST WOMEN (CEDAW). Body of experts set up in accordance with the stipulations of the 1979 **Convention on the Elimination of All Forms of Discrimination against Women** to monitor the implementation of the convention by its state parties. Like most other **human rights treaty bodies**, the committee makes nonbinding recommendations based on its review of mandatory country reports. The "suggestions and general recommendations" of the committee along with the comments of state parties are reflected in the committee's reporting to the **General Assembly**. Since 2000, an optional protocol to the convention allows the committee to receive individual complaints. *See also* GENDER; WOMEN.

COMMITTEE ON THE RIGHTS OF THE CHILD (CRC). Created in accordance with Article 43 of the **Convention on the Rights of the Child (CRC)**, the committee began operating in 1991. The committee is composed of independent experts elected by the state parties to the CRC. It monitors the implementation of the convention through a review of mandatory country reports. Its recommendations are not binding but its procedures are public and frequently involve the participation of **nongovernmental organizations (NGOs)** which can at any time submit information on individual cases. The committee may also request additional information from states to which they are obligated to respond in writing. The committee meets three times a year and reports on its activities to the **General Assembly** through the **Economic and Social Council (ECOSOC)**. *See also* CHILDREN; CHILDREN IN ARMED CONFLICTS; TREATY BODIES; UNITED NATIONS CHILDREN'S FUND (UNICEF).

COMMODITIES. Internationally traded unprocessed products of mining and agriculture. Speculation as well as climatic conditions and changing demand for and supply of raw materials result in wide fluctuations in the international prices of commodities. A key issue has been the relationship between the prices of primary commodities and those of manufactured goods, which triggers wide variations in the international prices of commodities.

Developing countries—many of which rely on a handful of commodities for their export earnings—are especially vulnerable to such fluctuations, and the linkages between commodity prices and exports and economic **development** have been the focus of considerable attention in various United Nations bodies since the 1950s and the source of continuing North-South tensions.

The problem was recognized in early studies of the **Economic Commission for Latin America and the Caribbean (ECLAC)** and the **Food and Agricultural Organization (FAO)** and debated in several conferences on individual commodities throughout the 1950s and 1960s. In 1964, the question of trade in commodities was included in the mandate of the **United Nations Conference on Trade and Development (UNCTAD)**. In order to minimize fluctuations in the prices of commodities and to mitigate their impact, developing countries have asked without success for the creation of an **Integrated Programme for Commodities (IPC)** comprising buffer stocks and individual commodity agreements of producers and consumers. *See also* DECLARATION ON THE ESTABLISHMENT OF A NEW INTERNATIONAL ECONOMIC ORDER (NIEO); NORTH-SOUTH DIALOGUE; TRADE AND DEVELOPMENT.

COMMON FUND FOR COMMODITIES. *See* INTEGRATED PROGRAMME FOR COMMODITIES (IPC).

COMMON HERITAGE OF MANKIND. First applied to the resources of the deep seabed, the concept refers to goods and values that provide common benefit to all and that are transmitted from one generation to future generations. The 1972 Stockholm **Declaration on the Human Environment**, the 1974 **Charter of Economic Rights and Duties of States**, the 1982 **United Nations Conference on the Law of the Sea**, the preamble to the 1982 World Charter for Nature and the 1987 **World Commission on Environment and Development** report include references to the principle. *See also* ANTARCTIC TREATY; CONVENTION ON BIOLOGICAL DIVERSITY (CBD, 1992); GLOBAL PUBLIC GOODS; OUTER SPACE TREATY (1967); SEABED AUTHORITY (INTERNATIONAL) (ISA).

COMMONWEALTH. Voluntary association of sovereign independent states (currently 53) that used to be British dominions, colonies, or protectorates subscribing to the idea that international peace and order, global economic **development**, and the rule of **international law** are essential to the security and prosperity of mankind. More specifically, the Commonwealth acts as a framework for supporting member countries in the **prevention** and resolution of their conflicts, the strengthening of democracy, the rule of law and **human rights**, and the promotion of economic growth and **sustainable development**. The Commonwealth is serviced by a secretariat located in London and enjoys observer status in the United Nations.

COMMONWEALTH OF INDEPENDENT STATES (CIS). Partial successor to the former Soviet Union created in 1991. Comprising all the former republics of the USSR except the Baltic States, the role of the Commonwealth of Independent States is to coordinate the foreign and economic policies of its members. Armenia, **Georgia** (confronted by a separatist movement in the region of Abkhazia), and **Tajikistan** (torn by a civil war) have accepted Russia's military protection under a loose United Nations mandate. The CIS has cooperated closely with the United Nations in a number of **peacekeeping** operations and was granted observer status in the United Nations in 1994. *See also* UNITED NATIONS MISSION OF OBSERVERS IN TAJIKISTAN (UNMOT, 1994–2000); UNITED NATIONS OBSERVER MISSION IN GEORGIA (UNOMIG, August 1993–present).

COMPREHENSIVE TEST BAN TREATY (CTBT). Adopted by the **General Assembly** on 10 September 1996 after three years of arduous negotiations in the **Conference on Disarmament (CD)**, the CTBT bans all nuclear explosions for military as well as civilian purposes. It will enter into force only after ratification of 44 states identified in the treaty that possess nuclear powers or research reactors. Several of these states have been reluctant to ratify the treaty because it fails to enjoin nuclear weapon states to dismantle their own nuclear arsenal. *See also* ARMS CONTROL; DISARMAMENT; NONPROLIFERATION OF NUCLEAR WEAPONS, TREATY ON THE (NPT, 1968); PARTIAL TEST BAN TREATY (PTBT, 1963).

CONCILIATION. Dispute settlement technique involving, as in the case of **enquiry**, the establishment of a fact-finding body. Going somewhat further than enquiry but not as far as **arbitration**, conciliation commissions may also recommend solutions that the parties are free to accept or reject. As is the case with enquiry, conciliation has acquired a multilateral dimension. In 1928, the **League of Nations** sponsored a convention requiring state parties to institute conciliation procedures based on permanent commissions. In 1990, the United Nations opened for signature a revised and expanded set of conciliation rules. *See also* IRAN-IRAQ WAR (1980–1988); JUDICIAL SETTLEMENT; MEDIATION; PEACEFUL SETTLEMENT OF DISPUTES; REGIONAL ARRANGEMENTS.

CONFERENCE OF THE COMMITTEE ON DISARMAMENT (CCD). Main United Nations forum for **disarmament** negotiations between 1969 and 1978. The CCD was superseded by the current **Conference on Disarmament (CD).** *See also* CONVENTION ON THE PROHIBITION OF THE DEVELOPMENT, PRODUCTION, AND STOCKPILING OF BACTERIOLOGICAL (BIOLOGICAL) AND TOXIN WEAPONS AND ON THEIR DESTRUCTION (1972).

CONFERENCE ON DISARMAMENT (CD). Established in 1979 as a result of the 1978 special session of the **General Assembly** on disarmament, which called for the creation of a single multilateral negotiating body in the United Nations. The Conference on Disarmament succeeds and supersedes a number of preexisting forums for **disarmament** negotiations with varying names and memberships. The CD currently has 66 members including the 5 major nuclear-weapons states (China, France, Russia, the United Kingdom, and the United States). The General Assembly frequently requests the CD to consider specific disarmament issues. In turn, the CD reports annually to the General Assembly. The Conference and its predecessor organizations have provided the multilateral setting for the negotiation of such major multilateral limitation and disarmament agreements as the **Nonproliferation of Nuclear Weapons Treaty (NPT)**, the **Convention on the Prohibition of the Development, Production, and Stockpiling of Bacteriological (Biological) and Toxin Weapons and on Their Destruction**, the **Convention on the Prohibition of the Development, Production, Stockpiling, and Use of Chemical Weapons and on Their Destruction**, and the **Comprehensive Test Ban Treaty (CTBT)**. *See also* ARMS CONTROL; ATOMIC ENERGY COMMISSION (AEC).

**CONFERENCE ON INTERNATIONAL ECONOMIC COOPER-
ATION (CIEC), 1975–1977.** First formal arrangement put in place
for the conduct of negotiations on North-South issues in the wake of
the 1974 General Assembly **Declaration on the Establishment of a
New International Economic Order.** The conference drew together
representatives of industrial countries (Australia, Canada, Japan,
Spain, Sweden, Switzerland, the United States, and a joint delegation
of the European Economic Community), 19 developing countries (6
each from Africa, Asia, and Latin America and Yugoslavia). The discussions were conducted in the framework of four commissions concerned with **energy**, raw materials and **trade**, **development** and
money, and finance, respectively.

The outcome of the 18-month-long negotiations was very modest,
developed countries agreeing only in principle to create a special $1
billion program to assist low-income **developing countries**, to establish a common fund for **commodities**, and to increase their **official
development assistance** to 0.7 percent of their gross domestic product. The conference ended in a stalemate on energy and financial
questions. No genuine and lasting agreement in fact emerged from
the CIEC, prompting developing countries to press for a resumption
of the **North-South dialogue** within the United Nations. *See also* IN-
TEGRATED PROGRAMME FOR COMMODITIES (IPC).

**CONFERENCE ON NGOs IN CONSULTATIVE STATUS
(CONGO).** Independent association of **nongovernmental organizations (NGOs)** in consultative status with the **Economic and Social
Council (ECOSOC)**, CONGO seeks to facilitate the participation of
NGOs in United Nations' debates and proceedings. One of its major
contributions is to have developed and promoted new and more extensive forms of NGO participation in United Nations global world
conferences.

CONFERENCES, UNITED NATIONS. *See* GLOBAL CONFER-
ENCES (UNITED NATIONS).

CONFLICT PREVENTION. Policies and techniques designed to
avoid the violent escalation of a dispute. The concept draws from and
expands on the practice of **preventive diplomacy** and includes such
measures as the establishment of **early warning** mechanisms based

on specific indicators to predict impending violence, the creation and monitoring of demilitarized zones, confidence-building measures, and the deployment of United Nations forces to forestall the outbreak of violence.

Increasing attention has been given in recent years to an even more comprehensive understanding of prevention focusing on the need to address the political, economic, and social root causes of conflict. Defined as "structural prevention," this approach calls for longer-term initiatives aiming at good governance, the eradication of **poverty**, and the elimination of inequalities as means to forestall the outbreak of violence. *See also* AGENDA FOR DEVELOPMENT; AGENDA FOR PEACE; PEACEKEEPING.

CONSENSUS. The drafters of the **United Nations Charter** seem to have contemplated a system of decision making through formal **voting**. In the **General Assembly**, "important decisions" require a two-third majority, all others a simple majority (Article 18). Procedural matters in the **Security Council** are to be disposed by affirmative votes of any 9 of its members (now 15), but in all other matters, the 9 members of the Council must include its permanent members. Decisions in the **Economic and Social Council (ECOSOC)** and the **International Court of Justice (ICJ)** are supposed to be made by majority votes (Articles 67 and 89 of the charter and Article 55 of the ICJ statute).

When in the mid-1960s, France, the Soviet Union, and its allies refused to pay their assessed part of the costs of the **United Nations Emergency Force (UNEF)** and the **United Nations Operation in the Congo (ONUC)**, they could have lost their vote in accordance with Article 17 of the charter. Negotiations conducted by **Secretary-General U Thant** led to an understanding that, following consultations among member states, decisions and resolutions could be considered to have been adopted if no objection had been voiced. Thus arose the now widespread practice of "consensus," which, in effect, means that a resolution under consideration is deemed to have been adopted if no delegation objects to it. The practice has frequently been resorted to by the Security Council and has spread to other United Nations organs such as ECOSOC, the **United Nations Conference on Trade and Development (UNCTAD)**, and UN-sponsored **global conferences**. Only a handful of the General Assembly's recommendations are adopted by formal votes, most of these being politically controversial.

The practice of consensus, in effect, gives a **veto** power to any state and since the mid-1980s, consensus has proved to be a powerful instrument in the hands of the major contributors to the United Nations **budget** to slow down and stabilize the rates of increase of UN-budgeted expenditures.

Reaching a consensus normally entails a lengthy process of negotiations involving informal meetings, the participation of regional and other **groups** such as the **Group of Seventy-Seven (G-77)** and the **European Union (EU)**, the designation of "contact groups" of representatives of regional groups, and other interested delegations.

CONSUMER PROTECTION. Wide array of national government policies and regulations intended to ensure that goods produced for the market are safe to use. In 1985, the United Nations **General Assembly** adopted nonbinding guidelines for consumer protection (Resolution 39/248 of 9 April 1985).

CONTAINMENT. A term coined by United States State Department officials under the **Truman** administration describing a set of policy measures and counterpressures designed to deter the Soviet Union's expansion. The term is now applied by strategists to describe methods used to prevent a rising local power from further expansion. *See also* BUSH, GEORGE W. (1946–); COLD WAR; COLLECTIVE SECURITY; REGIONAL ARRANGEMENTS; USE OF FORCE.

CONTRIBUTIONS. *See* BUDGET (UNITED NATIONS).

CONTROL MECHANISMS (INTERNAL AND EXTERNAL). Ultimately, member states of the United Nations have the final authority in monitoring and controlling the implementation of the programs and activities they mandate the organization to undertake. They do so primarily through the adoption of the United Nations **budget**. Notwithstanding the fact that the principles of economic rationality in the evaluation and measurement of the United Nations' "outputs" may not apply consistently to a politically driven organization, accountability is ensured through a variety of control mechanisms that have been set up since the early days of the United Nations' existence. The oldest mechanisms put in place by the **General Assembly** include the **Advisory Committee on Administrative and Budgetary Questions (ACABQ)** and the **United Nations Board of Auditors,** which were established in 1946. The **Joint Inspection Unit (JIU)** and the **Office of Internal Oversight Services (OIOS)** established respectively in 1966 and 1994 are two additional instruments for monitoring and evaluation. Continuing complaints about management and administrative lapses have led some observers to demand more effective mechanisms of accountability. *See also* OIL FOR FOOD PROGRAM (OFFP, 1997–2003).

CONVENTION AGAINST TORTURE AND OTHER CRUEL, INHUMAN, OR DEGRADING TREATMENT OR PUNISHMENT (UNITED NATIONS) (1984). Adopted by the **General Assembly** in 1984, this convention bans torture under all circumstances and establishes a **Committee against Torture (CAT)** to monitor its implementation. The convention defines torture as "any act by which severe pain or suffering, whether physical or mental, is intentionally inflicted on a person for such purposes as obtaining from him or a third person information or a confession." State parties must take effective legal and other measures to prevent torture and may not invoke a "state of emergency," external threats, or orders from a superior officer or authority to justify the use of torture. *See also* HUMAN RIGHTS; TREATY BODIES.

CONVENTION CONCERNING THE PROTECTION OF THE WORLD CULTURAL AND NATURAL HERITAGE. Convention adopted in 1972 under the auspices of the **United Nations Educational, Scientific, and Cultural Organization (UNESCO),** which entered into force in 1975. Its purpose is to protect natural and cultural sites of outstanding universal value and to preserve them for future generations. There are over 800 sites around the globe such as the Grand Canyon (United States), the Acropolis (Greece), Timbuktu (Mali), Angkor (Cambodia), the Taj Mahal (India), and the ancient city of Aleppo (Syria), which have received "World Heritage Site" status. *See also* CULTURAL HERITAGE.

CONVENTION ON BIOLOGICAL DIVERSITY (CBD, 1992). One of the major agreements painstakingly reached at the 1992 **United Nations Conference on the Environment and Development (UNCED)**, the convention has three main goals: the conservation of biological diversity, the sustainable use of its components, and the equitable sharing of the benefits from the use of genetic resources.

The convention's governing body is the Conference of Parties (COP) consisting of all governments that have ratified it. The COP reviews progress made under the terms of the convention, identifies new priorities, and draws up work plans for its members. Under the terms of the convention, governments are expected to develop national biodiversity strategies and to integrate them into broader national environment and development plans in such sectors as **forestry, agricultural development, fishing and fisheries**, and **energy**.

While there is a broad consensus on the desirability of preserving key plant and animal resources, some of the provisions of the convention have proved politically contentious. Such is the case for the principle of preventing the introduction and control of alien species that could threaten ecosystems. The idea of controlling the risks posed by organisms modified by biotechnology has run up against the opposition of **transnational corporations (TNCs)**, notably agribusinesses and the pharmaceutical industry. *See also* AGENDA 21; CARTAGENA PROTOCOL ON BIOSAFETY (2003).

CONVENTION ON CONTRACTS FOR THE INTERNATIONAL SALES OF GOODS (1980). Prepared by the **United Nations Commission on International Trade Law** and adopted by a diplomatic conference in 1980, this convention specifies the rules governing the formation of contracts for the international sale of goods and defines the substantive rights and obligations of buyers and sellers arising from the contract. *See also* FUNCTIONALISM; TRADE AND DEVELOPMENT.

CONVENTION ON INDIGENOUS AND TRIBAL PEOPLES (1989). Convention adopted by the **International Labour Organization (ILO)** (amending an earlier convention of 1957) setting the right of indigenous and tribal peoples to live in accordance with their cultures and traditions and "to decide their own priorities for the process of development as it affects their lives, beliefs, institutions, and spiritual well-being and the lands they occupy and otherwise use." The convention has exerted a degree of influence on the allocation and forms of international **development** assistance. *See also* BIOLOGICAL DIVERSITY; CULTURAL HERITAGE; INDIGENOUS PEOPLES; UNITED NATIONS PERMANENT FORUM FOR INDIGENOUS PEOPLES (UNPFIP).

CONVENTION ON THE ELIMINATION OF ALL FORMS OF DISCRIMINATION AGAINST WOMEN (1979). International bill of rights for **women** adopted by the **General Assembly** in 1979. The convention defines discrimination against women as "any distinction, exclusion, or restriction made on the basis of sex which has the effect or purpose of impairing or nullifying the recognition, enjoyment or exercise by women, irrespective of their marital status, on the basis of equality of women and men, of **human rights** and their fundamental freedoms in the political, economic, social, cultural, civil or any other field."

By accepting the convention, state parties commit themselves to incorporate the principle of equality of men and women in their legal system, abolish all discriminatory laws, and adopt appropriate ones preventing discrimination against women. They are also bound to submit national reports at least every four years to a **Committee on the Elimination of Discrimination against Women (CEDAW)**, on measures they have taken to comply with their treaty obligations. An optional protocol to the convention that entered into force in 2000 allows women from its states parties to make individual complaints to the committee. *See also* COMMISSION ON THE STATUS OF WOMEN (UNITED NATIONS) (CSW); TREATY BODIES.

CONVENTION ON THE PREVENTION AND PUNISHMENT OF THE CRIME OF GENOCIDE. Adopted by the **General Assembly** in 1948, the genocide convention entered into force in 1951. The convention prohibits genocide at all times whether during peace or war. In addition to the act of genocide, conspiracy, direct and public incitement, attempts to commit, or complicity in committing genocide are also punishable offenses. All persons who commit such acts must be punished whether they are constitutionally responsible rulers, public officials, or private individuals. The state parties also agree to enact legislation instituting effective penalties for persons guilty of genocide. Persons charged with genocide are to be tried by a competent tribunal of the state in which the act was committed or an international tribunal. In practice, domestic courts have rarely acted within a reasonable time frame. That is why the statutes of the **International Criminal Tribunal for the Former Yugoslavia (ICTY)** and the **International Criminal Tribunal for Rwanda (ICTR)** as well as the recently created **International Criminal Court (ICC)** statutes include the crime of genocide in the list of crimes over which they have jurisdiction. *See also* HUMAN RIGHTS.

CONVENTION ON THE PRIVILEGES AND IMMUNITIES OF THE UNITED NATIONS (1946). Granting privileges and immunities to diplomatic envoys is an old customary norm and practice of **international law** that was codified in the 1961 **Vienna Convention on Diplomatic Relations**. The purpose of diplomatic privileges, immunities, and exemptions, as described in the 1946 convention and in line with the provisions of the Vienna Convention, is not to benefit individuals themselves but to ensure the efficient performance of the functions of the United Nations and of the diplomatic permanent missions that represent states.

Under the 1946 Convention on the Privileges and Immunities of the United Nations, the UN enjoys a juridical personality (Article 1), which enables it to enter into contractual agreements. UN property and assets are immune from legal process (Article 2.2), and its premises are inviolable and immune from search, requisition, confiscation, expropriation, and any other form of interference whether by executive, administration, judicial, or legislative action (Article 2.3). The UN, its assets, income, and property are exempt from all direct taxes, customs duties, and import and export restrictions on articles for official use (Article 2.7). Differences in interpretation of the convention are to be referred to the **International Court of Justice (ICJ)** unless the parties agree otherwise (Article 8). The convention also spells out the rights and privileges of UN **personnel**. Annexes adopted separately but attached to the convention cover the rights and privileges of the **specialized agencies**. *See also* INTERNATIONAL CIVIL SERVICE.

CONVENTION ON THE PROHIBITION OF THE DEVELOPMENT, PRODUCTION, AND STOCKPILING OF BACTERIOLOGICAL (BIOLOGICAL) AND TOXIN WEAPONS AND ON THEIR DESTRUCTION (1972). Widely condemned at the end of World War I, the use of **bacteriological weapons** was prohibited under the 1925 **Geneva Protocol** for the Prohibition of the Use of Asphyxiating, Poisonous or Other Gases, and of Bacteriological Methods of Warfare. Negotiated in the **Conference on Disarmament (CD)**, subsequently adopted by the **General Assembly**, and opened for signature in 1972, this convention complements the protocol by prohibiting the development, production, stockpiling, acquisition, retention, and transfer of bacteriological weapons and requiring their destruction. The convention entered into force in 1975. Negotiations have been conducted for several years to incorporate into its provisions a verification system to monitor compliance. *See also* ARMS CONTROL; DISARMAMENT; WEAPONS OF MASS DESTRUCTION (WMDs).

CONVENTION ON THE PROHIBITION OF THE DEVELOPMENT, PRODUCTION, STOCKPILING, AND USE OF CHEMICAL WEAPONS AND ON THEIR DESTRUCTION (1997). Negotiated over a period of 12 years, this convention was adopted by the **Conference on Disarmament (CD)** in 1992 and entered into force in 1997. The treaty bans the use, development, production and stockpiling of chemical weapons and creates an international organization based in the Netherlands, the Organization for the Prohibition of Chemical Weapons, to verify state compliance through routine inspections and the collection of information on chemical facilities. *See also* ARMS CONTROL; CONVENTION ON THE PROHIBITION OF THE DEVELOPMENT, PRODUCTION, AND STOCKPILING OF BACTERIOLOGICAL (BIOLOGICAL) AND TOXIN WEAPONS AND ON THEIR DESTRUCTION (1972); DISARMAMENT; EVANS, GARETH (1944–); GENEVA PROTOCOL (1925); WEAPONS OF MASS DESTRUCTION (WMDs).

CONVENTION ON THE PROHIBITION OF THE USE, STOCKPILING, PRODUCTION, AND TRANSFER OF ANTIPERSONNEL MINES AND ON THEIR DESTRUCTION (1999). Opened for signature in 1997 and entered into force in March 1999, this treaty, also know as the **Ottawa Treaty** for the city where it was signed, was the result of the efforts of an unprecedented coalition of a number of governments, United Nations **Secretariat** officials, the **International Committee of the Red Cross (ICRC)**, and other **non-**

governmental organizations (NGOs) operating worldwide through a network known as the **International Campaign to Ban Landmines (ICBL)**.

The treaty imposes a ban on the use, development, production, stockpiling, and transfer of antipersonnel landmines and enjoins the states party to the convention to destroy all stockpiled **antipersonnel mines** and to clear all laid mines within a set time frame. The convention also provides for a system of annual reporting to the **secretary-general** of the United Nations on their implementation of the treaty. A review conference assessed the state of implementation of the treaty in 2004.

The convention was a major step toward a total ban on antipersonnel landmines. The production and international sale and transfer of antipersonnel landmines have almost stopped. Stockpiles are being destroyed. Mined areas are being cleared. Nevertheless, millions of landmines still lie in the ground throughout the world. Between 200 million and 215 million antipersonnel mines are still stockpiled by 78 countries. Over a dozen countries continue to produce antipersonnel mines, and **nonstate actors** or rebel groups still produce homemade landmines. Mine clearance operations are expensive ($1,000 per mine). Some 50 countries have not yet joined the treaty, including three of the permanent members of the Security Council (China, Russia, and the United States) and major producers are not part of the treaty.

The United Nations has been an active advocate of universal participation in the treaty. Its activities focus on assistance in mine clearance, especially in the context of its **peacekeeping** operations, assistance to victims, and educational and public information activities aimed at reducing the risk of injury from mines. The International Campaign to Ban Landmines was awarded the **Nobel Peace Prize** in 1997. *See also* ARMS CONTROL; DISARMAMENT.

CONVENTION ON THE RIGHTS OF THE CHILD (CRC, 1990). Adopted on 20 November 1989 and entered in force in 1990, the Convention on the Rights of the Child defines the rights of **children** in situations other than armed conflict (i.e., right to a nationality, freedom of expression, protection from ill treatment, etc.).

The CRC rests on four major principles that underpin its provisions: nondiscrimination; the best interests of the child; children have a right to life, survival, and development; and the views of children must be heard and respected. States party to the convention report every five years to the **Committee on the Rights of the Child (CRC)** on their obligations to adopt administrative, legislative, social, and educational measures for the implementation of the rights spelled out in the convention.

Two optional protocols were adopted in 2000 and entered into force in 2002 on **children in armed conflicts**. The former outlaws the compulsory recruitment of children under the age of 18 by government and nongovernment armed forces, the latter bans the sale of children, child prostitution, and child pornography. *See also* HUMAN RIGHTS; TREATY BODIES; UNITED NATIONS CHILDREN'S FUND (UNICEF).

CONVENTION RELATING TO THE STATUS OF REFUGEES AND STATELESS PERSONS (1951). Together with a 1967 additional Protocol on Refugees, the convention defines the criteria that make someone a **refugee**, spells out their legal status and rights, and determines the administrative and diplomatic procedures for their protection.

Under the terms of the convention, a refugee is a person "who owing to [a] well founded fear of being persecuted for reasons of race, religion, nationality, membership of a particular social group or political opinion, is outside the country of his nationality and is unable, or, owing to such fear, is unwilling to avail himself of the protection of that country; or who, not having a nationality and being outside the country of his former habitual residence as a result of such events, is unable or . . . unwilling to return to it." *See also* INTERNALLY DISPLACED PERSONS (IDPs); UNITED NATIONS HIGH COMMISSIONER FOR REFUGEES (UNHCR).

CONVENTIONAL ARMS REGISTER. Conventional arms are understood to include military forces other than nuclear, biological, and chemical weapons. In 1991, the **General Assembly** authorized the **secretary-general**, on the basis of information provided by member states, to establish and maintain a universal Register of Conventional

Arms including data on international arms transfers as well as information on military holdings and procurement through national production. The register features information on the following types of conventional arms: battle tanks, armored combat vehicles, large caliber artillery systems, combat aircraft, attack helicopters, warships, and missiles and missile systems. *See also* ARMS CONTROL; DISARMAMENT.

COORDINATION, UNITED NATIONS SYSTEM. Long-standing issue facing the United Nations virtually since its inception. The unbridled proliferation of economic, social, and developmental institutions driven by a political process that never rested on a solid political consensus regarding the contents and methods of **development** and the role of the United Nations therein, the emergence of complex peacekeeping operations and the spread of "operational" and "humanitarian" activities have historically combined in such a way as to create inconsistencies and disconnects throughout the United Nations system both at headquarters and in the field (and between headquarters and the field as well).

There are formal coordination mechanisms within the organization, notably the **Chief Executive Board (CEB)** and its predecessor body, the **Administrative Committee on Coordination (ACC)**. Furthermore, a degree of consistency has been achieved in regard to programs on the basis of the Millennium Development Goals of the 2000 **Millennium Declaration**. Nevertheless, criticisms of the organization persist, drawing attention to overlapping mandates, duplication, redundancies among intergovernmental and **secretariat** structures, a lack of priorities, and little if any budgetary and program joint planning, and prompting repeated calls for **reform**. *See* DEPUTY SECRETARY-GENERAL; ECONOMIC AND SOCIAL COUNCIL (ECOSOC).

COPYRIGHT. Legal provisions both national and international protecting **intellectual property rights**. The first UN organization to be involved in the international aspects of copyright was the **United Nations Educational, Scientific, and Cultural Organization (UNESCO)**, which throughout the late 1940s and early 1950s, served as the setting for the negotiation of a Universal Convention that went into force in 1956. This convention has been amended several times to extend to films, theater, radio, and television. The **World Intellectual Property Organization (WIPO)** and the **World Trade Organization (WTO)** are concerned with the developmental and trade aspects of copyrighting. *See also* ELECTRONIC COMMERCE (E-COMMERCE).

CORDIER, ANDREW (1901–1975). American educator and public official who served the United Nations from 1946 to 1962. As executive assistant to **Secretary-General Dag Hammarskjöld**, he was the chief UN negotiator in the 1960–1964 **United Nations Operation in the Congo (ONUC)**. Upon leaving the United Nations in 1962, he returned to academia. From 1968 to 1972, he was president of Columbia University.

CORDOVEZ, DIEGO (1935–). Foreign minister of Ecuador from 1988 to 1992, Diego Cordovez served the United Nations in various capacities for some 25 years. From 1981 to 1988, he was undersecretary-general for political affairs. In that capacity, he skillfully mediated and negotiated the agreement that led to the withdrawal of Soviet forces in **Afghanistan**. He has also served as special adviser to **Secretary-General Kofi Annan** in the **Cyprus question**.

COTE D'IVOIRE (2002–). Long reputed for its stability and prosperity, Cote d'Ivoire plunged into a state of quasi–civil war in September 2002 following an attempted coup turned rebellion in the northern part of the country. The intervention of French troops a month later led to a cease-fire agreement, but in November 2002 two new armed groups rose up in the western part of the country bordering Liberia. In January 2003, the government and insurgent groups entered into a peace accord calling for the establishment of a transitional government or reconciliation and the organization of elections in 2005. In May 2003, the **Security Council** set up the **United Nations Mission in Cote d'Ivoire (MINUCI)** to facilitate its implementation. The council also approved the establishment of a small staff in support of the **special representative of the secretary-general** to work on political, legal, civil affairs, civilian police, elections, humanitarian, and human rights issues.

The conflict may have "officially" ended, but, in effect, little progress has been made toward peace and reconciliation. With the peace accords floundering, the Security Council, acting under Chapter VII, decided in February 2004 to replace MINUCI with a new and stronger peacekeeping force, the **United Nations Operation in Cote d'Ivoire (UNOCI)**. Yet there is still no break in the political stalemate. Tensions remain high. The country is in effect partitioned, as rebel groups retain control over the northern and western regions. Sporadic violence continues with serious **human rights** violations committed by both government and rebel forces. The economy, on the decline since the mid-1980s, is partially paralyzed.

COUNCIL FOR NAMIBIA. *See* SOUTHWEST AFRICA.

CREDENTIALS COMMITTEE OF THE GENERAL ASSEMBLY. Subsidiary body of the **General Assembly** appointed at the beginning of each session of the assembly and consisting of nine of its members. The mandate of the Credentials Committee is to ascertain whether the members of the delegation representing a state have been duly appointed by its legal governmental authorities and to recommend their acceptance or rejection by the assembly. This procedure called "accreditation" is also used for **special and emergency special sessions of the General Assembly** as well as UN **global conferences**. Most of the time, it is a routine process. Controversies, however, have arisen in situations where the legality or legitimacy of the government was questioned. Such was the case of the representatives of the People's Republic of China after the overthrow of the government by the Communists in 1949. The credentials of South Africa's representatives were also rejected on the ground that **apartheid** made its government illegitimate. Likewise, disputes arose on the credentials of Cambodia's representatives after the ousting of the Khmer Rouge by Vietnam. *See also* CAMBODIA CONFLICT (1954–2003); CHINA REPRESENTATION IN THE UNITED NATIONS (1949–1971).

CRIME PREVENTION. Under the guidance of two commissions of the **Economic and Social Council (ECOSOC)**, the **Commission on Crime Prevention and Criminal Justice** and the **Commission on Narcotic Drugs**, the United Nations carries out a wide array of activities related to crime prevention focusing on the illicit trafficking of drugs, transnational organized crime, and, more recently, **terrorism**.

In 1998, the **General Assembly** held a **special session** on the world drug problem, which recognized that drug abuse was a global phenomenon that called for a significant reduction of the demand for and supply of drugs. In support of this objective, the United Nations Office on Drugs and Crime within the **secretariat** collects and disseminates internationally comparable drug abuse data assessing the magnitude and patterns of drug abuse at the country, regional, and global levels together with reports on global trends in illicit drug trafficking. The secretariat also provides assistance in the implementation of the **United Nations Convention against Transnational Organized Crime**, the **United Nations Convention against Corruption**, and the **United Nations Convention against the Illicit Traffic in Narcotic Drugs and Psychotropic Substances**. *See also* BUSINESS AND THE UNITED NATIONS; TRAFFICKING IN PERSONS; UNITED NATIONS CRIME CONGRESSES; UNITED NATIONS INTERREGIONAL CRIME AND JUSTICE RESEARCH INSTITUTE (UNICRI).

CRIMES AGAINST HUMANITY. As agreed by France, the United Kingdom, the United States, and the USSR in their 1945 agreement to prosecute and punish the leaders of the Axis states—Germany, Italy, and Japan—the term refers to "murder, extermination, enslavement, deportation, and other inhumane acts against any civilian population before or during the war; or persecution on political, racial, or religious grounds in execution of or in connection with any crime within the jurisdiction of the domestic law of the country where perpetrated." This definition has provided the basis for similar provisions found in the statutes of the ad hoc tribunals set up by the **Security Council** in the 1990s as part of the settlement of the **Bosnian**, **Cambodian**, **Rwandan**, and **Sierra Leone conflicts** and of the **International Criminal Court (ICC)**. A 1961 Declaration of the **General Assembly** banning the use of nuclear weapons asserts that their use constitutes a crime against humanity. In a 1996 **advisory opinion**, the **International Court of Justice (ICJ)** ruled that the use of **nuclear weapons** violated humanitarian law. *See also* CRIMES

AGAINST PEACE; INTERNATIONAL MILITARY TRIBUNAL FOR THE FAR EAST (1946–1948); INTERNATIONAL MILITARY TRIBUNAL FOR THE PROSECUTION AND PUNISHMENT OF THE MAJOR WAR CRIMINALS (NUREMBERG TRIBUNAL, 1945–1946); WAR CRIMES TRIBUNALS; WEAPONS OF MASS DESTRUCTION (WMDs).

CRIMES AGAINST PEACE. As understood by the Allied Powers in 1945 in their plans to prosecute war criminals, the term means the planning, preparation, initiation, or waging of an aggressive war or a war in violation of treaties, agreements, or international guarantees. Crimes against peace now fall under the jurisdiction of the **International Criminal Court (ICC)** but may not be prosecuted by the court until its states parties agree on a definition of the term. *See also* AGGRESSION; CRIMES AGAINST HUMANITY; INTERNATIONAL MILITARY TRIBUNAL FOR THE FAR EAST (1946–1948); INTERNATIONAL MILITARY TRIBUNAL FOR THE PROSECUTION AND PUNISHMENT OF THE MAJOR WAR CRIMINALS (NUREMBERG TRIBUNAL, 1945–1946).

CUBAN MISSILE CRISIS (1962). Dramatic **Cold War** confrontation between the United States and the Soviet Union triggered by the discovery by U.S. reconnaissance planes of missile-launching sites being constructed clandestinely in Cuba. The United States brought the matter to the attention of the **Security Council**, imposed a naval blockade on Cuba, and declared that any missile launched from Cuba would warrant a full-scale retaliatory attack by the United States against the Soviet Union. The Soviet Union was persuaded to remove all offensive weapons from the island thus bringing an end to the crisis. The United Nations played a relatively modest but significant role in its resolution. Both superpowers relied on the **secretary-general** and their ambassadors at the United Nations to channel informal proposals. Secretary-General **U Thant** is also credited with having provided the initial elements of the face-saving formula that enabled the Soviet Union to agree to the withdrawal of all missiles and equipment from Cuba. *See also* PREEMPTION; PRINCIPLES OF THE UNITED NATIONS; SELF-DEFENSE (RIGHT OF).

CULTURAL HERITAGE. Originally referring to the most monumental historical remnants of cultures, the term now extends to individual and collective acts of creation and representation (i.e., the performing arts, rites, festive events and the plastic arts) and processes of transmission of traditional skills and know-how, languages, and oral traditions. Reconciling universality and the preservation of cultures has been heightened by the standardization of culture associated with instantaneous planetary communication and **globalization**.

The **United Nations Educational, Scientific, and Cultural Organization (UNESCO)** is the UN agency primarily involved in these areas and has been instrumental in the development of international conventions prohibiting and preventing the illicit import, export, and transfer of cultural property and protecting "world heritage" sites. The **World Intellectual Property Organization (WIPO)** and the **World Trade Organization (WTO)** deal with patenting legal issues and trade related aspects of intellectual property rights. *See also* CONVENTION CONCERNING THE PROTECTION OF THE WORLD CULTURAL AND NATURAL HERITAGE; CONVENTION ON INDIGENOUS AND TRIBAL PEOPLES (1989); HAGUE CONVENTION FOR THE PROTECTION OF CULTURAL PROPERTY IN THE EVENT OF ARMED CONFLICT.

CULTURE AND DEVELOPMENT. The United Nations **Charter** states that "the United Nations shall promote . . . international cultural and educational cooperation" and the **Universal Declaration of Human Rights** says that each person is entitled to realize his "economic, social and cultural rights, indispensable to his dignity and the free development of his personality." As the main entity within the United Nations family concerned with culture, the **United Nations Educational, Scientific, and Cultural Organization (UNESCO)** has throughout its existence devoted considerable attention to strengthening a "culture of peace," that is to say a "process by which positive attitudes to peace, democracy and tolerance are forged through education and knowledge about different cultures." UNESCO seeks to protect the **cultural heritage** of nations, one of its major activities since 1959 when Egypt and Sudan requested international assistance to safeguard the monuments of Nubia. The UN and UNESCO proclaimed the period 1988–1997 a World Decade for Cultural Development.

The importance of the linkages between culture and **development**, however, has only recently been acknowledged as the process of **globalization** and the accompanying spread of a global consumer culture have posed with growing acuity the issue of the preservation of cultural identities. Increasing attention to **human rights** and a **right to development**, notably the rights of **indigenous peoples** also account for this growing interest in culture and development. As part of a World Decade for Cultural Development, a joint United Nations-UNESCO Independent World Commission on Culture issued a pioneering report "Our Creative Diversity" in 1995. The Commission drew from the **human development** concept advocated by the **United Nations Development Programme (UNDP)**, arguing that cultural growth and cultural diversity were an integral part of the broadening of choices to individuals that is at the heart of the process of development. *See also* UNITED NATIONS PERMANENT FORUM FOR INDIGENOUS PEOPLES (UNPFIP).

CYPRUS QUESTION (1960–). Cyprus, a British colony, was granted independence in 1960 under a constitutional arrangement of power sharing between the Greek majority of the population and the Turkish minority that precluded unification of the country with Greece (favored by the former) or partition supported by the latter. Large-scale fighting between the two communities nevertheless flared up and persisted throughout the early 1960s, leading Great Britain to bring the matter to the United Nations **Security Council**. In 1964, the Council established the **United Nations Peacekeeping Force in Cyprus (UNFICYP)** to act as a buffer between the two communities.

A military coup in 1974 brought to power officers reputed to favor unification with Greece, prompting Turkey to invade the island. In 1983, the Turkish Cypriots declared themselves independent from the Cypriot state and proclaimed the creation of a Turkish Republic of Northern Cyprus, which has been recognized only by Turkey.

Negotiations assisted by the United Nations, first by a mediator and then by a **special representative of the secretary-general**, have since continued intermittently and inconclusively while UNFICYP still contributes to an uneasy peace. Other organizations, including the **European Union (EU)**, have also tried, without success, to mediate a settlement. *See also* CORDOVEZ, DIEGO (1935–); MEDIA-TION; PEACEKEEPING.

– D –

DAYS-YEARS-DECADES (INTERNATIONAL). Since the early years of its existence, the United Nations has established a set of "days" and "years" to help focus attention on issues in which the organization has an interest or commitment. Their objectives are to raise awareness and concern for emerging or current issues through public information campaigns and statements by senior officials of the organization, to mobilize grassroots support, and to promote policy solutions. "Decades" are rarer occurrences and more ambitious undertakings insofar as they often define specific time frame goals, targets, and policies and provide for their periodic review and assessment.

International days are numerous. The following list is not exhaustive. 8 March: International Women's Day; 21 March: International Day for the Elimination of Racial Discrimination; 22 March: World Water Day; 7 April: World Health Day; 3 May: World Press Freedom Day; 21 May: World Day for Cultural Diversity for Dialogue and Development; 15 May: International Day of Families; 29 May: International Day of United Nations Peacekeepers; 31 May: World No-Tobacco Day; 5 June: World Environment Day; 26 June: International Day against Drug Abuse and Illicit Trafficking and International Day in Support of Victims of Torture; 29 June: World Refugee Day; 9 August: International Day of the World's Indigenous People; 21 September: International Day of Peace (formerly the opening day of the UN General Assembly, changed to a set date as of 2002); 16 October: World Food Day; 1 December: World AIDS Day, and 24 October: United Nations Day.

International years are less frequent and have been devoted, among others, to **refugees** (1959), **human rights** (1968), **education** (1970), racism, (1971), **population** (1974), **women** (1975), **children** (1979), **disabled persons** (1981), **youth** (1985), peace (1986), shelter for the homeless (1987), literacy (1990), **indigenous peoples** (1993), the **family** (1994), tolerance (1995), the oceans (1998), older persons

(1999), **dialogue among civilizations** (2001), mountains (2002), fresh water (2003), rice (2004), **microcredit** (2005), and **desertification** (2006).

Past "decades" have been concerned with **development** (1961–1970, 1971–1980, 1981–1991), racism and racial discrimination (1993–2003); **indigenous peoples** (1994–2003); and human rights education (1995–2004). Current decades focus on a culture of peace (2001–2010), the eradication of colonialism (2001–2010), the elimination of malaria (2001–2010), literacy (2003–2012), **education** (2005–2014), and **water** (2005–2015).

DEBT CRISIS (INTERNATIONAL). In the 1970s, many **developing countries** borrowed heavily from private banks and governments. Sharp increases in **energy** prices, declines in **commodity** prices, protectionist measures in the North, and a global economic slowdown in the 1980s stymied their capacity to generate enough internal growth and export earnings to service and repay their debts. As a result, the threat of default and debt renegotiation have since become a perennial concern of creditors and borrowers compounded, since the end of the **Cold War**, by the borrowing of Russia and Eastern European countries.

These discussions have centered primarily in the **World Bank** and the **International Monetary Fund (IMF)**. The world banking system rode out the 1980s crisis, large defaults have been avoided (with the exception of Argentina in 2001), and the provision of new loans and debt relief measures agreed by the **Group of Eight (G-8)** have stabilized the situation. Yet, the debt problem of numerous Third World countries (especially low-income countries) remains acute and its linkages with **foreign direct investment** and international **trade** is fraught with risks of international confrontations and financial and economic disorders. Southern countries still owe $2.5 trillion, the equivalent of a third of their annual gross national income. Sub-Saharan Africa's external debt is equal to two-thirds of its annual income. Latin America's debt servicing absorbs a third of its hard currency export earnings. Numerous UN studies suggest that countries have been compelled to divert resources away from social provisions to repay their debt thereby adversely impacting the poor, **women**, and **children**. Debt relief or outright cancellation are key demands of developing countries and a number of **nongovernmental organizations (NGOs)** like **Jubilee Research**. *See also* DEVELOPMENT; HEAVILY INDEBTED POOR COUNTRY INITIATIVE (HIPC); HUMAN RIGHTS; INTERNATIONAL CONFERENCE ON FINANCING FOR DEVELOPMENT (MONTERREY, MEXICO, 18–22 March 2002); RIGHT TO DEVELOPMENT.

DE CUELLAR, JAVIER PEREZ (1920–). *See* PEREZ DE CUELLAR, JAVIER (1920–).

DECLARATION BY UNITED NATIONS (1942). Statement endorsed by 26 nations reaffirming the principles of the **Atlantic Charter** and establishing the United Nations military alliance against the Axis powers. *See also* MOSCOW DECLARATION ON GENERAL SECURITY (1943).

DECLARATION ON THE ESTABLISHMENT OF A NEW INTERNATIONAL ECNOMIC ORDER (NIEO). The outcome of a 1974 **special session of the General Assembly**, this declaration reflects the aspirations of **developing countries** for a greater say in the definition of the broad parameters of **international trade**, finance, and monetary relations. Some of the demands contained in the NIEO—the creation of international mechanisms for stabilizing the prices of commodities, debt cancellation, and the regulation of multinational corporations through binding **codes of conduct**—presupposed a radically new international political and economic order and have met continuing resistance by most developed countries. Others—such as a reduction of protectionist measures in the North, preferential access for Southern products, and increased **finance for development**—only sought modifications in North-South relations. These issues are still debated in the **World Trade Organization (WTO)** and various United Nations forums, notably the **United Nations Conference on Trade and Development (UNCTAD)** and the follow-up to the 2002 **International Conference on Financing for Development**. *See also* DEBT CRISIS (INTERNATIONAL); DEVELOPMENT; INTEGRATED PROGRAMME FOR COMMODITIES (IPC); SOVEREIGNTY OVER NATURAL RESOURCES; TERMS OF TRADE.

DECLARATION ON THE GRANTING OF INDEPENDENCE TO COLONIAL COUNTRIES AND PEOPLES (1960). Major anti-colonialist manifesto unanimously adopted by the **General Assembly**. The declaration asserts that all peoples have a right to **self-determination**; should freely determine their political status; and pursue their economic, social, and cultural development. Stressing that alien domination was contrary to the United Nations **Charter**, the declaration further called upon colonial powers to immediately transfer all powers of government to dependent peoples. *See also* DECLARATION REGARDING NON-SELF-GOVERNING TERRITORIES; DECOLONIZATION; DEVELOPING COUNTRIES; HUMAN RIGHTS; SPECIAL COMMITTEE ON DECOLONIZATION.

DECLARATION ON THE HUMAN ENVIRONMENT. *See* UNITED NATIONS CONFERENCE ON THE HUMAN ENVIRONMENT (STOCKHOLM, 1972).

DECLARATION REGARDING NON-SELF-GOVERNING TERRITORIES. A broad normative statement of principle contained in Chapter XI of the **United Nations Charter** enjoining "Members of the United Nations which have or assume responsibilities for the administration of territories whose peoples have not yet attained a full measure of self-government" to exert their rule in such a manner as to promote their "well-being" and "self-government." The declaration also invited colonial powers to transmit to the **secretary-general** "information of a technical nature relating to economic, social, and educational conditions in the territories for "information purposes."

The declaration embodied a painstakingly reached compromise at the 1945 **San Francisco Conference** between the colonial powers, which saw it merely as a moral commitment, and those states that supported the goal of political independence for nonself-governing territories and endorsed the idea of a United Nations right of oversight in the administration of European colonies. *See also* DECLARATION ON THE GRANTING OF INDEPENDENCE TO COLONIAL COUNTRIES AND PEOPLES (1960); DECOLONIZATION; DOMESTIC JURISDICTION; HUMAN RIGHTS; MINORITIES, PROTECTION OF; SELF-DETERMINATION; SPECIAL COMMITTEE ON DECOLONIZATION.

DECLARATIONS. In the context of the United Nations, the term primarily refers to resolutions of the **General Assembly** solemnly asserting broad norms and principles deemed to be adhered to by the international community. UN-sponsored **global conferences** have also frequently resulted in the adoption of similar declarations.

The assembly has endorsed declarations about the rights of **children** (1959), **decolonization** (1960), the uses of **outer space** (1962), **racial discrimination** (1963), **disabled persons** (1975), torture (1975), **apartheid** (1977), **disarmament** (1980, 1990), **crime prevention** (1985), and **development** (1986).

As exhortatory rather than legislative documents, such declarations are not legally binding and remain the source of considerable controversy. Some of them, nevertheless, have acquired the status of quasi-international legal standards such as the **Universal Declaration of Human Rights** or the **Declaration on the Granting of Independence to Colonial Countries and Peoples**, which many consider sources of **international law**. Also, many declarations adopted by the assembly have paved the way for the conclusion of binding international treaties, as was notably the case in regard to the **Convention on the Rights of the Child**; the **Convention on the Elimination of All Forms of Discrimination against Women**; the **Convention against Torture and Other Cruel, Inhuman, or Degrading Treatment or Punishment**; and the **Convention on the Elimination of Racial Discrimination**. *See also* DECLARATION ON THE ESTABLISHMENT OF A NEW INTERNATIONAL ECONOMIC ORDER (NIEO); UNITED NATIONS CONFERENCE ON THE HUMAN ENVIRONMENT (STOCKHOLM, 1972).

DECOLONIZATION. When the United Nations was established in 1945, more than 750 million people—almost a third of the world population—lived under colonial rule. Articles 73 and 74 of the UN **Charter** set forth principles, including the right to **self-determination**, that have guided the United Nations in its decolonization efforts. The charter also established an international **Trusteeship System** and a **Trusteeship Council** that superseded the **mandate system of the League of Nations**.

These provisions were hotly contested by colonial powers, but more than 80 former colonies have since 1945 gained their independence or have freely joined an independent state. There are only a handful of nonself-governing territories remaining today, with fewer than 2 million people. The weakening of colonial powers confronted by the rising tide of nationalist movements was a determining factor contributing to the demise of European colonial empires. But the United Nations played a critical role in the collective delegitimization of colonial rule and in speeding the progress of decolonization. In 1960, the **General Assembly** adopted a **Declaration on the Granting of Independence to Colonial Countries and Peoples** and established two years later a special committee to monitor its implementation. In 1990 and 2001, the **General Assembly** also proclaimed two International Decades for the Eradication of Colonialism. *See also* ALGERIAN QUESTION; DECLARATION REGARDING NON-SELF-GOVERNING TERRITORIES; DEVELOPING COUNTRIES; GOA, DAMAN, AND DIU DISPUTE (1961); MINORITIES, PROTECTION OF; PORTUGUESE COLONIES; SPECIAL COMMITTEE ON DECOLONIZATION; TUNISIAN QUESTION.

DELL, SIDNEY (1918–1990). British development economist who started his career in 1947 in the **Department of Economic and Social Affairs** of the **secretariat**. When he retired some 40 years later, he headed the Center on Transnational Corporations, a unit within the secretariat concerned with the politically sensitive subject of the activities of **transnational corporations (TNCs) in developing countries**. A specialist in **trade** and industrialization questions, Dell was a prolific writer who tirelessly highlighted the benefits of multilateral cooperation and called upon industrial countries to take more responsibility for creating an environment favorable to Third World countries.

DE MELLO, SERGIO VIERA (1948–2003). Brazilian national who spent most of his career working for the Office of the **United Nations High Commissioner for Refugees (UNHCR)**. He served in various capacities in Lebanon, Bangladesh, Sudan, Cyprus, Mozambique, Peru, Rwanda, and Yugoslavia. After heading the Department of Humanitarian Affairs (later called the **Office for the Coordination of Humanitarian Affairs [OCHA]**), he led the UN operation in East

Timor and played an important role in the transition of the Indonesian province to independence. In 2002, he succeeded **Mary Robinson** as commissioner for human rights. In May 2003, Secretary-General Kofi Annan appointed De Mello as his special envoy of the UN in Iraq. Three months later, he was killed in a bomb attack on the United Nations headquarters in Baghdad.

DEMOCRATIC REPUBLIC OF THE CONGO (DRC). In August 1999, after more than five years of conflict, the governments of the Democratic Republic of the Congo, Angola, Namibia, Rwanda, Uganda, and Zimbabwe and the main Congolese opposition groups (the Rwanda-backed Congolese Democratic Assembly [RCD] and the Uganda-backed Movement for the Liberation of the Congo [MLC]) reached a cease-fire agreement. These so-called Lusaka Accords also set up a mechanism for the discussion of peace implementation and, in November 1999, the **United Nations Organization Mission in the Democratic Republic of the Congo (MONUC)** began monitoring the cease-fire and assisted in the disarmament, demobilization, and repatriation of foreign forces. In July 2003 the president of the DRC promulgated a transitional constitution providing for power-sharing arrangements.

Neighboring Rwanda and Uganda withdrew most of their troops in the second half of 2003. But an upsurge of fighting by armed groups and militias has gripped the eastern and northern parts of the country, fueled by long-standing ethnic tensions, and forcing the **Security Council**, in June 2003, to deploy an Interim Emergency Multinational Force (MNF) to reinforce MONUC's military presence. In subsequent resolutions, the council has further strengthened MONUC's mandate authorizing it to use all necessary means to fulfill its mandate in the Ituri district and ensure the protection of the civilian population and humanitarian workers throughout the territory of the DRC.

The Security Council's growing interventionist mood has not, however, stymied the fighting described by humanitarian agencies as "one of the bloodiest conflicts the world has known since the Second World War." In part, the conflict has been exacerbated and prolonged by the looting of the country's natural resources by both allies and opponents of the government, including military commanders and political leaders from Rwanda, Uganda, and Zimbabwe, which a Security Council–appointed UN panel of experts first reported on in late 2002. The council imposed an arms embargo in 2003 and has since repeated its earlier condemnations of the illegal activities taking place mainly in the DRC's mining areas and urged governments to help in ending the illegal trade in the countries' resources.

In any event, since 1999, an estimated 3.8 million people are thought to have been killed, the vast majority of them civilians. Violence in the region has caused massive displacements of populations—over 3 million according to United Nations Children's Fund (UNICEF) data—with **children** at high risk of becoming victims of various forms of exploitation. **Human rights** abuses—killings of unarmed civilians, torture, rape, and repression of political dissent—have become common currency. The **International Criminal Court (ICC)** chose the DRC as the focus of its first case as, in April 2004, the president of the DRC formally requested the ICC prosecutor to look into alleged war crimes, genocide, and **crimes against humanity**.

The socioeconomic situation in the rest of the country is equally catastrophic. Per capita gross domestic product is $90. Average life expectancy is only about 45 years. Only 25 percent of students attending school complete five years of primary school. 40 to 70 percent of the country's approximately 50 million inhabitants have no access to basic medical and **health** care. **HIV/AIDS** and other infectious diseases are widespread. Chronic food shortages affect several regions.

DEMOGRAPHY. Scientific discipline focusing on the study of "the number, structure and growth of world population from principally [a] quantitative point of view" and one of the long-standing and highly praised substantive activities of the **Department of Economic and Social Affairs (DESA)** in the United Nations **Secretariat**. *See also* COMMISSION ON POPULATION AND DEVELOPMENT (UNITED NATIONS); FUNCTIONALISM; POPULATION; POPULATION PROGRAMS OF THE UNITED NATIONS.

DENUCLEARIZATION. *See* NUCLEAR WEAPONS FREE ZONES (NWFZs).

DEPARTMENT FOR DISARMAMENT AFFAIRS (DDA). Upon recommendation of the **General Assembly**, a department for

disarmament affairs was created in 1982 within the UN **Secretariat**. This unit functioned for 10 years until 1992. The present Department for Disarmament Affairs was reestablished by the assembly in 1998. Its basic functions are to promote disarmament and nonproliferation and to strengthen disarmament regimes in regard to **weapons of mass destruction (WMDs)** and chemical and biological weapons. DDA also supports disarmament efforts in the area of conventional weapons, notably **antipersonnel landmines** and small arms. It oversees the work of regional centers concerned with peace and disarmament in Africa, Asia, and Latin America. *See also* UNITED NATIONS INSTITUTE FOR DISARMAMENT RESEARCH (UNIDIR).

DEPARTMENT OF ECONOMIC AND SOCIAL AFFAIRS (DESA). The broad mandate of this important unit of the United Nations **Secretariat** is to promote **sustainable development** mainly through the provision of **research** and policy analysis on economic, environmental, **gender**, **population**, and social issues. In its earlier years and through the leadership of such officials as **Philippe de Seynes** and the issuance of groundbreaking studies and reports like the *World Economic Survey*, the department played a key role in placing **development** at the center of the United Nations agenda. DESA still publishes widely respected and authoritative statistical and **demographic** yearbooks, manuals, and studies.

DEPARTMENT OF PEACEKEEPING OPERATIONS (DPKO). Unit within the United Nations **Secretariat** responsible for the planning, management, and direction of peacekeeping operations. DPKO also maintains contact with the **Security Council**, troop and financial contributors, and parties to a conflict in the implementation of Security Council mandates. Following issuance of the **Brahimi Report**, the department has undergone a major reorganization of its functions.

DEPARTMENT OF POLITICAL AFFAIRS (DPA). Within the UN **Secretariat**, this department provides advice and support to the **secretary-general**'s peace and security functions in the areas of **conflict prevention, postconflict peace building, peacemaking**, and **electoral assistance**.

DEPENDENCIA. Heterogeneous but influential body of scholarly analysis of the international economic system presenting its structure and mode of operation as causal factors in the exploitation of Southern countries and their persistent dependence on the wealthy industrial Northern countries. Its central proposition is that the relationship between advanced capitalist societies at the core of the world economy and the developing countries at the periphery is bound to be deleterious to the latter because of inherently unequal exchanges centered around skewed international **trade**, financial, and monetary rules. Several dependency writers such as **Fernando Henrique Cardoso** and **Celso Furtado** were close to the **Economic Commission for Latin America and the Caribbean (ECLAC)** and its first executive-secretary, **Raul Prebisch**, of Argentina. *See also* NEW INTERNATIONAL ECONOMIC ORDER (NIEO).

DEPUTY SECRETARY-GENERAL. High-level post created by the **General Assembly** at the end of 1997 as part of the reform of the United Nations to help manage secretariat operations and to ensure coherence of activities and programs, especially in the economic and social spheres. The effectiveness of this new office in meeting its stated purposes has received mixed reviews. *See also* CHIEF EXECUTIVE BOARD (CEB); COORDINATION, UNITED NATIONS SYSTEM; FRECHETTE, LOUISE (1946–); REFORM, UNITED NATIONS; UNITED NATIONS FUND FOR INTERNATIONAL PARTNERSHIPS (UNFIP).

DESERTIFICATION. A misnomer because the concept does not merely refer to the expansion of existing deserts. The phenomenon might better be described as land degradation, a process that occurs in dryland ecosystems as a result of human activities (such as over-exploitation, inappropriate land use, overgrazing, bad irrigation practices, etc.) and climatic variations. Over 250 million people are directly affected and some 1 billion are at risk in over 100 countries, most of them among the world's poorest. The problem was first raised at a 1977 United Nations Conference to Combat Desertification. Its persistence and continuing spread triggered further discussions at the 1992 **United Nations Conference on Environment and Development (UNCED)**, resulting in a recommendation to the

United Nations **General Assembly** to set up a mechanism for the elaboration of a multilateral convention to tackle the issue. *See also* AGENDA 21; NATURAL DISASTER; UNITED NATIONS CONVENTION TO COMBAT DESERTIFICATION (UNCCD, 1996).

DEVELOPING COUNTRIES. Term used synonymously with others like "emerging nations," "underdeveloped countries," "less developed countries," "Third World" and "Global South" to refer to non-Western countries of Asia, Africa, Latin America, and the Middle East sharing common characteristics in spite of cultural, political, and economic differences. Such characteristics include a wide incidence of **poverty**, high **population** growth rates, low levels of industrialization, widespread illiteracy and disease, as well as a general economic and technological dependence on the exports of primary products to the developed countries in return for finished products. Several of them gained their independence from colonial rule in the postwar era and face nation- and state-building problems.

With a few exceptions, individual developing countries tend to be minor players in international politics and, in order to increase their political leverage, are inclined to act collectively as a group through organizations like the **Nonaligned Movement (NAM)** and the **Group of Seventy-Seven (G-77)**. As their number dramatically swelled in the United Nations, developing countries endeavored throughout the 1960s and 1970s to reshape the political agenda of the organization, their major objective being to reduce their economic and political dependence on the industrial North. Since the **General Assembly**'s adoption of its **Declaration on the Establishment of a New International Economic Order**, the influence of developing countries has waned considerably in the face of developed countries' resistance and as a result of widening differences in their political, cultural, and economic conditions. The demands of the NAM and G-77, nevertheless, still overshadow the work of the United Nations. *See also* DECOLONIZATION; DEPENDENCIA; DEVELOPMENT; GLOBALIZATION; NORTH-SOUTH DIALOGUE; REFORM, UNITED NATIONS.

DEVELOPMENT. The meaning of the concept of development has undergone profound changes since it entered into the lexicon of the

United Nations in the late 1940s to the early 1950s. Originally, development was equated to "economic growth" as measured by increases in per capita income. The assumption was that free **trade** coupled with injections of private and public capital and **technical assistance** would create the conditions for an economic takeoff in developing countries and that the benefits of the resulting growth would "trickle down" to the bulk of their population.

Two decades later, in spite of impressive advances in many countries, particularly in Asia and Latin America, the growing number of "absolute poor" led to a reassertion of the importance of "social progress" and a renewed emphasis on **poverty** eradication as a fundamental objective of development. The shift in development thinking was highlighted by the Declaration on Social Progress adopted by the **General Assembly** in 1966 and the increasing emphasis placed by donor countries on the satisfaction of **basic needs** and the improvement of living standards in their lending policies.

During the 1980s, the prevailing concept of development was broadened by the recognition of the fundamental role of **women** as actors and beneficiaries in the economy and society. The mainstreaming of **gender** issues in development policies and the programs of aid agencies is now a well-recognized principle of national and international development strategies. United Nations–sponsored **global conferences** devoted to women have in no minor way contributed to this paradigmatic shift. In the mid-1980s and in the wake of the report of the **World Commission on Environment and Development**, environmental issues have also nudged their way into development thinking and led to concerns about the sustainability of the development process.

The return in the 1990s to a neo-liberal orthodoxy centered on the primacy of markets; the liberalization of trade, finance, and investment; together with the seemingly unstoppable process of **globalization** have triggered a new round of collective reflection on the understanding of development focused on the notion of **human security** advocated by the *Human Development Reports* of the **United Nations Development Programme (UNDP)**. The concept of human security remains controversial. Critics argue that it is tantamount to pouring old wine into new bottles and that it is too broad for concrete policy applications. Proponents, on the other hand, point to the rapid expansion of the range of security threats and find ammunition in the report of the **High-Level Panel on Threats, Challenges, and Change** which identifies several clusters of threats, beginning with economic and social threats: disease and **hunger**, **poverty** and unemployment, and **terrorism** and ethnic conflicts. *See also* DEVELOPING COUNTRIES; DEVELOPMENT COMMITTEE; GLOBAL PUBLIC GOODS; OFFICIAL DEVELOPMENT ASSISTANCE (ODA); UNITED NATIONS CONFERENCE ON TRADE AND DEVELOPMENT (UNCTAD).

DEVELOPMENT COMMITTEE. Known formally as the Joint Ministerial Committee of the Boards of Governors of the **World Bank** and the **International Monetary Fund (IMF)** on the Transfer of Real Resources to Developing Countries, the committee was established in 1974. Its mandate is to advise the governing bodies of the bank and the fund on **development** issues and on the financial resources required to promote economic development in **developing countries**. The Development Committee meets twice a year.

DEVELOPMENT FINANCE. *See* OFFICIAL DEVELOPMENT ASSISTANCE (ODA).

"DIALOGUE AMONG CIVILIZATIONS." A 1998 Iranian initiative purported to promote cultural awareness and understanding under the auspices of the United Nations. The proposal, primarily prompted by the Iranian government's efforts to gain stature and recognition within the Islamic world and normalize its relations with the West, triggered far-ranging diplomatic activities until 2001, which the **General Assembly** proclaimed the "United Nations Year of Dialogue among Civilizations." Several UN organizations, notably the **United Nations Educational, Scientific, and Cultural Organization (UNESCO)**, sponsored conferences, seminars, and meetings related to the dialogue and a personal representative of the **secretary-general** has endeavored to promote the idea. The General Assembly devoted two days of plenary meetings to the subject in the Fall of 2001, culminating in the adoption of a program of action, which it reviewed in 2005. In the wake of the events of 11 September 2001, the initiative has lost much of its momentum. *See also* PICCO, GIANDOMENICO (1948–).

DIGITAL DIVIDE. *See* INFORMATION TECHNOLOGY (IT).

DISABLED PERSONS. There are over 600 million persons—10 percent of the world population—believed to be affected by some form of disability and subjected to various forms of poverty, marginalization, and social exclusion. Two-thirds of them live in developing countries. Their number continues to increase as a result of civil wars, inadequate medical care, and **natural disasters**.

The work of the United Nations in support of disabled persons has considerably evolved over the years, first focusing in the early 1950s on disability prevention and rehabilitation and then, in the 1960s and 1970s, shifting to ways and means to promote their integration into society. The United Nations proclaimed 1981 the International Year of Disabled Persons and the following year adopted a World Program of Action concerning disabled persons that provides the basis for the UN current work in this field.

The organization's major objectives are how to support the participation of persons with disabilities in social life and development; to promote their equal access to employment, education, information, and goods and services; and to advance their **human rights**. Growing emphasis is being placed on the protection of the rights of people with disabilities to education, medical services, employment, and economic and social security. Two conventions developed under the auspices of the **International Labour Organization (ILO)** seek to promote equality of opportunity and treatment for persons with disabilities in vocational rehabilitation, training, and employment (Convention 159 adopted in 1983 and the 2001 Code of Practice on Managing Disability in the Workplace). The **General Assembly** is currently considering proposals for the adoption of a comprehensive international convention to "promote and protect the rights and dignity of persons with disabilities." See *also* DEVELOPMENT; SOCIAL INTEGRATION.

DISARMAMENT. In contrast to **arms control**, disarmament refers to the complete or partial reduction of armaments. The covenant of the **League of Nations** directed members of the League to reduce their national armaments to "the lowest point consistent with national safety." Interwar disarmament conferences during the late 1920s and early 1930s yielded only limited arms control agreements on arsenals and on navies and symbolic commitments such as the Kellog Briand Pact, which called upon its signatories to renounce war as an instrument and component of foreign policy. The rise of revisionist totalitarian systems in Germany, Italy, and Japan brought to a halt the League efforts to create an arms control regime, and the momentum toward general disarmament simply evaporated.

Not surprisingly, the United Nations **Charter** does not establish a special organ to negotiate disarmament issues, but the advent of **nuclear weapons**, which became known only after it had been signed, provided an immediate impetus to opening negotiations focused on arms limitation and disarmament. In its very first resolution, the General Assembly established an **Atomic Energy Commission (AEC)** to deal with the problems raised by the discovery of atomic energy and mandated it to make specific proposals for the elimination of nuclear weapons.

The **Cold War**, however, quickly stymied this negotiating machinery. The stalemate between the two major superpowers and the insistence of middle-level powers and developing countries through the **Nonaligned Movement (NAM)** to play a role pulled the negotiating process away from disarmament issues to the search for the proper forum where such disarmament talks could take place. Until 1957, the principal UN disarmament body was the **Disarmament Commission**, the successor body to the AEC. In subsequent years, the great powers agreed to enlarge the membership of the Disarmament Commission, which was rechristened first **Ten-Nation Committee on Disarmament**, then **Eighteen-Nation Committee on Disarmament**, then **Conference of the Committee on Disarmament (CCD)**, and, finally, **Conference on Disarmament (CD)**. After agreement was reached during the first **special session** of the United Nations **General Assembly** devoted to disarmament in 1978, the CD has become the single multilateral negotiating body of the international community At that session, the General Assembly also outlined an international disarmament program that would give priority to nuclear disarmament and increase the role of the members of the assembly vis-à-vis the permanent members of the Security Council. It also renewed calls for a general and comprehensive disarmament (GCD), which went unheeded. A second 1982 special session again failed to induce the major powers to discuss GCD.

GCD has however come to be increasingly perceived as utopian and unachievable and the political momentum has progressively shifted toward the arena of strategic arms control. A number of important multilateral arms control agreements were reached under the broad umbrella of the CD and its predecessor bodies, including the 1968 **Treaty on the Nonproliferation of Nuclear Weapons (NPT)**, the 1971 **Seabed Demilitarization Treaty**, the 1972 **Biological Weapons Convention (BWC)**, the 1977 **Environmental Modification Convention (ENMOD)**, the 1992 **Chemical Weapons Convention (CWC)**, and the 1996 **Comprehensive Test Ban Treaty (CTBT)**. Agreements have also been made about the creation of **nuclear weapons free zones**, and confidence building measures to strengthen international security. But bilateral arms control agreements involving reductions in strategic and intermediate nuclear armaments between the United States and the USSR have been negotiated outside the CD.

Following the demise of the Cold War and the disintegration of the Soviet Union, the proliferation of intrastate disputes in the 1990s has prompted new concerns for the illicit transfer and use of conventional arms, in particular **small arms and light weapons**, and the production and use of **antipersonnel landmines**. *See also* ANTARCTIC TREATY; BARUCH, BERNARD (1870–1965); CONVENTION ON THE PROHIBITION OF THE USE, STOCKPILING, PRODUCTION, AND TRANSFER OF ANTIPERSONNEL MINES AND ON THEIR DESTRUCTION (1999); CONVENTIONAL ARMS REGISTER; DAYS-YEARS-DECADES (INTERNATIONAL); ECONOMIC CONSEQUENCES OF DISARMAMENT; INDEPENDENT COMMISSION ON DISARMAMENT AND SECURITY ISSUES; INTERNATIONAL ATOMIC ENERGY AGENCY (IAEA); OUTER SPACE TREATY (1967); PARTIAL TEST BAN TREATY (PTBT, 1963); REGISTER OF CONVENTIONAL ARMS AND STANDARDIZED REPORTING OF MILITARY EXPENDITURES; UNITED NATIONS INSTITUTE FOR DISARMAMENT RESEARCH (UNIDIR); UNITED NATIONS MONITORING, VERIFICATION, AND INSPECTION COMMISSION (UNMOVIC); UNITED NATIONS SPECIAL COMMISSION (UNSCOM).

DISARMAMENT AND DEVELOPMENT. *See* ECONOMIC CONSEQUENCES OF DISARMAMENT.

DISARMAMENT COMMISSION (DC). Established in 1952 "under the **Security Council**" with the same membership as the **Atomic Energy Commission (AEC)**, which it replaced. Its mandate was to prepare plans, under international control, for the regulation, limitation, and balanced reduction of all armed forces and armaments; the elimination of **weapons of mass destruction (WMDs)**; and the effective control of atomic energy. *See also* DISARMAMENT.

DISASTER RELIEF. Provision of short-term assistance to people affected by famine, earthquakes, flooding, or other such natural disasters in the form of food, water, shelter, clothing, and other essentials. As such, disaster relief is distinct from humanitarian interventions, which are targeted at people affected by wars and internal strife. But the concept encompasses the idea of **prevention** or disaster preparedness, a set of long-range policies, measures, and programs designed to eliminate, mitigate, or prevent the occurrence of disasters. Such measures include, for example, the development of plans to minimize potential losses of life and damage and to organize effective rescue and relief operations, weather forecasting and warning, the education and training of the public, and the stockpiling of supplies. As such, international disaster relief is a complex process, as it involves a multiplicity of actors including governments, international agencies such as the **World Food Programme (WFP)** and the **United Nations High Commissioner for Refugees (UNHCR)**, and private charitable organizations such as the **International Committee of the Red Cross (ICRC)**. The coordination of their interventions in the field has always posed major challenges. This task was originally assigned to the **United Nations Disaster Relief Organization (UNDRO)** created in 1972. It is now assumed by the **Office for the Coordination of Humanitarian Affairs (OCHA)**. *See also* COORDINATION, UNITED NATIONS SYSTEM; EARLY WARNING; NATURAL DISASTER; WORLD CONFERENCE ON DISASTER REDUCTION (KOBE, HYOGO, JAPAN, 18–22 January 2005).

DISCRIMINATION. Article 55(c) of the United Nations **Charter** states that the United Nations "shall promote . . . respect for, and observance of, **human rights** and fundamental freedoms for all without distinction as to race, sex, language or religion." Throughout its existence, the United Nations has sought to address through conventions and **declarations** and other resolutions problems of discrimination arising from such factors as race, **gender**, linguistic or religious minority status, and disability, to cite only a few instances. In his reporting to intergovernmental bodies on **development**, the **secretary-general** has consistently stressed the need for all national societies to be "inclusive." *See also* APARTHEID; CONVENTION ON THE ELIMINATION OF ALL FORMS OF DISCRIMINATION AGAINST WOMEN (1979); DISABLED PERSONS; HUMAN DEVELOPMENT REPORT (HDR); INTERNATIONAL CONVENTION ON THE ELIMINATION OF ALL FORMS OF RACIAL DISCRIMINATION (1965); MIGRATION (INTERNATIONAL); MINORITIES, PROTECTION OF; REFUGEES; SOCIAL INTEGRATION.

DOMESTIC JURISDICTION. One of the most important principles shaping the activities and work of the United Nations. This principle is found in Article 2.7 of the United Nations **Charter**; which stipulates that nothing in the charter should be construed as to "authorize the United Nations to intervene in matters which are essentially within the domestic jurisdiction of any state."

What is the meaning of "intervene," what is the scope of the "domestic jurisdiction" of a state, and how are these determinations supposed to be made are questions that have stirred controversies from the very inception of the United Nations. For example, **apartheid** and the dismantling of colonial empires have been debated extensively within United Nations forums over the objections of South Africa and colonial powers, which invoked the domestic jurisdiction clause of the charter. These questions are still unsettled, although, in recent years, majorities in both the **Security Council** and the **General Assembly** have been increasingly inclined to broaden the scope of United Nations involvement in hitherto considered "essentially" domestic concerns as evidenced by such cases as the 1991 **Persian Gulf War**, the broadening of international **human rights** standards, and the growing acknowledgement that there are new global threats to peace and security. The principle still stands, nevertheless, as a reminder that no state is willing to surrender discretionary power to the organization. *See also* DECOLONIZATION; HIGH-LEVEL PANEL ON THREATS, CHALLENGES, AND CHANGE (HLP); HUMANITARIAN INTERVENTION; INTERNATIONAL COMMISSION ON INTERVENTION AND STATE SOVEREIGNTY; REFORM, UNITED NATIONS; SOVEREIGNTY.

DOMINICAN CRISIS (April–July 1965). Ruler of the country since 1930, General Rafael Trujillo was assassinated in 1961. A period of political turmoil followed, degenerating into civil war between right-wing and left-wing military forces. In April 1965, the United States massively intervened, dispatching a 24,000-strong force to the island. The intervention was initially justified as a means to protect endangered American lives, but subsequent official statements added the objective of preventing a Communist government from taking control. The matter quickly evolved into an East-West Cold War confrontation. The Soviet Union requested an urgent meeting of the **Security Council** to consider the armed intervention of the United States in the internal affairs of the Dominican Republic. The United States, meanwhile, successfully pressured the **Organization of American States (OAS)** into authorizing the dispatch of an Inter-American Peace Force including troops from five other Latin American countries that made up only one-sixth of the entire peace force. In effect, the United States recourse to the OAS precluded any action by the Security Council and circumvented the provisions of Article 53 of the charter, which stipulates that "no enforcement action shall be taken under regional arrangements or by regional agencies without the authorization of the Security Council." The involvement of the United Nations was limited to the dispatch at the request of the council of a representative of the **secretary-general** to report on the situation and, after July 1965, the council held no further meeting on the issue. *See also* PRINCIPLES OF THE UNITED NATIONS; REGIONAL ARRANGEMENTS; USE OF FORCE.

DULLES, JOHN FOSTER (1888–1959). U.S. secretary of state under President Dwight D. Eisenhower. He was one of the main architects of U.S. foreign policy during the **Cold War**. He served as a member of the U.S. delegation at the 1945 **United Nations Conference on International Organization** in San Francisco. *See also* CONTAINMENT.

DUMBARTON OAKS CONFERENCE AND PROPOSALS (August–October 1944). A series of meetings attended by the delegations of the United States, the United Kingdom, the Soviet Union, and China in the late summer and early fall of 1944 on proposals for a "general international organization" that had been prepared by the U.S. State Department and received the approval of key members of the U.S. Congress.

The Dumbarton Oaks Proposals emerging from these "conversations," or, as formally known, the Washington Conversations on International Peace and Security, called for a multipurpose organization primarily concerned with the maintenance of peace and security and the promotion of economic and social cooperation and international law. The proposals envisaged a system of progressive enforcement measures falling under the purview of a **Security Council** in which the major powers would have a determinant role and the creation of an **Economic and Social Council (ECOSOC)** dealing with economic and social questions under the authority of the **General Assembly** and exerting a loose degree of coordination over autonomous functional organizations.

No agreement could be reached on Security Council voting procedures, a matter that was later resolved at the **Yalta Conference**. Because of British opposition, the proposals made no provision with respect to **non-self-governing territories**. The text of the **Charter** of the United Nations was finalized at the 1945 **United Nations Conference on International Organization**. *See also* ATLANTIC CHARTER; DECLARATION BY UNITED NATIONS (1942); MOSCOW DECLARATION ON GENERAL SECURITY (1943); VETO.

– E –

EARLY WARNING. Wide variety of activities including research, information gathering, and analysis on the causes of conflicts for the early recognition and the detection of sociopolitical developments that might lead to conflicts. Early warning is thus designed to contribute to the formulation of rapid engagement action and **peace-building** strategies designed to prevent or mitigate potential conflicts.

The United Nations **Charter** and a 1988 **General Assembly** Declaration on the Prevention and Removal of Disputes and Situations and on the Role of the United Nations in This Field both urge the

United Nations to become involved "early in a dispute or situation" or "at any stage of a dispute or situation." The **secretary-general** (or his personal representatives and envoys) may personally perform this function through his **good offices** and **mediation**. In response to the growing need for the services of the secretary-general, **Javier Perez de Cuellar** set up an **Office for Research and Collection of Information (ORCI)** to provide him with early warning and policy recommendations. The office was dismantled by his successor **Boutros Boutros-Ghali** and its functions redistributed mainly to the **Department of Political Affairs**.

The **Office for the Coordination of Humanitarian Affairs (OCHA)** has developed a system of early warning for the monitoring of possible outbreaks of humanitarian crises and works closely with concerned **nongovernmental organizations (NGOs)**. Early warning mechanisms also exist or are being set for the early detection of **natural disasters** and environmental trends. Much of the policy-oriented research carried out by the **secretariat** in the economic and social sectors may be viewed as having early warning functions. *See also* AGENDA FOR PEACE; CONFLICT PREVENTION; DISASTER RELIEF; EARTHWATCH; GLOBAL ENVIRONMENTAL MONITORING SYSTEM (GEMS); ORGANIZATION FOR SECURITY AND COOPERATION IN EUROPE (OSCE); PREVENTIVE DIPLOMACY; SWISSPEACE; TELECOMMUNICATIONS; WORLD CONFERENCE ON DISASTER REDUCTION (KOBE, HYOGO, JAPAN, 18–22 January 2005).

EARTH COUNCIL. International **nongovernmental organization (NGO)** created in 1992 to promote the implementation of the **Earth Summit** agreements. Drawing its membership from the world's political, business, scientific, and nongovernmental communities, the council seeks to promote awareness of the need for more sustainable and equitable patterns of development and to build bridges of cooperation between **civil society** and governments. *See also* STRONG, MAURICE (1929–).

EARTH DAY. 5 June has been designated as "World Environment Day" by the **General Assembly**. *See also* DAYS-YEARS-DECADES (INTERNATIONAL).

EARTH SUMMIT. *See* UNITED NATIONS CONFERENCE ON ENVIRONMENT AND DEVELOPMENT (UNCED, RIO DE JANEIRO, 1992).

EARTHWATCH. Interagency mechanism created at the 1972 **United Nations Conference on the Human Environment** in Stockholm to exchange information, coordinate and spur environmental observation activities among UN organizations for integrated assessment, and **early warning** purposes. The **United Nations Environment Programme (UNEP)** provides the Earthwatch secretariat.

EAST TIMOR. *See* TIMOR-LESTE.

ECONOMIC AND SOCIAL COMMISSION FOR WESTERN ASIA (ESCWA). The political and military turmoil affecting the region long delayed the creation of ESCWA and has since considerably hampered its work. Established in 1973 in Beirut, Lebanon, the civil war forced the commission to move the seat of its activities to Baghdad, Iraq. The Iran-Iraq War compelled yet another relocation to Jordan. The commission's headquarters is now back in Beirut.

The present work of the commission gives priority to the facilitation of transboundary flows of goods, services, and persons in the context of globalization; poverty alleviation capacity and institution building; and the promotion of regional cooperation in the fields of agriculture, industry and transport, energy, water resources, the environment, and the development of statistics. The commission reports to the **Economic and Social Council (ECOSOC)**. *See also* REGIONAL COMMISSIONS.

ECONOMIC AND SOCIAL COUNCIL (ECOSOC). At the insistence of lesser powers at the 1945 **United Nations Conference on International Organization** in San Francisco, the Economic and Social Council was made one of the six principal organs of the United Nations. Originally composed of 18 members, ECOSOC was enlarged to 27 in 1965 and 54 in 1973 through United Nations **Charter** amendments. Members are elected by a two-thirds vote of the **General Assembly**, but in practice major industrial countries have been consistently reelected over the years. Until 1992, the council held two sessions annually. It now meets once a year alternately in New York and Geneva.

The broad mandate of ECOSOC is to act as a forum for the discussion of world economic and social issues and to further international cooperation for development through research studies and reports and the elaboration of multilateral conventions. (Article 62) The council also has the mandate to coordinate the activities of the **specialized agencies** (Articles 63 and 64).

ECOSOC carries out its work through a large number of subsidiary bodies: "functional" commissions dealing with statistics, **population**, social development, **human rights**, **women**, **narcotic drugs**, **crime prevention**, **science and technology for development**, **sustainable development**, and forests and five **regional commissions** (Europe, Latin America and the Caribbean, Asia and the Pacific, Africa, and Western Asia).

Other bodies reporting to ECOSOC include the **Committee for Programme and Coordination**, the **Committee on Nongovernmental Organizations**, the **United Nations Group of Experts on Geographical Names**, the Committee of Experts on the Transport of Dangerous Goods, the **Committee for Development Policy**, the **Meeting of Experts on the United Nations Programme in Public Administration and Finance**, the **Ad Hoc Group of Experts on International Cooperation in Tax Matters**, the **Committee on Energy and Natural Resources for Development**, the **United Nations Permanent Forum on Indigenous Peoples**, and the **United Nations Forum on Forests**. In addition, over 1,500 NGOs have consultative status with ECOSOC.

Since its inception, the functioning of the council has been hampered by political and organizational problems, prompting repeated calls for its abolition or efforts designed to "revitalize" it. The council has only a power of recommendation. Functioning under the authority of the General Assembly, its work has been overshadowed by the growing assertion of power of the assembly in the 1960s and 1970s. However, the scope of its agenda has expanded beyond manageable proportions. The integration and oversight of the activities of the **specialized agencies** stumbled against the bedrock of their political, administrative, and budgetary autonomy.

In spite of these obstacles, ECOSOC has produced useful albeit unheralded work originating most of the time from its subsidiary machinery. Its agenda has been streamlined and is now focused on the consideration of global thematic developmental issues, coordination matters, and humanitarian questions. Closer working relationships with the agencies have developed in spite of continuing territorial claims and turf battles through the interagency coordination mechanisms set up under the **Administrative Committee on Coordination (ACC)** (now the **Chief Executive Board [CEB]**). Since 1998, biennial joint meetings with the **Bretton Woods institutions (BWIs)**, coinciding with the gatherings of the **International Bank for Reconstruction and Development (IBRD)** and the **International Monetary Fund's (IMF)** governing bodies, have been organized to share views about developmental priorities and policies. *See also* COMMISSION FOR SOCIAL DEVELOPMENT (UNITED NATIONS); COMMISSION ON CRIME PREVENTION AND CRIMINAL JUSTICE (UNITED NATIONS); COMMISSION FOR HUMAN RIGHTS (UNITED NATIONS); COMMISSION ON NARCOTIC DRUGS (UNITED NATIONS); COMMISSION ON POPULATION AND DEVELOPMENT (UNITED NATIONS); COMMISSION ON SCIENCE AND TECHNOLOGY FOR DEVELOPMENT (UNITED NATIONS) (CSTD); COMMISSION ON SUSTAINABLE DEVELOPMENT (UNITED NATIONS) (CSD); COMMISSION ON THE STATUS OF WOMEN (UNITED NATIONS) (CSW).

ECONOMIC COMMISSION FOR AFRICA (ECA). The last to be established in the regional architecture of the UN regional machinery, the ECA began its operations in 1958. Located in Addis Ababa, Ethiopia, and comprising 53 members, the commission reports to the **Economic and Social Council (ECOSOC)** through the Conference of African Ministers Responsible for Economic and Social Development and Planning. Research and policy analysis on the economic and social conditions in Africa and advocacy and technical capacity for development are central to its work. The commission played a role in the creation of the **African Development Bank (AfDB)** and facilitated the creation of a number of subregional organizations including the **Economic Community of West African States**

(ECOWAS) and the Preferential Trade Area for Eastern and Southern Africa (COMESA) as well as several technical institutions concerned with banking and finance, technology, minerals, and remote sensing.

ECONOMIC AND SOCIAL COMMISSION FOR ASIA AND THE PACIFIC (ESCAP). Headquartered in Bangkok, Thailand, this **regional commission** of the **Economic and Social Council (ECOSOC)** was established in 1947 along with and like the **Economic Commission for Europe (ECE)**, originally to assist in the reconstruction of the countries devastated by the war. ESCAP progressively refocused its activities on the longer-term development needs of the region with particular attention to those of the poorest among them. Its program of work concentrates on poverty and emerging social issues; the development of statistics; trade and investment; transport and tourism; the environment and sustainable development; and information, communications, and space technology. ESCAP has encouraged the creation of a number of regional economic organizations, particularly the **Asian Development Bank (ADB).**

ECONOMIC COMMISSION FOR EUROPE (ECE). Set up in 1947 in Geneva, originally for the purpose of assisting in the reconstruction of war-torn Europe, the primary goal of the ECE is to encourage greater economic cooperation among its 55 member states. Professional organizations and other **nongovernmental organizations (NGOs)** take an active part in its activities.

For a long time, the activities of this **regional commission** of the **Economic and Social Council (ECOSOC)** were hampered by the **Cold War**. Soviet bloc countries did not participate in its technical work while the West disapproved of its all-European outlook. With the ebbing of East West tensions, the ECE was able to progressively enlarge and intensify its work. The main areas of ECE current activities are economic analysis; environment and human settlements; statistics; sustainable energy; trade, industry, and enterprise development; timber; and transport.

The work of the commission has also led to the adoption of several environmental conventions such as the Convention on Long Range Transboundary Air Pollution (1971), the Convention on Environmental Impact Assessment in a Transboundary Context (1991), the

Convention on the Protection and Use of Transboundary Watercourses and International Lakes (1992), the Convention on the Transboundary Effects of Industrial Accidents, and the Convention on Access to Information, Public Participation on Decision-making and Access to Justice in Environmental Matters (1998).

In addition, the commission has been active in the development of methodologies, definitions, and classifications of comparable statistics. Over 50 international transport agreements and conventions and over 100 vehicle regulations have been negotiated under its auspices, seeking to simplify border crossings and coordinate the development of road, rail, and inland waterway transport systems.

ECE publishes the *Economic Survey of Europe*, an annual authoritative analysis of economic developments and prospects of the region, and carries out technical assistance activities in support of countries in transition.

ECONOMIC COMMISSION FOR LATIN AMERICA AND THE CARIBBEAN (ECLAC). One of the five **regional commissions** reporting to the **Economic and Social Council (ECOSOC)**, the Economic Commission for Latin America (ECLA) was established in 1948 for the purpose of "raising the level of economic activity in Latin America" and to study the problems arising from the "economic maladjustments" in the world economy that affect the development of the subcontinent. Its membership (currently 33 members and 7 associate members) was enlarged in 1984 to include the Caribbean countries and it is known now as the Economic Commission for Latin America and the Caribbean.

Under the intellectual leadership of its first executive-secretary, Argentinian economist **Raul Prebisch** who later became the first head of the **United Nations Conference on Trade and Development (UNCTAD)**, ECLA economists developed influential ideas about dependency, center-periphery relations, and the decline in **terms of trade**, which durably shaped development thinking and provided the theoretical basis for the **New International Economic Order (NIEO)** proposals of the 1970s.

The commission continues to produce policy studies on a wide range of economic and social subjects including an annual *Survey of Economic and Social Conditions in America* and provides advisory services to governments. It contributed to the establishment of the Central American Common Market and the **Inter-American Development Bank**. *See also* DEPENDENCIA; TRADE.

ECONOMIC COMMUNITY OF WEST AFRICAN STATES (ECOWAS). Regional group of fifteen West African countries founded in 1975 to promote their economic integration in "all fields of economic activity, particularly industry, transport, telecommunications, energy, agriculture, natural resources, commerce, monetary and financial questions, social and cultural matters." Against all expectations, ECOWAS has proved more active and effective in the peace and security rather than the economic and social fields. Under the political leadership of Nigeria, ECOWAS has played an increasing role in United Nations **peacekeeping** operations, notably in **Sierra Leone**, **Liberia**, and, more recently, in **Burundi**, **Cote d'Ivoire**, and **Sudan**. *See also* REGIONAL ARRANGEMENTS; UNITED NATIONS MISSION IN COTE D'IVOIRE (MINUCI, May 2003–present); UNITED NATIONS OBSERVER MISSION IN LIBERIA (UNOMIL, September 1993–September 1997); UNITED NATIONS OBSERVER MISSION IN SIERRA LEONE (UNOMSIL, June 1998–October 1999).

ECONOMIC CONSEQUENCES OF DISARMAMENT. The link between **disarmament** and, initially, economic growth, and then, at the insistence of developing countries, **development**, is implied in Article 26 of the United Nations **Charter** which assigns to the **Security Council** the task "to promote the establishment and maintenance of international peace and security with the least diversion for armaments of the world's human and economic resources."

Proposals seeking to allocate resources released from reduced military spending to development have been repeatedly tabled for discussion throughout the history of the United Nations with no tangible results with the possible exception of President **Eisenhower**'s "Atoms for Peace" statement, which led to the establishment of the **International Atomic Energy Agency (IAEA)**.

Throughout the **Cold War**, the global arms race and high levels of military spending led the **General Assembly** to call for reductions in military expenditures and the reallocation of resources thus released to development. It did so, notably, in resolutions launching international "decades" devoted to development and disarmament. Likewise, a 1962 secretariat study entitled *The Economic and Social Consequences of Disarmament* made the case for allocating "an appropriate proportion" of financial resources released from disarmament measures to international aid.

The special session of the General Assembly marking the end of the first disarmament decade in 1978 again highlighted the links between arms expenditures and development and requested the **secretary-general** to convene an expert group to prepare a "forward looking and policy oriented report" on the economic and social consequences of the arms race and the possible conversion and deployment of resources released from military purposes through disarmament measures to economic and social development. The report of the group was issued in 1982.

A 1987 International Conference on Disarmament and Development offered yet another inconclusive opportunity to review the issue. Military expenditures did fall in the years following the end of the Cold War—at least until 1996—but flows of **Official Development Assistance** decreased, some attributing the failure of the so-called "peace dividend" to materialize to a lack of political will, others to the high costs of conversion, and still others to changing government priorities.

The shift in development thinking toward the concept of **human security** with its emphasis on the need for a more holistic understanding of security has fueled a continuing interest in the linkages between disarmament and development within the development community. But the spread of internal conflicts and **terrorism**, among other factors, have refocused the policy priorities of national governments in the North on issues of nonproliferation and **small arms** trafficking. *See also* DAYS-YEARS-DECADES (INTERNATIONAL); HIGH-LEVEL PANEL ON NEW THREATS, CHALLENGES, AND CHANGE (HLP); INDEPENDENT COMMISSION ON DISARMAMENT AND SECURITY ISSUES; UNITED NATIONS INSTITUTE FOR DISARMAMENT RESEARCH (UNIDIR).

ECONOMIC COOPERATION AMONG DEVELOPING COUNTRIES (ECDC). A set of policies designed to enhance cooperation among **developing countries**, especially through **trade** and the establishment of regional markets, the coordination of investment or production programs, and **capacity development** in order to minimize their overall dependence on industrial countries. These issues have been widely debated and dealt with at the **United Nations Conference on Trade and Development** but have achieved very mixed results. *See also* DEPENDENCIA; SOUTH COMMISSION.

EDUCATION. The 1948 **Universal Declaration of Human Rights** declares education to be a **human right** of everyone. The declaration states that education shall be free and compulsory, "at least in the elementary and fundamental stages" and further asserts that technical and professional education shall be made "generally available," while higher education is "equally accessible to all on the basis of merit." Subsequently, the right to education has been reaffirmed and elaborated in numerous international instruments, notably in the 1966 **International Covenant on Economic, Social, and Cultural Rights**.

At the time of the adoption of the declaration, illiteracy was widespread. Forty-two percent of the people living in Latin America, 63 percent in Asia, and 84 percent in Africa were believed to be illiterate. In the half century that has elapsed since then, primary school enrollments have expanded worldwide from 200 million to over 650 million. In Africa they increased tenfold, in Latin America six times, and in Asia five times. Notwithstanding this enormous expansion, which surpasses the historical experience of the industrial countries, the achievement of universal primary education remains a daunting task, as many disparities still need to be addressed. Overall, 115 million children of primary school age are still out of school. Children from poorer families are less likely to go to school and the lowest levels of attendance are found among **indigenous peoples** and other minority groups. One-third of the children living in Sub-Saharan Africa are out of school, in part a reflection of the impact of **HIV/AIDS**. Female enrollments have grown faster than male enrollments, but in all developing regions, except Latin America and the Caribbean and Eastern and Southeastern Asia, girls are less likely to remain in school.

National governments, universities, and research institutes have been the prime agents of worldwide change and progress in education. The United Nations' role has been mainly one of advocacy and promotion through the funding and development of a variety of education and training programs. The **United Nations Educational, Scientific, and Cultural Organization (UNESCO)** is the principal United Nations entity concerned with education. Its statistical work and, in particular, its estimates of the scope of illiteracy have done much to raise awareness of the scale and nature of the problem. UNESCO's efforts in the promotion of functional literacy and work-oriented training closely integrated with socioeconomic development are also important to note, as research has shown a close link between access to education and improved social indicators. The other **specialized agencies** of the United Nations provide a broad range of educational programs within their respective mandates, extending from traditional basic schooling to technical training for human resource development in such areas as public administration, agriculture, and health services. The **World Bank** recognized in the 1970s that education was an important tool for poverty reduction and has gradually broadened its support from secondary to vocational and technical education. The **United Nations Children's Fund (UNICEF)** devotes a large share of its annual program expenditures to education with special attention to basic education and girls' schooling. *See also* HEALTH; MILLENNIUM DECLARATION; TECHNICAL ASSISTANCE; UNITED NATIONS RELIEF AND WORKS AGENCY (UNRWA); WORLD CONFERENCE ON WOMEN (BEIJING, 4–15 September 1995).

EIGHTEEN-NATION COMMITTEE ON DISARMAMENT (ENDC). Main United Nations disarmament negotiating arena between 1962–1968.

EISENHOWER, DWIGHT D. (1890–1969). American army career officer who rose to the rank of commanding general of the victorious Allied forces in Europe during World War II. Elected to the presidency in 1952, Eisenhower sought to reduce the strains of the **Cold War**. In a 1953 speech to the United Nations **General Assembly**, he painted a dark picture of nuclear energy's destructive power and presented an "**Atoms for Peace**" blueprint for the civilian applications of nuclear energy. One of his proposals was a call to the Soviet Union to "make joint contributions from their stockpiles of normal uranium and fissionable materials to an International Atomic Energy Agency" that would then "devise methods whereby this fissionable material would be allocated to serve the peaceful pursuits of mankind." No effective international bank of nuclear materials was ever established, but one of the concrete programs emerging from the Eisenhower initiative was the creation, after two years of negotiations with the Soviet Union, of the **International Atomic Energy Agency (IAEA)**. *See also* ARMS CONTROL; DISARMAMENT.

EL SALVADOR CONFLICT (1972–1992). For almost two decades, the military government of El Salvador, allied with wealthy landowners, fought a bitter war against leftist rebels. The conflict came to an end in 1990 after representatives of the government and the insurgents met under the auspices of the UN **secretary-general** and reached an opening agreement on **human rights**. A ceasefire was declared in 1991 and a comprehensive settlement signed in 1992. The peace accords "aimed not only to bring about a cessation of conflict, but also to remove the original causes of the conflict and promote democratization and reconciliation among Salvadorans." The UN played an important role in supporting the peace negotiations and in the implementation of the peace accords. United Nations' observers were deployed in advance of the cease-fire to monitor the Human Rights Agreement and the **United Nations Observer Mission in El Salvador (ONUSAL)** was subsequently charged with verifying all aspects of the cease-fire and then of the peace accords. *See also* ARIAS, OSCAR (1941–); CENTRAL AMERICA CONFLICTS.

ELDERLY. *See* AGING.

ELECTORAL ASSISTANCE. In a broad sense, the United Nations has been involved in "electoral assistance" virtually since its inception through its advocacy of the **decolonization** process and promotion of the principles of **self-determination** and **human rights**. Since the end of the **Cold War**, the term has been used to refer to various types of assistance to member states in the organization of credible and legitimate democratic elections and strengthening of their institutional capacity to hold periodic elections over the long run. Such assistance is provided only at their request and is undertaken by the **Department of Political Affairs (DPA)**.

Electoral assistance activities thus understood include the conduct of needs assessment, designing electoral assistance project activities and support for international observer groups. **Technical assistance** is the most frequently requested type of electoral assistance and entails advice about electoral administration and planning, voter registration, election budgeting, review of electoral laws and regulations, training of election officials, voter and civic education, procurement of election materials, electoral dispute resolution, computerization of electoral rolls, boundary delimitation, and the like. Since 1989, the United Nations has received over 140 requests for electoral assistance.

ELECTRONIC COMMERCE (E-COMMERCE). Electronic commerce refers to all commercial transactions based on the electronic processing and transmission of data. The expansion of e-commerce hinges on a country's level of development of its telecommunication infrastructure, the skill level of its population, and the existence of a supportive legal and commercial environment. But it is already generally recognized that even though the bulk of Internet commerce is currently limited to business-to-business transactions rather than direct customer-to-business transactions, the growth of electronic commerce supported by the Internet could potentially spread to the entire spectrum of commercial activities, thereby providing further impetus to the **globalization** of commercial activities.

The spread of e-commerce carries with it significant benefits, among them direct access to distant markets, decreases in transaction costs, and low entry barriers. But doing business electronically poses significant challenges for governments related to **consumer protection**, national taxation, and **intellectual property** issues. At the international level, the expansion of e-commerce has blurred the distinction between domestic and foreign firms, thus making it difficult to determine the national jurisdiction under which such transactions fall. Ensuring legal consistency across all countries raises another set of issues. Finally, e-commerce poses the recurring problem of the North-South digital divide.

Since 1998, the **World Trade Organization (WTO)** has been carrying out a comprehensive program of work that seeks to clarify some of the key issues brought to the fore by the growth of e-commerce, focused on the fiscal implications of e-commerce, the relationship (and possible substitution effects) between e-commerce and traditional forms of commerce, the imposition of customs duties on electronic transmissions, patterns of competition, and questions of jurisdiction and applicable laws. The **United Nations Conference on Trade and Development (UNCTAD)** and the **World Bank** also carry out programs intended to facilitate **developing countries'** access to e-commerce. *See also* COPYRIGHT; INFORMATION TECHNOLOGY (IT); TRADE; TRADE-RELATED ASPECTS OF INTELLECTUAL PROPERTY RIGHTS (TRIPs); UNITED NATIONS COMMISSION ON INTERNATIONAL TRADE LAW (UNCITRAL).

EMPLOYMENT. The economic dislocations of the interwar period were fresh in the minds of the drafters of the United Nations **Charter** and, not surprisingly, they assigned an important role to the organization in the promotion of full employment. Originally focused on the war-torn countries of Europe, relevant United Nations efforts have progressively shifted to the needs of **developing countries**, where unemployment or underemployment rates have been and remain high, frequently averaging 50 percent of the work force. Full employment was identified as a core developmental objective by the 1995 Program of Action of the World Summit for Social Development, which proclaimed that "productive work and employment are central elements of development as well as decisive elements of human identity." Yet, at the end of 2002, the number of working poor, or workers living on $1 or less a day, returned to the level of 550 million recorded in 1998. To absorb new entrants into the labor market and reduce working poverty and unemployment, at least 1 billion new jobs are needed during the coming decade to reach the objective of the **Millennium Declaration** adopted by the heads of state during the 2000 **Millennium Assembly** to halve the number of people living in extreme poverty by 2015.

The **International Labour Organization (ILO)** is the principal entity within the United Nations system concerned with employment and labor issues. The right to work is recognized in Article 23 of the **Universal Declaration of Human Rights** and in Articles 6 and 7 of the **International Covenant on Economic, Social, and Cultural Rights (ICESCR)**.

ENERGY. Power derived primarily from either conventional sources (wood, water, coal, gas, oil) and new renewable sources (thermal and photovoltaic solar, wind biomass, geothermal, and ocean tides). Fuelwood and water and wind power were for a long time the only source of energy for mankind. In the 19th century, they were by and large, overtaken by coal. Gas and oil are now the prime source of energy, especially in the industrial countries of the North. Shortfalls in the supply of oil in the 1970s prompted interest in new and renewable sources of energy. But the cost of their development has slowed progress in their use. Nuclear fission, which many thought in the mid-1940s to be a cheap solution to rising demand in energy, has been downgraded in the wake of disasters in nuclear power plants in the United States and Russia and difficulties encountered in the safe disposal of nuclear wastes.

Energy development issues have by and large been treated in a multilateral setting outside of the United Nations, both by producer (in the **Organization of Petroleum Exporting Countries [OPEC]**) or consumer nations (in the **International Energy Agency [IEA]**). The role of the United Nations has been mainly limited to expert discussions about energy efficiency and its impact on the environment. The peaceful uses of nuclear energy has been the exclusive preserve of the **International Atomic Energy Agency (IAEA)**. *See also* COMMITTEE ON ENERGY AND NATURAL RESOURCES FOR DEVELOPMENT (CENRD); UNITED NATIONS CONFERENCE ON NEW AND RENEWABLE SOURCES OF ENERGY (NAIROBI, 1981); UNITED NATIONS DEVELOPMENT PROGRAMME (UNDP).

ENFORCEMENT ACTION. *See* SANCTIONS.

ENQUIRY. Traditional technique of dispute settlement involving the creation of an impartial commission to investigate and report on the facts over which the parties involved in the dispute disagree. Enquiry (or inquiry) is limited to a determination of the facts and does not include proposed terms of settlement; its findings may or may not be accepted by the parties.

Enquiry used to be dependent upon bilateral agreement between contending governments. Under the **League of Nations**, it gained a multilateral character. A controversial inquiry conducted by the League involved the Japanese occupation of Manchuria, a province of northeastern China in 1931. The report of the commission was sympathetic to China and triggered a debate within the League that led to the withdrawal of Japan from the organization. See *also* ARBITRATION; CONCILIATION; FACT-FINDING; JUDICIAL SETTLEMENT; MEDIATION; PEACEFUL SETTLEMENT OF DISPUTES; REGIONAL ARANGEMENTS.

ENVIRONMENT. In a 1968 resolution, the **Economic and Social Council (ECOSOC)** noted "the continued and accelerating impairment of the quality of the human environment caused by such factors as air and water pollution, erosion and other forms of soil deterioration, secondary effects of biocides, wastes and noise." In the council's view, intensified remedial action both at the national and international levels were urgently needed.

Since then, the involvement of the United Nations in environmental matters has grown exponentially. A major stepping stone in that process was the 1972 **United Nations Conference on the Human Environment**, which focused on the social and cultural needs to be factored into environmental protection planning, natural resources, and international cooperation policies. The creation of the **United Nations Development Programme (UNDP)** in 1972 was another important turning point for the United Nations, as the new program served as a key forum for an ongoing discussion of environmental issues. There, sharp differences of views along North-South lines became quickly apparent. Industrialized countries defined environmental issues primarily in terms of the formulation of preventive policies. Developing countries took the view that pollution was an unavoidable consequence of economic and industrial development, the control of which required financial assistance by Northern states. In its 1988 report, the **World Commission on Environment and Devel-**

opment (the Brundtland Commission) sought to reconcile these conflicting approaches through its advocacy of the concept of "**sustainable development**."

An important offshoot of the environmental work of the United Nations has been the elaboration of a large number of international agreements aiming at the protection of the environment, such as the 1987 **Montreal Protocol** concerned with the depletion of the ozone layer, the 1989 **Basel Convention on the Control of Transboundary Movements of Hazardous Wastes and Their Disposal**, the 1992 **United Nations Framework Convention on Climate Change**, the 1992 **Convention on Biological Diversity**, and the 1995 **United Nations Conference on Straddling Fishstocks and Highly Migratory Fish Stocks**, among others. In its 2004 report, the **High-Level Panel on Threats, Challenges, and Change** argued that threats to the environment constituted threats to international peace and security. *See also* ACID RAIN; AGENDA 21; DESERTIFICATION; EARLY WARNING; EARTHWATCH; ECONOMIC COMMISSION FOR EUROPE (ECE); ENERGY; ENVIRONMENT; ENVIRONMENTAL MODIFICATION CONVENTION (ENMOD, 1977); ENVIRONMENTAL SECURITY; FISHING AND FISHERIES; GLOBAL ENVIRONMENTAL MONITORING SYSTEM (GEMS); GLOBAL WARMING; UNITED NATIONS CONFERENCE ON ENVIRONMENT AND DEVELOPMENT (UNCED, RIO DE JANEIRO, 1992).

ENVIRONMENTAL MODIFICATION CONVENTION (ENMOD, 1977). Essentially the outcome of negotiations held in 1974–1975 by the United States and the USSR. A draft of the convention was submitted by the two countries to the United Nations **Conference of the Committee on Disarmament (CCD)** for further discussion. A slightly modified text emerged from the CDD that was transmitted to the **General Assembly** for its consideration and adoption.

Under the terms of the convention, its parties undertake not to engage in military or any other hostile use of environmental modification techniques having widespread, long-lasting, or severe effects as the means of destruction, damage, or injury to any other state party. The Convention entered into force in 1980. *See also* AGENDA 21;

ARMS CONTROL; DISARMAMENT; ECONOMIC CONSE-QUENCES OF DISARMAMENT; ENVIRONMENT; ENVIRON-MENTAL SECURITY; MONTREAL PROTOCOL ON SUB-STANCES THAT DEPLETE THE OZONE LAYER (1987); WEAPONS OF MASS DESTRUCTION (WMDs).

ENVIRONMENTAL SECURITY. The notion that environmental risks such as nuclear contamination, spent fuel and wastes, threats to energy resources, sudden disasters, and degradation or depletion of essential environmental resources may directly contribute to political and economic instability or international conflict. Both the 1972 **United Nations Conference on the Environment** and the **United Nations Conference on the Human Environment** established the principle that states must cooperate in jointly developing programs to manage the environment. See *also* AGENDA 21; ENVIRONMENT; ENVIRONMENTAL MODIFICATION CONVENTION (ENMOD, 1977); GOLAN HEIGHTS ISSUE; HIGH-LEVEL PANEL ON THREATS, CHALLENGES, AND CHANGE (HLP); MONTREAL PROTOCOL ON SUBSTANCES THAT DEPLETE THE OZONE LAYER (1987); PUGWASH CONFERENCES ON SCIENCE AND WORLD AFFAIRS (PUGWASH).

ETHNIC CLEANSING. Term coined to describe the forcible expulsion of Croats and Bosnian Muslims overrun by Serbs during the breakup of Yugoslavia that began in 1991. The term has evolved into a generic/legal notion referring to the elimination of ethnic groups from ethnically mixed regions through killing, rape, and other unlawful and forceful means. Ethnic cleansing has been made an international crime subject to the jurisdiction of the **International Criminal Court (ICC)**. *See also* GENOCIDE; RWANDA.

EUROPEAN UNION (EU). Regional organization formally established in 1993 but originating from the 1951 European Coal and Steel Community and the 1957 European Economic Community. The purpose of the EU is to promote cooperation in economic, social, and trade issues among its 25 members with a view to establishing a single market unifying all their economies through a common commercial policy, the reduction of differences among its richer and poorer members, and the stabilization of their currencies.

While the EU has been relatively successful in forging a unified policy on economic and trade issues, it has not been as effective in producing common political foreign policy positions. EU countries do try to coordinate their positions and often speak with a single voice on most questions in the United Nations. The EU has also become a major actor in and contributor to UN **peacekeeping** and humanitarian activities. However, member countries were divided over the 1991 and 2003 Persian Gulf Wars, future relations with Russia, and the post-1991 crises in the former Yugoslavia. The EU's protectionist policies, especially with respect to agriculture, have led to frictions with the United States and **developing countries**. Many countries in Africa, the Caribbean, and the Pacific (the so-called ACP countries) have entered into special agreements with the EU, granting them free access to the EU for virtually of all of their products. The EU has observer status in the United Nations.

EVANS, GARETH (1944–). Australian politician, member of Parliament for 21 years, and foreign minister from 1988 to 1996. He is best known for his role in helping develop the United Nations peace plan for **Cambodia** and bringing to a successful conclusion the negotiations over the **Chemical Weapons Convention**. In 2000–2001, he cochaired the **International Commission on Intervention and State Sovereignty**.

EVATT, HERBERT VERE (1894–1965). Australian politician and statesman who represented his country at the 1945 **United Nations Conference on International Organization** in San Francisco. During the United Nations **Charter** negotiations, Evatt fought for the rights of smaller powers and succeeded in broadening the role of the United Nations in social and economic affairs and the protection of human rights. Article 55 of the charter, which calls upon member states to work toward "higher standards of living, full employment and conditions of economic and social progress and development" has come to be known as "the Australian pledge." Evatt was elected president of the United Nations **General Assembly** in 1948, thus presiding over the United Nations' adoption of the **Universal Declaration of Human Rights**.

EXPANDED PROGRAMME OF TECHNICAL ASSISTANCE (EPTA). The outgrowth of an American proposal, the establishment of the Expanded Programme of Technical Assistance in 1949 empowered the United Nations to expand its hitherto modest **technical assistance** work. Under EPTA, the United Nations provided expert advice, training, and fellowships through projects designed to improve developing countries' health and educational facilities, land culture methods, communication and transportation facilities, and their financial and administrative procedures. EPTA was subsequently merged with the **Special United Nations Fund for Economic Development** into the **United Nations Development Programme**. *See also* OWEN, SIR DAVID (1904–1970).

EXPULSION FROM THE UNITED NATIONS. Article 6 of the UN **Charter** stipulates that a member of the United Nations that persistently violates principles contained in the charter may be expelled from the organization by the **General Assembly** on recommendation of the **Security Council**. In 1974, the council did receive a proposal for the expulsion of South Africa because of its **apartheid** policies. Three permanent members of the council vetoed the proposal (France, United Kingdom, and United States). In practice, no member of the organization has ever been expelled. Short of exclusion, the General Assembly has had recourse at the beginning of its annual sessions to rejecting the credentials of the representatives of some states (China and South Africa), thus preventing them from participating in its proceedings. *See also* CHINA REPRESENTATION IN THE UNITED NATIONS (1949–1971); CREDENTIALS COMMITTEE OF THE GENERAL ASSEMBLY.

– F –

FACT-FINDING. Common technique used in the **peaceful settlement of disputes** designed to collect accurate information about the allegations made by the parties involved. The deployment of fact-finding missions by the **Security Council**, the **Commission on Human Rights**, and other competent United Nations organs is a common practice, and the **secretary-general** is frequently asked to organize such missions. In

1991, the **General Assembly** adopted a declaration spelling out the common principles for fact-finding by the United Nations, the prerequisites for a decision to send fact-finding missions, and the conduct of fact-finding missions. See *also* CONCILIATION; ENQUIRY; GOOD OFFICES; JUDICAL SETTLEMENT; MEDIATION.

FALKLAND/MALVINAS (2 April–14 June 1982). Sovereignty over these 700-odd islands in the South Atlantic has been a source of tension between Argentina and Britain for over 200 years. The Argentinian long-standing claim to the "Islas Malvinas" and the decision to invade them in 1982 were based on the argument that Argentina was the regional heir to Spanish colonial possession of the islands. Furthermore, Spain had entered into an agreement with Great Britain in 1790 whereby the latter renounced any colonial ambitions in South America and adjacent islands. In contrast, Britain contended that the issue of sovereignty should be determined by the islanders through the exercise of their right to **self-determination** in accordance with the **Declaration on the Granting of Independence to Colonial Countries and Peoples** adopted by the United Nations **General Assembly** in 1960. Britain also invoked its right of individual and collective **self-defense** against **aggression** enshrined in Article 51 of the charter to justify its military operations against Argentina and eventual reoccupation of the islands. The British **veto** of a Security Council resolution calling for a cease-fire effectively prevented UN action and enabled Britain to finish the fighting on its own terms. The role of the General Assembly has been essentially limited to repeated calls to the two governments to settle their dispute by peaceful means.

FAMILY. Universally recognized as the basic unit of national societies, the family structure and functions have considerably changed over time and across nations and cultures. Through studies and advocacy, the United Nations has helped frame these issues in the context of the **development** process, **poverty** alleviation policies, and **human rights** concerns. The United Nations **General Assembly** proclaimed 1994 as the International Year of the Family to highlight the need to pay adequate attention to the family dimensions of development efforts and to recognize that the family is entitled to the widest possible protection and support. 15 May is the International Day of Families.

See also DAYS-YEARS-DECADES (INTERNATIONAL); GENDER; SOCIAL INTEGRATION.

FINANCE FOR DEVELOPMENT. It has always been understood that one of the major problems facing **developing countries** was their lack of capital for development purposes (because of their low savings rates and/or weak taxation capabilities) and that external flows of financial assistance were necessary to supplement their limited internal resources. Developed and developing countries agree on little else beyond those broad and imprecise parameters and development finance has turned into a perennial and intractable issue pitting North against South.

For most industrial countries, the gap in development finance was supposed to be filled primarily through international **trade** liberalization; government policies encouraging **foreign direct investment**; and internal reforms designed to enhance government effectiveness, accountability, and transparency. While agreeable in principle to these policies, developing countries argued in the early 1950s that priority should instead be placed on the creation of a capital development fund placed under the authority of the United Nations. The idea elicited stiff resistance from major potential donor countries and led to little practical result. Developing countries have since maintained that Northern governments should earmark 0.7 percent of their gross national product for **Official Development Assistance (ODA)**, a target enshrined in a 1960 resolution of the **General Assembly**. Very few donor countries have in fact met this target and the United States—the largest donor—does not consider it a legally binding commitment. Levels of ODA have, in any case, never been sufficient for meeting the basic development requirements of developing countries. After years of stagnation or decline throughout the 1990s, levels of ODA now seem to be on the rebound. In 2003, they amounted to some $68 billion. Although historically unprecedented both in nominal and real terms, this level of resources remains unsatisfactory, as several estimates by the **World Bank** and the **United Nations Development Programme** suggest that the resources required for meeting the goals of the **Millennium Assembly** would entail a doubling of current levels of ODA.

The resurgence of market-based solutions to the development challenges of developing countries have rekindled the North-South debate over the modalities of development finance and refocused attention on the role of foreign direct investment and international trade in the mobilization of financial resources for development. These and other related issues were addressed at the 2002 UN-sponsored **International Conference on Financing for Development**. It remains to be seen whether the "Monterrey consensus" that emerged from the conference is a genuine and durable consensus. *See also* GROUP OF TWENTY-FOUR (G-24); HEAVILY INDEBTED POOR COUNTRY INITIATIVE (HIPC).

FINANCIAL CRISES OF THE UNITED NATIONS. Virtually since its inception, the United Nations has been in a continuous state of financial crisis. Several factors account for this situation ranging from late payments by member states of their assessed contributions to a lack of synchronization between national budget cycles and the United Nations own cycle. But the root cause of the problem must be found in deep differences among member states over the programmatic priorities that should be assigned to the organization. For the wealthiest contributing countries, especially the United States, the UN should focus on security, humanitarian, and **human rights** issues. Conversely, developing countries take the view that the UN should focus on issues of economic and social **development**. Similarly, the former wish to strengthen the **Security Council** whereas the latter view the **General Assembly** as the prime policy making organ of the United Nations.

These underlying issues triggered the first major financial crisis of the United Nations in the early 1960s when the USSR, France, and other countries objected to the financing of the **United Nations Emergency Force (UNEF)** and the **United Nations Operation in the Congo (ONUC)** on the grounds that these were illegal **peacekeeping** operations under the terms of Article 43 of the charter, which gives primary responsibility to the Security Council for the maintenance of international peace and security. In response, the General Assembly authorized the United Nations to issue bonds for an amount not exceeding $200 million, to be redeemed in 25 annual installments. The sale of the bonds eased the crisis but did not resolve it. Nor did an **advisory opinion** of the **International Court of Justice (ICJ)** which ruled that the expenditures authorized by the Assembly for both UNEF and ONUC were "expenses of the Organization" that could be subject to compulsory assessment, since the ruling was rejected by the same countries that had objected to the establishment of UNEF and ONUC. The stalemate was resolved in 1964 by an agreement to have recourse to the practice of **consensus** that spared the delinquent contributors from losing their votes in the assembly (at the time no less than 25 states were in arrears in their payments). In 1965, another agreement was reached within the assembly making provision for the payment of voluntary contributions to help alleviate the United Nations' financial problems and, in 1973, the assembly decided that henceforth peacekeeping expenditures would be met through assessed contributions on the basis of a special scale outside of the UN regular **budget**.

For the next 20 years, the situation hardly improved as unpaid contributions for both the regular budget and the peacekeeping budget continued to grow. By 1984, the United Nations was owed close to $200 million. A new factor compounding the financial difficulties of the organization arose from the growing reluctance of the UN's major contributors to allow the steady growth of its budgets because of their increasing focus on activities supported by the developing countries under the **New International Economic Order (NIEO)**, which they objected to. The United States began to withhold its share of regular budget expenses for activities that it disagreed with. The dissolution of the USSR in 1991 and the emergence of a number of new successor states led to another wave of payments arrears; and new peacekeeping operations in **Cambodia, Somalia,** and the former Yugoslavia entailed expenses exceeding the UN regular budget. In early 1992, the UN was owed $1.9 billion. Four years later, the arrears of the United States had reached $1.6 billion.

Under such unrelenting pressure, the United Nations did carry out a major restructuring of its activities that involved large staff reductions and the practice of no-growth budgets.

In the wake of the 11 September terrorist attack, the United States has paid most of its arrears. But it is premature to predict that the United Nations has once and for all resolved its financial problems.

The lack of consensus among member states over the organization's priorities still remains unsolved and the United States Congress has made it clear that the United States' payments of its assessed contributions will remain contingent upon conditions set by itself. *See also* FINANCING OF THE UNITED NATIONS.

FINANCING OF THE UNITED NATIONS. United Nations funding comes from three different sources: assessed contributions to the regular **budget**, assessed contributions for **peacekeeping** operations, and voluntary contributions for **specialized agencies** and subsidiary organizations.

The **Committee on Contributions** determines every three years the scale of assessment for contributions to the regular budget on the basis of the countries' Gross National Product, which ranges from a maximum of 22 percent of the budget (USA) to a minimum of 0.001 percent (developing countries). Member countries also contribute to the peacekeeping operations budget. The level of their contributions is based on their assessed contributions to the regular budget, but account is also taken of the political responsibilities of the permanent members of the Security Council. Finally, member countries contribute on an entirely voluntary basis to the projects and activities of the UN specialized agencies and other subsidiary organizations of the United nations such as the **United Nations Development Programme**, the **United Nations Children's Fund (UNICEF)**, the **United Nations Population Fund (UNFPA)**, and the **World Food Programme (WFP)**. Eight countries contribute two-thirds of the United Nations' regular budget: the United States (22 percent), Japan (19.6 percent), Germany (9.4 percent), France (6.2 percent), the United Kingdom (5.3 percent), Italy (4.9 percent), Canada (2.5 percent), and Spain (2.4 percent). Since the early 1960s, the United Nations has faced repeated **financial crises** caused mainly by the failure of several member states to pay their dues.

FISHING AND FISHERIES. Fish is an important source of food, especially in **developing countries**. Overfishing as a result of technological advances and changes in fishing methods (high sea fishing in particular) and pollution have led to sharp declines in fish stocks. As traditional fishing communities have been increasingly affected, numerous disputes have flared up about fishing rights among states, some of them unilaterally extending the width of their territorial waters to a distance reaching 200 miles beyond their coastlines.

The 1982 **United Nations Convention on the Law of the Sea** has resolved—at least as far as the law goes—jurisdictional disputes over the rights and responsibilities of states in the exploitation of living resources. The sustainability of the exploitation of the oceans' fishing resources was an important subject of discussion at the 1992 **United Nations Conference on Environment and Development**. One of the outcomes of the conference was an agreement to open negotiations on the conservation and management of straddling fish stocks and highly migratory fish stocks. These negotiations were successfully completed in 1995 with the adoption of a **United Nations Conference on Straddling Fish Stocks and Highly Migratory Fish Stocks** supplementing the Convention on the Law of the Sea.

The **Food and Agricultural Organization** has been concerned with various aspects of fishing since the early 1950s. It publishes statistical data on fisheries, has assisted in the establishment of deep sea fishing training centers in developing countries and, in 1984, organized a major conference on fisheries. *See also* ENVIRONMENT; INTERGOVERNMENTAL OCEANOGRAPHIC COMMISSION (IOC).

FOOD AND AGRICULTURE ORGANIZATION (FAO). Founded in 1945, the Food and Agriculture Organization is one of the largest **specialized agencies** of the United Nations system with a budget of some $650 million and a staff of 3,700. Headquartered in Rome, the FAO maintains several regional and subregional offices and has a presence in some 80 countries. Its mission is to promote **agricultural development**, improved nutrition, **food security**, and bettering the conditions of rural population, thus "contributing toward an expanding world economy and ensuring humanity's freedom from **hunger**." *See also* AGRARIAN REFORM; COMMODITIES; FISHING AND FISHERIES; FORESTRY; INTERNATIONAL FUND FOR AGRICULTURAL DEVELOPMENT (IFAD); WORLD FOOD SUMMIT (13–17 November 1996).

FOOD SECURITY. According to the **World Food Summit**, food security is achieved when all people have physical and economic access to sufficient, safe, and nutritious food to meet their dietary needs. Today some 800 million people in developing countries—about 20 percent of the total population—are believed to be chronically undernourished. At the present pace in world **population** growth, this situation is likely to worsen in the years ahead. The problem is caused by low productivity in agriculture, high seasonal and year-to-year variability in food supplies, and lack of off-farm employment opportunities. It is in fact inextricably linked to the prevalence of **poverty** in the developing world.

Food security has been a long-standing priority of several United Nations organizations, notably the **Food and Agricultural Organization (FAO)** and the **International Fund for Agricultural Development (IFAD)**, which have launched programs designed to increase productivity, improve stability of supplies, and generate rural employment. The FAO has set up a Global Information and Early Warning System for Food and Agriculture, which is designed to give advance warning of impending food emergencies. *See also* AGRARIAN REFORM; AGRICULTURAL DEVELOPMENT; EARLY WARNING; GREEN REVOLUTION; HUNGER; UNITED NATIONS CONFERENCE ON THE LEAST DEVELOPED COUNTRIES (PARIS, 1981); WORLD FOOD SUMMIT (13–17 November 1996).

FOREIGN DIRECT INVESTMENT (FDI). Acquisition by the residents of one country of the ownership of the productive assets and tangible goods of another country such as factories and office buildings, extraction of minerals, and fuels and ownership of land. Increasing foreign investment is one measure of economic **globalization**. In 2004, FDI flows amounted to $612 billion globally. The largest flows of foreign investment occur between the industrialized countries (North America, North-West Europe, and Japan). But flows to nonindustrialized countries have been rising, suggesting that the Global South—or at least parts of it—may increasingly be integrated into the world economy. According to **United Nations Conference on Trade and Development (UNCTAD)** estimates, these flows stand currently at $255 billion.

After World War II, when many colonized countries gained independence, officials in the new governments believed that foreign ownership of productive assets was tantamount to a continuation of colonialism in economic form, as it implied external control, the potential export of profits abroad, and a possible erosion of state sovereignty. Many governments of newly independent countries thus sought to nationalize or nationalized foreign-owned industry. In recent years, with the increasing sway of the **Washington Consensus**, many developing countries have relaxed investment restrictions in order to attract foreign investors. The trend toward nationalization has been reversed. and many state enterprises have been privatized. In addition to foreign aid, attracting foreign direct investment through increased export earnings and a larger share of world trade has become an important strategy of developing countries for escaping poverty and stimulating internal growth. These policy changes have accordingly stimulated a surge in the flows of private capital to the Global South which rose sevenfold in the 1990s.

The impact of this infusion of foreign investment, critically important at a time of declining levels of **official development assistance**, remains nevertheless clouded by controversy and the notion that foreign direct investment is desirable for economic growth and poverty reduction is primarily a Northern idea, which many feel has been imposed on a recalcitrant South. Supporters of FDI argue that foreign investment brings capital and technology, skills, and increased employment and incomes. Critics of FDI suggest that it leads to dependent, or restricted, development and disrupts traditional ways of life and culture.

As a source of capital for economic development, FDI has been crucial to the success of China and other developing Asian countries. Yet its volume tends to fluctuate widely over time. In addition, while FDI flows are currently increasing in nonindustrial countries, they bypassed large parts of Africa, Latin America, and Asia from the 1970s down to the early 21st century. The latest available data suggest that FDI to the **Least Developed Countries** of the world increased but remain minuscule compared with the size of global flows or even flows to other developing countries. *See also* DEPENDENCIA; TRANSNATIONAL CORPORATIONS (TNCs).

FORESTRY. The management of forest ecosystems has become a major topical issue as it is increasingly recognized that forests play an essential role in preserving the world's environmental balance.

Forests are also important economically, as they are a significant source of wood products, food, and medicine.

The main UN entity concerned with forests is the **Food and Agriculture Organization**, which, since 1947, carries out periodic inventories providing information about such subjects as fuelwood resources, tropical deforestation, and forest fragmentation and biomass conditions. In the mid-1980s, the FAO, the **World Bank**, the **United Nations Development Program**, and the **World Resources Institute** collaborated in the design of a Tropical Forests Action program, in effect a framework for national policies for the sustainable utilization and exploitation of forests. Forestry-related issues were a major subject of discussion at the 1992 **United Nations Conference on Environment and Development**, which concluded with the adoption of a statement of principles on the management, conservation, and sustainable use of all forests.

The need for intensified international cooperation in the sustainable management and conservation of forests was recognized by the **Economic and Social Council** when, in 2000, it set up the **United Nations Forum on Forests** as one of its subsidiary bodies.

FRECHETTE, LOUISE (1946–). First **deputy secretary-general** of the United Nations who took office in March 1998 and served in that capacity until 2006 when she retired from UN service. A Canadian national and foreign affairs official, she served as permanent representative of Canada to the United Nations from 1995 to 1998. She chairs the Advisory Board of the **United Nations Fund for International Partnership**, has been extensively involved in the United Nations **reform** process and has sought to enhance the image of the United Nations in the economic and social fields.

FUNCTIONALISM. An approach to peace based on the assumption that rather than dealing with intractable security issues, states should instead seek to cooperate in technical areas — especially social and economic — of common concern. The further assumption of the theory is that habits of cooperation in one area will spill over into others, thus creating a cumulative process of mutual gains and confidence building. Much of this thinking provided the rationale for the creation of the **specialized agencies**. As the experience of the **United**

Nations Educational, Scientific, and Cultural Organization (UNESCO) and other specialized agencies shows, the distinction between technical (or functional) undertakings and political affairs proved illusory and prompted damaging charges of politicization that weakened the organizations concerned. *See also* MITRANY, DAVID (1888–1975).

FURTADO, CELSO (1920–2004). Brazilian economist who, with other economists like **Raul Prebisch** and **Victor Urquidi** in the **Economic Commission for Latin America and the Caribbean (ECLAC)**, where he worked from 1949 to 1957, helped develop influential ideas that shaped **development** thinking in the 1950s and 1960s. His studies exposed the various mechanisms of unequal exchange between North and South, argued for a fairer international economic order, and championed the active intervention of the state in developing economies. Furtado also served in the Committee for Development Planning (now the **Committee for Development Policy**) from 1979 to 1982. He was a member of the **South Commission** from 1987 to 1991.

– G –

GARCIA ROBLES, ALFONSO (1911–1991). Mexican diplomat who attended the 1945 **United Nations Conference on International Organization** in San Francisco conference. He became internationally known for his staunch support of nuclear **disarmament**. He played an instrumental role in the **denuclearization** of Latin America and the conclusion of the 1968 **Treaty on the Nonproliferation of Nuclear Weapons (NPT)**. Recipient of the **Nobel Peace Prize** in 1982. *See also* ARMS CONTROL.

GENDER. Conceptual approach that has gained a modicum of acceptance among governments and multilateral institutions and partially replaced traditional equality thinking between men and **women**. The gender perspective stresses the fact that the views, values, and experiences of men and women vary widely and are, by and large, "gender" determined. Both male and female views accordingly need to be equally heard and recognized in social, economic, and political decision making and planning. From this vantage point, the equal particpation of women in society is no longer merely a legitimate right but also a necessity that entails a profound restructuring of socioeconomic institutions—the **family**, the market, governments, and international organizations. This requires empowering women, that is to say, as the 1995 UN sponsored global conference on women in Beijing put it, "removing all the obstacles to women's participation in all spheres of public and private life through a full and equal share in economic, social, cultural, and political decision-making. This means that the principle of shared power and responsibility should be established between women and men at home, in the workplace, and in the wider national and international communities. Equality between women and men is a matter of human rights and a condition for social justice and is also a necessary and fundamental prerequisite for equality, development, and peace."

The UN has developed a gender empowerment measure (GEM), an index based on women's participation in political decision making, their access to professional opportunities, and their earning power. This indicator was launched in the 1995 **Human Development Report** published by the **United Nations Development Programme**. In a 2000 resolution, the **Security Council** called for the integration of women in all conflict resolution and postconflict resettlement, rehabilitation, and reconstruction processes. *See also* CONVENTION ON THE ELIMINATION OF ALL FORMS OF DISCRIMINATION AGAINST WOMEN (1979); INTERNATIONAL CONFERENCE ON POPULATION AND DEVELOPMENT (ICPD, CAIRO, 1994); MILLENNIUM DECLARATION; WORLD CONFERENCE ON WOMEN (BEIJING, 4–15 September 1995).

GENERAL AGREEMENT ON TARIFFS AND TRADE (GATT). Originally, a statement of principles that was part of the charter of the **International Trade Organization (ITO)**. The ITO never came into existence, but as of 1948, the General Agreement on Tariffs and Trade evolved into a mechanism for multilateral trade negotiations rounds to combat and roll back trade barriers. The seven-year-long Uruguay Round—the last in a series of five since GATT's inception—culminated in a final act establishing the **World Trade Organization (WTO)**.

GENERAL ASSEMBLY. One of the five principal organs of the United Nations. The mandate of the General Assembly covers the entire spectrum of the activities of the United Nations (Article 10 of the **charter**), but as a deliberative body, it can only discuss and make recommendations on general questions of a political, social, or economic character. It may not advise, however, on matters under consideration by the **Security Council**, unless the council requests it. Nevertheless, the assembly has broad powers of inquiry, study, and investigation (Articles 10–14), which it has liberally interpreted. The assembly supervises all the activities of the United Nations and reviews annual reports from the other principal organs of the United Nations. The **Economic and Social Council (ECOSOC)** and the **Trusteeship Council** carry out their activities under its authority. The assembly also considers and approves the **budget** of the organization and apportions the expenses among its members. It has the exclusive power to elect the nonpermanent members of the Security Council, all members of ECOSOC and the nonadministering members of the Trusteeship Council that are not permanent members of the Security Council. Acting upon a recommendation of the Security Council, the General Assembly appoints the **secretary-general** and votes the admission of new members. Finally, it has the power to propose **amendments** to the charter and to call for a general conference for charter revisions.

In recognition of the democratic principles of universality and state equality, each member of the assembly has one vote. Routine matters are decided by a simple majority. Matters of substance (the **budget**, the **scale of assessment**, the revision of the charter, trusteeship questions, the election of the nonpermanent members of the Security Council, and the admission of new members, for instance) require a two-thirds majority. Most of the time, the assembly has recourse to a **consensus** system that involves no formal voting. Other voting arrangements are in place in some of the **specialized agencies**, notably the **World Bank** and the **International Monetary Fund (IMF)**.

The General Assembly meets in regular annual sessions beginning the third Tuesday of September; **special and emergency sessions** are sometimes held on topics of international importance. These special meetings are frequently follow-up meetings to previous UN-sponsored **global conferences**. The assembly organizes its work in seven main committees dealing respectively with political, security, economic and financial, social and humanitarian, decolonization, administrative, and legal issues. It also has procedural, standing, and numerous ad hoc committees. In addition, the assembly together with ECOSOC is responsible for a number of UN programs and subsidiaries including the **United Nations Conference on Trade and Development (UNCTAD)**, the **United Nations Development Programme (UNDP)**, the **United Nations Children's Fund (UNICEF)**, the **United Nations Population Fund (UNFPA)**, and the **United Nations High Commissioner for Human Rights (UNHCHR)**, among others.

The large **membership** of the assembly and its intricate maze of subsidiary bodies have made it a rather unwieldy organ and prompted repeated calls for change and **reform** of its procedures and work methods. *See also* COMMITTEE ON CONFERENCES; COMMITTEE ON CONTRIBUTIONS; CREDENTIALS COMMITTEE ON THE GENERAL ASSEMBLY; GENERAL COMMITTEE.

GENERAL COMMITTEE. Committee of the **General Assembly** that includes the president and vice presidents of the assembly and the chairs of its committees. The business of the committee is purely procedural, as it focuses on reviewing the agenda, allocating individual items to the main committees, and advising the president of the assembly in the determination of the evolving priority of agenda items.

GENERAL SYSTEM OF PREFERENCES (GSP). Negotiated under the auspices of the **United Nations Conference on Trade and Development (UNCTAD)** and introduced in 1971, the General System of Preferences was designed to allow industrialized countries to grant nonreciprocal tariff reductions to developing countries as exceptions to the principle of most-favored-nation treatment provided for in the **General Agreement on Tariffs and Trade (GATT)**. The underlying idea is to help developing countries industrialize. *See also* WORLD TRADE ORGANIZATION (WTO).

GENEVA CONVENTIONS (1949) AND ADDITIONAL PROTOCOLS (1977). The core of international **humanitarian law**. The four Geneva Conventions and the protocols that strengthen their provisions not only codify state practice and earlier treaties on the methods of international warfare, they also establish a right of relief for combatants and civilian populations. The conventions specify the rules applicable for the treatment of the wounded, shipwrecked, prisoners, and civilians in international armed conflicts.

GENEVA PROTOCOL (1925). International agreement banning the use of chemical, biological, or bacteriological weapons. The protocol was an effort to prevent the utilization of such weapons, as had been the case in World War I, but it did not address the issues of their production and stockpiling. United Nations efforts beginning in 1969 led to the adoption of two separate conventions prohibiting the development, production, and stockpiling of biological and chemical weapons, the **Convention on the Prohibition of the Development, Production, and Stockpiling of Bacteriological (Biological) and Toxin Weapons and on Their Destruction** and the **Convention on the Prohibition of the Development, Production, Stockpiling, and Use of Chemical Weapons and on Their Destruction**, which entered into force in 1975 and 1997. *See also* ARMS CONTROL; WEAPONS OF MASS DESTRUCTION (WMDs).

GENOCIDE. The **Convention on the Prevention and Punishment of the Crime of Genocide** defines genocide as "any of the following acts committed with intent to destroy, in whole or in part, a national, ethnic, racial, or religious group, as such: . . . killing members of the group; . . . causing serious bodily or mental harm to members of the group; . . . deliberately inflicting on the group conditions of life calculated to bring about its physical destruction, in whole or in part; . . . imposing measures intended to prevent births within the group; . . . forcibly transferring children of the group to another group." This definition has been incorporated in the statutes of the ad hoc **International Criminal Tribunal for the Former Yugoslavia (ICTY)** and the **International Criminal Tribunal for Rwanda (ICTR)** set up to deal with atrocities committed in the former Yugoslavia and **Rwanda** and the permanent **International Criminal Court (ICC)**.

GEORGIA CONFLICT. Absorbed into the Russian empire in the 19th century and independent for three years (1918–1921), following the Russian revolution, Georgia was forcibly incorporated into the Soviet

Union until its dissolution in 1991. In April of that year, Georgia declared its independence. Several areas, including Abkhazia and South Ossetia, have since become embroiled in disputes with Russian-supported separatists that have led to armed conflict and interethnic violence. Ethnic Armenian groups also seek greater autonomy and closer ties with Armenia.

In 1993, the Security Council established the **United Nations Observer Mission in Georgia (UNOMIG)** to verify compliance with a cease-fire agreement concluded by the government of Georgia and Abkhaz insurgents. UNOMIG's mandate was almost immediately invalidated as hostilities resumed accompanied by large displacements of civilian populations and widespread violations of **human rights**. After several rounds of difficult negotiations chaired by a special envoy of the **secretary-general**, the Georgian and Abkhaz sides reached a new cease-fire agreement in mid-1994 providing for the deployment of a peacekeeping force of the **Commonwealth of Independent States (CIS)** to monitor compliance with the agreement. Under the terms of the new agreement, UNOMIG monitors its implementation and observes the operation of the CIS force. Since then, the peace process has by and large remained stalled.

GLOBAL COMMISSION ON INTERNATIONAL MIGRATION (GCIM). In his 2002 report on United Nations **reform**, the **secretary-general** identified **migration** as a priority issue for the international community. Subsequent internal work within the **secretariat** pointed to the need to further explore various aspects of international migration, notably the **human security** of migrants, the socioeconomic consequences of labor migration, the impact of migration on development, asylum and migrant integration issues, and the state of international cooperation. The idea of an independent global commission looking into gaps in current policy approaches to migration and examining interlinkages with other issues also arose from this work. Sweden and Switzerland have taken the lead in the establishment of such a commission, which began operation in early 2004. Comprised of 18 internationally recognized members drawn from all regions and bringing a wide range of migration perspectives and expertise, the commission organized broad-based regional consultations with governments, **nongovernmental organizations (NGOs)**, regional organizations, media, the corporate sector, migrant associations, and trade unions. Its final report was issued in late 2005 and made recommendations designed to strengthen the international governance of international migration. *See also* INDEPENDENT COMMISSIONS; INTERNATIONAL LABOUR ORGANIZATION (ILO); INTERNATIONAL ORGANIZATION FOR MIGRATION (IOM).

GLOBAL COMPACT. First aired by the **secretary general** in 1999, the compact was formally launched at United Nations headquarters on 26 July 2002. The project invites world business leaders to respect **human rights** standards and international labor norms and principles and to protect the **environment** in their corporate practices and policies. In contrast to the regulatory **"codes of conduct"** bitterly debated in UN forums in the 1970s, the scheme is entirely voluntary and relies on public accountability and self-interest as catalysts toward responsible global corporate responsibility. The operation of the Global Compact includes the convening of "policy dialogues" with the participation of labor, business, **nongovernmental organizations (NGOs)**, the UN, and governments on current problems. Topics discussed hitherto have included the role of the private sector in zones of conflict and business and sustainable development. Private corporations are also invited to share instances of their practices on the Global Compact web portal. Local networks for information exchange are being established. The expectation is that these activities will be translated into field projects. *See also* INTERNATIONAL LABOUR ORGANIZATION (ILO); TRANSNATIONAL CORPORATIONS (TNCs); UNITED NATIONS ENVIRONMENT PROGRAMME (UNEP); UNITED NATIONS HIGH COMMISSIONER FOR HUMAN RIGHTS (UNHCHR).

GLOBAL CONFERENCES (UNITED NATIONS). Special meetings convened by the **General Assembly** to direct attention to emerging or current issues of concern to the international community. Their focus has been primarily on a wide range of developmental topics including **transnational organized crime**, **trade**, **employment**, **water**, **population**, **urbanization**, **women**, **human rights**, **sustainable development**, **information technology**, **science and technology**, **education**, and **natural disaster** prevention. A smaller number of them have dealt with peace and security issues such as **disarmament**, **antipersonnel landmines**, and **small arms**. UN global conferences have been criticized for being expensive and ineffectual policy making instruments and "conference fatigue" has led in recent years to the practice of convening special sessions of the General Assembly to review and assess their outcomes. UN global conferences have nevertheless played useful norm-setting functions. They have served as **early warning** mechanisms, provided new space for the participation of **civil society** in UN state-dominated multilateral policy deliberations, and contributed to better prioritizing in the work of the organization.

GLOBAL ENVIRONMENTAL FACILITY (GEF). The only new funding source to emerge from the 1992 **Earth Summit**, the Global Environmental Facility, after a three-year pilot phase, was formally launched in 1994. GEF funds projects falling under the 1992 **Convention on Biological Diversity**, the 1994 **United Nations Framework Convention on Climate Change**, and the 1996 **United Nations Convention to Combat Desertification**. During its first decade of operation, GEF allocated over $4 billion supplemented by $11 billion in cofinancing for more than 1,000 projects in 171 developing and transition countries. It is governed by a 32-member board representing 16 developing countries, 14 developed countries, and 2 countries with transitional economies.

GLOBAL ENVIRONMENTAL MONITORING SYSTEM (GEMS). Established in 1975 as part of the **United Nations Environment Programme**'s **Earthwatch** as a collaborative effort of the United Nations system to assess and monitor **environmental** pollution and to serve as an **early warning** instrument on emerging issues of potential international importance.

GLOBAL GOVERNANCE. Imprecise but nowadays widely used term referring to rules, norms, structures, and institutions designed to address problems and issues transcending national boundaries such as international crime, environmental degradation, and **human rights** violations. The term does not imply the existence of centralized command structures, which is central to the concept of **world government**. Nor does it refer solely to formal institutions and organizations through which international affairs are managed. The United Nations and national governments are essential actors in the conduct of global governance but other **nonstate actors** are involved. The increasing **interdependence** of the world economy, **globalization**, and the proliferation of internal conflicts in the post–**Cold War** period have heightened demands for global governance arrangements and severely tested the functioning capacity of the United Nations. *See also* COMMISSION ON GLOBAL GOVERNANCE; GLOBAL PUBLIC GOODS.

GLOBAL POLICY FORUM (GPF). New York–based **nongovernmental organization (NGO)** with consultative status in the **Economic and Social Council (ECOSOC)** created in 1993. GPF's mission is to promote accountability of global decisions, educate and mobilize for global citizen participation, and advocate on international peace and justice issues. GPF monitors United Nations **Security Council** activities and has been especially active on **Iraq**-related issues. GPF also organizes international conferences on social and economic policy with particular attention to corporate accountability, the UN **Global Compact, finance for development**, and the reform of the **International Monetary Fund (IMF)**.

GLOBAL PUBLIC GOODS. International public goods are benefits that provide utility or satisfy needs and wants that reach across countries, population groups, and generations. Peace, good **governance**, a safe and clean **environment**, and **health** quality are instances of public goods. Activities that contribute to the production of public goods, such as **conflict prevention, peacekeeping**, crime reduction, and the eradication or control of disease, are likewise public goods. The concept has been used as a rationale for international cooperation through international organizations, the argument being that since all countries benefit from public goods, they should contribute to their cost and production. *See also* DEVELOPMENT; GLOBAL GOVERNANCE.

GLOBAL WARMING. There is increasing evidence that Earth's climate has changed over the last century. Since the beginning of the 20th century, Earth's mean surface temperature increased by about

1.1°F, the greatest warming trend observed in the past 400 to 600 years. Over the last 40 years, for which there are reliable data, the temperature increased by about 0.5°F. Mountain glaciers are receding, and the Arctic ice pack has lost about 40 percent of its thickness. Global sea levels have been rising about three times faster over the past 100 years compared with the previous 3,000 years.

If these climatic trends continue unchecked, global warming may result in major disruptive changes in the human and natural habitats. The most severe consequences of global warming include a faster rise in sea level, threatening low-lying coastal areas and small island developing countries; more heat waves and droughts, which may result in conflicts over water resources; more extreme weather events, producing floods and property destruction; and a wider spread of infectious diseases.

Global warming results primarily from human activities—deforestation and the burning of fossil fuels (coal, oil, and gas)—which release carbon dioxide (CO_2) and other heat-trapping gases and particles (methane and nitrous oxides) into the air. As such, the problem of global warming is a transboundary issue, affecting all nations and the whole environment. Reducing these emissions through the use of renewable energy resources and energy-efficient technologies and curbing the consumption of fossil fuels is an internationally accepted first step in stopping global warming. The policy modalities to reach this objective have however raised contentious and by and large unresolved North-South disputes as well as confrontations between the United States and both the **European Union** and **developing countries**. *See also* ACID RAIN; CLIMATE CHANGE; COMMISSION ON SUSTAINABLE DEVELOPMENT (UNITED NATIONS) (CSD); ENERGY; ENVIRONMENT; HEALTH; KYOTO PROTOCOL; WATER.

GLOBALIZATION. Multidimensional and ongoing process driven by trade liberalization, increased capital flows across borders, and the spread of information and communication technology leading to greater worldwide cultural, political, technological, and economic integration across traditional territorial state boundaries.

Globalization has its roots in the intercontinental spread of Buddhism, Christianity, and Islam; the rise of ancient empires and trade routes; the mercantile age of colonization; and the industrial and transportation revolutions of the 18th and 19th centuries. Contemporary globalization, however, is different from earlier phases in its scope, pace, and magnitude. To the extent that it has brought about rapidly expanding worldwide flows of goods, services, capital, information, and people and contributed either to the strengthening or emergence of **nonstate actors** such as **transnational corporations** and global social movements, globalization poses fundamental challenges to the present world order, which remains grounded on territorially based sovereign states. The widely different capacities of **developing countries** to participate in the process of globalization, share in its economic benefits, and respond to its disruptive impact has become a major source of North-South controversy. As documented in numerous United Nations reports and studies such as the **Human Development Report**, globalization appears to have aggravated social and economic inequalities both within and among nations. *See also* INFORMATION TECHNOLOGY (IT); MILLENNIUM DECLARATION; SOVEREIGNTY; TELECOMMUNICATIONS; TRANSNATIONAL CORPORATIONS (TNCs); WORLD SUMMIT ON THE INFORMATION SOCIETY (WSIS) (GENEVA, 10–12 December 2003/TUNIS, TUNISIA, 16–18 November 2005).

GOA, DAMAN, AND DIU DISPUTE (1961). "Overseas province" of Portugal until 1961 when it was forcibly seized by India. The Indian military action posed an interesting problem in regard to the United Nations **Charter** provisions prohibiting the **use of force**. Was it an act of aggression as suggested by a **Security Council** resolution calling for a cease-fire and the withdrawal of Indian forces, which was vetoed by the Soviet Union? Or did Portugal's centuries-old occupation constitute an act of "permanent **aggression**" as India argued, thus justifying a military action intended to remove one of the last vestiges of colonialism? The issue was less legal than moral and political, as its disposition showed the increasing anticolonial mood of the majority of **developing countries** entering the United Nations at the time. *See also* DECLARATION ON THE GRANTING OF INDEPENDENCE TO COLONIAL COUNTRIES AND PEOPLES (1960); DECOLONIZATION; SELF-DETERMINATION.

GOLAN HEIGHTS ISSUE. The Golan Heights, previously known as the Syrian Heights, are a plateau on the border of Israel, Lebanon,

Jordan, and Syria. During the 1973 Yom Kippur War, the Israeli army captured the heights and placed it under military administration. The Israeli Parliament annexed the land in 1981. Neither the UN nor any other country has recognized this annexation, and the Golan Heights are considered to be Syrian territory under Israeli military occupation.

Israel and Syria signed a cease-fire agreement in 1974 that left the heights in Israeli hands with a demilitarized zone separating the two sides. Syria has always demanded a full Israeli withdrawal from all of the Golan Heights. Successive Israeli governments have expressed support for some Israeli withdrawal from the Golan without specifying the extent of this withdrawal. Israel insists that any agreement with Syria must include fully normalized diplomatic and economic relations. The **United Nations Disengagement Observer Force (UNDOF)** was established in 1974 to supervise the implementation of the 1974 Israeli-Syrian agreement. Syria and Israel still contest the ownership of the heights but have not used overt military force since 1974. The great strategic value of the heights both militarily and as a source of **water** means that a deal is uncertain. *See also* ARAB-ISRAELI CONFLICT; ENVIRONMENTAL SECURITY.

GOOD OFFICES. Mediation and good offices are virtually interchangeable notions, both in effect referring to the methods of peaceful settlement of disputes spelled out in Chapter VI of the charter. Good offices is not specifically mentioned in the charter but has become a widely used practice (with varying degrees of success) of the **secretary-general** in **early warning** and **conflict prevention**, management, and resolution. Numerous United Nations **peacekeeping** operations have included a good office component. *See also* ARBITRATION; CONCILIATION; ENQUIRY; JUDICIAL SETTLEMENT; PEACEMAKING; POSTCONFLICT PEACE BUILDING; UNITED NATIONS GOOD OFFICES MISSION IN AFGHANISTAN AND PAKISTAN (UNGOMAP, October 1988–March 1990).

GORBACHEV, MIKHAIL (1931–). General Secretary of the Communist Party from 1985 to 1991. He served as president of the USSR in 1990–1991. His policies of "glasnost" (openness) and "perestroika" (reform) at home and his allowing the peaceful breakaway of the countries of Eastern Europe are credited with helping end the

Cold War. A 1991 coup by party hardliners failed, but Gorbachev lost much of his political clout and he was forced to resign. He was awarded the **Nobel Peace Prize** in 1990.

GRANT, JAMES P. (1922–1995). Energetic head of the **United Nations Children's Fund (UNICEF)** from 1980 to 1995. He helped mobilize international, national, and local initiatives in support of a worldwide campaign to save children's lives through immunization, oral rehydration therapy, and breastfeeding. By the end of the 1980s, these simple life-saving techniques were estimated to have saved 12 million lives. They are still in use. Grant also played a determinant role in securing the adoption by the **General Assembly** in 1989 of the **Convention on the Rights of the Child**.

GREEK QUESTION (1946–1951). At the end of World War II, civil war broke out between the central government of Greece against communist insurgents, the former supported by the West, the latter by the Soviet bloc. The **Security Council** set up a commission to investigate charges and countercharges regarding border violations and assistance to the guerrillas. The findings of the commission's report were vetoed by the Soviet Union and the question removed from the council's agenda. The **General Assembly** thereupon set up a small observer group, the United Nations Special Committee on the Balkans (UNSCOB) to monitor on the scene border violations by Soviet bloc countries in support of leftist Greek guerrillas along the northern frontiers of Greece. Together with the **United Nations Truce Supervision Organization (UNTSO)** and the **United Nations Military Observer Group in India and Pakistan (UNMOGIP)**, the functions of UNSCOB foreshadow those assigned later to many **peacekeeping** operations. The process through which it was established also prefigures the use of the **Uniting for Peace Resolution**.

GREEN REVOLUTION. Term referring to a major increase in crop yields resulting from the use of genetically created, high-yield varieties of wheat, rice, and corn and reliance on extensive irrigation and the use of pesticides. After stunning production improvements in such countries as the Philippines, India, Pakistan, and Sri Lanka, production peaked in the early 1980s and declined subsequently, while at the same time some of the negative consequences of the Green

Revolution came to the fore, such as long-term soil degradation, distribution problems, and widening social disparities among grain producers, grain brokers, and consumers. These issues have spurred interest in the applications of biotechnology to **food security**.

GREENPEACE INTERNATIONAL. Influential, independent **nongovernmental organization (NGO)** set up in 1971 to campaign against environmental degradation. Now active throughout the world in some 40 countries, Greenpeace seeks to achieve its objectives through a variety of means ranging from research, public debate, lobbying, and quiet diplomacy to higher profile nonviolent methods targeted at governments and corporations. Focusing on threats to the planet's biodiversity and the **environment**, Greenpeace is active in the fields of **climate change**, forest conservation, the preservation of the **oceans'** living resources, genetic engineering, and sustainable trade.

GROUP OF EIGHT (G-8). A group of Northern industrial rich countries that meets annually to coordinate their economic, monetary, and **trade** policies and relations. Originally composed of the United States, Great Britain, France, Japan, and West Germany in 1985, the group was formalized when Canada and Italy joined shortly after and renamed G-8 in 1997 when Russia was invited to participate in its discussions. Over the years, its agenda has broadened considerably to encompass security and **development** issues. The group operates independently from the United Nations.

GROUP OF SEVENTY-SEVEN (G-77). Loose coalition of now over 120 countries, predominantly developing ones, that articulates and presses for their collective economic interests within the **United Nations**. Created in 1964, the G-77 used its voting power to convene a **United Nations Conference on Trade and Development (UNCTAD)**, which subsequently became a permanent UN organization. Ten years later, the group used its numerical majority in the **General Assembly**, leading it to proclaim a **Declaration on the Establishment of a New International Economic Order (NIEO)**. The **debt crisis** of the 1980s, the growing sway of neoliberal views of development in the 1990s, and sheer internal divisions have weakened the capacity of the group to shape UN development activities.

GROUP OF TWENTY-FOUR (G-24). Formally known as the Inter-governmental Group of Twenty-Four on International Monetary Affairs, this group of 24 African, Latin American, and Asian countries was established in 1971 to coordinate and define the position of **developing countries** on monetary and development finance issues. The G-24 meets twice a year in conjunction with meetings of the **International Monetary Fund (IMF)** and the **World Bank**.

GROUPS AND GROUPINGS. The day to day business and proceedings of a multilateral organization like the United Nations involving the participation of 191 theoretically sovereign and equal member states is very much influenced by groups of states brought together because they share similar or converging interests and/or seek allies and supporters to influence the decision-making process. An early and still relevant practical incentive to the emergence of groups is the institutionalized system of rotating elective chairmanships and offices within each organ of the United Nations. The purpose of the regional groups—for Africa, Asia, Latin America and the Caribbean, Eastern Europe, and Western Europe—which sprang up almost immediately after the creation of the organization, was and continues to be to serve as consultative mechanisms for the selection and nomination of candidates for elective office (i.e., the nonpermanent seats of the **Security Council** and the presidency of the **General Assembly** and its various committees).

The **Cold War** subsequently fueled the creation of new groups such as the Eastern and Western blocs. These are playing a decreasing role in the post–Cold War era. But other groups like the **Nonaligned Movement (NAM)** and the **Group of Seventy-Seven (G-77)** or more recently, the **Alliance of Small Island States (AOSIS)**, which all emerged in the context of the **North-South dialogue**, still influence the proceedings of UN intergovernmental bodies.

These groups should not be confused with political organizations like the **Organization of the Islamic Conference (OIC)**, the **Arab League**, and the **European Union**, which also seek to present joint collective positions. Nor should they be confused with "informal" or temporary groups—"working groups," "editorial committees," and "Friends of the President," that come into existence in the course of major multilateral conferences like the **United Nations Conference on the Law of the Sea (UNCLOS)**.

The existence of group structures within the United Nations has been a long-standing subject of controversy, some arguing that it facilitates the negotiating process among groups, others that it hinders it by encouraging **consensus** on minimal common grounds. Blessing or curse, the proliferation of groups and groupings within the United Nations is a fixed characteristic of multilateral diplomacy. It is likely to remain a key fixture of the organization as it enables small and weaker states to articulate and press for their demands. *See also* GROUP OF EIGHT (G-8); GROUP OF TWENTY-FOUR (G-24).

GUATEMALA CONFLICT (1960–1995). Longest running conflict in the American hemisphere, which caused the displacement of more than a million persons and cost an estimated 200,000 lives. After more than three decades of violence, the civil war was brought to an end by an agreement mediated by the United Nations between the government and leftist rebels. The implementation of the accords was overseen by the **United Nations Verification Mission in Guatemala (MINUGUA)**. While open armed conflict has ended, the root causes of the conflict—social inequality, widespread poverty, ethnic exclusion of indigenous peoples, the prevalence of corruption and lack of accountability in state institutions—remain by and large unaddressed. Serious **human rights** abuses are still a concern. The advocacy work of numerous **nongovernmental organizations (NGOs)**, special rapporteurs of the **Commission for Human Rights**, and **special representatives** of the **secretary-general** have helped focus official attention on the issue. *See also* ARIAS, OSCAR (1941–); CENTRAL AMERICA CONFLICTS.

– H –

HABITAT. *See* COMMISSION ON HUMAN SETTLEMENTS (UNITED NATIONS); UNITED NATIONS CENTRE ON HUMAN SETTLEMENTS (UNCHS or HABITAT); UNITED NATIONS CONFERENCE ON HUMAN SETTLEMENTS (HABITAT I, VANCOUVER, 1976); UNITED NATIONS CONFERENCE ON HUMAN SETTLEMENTS (HABITAT II, ISTANBUL, 1996).

HAGUE CONVENTION FOR THE PROTECTION OF CULTURAL PROPERTY IN THE EVENT OF ARMED CONFLICT.

First international treaty adopted in 1954 calling for measures designed to lessen the consequences of armed conflict for cultural heritage. The convention is complemented by two protocols. One prohibits the export of cultural property from an occupied territory and requires its return to the territory of the state from which it was removed. The other reaffirms the "immunity" of cultural property in times of war or occupation and establishes the "individual criminal responsibility" of perpetrators of crimes against culture. The **United Nations Educational, Scientific, and Cultural Organization (UNESCO)** is the depository of the convention and supervises its implementation. *See also* CONVENTION CONCERNING THE PROTECTION OF THE WORLD CULTURAL AND NATURAL HERITAGE; CONVENTION ON INDIGENOUS AND TRIBAL PEOPLES (1989); CULTURAL HERITAGE.

HAITI. In 1990, the Haitian government requested the United Nations to supervise the first free elections being planned after the fall of the Duvalier dictatorship. With the approval of the **General Assembly**, a **United Nations Observer Group for the Verification of the Elections in Haiti (ONUVEH)** duly certified that the election of President Jean-Bertrand Aristide in January 1991 had taken place under free and democratic conditions. In September 1991, however, Aristide was overthrown in a military coup and went into exile. At the prompting of the **Organization of American States (OAS)**, which had imposed a trade embargo on Haiti, the General Assembly demanded the immediate restoration of the Aristide government and the full observance of human rights in Haiti. In April 1993, acting upon a suggestion of the **secretary-general**, the Assembly authorized the deployment of an **International Civilian Mission in Haiti (MICIVIH)** to verify respect for **human rights**. Two months later, the **Security Council** imposed a worldwide fuel and arms embargo on Haiti. When MICIVIH was expelled in July 1994, the council authorized military intervention, and in September 1994, a U.S.-led multinational force entered Haiti, removing the de facto military government and restoring elected officials.

From 1994 to 2003, the UN and the OAS have thus undertaken no less than 10 separate and joint missions in Haiti. These operations have been primarily concerned with the professionalization of the police, the strengthening of the judiciary, and the promotion of human rights. At the same time, the United Nations initiated humanitarian and reconstruction activities under the guidance of a **United Nations Development Programme (UNDP) resident coordinator** who also acted as deputy to the special representative of the secretary-general.

None of these interventions, however, succeeded in resolving the political and socioeconomic problems that have plagued the country for decades. In February 2004, the situation deteriorated dramatically. Armed rebels and criminal gangs took over several towns in the northern part of the country. In spite of the resignation and departure of President Aristide, violence continued unabated, leading the Security Council to authorize the deployment of a multinational force to restore law and order in the capital. On 30 April 2004, the council set up under Chapter VII the **United Nations Stabilization Mission in Haiti (MINUSTAH)**. The new mission took over from the multinational force. Its aims are to secure a stable environment within which the constitutional and political process in Haiti could take place and to assist a transitional government in the reform of the Haitian national police and the implementation of comprehensive and sustainable disarmament, demobilization, and reintegration programs.

The prompt intervention of the United Nations may have avoided a humanitarian catastrophe. But the country has neither the necessary resources nor the infrastructure to cope with its recovery needs, meet its formidable developmental challenges (Haiti is the poorest nation in the Western hemisphere), and resolve political issues arising from the long-standing practices of successive predatory regimes. These long-term issues have prompted the secretary-general to call for an international presence of some 20 years. *See also* INTERNATIONAL CIVILIAN MISSION SUPPORT IN HAITI (MICAH, 1999–2001); UNITED NATIONS CIVILIAN POLICE MISSION IN HAITI (MIPONUH, December 1997–March 2000); UNITED NATIONS MISSION IN HAITI (UNMIH, September 1993–June 1996); UNITED NATIONS SUPPORT MISSION IN HAITI (UNSMIH, 1996–1997); UNITED NATIONS TRANSITION MISSION IN HAITI (UNTMIH, August–November 1997).

HAMMARSKJÖLD, DAG HJALMAR (1905–1961). Second **secretary-general** of the United Nations from April 1953 until his accidental death in a plane crash while on a mission in the Congo on

18 September 1961. His reputation for intellectual integrity, diplomatic skills, and political independence gave him the authority not only to broaden significantly the functions of the office but also to initiate new practices, which have durably shaped the work of the organization. In this process, he was assisted by a few chosen men, such as **Ralph Bunche**, **Brian Urquhart**, **Andrew Cordier**, **Philippe de Seynes**, and **C. V. Narashiman**, who shared his exacting standards for duty and service to the organization.

In his view, the United Nations was not merely a "static conference machinery" but a "dynamic instrument of international cooperation." The philosophy and rationale of **peacekeeping** (he was responsible with Canadian prime minister **Lester Pearson** for the mounting of the **United Nations Emergency Force [UNEF]**, the first UN peacekeeping operation, and he organized the **United Nations Observer Group in Lebanon [UNOGIL]**), the conduct of what he termed **quiet diplomacy** or **preventive diplomacy** (he obtained the release of 15 American flyers detained by the People's Republic of China) and his extensive use of personal representatives and envoys in the settling of political disputes are some of the major aspects of his legacy.

In 1960, invoking Article 99 of the UN Charter, he placed the question of the **Congo** on the agenda of the Security Council and urged it to act "with utmost speed," a request that eventually led to the launching of the controversial **United Nations Operation in the Congo (ONUC)**.

HAQ, MAHBUL UL (1934–1999). Pakistani development economist and statesman who was Pakistan's minister of Finance, Planning and Commerce from 1982 to 1988. Prior to that, Haq had worked at the **World Bank** from 1970 to 1982, where he endeavored to steer the institution's lending policies toward **poverty** alleviation programs and increased allocations for small farm production, nutrition, **education**, **water** supply, and other social sectors. In 1989, he joined the **United Nations Development Programme (UNDP)** as special adviser to the UNDP Administrator. There, until 1995, with other development economists such as **Richard Jolly** and **Amartya Sen**, he played a critical intellectual and organizational leadership role in the creation and launching of UNDP's influential **Human Development Report**

(HDR). His 1976 book *The Poverty Curtain* foreshadowed the basic needs and human security approaches that shape the **development** thinking underpinning the HDR.

HAZARDOUS WASTES. *See* BASEL CONVENTION ON THE CONTROL OF TRANSBOUNDARY MOVEMENT OF HAZARDOUS WASTES AND THEIR DISPOSAL (1989).

HEADQUARTERS, UNITED NATIONS. New York was chosen by the **General Assembly** as the location of the permanent headquarters of the United Nations in 1946. The original plan was to use the grounds of the 1939 World's Fair but the project failed to materialize. American industrialist and philanthropist **John D. Rockefeller Jr.** offered the United Nations a donation of over $8.5 million to purchase a property for the organization headquarters in Manhattan. An 18-acre plot where there were only decaying buildings and old slaughterhouses was used to build the UN's headquarters.

The design of the United Nations complex was drawn by a team of international architects. Construction began in 1949 and was completed four years later. The present structure consists of a complex with four buildings: the 39-story **secretariat** building, home of the UN's administration, the **General Assembly** building, the conference building, and the **Dag Hammarskjöld** Library. Adjacent to the United Nations complex is a small public park bordering the East River featuring artworks donated by many countries.

The expansion of the administrative machinery of the United Nations until the 1990s forced the organization to rent additional premises in other buildings located in its vicinity. More recently, however, the aging of the 1950s structures has prompted calls for their renovation. Various plans are now being considered including the construction of a new 35-story building on a site adjacent to the present location of the United Nations.

Along with New York, the United Nations has three additional "headquarters" in Geneva, Nairobi, and Vienna. The UN presence in these three countries is the result of historical antecedents (Geneva used to be the seat of the **League of Nations**) and/or of demands by host governments keen on enhancing their international credentials.

The United Nations in Geneva is one of the busiest intergovernmental conference centers in the world. Over 10,000 UN staff work there—the largest concentration of United Nations personnel in the world, higher than New York—either with the United Nations Office in Geneva (which is technically part of the UN Secretariat) or the numerous **specialized agencies** and programs located in and around Geneva. The following units of the secretariat are located in Geneva: the **Economic Commission for Europe (ECE)**, the **Joint Inspection Unit (JIU)**, the **United Nations High Commissioner for Human Rights (UNHCHR)**, the **United Nations High Commission for Refugees (UNHCR)**, the **United Nations Institute for Disarmament Research (UNIDIR)**, the **United Nations Institute for Training and Research (UNITAR)**, the **United Nations Research Institute for Social Development (UNRISD)**, and the **United Nations Conference on Trade and Development (UNCTAD)**. The specialized agencies headquartered in Geneva include the **International Labour Organization (ILO)**, the **International Telecommunications Union (ITU)**, the **World Health Organization (WHO)**, and the **World Intellectual Property Organization (WIPO)**.

The Vienna International Center (VIC), known as UNO City, opened on 23 August 1979 and is rented to the United Nations for 99 years at a symbolic rate of one Austrian schilling annually. The operational costs of the buildings are borne by the UN. With more than 4,000 employees, the VIC is an important international diplomatic meeting center. The following organizations are based at the VIC: the United Nations Office at Vienna, which provides administrative support to the different bodies and institutions housed in the VIC and represents the **secretary-general** in the host country, the Office for Outer Space Affairs, the United Nations **Office for Drug Control and Crime Prevention (UNODC)**, the secretariat for the **United Nations Commission on International Trade Law (UNCITRAL)**, the **United Nations Industrial Development Organization (UNIDO)**, and the **International Atomic Energy Agency (IAEA)**.

There are currently over 20 organizations of the United Nations system maintaining offices located in Nairobi, the most important ones being the **United Nations Environment Programme (UNEP)** and **Habitat**. All in all, the United Nations organizations in Kenya employ over 2,500 staff members.

Other capitals of the world host United Nations agencies. The **World Maritime Organization (WMO)** is located in London, the **United Nations Educational, Scientific, and Cultural Organization (UNESCO)** in Paris, the **United Nations World Tourism Organization (UNWTO)** in Madrid, the **International Civil Aviation Organization (ICAO)** in Montreal, the **Food and Agriculture Organization (FAO)** and the **World Food Programme (WFP)** in Rome, and the **United Nations University (UNU)** in Tokyo.

The sites that make up the United Nations headquarters are considered international territory, which means that diplomats (and the international staff depending on the agreements entered into by the United Nations with the host country) working there are immune from prosecution by local courts. The New York, Geneva, and Vienna premises of the United Nations can be visited through guided tours. Since their inception in 1952, 38 million visitors have taken a guided tour of the United Nations New York headquarters. Children and students constitute over 40 percent of the visitors. *See also* CONVENTION ON THE PRIVILEGES AND IMMUNITIES OF THE UNITED NATIONS (1946); PERSONNEL QUESTIONS.

HEALTH. In just two generations, the world has achieved unprecedented progress in health care. Smallpox has been eradicated (at the modest cost of $300 million). Malaria has been pushed back. Polio is near extinction. Child mortality rates have fallen dramatically and 1 billion more people have gained access to clean drinking **water**. At the same time, however, daunting challenges remain. The gap in life expectancy between the richest and poorest countries is 30 years. Nearly all child deaths occur in **developing countries**, a large number of them in Africa. Tuberculosis has surged again. The spread of **HIV/AIDS** has led to significant declines in life expectancy and is eroding the health and development gains of the previous 50 years in many countries.

Health was an early concern of the **League of Nations**. Within the constellation of UN agencies, the **World Health Organization (WHO)** is the primary entity involved. It has played a leading role in the improvement of worldwide health standards throughout the past half century. Several other United Nations agencies also deal with health-related issues, notably the **United Nations Population Fund**

(UNFPA) and the **United Nations Children's Fund (UNICEF)**. *See also* ALMA-ATA HEALTH DECLARATION (1978); MILLENNIUM DECLARATION; WORLD CONFERENCE ON WOMEN (BEIJING, 4–15 September 1995).

HEAVILY INDEBTED POOR COUNTRY INITIATIVE (HIPC). Scheme launched in 1996 by rich donor nations through the **International Monetary Fund (IMF)** and the **World Bank** designed to reduce the external debt of the most indebted developing countries. The HIPC has been criticized by many **nongovernmental organizations (NGOs)**, notably **Oxfam** and **Jubilee Research**, for being "halfhearted," "inadequate," and unduly "piecemeal." In the view of these organizations, several least-developed countries with significant debt burdens have not been included in the initiative. The threshold levels to measure debt sustainability are arbitrary and still too high. The debt reduction is too small and unlikely to release funds for social development purposes, and the conditionalities set by the World Bank and the IMF have slowed down the process. Only a handful of countries have actually "graduated" from the program, leading to repeated calls for "deeper," "broader," and "faster debt relief" measures, which donor countries are beginning to respond to. *See also* DEBT CRISIS (INTERNATIONAL); FINANCE FOR DEVELOPMENT.

HERITAGE FOUNDATION. American think tank created in 1973 to promote policies based on free enterprise, limited government, and a strong national defense. Generally critical of the United Nations and multilateralism, the foundation was especially influential in shaping some of the decisions of the Ronald Reagan administration, notably the withholding of some of the United States assessed contributions to the regular **budget** of the United Nations and the decision to withdraw from the **United Nations Convention on the Law of the Sea** and the **United Nations Educational, Scientific, and Cultural Organization (UNESCO)**. *See also* KIRKPATRICK, JEAN (1926–).

HIGH-LEVEL PANEL ON THREATS, CHALLENGES, AND CHANGE (HLP). A Group of eminent persons constituted by the **secretary-general** in the wake of the controversies provoked by the U.S.-led 2003 military intervention in **Iraq** and its justification on the basis of the doctrine of **preemption**, which many saw as a rejection of **multilateralism** and a marginalization of the United Nations.

The group was requested to make recommendations and propose practical and credible measures "ensuring effective collective responses to the common security problems and challenges facing Member States." In its report issued in December 2004, the panel argued that "any event or process that leads to large scale death or lessening of life chances and undermines states as the basic unit of the international system, is a threat to international security." On that basis, the group identified six clusters of global threats (without prioritizing them) with which the world must be concerned now and in the decades ahead: economic and social threats including poverty, infectious diseases, and environmental degradation; interstate conflict; internal conflict, particularly civil war, genocide, and other large-scale atrocities; nuclear, radiological, chemical, and biological weapons; terrorism; and transnational organized crime.

In order to maximize the UN's capacity to respond to these various threats, the panel proposed various institutional and procedural **reform**s designed to strengthen the effectiveness of the **General Assembly**, simplify the cumbersome nature of the UN economic programs and machinery and, most controversially, correct the broadly perceived lack of representativeness of the **Security Council**.

One of the most politically sensitive issues before the HLP was the question of determining when a state can legitimately use force against another. In reference to the Bush doctrine of preemptive strike, the panel warned that "allowing one to so act is to allow all," and while producing neither a rewriting nor a reinterpretation of Article 51 of the United Nations Charter, it did provide for guidelines for the legitimate **use of force** by members of the United Nations. The panel thus considers preventive wars against non-imminent threats potentially justifiable. But the decision to use force, most particularly in regard to **terrorism**, should meet several tests: the threat has to be serious; force should be used only as a last resort; and it should be proportionate to the threat.

In this context, the panel proposed a useful definition of terrorism, which it describes as "any action that is intended to cause death or serious bodily harm on civilians or noncombatants when the purpose of such an act by its nature or context, is to intimidate a population, or to compel a government or an international organization to do or to abstain from doing any act." The report also deals with what it sees as a "cascade of nuclear proliferation" in the near future and recommends creating incentives for countries to stop enriching uranium.

The High-Level Panel report is remarkable for its endorsement of a right of **humanitarian intervention**. The panel thus ruled firmly that the rights of individuals take precedence over the rights of states and that the international community has not only a right to override state **sovereignty** but also the responsibility to protect the **human rights** of the victims, especially in cases of major breaches of **humanitarian law**, such as the **genocide** in **Rwanda** or **ethnic cleansing** in **Kosovo**.

On the question of **Security Council** reform, the panel merely proposed two alternatives already on the negotiating table: the first would give six countries (Germany, Japan, India, Brazil, and two African counties) permanent seats without a right of **veto** and create three extra nonpermanent seats, thus bringing the total number of seats of the council to 24. The second scenario would expand the council by the same number of seats by creating a new tier of members serving four years that could be immediately reelected above the current layer of two-year members, which cannot be reelected. *See also* ANNAN, KOFI (1938–); COLLECTIVE SECURITY; DOMESTIC JURISDICTION; HUMAN SECURITY; SELF-DEFENSE, RIGHT OF; REFORM, UNITED NATIONS.

HIV/AIDS. An estimated 40 million people, including 2.5 million children live with HIV/AIDS. In 2002, 5 million people were infected with HIV and over 3 million died (500,000 of whom were children). The African continent is the most immediately affected region. By 2010, about 50 million children in sub-Saharan Africa will be orphans, having lost one or both parents to AIDS. Current projections suggest that 45 million people will become infected with the virus in 126 low- and middle-income countries between 2002 and 2010. More than 40 percent of those infections may occur in Asia and the Pacific.

While the epidemic is worsening in parts of Africa and Asia, significant progress has been made in controlling it in most of Europe and North America. An important reason for this situation is the availability and affordability of treatment and, more generally, inequalities among countries in the global pharmaceutical market and in national science and technology infrastructures. Poorer countries cannot afford expensive drug therapies or produce them because of their lack of manufacturing capacity. International property rights are another obstacle in their access to cheaper generic equivalents.

Global spending—both bilateral and multilateral—has risen 15-fold since 1996 to nearly $5 billion but remains inadequate. According to the **Joint United Nations Programme on HIV/AIDS**, the world would need $20 billion annually by 2007 to fight AIDS effectively. In the course of a debate on the special challenges facing Africa in January 2000, the **Security Council** discussed the spread of HIV/AIDS, thus signaling that a health issue could be part of a broader security concern. A **General Assembly** Special Session on HIV/AIDS in June 2001 set targets for reversing the spread of the epidemic. *See also* CONVENTION ON BIOLOGICAL DIVERSITY (CBD, 1992); INTELLECTUAL PROPERTY RIGHTS (IPRs); MILLENNIUM DECLARATION; TRANSNATIONAL CORPORATIONS (TNCs); TRADE-RELATED ASPECTS OF INTELLECTUAL PROPERTY RIGHTS (TRIPs).

HOFFMAN, PAUL (1891–1974). U.S. industrialist and former administrator of the Marshall Plan. The first administrator of the **United Nations Development Programme (UNDP)** from 1966 until his retirement in 1972, he forcefully and durably shaped the developmental work of the programme.

HULL, CORDELL (1871–1955). American politician, lawyer, and diplomat and by many considered the "Father of the United Nations." Secretary of state from 1933 to 1944, he participated in some of the wartime Allies conferences and initiated preparations of blueprints for an international organization dedicated to the maintenance of peace and security, which served as a basis for discussions on the United Nations **Charter** at the 1944 **Dumbarton Oaks Conference** and the 1945 **United Nations Conference on International Organization** in San Francisco. Hull was the 1945 recipient of the **Nobel Peace Prize**. *See also* PASVOLSKY, LEO.

HUMAN DEVELOPMENT REPORT (HDR). Influential annual report launched in 1990 by the **United Nations Development**

Programme (UNDP) under the leadership of Pakistani economist and finance minister **Mahbul ul Haq** with strong intellectual support from Indian Nobel Laureate for Economics **Amartya Sen**. The report, translated into a dozen languages and launched in more than 100 countries annually, has contributed to major shifts in development thinking, emphasizing through the development and analysis of various indexes—the **Human Development Index (HDI)**, the Gender Related Development Index, the Gender Empowerment Measure, and the Human Poverty Index—that the goal of development is not merely to increase national income but to create an environment in which people can develop their full potential and lead productive lives in accord with their needs and interests. Using life expectancy, literacy, average number of years of schooling and income, the HDI provides a more comprehensive yardstick of welfare and security than economic indicators like per capita income. Its underlying assumption is that "more is not better" as countries with similar per capita income may not be equally effective in translating economic prosperity into better lives for peoples. *See also* BASIC HUMAN NEEDS; HUMAN SECURITY; JOLLY, SIR RICHARD (1934–).

HUMAN RIGHTS. Article 1, paragraph 3 of the **Charter** of the United Nations stipulates that one of the principal tasks of the organization is to promote and encourage respect for human rights and for fundamental freedoms for all without distinction as to race, sex, language, or religion. The United Nations promotes human rights through a variety of approaches, first and foremost through cataloging and codifying human rights, but also through the training of national armed forces, police forces, and the legal profession and the provision of advisory services for the incorporation of international human rights norms and standards in national legislation. An indication of the increasing salience of the protection and promotion of human rights by the United Nations can be found in the 1993 decision of the **General Assembly** to create the post of **United Nations High Commissioner for Human Rights (UNHCHR)**.

In assessing the human rights work of the United Nations, a distinction has to be made between charter-based and treaty-based human rights bodies. The former—such as the **Commission for Human Rights**, an intergovernmental subsidiary body of the **Economic**

and Social Council—derive their existence from provisions contained in the Charter of the United Nations and have broad human rights mandates. The latter derive their existence from provisions contained in specific legal instruments, have more narrow mandates, and address a limited audience (i.e., the countries that have ratified these instruments). These treaties include the two International Covenants of 1966—on civil and political rights and economic, social, and cultural rights respectively—which translated the principles set forth in the 1948 **Universal Declaration of Human Rights** into specific rights, the **International Convention on the Elimination of All Forms of Racial Discrimination** (1965), the **Convention on the Elimination of All Forms of Discrimination against Women** (1979), the **Convention against Torture and Other Cruel, Inhuman, or Degrading Treatment or Punishment** (1984), the **Convention on the Rights of the Child** (1989), and the **International Convention on the Protection of the Rights of All Migrant Workers and Members of Their Families** (2003).

Seven committees of independent experts established under the principal human rights treaties (also referred to as "treaty-monitoring bodies") monitor the implementation of the respective treaties by reviewing states parties reports submitted under their provisions. They are the **Committee on Economic, Social, and Cultural Rights**; the **Committee on the Elimination of Discrimination against Women**; **Human Rights Committee**, the **Committee against Torture**; the **Committee on the Rights of the Child**; the **Committee for Elimination of Racial Discrimination**; and the Committee on Migrant Workers. Four of these committees also accept and render views on individual complaints of human rights violations.

While contemporary human rights law promoted by the United Nations is impressive in scope and coverage, its inherent weakness is that its implementation is not self executing and is left in the hands of governments. Instances of inconsistencies and "double standards" in the functioning of the UN human rights machinery have not been infrequent and led to the creation of a **Human Rights Council** in 2006, replacing the much criticized Commission for Human Rights. *See also* APARTHEID; CHILDREN IN ARMED CONFLICTS; DAYS-YEARS-DECADES (INTERNATIONAL); INTERNATIONAL LABOUR ORGANIZATION (ILO); MINORITIES,

PROTECTION OF; SELF-DETERMINATION; TRANSNATIONAL CORPORATIONS (TNCs); WORLD CONFERENCE ON WOMEN (BEIJING, 4–15 September 1995).

HUMAN RIGHTS COMMITTEE (HRC). Established in accordance with the 1966 **International Covenant on Civil and Political Rights (ICCPR)**, this committee of experts monitors the implementation of the covenant by its states parties and submits annual reports on its findings to the **Economic and Social Council (ECOSOC)** and the **General Assembly**. The committee examines periodic mandatory reports submitted by states parties and may receive and consider complaints by parties alleging that another state party is not fulfilling its obligations. It may also receive communications from individuals who claim to be victims of a violation by the participant state under whose jurisdiction they are. *See also* HUMAN RIGHTS; UNIVERSAL DECLARATION OF HUMAN RIGHTS (UDHR, 1948).

HUMAN RIGHTS COUNCIL. Acting on a recommendation of the **secretary-general** and after months of protracted debates, the **General Assembly** created in 2006 a Human Rights Council replacing the **Commission for Human Rights (CHR)**, whose credibility had been damaged for accommodating among its members states known for their human rights abuses and double-standards and inconsistencies in its monitoring and application of **human rights** norms and standards. The purpose of the **reform** is to preserve the strengths of the CHR while including innovations designed to address its weaknesses.

The new panel remains in Geneva, its membership shrinking to 47 members (from 54 for CHR). It is a quasi-permanent body meeting for at least three sessions per year for a total duration of no less than 10 weeks (the CHR met in annual six-week long sessions) and reporting directly to the General Assembly. The council's members are elected to three-year terms by a majority of the entire assembly rather than by a majority of the smaller **Economic and Social Council (ECOSOC)**. They can be reelected for only a second term. One major difference with the defunct CHR is a provision requiring members of the council to undergo a review of their human rights records. In addition, a two-thirds majority vote by the General Assembly may suspend the rights of membership in the council of any member committing "gross and systematic" human rights violations.

HUMAN RIGHTS WATCH (HRW). Independent international **nongovernmental organization (NGO)** created in 1978 to redress abuses of **human rights**. Headquartered in New York, HRW's human rights advocacy strategy primarily relies on fact-finding investigations into human rights abuses by government and **nonstate actors** worldwide and a large body of publications as tools to generate public attention and mobilize diplomatic and economic pressures on human rights offenders. Originally, HRW focused its activities on civil and political rights but it has paid increasing attention to addressing economic, social, and cultural rights. HRW played a key role in the campaigns to ban **antipersonnel landmines,** to stop the use of **children in armed conflicts**, and to establish the **International Criminal Court (ICC).** *See also* AMNESTY INTERNATIONAL (AI); CIVIL SOCIETY; NONSTATE ACTORS.

HUMAN SECURITY. Broad concept related to the notion of human development promoted by the **United Nations Development Programme (UNDP),** which focuses on the need to create and sustain societies that enable individual human beings to realize their full potential. For that purpose, individuals should be protected against threats arising not only from conflicts and war but also from nonmilitary threats such as **poverty**, environmental degradation, illicit drug trafficking, and infectious diseases. *See also* HIGH-LEVEL PANEL ON THREATS, CHALLENGES, AND CHANGE (HLP); HUMAN DEVELOPMENT REPORT (HDR); INDEPENDENT WORKING GROUP ON THE FUTURE OF THE UNITED NATIONS.

HUMAN SETTLEMENTS. *See* URBANIZATION.

HUMANITARIAN AGENCIES. Although the United Nations has long been involved in the provision of relief in man-made or natural disasters, it has been increasingly called in the post–**Cold War** era to respond to the socioeconomic needs arising from civil wars and emergencies. In 1992, a Department of Humanitarian Affairs (restructured in 1998 into the **Office for the Coordination of Humanitarian Affairs [OCHA]**) was created to coordinate international humanitarian relief. Other United Nations bodies also involved in humanitarian crises include the **United Nations Development**

Programme, the **United Nations High Commissioner for Refugees (UNHCR)**, the **United Nations Children's Fund (UNICEF)**, the **World Food Programme (WFP)**, the **United Nations High Commissioner for Human Rights (UNHCHR)**, as well as several **specialized agencies** such as the **Food and Agriculture Organization (FAO)** and the **World Health Organization (WHO)**. The outbreak of internal armed conflicts has also drawn in the participation of numerous **nongovernmental organizations (NGOs)**. *See also* RED CROSS, THE.

HUMANITARIAN ASSISTANCE. Provision of external aid in response to as well as to prevent, mitigate, and prepare for humanitarian emergencies. As defined, humanitarian assistance is a long-standing activity of the United Nations that can be traced back to the work of the **International Refugee Organization (IRO)** and the **United Nations Children's Fund (UNICEF)**. The United Nations role in humanitarian assistance to people impacted by natural and man-made disasters expanded rapidly only after the creation in 1972 of the **United Nations Disaster Relief Organization (UNDRO)**, a forerunner of the Department of Humanitarian Affairs (later called the **Office for the Coordination of Humanitarian Affairs [OCHA]**) set up in 1992. Today, virtually the entire UN system participates in this enterprise.

Although apparently well embedded now within the United Nations mandate, the humanitarian work of the organization poses major operational issues arising primarily from tensions between the norms of sovereignty and noninterference, defended primarily by Southern countries and China, and a right to intervene or right of access in the delivery of humanitarian aid advocated mostly by Northern countries. The age old humanitarian principles of humanity, impartiality, and neutrality articulated over a century ago by the **International Committee of the Red Cross (ICRC)** have also proved ill-suited to the dynamics of the internal conflicts the United Nations has been increasingly drawn into. *See also* FOOD AND AGRICULTURE ORGANIZATION (FAO); HUMANITARIAN AGENCIES; HUMANITARIAN INTERVENTION; INTERNATIONAL COMMISSION ON INTERVENTION AND STATE SOVEREIGNTY; NORTH KOREA; OFFICE FOR THE COORDINATION OF HUMANITARIAN AFFAIRS (OCHA); RED CROSS,

THE; UNITED NATIONS DEVELOPMENT PROGRAMME (UNDP); UNITED NATIONS EDUCATIONAL, SCIENTIFIC, AND CULTURAL ORGANIZATION (UNESCO); UNITED NATIONS HIGH COMMISSIONER FOR REFUGEES (UNHCR); WORLD FOOD PROGRAMME (WFP); WORLD HEALTH ORGANIZATION (WHO).

HUMANITARIAN INTERVENTION. International law prohibits "interventions" by any state within the territory of another without that state's consent, including in cases of internal wars. These prohibitions, which are a corollary of the principle of the sovereign equality of states are reaffirmed in the **Charter** of the United Nations as part of its general prohibition of the **use of force** (subject only to a right of individual and **collective self-defense**).

Since the end of the **Cold War**, the **Security Council** has authorized military interventions for humanitarian purposes in **Iraq, Somalia, Haiti**, and **Timor-Leste**, among other cases, on the grounds that such actions were justified in situations of internal conflict or war because they were accompanied by war crimes, massive **human rights** violations and other crimes against humanity that threatened peace and security and, therefore, fell within the jurisdiction and were the responsibility of the council under Chapter VI and VII of the UN Charter. The argument that humanitarian intervention is permissible if authorized by the Security Council has raised further questions about the legality of such actions as the collective intervention in **Kosovo** led by the **North Atlantic Treaty Organization (NATO)**,which was undertaken without explicit Security Council approval. *See also* HIGH-LEVEL PANEL ON THREATS, CHALLENGES, AND CHANGE (HLP); INDEPENDENT INTERNATIONAL COMMISSION ON KOSOVO; INDEPENDENT WORKING GROUP ON THE FUTURE OF THE UNITED NATIONS; INTERNATIONAL COMMISSION ON INTERVENTION AND STATE SOVEREIGNTY; REFORM, UNITED NATIONS; SOVEREIGNTY.

HUMANITARIAN LAW. Body of rules in **international law** that, in times of international armed conflicts, seek to protect persons who are not or no longer are taking part in hostilities and restrict the methods of warfare employed. International humanitarian law is rooted in the "law of armed conflict," which developed progressively since medieval times through the practice of states. It is codified in a number of international treaties, declarations, and conventions. The most important sources of international humanitarian law, so strictly defined, are found in the four 1949 **Geneva Conventions** and the two 1977 Protocols attached to them. Other international legal instruments prohibiting the use of certain weapons and protecting categories of peoples and goods include the 1954 **Hague Convention for the Protection of Cultural Property in the Event of Armed Conflict** (plus its protocols), the 1972 **Biological Weapons Convention**, the 1980 **Chemical Weapons Convention** and its protocols, the 1993 **Chemical Weapons Convention**, the 1999 **Convention on the Prohibition of the Use, Stockpiling, Production, and Transfer of Antipersonnel Mines and on Their Destruction**, and the 2000 optional protocol to the **Convention on the Rights of the Child**.

While international humanitarian law applies in situations of armed conflicts, **human rights** law generally seeks to protect the individual at all times. Reflecting the fact that a large number of conflicts are internal, international humanitarian law has evolved to encompass a body of international law related to human rights and the rights of civilian victims and nonarmed persons such as **refugees, internally displaced persons, women**, and **children** in noninternational armed conflicts. Such a development was foreshadowed in a provision common to the four Geneva Conventions, which calls for the humane treatment of all persons not taking part in hostilities and prohibits acts of violence to life and persons such as murder, mutilation, cruel treatment and torture, the taking of hostages, and the passing of sentences and carrying out of executions without previous judgment by a regularly constituted court. The 1977 Second Protocol relating to the Protection of Victims of Noninternational Armed Conflicts extends these fundamental rights to the protection of victims of noninternational armed conflicts and reinforces the fundamental rights of children and the right to protection from gender violence and from slavery. *See also* INTERNATIONAL COVENANT ON CIVIL AND POLITICAL RIGHTS (ICCPR, 1966); INTERNATIONAL COVENANT ON ECONOMIC, SOCIAL, AND CULTURAL RIGHTS (ICESCR, 1966); UNIVERSAL DECLARATION OF HUMAN RIGHTS (UDHR, 1948).

HUMPHREY, JOHN (1905–1995). Canadian lawyer and scholar who was appointed in 1946 as the first director of the Human Rights Division in the United Nations Secretariat. In that capacity, he was one of the principal drafters of the **Universal Declaration of Human Rights**. He remained with the UN for 20 years and during that period oversaw the elaboration of major **human rights** instruments. Upon retirement in 1966 he resumed his teaching career and continued to actively promote human rights causes.

HUNGARIAN CRISIS (1956). Just at the moment when the United Nations was trying to resolve the **Suez Canal crisis**, turmoil erupted in Hungary where a popular uprising forced a new government to pledge greater freedom and appeal for the withdrawal of Soviet troops. Within days, Soviet troops crushed all resistance, seized the new Hungarian leaders, and installed a new government subservient to Moscow. Soviet **vetoes** blocked **Security Council** action. The **General Assembly** thereafter called upon the USSR to desist forthwith from any form of intervention in the internal affairs of Hungary and to withdraw all its forces without delay, but its appeals as well as resolutions adopted in subsequent years went unheeded. *See also* UNITING FOR PEACE RESOLUTION (1950).

HUNGER. Close to one billion people across the world, most of them in **developing countries**, suffer from hunger, a term referring to undernutrition (the absence of food proteins and caloric energy); micronutrient deficiencies (dietary shortages of iron, iodine, and vitamin A); and nutrient-depleting illnesses such as diarrhea, measles, and malaria.

Limited progress has been made in reducing the incidence of hunger over the past decades. Outright famine and starvation have by and large disappeared. But according to estimates of the **Food and Agricultural Organization (FAO)**, the number of undernourished shrank from 817 million in 1990–1992 to 798 million in 1999–2001, a reduction of only 2.1 million per year. Regionally, the number of undernourished declined in Asia and the Pacific and in Latin America but increased in Africa South of the Sahara. To achieve the 1996 **World Food Summit** target of halving the number of undernourished people by 2015 from their number in 1990–1992, annual worldwide reductions of 26 million would be required.

It is generally recognized that world agricultural production may be sufficient to provide a growing world population with enough food. The principal problem is one of distribution, i.e., of access to the available global food supply. The continued growth in food production, however, hinges on a set of interrelated factors, including environmental factors (losses of farmland, limits to freshwater supplies, erosion and degradation of soils, and declining genetic diversity); scientific and technological considerations (improved seeds, fertilizers, and pesticide and genetic engineering); and socioeconomic constraints such as inadequate markets, infrastructure, and research investment and limited access by poor farmers to land capital and technology. Economists also argue that if poor people had greater purchasing power, more food would be produced and made available. Hunger is thus inextricably linked to the prevalence of poverty, and its elimination depends in no small way on poverty reduction strategies, notably **agrarian reform**, a politically explosive issue in many developing countries. Hunger also has man-made causes: war, political turbulence, civil conflict, and social unrest, as is the case in such countries as **Sudan**, Colombia, and **Liberia**.

The elimination of hunger has been a long-standing development goal of the United Nations, which can be traced back to discussions taking place in the **Economic and Social Council (ECOSOC)** in the late 1940s and early 1950s on land and agrarian reform. The major UN entities involved in hunger-related activities include the FAO and the **International Fund for Agricultural Development (IFAD)**. The **World Food Programme (WFP)** also plays an important role, especially in man-made and natural humanitarian crises. The **United Nations Children's Fund (UNICEF)** does have an extensive participation in such crises, but its work is more development oriented. *See also* AGRICULTURAL DEVELOPMENT; DESERTIFICATION; ENVIRONMENT; FOOD SECURITY; MILLENNIUM DECLARATION.

– I –

ILLITERACY. Considerable progress has been made in the elimination of illiteracy since a survey conducted by **United Nations Educational, Scientific, and Cultural Organization (UNESCO)** in the early 1960s concluded that two-fifth of the world's adults were illiterate. But in large part as a result of **population** growth in developing countries, in absolute terms, the number of illiterate people in the world has continued to increase and was estimated, in 1995, to reach 1 billion worldwide, two-thirds of them **women**.

Education for all, a normative goal advocated by UNESCO and recognized as an individual human right by the **Universal Declaration of Human Rights** and the **International Covenant on Economic, Social, and Cultural Rights** remains a far distant objective. Overall, 80 percent of school-age children in the developing regions are enrolled in primary school. But more than 115 million children of primary school age are still out of school. One-third of children in Africa are out of school, and in Southern Asia, Oceania, and Western Asia enrollments are lagging.

One of the goals of the **Millennium Development Declaration** calls for the achievement of universal primary education and to ensure that by 2015 boys and girls will be able to complete a full course of primary schooling. The objective is not altogether unrealistic, but achieving it requires dramatically scaled-up efforts in sub-Saharan Africa, Southern Asia, and Oceania. Maintaining such high levels of enrollment in the long run is another looming challenge, especially in those countries where **HIV/AIDS** has killed significant numbers of trained teachers.

INDEPENDENT COMMISSION ON DISARMAMENT AND SECURITY ISSUES. Also known as the Palme Commission, after its chairman, former prime minister Olaf Palme of Sweden, this group of eminent persons representing the **North Atlantic Treaty Organization (NATO)**, the **Warsaw Pact**, and **developing countries** endeavored to elaborate guiding principles for global **disarmament** and **arms control** supplementing the concept of security elaborated in the **Independent Commission on International Development Issues** (the Brandt Commission). Its report (*Common Security: A Blueprint for Survival*) was issued in 1982 and called for new modes of multilateral cooperation through the United Nations in dealing with nuclear disarmament issues. In 1982, the expert group did issue a report *The Relationship between Disarmament and Development*, which generated considerable interest and research, as it was the first comprehensive attempt to investigate systematically the various dimensions of the relationship between disarmament and development. Drawing from commissioned studies, it concluded, on the basis of alternative scenarios of the world economy until the year 2000 with varying shares of military outlays in GNPs, that even modest resources released through disarmament could make a significant contribution to global economic prospects. Its recommendations also dealt with the relationship between disarmament and development. *See also* COMMISSION ON GLOBAL GOVERNANCE; COMMISSION ON INTERNATIONAL DEVELOPMENT (PEARSON COMMISSION); ECONOMIC CONSEQUENCES OF DISARMAMENT; INDEPENDENT COMMISSIONS; INDEPENDENT WORKING GROUP ON THE FUTURE OF THE UNITED NATIONS; INTERNATIONAL COMMISSION ON INTERVENTION AND STATE SOVEREIGNTY; SOUTH COMMISSION; REFORM, UNITED NATIONS.

INDEPENDENT COMMISSION ON INTERNATIONAL DEVELOPMENT ISSUES (ICIDI). Panel of international leaders led by former German chancellor Willy Brandt that produced influential reports in the early 1980s setting out comprehensive global strategies for **food**, aid, **environment**, **international trade**, finance, and monetary reform designed to enable **developing countries** to eradicate poverty and become equal trading partners with developed nations. The two reports *North South* (1980) and *Common Crisis* (1983) emphasize the interdependence of Northern and Southern countries and the need to address the world's problems collectively. In many respects, they foreshadowed some of the 1987 findings and recommendations of the World Commission on Environment and Development's report. *See also* COMMISSION ON INTERNATIONAL DEVELOPMENT (PEARSON COMMISSION); INDEPENDENT COMMISSIONS; NORTH-SOUTH DIALOGUE; SOUTH COMMISSION; WORLD COMMISSION ON THE SOCIAL DIMENSIONS OF GLOBALIZATION.

INDEPENDENT COMMISSIONS. Groups of independent experts and politically notable personalities representative of all regions of the world that sprang up from the late 1970s to address cross-national "common interests of survival" and to recommend appropriate remedial policies. The 1969 **Commission on International Development** (the Pearson Commission) was an early precursor of subsequent commissions such as the **Independent Commission on International Development Issues** (the Brandt Commission), the **Independent Commission on Disarmament and Security**, the **South Com-**

mission, the **Commission on Global Governance**, the **Independent Working Group on the Future of the United Nations** system, the **International Commission on Intervention and State Sovereignty**, the **Global Commission on International Migration**, and the **World Commission on Environment and Development (Brundtland Commission)**.

The origins, mandates, funding, and functions of these bodies vary considerably. But they all enjoy a significant degree of political independence that confers them legitimacy and credibility. The recommendations contained in their reports are usually grounded on the assumption that the growing **interdependence** of nations in the context of a globalizing world creates an institutional deficit in the international cooperation architecture that must be corrected. Notwithstanding the notable exception of the Brundtland Commission, the impact of their prescriptions has been uneven and generally minimal. Their influence—in terms of reshaping the architecture of global governance and mobilizing political support for new policy initiatives—has been mixed. *See also* HIGH-LEVEL PANEL ON THREATS, CHALLENGES, AND CHANGE (HLP); INDEPENDENT INTERNATIONAL COMMISSION ON KOSOVO; INDEPENDENT WORKING GROUP ON THE FUTURE OF THE UNITED NATIONS; MULTILATERALISM; REFORM, UNITED NATIONS.

INDEPENDENT INTERNATIONAL COMMISSION ON KOSOVO. Created on the initiative of the Swedish government in the aftermath of the military intervention in Kosovo, this group of 11 experts addressed the origins of the **Kosovo question**, assessed the merits of the North Atlantic Treaty Organization (NATO) campaign, and offered various options for the future of Kosovo ranging from outright independence to the creation of a United Nations protectorate for an indefinite number of years. In its final report issued in 2000, the Commission found that NATO's intervention was illegitimate and urged the United Nations to "close the gap between legality and legitimacy" by preparing a new framework for intervention. *See also* HUMANITARIAN INTERVENTION; INDEPENDENT COMMISSIONS; INDEPENDENT WORKING GROUP ON THE FUTURE OF THE UNITED NATIONS; INTERNATIONAL COMMISSION ON INTERVENTION AND STATE SOVEREIGNTY; REFORM, UNITED NATIONS.

INDEPENDENT WORKING GROUP ON THE FUTURE OF THE UNITED NATIONS. Convened under the auspices of the Ford Foundation and at the initiative of **Secretary-General Boutros Boutros-Ghali**, this 12-member group (5 from developing countries, 2 from Eastern Europe, 5 from Western countries) offered recommendations to enable the United Nations to cope with the growing significance of transboundary problems arising from the process of **globalization**. While underlining the responsibilities of its member states in constraining the scope and competence of the United Nations, the group's proposals aim at a more democratic organization within the framework of the notion of "**human security**." Most particularly, the group recommended the establishment of two new principal organs of the UN, a UN Social Council and a UN Economic Council, acting concurrently with a revamped and more democratic **Security Council**. *See also* INDEPENDENT COMMISSIONS; REFORM, UNITED NATIONS.

INDIA-PAKISTAN DISPUTE (1948–). *See* KASHMIR DISPUTE (1948–).

INDIGENOUS PEOPLES. The term designates broadly the descendants of inhabitants of lands encroached upon by European empire building and colonial settlement and now living on the margins of modern state societies. In other cases, there are peoples who have been pushed back—often into the mountains or wastelands—by new waves of social invaders and immigrants. The surviving communities of the Inuit and Aleut of the Arctic, the Aborigines of Australia, the Maori of New Zealand, the tribal peoples of Asia are instances of such culturally distinct groups regarded as "indigenous."

An estimated 350 million peoples labeled "indigenous" live throughout the world, existing under severe conditions of relative deprivation, subjected to discrimination and exclusion, displaced from their traditional lands, and denied their cultural identities. International concern for the promotion of indigenous peoples' rights appears to be growing, albeit haltingly so. A **United Nations Permanent Forum for Indigenous Peoples** was established in 2000 by the **Economic and Social Council (ECOSOC)**, providing a setting for the discussion of various issues of concern to indigenous populations, ranging from their rights over their lands and natural resources to **education** and **health** conditions. A United Nations Declaration spelling out their rights is being drafted. Their condition is also reviewed by the **Commission for Human Rights** and monitored by one of its special rapporteurs. *See also* MINORITIES, PROTECTION OF.

INDONESIAN QUESTION (1945–1949). One of the earliest **decolonization** issues to reach the United Nations. Between 1945 and 1949, Indonesia sought to achieve independence from the Netherlands. In the course of this armed struggle, the **Security Council** arranged several cease-fires in the field and maintained, between 1947 and 1951, a small group of military observers, which also assisted in the negotiations. Continuing diplomatic and economic pressures on the Dutch, especially from the United States, paved the way to a final settlement of the dispute and an agreement on independence was concluded in December 1949. A subsequent controversy flared up about Western New Guinea, which the Dutch refused to relinquish. The dispute was mediated by the United Nations and resolved through the **United Nations Temporary Executive Authority**. *See also* MEDIATION; PEACEKEEPING.

INFORMATION TECHNOLOGY (IT). Information technology breakthroughs beginning in the second half of the 19th century have provided repeated opportunities for improved modes of coordination and cooperation among nations primarily concerned with the creation of regulatory regimes, equipment standardization, and uniform operating rules. The creation of the International Telegraph Union (ITU) in 1865 was intended to provide a regulatory framework for the continuing expansion of telegraph networks. A Radiotelegraph Conference held in 1906 resulted in the adoption of an International Radiotelegraph Convention regulating wireless telegraphy. With the rapid expansion of telecommunications, the old ITU was revamped in 1947 and became a **specialized agency** of the United Nations under the name of **International Telecommunications Union (ITU)**. With the launch of the first satellite in orbit around Earth and the consequent development of satellite communications, the ITU became the focal forum for allocating frequencies to various space services.

The current and still unfolding IT revolution has been triggered by the rapid spread of communication technologies, including the home computer to the Internet, e-mail, and the fax machine. The growing use of these technologies has created new ways of disseminating knowledge and education; changed economic, financial, and business transactions and practices; and altered many of the ways governments function. IT also has the potential capacity to improve the living conditions of millions of peoples around the globe and the competitiveness of **developing countries** in the world economy. In the short term, however, it has heightened the technological disparities between North and South, creating the so-called "digital divide," as most developing countries lack the infrastructure and/or do not have the resources that would give them access to the use of IT applications.

As noted, the role of the United Nations has for a long time focused primarily on the development of regulatory regimes for information technology. More recently, and with the assistance of the private sector, the organization has shifted to promoting the acquisition of new technologies by developing countries. One of the key objectives of the 2005 **World Summit on the Information Society** held in Tunis under the aegis of the ITU was to develop international cooperation policies for bridging the digital divide. *See also* ELECTRONIC COMMERCE (E-COMMERCE); GLOBALIZATION; SCIENCE AND TECHNOLOGY FOR DEVELOPMENT.

INSTITUTE FOR GLOBAL POLICY (IGP). Policy research arm of the **World Federalist Movement** set up in 1983 as a peace education instrument to promote a better understanding of the United Nations and other international organizations. IGP research focuses on federalist political philosophy and the promotion of international peace and security, **global governance**, international democracy and world federalism, proposals on the establishment of a UN parliamentary assembly, **weighted voting** in international decision making, and the **reform** of the UN and the **Security Council**.

INTEGRATED PROGRAMME FOR COMMODITIES (IPC). The centerpiece of the demands of developing countries contained in the **New International Economic Order**. Inspired by the research and program of action forged by **Raul Prebisch**, first in his capacity as the executive secretary of the **United Nations Commission for Latin America and the Caribbean (ECLAC)** in the 1950s and then as the first head of the **United Nations Conference on Trade and Development (UNCTAD)**, the IPC stipulated that agreements for 18 **commodities** would be negotiated by producing and consuming countries with the principal aims of avoiding excessive price fluctuations and stabilizing commodity prices at levels remunerative to producers and equitable to consumers. In conjunction with the IPC, a "Common Fund" would help stabilize prices when they either fell below or climbed too high above the negotiated price targets through buffer stocks operated under the IPC.

Only a handful of commodity agreements were ever agreed upon and they either collapsed or became inoperative as a result of producer and consumer country clashing interests. Northern countries rejected the pleas of Southern countries for the establishment of a $10 billion common fund acquiescing only to fund a modestly endowed institution with functions limited to **technical assistance**, which operates from the Netherlands.

INTELLECTUAL PROPERTY RIGHTS (IPRs). Legal term referring to the rights given to persons over the creations of their minds. IPRs usually give the creators an exclusive right over the use of their creations for a certain lapse of time. Intellectual property rights broadly fall into two major categories. One, **copyrights**, such as the rights of authors of literary and artistic works (books, musical compositions, paintings, sculpture, computer programs, and films), the rights of performers (actors, singers, and musicians) as well as those of producers of sound recordings and broadcasting organizations; and two, industrial property rights intended to protect and stimulate innovation and the design and creation of technology such as inventions (protected by patents), industrial designs, and trade secrets.

Intellectual property plays an important role in an increasingly broad range of areas extending from the Internet to health care to numerous aspects of science and technology. For example, the interests of patent owners of pharmaceutical drugs have clashed with the public health concerns generated by the need of countries deeply affected by **HIV/AIDS** for affordable generic medicine. The expansion of the

Internet and **electronic commerce** has underlined the challenges involved in seeking to encourage the dissemination and exploitation of creative works of knowledge and, at the same time, to protect the rights of creators. A particularly sensitive issue that has surfaced in recent years is the preservation, management, and sustainable use of genetic resources and of associated traditional knowledge as well as the sharing of the benefits that they offer in pharmaceutical, chemical, and agricultural research. Another source of contentious debate relates to the **Trade-Related Aspects of Intellectual Property Rights (TRIPs),** which make protection of intellectual property rights an integral part of the multilateral trading system as embodied in the **World Trade Organization (WTO).**

How to balance the legitimate interests of rights holders and those of users has become a **North-South** issue in **international trade.** Developed, rich countries have insisted on strengthening intellectual property rights on the grounds that they are essential to provide incentives for invention and creation. Southern countries take the view that property rights unduly reward powerful **transnational corporations (TNCs)** and aggravate North-South inequalities in the applications of science and technology for development by privatizing the ownership of information. *See also* CONVENTION ON BIOLOGICAL DIVERSITY (CBD, 1992); WORLD INTELLECTUAL PROPERTY ORGANIZATION (WIPO).

INTER-AMERICAN DEVELOPMENT BANK (IDB). The oldest and largest regional multilateral development institution established in 1959 to promote the economic and social development of Latin America and the Caribbean. In the past, the bank's lending focused on the productive sectors of **agriculture** and industry; the physical infrastructure sectors of **energy** and transportation; and the social sectors of environmental and public health, education, and urban development. Current lending priorities focus on **poverty** reduction and social equity and the **environment**. The bank's affiliates promote private sector development, mainly in the microenterprise sector and small- and medium-scale companies. By the end of 2002, the bank had approved over $118 billion in loans and guaranteed finance projects with investments totaling $282 billion. *See also* AFRICAN DEVELOPMENT BANK (AfDB); ASIAN DEVELOPMENT BANK (ADB); MULTILATERAL DEVELOPMENT BANKS (MDBs).

INTERDEPENDENCE. The driving forces shaping current world politics—international finance, **international trade** and commerce, environmental **pollution**, the **information technology** revolution, and the growing role of transnational **nonstate actors** like **nongovernmental organizations (NGOs)** and **transnational corporations (TNCs)**—are increasingly linking states in a wide ranging web of expanding interactions. These processes create conditions of "interdependence" in the sense that states as well as peoples are increasingly affected by decisions made by others beyond their national boundaries. Interdependence may thus be symmetric if all sets of actors are affected equally in a pattern of mutual dependence. It may also be asymmetric if the vulnerability of one set of actors is greater than that of another. North-South political and economic relations may be described as asymmetric. *See also* GLOBALIZATION; INDEPENDENT COMMISSIONS; MULTILATERALISM.

INTERGOVERNMENTAL OCEANOGRAPHIC COMMISSION (IOC). Autonomous body within the **United Nations Educational, Scientific, and Cultural Organization (UNESCO)** established in 1960 to promote the sharing of knowledge and practical research on the nature and utilization of the resources of the **oceans** and coastal areas with particular attention to marine environmental protection, **fishing, fisheries**, and ecosystems, **climate change**, ocean observing and monitoring, and disaster mitigation.

INTERNALLY DISPLACED PERSONS (IDPs). The term designates persons forced to flee or leave their homes for a variety of reasons, most commonly armed conflict, violence, violations of **human rights**, and natural or man-made disasters *within* their own countries. When first assessed in 1982, the magnitude of the problem of internal displacement was estimated to involve some 1.2 million persons in a dozen countries. Ten years later, the **secretary-general** reported to the **Commission for Human Rights** that the number had risen to 24 million. Nowadays, there are an estimated 25 million IDPs in some 50 countries. The explosion in the number of IDPs relates to a large extent to the dynamics of post–**Cold War** politics, as ethnic, religious, class, and social cleavages, which had been suppressed or controlled during the Cold War, came to the fore when the nature of war shifted from interstate confrontations to predominantly intercommunal conflict.

Insofar as IDPs do not cross state borders, they cannot benefit from the rights and status provided by international **refugees** law and the protection and assistance of the Office of the **United Nations High Commissioner for Refugees (UNHCR)**. They are nevertheless protected by international **humanitarian law** and can receive the assistance of humanitarian agencies. Government sensitivity about interference in their internal affairs being at the heart of the issue, a special mechanism was set up to monitor this human rights problem. Since 1992, a representative of the secretary-general serves as an advocate or "ombudsman" for IDPs and reports to the Commission for Human Rights. The representative of the secretary-general has developed "Guiding Principles on Internal Displacement" intended for national authorities, **nongovernmental organizations (NGOs)**, and **nonstate actors** that set forth the rights and guarantees applying to IDPs. *See also* INTERNATIONAL COMMISSION ON INTERVENTION AND STATE SOVEREIGNTY; PRINCIPLES, OF THE UNITED NATIONS.

INTERNATIONAL ALERT. Independent, London-based **nongovernmental organization (NGO)** established in 1985 by a group of **human rights** advocates concerned about the fact that the denial of human rights often led to internal armed conflicts that in turn undermined efforts to protect individual and collective human rights and to promote sustainable development. International Alert operates in over 20 countries and territories, works with governments, the **European Union**, and the United Nations in an effort to shape both policy and practice in building sustainable peace and carries out public awareness work activities. Its regional work is based in the African Great Lakes, West Africa, the Caucasus, Colombia, Sri Lanka, Nepal, and the Philippines. Its advocacy work focuses on **business**, **humanitarian assistance** and **development**, **gender**, security, and postconflict reconstruction.

INTERNATIONAL ATOMIC ENERGY AGENCY (IAEA). Established in 1957 as an autonomous organization under the aegis of the United Nations following a 1953 proposal by President **Dwight D. Eisenhower** to create an international body to control and develop the use of atomic energy. The agency assists its members in planning for and using nuclear science and technology for peaceful purposes, develops nuclear safety standards, and verifies through its inspection system state compliance with their obligations under the **Treaty on the Nonproliferation of Nuclear Weapons** and other nonproliferation agreements. The agency has played a controversial role in the verification of the disarmament measures imposed on Iraq by the **Security Council** after the 1991 **Persian Gulf War**. See also ARMS CONTROL; "ATOMS FOR PEACE"; DISARMAMENT; WEAPONS OF MASS DESTRUCTION (WMDs).

INTERNATIONAL BANK FOR RECONSTRUCTION AND DEVELOPMENT (IBRD). Better known as the World Bank, plans for the establishment of such a bank were made at the 1944 **Bretton Woods Conference**, and the IBRD formally came into existence a year later. Technically, the bank is a **specialized agency** of the United Nations, but it is largely independent, as it is governed by a board of governors with votes allocated according to capital subscription. The bank makes loans to member nations and private investors to facilitate productive investment and to encourage foreign trade. To date, it has made loans amounting cumulatively to an approximate total of $360 billion.

Together with its sister organization, the **International Monetary Fund (IMF)**, the bank was part of an overall scheme designed to restore a viable and expanding world economy, freer trade, and the avoidance of world depressions. The original focus of the bank's activities was on the reconstruction of Europe but rapidly shifted to the developmental concerns of **Third World** countries. The work of the bank has been a perennial subject of controversy, critics complaining that it seeks to impose a free market system on them and that the projects it finances are environmentally destructive and skewed in favor of middle-income countries. In response to such criticisms, the bank has made significant changes in its lending policies moving from large-scale infrastructural projects to a focus on **poverty** eradication and **debt** alleviation. The bank issues numerous publications, including the important annual *World Development Report*. *See also* INTERNATIONAL DEVELOPMENT ASSOCIATION (IDA); INTERNATIONAL FINANCE CORPORATION (IFC); MCNAMARA, ROBERT S. (1916–); MULTILATERAL INVESTMENT GUARANTEE AGENCY (MIGA); WASHINGTON CONSENSUS.

INTERNATIONAL CAMPAIGN TO BAN LANDMINES (ICBL). Broad coalition of veterans organizations, **human rights** groups, handicapped rights groups, public health groups, and **arms control** groups created in 1992, which played a significant role in securing the adoption of the 1997 **Ottawa Treaty** banning the use, production, stockpiling, sale, transfer, or export of **antipersonnel mines.** Since then, the ICBL has continued its advocacy campaigns pressing for the signing, ratification, implementation, and monitoring of the treaty, increased resources for humanitarian demining, mine awareness programs, and increased resources for landmine victim rehabilitation and assistance. The success of the ICBL has spearheaded the emergence of similar networks, such as the International Action Network on Small Arms, which came into existence in 1999 with the aim of curbing the accumulation and trafficking in small arms. The ICBL was awarded the Nobel Peace Prize in 1997. *See also* CIVIL SOCIETY; NONGOVERNMENTAL ORGANIZATIONS (NGOs).

INTERNATIONAL CHAMBER OF COMMERCE (ICC). Influential world business organization set up in 1919 to promote trade, investment, and free market enterprise. Headquartered in Paris and composed of national committees and groups, the ICC has a broad range of activities in such areas as international **trade, intellectual property**, taxation, insurance, marketing, advertising, **environment**, air and maritime transport, and banking. The ICC threw its weight in support of the United Nations when the organization was founded in 1945 but became increasingly critical and hostile when regulatory and interventionist schemes evolved into the prevailing conventional development wisdom in the 1970s. Relations with the United Nations have markedly improved with the demise of the **New International Economic Order**. The ICC was among the earliest business supporters of the **Global Compact**.

INTERNATIONAL CIVIL AVIATION ORGANIZATION (ICAO). A **specialized agency** of the United Nations system set up in 1947 and headquartered in Montreal. Its purpose is to encourage the development of guiding principles and techniques of international **air transport** and to promote and conduct both planning and development of international air navigation. Its work focuses on such matters as air traffic control, safety standards for aircraft, and the licensing of pilots. *See also* FUNCTIONALISM.

INTERNATIONAL CIVIL SERVICE. Staffing concept that has its origins in the **League of Nations** and is embedded in key provisions of the United Nations Charter. Article 100 of the charter stipulates that "In the performance of their duties the **secretary-general** and the staff shall not seek or receive instructions from any government or from any other authority external to the Organization." In addition, "They shall refrain from any action which might reflect on their position as international officials responsible to the Organization." In turn, each member state "undertakes to respect the exclusively international character of the responsibilities of the secretary-general and the staff and not to seek to influence them in the discharge of their responsibilities."

Lauded as "one of the most important and promising developments of the twentieth century" by Secretary-General **Trygve Lie**, the notion of an independent international civil service, whose members perform their functions free from any national influence and solely in the interest of the organization, while enshrined in the UN Staff Rules and Regulations and the **Convention on the Privileges and Immunities of the United Nations**, has nevertheless been repeatedly flouted by member states. Between 1951 and 1953, the United States forced the resignation of more than 40 UN officials on account of their alleged "anti-American activities." The Soviet Union portrayed the independence of the international civil service as a mere "fiction." In fact, virtually all members of the organization have sought to secure as many posts as possible for their nationals, prompting recurrent complaints of improper attempts to influence personnel decisions by successive secretaries-general.

With the end of the **Cold War**, these problems have lost some of their acuity but others have cropped up in the wake of the organization's growing involvement in internal conflicts, especially the increasing security risks facing UN staff in the field. The display of the United Nations flag and other symbolic paraphernalia of the organization had traditionally ensured a reasonable degree of safety for its personnel. But the image of neutrality that they projected can no longer be taken for granted, as UN staff have more and more been the target of attacks, physical assault, armed robbery, kidnapping, and murder. This qualitative change in perception was dramatically underlined by the attack on 19 August 2003 on the United Nations headquarters in Baghdad, which brought home the painful message that the organization, while continuing to be confronted by traditional threats of criminal activity and the collateral effects of social disorder, must now also cope with the threat of deliberate direct attacks.

A related issue is the integrity of the international civil service, which has come under scrutiny in the wake of a number of financial irregularities uncovered in the implementation of the **Oil for Food Program**. *See also* PERSONNEL QUESTIONS; UNITED NATIONS SYSTEM STAFF COLLEGE.

INTERNATIONAL CIVILIAN MISSION IN HAITI (MICIVIH, 1993–1999). A joint undertaking of the United Nations and the **Organization of American States** authorized by the **General Assembly** to monitor and promote respect for **human rights** in **Haiti**. MICIVIH was set up at the request of Haitian president Jean-Bertrand Aristide, who was ousted from power by a military coup. After the return of constitutional rule in 1994, the mandate of the mission was expanded to include institution building. *See also* INTERNATIONAL CIVILIAN MISSION SUPPORT IN HAITI (MICAH, 1999–2001); UNITED NATIONS CIVILIAN POLICE MISSION IN HAITI (MIPONUH, December 1997–March 2000); UNITED NATIONS MISSION IN HAITI (UNMIH, September 1993–June 1996); UNITED NATIONS OBSERVER GROUP FOR THE VERIFICATION OF ELECTIONS IN HAITI (ONUVEH); UNITED NATIONS STABILIZATION MISSION IN HAITI (MINUSTAH, April 2004–present); UNITED NATIONS SUPPORT MISSION IN HAITI (UNSMIH, 1996–1997); UNITED NATIONS TRANSITION MISSION IN HAITI (UNTMIH, August–November 1997).

INTERNATIONAL CIVILIAN MISSION SUPPORT IN HAITI (MICAH, 1999–2001). Approved by the **General Assembly**, the International Civilian Support Mission in **Haiti** was designed to consolidate the results achieved by its predecessor missions in the promotion of **human rights** and the strengthening of the Haitian police and judiciary. *See also* INTERNATIONAL CIVILIAN MISSION IN HAITI (MICIVIH, 1993–1999); UNITED NATIONS CIVILIAN

POLICE MISSION IN HAITI (MIPONUH, December 1997–March 2000); UNITED NATIONS MISSION IN HAITI (UNMIH, September 1993–June 1996); UNITED NATIONS OBSERVER GROUP FOR THE VERIFICATION OF ELECTIONS IN HAITI (ONUVEH); UNITED NATIONS STABILIZATION MISSION IN HAITI (MINUSTAH, April 2004–present); UNITED NATIONS SUPPORT MISSION IN HAITI (UNSMIH, 1996–1997); UNITED NATIONS TRANSITION MISSION IN HAITI (UNTMIH, August–November 1997).

INTERNATIONAL COMMISSION OF JURISTS (ICJ). Nongovernmental organization (NGO) founded in 1952 and headquartered in Geneva. Its membership is composed of eminent jurists representative of the different legal systems of the world. The commission focuses its work on the promotion of **international law** and principles that advance **human rights**. Reputed for its impartiality and objectivity, it provides legal expertise and advice to the **Commission for Human Rights**.

INTERNATIONAL COMMISSION ON INTERVENTION AND STATE SOVEREIGNTY. Group of experts set up in 2000 with the assistance of the government of Canada to inquire into ways and means whereby the international community could and should respond to massive violations of humanitarian norms and principles in the context of respect for the sovereign rights of states. Shaped by the experience of **Rwanda**, the **Bosnian** conflict, and **Kosovo**, the basic idea emerging from their lengthy and thoughtful report is that sovereign states have a responsibility to protect their citizens and when they are unwilling or unable to do so, that responsibility should be borne by the broader community of states. The idea has been embraced by the **secretary-general** and the **High-Level Panel on Threats, Challenges, and Change**. The latter describes it as an "emerging norm" implicitly suggesting that the principle is not yet universally accepted. *See also* HUMANITARIAN INTERVENTION; INDEPENDENT INTERNATIONAL COMMISSION ON KOSOVO; SOVEREIGNTY; REFORM, UNITED NATIONS.

INTERNATIONAL COMMITTEE OF THE RED CROSS (ICRC). Founded in 1863 to provide relief for soldiers wounded in battle, the International Committee of the Red Cross is a Swiss-based organization with an international status recognized in the 1949 **Geneva Convention**. The ICRC provides legal protection to military and civilian victims of international conflicts and civil wars. It has played and continues to play a significant role in the development and codification of **humanitarian law**. The ICRC has observer status at the United Nations. *See also* CONVENTION ON THE PROHIBITION OF THE USE, STOCKPILING, PRODUCTION, AND TRANSFER OF ANTIPERSONNEL MINES AND ON THEIR DESTRUCTION (1999); HUMANITARIAN AGENCIES; RED CROSS, THE.

INTERNATIONAL CONFERENCE ON FINANCING FOR DE-VELOPMENT (MONTERREY, MEXICO, 18–22 March 2002). The culmination of a four-year-long preparatory process, the Monterrey Conference was the first UN-sponsored **global conference** on financial and development issues, bringing together representatives of finance ministers; leaders from the private sector; intergovernmental financial, trade, and monetary organizations; and civil society. The conference recognized the link between financing for development and the objectives of the **Millennium Declaration**. Achieving these goals, the conference concluded, required new partnerships between developed and developing countries, together with innovative approaches to public-private relationships.

The final document adopted by the conference—the so-called Monterrey Consensus—calls for an ongoing process of negotiations and consultations within the United Nations and the **Bretton Woods institutions** on virtually all policy issues that had been for decades on the agenda of the **North-South dialogue**, notably the mobilization of domestic resources; **foreign direct investment** and other private flows; **international trade**; increases in financial and **technical assistance**; external **debt**; and the reform of the international monetary, financial, and trade systems. *See also* BUSINESS COUNCIL FOR THE UNITED NATIONS (BCUN); WORLD SUMMIT ON THE INFORMATION SOCIETY (WSIS) (GENEVA, 10–12 December 2003/TUNIS, TUNISIA, 16–18 November 2005).

INTERNATIONAL CONFERENCE ON POPULATION (BUCH-AREST, 1974). One of the world conferences sponsored by the United Nations in the field of population. Primarily concerned with encouraging national and international policies to slow down the rate of world population growth, the conference did recognize the existence of a global population problem and, more hesitantly so, that demographic policies could not succeed unless they were integrated in socioeconomic development considerations. Taking place amid proposals for a **New International Economic Order**, Third World countries interpreted Western insistence on population control as a substitute for necessary financial aid and argued that the solution to population growth lay in equitable development. *See also* COMMISSION ON POPULATION AND DEVELOPMENT (UNITED NATIONS); INTERNATIONAL CONFERENCE ON POPULATION (MEXICO, 1984); INTERNATIONAL CONFERENCE ON POPULATION AND DEVELOPMENT (ICPD, CAIRO, 1994); POPULATION PROGRAMS OF THE UNITED NATIONS; UNITED NATIONS POPULATION DIVISION.

INTERNATIONAL CONFERENCE ON POPULATION (MEXICO, 1984). Second major conference organized by the United Nations on **population** issues. It was marked by a shift in leadership from North to South over matters and methods of world population control as the declaration emerging from the conference confirmed that development and family planning are mutually reinforcing rather than competitive approaches to lowering population growth. *See also* COMMISSION ON POPULATION AND DEVELOPMENT (UNITED NATIONS); INTERNATIONAL CONFERENCE ON POPULATION (BUCHAREST, 1974); INTERNATIONAL CONFERENCE ON POPULATION AND DEVELOPMENT (ICPD, CAIRO, 1994); POPULATION PROGRAMS OF THE UNITED NATIONS; UNITED NATIONS POPULATION DIVISION.

INTERNATIONAL CONFERENCE ON POPULATION AND DEVELOPMENT (ICPD, CAIRO, 1994). Third in a series of world conferences on population issues organized by the United Nations. Whereas previous conferences had focused on demographics and birth control, the Cairo conference reached a fragile consensus underlining the need to integrate population concerns into economic and social policies and emphasized the centrality of the role of **women** in the population-development policy agenda. The Vatican and Latin American states expressed reservations on the provisions of the plan adopted by the conference on abortion and contraception issues. Several Muslim countries also expressed reservations on matters related to the status and rights of women. Nevertheless, the conference set the specific goal of making family planning universally available by 2015 and to provide women with expanded access to education and health services and to employment opportunities by the same year. *See also* COMMISSION ON POPULATION AND DEVELOPMENT (UNITED NATIONS); GLOBAL CONFERENCES (UNITED NATIONS); INTERNATIONAL CONFERENCE ON POPULATION (BUCHAREST, 1974); INTERNATIONAL CONFERENCE ON POPULATION (MEXICO, 1984); MILLENNIUM DECLARATION; POPULATION PROGRAMS OF THE UNITED NATIONS; UNITED NATIONS POPULATION DIVISION; UNITED NATIONS POPULATION FUND (UNFPA).

INTERNATIONAL CONVENTION ON THE ELIMINATION OF ALL FORMS OF RACIAL DISCRIMINATION (1965). Legal instrument building upon a 1963 declaration of the **General Assembly**. Under the terms of its sweeping but not altogether effective provisions, states parties pledge to engage in no act or practice of racial discrimination and to refrain from sponsoring, defending, or supporting racial discrimination. They are also bound to review national and local policies and to amend laws and regulations creating or perpetuating racial discrimination. They must also prohibit racial discrimination by persons, groups, and organizations and encourage integrationist or multiracial organizations and movements and other means of eliminating barriers between races. The implementation of the convention is monitored by a **Committee on the Elimination of Racial Discrimination**. *See also* HUMAN RIGHTS; TREATY BODIES.

INTERNATIONAL CONVENTION ON THE PROTECTION OF THE RIGHTS OF ALL MIGRANT WORKERS AND MEMBERS OF THEIR FAMILIES (2003). Adopted without a vote by the **General Assembly** in 1990 after 10 years of negotiations and entered into force in 2003, this treaty provides a comprehensive framework for the protection of **migrants** by transit, sending, and host countries. The convention does not create new rights for migrants but seeks to guarantee equality of treatment and the same working conditions for migrants and nationals.

The implementation of the convention is overseen by an expert committee. So far, countries that have ratified the convention are primarily countries of origin of migrants. No Western migrant-receiving country has yet ratified the convention, although the majority of migrant workers (nearly 100 million out of a total of 175) live in Europe and North America. *See also* HUMAN RIGHTS; INTERNATIONAL LABOUR ORGANIZATION (ILO); TREATY BODIES.

INTERNATIONAL COUNCIL FOR SCIENCE (ICSU). Originally called the International Council for Scientific Unions. **Nongovernmental organization (NGO)** created in 1931 to promote the participation of scientists in programs addressing major international issues. The ICSU has close ties with the **specialized agencies** and the **United Nations Educational, Scientific, and Cultural Organization (UNESCO)** in particular. It plays an important role in the implementation of the **United Nations Framework Convention on Climate Change (UNFCCC)**. *See also* WORLD CLIMATE RESEARCH PROGRAM (WCRP).

INTERNATIONAL COURT OF JUSTICE (ICJ). Established under Chapter XIV of the United Nations **Charter**, the ICJ is the principal judicial organ of the United Nations. It is composed of 15 judges elected by the **General Assembly** and the **Security Council** for nine-year terms. The seat of the Court is in The Hague.

The court began work in 1946 replacing the Permanent Court of International Justice, which had functioned under the aegis of the **League of Nations**. It operates under a statute that is largely similar to that of its predecessor and that is an integral part of the Charter of the UN.

The ICJ renders decisions on disputes between states that have accepted its jurisdiction. It may also give **advisory opinions** on the interpretation of treaties or any other question of international law. This procedure is opened only to the principal organs of the United Nations and the **specialized agencies** of the UN. The reluctance of member states of the UN to have recourse of judicial settlement by and large accounts for the court's relatively scanty caseload. *See also* JUDICIAL SETTLEMENT; NICARAGUA QUESTION; NUCLEAR

WEAPONS (PROHIBITION OF THE USE); SOUTHWEST AFRICA; UNITED NATIONS AOUZOU STRIP OBSERVER GROUP (UNASOG, April–June 1994); WEAPONS OF MASS DESTRUCTION (WMDs); WESTERN SAHARA DISPUTE (1976).

INTERNATIONAL COVENANT ON CIVIL AND POLITICAL RIGHTS (ICCPR, 1966). This covenant was adopted by the **General Assembly** in 1966 and entered into force in 1976. Together with the **International Covenant on Economic, Social, and Cultural Rights**, it complements the general framework of internationally recognized human rights established in the 1948 **Universal Declaration of Human Rights**.

Some of the principal individual civil and political rights are the right to life, liberty, and freedom of movement; assembly and association; equality before the law; privacy; physical and mental well-being; freedom of thought, conscience, and expression; the right to own property; and the right to participate in the political affairs of the country. The covenant forbids torture and inhuman or degrading treatment; slavery or involuntary servitude; arbitrary arrest and detention; and propaganda advocating either war or hatred based on race, religion, national, origins, or language. It also restricts the death penalty to the most serious crimes and prohibits it entirely for people under 18 of age.

The covenant permits governments to temporarily suspend some of these rights in cases of civil emergency and establishes a United Nations **Human Rights Committee** to monitor its implementation. An optional protocol to the covenant allows the **Commission for Human Rights** to investigate complaints of human rights violations from individuals belonging to state parties.

INTERNATIONAL COVENANT ON ECONOMIC, SOCIAL, AND CULTURAL RIGHTS (ICESCR, 1966). This treaty, finalized together with the **International Covenant on Civil and Political Rights**, clarifies the basic economic, social, and cultural rights that individuals are entitled to. These include the right to work under favorable conditions; to wages sufficient to support a minimum standard of living; to form trade unions and strike; to social security; to adequate standards of living; to physical and mental health; to free primary education; and to copyright, patent, and trademark protection for intellectual property. In addition, the covenant forbids the exploitation of **children**.

The Covenant entered into force in 1976 and requires states parties to submit annual reports on their progress in providing for these rights to the **secretary-general**, who in turn transmits them to the **Economic and Social Council**. *See also* COMMITTEE ON ECONOMIC, SOCIAL, AND CULTURAL RIGHTS (CESCR).

INTERNATIONAL CRIMINAL COURT (ICC). The idea of creating a permanent International Criminal Court was first considered in 1948 by the **International Law Commission**, but no action was taken on the commission's favorable assessment and recommendation, primarily as a result of differences arising from **Cold War** power struggles. The post–Cold War explosion of internal conflicts and civil wars led the **Security Council** to create ad hoc tribunals to address war crimes in the former Yugoslavia, Rwanda, and Sierra Leone. In 1995, the **General Assembly** established a preparatory committee charged with drafting the statute of an International Criminal Court. Drawing from the 1948 Genocide Convention and the experience of the Nuremberg and Tokyo tribunals, the **International Criminal Tribunal for the Former Yugoslavia (ICTY)**, and the **International Criminal Tribunal for Rwanda (ICTR)**, the committee completed its work two years later. In 1998, its proposals were endorsed by a full diplomatic conference in Rome by a vote of 120 to 7, with 21 countries abstaining, as no consensus could be reached at the conference on the ICC's jurisdiction over individuals.

Under the terms of its statute, the states parties as well as the UN **Security Council** can refer situations to the court for investigation. The court has jurisdiction over individuals having committed the most serious crimes, including genocide, mass murder, enslavement, rape, torture, and, once it is defined, the crime of **aggression**. Having received the necessary number of ratifications, the treaty took effect on 1 July 2002. Seated in The Hague, the court was officially inaugurated on 3 March 2003. *See also* GENOCIDE; INTERNATIONAL MILITARY TRIBUNAL FOR THE FAR EAST (1946–1948); INTERNATIONAL MILITARY TRIBUNAL FOR THE PROSECUTION AND PUNISHMENT OF THE MAJOR WAR CRIMINALS

(NUREMBERG TRIBUNAL, 1945–1946); WAR CRIMES TRI-BUNALS.

INTERNATIONAL CRIMINAL TRIBUNAL FOR RWANDA (ICTR). Set up in 1994 by the **Security Council** to try persons accused of **genocide** and serious violations of **international humanitarian law** between 1 January and 31 December 1994. The ICTR has been the target of criticisms similar to those addressed toward the **International Criminal Tribunal for the Former Yugoslavia (ICTY)**. It is located in Arusha, Tanzania. *See also* HUMAN RIGHTS; HUMANITARIAN LAW; INTERNATIONAL CRIMINAL COURT (ICC); SPECIAL COURT FOR SIERRA LEONE; WAR CRIMES TRIBUNALS.

INTERNATIONAL CRIMINAL TRIBUNAL FOR THE FORMER YUGOSLAVIA (ICTY). Established in 1993 by the **Security Council** to try four clusters of offenses: grave breaches of the **Geneva Conventions**, violations of the law and customs of war, genocide, and crimes against humanity committed on the territory of the former Yugoslavia since 1991. Seated in The Hague, the legality of its establishment was initially questioned, prompting at the time renewed calls for the creation of a permanent **International Criminal Court (ICC)**. Although a number of major defendants have been brought to trial, including former president Slobodan Milosevic, the tribunal has been criticized for the lack of consistency in its judgments and the slowness of its proceedings. *See also* HUMAN RIGHTS; HUMANITARIAN LAW; INTERNATIONAL CRIMINAL TRIBUNAL FOR RWANDA (ICTR); SPECIAL COURT FOR SIERRA LEONE; WAR CRIMES TRIBUNALS.

INTERNATIONAL DEVELOPMENT ASSOCIATION (IDA). Established in 1960 as an affiliate of the **World Bank**, the IDA provides interest-free credits to the poorest among developing countries. Its loans (cumulatively $135 billion until now) are targeted at the provision of basic services such as education, health care, clean water, and sanitation. The IDA also supports reforms and investment aimed at employment creation and increased productivity. See also INTERNATIONAL BANK FOR RECONSTRUCTION AND DEVELOP-

MENT (IBRD); INTERNATIONAL FINANCE CORPORATION (IFC); WORLD BANK GROUP.

INTERNATIONAL DEVELOPMENT STRATEGY (IDS). Term referring to the set of goals, national and international policies, and benchmarks promoted by the United Nations for the four successive development decades that it proclaimed since 1961. *See also* DAYS-YEARS-DECADES (INTERNATIONAL); MILLENNIUM DECLARATION.

INTERNATIONAL ENERGY AGENCY (IEA). International organization established in 1974 in response to the oil shocks of the 1960s to early 1970s by oil-consuming industrialized countries. The functions of the organization located in Paris are to assist its members in coping with disruptions in the supply of oil, promote efficient national **energy** policies, exchange information on energy markets, and encourage the development of alternative sources of energy.

INTERNATIONAL FINANCE CORPORATION (IFC). Established in 1956 as a member of the **World Bank Group**, the IFC is the largest multilateral source of loan and equity financing for private enterprise in developing countries. It provides long-term loans, guarantees, and risk management as well as advisory services. Its current committed portfolio amounts to some $21 billion. *See also* INTERNATIONAL DEVELOPMENT ASSOCIATION (IDA).

INTERNATIONAL FUND FOR AGRICULTURAL DEVELOPMENT (IFAD). Established in 1977 as the 13th **specialized agency** of the United Nations, the IFAD is an offshoot of a United Nations **global conference**, the World Food Conference that was held in Rome in 1974. The conference coincided with large-scale famine in the African Sahel and concluded that food and nutrition problems were less the result of occasional crop failures than deep-seated developmental and poverty issues.

IFAD was accordingly given the task to provide loans on highly concessional terms to the poorest people in the poorest areas: small farmers, artisans, fishermen, nomadic herdspeople, rural landless, and poor rural women. The fund is jointly funded by Western countries, which contribute 60 percent of its budget, and oil-exporting nations belonging to the **Organization of Petroleum Exporting Countries (OPEC)**, which contribute 40 percent. *See also* FOOD SECURITY.

INTERNATIONAL LABOUR ORGANIZATION (ILO). The International Labour Organization came into existence in 1919 as an autonomous institution associated with the **League of Nations**. In 1946, it became the United Nations' first specialized agency.

The ILO's goals are to improve working and living conditions, to defend **human rights,** and to promote productive employment. The ILO differs from other **specialized agencies** because of its tripartite structure. Each national delegation has four members: two government representatives, one worker's delegate, and one employer's delegate.

The ILO carries out extensive operational programs and educational and research work. Its main function is the elaboration and adoption of international conventions and recommendations, setting norms and standards on basic labor rights such as freedom of association, the right to organize, collective bargaining, abolition of forced labor, equality of opportunity and treatment, and other work-related issues pertaining, for instance, to **migrants** or **indigenous peoples**. Each member state having ratified ILO conventions must provide periodic reports describing the measures taken to implement their provisions, which are reviewed for comments and observations by a body of independent jurists. *See also* EMPLOYMENT.

INTERNATIONAL LAW. Principles, customs, and rules governing the conduct of states and international organizations and, increasingly, individuals and other **nonstate actors**. In comparison to national legal systems, international law is primitive, as the principle of **sovereignty** restricts its effective enforcement. Yet, the United Nations has provided the setting for the negotiations of numerous international declarations, conventions, and treaties that have considerably expanded the scope of international legal standards and norms, especially in regard to the **environment**, economic relations, and **human rights**. *See also* INTERNATIONAL COURT OF JUSTICE (ICJ); INTERNATIONAL CRIMINAL COURT (ICC); INTERNATIONAL LAW COMMISSION (ILC); INTERNATIONAL TRI-

BUNAL FOR THE LAW OF THE SEA; JUDICIAL SETTLE-
MENT; UNITED NATIONS COMMISSION ON INTERNA-
TIONAL TRADE LAW (UNCITRAL); UNITED NATIONS CON-
VENTION ON THE LAW OF THE SEA (UNCLOS, 1982); WAR
CRIMES TRIBUNALS.

INTERNATIONAL LAW COMMISSION (ILC). Established in November 1947 by the **General Assembly**, the mandate of the International Law Commission is to promote the progressive development
and codification of **international law**. The commission's work has
focused on the preparation of drafts on topics of international public
law, such as the regime of the high seas and territorial waters, the law
of treaties, arbitral procedures, and succession of states in respect to
treaties. Topics may be chosen by the commission and approved or
suggested by the General Assembly or the **Economic and Social
Council (ECOSOC)**. When the commission completes its draft articles on a particular topic, the General Assembly usually convenes an
international conference to incorporate them into a convention
opened to states for signature. An important achievement of the commission has been the preparation of a draft statute for an **International Criminal Court (ICC)** that provided the basis for the negotiations that led to the creation of the court in 1998. The commission
has also produced treaties on the reduction of statelessness, diplomatic and consular relations, the law of treaties, and succession of
states in respect of treaties. *See also* VIENNA CONVENTION ON
DIPLOMATIC RELATIONS (1961); VIENNA CONVENTION ON
THE LAW OF TREATIES.

INTERNATIONAL MARITIME ORGANIZATION (IMO). Established in 1948, the IMO is a **specialized agency** of the UN that began operations in 1959. Its goal is to improve the safety of international **shipping** and to prevent marine **pollution** from ships through
the development of international regulatory standards. Assessed contributions of member states to the IMO budget are based primarily on
the tonnage of their merchant fleet, a formula different from that used
in other United Nations intergovernmental bodies. *See also* FUNC-
TIONALISM; VOTING.

INTERNATIONAL MEETING TO REVIEW THE IMPLEMEN- TATION OF THE PROGRAMME OF ACTION FOR THE SUS- TAINABLE DEVELOPMENT OF SMALL ISLAND DEVEL- OPING STATES (PORT-LOUIS, MAURITIUS, 10–14 January 2005). Follow-up meeting to the 1994 **United Nations Conference on the Sustainable Development of Small Developing States** primarily intended to win international recognition of the vulnerabilities of small islands and mobilize political and financial support for their sustainable development.

The major outcome document of the conference, the Mauritius Strategy for further implementation of the Barbados Program of Action, emphasizes that small island developing States (SIDS) "are located among the most vulnerable regions in the world in relation to the intensity and frequency of natural and environmental disasters and their increasing impact, and face disproportionately high economic, social and environmental consequence." On trade issues, the Mauritius Strategy recognizes that "most small island developing States, as a result of their smallness, persistent structural disadvantages and vulnerabilities, face specific difficulties in integrating into the global economy." The document also recognizes "the importance of intensifying efforts to facilitate the full and effective participation" by small island developing States "in the deliberations and decision-making process of the **World Trade Organization (WTO)**." On **climate change**, the strategy indicates "that they [SIDs] are already experiencing major adverse effects of climate change" and that "adaptation to adverse impacts of climate change and sea-level rise remains a major priority" for them. A "Declaration" appended to the strategy reiterates that international trade is "important for building resilience and the sustainable development" of SIDS, and calls upon international institutions, including financial institutions, to "pay appropriate attention to the structural disadvantages" of SIDS. *See also* AGENDA 21; WORLD CONFERENCE ON DISASTER REDUCTION; UNITED NATIONS CONFERENCE ON ENVIRONMENT AND DEVELOPMENT (UNCED, RIO DE JANEIRO, 1992).

INTERNATIONAL MILITARY TRIBUNAL FOR THE FAR EAST (1946–1948). Tribunal established by the Allies in 1946 to bring to trial Japanese officials suspected of war crimes and crimes against humanity. The tribunal followed the principles set forth by the **International Military Tribunal for the Prosecution and Punishment of the Major War Criminals**, or Nuremberg Tribunal. *See also* WAR CRIMES TRIBUNALS.

INTERNATIONAL MILITARY TRIBUNAL FOR THE PROSECUTION AND PUNISHMENT OF THE MAJOR WAR CRIMINALS (NUREMBERG TRIBUNAL, 1945–1946). The first modern international criminal court constituted by victorious Allied powers after their defeat of the Axis Powers. Another similar court—the **International Military Tribunal for the Far East**—was set up to try Japanese war criminals. The German defendants were tried for crimes against peace, crimes against humanity, and war crimes. The court's judgment was based in part on the principle that political leaders waging an aggressive war incur criminal responsibility under **international law** and cannot invoke internal laws for their defense.

The charges of crimes against humanity and individual liability have been criticized by some as constituting retroactive legislation and "victor's justice." The legal debate notwithstanding, the judgment of the Nuremberg Tribunal constituted a precedent for the future that paved the way to the creation of the **International Criminal Tribunal for the Former Yugoslavia** and the **International Criminal Court**. It was endorsed by the **General Assembly** in 1946 and the **International Law Commission**, which was asked by the assembly in 1947 to prepare a draft code relating to the Nuremberg principles. *See also* CRIMES AGAINST HUMANITY; CRIMES AGAINST PEACE; INTERNATIONAL CRIMINAL TRIBUNAL FOR RWANDA (ICTR); SPECIAL COURT FOR SIERRA LEONE; WAR CRIMES TRIBUNALS.

INTERNATIONAL MONETARY FUND (IMF). Created at the 1944 **Bretton Woods Conference** with a view to avoiding a repetition of the disastrous economic policies that had contributed to the Great Depression of the 1930s, the IMF was intended to promote international monetary cooperation, to facilitate the expansion and balanced growth of international trade, to assist in the establishment of a multilateral system of payments, and to make its resources available under adequate safeguards to members experiencing balance of payment difficulties. The 1971 U.S. decision to suspend fixed exchange rates between the U.S. dollar and gold weakened the impact of exchange-rate management on the workings of the world economy. But the fund has gained a larger role in shaping its members' macroeconomic policies in the wake of the rise in oil prices in the 1970s and the international **debt** problems that have since the 1980s affected **developing countries**.

Along with the World Bank and some of the other **specialized agencies** of the United Nations, the IMF operates on a system of **weighted voting**. Votes are allocated according to the amount of money each country has paid into the fund, which is referred to as its "quota." Quotas are reviewed periodically and generate the pool of money from which member countries may borrow and the total amount of credit a member is eligible to receive.

A most controversial aspect of the fund's activities is the "conditionality" of its loans. Members may borrow money only if they introduce "structural adjustment measures" to reduce their deficits. These typically include currency devaluations; reductions in budget deficits through cuts in public spending, subsidies, and price controls; raising taxes; restructuring public enterprises; the elimination of foreign exchange and trade controls; and structural reforms in the agriculture and financial sectors. In response to widespread criticisms that the adjustment measures increased the incidence of **poverty** and were ill suited, the fund has softened the terms of the conditionality of its loans.

INTERNATIONAL ORGANIZATION FOR MIGRATION (IOM). Intergovernmental institution tracing its origins to a 1951 organization set up to resettle European displaced persons, refugees, and migrants (the Intergovernmental Committee for European Migration). The IOM has since grown into a multitask entity with offices and operations on every continent. Its functions encompass a wide variety of activities designed to assist governments and civil society through rapid humanitarian responses to sudden migration flows, post-emergency return and reintegration programs, assistance to migrants in distress, and research related to migration management.

While not part of the United Nations system, IOM maintains close ties with UN bodies and operational agencies. IOM currently assists some 12 million migrants. It has provided assistance to third-country nationals fleeing the conflict in Iraq, and in **Kosovo**, its work has evolved from emergency response to long-term activities in support of population stabilization. Working with the United Nations and the government of **Sudan**, it is currently assisting internally displaced persons in the Darfur Western region of the country. IOM has carried out out-of-country registration and voting programs in recent elections held in **Afghanistan**, Pakistan, and Iran.

INTERNATIONAL PEACE ACADEMY (IPA). Independent, international think tank promoting the prevention and settlement of armed conflicts between and within states through applied policy research and development. The International Peace Academy works closely with the United Nations, regional and other international organizations, governments, and **nongovernmental organizations (NGOs)**, as well as with parties to conflicts in selected cases. It also draws from a worldwide network of government and **business** leaders, scholars, diplomats, military officers, and leaders of **civil society** in its policy research projects.

Originally primarily concerned with peace and security issues, notably **peacekeeping**, the IPA progressively broadened the scope of its programs to an exploration of strategies for **conflict prevention**, conflict management, and **peace building**. The United Nations remains the principal focal point of its research, but the IPA has also examined the role of subregional and regional organizations, the **Bretton Woods institutions**, NGOs, and private sector actors. Its most recent programs focus on ways and means to enhance the security infrastructure in Africa, to strengthen the nexus between security and development programming, and to assess the UN's state-building efforts. *See also* RIKHYE, INDAR JIT (1920–).

INTERNATIONAL REFUGEE ORGANIZATION (IRO). Agency of the United Nations set up in 1946 for assisting in the care, repatriation, and resettlement of **refugees** in war-torn Europe. The IRO brought to completion some of the work previously undertaken by the **United Nations Relief and Rehabilitation Administration** and was disbanded in 1952. Its activities were taken over by the Office of the **United Nations High Commissioner for Refugees (UNHCR)**.

INTERNATIONAL RESCUE COMMITTEE (IRC). Founded in 1933, the International Rescue Committee is a **nongovernmental organization (NGO)** providing relief, rehabilitation, protection, postconflict development, and resettlement services for those uprooted or affected by violent conflict and political repression. The IRC works in some 25 countries, focusing on rebuilding shattered communities; the rehabilitation of health care, water, and sanitation systems; the reunification of families; the establishment of schools; the training of teachers; the strengthening of the capacity of local organizations and institutions; the development of civil society and good-governance initiatives; and the promotion of human rights.

INTERNATIONAL RESEARCH AND TRAINING INSTITUTE FOR THE ADVANCEMENT OF WOMEN (INSTRAW). Autonomous research organization within the United Nations carrying out research and training programs to help integrate and mobilize women in development. Located in Santo Domingo (Dominican Republic) the institute has been experiencing financial difficulties threatening its viability.

INTERNATIONAL TELECOMMUNICATIONS UNION (ITU). Originally founded in 1864 under the name of International Telegraph Union to coordinate the operation of **telecommunication** networks and services, the union became a **specialized agency** of the United Nations under its present name in 1947. Its membership is unique, as it encompasses telecommunication policy makers and regulators, network operators, equipment manufacturers, hardware and software developers, regional standard-making organizations, and financing institutions. The ITU's research, standard setting, and radio frequency allocation and management activities have helped foster the growth of new technologies and facilitated the operation of radio-based systems like cellular phones, aircraft and maritime navigation systems, scientific research stations, satellite communications systems, and radio and television broadcasting. Its work has increasingly focused on telecommunication development in developing countries. The Union sponsored a **World Summit on the Information Society** that was held in 2005. *See also* INFORMATION TECHNOLOGY (IT).

INTERNATIONAL TRADE. *See* GENERAL AGREEMENT ON TARIFFS AND TRADE (GATT); GLOBALIZATION; INTERNATIONAL TRADE CENTRE (ITC); INTERNATIONAL TRADE ORGANIZATION (ITO); LIBERAL INTERNATIONALISM; TRADE AND DEVELOPMENT; UNITED NATIONS CONFERENCE ON TRADE AND DEVELOPMENT (UNCTAD); WASHINGTON CONSENSUS; WORLD TRADE ORGANIZATION (WTO).

INTERNATIONAL TRADE CENTRE (ITC). Technical cooperation body created in 1964 under the aegis of the now defunct **General Agreement on Tariffs and Trade (GATT).** Jointly funded by the **United Nations Conference on Trade and Development (UNCTAD)** and the **World Trade Organization (WTO)**, the ITC assists businesses in the understanding of WTO rules, strengthening their competitiveness and developing trade promotion strategies.

INTERNATIONAL TRADE ORGANIZATION (ITO). After preliminary negotiations in London and Geneva, a draft charter for an ITO was agreed on at the United Nations Conference on Trade and Employment at Havana, Cuba, in 1948. The new ITO would have functioned as a **specialized agency** of the United Nations and provided a multilateral framework for the orderly expansion of a free-trading international system. Proposed by the United States, the ITO was supposed to complement the work of the **Bretton Woods institutions**. The project was attacked by lobbyists and pressure groups in the U.S. Congress as a threat to American sovereignty and a communist plot. Fears that American producers would not be able to compete with low-wage producers abroad prevailed and the project quietly died in the United States Senate. *See also* GENERAL AGREEMENT ON TARIFFS AND TRADE (GATT).

INTERNATIONAL TRIBUNAL FOR THE LAW OF THE SEA. Established in accordance with the 1982 **United Nations Convention on the Law of the Sea**, this judicial body adjudicates disputes among the parties to the Convention. Located in Hamburg, Federal Republic of Germany, the tribunal became operational in 2002.

IRAN HOSTAGE CRISIS (4 November 1979–20 January 1981).
Mass demonstrations forced the Shah of Iran, a close ally of the United States to flee the country in January 1979. Following the establishment of an Islamic regime under the virulently anti-American Ayatollah Ruhollah Khomeini, demonstrators attacked and seized the United States embassy in Tehran while Iranian security forces stood by failing to intervene. Most of the hostages were kept for more than 14 months until 20 January 1981.

Initially the Iranian government denied that the embassy takeover had been an official action of the government. But in February 1980, Iran issued a set of demands in return for freeing the hostages, including the return of the deposed Shah to Iran (who had been admitted to the United States for medical treatment) and other diplomatic gestures, notably an apology for prior American actions in Iran and a promise not to interfere in the future. Early on in the crisis, President **Jimmy Carter** applied economic and diplomatic pressure on Iran, ending oil imports from Iran, expelling a number of Iranians in the United States, and freezing some $8 billion of Iranian assets in the United States. Washington also brought the matter to the **International Court of Justice (ICJ)**, which ruled that the Iranian government was indirectly responsible for its omission to protect the embassy. In accordance with the Vienna Convention on Diplomatic Relations, the court also determined that Iran had an obligation to restore the embassy to the United States and to make reparation.

After an abortive military rescue attempt by the United States, the matter was finally settled by an agreement mediated by the Algerian government, which, in turn, led to the establishment of an ad hoc tribunal to deal with outstanding claims between the two countries by **arbitration**.

IRANIAN QUESTION (1946). One of the first **Cold War** skirmishes in the **Security Council**. Iran brought the issue to the council on the grounds that the Soviet Union had failed to withdraw troops from the country at the end of World War II as had been agreed earlier by the Allies. The USSR eventually withdrew its troops and the matter was dropped from the council's agenda.

IRAN-IRAQ WAR (1980–1988). Protracted and bloody conflict triggered by a territorial dispute over a waterway forming the boundary between Iraq and Iran. The war ended in a stalemate but entailed millions of casualties and severe economic damage to both countries. It was also marked by the use of chemical weapons. For a long time, cease-fire appeals by the **Security Council** and the **General Assembly** went unheeded. Several **mediation** efforts by a **special representative of the secretary-general** failed and so did **conciliation** efforts by the **Nonaligned Movement (NAM)**. Sheer exhaustion, the implicit threat of a mandatory arms embargo by the Security Council, and the personal involvement of Secretary-General **Perez de Cuellar** prompted the two warring countries to bring an end to the fighting and accept a cease-fire supervised by United Nations peacekeepers. Comprehensive peace negotiations mediated by the secretary-general ended in a final peace agreement in 1991. *See also* UNITED NATIONS IRAN-IRAQ MILITARY OBSERVER GROUP (UNIIMOG, 9 August 1988–February 1991).

IRAQ. Formed out of three former regions of the Ottoman Empire (Mosul, Baghdad, and Basra), Iraq became a British mandate at the end of World War I. Iraq joined the **League of Nations** and was recognized as a sovereign state after independence from British control in 1932. A popular revolution overthrew the British-installed Hashemite monarchy in 1958, and after a series of coup attempts, the Arab Socialist Baath Party came to power in 1968. Saddam Hussein, a key figure in the Baath Party, acceded to the presidency and control of the country in 1979. Saddam's rule lasted throughout the **Iran-Iraq War (1980–1988)**, killing millions of people on both sides, and ending in a stalemate. The country was involved in two other wars in 1991 and 2003 which eventually resulted in the overthrow of the regime and the trial of its political leaders for crimes against its civilian populations by an ad hoc Iraqi tribunal. *See also* PERSIAN GULF WAR, FIRST (January–February 1991); PERSIAN GULF WAR, SECOND (March–April 2003).

ITALIAN COLONIES (1949–1951). One of the first **decolonization** issues to reach the United Nations and a rare case of peaceful disposition of a colonial problem through the direct involvement of the **General Assembly**. In their peace treaty with Italy during World War II, France, the Soviet Union, the United Kingdom, and the United States had agreed that the assembly would decide on the future status of the Italian colonies if they could not agree among themselves over the matter. Unable to settle their differences, the issue became the responsibility of the assembly, which reviewed it in several of its sessions. The deliberations of the assembly eventually paved the way to Libya's independence in 1951. Somaliland was placed under Italian Trusteeship until 1960 when it achieved independence. Eritrea was associated in a federal arrangement with Ethiopia but became independent in 1993. *See also* SELF-DETERMINATION; TRUSTEESHIP SYSTEM.

– J –

JACKSON, SIR ROBERT (1911–1991). Australian official with an extensive experience of development issues in Asia. He first served the United Nations as senior deputy director-general of the **United Nations Relief and Rehabilitation Administration (UNRRA)** from 1945 to 1947, overseeing its operations in Europe. He subsequently supervised the transfer of UNRRA's residual functions to the **World Health Organization (WHO)** and the **Food and Agriculture Organization (FAO)** and assisted in the establishment of the **International Children's Emergency Fund (UNICEF)**. Thereafter, he was appointed assistant secretary-general for Coordination in the UN (1948), special consultant to the Administrator of the **United Nations Development Programme (UNDP)** (1963–1971), and undersecretary-general in charge of the United Nations Relief Operation in Bangladesh (1972–1974).

Sir Robert is best known for authoring a study of the United Nations development system at the request of the UNDP's governing bodies. The report's sweeping criticisms of the excessive complexity of the UN **technical assistance** machinery and the shortcomings of UN agency assistance programs and their lack of coordination triggered considerable controversy both inside and outside the United Nations. But its recommendations paved the way to a significant decentralization of authority from headquarters to UNDP field offices, which was designed to make UNDP technical assistance more closely linked to the development objectives of recipient countries. *See also* REFORM, UNITED NATIONS.

JARRING, GUNNAR (1907–). Swedish diplomat who became Sweden's ambassador to the United Nations in 1954 and later served as ambassador to the United States and the Soviet Union. From 1967 to 1990 he was **special representative** to the United Nations **secretary-general** on the Middle East, seeking to mediate the **Arab-Israeli conflict**.

JOINT INSPECTION UNIT (JIU). Oversight body created in 1966 by the **General Assembly** to conduct independent assessments of UN activities. Its mandate is to make recommendations to the assembly on ways and means to improve financial and management practices within the United Nations system. Dissatisfaction with the effectiveness of its oversight contributed to the establishment of a new watchdog body within the **secretariat** in the early nineties. *See also* BERTRAND, MAURICE (1922–); CONTROL MECHANISMS (INTERNAL AND EXTERNAL); OFFICE OF INTERNAL OVERSIGHT SERVICES (OIOS).

JOINT UNITED NATIONS PROGRAMME ON HIV/AIDS (UNAIDS). Established in 1994 by a resolution of the **Economic and Social Council (ECOSOC)** and launched in January 1996, UNAIDS is a voluntarily funded interagency program set up in 1996 to assist national governments in their efforts to address the socioeconomic factors driving the HIV/AIDS epidemic. Cosponsored by the **United Nations High Commissioner for Refugees (UNHCR)**, the **United Nations Children's Fund (UNICEF)**, the **United Nations Development Programme (UNDP)**, the **United Nations Population Fund (UNFPA)**, the **United Nations Educational, Scientific, and Cultural Organization (UNESCO)**, the **World Health Organization (WHO)**, the **World Bank (WB)**, the **United Nations Office on Drug Control and Crime (UNODC)**, and the **International Labour Organization (ILO)**, UNAIDS has an annual budget of $60 million and is guided by a coordinating board comprising representatives of governments, UNAIDS' cosponsors, and **nongovernmental organizations (NGOs)**. UNAIDS operates mainly through the country-based staff of its cosponsors in theme groups, sharing information, planning and monitoring coordinated action, and deciding on joint financing of AIDS activities in consultation with the host government. Its objectives are to prevent the spread of AIDS, provide care and support for those infected and affected by the disease, reduce the vulnerability of individuals and communities to HIV/AIDS, and to alleviate the socioeconomic and human impact of the epidemic. One of its key functions is to gather, analyze, and disseminate information on the evolving epidemic and on the global response to it. *See also* COORDINATION, UNITED NATIONS SYSTEM.

JOLLY, SIR RICHARD (1934–). British development economist who combined operational experience with research and teaching. He started his career in development in the 1970s as head of the Institute for Development Studies at the University of Sussex. As a member of the United Nations **Committee for Development Policy (CDP)** (then known as Committee for Development Planning) and thereafter as deputy executive director of the **United Nations Children's Fund** in the 1980s, Jolly and his colleagues offered systematic critiques of existing structural adjustment and development policies that, in their view, were unduly centered on economic models. In so doing they spearheaded efforts to direct attention to the needs of **children**, **women**, and the poor in the making of economic adjustment policies. Joily's groundbreaking study "Adjustment with a Human Face" and advocacy work contributed to shift the concept of **development** away from a purely economic focus to a more people-centered approach, thus paving the way to the notion of human development encapsulated in the **Human Development Report (HDR)** of the **United Nations Development Programme (UNDP)**, which he coordinated from 1996 to 2000. Jolly also championed the so-called 20/20 Initiative, which called for developing and donor countries to devote 20 percent of government budgets and 20 percent of aid allocations, respectively, to basic social services. This proposal was endorsed by the 1995 **World Summit for Social Development**. *See also* HAQ, MAHBUL UL (1934–1999).

JUBILEE RESEARCH. British based **nongovernmental organization (NGO)** describing itself as "not just an economic think-tank . . . (but) a think-and-do tank" advocating a 100 percent cancellation of the unpayable and uncollectable debts of developing countries and the democratization of international financial activities of governments and multilateral institutions. Jubilee Research grew out of Jubilee 2000, which throughout the 1990s orchestrated a worldwide campaign that was critical of the **International Monetary Fund**'s **(IMF)** structural adjustment programs and brought pressure to bear on the leaders of the **Group of Eight (G-8)** (then 7) to "cancel the unpayable debts of the poorest countries by the year 2000, under a fair and transparent process." There were Jubilee 2000 campaigns in more than 60 countries around the world, and by the end of the campaign, 24 million signatures had been gathered for the Jubilee 2000 petition. The G-8 leaders have since committed themselves to writing off $100 billion of poor-country debts, and debt has been pushed onto the global political agenda. Jubilee 2000 and Jubilee Research have earned the reputation for providing up-to-date, accurate research, analyses, news, and data on international debt and finance. *See also* DEBT CRISIS (INTERNATIONAL); HEAVILY INDEBTED POOR COUNTRY INITIATIVE (HIPC).

JUDICIAL SETTLEMENT. Like **arbitration**, judicial settlement or adjudication is a method of peaceful settlement of disputes leading to binding decisions. Adjudication, in contrast to arbitration, which relies on ad hoc procedures and judges selected for each individual case, involves awards and judgments made by a preconstituted and permanent international tribunal on the basis of **international law**. The first such tribunal was established in 1920 when the **League of Nations** created the Permanent Court of International Justice (PCIJ). The PCIJ functioned until 1940 and was replaced seven years later by the **International Court of Justice (ICJ)**, one of the major organs of the United Nations. The jurisdiction of both courts is based on voluntary acceptance by litigating parties. International adjudication is thus a limited and imperfect effort to transpose some of the stability and regularity associated with domestic national legal systems to the settlement of disputes at the international level. *See also* CONCILIATION; ENQUIRY; MEDIATION; REGIONAL ARRANGEMENTS.

– K –

KASHMIR DISPUTE (1948–). India and Pakistan became independent in 1947, and under a partition scheme agreed to with Great

Britain, the autonomous state of Kashmir, populated by a majority of Muslims but ruled by a Hindu maharajah, was to be given the option of joining either Pakistan or India or becoming independent. Faced with Muslim unrest, the Kashmir ruler asked for Indian military assistance and announced the accession of Kashmir to India. Large-scale hostilities immediately erupted as Pakistani troops also intervened. The **Security Council** established a commission to investigate and mediate the dispute. In 1949, the commission was able to secure a truce supervised by the **United Nations Military Observer Group in India and Pakistan (UNMOGIP)** as well as acceptance in principle of a plebiscite to resolve the accession problem. The plebiscite has never been held, India taking the position that Kashmir has become a permanent member of the Indian Union, and Pakistan demanding the organization of a plebiscite. Renewed fighting between India and Pakistan flared up again in 1965 and 1971, and many fear that tensions between the two countries over Kashmir could escalate into a nuclear war.

KATANGA. Mineral rich province of the **Democratic Republic of the Congo** that was prevented from seceding through the intervention of the **United Nations Operation in the Congo (ONUC)**.

KIRKPATRICK, JEAN (1926–). American university educator who served as U.S. ambassador to the United Nations under President Ronald Reagan from 1980 to 1984. An ardent anticommunist, she is famous for her "Kirkpatrick doctrine," which advocated U.S. support of authoritarian governments around the world and unflagging opposition to Third World demands for a **New International Economic Order**. *See also* HERITAGE FOUNDATION.

KLEIN, LAWRENCE (1920–). American economist who drew from the work of **Jan Tinbergen** and developed economic models to forecast the development of business fluctuations and study the effects of government economic policies. He created **Project LINK**, so-called because it links models of the world's countries to measure and assess the effect of changes in one economy on others. Initially based at the University of Pennsylvania, Project LINK is now administered by the United Nations **Department of Economic and Social Affairs**.

KOREAN WAR (25 June 1950–27 July 1953). At the end of World War II, Korea was divided into two zones of occupation: **North Korea** and South Korea under Soviet and American control, respectively. As Cold War tensions rose, rival governments were installed in 1948 and relations between them became increasingly strained. On 25 June 1950, North Korean communist forces invaded South Korea. The same day, in the absence of the Soviet Union, the **Security Council** quickly condemned the **aggression**, called for a cease-fire and asked UN members to assist South Korea. On 27 June, President **Harry S. Truman** ordered U.S. forces into Korea. Several other nations joined the U.S. military effort. Upon the return of the Soviet Union to the council, the USSR vetoed any further possible attempts by the council to direct and coordinate the collective measures it had adopted to repel the North Korean attack. The United States proposed that the **General Assembly** assume the responsibility of dealing with such situations when the Security Council was prevented from acting by **vetoes**. Under the terms of its **Uniting for Peace Resolution**, the assembly thus dealt with the Communist Chinese intervention in Korea in late 1950, declared China guilty of aggression, recommended collective economic measures, and called upon all states to continue to lend every assistance to the United Nations action in Korea. An armistice was signed in 1953, bringing the fighting to an end. *See also* COLLECTIVE SECURITY; SANCTIONS; UNITED NATIONS KOREAN RECONSTRUCTION AGENCY (UNKRA).

KOSOVO QUESTION. Until 1989, Kosovo was an autonomous province within the state of **Yugoslavia**. That autonomy was revoked by President Slobodan Milosevic on the grounds that the Serb minority in Kosovo was at risk. The situation further deteriorated when men and arms started flowing from neighboring Albania in support of an insurgent group in Kosovo, the Kosovo Liberation Army. Large-scale Yugoslav attacks on the KLA and ethnic Albanians resulted in more than 200,000 Kosovar refugees and displaced persons in 1998. The **Security Council**, in resolutions invoking Chapter VII of the United Nations **Charter**, regretted the loss of life and qualified the situation as a threat to regional peace and security but was unable to take further action. Ostensibly to put an end to the killing of the innocent by the Yugoslav army and police forces in Kosovo, the **North**

Atlantic Treaty Organization (NATO) launched in March 1999 an eleven-week-long campaign of air bombardment on Yugoslavia to force a withdrawal of its forces from Kosovo, enable the return of refugees, and pave the way to a political settlement. The legality of the NATO military intervention under the provisions of the United Nations on the **use of force** and international **humanitarian law** is still debated.

With the subsequent establishment of the **United Nations Interim Administration Mission in Kosovo (UNMIK)**, the Security Council has in effect placed Kosovo under a UN protectorate. UNMIK is seeking to build democratic institutions, organize free and fair elections, protect the rights of minorities, establish an impartial legal system, and create a functioning economy before the province's final status is determined. But the underlying cause of the conflict has not been addressed and, for all intents and practical purposes, Kosovo remains ethnically segregated. Most Serbs live either in enclaves or in the northern part that abuts Serbia proper, and UNMIK police and NATO troops provide tenuous security. The UN Security Council, has called for "substantial autonomy and meaningful self-determination for Kosovo." But ethnic Albanians want outright independence or wish to be integrated into a Greater Albania, while the Serb minority (10 percent of the population) would like to return to Serbian rule. In addition to its unresolved political status, Kosovo is saddled with a stalled economy afflicted by rates of unemployment as high as 70 percent. Over 50 percent of the population lives below the national poverty line. *See also* HUMANITARIAN INTERVENTION; INDEPENDENT INTERNATIONAL COMMISSION ON KOSOVO; PEACEKEEPING; TRANSITIONAL ADMINISTRATION.

KYOTO PROTOCOL. Additional legal provision to the 1992 **United Nations Framework Convention on Climate Change (UNFCCC)** agreed to in 1997. The protocol, which came into force in 2005 following ratification by Russia, calls on industrialized countries to reduce their combined emissions of six major greenhouse gases during the five-year period extending from 2008 to 2012 to below 1990 levels. The **European Union** and Japan are to cut these emissions by 8 percent and 6 percent respectively. The United States is not a party to the protocol. *See also* CLIMATE CHANGE; GLOBAL WARMING.

Secretary-General Trygve Lie (1946–1952), Secretary-General Dag Hammarskjöld (1953–1961), Secretary-General U Thant (1961–1971), Secretary-General Kurt Waldheim (1972–1981), and Secretary-General Javier Perez de Cuellar (1982–1991). Courtesy of United Nations Office in Geneva Phototheque

Secretary-General Boutros Boutros-Ghali (1992–1996). Courtesy of United Nations Office in Geneva Phototheque

Secretary-General Kofi Annan (1996–2006). Courtesy of United Nations Office in Geneva Phototheque

San Francisco Conference (1945). Courtesy of United Nations Office in Geneva Phototheque

First General Assembly (1946). Courtesy of United Nations Office in Geneva Phototheque

Security Council meeting on Haiti (1994). Courtesy of United Nations Office in Geneva Phototheque

International Court of Justice in The Hague. Courtesy of United Nations Office in Geneva Phototheque

Talks on Cyprus with Glafcos Clerides, Rauf Denktash, and Kofi Annan (1977). Courtesy of United Nations Office in Geneva Phototheque

United Nations humanitarian assistance in Cyprus (1974). Courtesy of United Nations Office in Geneva Phototheque

United Nations Protection Force in Bosnia Herzegovina (1994). Courtesy of United Nations Office in Geneva Phototheque

United Nations Operation in Mozambique (1994). Courtesy of United Nations Office in Geneva Phototheque

Monitoring elections in Mozambique (1994). Courtesy of United Nations Office in Geneva Phototheque

Refugee camp with Russian refugees. Courtesy of United Nations Office in Geneva Phototheque

UNICEF literacy class in Nigeria. Courtesy of UNICEF (UNOG Phototheque)

Milk distribution by FAO in the Philippines. Courtesy of FAO (UNOG Phototheque)

– L –

LABOR. *See* EMPLOYMENT; INTERNATIONAL LABOUR OR-
GANZATION (ILO).

LAGOS PLAN OF ACTION (1980). A continent-wide effort by
African governments under the aegis of the Organization for African
Unity to forge a long-term comprehensive strategic approach to the
development of Africa. Launched in 1980, the Lagos Plan of Action
rested on the twin requirements of the integration of Africa's physi-
cal, institutional, social, and production structures and the gradual es-
tablishment of an African common market. Neither of these goals
was reached, prompting the search for new regional and international
blueprints for cooperation. *See also* AFRICAN ECONOMIC CON-
DITIONS; NEW PARTNERSHIP FOR AFRICA'S DEVELOP-
MENT (NEPAD); UNITED NATIONS NEW AGENDA FOR THE
DEVELOPMENT OF AFRICA (UN-NADAF); UNITED NATIONS
PROGRAMME OF ACTION FOR AFRICA'S ECONOMIC RE-
COVERY (UN-PAARD, 1986–1990).

LANDLOCKED COUNTRIES. Group of countries that have no
coastline. There are 42 such countries in the world that are placed in
a disadvantageous position insofar as they are cut off from sea resources such as fishing. More importantly, they are disconnected
from seaborne trade and depend on transit countries to gain access to
seaports and international markets. Their reliance on a limited number of commodities and their remoteness from world markets make
landlocked countries as a group the poorest among **developing countries**. Afghanistan, Armenia, Azerbaijan, Bhutan, Bolivia, Botswana,
Burkina Faso, Burundi, Central African Republic, Chad, Ethiopia,
Kazakhstan, Kyrgyzstan, Laos, Lesotho, Malawi, Mongolia, Nepal,
Niger, Paraguay, Rwanda, Swaziland, Tajikistan, Turkmenistan,
Uganda, Uzbekistan, and others have been classified by the United
Nations as landlocked countries.

The special situation and developmental needs of landlocked
countries have been recognized and in part addressed in a number of
international legal instruments, notably in a 1965 Convention on

Transit Trade of Landlocked States and the **United Nations Convention on the Law of the Sea (UNCLOS, 1982)**. In 2003, at the request of the **General Assembly**, an international ministerial conference was held in Kazakhstan that resulted in the adoption of an international program of action to deal with the continuing problems faced by landlocked and transit countries. In 2002, the **secretary-general** appointed a special envoy to undertake advocacy work and mobilize financial and political support for landlocked countries, the **least developed countries**, and **small island developing states**.

LANDMINES. *See* ANTIPERSONNEL MINES.

LAW OF THE SEA. *See* UNITED NATIONS CONVENTION ON THE LAW OF THE SEA (UNCLOS, 1982).

LAWYERS' COMMITTEE ON NUCLEAR POLICY (LCNP). American **nongovernmental organization (NGO)** founded in 1981 to promote peace and **disarmament** in the United Nations and the **International Court of Justice** through national and **international law**. The LCNP provides legal information and resources in the form of books, articles, and discussion papers to policy makers, diplomats, lawyers, legal scholars, and lay people, and the media on **disarmament** and **international law**.

LEAGUE OF ARAB STATES. *See* ARAB LEAGUE.

LEAGUE OF NATIONS (1919–1946). International organization established in 1919 as part of the Treaty of Versailles which formally brought World War I to an end. The League's main objectives were to preserve peace through **arbitration, conciliation**, and a system of **collective security** and to promote improved economic and social living conditions worldwide. The League was successful in dealing with minor conflicts throughout the 1920s. The divisions and wavering of France and Great Britain, its main supporters; the aloofness of the United States, which never joined; and the revival of nationalism in the wake of the world economic crisis of the 1930s contributed, among other factors, to its failure to prevent and roll back Japan's annexation of Manchuria in 1931–1933, Italy's invasion of Abyssinia in

1934–1936, and Germany's subsequent territorial ambitions in Europe. The League was thus unable to prevent the outbreak of World War II. Many of its economic and social activities foreshadow those undertaken by the United Nations. The League was officially dissolved on 18 April 1946. *See also* MANDATE SYSTEM OF THE LEAGUE OF NATIONS.

LEAST DEVELOPED COUNTRIES (LDCs). The poorest countries among **developing countries**. They share common socioeconomic conditions and characteristics including low per capita income; serious deficiencies in levels of nutrition, **health**, **education**, and literacy; and economic vulnerability as measured by the instability of their agricultural production and the concentration of their merchandise exports.

The LDCs' situation is monitored in periodic reports of the **United Nations Conference on Trade and Development**. Every three years, the **Committee for Development Policy** draws up a list of LDCs on the basis of set criteria. As such, the LDCs may claim special and preferential treatment by bilateral and multilateral donors. Several global conferences have been convened by the United Nations in order to generate international attention and action to reverse their deteriorating socioeconomic conditions. The latest conference was held in Brussels in 2001. *See also* UNITED NATIONS CONFERENCE ON THE LEAST DEVELOPED COUNTRIES (PARIS, 1981).

LEBANESE CRISIS (1958). In May 1958, civil conflict between Muslims and Christians assumed the proportions of a civil war and led the Lebanese government to request the **Security Council** to consider its complaint "in respect of a situation arising from the intervention of the United Arab Republic in the internal affairs of Lebanon, the continuance of which is likely to endanger the maintenance of international peace and security." The Lebanese government also accused the United Arab Republic of encouraging and supporting the rebellion by the supply of large quantities of arms to subversive elements in Lebanon and by the infiltration of armed personnel from Syria into Lebanon.

In June, the council dispatched to Lebanon the **United Nations Observation Group in Lebanon (UNOGIL)** so as to ensure that there was no illegal infiltration of personnel or supply of arms or other matériel across the Lebanese borders.

LEONTIEF, WASSILY (1906–1999). Russian-born American economist who won the **Nobel Peace Prize** for Economics in 1973. One of his major contributions was that he developed an input-output method of economic analysis that could be used for national planning and forecasting purposes and had the potential of practical policy applications for steering the **North-South dialogue** and economic relations.

LEWIS, SIR ARTHUR (1915–1991). Development economist born in St. Lucia who taught in Great Britain and the United States. He received the **Nobel Prize** in economics for his work on the determinants of economic growth rates, notably the unlimited supply of labor deriving from population pressures, which keeps wages down, generates high profits, and results in the emergence of dual economies. From 1957 to 1963, Arthur Lewis was deputy managing director of the **Special United Nations Fund for Economic Development (SUNFED)**, a forerunner of the **United Nations Development Programme (UNDP)**.

LEWIS, STEPHEN (1937–). Canadian politician and diplomat who served as ambassador to the United Nations from 1984 to 1988. He was deputy executive director of the **United Nations Children's Fund (UNICEF)** from 1995 to 1999. Since 2001, he has served as the secretary-general's special envoy for **HIV/AIDS** in Africa.

LIBERAL INTERNATIONALISM. An approach to international peace and security rooted in 19th-century European political thinking first publicly proposed by U.S. president **Woodrow Wilson** as a general framework for the settlement of World War I. Liberal internationalism posited that the international order had been corrupted by the rise of undemocratic leaders and the practice of balance-of-power politics in interstate relations. The spread of democracy worldwide associated with strong support for a broad interpretation of civil liberties for freedom of expression and religious toleration together with the deregulation and opening of national economies, the freeing of international markets, and creation of multipurpose international organizations would enhance closer contacts between peoples and nations and promote economic growth, social progress, and shared prosperity, thus creating conditions conducive to international peace and stability. Much of this thinking shaped the drafting of the **Charter** of the United Nations. Contested by **developing countries** throughout the decades of the 1960s and 1970s, liberal internationalism has resurfaced in the post–**Cold War** years as an influential ideology providing the basis for many of the development prescriptions of the **Washington Consensus**. It still remains controversial, especially in the field of international **trade**. *See also* HULL, CORDELL (1871–1955); NEW INTERNATIONAL ECONOMIC ORDER (NIEO).

LIBERIA CONFLICT (1980–2003). Founded in 1847 by freed American slaves, Liberia's political life, economy, and society has long been dominated by these "Americano-Liberians." Deep-seated tensions between "Americano-Liberians" and the various ethnic groups living in the area before their arrival helped spark a bloody civil conflict in 1980 marked by a succession of military coups and ongoing ethnic strife. Several attempts at **mediation** by the **Economic Community of West African States (ECOWAS)** failed. The **Security Council** imposed an armed embargo on Liberia in 1992 and, following a peace agreement brokered by ECOWAS, authorized the establishment of the **United Nations Observer Mission in Liberia (UNOMIL)**.

Persisting tensions between the government and opposition parties, systematic abuses of human rights, and the exclusion and harassment of political opponents stymied the process of national reconciliation and contributed to the resumption of civil war. In 1999, Liberia was accused of fomenting war in neighboring **Sierra Leone** by arming insurgency groups in exchange for diamonds. In 2001, the United Nations **Security Council** imposed **sanctions** on Liberian diamonds and issued a travel ban on Liberian government officials in response to its continuing support of the rebel insurgency in Sierra Leone. Two years later, the council banned the import of log and timber products originating from Liberia.

Besieged by several rebel groups, the government collapsed in 2003. On 17 June 2003, a cease-fire agreement brought to an end Liberia's long civil war. Three months later, the Security Council dispatched a new 15,000-troop **peacekeeping** operation in addition to 1,000 civilian police officers, the **United Nations ObserverMission in Liberia (UNOMIL)**, to support the implementation of the cease-fire agreement. The main mechanisms for the implementation of the peace process are in place: a transitional government was set up in October 2003 and elections took place in October–November 2005. The delivery of **humanitarian assistance** has become possible as UNOMIL is progressively extending and consolidating its control.

But the country is economically bankrupt and faces a catastrophic humanitarian situation. Over 250,000 persons have lost their lives since the conflict began. At least half of the dead have been civilian noncombatants, and more than 1.3 million people have been uprooted. At the end of the fighting, an estimated 350,000 Liberians were displaced, living in temporary camps with inadequate basic services. Some 38,000 fighters are believed to have been involved in the conflict, including 15,000 children and 2,000 women. *See also* CHILDREN IN ARMED CONFLICTS.

LIE, TRYGVE HALVDEN (1896–1968). Norwegian labor and political leader who headed his delegation at the 1945 **United Nations Conference on International Organization** in San Francisco and became the first United Nations **secretary-general** from 1946 to 1953. Rising **Cold War** tensions stymied Lie's efforts to play an independent leadership role and to act as a bridge between East and West. His public stands alternatively antagonized either the USSR or the United States, and he incurred the uncompromising wrath and opposition of the former after labeling the attack of North Korea on South Korea an **aggression** in violation of the principles of the United Nations **Charter** and calling upon the **Security Council** to take steps necessary to reestablish peace in the **Korean War**.

Soviet vetoes in the Security Council blocked his reappointment for a second term in office and the council could not agree on a successor. In a move of dubious legality under the terms of the charter, the **General Assembly** extended his tenure for three years. Lie faced continued Soviet criticism and ostracism. At the same time, he elicited broad opprobrium when in 1952 he allowed the United States to use United Nations premises to carry out loyalty investigations of American nationals employed by the organization and dismissed a number of them. These actions were widely perceived as breaches to the independence of the **secretariat**. Lie resigned in the fall of 1952 and thereafter took up several ministerial posts in his country.

While his tenure was marred by unending political controversies, Lie did establish precedents that enabled future incumbents to exert a degree of political leadership in world affairs. His practice of submitting oral and written reports to the Security Council, for example, was extensively used by his successors. *See also* CONVENTION ON PRIVILEGES AND IMMUNITIES OF THE UNITED NATIONS (1946); INTERNATIONAL CIVIL SERVICE; KOREAN WAR (25 June 1950–27 July 1953).

LOCKERBIE INCIDENT (1988). On 21 December 1988, an American airliner was blown up flying over Lockerbie, Scotland. All 270 passengers as well as 11 people on the ground were killed. After a three-year joint investigation by Scottish, European, and American authorities, indictments for murder were issued in 1991 against two Libyan nationals, an intelligence officer and the head of the Libyan Arab Airlines station in Malta. Libya refused to extradite the men, citing the Libyan constitution's ban on extraditing citizens to stand trial overseas and expressing fear that the pair might not receive a fair trial in either a British or American court of law. The United States and Great Britain brought the matter to the **Security Council** and persuaded it to impose **sanctions** against Libya in 1992 and 1993, barring direct flights in and out of Libya, forbidding the sale of arms and spare parts for oil refineries, and freezing some of Libya's overseas assets. After protracted negotiations, in 1999, Libya accepted that the trial be held in a neutral country by a panel of Scottish judges. UN sanctions were lifted just before the trial took place in the Netherlands, resulting in the conviction of one of the accused.

The Lockerbie case is often cited as one of the rare instances of the successful application of sanctions by the United Nations. Their success is attributed to the enormous toll of the trade embargo on the Libyan economy and the eagerness of the Libyan government to revive the country's economy.

– M –

McNAMARA, ROBERT S. (1916–). American businessman and politician who was U.S. secretary of defense from 1961 to 1968. Growing doubts about the conduct of the Vietnam War led him to resign. In 1968 he became president of the **World Bank**. Throughout his tenure, he endeavored to shift the lending policies of the bank from their initial emphasis on infrastructural projects to a greater focus on **poverty** alleviation.

MACEDONIA. *See* UNITED NATIONS PREVENTIVE DEPLOYMENT FORCE (UNPREDEP, 1995–1999).

MALIK, CHARLES (1906–1987). Lebanese scholar, educator, politician, and diplomat. He represented Lebanon at the 1945 **United Nations Conference on International Organization** in San Francisco and played a key role in the drafting of the **Universal Declaration of Human Rights (UDHR)**.

MANDATE SYSTEM OF THE LEAGUE OF NATIONS. Arrangements inspired by **President Woodrow Wilson**'s peace proposals that were incorporated in the Covenant of the **League of Nations** whereby colonial territories taken from Germany and Turkey, such as Palestine and **Southwest Africa**, would be administered by the victors under supervision of the League. Article 22 of the covenant stipulated that the "well-being and development" of the peoples concerned was "a sacred trust of civilization" accepted by "advanced nations" serving as "Mandatories on behalf of the League." It also provided for a permanent commission of private experts to receive and examine the annual reports of the Mandatories and to advise the Council of the League on all matters relating to the observance of the mandates. Many may today find the language of the covenant unduly pervaded by the patronizing imperial notion of the "white man's burden." But the covenant did establish the principle that colonial powers were accountable to the international community (albeit in limited ways) for their treatment of subjected peoples. The **Trusteeship System** of the United Nations laid down in the United Nations **Charter** is a virtual carbon copy of the League's Mandates. *See also* DECLARATION REGARDING NON-SELF-GOVERNING TERRITORIES; DECOLONIZATION; SELF-DETERMINATION.

MEADE, JAMES E. (1907–1995). English economist, recipient of the Nobel Prize in 1977 for his contributions to the theory of **international trade** and international capital movements. Meade believed that governments should take strong measures to promote equality of income arguing that fiscal and monetary policy tools were essential in achieving the goals of full employment and equilibrium in balance of payments. Meade also examined the conditions under which free trade made a country better off, concluding that a carefully chosen dose of protectionism could improve a nation's economic well-being. *See also* TRADE AND DEVELOPMENT.

MÉDECINS SANS FRONTIÈRES (MSF). International **nongovernmental organization (NGO)** created in 1971 in reaction to the unwillingness or incapacity of the international community to intervene collectively to prevent or alleviate the mass suffering of populations in danger during the Nigerian Civil War in 1968. MSF has since grown into a worldwide organization capable on short notice of fielding volunteer teams providing nutritional help, immunizations, and other emergency medical services in humanitarian crisis situations. MSF has consultative status in the **Economic and Social Council (ECOSOC)**, and was awarded the **Nobel Peace Prize** in 1999. *See also* HUMANITARIAN AGENCIES.

MEDIATION. Widely used mode of negotiation in conflict resolution in which the parties to a conflict seek the assistance of, or accept an offer to help from, a private individual, a group, or an international organization to find a mutually agreeable solution to their conflict. Mediators may act as channels of communications and may propose compromise solutions based on their assessment of each side's demands and interests. But their intervention can only take place at the request of the contending parties, which also have the ultimate power to decide. In that sense, mediation differs from **arbitration** and **adjudication**.

Drawing its authority from Article 33 of the charter, the United Nations is probably the most important mediator on the world scene, as suggested by the increasingly large number of disputes in which the **secretary-general** intervenes personally or through his **special representatives** and envoys. This type of mediation, however, is not necessarily the most successful, as it frequently deals with intractable issues where the chances of effective mediation are slim and actors show little willingness to moderate their claims. In contrast, small states and regional organizations such as the **Organization of African Unity (OAU)**, the **Organization of American States (OAS)**, and the **Economic Community of West African States (ECOWAS)** seem to have a better record in effecting successful outcomes in international mediation. *See also* CONCILIATION; CYPRUS QUESTION (1960–); INDONESIAN QUESTION (1945–1949); IRAN-IRAQ WAR (1980–1988); JUDICIAL SETTLEMENT; PEACEFUL SETTLEMENT OF DISPUTES; REGIONAL ARRANGEMENTS.

MEETING OF EXPERTS ON THE UNITED NATIONS PROGRAMME IN PUBLIC ADMINISTRATION AND FINANCE. Expert group (recently renamed the Committee of Experts on Public Administration) that, under the authority of the **Economic and Social Council (ECOSOC)**, advises the council and the **secretary-general** on issues of public administration and finance for development in developing countries. With the growing interest in market forces in development in the 1990s, political support for the group waned and some member states called for its dissolution. After considerable wrangling, the terms of reference of the group were overhauled and, since 2000, the group has been concerned with the role and functioning of the state in responding to and encouraging the process of **globalization**. Building the requisite national capacities of governance and public administration to meet the challenges of globalization is an important focus of the group's work. The group generally meets once a year and is serviced by the **Department of Economic and Social Affairs (DESA)**.

MEMBERSHIP (UNITED NATIONS). The United Nations is today virtually a universal organization. This was not the case when the organization was created, as it was originally open only to "peace loving" states (a reference to states that had declared war on the Axis Powers during World War II) and states that were "able and willing to carry out" the obligations arising from the United Nations **Charter** provisions (a reference to their capacity to afford the costs of membership).

The **Cold War** slowed down but did not stop the admission of new members. The relaxation of East-West tensions opened the door wide and the UN now welcomes all newcomers including mini states like

Lichtenstein and Monaco. Exceptions to this pattern were the cases of partitioned states—a legacy of the Cold War—such as Germany, Vietnam, and Korea, which were admitted only in 1973, 1977, and 1991, respectively, under different formulas. The case of China was always treated as an issue of credentials rather than admission until 1971 when the **General Assembly** recognized the People's Republic of China as the sole legitimate holder of China's seat.

National liberation movements and groups like the Palestine Liberation Organization, regional intergovernmental organizations like the **European Union (EU)** and the **African Union (AU)**, and quasi states like the Holy See enjoy "observer status," which gives them a virtually unlimited access to UN meetings and proceedings without a right to vote.

The mass entry of states from Asia and Africa reshaped the UN agenda and their numerical majority contributes to the persistence of the North-South cleavages affecting its priorities. *See also* CHINA REPRESENTATION IN THE UNITED NATIONS (1949–1971); CREDENTIALS COMMITTEE OF THE GENERAL ASSEMBLY; DEVELOPING COUNTRIES; GROUP OF SEVENTY-SEVEN (G-77); NONALIGNED MOVEMENT (NAM).

METEOROLOGY. *See* WORLD METEOROLOGICAL ORGANIZATION (WMO).

MICROCREDIT. Provision of small loans to finance small-scale enterprises run by poor families and individuals who would otherwise be unable to receive credit from conventional banks because of their socioeconomic conditions. Microcredit has received increasing political attention from the international donor community and in United Nations forums, and it has proved to be an effective tool for improving the welfare of **women** and the rural poor. The year 2005 has been proclaimed International Year of Microcredit by the **General Assembly**.

MIDDLE EASTERN SITUATION. *See* ARAB-ISRAELI CONFLICT.

MIGRANT WORKERS. *See* MIGRATION (INTERNATIONAL).

MIGRATION (INTERNATIONAL). Migrants are persons taking up residence temporarily or permanently outside their country. Most frequently, the term refers to migrant workers. More specifically, the United Nations **International Convention on the Protection of the Rights of All Migrant Workers and Members of Their Families** defines a migrant worker as "a person who is to be engaged, is engaged or has been engaged in a remunerated activity in a State of which he or she is not a national."

According to UN estimates, there are more than 170 million international migrants. The United States, India, Pakistan, France, Germany, Canada, Saudi Arabia, Australia, the United Kingdom, and Iran are among the countries receiving the largest number of migrants. Bangladesh, Sri Lanka, Pakistan, and India generate the largest numbers of migrants. In some countries like Qatar and the United Arab Emirates, migrants represent more than 70 percent of the entire population. In Western Europe and the United States, migrants constitute 10 percent of the overall population. In terms of gender distribution, recent studies have drawn attention to an increasing pattern of feminization of migration as female migrants move abroad as wage earners rather than as accompanying family members.

The growth of the global population of migrants appears to be accelerating. Some attribute this phenomenon to the **globalization** of production and services and the liberalization of **international trade**, which have adversely impacted national economies and motivated large numbers of people to leave their countries of origin. Others single out the persistence of **poverty**, armed conflicts, and racism as root causes of international migration. In any event, the free flow of capital, information, and services has not been accompanied by relatively free flows of peoples. Restrictive migration policies by receiving countries and their reluctance to grant migrants employment, health care, education, housing, legal protection, and trade union rights similar to those enjoyed by their nationals have raised contentious internal as well as international issues concerning the **human rights** of migrants.

Several United Nations entities are engaged with the subject of international migration in the context of their respective mandates. These include the **General Assembly**, which in 1990 adopted the international convention mentioned earlier, the **Commission on Human Rights**, which in 1999 appointed a special rapporteur on the Human Rights of Migrants; the **Department of Economic and Social Affairs (DESA)** within the UN **Secretariat**; and the **United Nations High Commissioner for Human Rights (UNHCHR)**. The **United Nations Educational, Scientific, and Cultural Organization (UNESCO)** is concerned with the promotion of migrants' social integration and the protection of cultural diversity in host countries. The **International Labour Organization (ILO)** has also set in place two conventions granting equal treatment between nationals and nonnationals in social security and prohibiting abusive conditions of work. Extensive discussions about the protection of migrants took place in the 1993 **World Conference on Human Rights** and the 2001 **World Conference against Racism, Racial Discrimination, Xenophobia, and Related Intolerance**. Increasing attention is being given to the links between migrants and **refugees**, an issue that raises controversial questions about the applicability of political and civil rights for migrants and the indivisibility of political, civil, social, economic, and cultural rights. The issue has been rekindled by the issue of **terrorism**, as a number of governments have equated efforts to curb illegal immigration with the international campaign against terrorism. *See also* GLOBAL COMMISSION ON INTERNATIONAL MIGRATION (GCIM); INTERNATIONAL ORGANIZATION FOR MIGRATION (IOM).

MILITARY STAFF COMMITTEE. The only subsidiary body of the **Security Council** specifically mentioned in Articles 26 and 47 of the United Nations **Charter**. Its role was to advise and assist the council on all questions relating to its military requirements, including the employment, command, and strategic direction of any armed forces placed at its disposal, as well as the regulation of armaments and possible **disarmament**. Disagreement among the major powers over the size and character of their respective contributions to the establishment of standby military forces that would enable the Security Council to take military action on its own prevented the creation of a permanent UN standing force. The committee still meets regularly but effectively ceased to function in 1948. Its assigned planning and strategic functions have been taken over by other organs of the United Nations, notably the **Department of Peacekeeping Operations (DPKO)**. *See also* COLLECTIVE SECURITY.

MILLENNIUM ASSEMBLY. Large gathering of world government leaders, representatives of **civil society** and religious and spiritual leaders at United Nations headquarters convened in September 2000 at the suggestion of **Secretary-General Kofi Annan** to discuss the major issues facing the UN and its role in the 21st century. Discussions, based in part on a seminal report of the secretary-general outlining his vision of the role of the organization, resulted in a **Millennium Declaration** identifying a number of development objectives and policies aimed at ensuring that globalization becomes a positive and inclusive force. *See also* GLOBAL COMPACT.

MILLENNIUM DECLARATION. Formal statement adopted at the 2000 **Millennium Assembly** assigning priority to international policies designed to make **globalization** socially more inclusive and to eradicate **poverty** in the developing world. The declaration contains quantified and measurable goals and objectives related to poverty eradication (halve the proportion of people whose income is less than $1 a day and suffer from hunger between 1990 and 2015), **health** (reduce by three-quarters, between 1990 and 2015 maternal mortality), **education** (achieve universal primary schooling by 2015), **gender** equality (eliminate gender disparity in primary and secondary education), child mortality (reduce by two-thirds, between 1990 and 2015, the under-five mortality rate), HIV/AIDS, and environmental sustainability. **World Bank** estimates suggest that the additional foreign aid required to reach these goals by 2015 is between $40 billion and $60 billion a year. *See also* OFFICIAL DEVELOPMENT ASSISTANCE (ODA).

MILLENNIUM DEVELOPMENT GOALS (MDGs). *See* MILLENNIUM DECLARATION.

MINORITIES, PROTECTION OF. Virtually all states include groups of people whose ethnic, linguistic, or religious identity differs from the majority population. Relations between minority groups and between minority and majority populations are often strained to the point of triggering internal disturbances or armed conflicts, with frequent adverse consequences for international peace and security.

World War I was in part caused by unresolved issues related to the status of minorities, prompting President **Woodrow Wilson** to advocate a right of **self-determination** as one of the principles to govern a durable postwar political settlement. Whenever the principle of "one nation-one state" proved infeasible, provisions were made in the 1919–1920 bilateral treaties between the Allied and Associated Powers and the states of Eastern Europe and the Balkans for the protection of minorities and their linguistic, cultural, and religious rights. These stipulations were to be monitored by the **League of Nations**, but the system fell into desuetude with the rise of totalitarian regimes in the 1930s.

The Charter of the United Nations (Articles 1 and 55) posits a right to nondiscrimination that was subsequently recognized in the 1948 **Universal Declaration of Human Rights (UDHR)**, the 1966 **International Covenant on Civil and Political Rights (ICCPR)** (Articles 2 and 26), the 1966 **International Covenant on Economic, Social, and Cultural Rights (ICESCR)** (Article 2), the 1989 **Convention on the Rights of the Child (CRC)** (Article 2), and the 1965 **International Convention on the Elimination of All Forms of Racial Discrimination** (Article 2). These instruments prohibit discrimination on the basis of race, language, religion, national or social origin, and birth. Together with a nonbinding 1992 Declaration of the **General Assembly** on the Rights of Persons Belonging to National or Ethnic, Religious and Linguistic Minorities, they also establish special rights for minorities enabling them to preserve their identity, traditions, culture and language, exercise their religion and participate in the political, social, and economic life of the state they reside in. The principal obligation of the states parties to these human rights conventions is to adopt legislation and other appropriate legal and administrative measures for the protection of minorities' rights. Their policies are monitored by the **treaty bodies** established in accordance with the provisions of the conventions through periodic reports and the examination of individual complaints.

The 1960 **Declaration on the Granting of Independence to Colonial Countries and Peoples** does recognize a right to self-determination, which it construes as the right of peoples to freely decide on their political status and social, economic, and cultural development.

At the same time, however, it deems any attempt to destroy the national unity or territorial integrity of a state incompatible with the aims of the United Nations. In practice, then, self-determination has been understood as applying only to peoples under colonial domination.

However impressive the mechanisms set up by the United Nations for the protection of minorities—especially in comparison with the dismaying experience of the League of Nations—they have not brought about lasting solutions to the problems of nation building and the protection of minorities as evidenced by the explosion of ethnonationalisms and civil wars in the post–Cold War era. Neither can they be viewed as a prelude to a firmly established right of the international community to intervene in sovereign states to protect their minorities. *See also* DECLARATION REGARDING NON-SELF-GOVERNING TERRITORIES; DECOLONIZATION; HIGH-LEVEL PANEL ON THREATS, CHALLENGES, AND CHANGE (HLP); HUMAN RIGHTS; INDIGENOUS PEOPLES; INTERNATIONAL COMMISSION ON INTERVENTION AND STATE SOVEREIGNTY.

MITRANY, DAVID (1888–1975). Romanian-born political economist widely regarded as one of the intellectual architects of "**functionalism**," an approach to peace that holds that international cooperation in technical and sectoral areas has a "spillover" effect resulting in a reduction of regional and global tensions and increased political integration. The **European Union (EU)** and the UN **specialized agencies** are instances of international institutions grounded on functionalist thinking.

MONTERREY CONSENSUS. *See* INTERNATIONAL CONFERENCE ON FINANCING FOR DEVELOPMENT (MONTERREY, MEXICO, 18–22 March 2002).

MONTREAL PROTOCOL ON SUBSTANCES THAT DEPLETE THE OZONE LAYER (1987). The 1985 Vienna Convention for the Protection of the Ozone Layer established mechanisms for international cooperation in research into the **ozone layer** and the effects of ozone-depleting chemicals (ODCs). The discovery of an ozone hole in the Antarctic region spurred further negotiations, which led to the adoption of a protocol that was agreed at the headquarters of the **International Civil Aviation Organization (ICAO)** in Montreal in 1987. The Protocol calls for the reduction and phased elimination of man-made ODCs. It is successfully implemented as it proved fairly easy to develop substitute methods to replace ozone-depleting chemicals. *See also* CLIMATE CHANGE; GLOBAL WARMING; KYOTO PROTOCOL; UNITED NATIONS FRAMEWORK CONVENTION ON CLIMATE CHANGE (UNFCCC).

MORSE, FRANK BRADFORD (1921–1994). American politician who served in the U.S. Congress from 1961 to 1972. In 1972, he joined the United Nations as undersecretary-general for political and General Assembly affairs. From 1976 to 1986, Morse headed the **United Nations Development Programme (UNDP).**

MOSCOW DECLARATION ON GENERAL SECURITY (1943). Statement issued by China, Great Britain, the United States, and the Soviet Union that pledged to continue their wartime cooperation "for the organization and maintenance of peace and security" and recognized "the necessity of establishing at the earliest practical date a general international organization." *See also* ATLANTIC CHARTER; DECLARATION BY UNITED NATIONS (1942); YALTA CONFERENCE (1945).

MOZAMBIQUE CONFLICT (1982–1992). In 1962, several anti-colonial political groups formed the Front for the Liberation of Mozambique (FRELIMO) and initiated an armed campaign against Portuguese colonial rule in September 1964. After 10 years of sporadic warfare and Portugal's return to democracy, FRELIMO took control of the capital in April 1974 and the country became independent two months later as a one-party Socialist state receiving substantial international aid from Cuba and the Soviet Union. In 1982, with the support of South Africa, the Mozambican National Resistance (RENAMO), an anti-Communist group, launched a series of attacks plunging the country into civil war. In 1990, with **apartheid** crumbling in South Africa, and support for RENAMO by South Africa and the United States drying up, the first direct talks between the FRELIMO government and RENAMO were held. In November 1990 a new constitution was adopted making Mozambique a multiparty state, with periodic elections and guaranteed democratic rights. A UN-mediated peace agreement was signed in Rome between the president of Mozambique and the RENAMO leader that formally took effect on 15 October 1992. The **United Nations Operation in Mozambique (UNOMOZ)** was set up by the **Security Council** to oversee the country's transition to democracy. The last UNOMOZ contingents departed in early 1995. *See also* PORTUGUESE COLONIES.

MULTILATERAL DEVELOPMENT BANKS (MDBs). Specialized regional or subregional and private financial institutions patterned along the model of the **World Bank** providing concessional long-term loans and grant financing for technical assistance, advisory services, and project preparation. The political dynamics that led to the creation of the **Inter-American Development Bank (IDB)**, the **Asian Development Bank (ADB)**, and the **African Development Bank (AfDB)** varied from one region to the next, accounting for significant differences in their governance, finance, and lending priorities. These differences have considerably narrowed over time, as the establishment of the Regional Development Banks (RDBs) reflect a common aspiration of **developing countries** toward greater regional cooperation and integration. They also represent the collective demand of Southern countries for greater access to development finance in the context of the postwar order typified by the **Bretton Woods institutions**, in which voting shares and decisional outcomes are heavily weighted in favor of industrial countries. The **Economic Commission for Africa (ECA)** and the United Nations **Economic and Social Commission for Asia and the Pacific (ESCAP)** played an instrumental role in the setting up of the ADB and the AfDB.

MULTILATERAL INVESTMENT GUARANTEE AGENCY (MIGA). Established in 1988 as one of the **World Bank Group**, MIGA promotes foreign investment in developing and transitional economy countries by providing guarantees to foreign investors against noncommercial losses such as expropriation, currency inconvertibility, and transfer restrictions.

MULTILATERALISM. Approach to international relations relying on modes of cooperation among three or more states working together through formal international institutions. The United Nations can be portrayed as a multilateral institution, and the multilateral architecture set up at the end of World War II comprised a wide array of such international organizations devoted to the maintenance of peace and security and the promotion of economic and social development.

The postwar multilateral system has expanded into a multiplicity of international organizations both within and outside the United Nations in response to the growing **interdependence** of peoples and states, the rise of transnational global issues, and the increasing involvement of **nonstate actors**. Since the end of the Cold War, multilateralism has encountered mounting challenges from the growing inclination of the United States to act unilaterally and to reject such multilateral agreements as the **Kyoto Protocol**, the **International Criminal Court (ICC)**, and the Ottawa **antipersonnel landmine** treaty. *See also* HIGH-LEVEL PANEL ON THREATS, CHALLENGES, AND CHANGE (HLP).

MULTINATIONAL CORPORATIONS (MNCs). *See* TRANSNATIONAL CORPORATIONS (TNCs).

MYRDAL, ALVA (1902–1986). Swedish social scientist, politician, and diplomat. For a number of years, she represented Sweden in the United Nations **General Assembly**, where she played an active role in **disarmament** discussions, endeavoring to bring pressure to bear on the United States and the USSR to show greater concern for concrete disarmament measures. She was married to **Gunnar Myrdal**.

MYRDAL, GUNNAR (1898–1987). Swedish economist, sociologist, and public official. Author of a pioneering study on race relations in the United States, he served as executive secretary of the **Economic Commission for Europe (ECE)** from 1947 to 1957. He was an articulate advocate of greater assistance to **developing countries**. He was married to **Alva Myrdal**.

– N –

NAMIBIAN QUESTION. *See* SOUTHWEST AFRICA.

NANSEN, FRIDTJOF (1861–1930). Norwegian explorer, scientist, diplomat, politician, and first high commissioner for refugees of the **League of Nations**. Throughout the post–World War I years and until his death, he played a leading role in international humanitarianism, both inside and outside the League, in the repatriation of exprisoners of war, the provision of relief to millions of **refugees** and victims of famine, and in setting up a number of international organizations devoted to their interests. One of his achievements was the creation in 1922 of a travel document—the so-called Nansen passport—issued by national governments to refugees on recommendation of the high commissioner, which serves as the equivalent of a regular passport.

NARASHIMAN, C. V. (1915–2003). Indian senior civil servant who joined the United Nations in 1959 as head of the **Economic Commission for Asia and the Far East (ECAFE)**. Secretary-General **Dag Hammarskjöld** brought him to New York as his chef de cabinet. He remained in that post for 18 years, continuing with **U Thant** and **Kurt Waldheim** and playing a leading role in the institutional development of the United Nations, notably in the establishment of several institutions such as the **United Nations Conference on Trade and Development (UNCTAD)** and the **United Nations Industrial Development Organization (UNIDO)**.

NARCOTIC DRUGS. Natural and synthetic addictive substances affecting moods and thought processes. Their harmful effects prompted the adoption of several conventions under the **League of Nations** seeking to regulate the manufacture, trade, and distribution of narcotics. This normative work has been further expanded by the United Nations, culminating in the adoption in 1961 of a single convention subsuming all previous conventions. This instrument was complemented by a 1988 **United Nations Convention against Illicit Traffic in Narcotic Drugs and Psychotropic Substances**. The **General Assembly** devoted one of its **special sessions** to narcotic drugs. *See* *also* COMMISSION ON NARCOTIC DRUGS (UNITED NATIONS); CRIME PREVENTION; UNITED NATIONS OFFICE ON DRUG CONTROL AND CRIME (UNODC).

NATURAL DISASTER. The term refers to sudden upheavals of nature (earthquakes, flooding, or volcanic eruptions) as opposed to man-made disasters (technological disasters, environmental pollution) or slowly developing phenomena such as droughts and **desertification**, which may be caused or aggravated by human actions such as excessive land use and deforestation.

Whether slow or sudden, natural disasters cause extensive destruction, death, and suffering. Data from reinsurance companies in 2003 show the occurrence of around 700 disasters, with over 50,000 people killed and economic losses rising to over $60 billion from $55 billion in 2002. Developing countries are disproportionately affected, the underlying problem of growing vulnerability to natural hazards being partly related to **development** activities and in particular the persistence and prevalence of **poverty**.

The United Nations has devoted increasing attention to the alleviation of the human consequences of natural disasters, beginning with the creation of the **United Nations Disaster Relief Organization (UNDRO)** in 1972 and the establishment of a number of **early warning systems**. The International Decade for Natural Disaster Reduction (1990–1999) also helped raise awareness among local communities, governments, and international organizations on risk-reduction needs. But poverty-reduction and development strategies still do not appear to fully take account of the need to reduce risk and vulnerability to natural and technological hazards. *See also* DAYS-YEARS-DECADES (INTERNATIONAL); DISASTER RELIEF; OFFICE FOR THE CO-ORDINATION OF HUMANITARIAN AFFAIRS (OCHA); SMALL ISLAND DEVELOPING STATES (SIDS); WORLD CONFERENCE ON DISASTER REDUCTION (KOBE, HYOGO, JAPAN, 18–22 January 2005); WORLD CONFERENCE ON NATURAL DISASTER REDUCTION (YOKOHAMA, JAPAN, 1994).

NATURAL RESOURCES. A nation's basic physical resources, such as oil, gas, coal, water, minerals, and arable land for food and commodity production. The availability of and access to natural resources are essential conditions of economic growth and development. Debates over natural resources within the United Nations have thus initially focused on issues of control, with the **General Assembly** adopting in 1973 a highly controversial **Charter of Economic Rights and Duties of States** that affirmed the developing countries' "full sovereignty" over their natural resources. The **codes of conduct** for **transnational corporations** discussed throughout the 1970s and 1980s in various UN forums also reflect the same concerns. More recently and as a result of renewed attention to market forces in the development process, attention has shifted to the role of **foreign direct investment** in the exploitation of natural resources in the developing world.

An issue that emerged in the 1990s was the linkages between group competition over natural resources (for instance, diamonds, gold, timber, and oil) and the outbreak and perpetuation of internal conflicts. High dependence on natural resources, as the cases of the civil wars in **Angola**, **Congo**, **Sierra Leone**, and **Liberia** illustrate, is now viewed as a major cause of conflict, especially as this reliance coincides with patterns of poor governance, lack of accountability, widespread poverty, and sharp social inequalities. The issue of natural resources has accordingly moved again to the forefront of discourse on **conflict prevention**, **peace building**, and long-term **development**. *See also* COMMITTEE ON ENERGY AND NATURAL RESOURCES FOR DEVELOPMENT (CENRD); GLOBAL COMPACT; PEACE-BUILDING COMMISSION; SOVEREIGNTY OVER NATURAL RESOURCES; TRANSNATIONAL CORPORATIONS (TNCs).

NEW AND RENEWABLE SOURCES OF ENERGY. The oil "shocks" of the 1960s and early 1970s triggered interest in alternative and nontraditional fossil fuels like peat; biomass; oil sands; geothermal energy; marine energy; solar, wind, and hydropower; and draft animals. In 1961, the **Economic and Social Council (ECOSOC)** convened an international conference that focused primarily on solar energy issues. Twenty years later, the United Nations sponsored another major conference on new and renewable sources of energy that resulted in the creation in 1982 by the **General Assembly** of a Committee on the Development and Utilization of New and Renewable Sources of Energy. This committee was merged in 1998 with the Committee on Natural Resources into a **Committee on Energy and Natural Resources for Development (CENRD)**. Political interest in the subject has widely fluctuated over time driven, in particular, by the variations in oil supply and prices.

NEW INTERNATIONAL ECONOMIC ORDER (NIEO). Manifesto adopted by the **General Assembly** at its sixth special session in 1974 at the prodding of **developing countries**, which sought to introduce far-reaching changes in the world economy. The demands contained in the NIEO stem from the growing concerns of developing countries that had argued throughout the 1950s and 1960s within the framework of the **Nonaligned Movement (NAM)** and the **United Nations Conference on Trade and Development (UNCTAD)** for structural changes in the world economy, fairer terms of trade, and greater flows of **finance for development** on more liberal terms. The resistance of developed countries, which insisted that any economic change should be discussed in the **Bretton Woods institutions**, and the success of the **Organization of Petroleum Exporting Countries (OPEC)** in increasing petroleum prices substantially in 1973 were the catalysts that brought together and spurred the loose coalition of developing countries to press for adoption by the assembly of a **Charter of Economic Rights and Duties of States** and of a **Declaration on the Establishment of a New International Economic Order**.

The specific measures called for in the NIEO include the adoption of an integrated approach to the management and pricing of core commodities to reduce excessive price and supply fluctuations and maintain commodity prices in real terms; the indexation of developing-country export prices to rising prices of developed countries' manufactured exports; reaching the target of 0.7 percent of the gross national product (GNP) of the developed countries in **Official Development Assistance (ODA)**; the negotiated redeployment of some developed countries' industries to developing countries; the lowering of tariffs on the exports of manufactures from developing countries; and the establishment of mechanisms for the transfer of technology to developing countries.

The General Assembly devoted two other special sessions to a review of the implementation of the NIEO in 1980 and 1990. But the

South's lack of effective power in world politics, divergent interests among developing countries, the crushing debt burden that affected several Southern countries in the 1980s, and the sheer costs involved in putting into effect the measures advocated in the NIEO simply led to its political demise. *See also* INTEGRATED PROGRAMME FOR COMMODITIES (IPC); WASHINGTON CONSENSUS.

NEW PARTNERSHIP FOR AFRICA'S DEVELOPMENT (NEPAD). The latest in a series of multilateral blueprints to promote growth and development in Africa. Adopted under the aegis of the **African Union (AU)**, the New Partnership for Africa's Development rests on the idea of reciprocal promises of good governance reform by African governments in return for commitments by industrialized countries for greater **Official Development Assistance (ODA)**, **foreign direct investment (FDI)**, market access for African goods, and **debt** relief and cancellation. *See also* AFRICAN ECONOMIC CONDITIONS; LAGOS PLAN OF ACTION; UNITED NATIONS PROGRAMME OF ACTION FOR AFRICAN ECONOMIC RECOVERY AND DEVELOPMENT (UN-PAARD, 1986–1990); UNITED NATIONS NEW AGENDA FOR THE DEVELOPMENT OF AFRICA (UN-NADAF).

NEW WORLD INFORMATION AND COMMUNICATION ORDER (NWICO). Politically controversial proposals emanating from the **United Nations Educational, Scientific, and Cultural Organization (UNESCO)** in the late 1970s that sought to eliminate North-South imbalances and disparities in worldwide communication and information flows. While Southern countries presented these proposals as an effort to overcome stereotyped thinking and to promote more understanding of diversity and plurality, developed countries perceived them as attempts to regulate the media and professional organizations and threats to freedom of information. This divisive debate contributed to the withdrawal of several countries from UNESCO in the early 1980s. UNESCO has since considerably scaled down its activities in this field, limiting its work primarily to the discussion of recurrent technical world reports in the areas of communication, information, and informatics and, only secondarily, to their social and economic implications. *See also* NEW INTERNATIONAL ECONOMIC ORDER (NIEO).

NICARAGUA QUESTION. The Nicaraguan Somoza dynasty ended in 1979 with a massive uprising led by the Sandinista National Liberation Front (FSLN), which had conducted a low-level guerrilla war against the Somoza regime since the early 1960s.

The FSLN established an authoritarian dictatorship soon after taking power and U.S.-Nicaraguan relations deteriorated rapidly as the regime nationalized many private industries, confiscated private property, and supported Central American guerrilla movements. Washington suspended aid to Nicaragua in 1981. The Ronald Reagan administration provided assistance to the Nicaraguan resistance, the so-called Contras, and in 1985 imposed an embargo on U.S.-Nicaraguan trade.

Nicaragua took the United States to the **International Court of Justice (ICJ)**, which rendered a judgment in 1986 clarifying a number of legal issues pertaining to the **use of force**. The court held that the United States had broken international law by aiding the Contras. The ICJ thus emphasized that participation in a civil war by "organizing or encouraging the organization of irregular forces or armed bands . . . for incursion into the territory of another state" and by "participating in acts of civil strife . . . in another State" was not only an act of illegal intervention in the domestic affairs of a foreign state, but also a "violation of the principle of the prohibition of the use of force" contained in the United Nations **Charter**.

In any event, in response to both domestic and international pressure, the Sandinista regime entered into negotiations with the Nicaraguan resistance and agreed to nationwide elections in February 1990. In these elections, which were proclaimed free and fair by the **United Nations Observer Mission for the Verification of Elections in Nicaragua (ONUVEN)**, Nicaraguan voters elected as their president the candidate of the National Opposition Union, Violeta Barrios de Chamorro. *See also* ARIAS, OSCAR (1941–); CENTRAL AMERICA CONFLICTS.

NOBEL PEACE PRIZE. Awards given each year to persons or institutions that have contributed to the preservation of peace or interstate cooperation. The Nobel Peace Prize has been awarded to **Ralph Bunche** in 1950 for his mediation efforts in the Middle East conflict, **Secretary-General Dag Hammarskjöld** in 1961 for his peace efforts in the Congo, Secretary-General **Kofi Annan** in 2001, the

United Nations High Commissioner for Refugees (UNHCR) in 1954 and 1981; UN peacekeepers in 1988 and the UN itself (2001).

Two development agencies, the **United Nations Children's Fund (UNICEF)** and the **International Labour Organization (ILO)**, were recognized in 1965 and 1969, respectively. The prize was awarded to the **International Atomic Energy Agency (IAEA)** and its chief, Mohamed El Baradei in 2005. Several economists who were UN staffers or contributed to UN activities were Nobel laureates in economics, notably **Lawrence Klein, Wassily Leontief, W. Arthur Lewis, James E. Meade, Gunnar Myrdal, Jan Tinbergen**, and **Sir Richard Stone**.

Other Nobel laureates include **John Boyd Orr**, the first director general of the **Food and Agricultural Organization (FAO)**; **Alva Myrdal**, who worked at the **United Nations Educational, Scientific, and Cultural Organization (UNESCO)**; **Lester Pearson** (1957) for his role in the launching of **peacekeeping** operations; **Rene Cassin** (1968) for the drafting of the **Universal Declaration of Human Rights (UDHR)**; and **Alfonso Garcia Robles** (1982), who spearheaded **disarmament** negotiations.

A number of **nongovernmental organizations (NGOs)** have also been awarded the prize for their work in their respective fields of activities: **Amnesty International (AI)**, **International Campaign to Ban Landmines (ICBL)**, **Médecins Sans Frontières (MSF)**, and **Pugwash Conferences on Science and World Affairs (PUGWASH)**.

NONALIGNED MOVEMENT (NAM). Loosely structured coalition of Asian and African states that came into existence in 1961 to fight colonialism and advocate neutral policies in the context of the **Cold War**. The NAM's highest authority is its Conferences of Heads of States or Governments, which meets every four years in various locations. In addition, it holds regular meetings at the Foreign Ministers level. The standing machinery of the NAM remains limited to a Coordinating Bureau of Nonaligned Countries and a Standing Committee for Economic Cooperation, which, among other things, work out common positions on issues debated in the United Nations.

In spite of internal divisions and squabbles, the Nonaligned Movement, in concert with the **Group of Seventy-Seven (G-77)**, played one superpower off the other and was able to exert a degree of influence in the United Nations. The policies advocated by the NAM include the right of peoples who are not yet free to **self-determination** and independence, the respect of the sovereignty and independence of all states, and the right of all states to equal participation in international affairs including sharing in the benefits of economic **development**.

The end of the Cold War sharply eroded the NAM's political leverage in United Nations forums. But persisting political and economic dependence on the North and fears of a further marginalization in an increasingly globalized and unequal world account for its continuing existence.

NONGOVERNMENTAL LIAISON SERVICE (NGLS). A jointly financed, interagency unit supported by several United Nations agencies, programs, and funds and bilateral donors. Created in 1975 at the initiative of the **United Nations Development Programme (UNDP)** and the United Nations Department of Public Information, the purpose of the NGLS is to promote greater mutual understanding and cooperation between the UN system and **nongovernmental organizations (NGOs)**. It has played a significant role in supporting NGOs' work around major UN conferences, with a focus on sustainable human development, the environment and development, the global economy, and Africa's development issues. The NGLS has a broad outreach and publication program. Its website is an invaluable source of timely information about the current work of the United Nations system in development.

NONGOVERNMENTAL ORGANIZATIONS (NGOs). Special-purpose associations of individuals or groups created by means other than an agreement among states. It is estimated that the number of internationally active NGOs exceeds 35,000. NGOs fulfill a wide variety of functions ranging from advocacy, research, and information to the provision of humanitarian assistance. Examples of NGOs engaging in political activities across national borders include **Amnesty International (AI)**, the **International Campaign to Ban Landmines (ICBL)**, the **International Committee of the Red Cross (ICRC)**, and **Médecins Sans Frontières (MSF)**. In recognition of their role, some NGOs are granted special status in the **Economic and Social Council (ECOSOC)** and numerous **specialized agencies**. Many

NGOs have developed informal consultative arrangements with the **Security Council** and the **Commission for Human Rights**. *See also* ACADEMIC COUNCIL ON THE UNITED NATIONS SYSTEM (ACUNS); BUSINESS COUNCIL FOR THE UNITED NATIONS (BCUN); CARE INTERNATIONAL (CARE); CARITAS INTERNATIONALIS; CARNEGIE ENDOWMENT FOR INTERNATIONAL PEACE; COMMITTEE ON NONGOVERNMENTAL ORGANIZATIONS; EARTH COUNCIL; GREENPEACE INTERNATIONAL; HUMAN RIGHTS WATCH (HRW); INTERNATIONAL ALERT; LAWYERS' COMMITTEE ON NUCLEAR POLICY (LCNP); NONGOVERNMENTAL LIAISON SERVICE (NGLS); OXFAM; PANEL OF EMINENT PERSONS ON UNITED NATIONS–CIVIL SOCIETY RELATIONS; PLANNED PARENTHOOD; POPULATION COUNCIL; PUGWASH CONFERENCES ON SCIENCE AND WORLD AFFAIRS (PUGWASH); RED CROSS, THE; SAVE THE CHILDREN; SOCIETY FOR INTERNATIONAL DEVELOPMENT (SID); SWISSPEACE; THIRD WORLD NETWORK (TWN); TRANSPARENCY INTERNATIONAL (TI); UNITED NATIONS ASSOCIATION OF THE UNITED STATES OF AMERICA (UNA-USA); WORLD COUNCIL OF CHURCHES (WCC); WORLD FEDERALIST MOVEMENT (WFM); WORLD FEDERATION OF UNITED NATIONS ASSOCIATIONS (WFUNA); WORLD RESOURCES INSTITUTE (WRI).

NONINTERVENTION. *See* PRINCIPLES, OF THE UNITED NATIONS.

NONPROLIFERATION OF NUCLEAR WEAPONS, TREATY ON THE (NPT, 1968). Centerpiece of a series of international treaties and multilateral inspections aimed at halting the spread of nuclear weapons. Debated and negotiated for seven years in the **Eighteen-Nation Disarmament Committee**, the NPT was eventually concluded and approved by the **General Assembly** in 1968. It entered into force in 1970.

The treaty defines "nuclear-weapons states" as countries that detonated a nuclear device before 1967, for example, the United States, Russia, Great Britain, France, and China. All other countries are treated as "nonnuclear weapons states" and under the NPT, these countries may neither manufacture nor receive nuclear explosives. In addition, they agree to accept the **International Atomic Energy Agency**'s **(IAEA)** inspections and monitoring of all their peaceful nuclear activities.

The NPT originally entered into force for a period of 25 years. In 1995, its signatories agreed to extend the treaty indefinitely without conditions. Several major states deemed to have nuclear potential have not ratified the NPT, notably Israel, India, and Pakistan. *See also* COMPREHENSIVE TEST BAN TREATY (CTBT); DISARMAMENT.

NON-SELF-GOVERNING TERRITORIES. *See* DECLARATION REGARDING NON-SELF-GOVERNING TERRITORIES.

NONSTATE ACTORS. By and large, international relations consists of the relations between states. In recent decades, however, actors other than state officials and government representatives operating within states or across state borders have played an increasingly regular part in global politics, interacting with governments and affecting political outcomes. Known as "nonstate" or "transnational" actors, they include the national liberation or guerrilla movements that sprang up during the **decolonization** process; international intergovernmental organizations like the United Nations, the **North Atlantic Treaty Organization (NATO),** and the **European Union (EU)**; national **nongovernmental organizations (NGOs)** with significant international activities, such as **Médecins Sans Frontières (MSF)** and the Sierra Club, based in France and the United States, respectively; international nongovernmental organizations such as **Amnesty International (AI)** and the **International Chamber of Commerce (ICC)**; multinational or **transnational corporations (TNCs)**, such as Shell and General Motors; and networks of individuals and groups involved in illicit trading in arms and drugs and **terrorism**. The proliferation and growing importance of nonstate actors is a distinctive feature of contemporary world affairs.

NONUSE OF FORCE. One of the key **principles** of the United Nations **Charter**, enjoining member states of the organization to refrain from the use of force in their international relations and have recourse to **peaceful settlement** methods in the resolution of their disputes. The concrete implementation of the principle has been discussed with little tangible results by a Special Committee on Enhancing the Effectiveness of the Principle of the Nonuse of Force in International Relations set up in 1978 by the **General Assembly**. The assembly also adopted in 1987 a declaration bearing the same name. The unilateral use of force in the 2003 second **Persian Gulf War** has rekindled the debate and prompted the search for more precise criteria for the legitimate use of force. *See also* HIGH-LEVEL PANEL ON THREATS, CHALLENGES, AND CHANGE (HLP); NUCLEAR WEAPONS, PROHIBITION ON THE USE; SELF-DEFENSE, RIGHT OF; USE OF FORCE.

NORTH ATLANTIC TREATY ORGANIZATION (NATO, 1949). A military defense organization set up during the **Cold War** as a counterweight to the Soviet Union and its Eastern European allies. With the demise of the Cold War, NATO's original function became irrelevant and the organization has since sought to redefine its mission. In this context, it has played a role in a number of **peacekeeping** operations, notably in the former Yugoslav Republic of **Macedonia** and in **Afghanistan**. Its bombing campaign against Serbia in the **Kosovo** crisis elicited a major legal and moral controversy.

NORTH KOREA. Little known but important instance of United Nations provision of **humanitarian assistance**. Self-imposed political isolation; catastrophic droughts, floods, and soil erosion in the 1990s; and a long-lasting economic downturn have combined to cripple the Peoples' Democratic Republic of Korea (DPRK) **food security** system and turned it into a food deficit country. Some 6.5 million people—a quarter of the total population—live at subsistence level and are dependent on the assistance provided by the **World Food Programme (WFP)** through food delivery and food for work programs. WFP's emergency operation entails the yearly delivery of some 500,000 tons of food, valued at $200 million. The **United Nations Children's Fund (UNICEF)** has also participated in this process, focusing on the health needs of children and pregnant women, which it has targeted in immunization campaigns. Substantial gains have been made in a decade of humanitarian intervention. But if international assistance staved off widespread famine, malnutrition remains a problem and the country still requires considerable development assistance that has not been forthcoming. *See also* DISASTER RELIEF.

NORTH-SOUTH DIALOGUE. Shorthand term referring to the on-and-off discussions that pit the rich industrial Northern countries against the poor and economically weak countries of the Southern Hemisphere, in and out of the United Nations over the past three to four decades. The beginning of this "dialogue" can be traced back to the **Conference on International Economic Cooperation (CIEC)**, which was held in Paris from 1975 to 1977. Developing countries were not satisfied by the outcome of CIEC. Still energized by the **Declaration on the Establishment of a New International Economic Order**, they pressed for a resumption of these negotiations within the United Nations, a demand that was rejected by developed countries, which argued that the proper framework for such negotiations was not the United Nations but the **Bretton Woods institutions**. In subsequent years, the so-called North-South dialogue was no more than an endless and inconclusive series of discussions about where negotiations should take place and on what subjects, culminating in the adoption each year of ineffective exhortations by the **General Assembly**.

This fruitless process was taken over by events, notably the **debt crisis** of the 1980s and the subsequent rise of market-oriented developmental policies. The **global conferences** sponsored by the United Nations in the 1990s have, however, increasingly provided the setting for developing countries to continue pressing for their demands and reaching agreement on some of the matters left unresolved by the 1975 Paris conference. Of particular—though not necessarily conclusive—significance in this regard is the 2002 **International Conference on Financing for Development** and discussions taking place within the **World Trade Organization (WTO)**, which some observers view as steps away from "dialogue" to serious negotiations. *See also* INDEPENDENT COMMISSION ON INTERNATIONAL DEVELOPMENT ISSUES (ICIDI); SOUTH CENTER.

NUCLEAR ENERGY, PEACEFUL USES. *See* INTERNATIONAL ATOMIC ENERGY AGENCY (IAEA).

NUCLEAR WEAPONS, PROHIBITION ON THE USE. In 1961, the **General Assembly** issued a declaration banning the use of nuclear weapons. The resolution was adopted by 55 votes for (the USSR and its allies and Third World countries) to 20 against (16

Western European countries, China, and 3 Central American countries). Twenty-six countries abstained (such as Austria and the Scandinavian countries).This visible lack of political consensus explains why the proposal to hold a special conference on the subject never got off the ground.

In the 1990s, the **World Health Organization (WHO)** and the assembly brought the question of the use of nuclear weapons to the **International Court of Justice (ICJ)**. The court dismissed the request of the WHO for an advisory opinion on whether international law permits the threat or use of nuclear weapons on the ground that the subject matter was outside the scope of the WHO. In response to the assembly request, the court ruled that the threat or use of nuclear weapons would generally be contrary to the rules of **international law** applicable in armed conflicts. The decision was reached by the narrowest margin.

NUCLEAR WEAPONS FREE ZONES (NWFZs). Regional agreements calling for the demilitarization and denuclearization of specific geographical areas designed to strengthen the nonproliferation regime established under the 1959 **Antarctic Treaty**, the 1967 **Outer Space Treaty**, the 1968 **Comprehensive Test Ban Treaty (CTBT)**, and the 1971 **Seabed Demilitarization Treaty**. NWFZs have been established in Latin America, the South Pacific, South East Asia, and Africa. *See also* ARMS CONTROL.

NUREMBERG TRIBUNAL. *See* INTERNATIONAL MILITARY TRIBUNAL FOR THE PROSECUTION AND PUNISHMENT OF THE MAJOR WAR CRIMINALS (NUREMBERG TRIBUNAL, 1945–1946).

– O –

OBSERVATION MISSIONS, UNITED NATIONS. Variously known as observer groups or military observers, the purpose of these **peacekeeping** missions is to observe the implementation of cease-fires on the ground and to ensure that all parties adhere to the terms of their agreement. UN military observers have thus been deployed between the new state of Israel and its Arab neighbors and in Kashmir between India and Pakistan, Other similar operations have been stationed in the **Aouzou Strip**, Lebanon, Yemen, the borders between Iraq and Iran and Iraq and Kuwait, Central American countries, **Angola**, **Rwanda**, **Georgia**, **Liberia**, **Tajikistan**, Ethiopia and Eritrea, Macedonia, Croatia, **Haiti**, the Central African Republic, **Sierra Leone**, and the **Democratic Republic of the Congo**. *See also* UNITED NATIONS INDIA-PAKISTAN OBSERVATION MISSION (UNIPOM); UNITED NATIONS IRAN-IRAQ MILITARY OBSERVER GROUP (UNIIMOG, 9 August 1988–February 1991); UNITED NATIONS IRAQ-KUWAIT OBSERVATION MISSION (UNIKOM, April 1991–October 2003); UNITED NATIONS MILITARY OBSERVER GROUP IN INDIA AND PAKISTAN (UNMOGIP, 1949–present); UNITED NATIONS MISSION OF OBSERVERS IN TAJIKISTAN (UNMOT, 1994–2000); UNITED NATIONS OBSERVATION GROUP IN LEBANON (UNOGIL, June–December 1958); UNITED NATIONS OBSERVER GROUP FOR THE VERIFICATION OF ELECTIONS IN HAITI (ONUVEH); UNITED NATIONS OBSERVER GROUP IN CENTRAL AMERICA (ONUCA, 7 November 1989–16 January 1992); UNITED NATIONS OBSERVER MISSION FOR VERIFICATION OF THE ELECTIONS IN NICARAGUA (ONUVEN, 1988); UNITED NATIONS OBSERVER MISSION IN ANGOLA (MONUA, June 1997–February 1999); UNITED NATIONS OBSERVER MISSION IN BOUGAINVILLE (UNOMB, 1 January 2004–30 June 2005); UNITED NATIONS OBSERVER MISSION IN EL SALVADOR (ONUSAL, July 1991–April 1995); UNITED NATIONS OBSERVER MISSION IN GEORGIA (UNOMIG, August 1993–present); UNITED NATIONS OBSERVER MISSION IN LIBERIA (UNOMIL, September 1993–September 1997); UNITED NATIONS OBSERVER MISSION IN SIERRA LEONE (UNOMSIL, June 1998–October 1999); UNITED NATIONS OBSERVER MISSION IN UGANDA-RWANDA (UNOMUR, June 1993–September 1994); UNITED NATIONS ORGANIZATION MISSION IN THE DEMOCRATIC REPUBLIC OF THE CONGO (MONUC, February 2000–present); UNITED NATIONS TRUCE SUPERVISION ORGANIZATION (UNTSO, 1948–present).

OCEANS. The oceans cover more than 76 percent of Earth's surface and play a critical role in shaping and sustaining our daily lives: they control climate and weather conditions; they host shipping, transportation, recreation, and tourism; and they are a source of food, minerals, and energy. The growth of the world population, especially in coastal zones, however, is increasingly posing threats to the oceans, ranging from deleterious land-based activities such as industrial, sewage, and agricultural effluents and the excessive exploitation of fish stocks to aquaculture and polluting agents used on ships.

One of the functions of the **United Nations Environment Programme (UNEP)** is to assist in the protection of the oceans and seas and promote the environmentally sound use of marine resources through education, training, research, and the development of normative multilateral interstate cooperation agreements. Several **specialized agencies** of the United Nations have activities related to the oceans, notably, the **United Nations Educational, Scientific, and Cultural Organization (UNESCO)**, the **International Maritime Organization (IMO)**, and the **World Meteorological Organization (WMO)**. *See also* UNITED NATIONS CONVENTION ON THE LAW OF THE SEA (UNCLOS, 1982).

OFFICE FOR RESEARCH AND COLLECTION OF INFORMATION (ORCI). Unit of the United Nations **Secretariat** set up by **Secretary-General Javier Perez de Cuellar** to collect and analyze information to provide **early warning** and policy recommendations to the secretary-general. ORCI was also assigned to develop a quantitative system, based on early-warning indicators and computer models, for the prediction of crises. The functioning of the office was plagued by the hostility of major member states, a shortage of manpower and resources, and a paralyzing bureaucratic separation between early-warning advice and policy action. It was eventually dismantled by Secretary-General **Boutros Boutros-Ghali** and its functions reallocated within the **Department of Political Affairs (DPA)**. *See also* CONFLICT PREVENTION; PREVENTIVE DIPLOMACY.

OFFICE FOR THE COORDINATION OF HUMANITARIAN AFFAIRS (OCHA). The increasing involvement of the United Nations in multidimensional and complex emergencies following the end of the **Cold War** led to the creation in 1992 of the UN Department of Humanitarian Affairs for the purpose of addressing the need of better coordination among governments, **nongovernmental organizations (NGOs)**, UN **specialized agencies**, and individuals involved in humanitarian crises. The department was renamed Office for the Coordination of Humanitarian Affairs in 1998.

OCHA's mandate is to coordinate international humanitarian responses to complex emergencies and to provide the humanitarian community with support in policy development. The office also plays an advocacy role through the dissemination of information and analysis. OCHA's monitoring and **early-warning** function, contingency work, and efforts to mobilize donor support through yearly "consolidated appeals" have proved useful. But its coordinating mandate has yielded mixed results and underfunding has hampered its work. Widely uneven donor responses to emergency relief have been another obstacle. *See also* DAYS-YEARS-DECADES (INTERNATIONAL); HUMANITARIAN AGENCIES; HUMANITARIAN ASSISTANCE; HUMANITARIAN LAW; NATURAL DISASTER; UNITED NATIONS DISASTER RELIEF ORGANIZATION (UNDRO); WORLD CONFERENCE ON DISASTER REDUCTION (KOBE, HYOGO, JAPAN, 18–22 January 2005); WORLD CONFERENCE ON NATURAL DISASTER REDUCTION (YOKOHAMA, JAPAN, 1994).

OFFICE OF INTERNAL OVERSIGHT SERVICES (OIOS). Established by the **General Assembly** in 1994 to assist the **secretary-general** in the performance of his internal oversight responsibilities. Modeled after a budget watchdog body of the United States Congress, OIOS monitors, audits, investigates, inspects, and evaluates the United Nations Secretariat and the organization's funds and programs with a view to enhancing their accountability, transparency, and efficiency. OIOS reports regularly to the assembly on its findings. In its first ten years of existence, OIOS claims to have exposed waste and fraud in the value of some $300 million, half of which was recovered and saved. *See also* CONTROL MECHANISMS (INTERNAL AND EXTERNAL).

OFFICE OF THE OMBUDSMAN. Office created by the **General Assembly** in 2001 to address employment-related problems of staff

members within the **secretariat**. *See also* PERSONNEL QUES-
TIONS.

OFFICE OF THE UNITED NATIONS HIGH COMMISSIONER FOR REFUGEES. *See* UNITED NATIONS HIGH COMMIS-
SIONER FOR REFUGEES (UNHCR).

OFFICIAL DEVELOPMENT ASSISTANCE (ODA). Economic or technical assistance extended by governments and their agencies and multilateral institutions on a "concessional" basis—meaning that all or part of each transaction is a grant or is loaned at favorable interest rates or repayment terms—for the promotion of the economic and social development of **developing countries**. In 1961, the **General Assembly** proclaimed the 1960s as the "United Nations Development Decade" (the first in a series of five successive international decades proclaimed by the assembly) that called for a concerted array of international and national measures to accelerate growth in developing countries. Each development decade has asked developed countries to devote 0.7 percent of their gross national product as a target for their annual official assistance. This target has been met only by a handful of Northern countries. The **Organization for Economic Cooperation and Development (OECD)** monitors ODA annual flows.

OGATA, SADAKO (1927–). Japanese scholar and diplomat who represented her country in the **Commission for Human Rights**, the **United Nations Children's Fund (UNICEF)**, and the **General Assembly**. As **United Nations High Commissioner for Refugees (UNHCR)** from 1991 to 2000, she profoundly reshaped and considerably expanded the mandate of her agency as it increasingly became involved in internal conflicts.

OIL FOR FOOD PROGRAM (OFFP, 1997–2003). Authorized in 1995 by the **Security Council** in the wake of the 1991 Persian **Gulf War**, this program allowed **Iraq**, under United Nations supervision, to sell oil to purchase civilian supplies. It was designed as a temporary measure to alleviate civilian suffering arising from the **sanctions** imposed on Iraq by the Security Council.

From 1995 to 2003, Iraq sold more that $65 billion in oil through the program and issued $38 billion in letters of credit to purchase humanitarian goods and equipment. The $27 billion balance was used to cover Gulf War reparations, UN administrative and operational costs for the program, and the expenditures incurred by the **International Atomic Energy Agency (IAEA)** and the **United Nations Monitoring, Verification, and Inspection Commission (UNMOVIC)** weapon inspection programs. In financial terms, the OFFP was the largest program ever administered by the United Nations. Several UN agencies, including the **United Nations Educational, Scientific, and Cultural Organization (UNESCO)**, the **World Health Organization (WHO)**, the **International Telecommunications Union (ITU)**, the **United Nations Children's Fund (UNICEF)**, the **United Nations Development Programme (UNDP)**, the **World Food Programme (WFP)**, and the **United Nations Centre on Human Settlements (UN-Habitat)**, were involved in its implementation. Before the American led invasion of Iraq in March 2003, some 893 international staff and 3,600 Iraqis worked for the program in Iraq.

Portrayed as "most complex," "most unusual," and "unprecedented," the seven-year-long program almost immediately after its closing was the target of allegations of improprieties in its management and administration. They have since ballooned into a partisan political debate that has given additional fodder to critics of the United Nations, cast a long shadow over the authority and leadership of **Secretary-General Kofi Annan**, and triggered another round of calls for **reforms**.

Notwithstanding the political fracas over its management, the Oil for Food Program did succeed in its humanitarian objective. The program enabled the import of enough food to feed 27 million Iraqis. All Iraqi residents were entitled to receive a monthly Oil-for-Food basket and 60 percent of the population is believed to have been totally dependent on it. In addition, the program led to significant improvements in the health care delivery services of the country.

OPTIONAL CLAUSE. The **International Court of Justice (ICJ)** adjudicates cases only with the consent of the states involved. Under a provision of the Statute of the IC—the so-called "optional clause" because they are not required to do so—states may confer on the ICJ a degree of compulsory jurisdiction before the occurrence of a dispute by depositing a declaration to that effect with the **secretary-general** of the United Nations. Many states have accepted the optional clause albeit with reservations, generally excluding disputes that they consider domestic issues. For example, the 1946 U.S. declaration of acceptance was ratified by the Senate with the italicized provision that excluded "disputes with regard to matters that are essentially within the domestic jurisdiction of the United States *as determined by the United States of America.*"

ORGANIZATION FOR ECONOMIC COOPERATION AND DEVELOPMENT (OECD). Originally founded in 1948 to coordinate the distribution of the funds donated to European countries for their economic recovery under the Marshall Plan, the Organization for European Economic Cooperation took its current name in 1961 to reflect its broadened and new mandate to promote economic growth among its members, contribute to the expansion of world trade, and extend aid to developing countries. *See also* OFFICIAL DEVELOPMENT ASSISTANCE (ODA).

ORGANIZATION FOR SECURITY AND COOPERATION IN EUROPE (OSCE). Regional security organization encompassing states from Europe, Central Asia, and North America that emerged from the 1973 Conference on Security and Cooperation in Europe (CSCE) in Helsinki. Formalized in 1995 and headquartered in Vienna, the OSCE is a multilateral institution aiming at transforming Europe's system of antagonistic military alliances into a transcontinental regime of cooperation in military, economic, and political matters. Its activities deal with **arms control, preventive diplomacy** and **early warning**, election monitoring, security-building measures, **human rights**, democratization, and economic and **environmental security**. It has been involved in several UN **peacekeeping** operations, including **Bosnia-Herzegovina, Georgia**, and **Kosovo**. *See also* UNITED NATIONS CIVILIAN POLICE SUPPORT GROUP (UNPSG); UNITED NATIONS MISSION OF OBSERVERS IN TAJIKISTAN (UNMOT, 1994–2000).

ORGANIZATION FOR THE PROHIBITION OF CHEMICAL WEAPONS (OPCW). *See* CONVENTION ON THE PROHIBITION OF THE DEVELOPMENT, PRODUCTION, STOCKPILING, AND USE OF CHEMICAL WEAPONS AND ON THEIR DESTRUCTION (1997).

ORGANIZATION OF AFRICAN UNITY (OAU). Created in 1963, the main purposes of the Organization of African Unity were to support **self-determination** and **decolonization** in the African continent, to promote solidarity among African states, and to encourage their cooperation in political, security, and development matters. The OAU played a significant role in bringing about the independence of **Southwest Africa** and in the elimination of **apartheid** in South Africa. It also contributed in minor ways to United Nations peacekeeping efforts in **Somalia, Liberia**, and **Mozambique**. In 2000, the OAU was superseded by the **African Union (AU)**.

ORGANIZATION OF AMERICAN STATES (OAS). Regional organization established in 1948 and headquartered in Washington, D.C. The purpose of the Organization of American States is to strengthen peace and security on the continent; to promote and consolidate representative democracy; and to enhance the economic, social, and cultural development of its members. Since the 1970s, however, the OAS has shifted its priorities to the promotion of **human rights** and development. The organization has observer status in the United Nations and has played a significant role in supporting the **peacekeeping** and human rights work of the United Nations, especially in **Haiti** and **Central America**. *See also* DOMINICAN CRISIS (April–July 1965); REGIONAL ARRANGEMENTS; UNITED NATIONS STABILIZATION MISSION IN HAITI (MINUSTAH, April 2004–present).

ORGANIZATION OF ARAB PETROLEUM EXPORTING COUNTRIES (OAPEC). Established in 1968 by the governments of Saudi Arabia, Kuwait, and Libya to protect the interest of its Arab members in their relations with the oil importing countries and foreign oil companies. It is headquartered in Kuwait. *See also* ORGANIZATION OF PETROLEUM EXPORTING COUNTRIES (OPEC).

**ORGANIZATION OF PETROLEUM EXPORTING COUN-
TRIES (OPEC).** Intergovernmental organization created in 1960 intended to coordinate the oil policies of its member countries and to
stabilize prices in international oil markets. OPEC was able to impose several increases in oil royalties and taxes throughout the 1970s.
But its subsequent attempts to impose production ceilings and to stabilize prices met with mixed results because of disagreements among
its members over the level of their respective production quotas.
OPEC's initial successes encouraged the short-lived belief that the
formation of similar **commodity** organizations among **developing
countries** could enhance their bargaining power in the **North-South
dialogue**. *See also* DECLARATION ON THE ESTABLISHMENT
OF A NEW INTERNATIONAL ECONOMIC ORDER (NIEO).

ORGANIZATION OF THE ISLAMIC CONFERENCE (OIC). Intergovernmental organization set up in 1971 to promote solidarity
among its Islamic member states and to strengthen their cooperation
in political, economic, social, cultural, and scientific matters. The
OIC has observer status in the United Nations.

ORR, JOHN BOYD (1880–1971). Scottish doctor and biologist. He
received the **Nobel Peace Prize** in 1949 for his scientific research on
nutrition and his work for the United Nations **Food and Agriculture
Organization (FAO)**. The first director-general of the FAO, he resigned after his comprehensive plans for improving food production
and its equitable distribution failed to win approval.

OTTAWA TREATY. *See* CONVENTION ON THE PROHIBITION
OF THE USE, STOCKPILING, PRODUCTION, AND TRANSFER
OF ANTIPERSONNEL MINES AND ON THEIR DESTRUCTION
(1999).

OTUNNU, OLARA (1950–). Ugandan lawyer, politician, and diplomat. Olara Otunnu served as Uganda's Permanent Representative to
the United Nations from 1980 to 1985. He was minister for foreign
affairs of Uganda from 1985 to 1986. From 1997 to 2005, he was
special representative of the secretary-general for **Children in
Armed Conflicts** and, in that capacity, acted as a strong advocate of
war-affected children.

OUTER SPACE. As a result of scientific and technological innovations, Soviet-American rivalry during the **Cold War** gradually extended to outer space, climaxing in 1957 with the launching of the first artificial satellite by the Soviet Union. This development profoundly affected military and political capabilities concerning the uses of outer space and brought to the fore the need to prevent a further extension of national rivalries and the arms race into outer space.

Over the years, the **General Assembly** has adopted several treaties and declarations on various aspects of the peaceful uses of outer space, including the activities of states in the exploration and use of outer space, the rescue and return of astronauts and objects launched into outer space, international liability for damage caused by outer space objects, and the registration of objects launched into outer space. In 1959, the assembly created a **United Nations Committee on the Peaceful Uses of Outer Space (COPUOS)** to promote international cooperation regarding this subject. Within the secretariat, the Office for Outer Space follows legal, technical, technological, and scientific developments in order to provide information and advice to member states. It also assists developing countries in the uses of space technology for developmental purposes. *See also* OUTER SPACE TREATY (1967).

OUTER SPACE TREATY (1967). Formally known as the Treaty on Principles Governing the Activities of States in the Exploration and Use of Outer Space, Including the Moon and Other Celestial Bodies, this treaty was based on a 1962 declaration of the **General Assembly** and entered into force in 1967. It provides the basic legal framework of international space law by proclaiming that the exploration and use of **outer space** shall be carried out for the benefit of humankind and that outer space is not subject to national appropriation by claims of sovereignty or occupation. The treaty also prohibits states to place nuclear weapons and other weapons of mass destruction in orbit or on celestial bodies and stipulates that the moon and other celestial bodies shall be used exclusively for peaceful purposes. *See also* ARMS CONTROL; COMMON HERITAGE OF MANKIND; DISARMAMENT.

OWEN, SIR DAVID (1904–1970). British diplomat and one of the principal architects of United Nations economic and social assistance to developing countries. He served as assistant secretary-general for economic affairs in the UN Secretariat from 1946 until 1952 when he took charge of the **Expanded Programme of Technical Assistance (EPTA)**. His long-lasting accomplishment was the establishment of a network of "resident representatives" of EPTA in countries receiving technical assistance to oversee projects and act as contact points between EPTA, recipient governments, and the specialized agencies that they also represented. This system still survives today as the **United Nations Development Programme's (UNDP) Resident Representatives**. *See also* COORDINATION, UNITED NATIONS SYSTEM.

OXFAM. Humanitarian agency based in the United Kingdom and devoted to "the relief of suffering arising as a result of wars or of other causes in any part of the world." OXFAM grew out of a group set up in 1942 to persuade the British government to allow essential humanitarian supplies through the blockade it had imposed on Nazi-occupied Greece. From a small local charity organization, OXFAM has evolved into a major national and international humanitarian actor. Emergency relief and rehabilitation is still one of its main activities. In the 1980s, the organization was active in the Horn of Africa and, in the 1990s, it provided **humanitarian assistance** to affected civilians in all sides of the wars in the former Yugoslavia and the Great Lakes region of Central Africa. At the same time, OXFAM has increasingly dedicated itself to policy research on the structural causes of **poverty** in the Third World (for instance the external **debt** burden of **developing countries**, unfair terms of **trade**, and inappropriate agricultural policies) and intensified its lobbying of governments, the United Nations, and regional organizations such as the **African Union (AU)** to promote development and humanitarian causes.

OZONE LAYER. Term designating the belt of unstable oxygen gases situated 15–50 kilometers above Earth's surface, shielding it from the sun's ultraviolet radiation. *See also* CLIMATE CHANGE; GLOBAL WARMING; MONTREAL PROTOCOL ON SUBSTANCES THAT DEPLETE THE OZONE LAYER (1987); UNITED NATIONS ENVIRONMENT PROGRAMME (UNEP); UNITED NATIONS FRAMEWORK CONVENTION ON CLIMATE CHANGE (UNFCCC); WORLD METEOROLOGICAL ORGANIZATION (WMO).

– P –

PALESTINE. See ARAB-ISRAELI CONFLICT; REFUGEES; UNITED NATIONS RELIEF AND WORKS AGENCY (UNRWA).

PALME COMMISSION. *See* INDEPENDENT COMMISSION ON DISARMAMENT AND SECURITY ISSUES.

PANEL OF EMINENT PERSONS ON UNITED NATIONS–CIVIL SOCIETY RELATIONS. In his September 2002 report on UN **reform, Secretary-General Kofi Annan** noted that due to their "explosive growth," the system for facilitating the interaction between the United Nations and **nongovernmental organizations (NGOs)** was "showing signs of strains." The capacity of the United Nations to manage the growing demand of NGOs to participate in meetings, the standardization of accreditation procedures, and the need for a better balance in participation between NGOs from industrialized countries and those from developing countries were some of the challenges facing the United Nations. How these challenges could be met was the key question that a Panel of Eminent Persons on UN-Civil Society Relations set up by the secretary-general in early 2003 was asked to consider.

The advisory group, chaired by former Brazilian president **Fernando Henrique Cardoso**, reported a year and a half later. In its report, the group stressed the importance of **civil society** and other constituencies to the United Nations because their experience and social connections could help the UN do a better job, improve its legitimacy, identify priorities, and connect it with public opinion. Arguing that **multilateralism** was changing and was increasingly shaped by ad hoc coalitions geared to specific goals, the group presented 30 reform proposals, some of which the secretary-general himself would have the authority to act on, while others would require intergovernmental approval. These proposals essentially aim at strengthening the participation of civil society organizations in UN processes, including the **Security Council**. *See also* REFORM, UNITED NATIONS.

PARTIAL TEST BAN TREATY (PTBT, 1963). Concern about the proliferation of nuclear weapons, the contamination of the environment, and the radioactive fallout risks associated with nuclear testing can be traced back to the early 1950s. President Dwight D. Eisen-hower's "**Atoms for Peace**" speech to the United Nations **General Assembly** in 1953 and a 1954 Indian proposal for a complete ban on testing nuclear weapons are manifestations of this concern. For years the issue dragged on. Negotiations involving primarily the United States and the Soviet Union stalemated over ways and means to ade-quately verify the implementation of such a ban. The two countries eventually reached agreement in 1963 over a Partial Test Ban Treaty prohibiting nuclear tests in the atmosphere, under the sea, and in outer space but still allowing underground testing. The hope was that the accord would lead to achieving a **Comprehensive Test Ban Treaty (CTBT)** prohibiting all testing in any environment and with any yield. A CTBT was concluded in 1996. *See also* ARMS CON-TROL; CONFERENCE ON DISARMAMENT (CD); DISARMA-MENT; NONPROLIFERATION OF NUCLEAR WEAPONS, TREATY ON THE (NPT, 1968); WEAPONS OF MASS DE-STRUCTION (WMDs).

PASVOLSKY, LEO (1893–1953). American economist of Russian origin considered by many the main architect of the United Nations **Charter**. He joined the United States Department of State in 1936 where he worked until 1946. There, as special assistant to Secretary of State **Cordell Hull**, he crafted and shepherded the blueprints for a postwar international organization that led to the proposals submitted by the American delegation at the 1944 **Dumbarton Oaks Conver-sations**. He played a key role at the 1945 San Francisco **United Na-tions Conference on International Organization** in the formation of a consensus over the final text of the charter. Likewise, he was a leading advocate of President **Truman**'s administration throughout the ratification hearings of the United States Senate.

PEACE BUILDING. *See* POSTCONFLICT PEACE BUILDING.

PEACE-BUILDING COMMISSION. The deployment of UN peace enforcement and peacekeeping forces is essential to the termination of internal violent conflicts. However, traditional **peacekeeping** ac-tivities cannot by themselves prevent the outbreak of new hostilities, and because the underlying socioeconomic problems that led to the conflict are not dealt with in a sustained manner, half the countries emerging from violent conflict relapse into violence within a five-year time span. Acting on proposals made by the **High-Level Panel on Threats, Challenges, and Change** and **Secretary-General Kofi Annan**, the **General Assembly**, and the **Security Council** jointly set up in late December 2005 a new intergovernmental advisory body, the Peace-Building Commission, to advise the council on country-specific postconflict activities needed to strengthen their socioeconomic foundations for sustainable peace and development.

Acting on the basis of consensus, the main purposes of the commission will be to suggest and propose integrated strategies for postconflict peace building, recovery, and sustainable development; to focus attention on the reconstruction and institution-building efforts necessary for recovery; and to provide recommendations and information to improve United Nations coordination. The commission's agenda is to be set at the request of the Security Council, the **Economic and Social Council (ECOSOC)**, the secretary-general, or member states on the "verge of lapsing or relapsing into conflict." The commission will have an Organizational Committee comprising seven Security Council members, including permanent members; seven members of ECOSOC elected from regional groups, with due consideration to those countries that have experienced postconflict recovery; five top providers of assessed contributions to United Nations budgets and of voluntary contributions to United Nations funds, programs, and agencies; five top providers of military personnel and civilian police to United Nations missions; and seven members elected by the assembly.

PEACEFUL SETTLEMENT OF DISPUTES. Safeguarding international peace and security was the primary purpose assigned to the United Nations by the drafters of the United Nations **Charter**. The **Security Council**, under Chapter VII of the charter, is the sole organ of the United Nations empowered to determine the existence of any threat to the peace, breach of the peace, or acts of aggression and to make binding decisions to impose military and nonmilitary **sanctions**. At the same time, all members of the United Nations have the prior obligation to "settle their international disputes by peaceful means in such a manner that international peace and security, and justice, are not endangered." (Article 2, paragraph 1). Under Chapter VI of the charter, both the Security Council and the **General Assembly** (as long as the council is not exercising jurisdiction over a question) may *recommend*, not impose, procedures or terms of settlement through traditional techniques of disputes settlement, such as negotiation, **enquiry, fact-finding, good offices, mediation, conciliation, arbitration, judicial settlement**, and resort to **regional arrangements**. These techniques are listed in Article 33, paragraph 1 of the charter. *See also* COLLECTIVE SECURITY; PRINCIPLES OF THE UNITED NATIONS.

PEACEKEEPING. The term *peacekeeping* is not found in the United Nations **Charter**. Its main intellectual architects, Canadian prime minister **Lester Pearson**, Secretary-General **Dag Hammarskjöld**, and his aide **Ralph Bunche**, described it as belonging to "Chapter VI and a Half" of the charter, between traditional methods of conflict resolution such as **mediation** and **fact-finding** (Chapter VI) and more coercive actions such as embargoes and military intervention (Chapter VII).

First used to describe the activities of the 1957 **United Nations Emergency Force (UNEF I)**, peacekeeping has in effect come to include missions that are very different from one another. Originally, peacekeeping meant the interposition of a neutral, lightly armed military force between two states having reached a cease-fire so as to monitor truces and troop withdrawals and provide buffer zones. Used during the **Cold War**, the technique required the consent of the parties involved and was intended to discourage a renewal of hostilities while providing an environment conducive to the settlement of their dispute.

Since the end of the Cold War, peacekeeping has encompassed missions with multiple tasks performed by military and civilian personnel, ranging from **preventive deployment** to **humanitarian assistance**, peace enforcement, and **peace building**. Such complex peacekeeping operations have increasingly been carried out in cooperation with **regional organizations** and involve the participation of **civil society** organizations. The costs of peacekeeping operations are apportioned by the **General Assembly** on a special scale of assessment based on the relative economic wealth of member states, with the permanent members of the Security Council required to pay a larger share. Many countries have voluntarily made additional resources available in the form of transportation, supplies, and personnel. *See also* AGENDA FOR PEACE; BRAHIMI REPORT; BUDGET (UNITED NATIONS); PEACEKEEPING OPERATIONS, SPECIAL COMMITTEE ON; SCHACHTER, OSCAR (1915–2003); URQUHART, SIR BRIAN (1919–).

PEACEKEEPING OPERATIONS, SPECIAL COMMITTEE. Committee established by the **General Assembly** in 1965 in the wake of the financial crisis triggered by the **United Nations Operation in the Congo (ONUC)** to study all aspects of **peacekeeping** including methods of financing services and personnel that member states might make available to the organization. The committee is still in existence, but its deliberations have produced few if any tangible results. *See also* BRAHIMI REPORT.

PEACEMAKING. Term coined by **Secretary-General Boutros Boutros-Ghali** in his **Agenda for Peace** referring to a range of activities designed to bring parties together in forging an actual settlement agreement by peaceful means as spelled out in Chapter VI of the United Nations **Charter** on the **peaceful settlement of disputes**. *See also* ARBITRATION; CONCILIATION; CONFLICT PREVENTION; ENQUIRY; GOOD OFFICES; JUDICIAL SETTLEMENT; MEDIATION; PEACEKEEPING; POSTCONFLICT PEACE BUILDING; REGIONAL ARRANGEMENTS.

PEARSON, LESTER (1897–1972). Canadian politician and diplomat, Lester Pearson played an active role in the work of the United Nations and was elected president of the seventh UN General Assembly. He headed the **Commission on International Development**. In 1957 he was awarded the **Nobel Peace Prize** for his role in the conception and establishment of the first **United Nations Emergency Force (UNEF I)**. *See also* PEACEKEEPING; SUEZ CANAL CRISIS (1956–1957).

PEARSON COMMISSION. *See* COMMISSION ON INTERNATIONAL DEVELOPMENT (PEARSON COMMISSION).

PEREZ DE CUELLAR, JAVIER (1920–). Fifth **secretary-general** of the United Nations from 1982 to 1991. A lawyer and highly respected career diplomat, he joined the Peruvian diplomatic service in 1944 and was a member of the Peruvian delegation at the first session of the General Assembly in 1946. He was subsequently posted in France, the United Kingdom, Bolivia, and Brazil and later served as ambassador to Switzerland, the Soviet Union, Poland, and Venezuela. In 1971, he was appointed permanent representative of Peru to the United Nations and headed his country's delegation to all sessions of the assembly until 1975. In 1973 and 1974, he represented Peru in the Security Council. From 1975 to 1977, Secretary-General **Kurt Waldheim** appointed him as his special representative and, from 1979 to 1981, undersecretary-general for special political affairs.

As secretary-general of the United Nations, he earned praise for his quiet, unassuming, and patient negotiating style. He sought to mediate the conflict between Argentina and Great Britain over the **Falkland/Malvinas** Islands and played a more effective role in promoting peace and security in **Central America conflicts**. Likewise, the thawing of the **Cold War** enabled him to intercede successfully in the negotiations that brought about the independence of **Southwest Africa** (Namibia) and the conclusion of a cease-fire in the **Iran-Iraq War (1980–1988)**. Through his interventions, the conflict between Morocco, the Polisario Front, and Algeria in the **Western Sahara dispute** abated, and the terms of its settlement were worked out, although they still remain to be implemented.

PEREZ-GUERRERO, MANUEL (1911–1985). Venezuelan statesman. He started his international career in the mid-1930s with the **League of Nations** and later held numerous high-level positions in the United Nations, notably as secretary-general of the **United Nations Conference on Trade and Development (UNCTAD)**. He played a decisive role in the creation of the **Organization of Petroleum Exporting Countries (OPEC)** in 1960 and was one of the key leaders of the **Group of Seventy-Seven (G-77)** in the **North-South dialogue** in the 1960s and 1970s.

PERMANENT COURT OF ARBITRATION (PCA). Arbitral body that commenced operations in 1913 and still functions at its seat in the Hague. Strictly speaking it is not a court but rather a panel of international experts from which states parties select individuals to arbitrate their disputes. Seldom used, its role has been further eclipsed by the creation of the **League of Nations' Permanent Court of International Justice (PCIJ)** and the United Nations **International Court of Justice (ICJ)**. It was used nevertheless in the settlement of the 1979 **Iran hostage crisis**. *See also* ARBITRATION.

PERMANENT COURT OF INTERNATIONAL JUSTICE (PCIJ). Judicial arm of the **League of Nations**. Its statute and mode of operation were broadly similar to those of the United Nations' **International Court of Justice (ICJ)**.

PERMANENT MISSIONS TO THE UNITED NATIONS. Nearly all member states of the United Nations maintain "permanent missions" to the United Nations in New York and its offices in Geneva and Vienna. The head of the mission—normally with the rank of ambassador—and the staff of the mission—of varying size depending on the interests and resources of the state—perform the traditional diplomatic functions of representation, negotiation, information gathering, and reporting. Their tasks relate primarily to matters on the agenda of the United Nations but may also extend to issues of a bilateral nature.

PERSIAN GULF WAR, FIRST (January–February 1991). In August 1990, Iraqi military forces invaded and occupied Kuwait thus sparking the first Gulf War. The **Security Council** passed no less than 12 resolutions condemning the invasion. In its last resolution (660), the council authorized the use of force if Iraq did not withdraw unconditionally by 15 January 2001. A broad-based U.S.-led coalition attacked Iraq two days after that date. After five weeks of intensive air and land operations, Iraqi forces were expelled from Kuwait.

According to the terms of the April 6 provisional truce and permanent cease-fire that ended the war, Iraq agreed to pay reparations to Kuwait, reveal the location of its stockpiles of chemical and biological weapons, and eliminate weapons of mass destruction. The Iraqi government also agreed to allow United Nations inspectors to search for unauthorized weapons in Iraq and for the coalition allies to enforce "No-Fly Zones" over northern and southern Iraq in order to protect rebellious Kurds and Shiite Muslim minorities from air strikes by the Iraqi air force.

The comprehensive economic sanctions against Iraq imposed by the Security Council on 6 August 1990, just after the Iraqi invasion of Kuwait, were kept in place as leverage to press for Iraqi **disarmament** and other goals. The sanctions remained in place thereafter, despite a harsh impact on Iraqi civilians, mitigated in part by a UN **Oil for Food Program (OFFP)** that started in late 1997. The program was brought to a close following the U.S.-led invasion of Iraq in March 2003. *See also* AGGRESSION; COLLECTIVE SECURITY; PERSIAN GULF WAR, SECOND (March–April 2003); RIO DECLARATION ON ENVIRONMENT AND DEVELOPMENT (1992); SANCTIONS; UNITED NATIONS MONITORING, VERIFICATION, AND INSPECTION COMMISSION (UNMOVIC); UNITED NATIONS SPECIAL COMMISSION (UNSCOM).

PERSIAN GULF WAR, SECOND (March–April 2003). After months of threats and a long military buildup and, on the basis of changing assertions that **Iraq** was supporting international **terrorism**, had failed to abide to the terms of the 1991 cease-fire by developing and hiding **weapons of mass destruction (WMDs)**, and refused to cooperate with United Nations weapons inspections, the United States and its military ally, Great Britain, attacked Iraq on 20 March 2003. The military campaign cut short UN arms inspections and was launched without the explicit approval of the **Security Council** after a war-sanctioning resolution failed to gain support in the council.

The invasion of Iraq removed Saddam Hussein's regime from power. A new political regime is being put in place and the occupation forces are encountering stiff armed resistance. The international community remains deeply divided over the legality of the war under **international law** as the claims about Iraqi weapons threats and terror links have proven false.

Two months after the outbreak of the war, UN **Secretary-General Kofi Annan** appointed a **special representative** for Iraq and the UN assumed minor responsibilities there. In August 2003, the bombing of United Nations headquarters in Baghdad killed 15 UN staff including Special Representative **Sergio Viera de Mello**. The UN then pulled out of Iraq but in February 2004 agreed to send a mission to the country, to help construct a new interim government and in the planning of national elections. A more substantial role for the United Nations appears unlikely as long as the occupation lasts, and for the time being, the UN role in the country involves assisting and advising on the political transitional process and helping to restore basic services and infrastructure. *See also* AGGRESSION; BUSH, GEORGE W. (1946–); COLLECTIVE SECURITY; HIGH-LEVEL PANEL ON THREATS, CHALLENGES, AND CHANGE (HLP); INTERNATIONAL ATOMIC ENERGY AGENCY (IAEA); PERSIAN GULF WAR, FIRST (January–February 1991); PREEMPTION; USE OF FORCE.

PERSONNEL QUESTIONS. The staff regulations governing the **Secretariat** of the **League of Nations** and of the United Nations were inspired by the British concept of an independent civil service and its principles of command and control, seniority, independence, and merit. As Article 101 of the United Nations **Charter** states, "the paramount consideration in the employment of staff and in the determination of conditions of services is the necessity of securing the highest standards of efficiency, competence and integrity." The same article, however, also stipulates that "due regard is also to be paid to the importance of recruiting staff on as wide a geographical basis as possible." The drafters of the charter did understand that there was a potential conflict between these two objectives but they believed they could "in large measure be reconciled."

As long as the organization's mandate was limited to the servicing of UN deliberative bodies and its staff needs entailed little more than competence in public information, legal issues, conference servicing, and administration, the inconsistency did not produce major difficulties. As the organization's membership started to grow in the 1960s and 1970s and its functions expanded to include technical assistance, peacekeeping, and humanitarian work, tensions began to appear between the two objectives of the charter. It became clear at that time that the notion of an independent meritocracy was not universally shared as patronage and geographical distribution started to prevail over merit considerations. The hierarchical culture of the secretariat and the proliferation of **control mechanisms** have also proved ill suited to the prompt decision making required in field situations while hampering rapid recruitment.

Numerous reform schemes have thus been entertained throughout the years. An important innovation, spearheaded by **Maurice Bertrand**, a French public administration specialist and member of the **Joint Inspection Unit (JIU)**, was the introduction in the late 1960s of a system of recruitment based on competitive examination held on the basis of occupational groups. The slow but expanding scope of application of the system has significantly helped resolve the tensions between geographical representation and the need for quality staff. The latest and most recent set of reform proposals for human resource management were initiated by **Secretary-General Kofi Annan** in his first term. They cover virtually all aspects of personnel policies including planning, recruitment, placement, promotion, mobility, career development, and conditions of service.

With its growing presence in the field and involvement in internal conflicts, the issue of safety of United Nations personnel has become a growing concern, especially after the 2003 bombing of the United Nations headquarters in Baghdad. A 1999 Convention on the Safety of United Nations and Associated Personnel adopted by the **General Assembly** requires states parties to take all necessary measures to protect United Nations staff and to cooperate in the prevention of crimes committed against them.

The United Nations Secretariat employs some 7,500 staff members under the regular **budget** and nearly an equal number under special funding. The UN system as a whole, the United Nations and its related programs and **specialized agencies**, including the World Bank and the International Monetary Fund, employs some 61,000 people. When the United Nations started operations in 1946, it had a staff of some 300 persons. *See also* CONVENTION ON THE PRIVILEGES AND IMMUNITIES OF THE UNITED NATIONS (1946); INTERNATIONAL CIVIL SERVICE; SAFETY OF UNITED NATIONS PERSONNEL.

PICCO, GIANDOMENICO (1948–). Italian United Nations senior official who was assistant secretary-general for political affairs from 1973 to 1992. He played an important role in the negotiations that led to a cease-fire between Iran and Iraq in 1988. He represented the

secretary-general in the negotiations of the 1988 Geneva Accords on **Afghanistan** and since then he has acted as special representative of the secretary-general for the United Nations Year of **Dialogue Among Civilizations**. *See also* IRAN-IRAQ WAR; MEDIATION.

PLANNED PARENTHOOD. Oldest of several **nongovernmental organizations (NGOs)** active in family planning. Founded in 1948 and headquartered in London. *See also* GLOBAL CONFERENCES (UNITED NATIONS); POPULATION; UNITED NATIONS POPULATION FUND (UNFPA).

PLEDGING CONFERENCES. Intergovernmental conferences meeting sponsored by the United Nations for the purpose of enabling governments to announce their voluntary contributions to UN development and humanitarian activities.

POLLUTION. Broadly speaking, the addition of dangerous chemical substances to the environment. It is the subject of increasing international cooperation through the United Nations, especially since the 1972 **United Nations Conference on the Human Environment** in **Stockholm**. *See also* AIR POLLUTION; ECONOMIC COMMISSION FOR EUROPE (ECE); ENVIRONMENT; INTERNATIONAL MARITIME ORGANIZATION (IMO); UNITED NATIONS ENVIRONMENT PROGRAMME (UNEP).

POPULATION. A major policy concern of the United Nations since 1946. Since the early days of the organization, UN organs (notably the **Commission on Population and Development** and the **Statistical Commission** of the **Economic and Social Council [ECOSOC]**) have carried out analytical studies of world population. In 1950, the United Nations conducted the first world population census, which warned about a forthcoming population explosion in the world. The study's findings triggered the convening of world expert conferences in 1954 and 1965, which discussed and recommended ways and means to limit future population growth through family planning. In that context and to assist in this process, the **secretary-general**, at the request of the **General Assembly**, set up in 1967 a United Nations Fund for Population Activities, since renamed the **United Nations Population Fund (UNFPA)**.

The United Nations has subsequently sponsored the organization of intergovernmental **global conferences** on population issues at 10-year intervals. The conferences have highlighted the linkages between population growth and **development**. The policy focus now is less on controlling the expansion of the world population, which has considerably slowed down, but on better access to and awareness of family planning to women, reproductive health as a **human right**, the **HIV/AIDS** pandemic, the economic and socioeconomic consequences of the **aging** of populations, and international **migration**. *See also* PLANNED PARENTHOOD; POPULATION COUNCIL; POPULATION PROGRAMS OF THE UNITED NATIONS.

POPULATION COUNCIL. New York–based worldwide organization established in 1972 that carries out biomedical research on human reproduction, new methods of contraception, population policies, family planning, and reproductive health. Has close ties with the **United Nations Population Fund (UNFPA)**.

POPULATION PROGRAMS OF THE UNITED NATIONS. From its inception, the United Nations has carried out extensive activities in this field under the authority of the **Economic and Social Council (ECOSOC)** and the **Commission on Population and Development** and, within the **secretariat**, the support of the **United Nations Population Division**. Initially, the work of the United Nations was limited to information gathering, demographic analysis, and **technical assistance** in census methods. One of the outcomes of this authoritative work was to draw attention to the rapid expansion of the world **population**, to changes in its North-South distribution, and to the rapid increase in the number of older persons.

As a result of the **global conferences** sponsored at 10-year intervals by the United Nations on population issues since 1954, the scope of the United Nations' work on **demography** has expanded to encompass developmental, **gender**, and **human rights** policy concerns. No longer defined simply in terms of fertility reduction, population issues are now framed in the context of the **development** process, women's equality and empowerment, safe reproductive **health**, and the expansion of **education** for girls. The **regional commissions**, the **United Nations Population Fund (UNFPA)**, the **United Nations Children's Fund (UNICEF)**, the **World Health Organization (WHO)**, and the

World Bank also carry out population programs within their respective mandates. See also AGING; DEVELOPMENT; HEALTH; MIGRATION (INTERNATIONAL); POPULATION; UNITED NATIONS POPULATION FUND (UNFPA).

PORTUGUESE COLONIES. Portugal was the first European nation to extend its sway over a worldwide colonial empire, which in the 16th century extended from Brazil in Latin America to **Angola** and **Mozambique** in Africa to Macau in Asia. When the United Nations was founded, Portugal retained control over only a handful of territories. Throughout the 1950s and 1960s, Portugal steadfastly resisted United Nations **decolonization** efforts, declaring its remaining colonies to be "overseas provinces of the mother country" while at the same time trying to suppress by military means the independence movements that sprang up in several of them and encouraging immigration to the colonies when many other European nations were beginning to grant independence to their own. It was only after a 1974 coup d'etat overthrew the conservative regime of Antonio de Oliveira Salazar in mainland Portugal that the new regime, bowing to United Nations pressures, swiftly granted independence to most of its colonies, notably Angola, Mozambique, Cape Verde, and Guinea-Bissau.

Unlike the majority of former Portuguese colonies, the Azores did not have an armed struggle for independence. In 1976 the Azores became an autonomous region with its own government. The islands' autonomy revolves around responsibility for the economy, with education, health, the army, police, and judiciary controlled directly by the national government in Lisbon. Negotiations between the People's Republic of China and Portugal for the return of Macau to Chinese sovereignty began in 1985, resulting in a 1987 agreement to return Macau to the Chinese as a special administrative region (SAR) of China on 20 December 1999. *See also* TIMOR-LESTE.

POSTAL SERVICES (UNITED NATIONS). In agreement with United States postal authorities, the United Nations has been issuing stamps in US denominations since 1951. Similar agreements with the Swiss and Austrian postal services, concluded in 1968 and 1979, respectively, have enabled the organization to also issue stamps from its Geneva and Vienna offices. These stamps are valid for postage only when used from the UN in New York, Geneva, and Vienna. They reflect the work of the United Nations and its affiliated organizations, illustrate their aims and achievements, and commemorate significant events in their activities.

POSTCONFLICT PEACE BUILDING. Set of interrelated and coordinated short- and long-term multiagency and multilevel interventions and measures in many recent United Nations peacekeeping operations designed to create a stable environment in post-war-torn societies and to forestall the reemergence of destructive processes that in the first place created the conditions for the outbreak of a civil conflict.

The term was coined by **Secretary-General Boutros Boutros-Ghali** in his **Agenda for Peace** as an approach to both postconflict settlement and **conflict prevention** practices complementing the **peacekeeping** and **peacemaking** activities of the United Nations. The range of postconflict activities undertaken in United Nations peacekeeping operations include reconciliation measures, the demobilization of former combatants and their reintegration in society, **electoral assistance**, the reestablishment of the rule of law, the provision of public security through the training of an adequate police force and a functioning judiciary, the repatriation and resettlement of **refugees** and **internally displaced persons**, the reconstruction of **civil society**, **antipersonnel landmine** clearance, and the rebuilding of the economy through long-term economic assistance. The United Nations has run peace-building missions in **Cambodia**, **East Timor**, **El Salvador**, **Liberia**, **Mozambique**, **Namibia**, **Nicaragua**, and **Timor-Leste**, among others. *See also* PEACE-BUILDING COMMISSION.

POVERTY. The **Charter of the United Nations** originally enjoined the organization to promote "higher standards of living, full employment, and conditions of economic and social progress." On that basis and with the mass entry of **developing countries** in the 1960s, the United Nations vastly expanded the scope of its activities in **development**. Poverty eradication is now one of its overriding objectives.

"Well-being" is a highly subjective and culturally driven value, but poverty is widely understood today as the nonfulfillment of preferences and the nonsatisfaction of basic needs. Deprivation, social exclusion, personal capability failure, powerlessness, and vulnerability are dimensions of poverty measurable by social and economic indicators such as the human development index developed by the **United Nations Development Programme (UNDP)**.

The **World Bank** defines poverty in terms of individual consumption levels of less than one and two dollars a day. This rather conservative indicator based on purchasing power parity techniques to facilitate comparisons across countries shows that over a billion people, a quarter of the population of the developing world, now live on below one dollar a day. Close to three billion people—half the total world population live on below two dollars a day. *See also* HIGH-LEVEL PANEL ON THREATS, CHALLENGES, AND CHANGE (HLP); HUMAN DEVELOPMENT REPORT (HDR); HUMAN SECURITY; HUNGER; MILLENNIUM DECLARATION.

PREBISCH, RAUL (1901–1986). Argentinian economist and banker. As executive secretary of the **Economic Commission for Latin America and the Caribbean (ECLAC)** from 1948 to 1962, he argued that the **terms of trade** for developing countries had been declining since the beginning of the century, thus dragging them into a state of "dependency" upon developed countries. As producers of raw materials for First World countries and recipients of their manufactured products, developing countries locked themselves into an unequal "center-periphery" relationship. Only major structural changes in international economic relations, to be achieved through collective action, could reverse this process. His views, which rationalized internal state control of markets and import-substitution strategies, were articulated in numerous studies of the commission and provided the rationale for the creation of the **Group of Seventy-Seven (G-77)** and of the **United Nations Conference on Trade and Development (UNCTAD)**. From 1964 to 1969, Prebisch was the first secretary-general of UNCTAD. *See also* INTEGRATED PROGRAMME FOR COMMODITIES (IPC); NEW INTERNATIONAL ECONOMIC ORDER (NIEO); TRADE AND DEVELOPMENT; SINGER, HANS (1910–2005).

PREEMPTION. Defined as the anticipatory **use of force** in the face of an imminent attack, preemption has long been accepted as legitimate and appropriate under **international law**. Thus, under Article 51 of the United Nations **Charter**, member states may invoke a right of **self-defense** only until the **Security Council** has undertaken measures against an aggressor.

However, no political or legal consensus has ever been achieved over the point in time from which measures of self-defense against an armed attack may be taken. Nor is there any agreement over what constitutes a "threat" or "armed attack" that might trigger the anticipatory use of force in self-defense. In the 1962 **Cuban Missile Crisis**, the United States premised its self-defense stand and decision to impose a quarantine on Cuba on an acknowledged anticipatory self-defense, since the presence of nuclear missiles on the Caribbean island posed an imminent and immediate threat to the United States. The legality of the U.S. military blockade was questioned because it had not received the prior approval of the council.

The 11 September 2001 terrorist attacks on the United States have rekindled the debate over the outer limits of self-defense and preemption. The day after the attack, the Security Council adopted a resolution that recognized the "inherent right of individual or collective self-defense" and expressed its readiness "to combat all forms of terrorism." In a subsequent statement to a joint session of Congress, U.S. President **George W. Bush** vowed to hold responsible the terrorists as well as those who harbor them. On that basis and on the ground that the Taliban regime had allowed the territory of **Afghanistan** to be used as a base of operation by terrorists, the United States initiated a military campaign in Afghanistan designed to prevent and deter similar further attacks. Thus, anticipatory self-defense has been brought to a new plateau in the sense that an open-ended war has been undertaken by the United States against individuals, **nonstate actors**, and states that may be subjected to "accountability" tests if they are suspected to aid, support, or harbor terrorists.

The preemption concept was subsequently elaborated in a National Security Strategy paper that threatened to attack so-called "rogue states" that posed a danger to the United States even if they could not demonstrably be tied to the activities of global terrorist organizations. The paper also argued that the spread of **weapons of mass destruction (WMDs)** technology to states with a history of **aggression** created unacceptable levels of risk to the United States and provided "a compelling case for taking anticipatory actions to defend ourselves, even if uncertainty remains as to the time and place of the enemy's attack." This doctrine was used to justify the U.S.-led intervention against **Iraq** in 2003 and has since generated considerable debate, many viewing it as a manifestation of the demise of the postwar **multilateralism** enshrined in the United Nations Charter. A panel of eminent persons set up by **Secretary-General Kofi Annan** in 2003 has sought to define broad guidelines for the use of self-defense. *See also* HIGH-LEVEL PANEL ON THREATS, CHALLENGES, AND CHANGE (HLP); PERSIAN GULF WAR, SECOND (March–April 2003).

PREVENTIVE DEPLOYMENT. Refers to the stationing of peacekeepers who act as a deterrent force designed to forestall the escalation of an incipient emerging conflict into acute violence. Troops in preventive deployment monitor and report on activities that may undermine stability, such as arms smuggling; may intervene to prevent abuses against civilian populations; and assist in the delivery of humanitarian assistance and social services. The **United Nations Peacekeeping Force in Cyprus (UNFICYP)** and the **United Nations Angola Verification Mission (UNAVEM I, II)** were peacekeeping operations with a preventive deployment component. Another example is the **United Nations Preventive Deployment Force (UNPREDEP)** that monitored **Macedonia**'s borders with Albania and Serbia.

PREVENTIVE DIPLOMACY. Concept coined by **Secretary-General Dag Hammarskjöld** originally referring to steps that could be taken by the United Nations or the secretary-general under Chapter VI of the charter in order to insulate local conflicts from **Cold War** antagonisms. The earlier **peacekeeping** operations undertaken by the United Nations are instances of preventive diplomacy. The term has acquired a broader meaning encompassing measures designed to prevent the outbreak or an escalation of conflicts. Such measures include confidence-building measures, **fact-finding**, **early warning**, **preventive deployment**, demilitarized zones. *See also* AGENDA FOR PEACE.

PREVENTIVE OR ENFORCEMENT ACTION. Under the United Nations **Charter**, the United Nations may take "preventive or enforcement action" for the maintenance of international peace and security. Such measures may include actions by the **Security Council** pursuant to Chapter VI of the charter on the **peaceful settlement of disputes** and Chapter VII, "action with respect to threats to the peace, breaches to the peace and acts of **aggression**." *See also* AGENDA FOR PEACE; PREVENTIVE DIPLOMACY; SANCTIONS.

PRINCIPLES OF THE UNITED NATIONS. To achieve its purposes—the maintenance of peace and security, the development of friendly relations, international cooperation in economic and social matters—the United Nations **Charter** sets forth a number of principles for the guidance of its members and the organs of the United Nations. Most of them are found in Article 2 of the charter and include: the sovereign equality of all members and the related notion that the organization may not intervene in any matters that are essentially within the **domestic jurisdiction** of a state; all members must settle their international disputes by peaceful means and refrain from the threat or use of forces; and all members must support the preventive and enforcement actions of the United Nations and refrain from assisting states that are the objects of such actions. Respect for **human rights**, the right of **self-determination**, and the right of individual and **collective self-defense** are other principles found in miscellaneous provisions of the charter. *See also* COLLECTIVE SECURITY; PREEMPTION; SELF-DEFENSE, RIGHT OF; USE OF FORCE.

PRIVATE PETITIONS. Procedures enabling individuals to lodge complaints about violations of their rights to the committees supervising the implementation of the **International Covenant on Civil and Political Rights**, the **Convention against Torture**, the **International Convention on the Elimination of All Forms of Racial Discrimination**, and the **Convention on the Elimination of All Forms of Discrimination against Women**. Such cases can generally only be lodged by the victim of an alleged violation after she or he has exhausted any remedies that are available at the national level. The proceedings follow an adversarial procedure and the outcome is a decision by the committee in the form of a judicial decision. These decisions are not legally binding on the state concerned. *See also* COMMITTEE AGAINST TORTURE (CAT); COMMITTEE FOR

THE ELIMINATION OF RACIAL DISCRIMINATION (CERD); COMMITTEE ON THE ELIMINATION OF DISCRIMINATION AGAINST WOMEN (CEDAW); HUMAN RIGHTS COMMITTEE (HRC).

PRIVILEGES AND IMMUNITIES OF THE UNITED NATIONS. *See* CONVENTION ON THE PRIVILEGES AND IMMUNITIES OF THE UNITED NATIONS (1946).

PROJECT LINK. International network of more than 60 national and international economic research institutions and organizations providing global, regional, and national economic forecasts and economic policy analysis based on an integrated global econometric model. Project LINK also provides a forum for semiannual meetings of participating organizations to discuss the short-term global economic outlook and related economic policy issues and serves as a resource to assist in the development of a capacity for economic forecasting and analysis in **developing countries**. The system was founded under the intellectual leadership of **Lawrence Klein** and is coordinated jointly by the University of Toronto and the United Nations **Department of Economic and Social Affairs (DESA)**. *See also* COMMITTEE FOR DEVELOPMENT POLICY (CDP); TINBERGEN, JAN (1903–1994).

PRONK, JAN (1940–). Prominent Dutch politician and government official who served three times as minister for development cooperation and, more recently, as minister of the environment. A well-known advocate of multilateral policies for sustainable economic and environment development, Pronk was deputy secretary-general of the **United Nations Conference on Trade and Development (UNCTAD)** from 1980 to 1985. He also was the **secretary-general**'s special envoy for the 2002 **World Summit on Sustainable Development (WSSD)**. Since 2004, he has been the special representative of the secretary-general for the **Sudan**.

PUERTO RICAN QUESTION. Colony of Spain annexed by the United States in the wake of the 1898 Spanish American War, Puerto Rico was initially considered a **non-self-governing territory** within the meaning of the charter's **Declaration Regarding Non-Self-Governing Territories**. In 1952, Puerto Rico acquired "Commonwealth" status within the United States and was removed from the list of nonself-governing territories. Nevertheless, since the early 1970s, the General Assembly's **Special Committee on Decolonization** has considered the island a non-self-governing territory and adopted numerous resolutions supporting the right of Puerto Ricans to **self-determination** and independence from the United States. *See also* DECLARATION ON THE GRANTING OF INDEPENDENCE TO COLONIAL COUNTRIES AND PEOPLES (1960); DECOLONIZATION.

PUGWASH CONFERENCES ON SCIENCE AND WORLD AFFAIRS (PUGWASH). Worldwide **nongovernmental organization (NGO)** created in 1957 that was designed to bring together scholars and public policy makers concerned about global security threats arising from the **Cold War**. During that period, Pugwash acted as one of the unofficial channels of communication between the United States and the USSR. In addition, the organization played a significant substantive role in the preparations and negotiations of the 1963 **Partial Test Ban Treaty (PTBT)**, the 1968 **Treaty on the Nonproliferation of Nuclear Weapons (NPT)**, the 1972 Antiballistic Missile Treaty (ABMT), the 1972 **Biological Weapons Convention (BWC)**, and the 1993 **Chemical Weapons Convention (CWC)**. Since the end of the Cold War and the relaxation of international tensions that followed, Pugwash has continued to work on **arms control** issues, notably conventional weapons reductions and restructuring, space weapons, and bacteriological and chemical weaponry. But it has also broadened its activities to include disarmament-related environmental and developmental issues. In 1995, Pugwash was awarded the **Nobel Peace Prize**. *See also* ENVIRONMENTAL SECURITY; NONSTATE ACTORS.

– Q –

QUIET DIPLOMACY. Multilateral public diplomacy as it is practiced in the United Nations has many of the characteristics of national legislative processes. Its merits have been debated for a long time. Some argue that public discussion of world issues may contribute to an easing of tensions and to progress toward accommodation or agreement, others that they can just as readily be used for propaganda purposes or home consumption and hinder the process of **peacemaking**. In actual practice, speeches, votes, and other public proceedings have in effect supplemented the informal procedures of private parliamentary diplomacy, or **preventive diplomacy**, as **Secretary-General Dag Hammarskjöld** called it. The charter recognizes the value of conventional diplomacy in its chapter on the **peaceful settlement of disputes** by highlighting the importance of such traditional techniques of diplomacy as **enquiry**, **good offices**, and **mediation**.

– R –

RACIAL DISCRIMINATION. In accordance with the **Charter** of the United Nations, all members of the organization accept the obligation to pursue the realization of **human rights** and fundamental freedoms for all, without distinction as to race, sex, language, or religion. The 1948 **Universal Declaration of Human Rights (UDHR)**, in its Article 1, further amplifies this by stating that all human beings are born free and equal in dignity and rights and the **Convention on the Prevention and Punishment of the Crime of Genocide** declares genocide an international crime.

Driven by the expanding numerical majority of **Third World** countries, United Nations debates throughout the 1950s and 1960s, focused on racial discrimination in **non-self-governing territories** and **apartheid** in South Africa and Southern Rhodesia, culminating in 1965 and 1971, respectively, in the adoption by the **General Assembly** of the **International Convention on the Elimination of All Forms of Racial Discrimination** and the International Convention on the Suppression and Punishment of the Crime of Apartheid.

In spite of the demise of European colonial empires and of the apartheid regime, the issue of racial discrimination has remained high on the agenda of the United Nations, fed by continuing regional disputes such as the **Arab-Israeli conflict** and lingering feelings of economic exploitation among **developing countries** by the Northern states. In 1968, shortly before the convention entered into force, the first International Conference on Human Rights, meeting in Tehran, called for the criminalization of racist and Nazi organizations. On 11 December 1969, the General Assembly designated 1971 as the International Year for Action to Combat Racism and Racial Discrimination to "be observed in the name of the ever-growing struggle against racial discrimination in all its forms and manifestations and in the name of international solidarity with those struggling against racism." In follow-up to the Year, the General Assembly designated the 10-year period beginning on December 1973 as the Decade for Action to Combat Racism and Racial Discrimination. The program for the Decade was primarily focused on a worldwide education campaign. The assembly has since proclaimed two other "decades" (1983–1992 and 1994–2003) with similar objectives. In addition, the United Nations has held three world conferences concerned with an ever widening range of racial discrimination issues in 1978, 1983, and 2001, encompassing racial or ethnic exclusion or intolerance; hatred; terror or systematic denials of human rights and fundamental freedoms; gender discrimination; and violations of the rights of **refugees**, immigrants, and **migrant workers**. *See also* PRIVATE PETITIONS; TREATY BODIES; WORLD CONFERENCE AGAINST RACISM, RACIAL DISCRIMINATION, XENOPHOBIA AND RELATED INTOLERANCE (DURBAN, SOUTH AFRICA, 2001); WORLD CONFERENCE ON HUMAN RIGHTS (VIENNA, 1993).

RAMPHAL, SIR SHRIDATH (1928–). National of Guyana with a long-standing involvement in work for international peace, **disarmament**, and **development**. An unapologetic advocate of **Third World** causes, he was **secretary-general** of the **commonwealth** from 1975 to 1990 and played an important role in the **North-South dialogue**. A strong supporter of the United Nations, he served in the 1980s on several **independent commissions** that reported on global issues — the **Independent Commission on International Development Issues (ICIDI)**, the **Independent Commission on Disarmament and Security Issues**, the **World Commission on Environment and Development**, and the **South Commission**. In 1995, he cochaired the **Commission on Global Governance**, with the then prime minister of Sweden, **Ingvar Carlsson**.

RAW MATERIALS. *See* COMMODITIES.

RED CROSS, THE. International movement comprising three types of independent institutions: the National Red Cross and Red Crescent Societies, the International Federation of Red Cross and Red Crescent Societies, and the **International Committee of the Red Cross (ICRC)**. Each institution is autonomous but shares the same principles of humanitarianism: impartiality, neutrality, independence, and voluntary service. Their humanitarian mission is to protect the lives of victims of war and internal conflicts, undertake international relief activities, and promote and strengthen **humanitarian law**. *See also* HUMANITARIAN AGENCIES.

REFORM, UNITED NATIONS. Would-be reformers of the United Nations as well as blueprints for change are legion. But political disagreements over the purposes and priorities of the organization have made formal reforms in the UN architecture virtually impossible (the **charter** was amended only once in 1965). Incremental change has been the prevailing pattern, with innovations originating from initiatives of the **secretary-general** or the political process. **Peacekeeping** is one such innovation. *See also* AMENDMENT (UNITED NATIONS CHARTER); ECONOMIC AND SOCIAL COUNCIL (ECOSOC); GENERAL ASSEMBLY; INDEPENDENT COMMISSIONS; PANEL OF EMINENT PERSONS ON UNITED NATIONS–CIVIL SOCIETY RELATIONS; REVIEW OF THE UN CHARTER; SECURITY COUNCIL; SPECIAL COMMITTEE ON THE CHARTER OF THE UNITED NATIONS AND ON THE STRENGTHENING OF THE ROLE OF THE ORGANIZATION; STRONG, MAURICE (1929–); WORLD GOVERNMENT.

REFUGEES. Refugee problems in Europe during and immediately after the end of World War II were the concern of two temporary organizations, the **International Refugee Organization (IRO)** and the **United Nations Relief and Rehabilitation Administration (UNRRA)**. The scale and scope of the problem prompted the subsequent establishment of the **United Nations Children's Fund (UNICEF)** and the Office of the **United Nations High Commissioner for Refugees (UNHCR)**.

The number of refugees has widely varied over time but swelled in the 1990s with the explosion of ethnic conflicts, notably in Bosnia, Central Africa, and Rwanda. Current estimates place the total number of refugees in the world assisted by the UNHCR to some 20 million people. The largest refugee population is that of Palestinians, estimated to be 4 million people, who are cared for since 1948 by the **United Nations Relief and Works Agency (UNRWA)**. Refugees are protected under the terms of the 1951 **Convention Relating to the Status of Refugees and Stateless Persons**. *See also* HUMAN RIGHTS; INTERNALLY DISPLACED PERSONS (IDPs).

REGIONAL ARRANGEMENTS. The United Nations Charter assigns to the **Security Council** a primary responsibility in the maintenance of peace and security, especially in regard to **preventive or enforcement actions**. At the same time, Chapter VIII of the charter makes provision for regional organizations to resolve disputes and maintain peace. Article 52 encourages regional organizations to initiate procedures for the **peaceful settlement of disputes**. Article 53 stipulates that the Security Council shall utilize such regional arrangements for enforcement action under its authority and that regional arrangements or agencies may not take enforcement action without its authorization.

Cold War rivalries led to a vast expansion of collective **self-defense** alliances under Article 51, as evidenced by the creation of the **North Atlantic Treaty Organization (NATO)**, the Warsaw Pact, the **Arab League**, and the **Organization of African Unity (OAU)**. This system of multilateral arrangements virtually disappeared with the end of the Cold War. Nevertheless, regional organizations have now acquired new and significant roles in the field of **peacekeeping**. In Liberia, the **United Nations Observer Mission in Liberia (UNOMIL)** was the first UN peacekeeping operation undertaken in 1990 in cooperation with an operation already established by a regional organization, the Military Observer Group (ECOMOG) set up by the **Economic Community of West African States (ECOWAS)**. In Bosnia and Herzegovina, the **European Union** took over from the **United Nations Mission in Bosnia and Herzegovina (UNMIBH)** in 2002. In Georgia, the United Nations cooperates with the **Organization for Security and Cooperation in Europe (OSCE)** and the peacekeeping force of the **Commonwealth of Independent States (CIS)**. In Kosovo, NATO forces ensure overall security, while the United Nations is responsible for civil administration and **humanitarian assistance**, democratization and institution building is directed by the OSCE, and economic reconstruction by the European Union. *See also* AGGRESSION; DOMINICAN CRISIS (April–July 1965); HAITI; POSTCONFLICT PEACE BUILDING; UNITED NATIONS CIVILIAN POLICE SUPPORT GROUP (UNPSG).

REGIONAL COMMISSIONS. Article 68 of the United Nations **Charter** provides for the creation of commissions under the authority of the **Economic and Social Council (ECOSOC)**. Extensions of ECOSOC at the regional level, the main purpose of the regional commissions is to support the economic and social development of the member states in the region, foster regional integration, and promote cooperation among the member states.

The commissions' membership normally includes states located in the region but also other countries with special interests in the region: Canada and the United States sit in the **Economic Commission for Europe (ECE)**; France and the United States are members of the **Economic and Social Commission for Asia and the Pacific (ESCAP)**; and Israel belongs to the ECE. **Non-self-governing territories** enjoy "associate membership," and such is the case for Anguilla, Aruba, the British Virgin Islands, Montserrat, the Netherlands Antilles, Puerto Rico, and the U.S. Virgin Islands in the **Economic Commission for Latin America and the Caribbean (ECLAC)**; French Polynesia, New Caledonia, and Guam in ESCAP.

All regional commissions report annually to ECOSOC, publish annual economic surveys of major economic and social developments in their regions, and engage in technical assistance. Their financial resources derive from the UN regular **budget** and are supplemented by additional specific project contributions from governments. They have frequently spearheaded efforts to create regional integration schemes including regional banks, common markets, and free trade areas. *See also* ECONOMIC COMMISSION FOR AFRICA (ECA); ECONOMIC AND SOCIAL COMMISSION FOR WESTERN ASIA (ESCWA); MULTILATERAL DEVELOPMENT BANKS (MDBs).

REGIONAL DEVELOPMENT BANKS (RDBs). *See* MULTILATERAL DEVELOPMENT BANKS (MDBs).

REGIONAL GROUPS. *See* GROUPS AND GROUPINGS.

REGISTER OF CONVENTIONAL ARMS AND STANDARDIZED REPORTING OF MILITARY EXPENDITURES. An arrangement whereby governments provide information on a voluntary basis on their transfers to other states of major weapons including battle tanks, armored combat vehicles, large caliber artillery, combat aircraft, attack helicopters, warships, and missiles and missile launchers. The data are collected and published annually by the United Nations. *See also* ARMS CONTROL; DEPARTMENT FOR DISARMAMENT AFFAIRS (DDA); DISARMAMENT.

RESEARCH. If research is defined as the gathering of information for policy analysis and recommendation, then virtually the entire United Nations system is engaged in such "research," ranging from the compilation of demographic and trade statistics to analytical reports on the status and condition of women to socioeconomic projections and technical studies on telecommunications and civil aviation safety. The United Nations has a large publication program designed to disseminate this material. All the departments dealing with political issues within the **secretariat** of the United Nations have "lessons learned," **early warning**, and other "policy analysis" units that undertake policy evaluations and assessments for their senior management and the **secretary-general**.

In some cases, the need has arisen for independent analysis insulated from day-to-day political pressures and concerns. It is with this objective in mind that such institutions as the **United Nations Institute for Training and Research (UNITAR)**, the **United Nations Institute for Disarmament Research (UNIDIR)**, and the **United Nations University (UNU)** were set up. The work of these organizations, which enjoy a large degree of autonomy within the framework of the United Nations, focuses on enhancing the understanding of current or emerging global issues on the agenda of the organization. They also carry out training activities. *See also* FUNCTIONALISM;

INTERNATIONAL RESEARCH AND TRAINING INSTITUTE FOR THE ADVANCEMENT OF WOMEN (INSTRAW); OFFICE FOR RESEARCH AND COLLECTION OF INFORMATION (ORCI); UNITED NATIONS INTERREGIONAL CRIME AND JUSTICE RESEARCH INSTITUTE (UNICRI); UNITED NATIONS RESEARCH INSTITUTE FOR SOCIAL DEVELOPMENT (UNRISD); UNITED NATIONS SYSTEM STAFF COLLEGE.

RESIDENT COORDINATORS. *See* RESIDENT REPRESENTATIVES.

RESIDENT REPRESENTATIVES. Variously known as "country representatives," "resident coordinators," or simply "resident representatives," the main function of these officials of the **United Nations Development Programme (UNDP)** is to coordinate the UN's operational activities among the various agencies of the UN at the country level. Their origins can be traced back to mechanisms of coordination set up in the context of the **Expanded Programme of Technical Assistance (EPTA)**. In many cases of human disasters, natural catastrophe and complex emergency situations, the resident representative also acts as humanitarian coordinator for the UN system. *See also* COORDINATION, UNITED NATIONS SYSTEM; HUMANITARIAN ASSISTANCE; NATURAL DISASTER; OWEN, SIR DAVID (1904–1970).

REVIEW OF THE UNITED NATIONS CHARTER. In a concession to smaller nations, the big powers agreed at the 1945 **United Nations Conference on International Organization** in San Francisco that the **General Assembly** would hold a "General Conference" to review the charter in 1955. As required by Article 109 of the charter, the assembly placed the question on its agenda at its 10th session. But there was no substantial support at the time for holding such a conference, nor did any country submit any proposal for amending the charter. The general feeling was that, in the context of the **Cold War**, it would be futile to seek to formally change the provisions of the charter (especially the **veto**) in the absence of agreement among the permanent members of the **Security Council**. *See also* AMENDMENT (UNITED NATIONS CHARTER); REFORM, UNITED NATIONS.

RHODESIAN QUESTION. In 1953, the United Kingdom attempted to create a federation consisting of the current nations of Zimbabwe, Zambia, and Malawi (at the time called Southern Rhodesia, Northern Rhodesia, and Nyasaland respectively). The federation was dissolved a year later upon the independence of Malawi and Zambia. Southern Rhodesia remained a British colony and came to be known simply as Rhodesia. The British government adopted a policy known as No Independence before Majority Rule, but in 1965, the Rhodesian white minority government unilaterally proclaimed the country's independence. The move was internationally condemned and the **Security Council** imposed increasingly stringent **sanctions** against the white regime. In 1966, for the first time ever, the council applied mandatory sanctions under Chapter VII of the United Nations **Charter**, limited at first to an arms embargo, oil, and Rhodesian exports and subsequently expanded to all of Rhodesia's economic relations. The impact of the sanctions combined with the pressures of internal civil war and British efforts to mediate the conflict eventually led to a settlement. After multiracial elections, power was transferred to the black majority in 1980 and Rhodesia became independent under the name of Zimbabwe.

RIGHT TO DEVELOPMENT. Principle enshrined in a nonbinding 1986 resolution of the **General Assembly** positing that "every human person and all peoples are entitled to participate in, contribute to, and enjoy economic, social, cultural, and political development, in which all human rights and fundamental freedoms can be fully realized." The Declaration and Program of Action adopted by the 1993 **World Conference on Human Rights** in Vienna reaffirmed that the right to development was a "universal and inalienable right and an integral part of fundamental human rights."

The concept has been a continuing source of sharp disagreement among governments, largely along North-South lines. Some argue that the right to development simply reflects the need to strike a better balance between political and civil rights and economic, social, and cultural rights in accordance with the principle of the indivisibility of **human rights**. Others object to the idea that a right to development implies an obligation on the part of states to create national and international conditions favorable to its realization. The still raging controversy has centered on such issues as whether extreme poverty, the structural adjustment programs of the **International Monetary Fund (IMF)**, external **debt**, and **globalization** constitute obstacles that prevent the peoples of developing countries from achieving a collective right to adequate **food**, housing, **education**, **employment**, and **health**.

RIKHYE, INDAR JIT (1920–). Senior military officer in the Indian Army who devoted most of his professional life to UN **peacekeeping** operations. He was in command of the first **United Nations Emergency Force (UNEF I)** from 1958 to 1960. Military adviser to the **secretary-general** for the next eight years, he was involved in the 1960 Congo crisis; the decolonization of West Irian, Rwanda, and Burundi; and the **Cuban Missile Crisis**. As commander of the second UN peacekeeping operation in Egypt (**United Nations Emergency Force II**), he was in the center of the controversial UN decision to pull out of the Sinai when the government of Egypt withdrew its consent to the force. Upon retirement from UN service, Rikhye helped establish and led for 20 years the **International Peace Academy (IPA)**, a think tank initially concerned primarily with research and training in peacekeeping.

RIO DECLARATION ON ENVIRONMENT AND DEVELOPMENT (1992). Collection of 21 principles expanding on those adopted at the 1972 Stockholm **United Nations Conference on the Human Environment**, notably in regard to the general duty of states not to cause damage to the environment of other states. The Rio Declaration establishes the principle of the "common but shared responsibilities" of developed and developing countries in the preservation of the environment. Another principle—probably reflecting the environmental devastation caused by Iraqi armed forces in the 1990 **Persian Gulf War**—enjoins states to "respect international law providing protection for the environment in times of armed conflict."

ROBINSON, MARY (1944–). Second **United Nations High Commissioner for Human Rights (UNHCHR)** from 1997 to 2002, Mrs. Robinson came to the United Nations after a distinguished seven-year tenure as president of Ireland, during which she paid special attention to the needs of **developing countries**. A strong advocate of **human rights**, she gave priority to integrating human rights concerns into the activities of the United Nations and reoriented the work of her office at the country and regional levels.

ROBLES, ALFONSO GARCIA (1911–1991). *See* GARCIA ROBLES, ALFONSO (1911–1991).

ROCKEFELLER, JOHN D., JR. (1874–1960). American banker and philanthropist who became one of the largest real estate holders in New York City in the interwar period. He purchased and donated the land on which the **United Nations headquarters** was built.

ROMULOS, CARLOS (1899–1986). Philippine statesman, writer, and veteran of UN affairs. He signed the **Bretton Woods Agreement** for the Philippines in 1944 and led the Philippine delegation at the 1945 **United Nations Conference on International Organization** in San Francisco where he successfully pressed for the inclusion of clauses in the charter calling for **self-determination** and independence in European colonial empires. He headed the Philippines delegation to the first session of the United Nations **General Assembly** and to succeeding sessions. In 1949, he was elected president of the General Assembly.

ROOSEVELT, ELEANOR (1884–1962). Humanitarian and civic leader who promoted the welfare of youth, black Americans, the poor, and **women** at home. After the death of her husband, President **Franklin D. Roosevelt** in 1945, she became a delegate to the United Nations **General Assembly**, focusing her activities on humanitarian, social, and cultural issues. She played a key role in the drafting of the **Universal Declaration of Human Rights (UDHR)**.

ROOSEVELT, FRANKLIN DELANO (1882–1945). Thirty-second president of the United States from 1933 to 1945. During the war years, he initiated a series of meetings and conferences that eventually led to the creation of the United Nations and some of its **specialized agencies**, notably the **Food and Agriculture Organization (FAO)**, the **International Bank for Reconstruction and Development (IBRD)**, and the **International Monetary Fund (IMF)**. Roosevelt eventually deferred to his secretary of state **Cordell Hull**'s insistence on the need for a universal international organization. But he remained adamant on granting the big powers a central role in the peace and security functions of the United Nations. *See also* AT-LANTIC CHARTER; BRETTON WOODS CONFERENCE AND AGREEMENT (1944); DUMBARTON OAKS CONFERENCE AND PROPOSALS (August–October 1944); MOSCOW DECLA-RATION ON GENERAL SECURITY (1943); ROOSEVELT, ELEANOR (1884–1962); YALTA CONFERENCE (1945).

RUGGIE, JOHN (1944–). Distinguished American academic who served as a senior advisor to **Secretary-General Kofi Annan** from 1997 to 2001, assisting him in the positioning of the United Nations in such issues as UN-U.S. relations, UN relations with the global **business** community, and the reform of the organization. He played a key role in the conception and launching of the secretary-general's **Global Compact** as well as in the preparations of the 2000 **Millennium Assembly** and the drafting of the **Millennium Declaration**.

RURAL DEVELOPMENT. Approach to **development** stressing the objective of increased food production and **food security**. **Agenda 21**, adopted at the **United Nations Conference on Environment and Development (UNCED)**, emphasizes that achieving these objectives require **education**, economic incentives, appropriate and new technologies, a better management of natural resources, the protection of the **environment**, and the generation of productive **employment**. **Agrarian reform**, broad-based participation, income diversification, and land conservation are the key policy tools to rely upon. *See also* AGRICULTURAL DEVELOPMENT; FOOD AND AGRICULTURE ORGANIZATION (FAO); FOOD SECURITY; HUNGER; UNITED NATIONS CONFERENCE ON THE LEAST DEVELOPED COUNTRIES (PARIS, 1981); WORLD FOOD SUMMIT (13–17 November 1996).

RWANDAN CONFLICT. Small landlocked country in the Great Lakes Region of Central Africa bordered by Uganda, **Burundi**, the **Democratic Republic of the Congo**, and Tanzania. In 1895, Rwanda, like Burundi, became a German colony. After Germany's defeat in World War I, Rwanda was taken over by Belgium with a **League of Nations mandate**. After World War II, Rwanda became a

United Nations **Trust Territory** with Belgium as the administrative authority.

Historically, the country has been beset by ethnic tensions arising from the traditionally unequal relationship between the dominant Tutsi minority and the majority Hutus. These tensions were exacerbated by Belgian colonial rule, and an increasingly restive Hutu population revolted in November 1959 overthrowing the Tutsi monarchy. Two years later, the Hutu-dominated party won an overwhelming victory in a UN-supervised referendum and took power in 1962 following a United Nations **General Assembly** resolution terminating the Belgian trusteeship.

During the 1959 revolt and its aftermath, more than 160,000 Tutsis fled to neighboring countries. After independence, thousands more Tutsis were killed, and some 150,000 driven into exile in neighboring countries. These exiles formed the backbone of a rebel force, the Rwandan Patriotic Front (RPF), which invaded Rwanda in 1990 from its bases in Uganda. The war came to a shaky end in 1992 when the Hutu government and the RPF signed a cease-fire agreement authorizing a neutral military observer group under the auspices of the **Organization of African Unity (OAU)** and providing for power sharing arrangements. The shooting down of the plane carrying Hutu president Juvenal Habyarimana and his Burundian counterpart near Kigali put an end to the political and military truce and triggered in April 1994 what appeared to be a coordinated attempt by Hutus to exterminate the Tutsi population. In response, the Tutsi-led Rwandan Patriotic Front intensified its military campaign to control the country. The RPF achieved its objective in July 1994 with its capture of the capital, Kigali, while French peacekeepers occupied the southwest part of the country. The war was over, but by then, 800,000 Tutsis and moderate Hutus had been massacred; a million Rwandans had been displaced internally; and some 2 million Hutus, including some of those responsible for the genocide, had taken refuge in neighboring Burundi, Tanzania, Uganda, and the former Zaire, as they feared Tutsi retribution.

Most of the refugees have returned to Rwanda, but about 10,000 remain in the neighboring **Democratic Republic of the Congo (DRC)** and have formed an insurgency force bent on retaking Rwanda, prompting the Kigali government to invade refugee camps dominated by Hutu militiamen and to support insurgent forces fighting the DRC government. Rwanda withdrew its forces from the DRC in late 2002 after signing a peace deal with Kinshasa. But tensions continue to simmer, with Rwanda accusing the Congolese army of aiding Hutu rebels in eastern DRC.

In spite of repeated and documented warnings, the international community stood by on the sidelines and remained uninvolved both in the stages preceding the crisis and throughout the genocide. The size of the UN force on the ground was in fact decreased after the murder of 10 Belgian peacekeepers and brought back to strength only after the RPF victory in order to help maintain public order and restore basic services.

The ruling RPF faces major legitimacy challenges. In 2003, the government won elections marred by fraud, arrests, intimidation, and appeals to ethnic fears and loyalties. Citing the need to avoid another genocide, the government has suppressed dissent and limited the exercise of civil and political rights. The persistence of the Hutu extremist insurgency across the border and the government's opposition to investigations of RPF crimes by the United Nations **International Criminal Tribunal for Rwanda (ICTR)** are manifestations of the Tutsis' precarious hold on power. Ethnic reconciliation remains a distant goal to achieve, as close to 100,000 individuals remain in custody awaiting trial on charges relating to the 1994 genocide. In addition, the government's involvement in the neighboring Democratic Republic of the Congo has elicited accusations of illegal Rwandan exploitation of DRC **natural resources** and mild rebukes of the **Security Council**. *See also* TRUSTEESHIP SYSTEM; UNITED NATIONS ASSISTANCE MISSION IN RWANDA (UNAMIR, October 1993–March 1996); WAR CRIMES TRIBUNALS.

– S –

SACHS, JEFFREY (1954–). American economist specializing in **globalization**-related issues, **poverty** reduction policies, **health** and development, and transitions to market economies. He served as economic advisor to governments in Latin America, Eastern Europe, the former Soviet Union, Asia, and Africa and to a number of United

Nations agencies. As a special advisor to the **secretary-general**, he has been an indefatigable advocate of the goals of the **Millennium Declaration**.

SADIK, NAFIS (1929–). National of Pakistan who started her career as a civilian doctor in Pakistani military hospitals and spent her lifetime calling attention to the importance of addressing the needs of **women** and of involving women directly in the making of **development** and **population** policies and programs. In 1964, Dr. Sadik headed the health section of the Pakistan government's planning commission. There, she was the primary architect of Pakistan's first population policy program. She later served as the deputy director-general and then director general of the Pakistan Central Planning Council. From 1987 to 2000, Dr. Sadik was executive director of the **United Nations Population Fund (UNFPA)**, with the rank of undersecretary-general. One of her major achievements was the organization of the **International Conference on Population and Development (ICPD)**, held in Cairo in 1994, which resulted in a 20-year Programme of Action linking women's **health**, global population control, and development.

SAFETY OF UNITED NATIONS PERSONNEL. In accordance with the 1946 **Convention on the Privileges and Immunities of the United Nations**, all employees of the United Nations and its **specialized agencies** enjoy functional immunity in the state members of the organization. The growing involvement of the United Nations in internal conflicts and its expanding role in unstable humanitarian crises has led to an increasing number of physical attacks on United Nations personnel, which prompted the **General Assembly** in 1993 to initiate the drafting of a Convention on the Safety and Security of United Nations and Associated Personnel. The convention was duly completed a year later and entered into force in 1999. *See also* PERSONNEL QUESTIONS.

SAN FRANCISCO CONFERENCE. *See* UNITED NATIONS CONFERENCE ON INTERNATIONAL ORGANIZATION.

SANCTIONS. In dealing with peace and security issues, the **Security Council** may use a broad range of techniques including deliberation, investigation, recommendation, **mediation**, the interposition of a **peacekeeping** force, and lastly economic and military sanctions. The United Nations **Charter** does not use the term; Article 39 simply states that the council shall take "measures" to maintain or restore international peace and security. Such measures have included arms, commodities, and oil embargoes; travel bans; partial assets freezes; economic blockades; and more comprehensive measures. Their purpose also varies widely. Sanctions may be designed to contain a conflict; to encourage compromise by parties to a conflict; or to force a state to withdraw from a territory, hand over suspects, or cease active hostilities.

Until the end of the **Cold War**, the Security Council imposed sanctions only twice, against Southern Rhodesia (1966–1979) and South Africa (1977–1994). Since then, sanctions have been imposed with increasing frequency against a dozen states: **Iraq** and occupied Kuwait (1990–2003), the Federal Republic of Yugoslavia (1991–1996 and 1998–2001), Somalia (1992–), Libya (1992–2003), **Liberia** (1992–2001, 2001–), **Haiti** (1993–1994), **Angola** (1993–), **Rwanda** (1994–1996), **Sudan** (1996–2001), **Sierra Leone** (1997–), **Afghanistan** (1999–), Eritrea and Ethiopia (2000–2001).

A recent trend in the design of sanctions has been to make them more targeted on individuals, groups of individuals, and particular products (oil, diamonds, and timber) used to finance internal conflicts. Whether sanctions "work" and are successful in meeting their stated purposes remains a matter of controversy. It is unclear, for example, whether the humanitarian crisis experienced by Iraq in the 1990s can be attributed to the sanctions applied against it or to government policy choices. *See also* AGGRESSION; APARTHEID; COLLECTIVE SECURITY; LOCKERBIE INCIDENT (1988); PREVENTIVE OR ENFORCEMENT ACTION; PREVENTIVE DEPLOYMENT; RHODESIAN QUESTION.

SANITATION. *See* WATER.

SAVE THE CHILDREN. Leading international relief and **development nongovernmental organization (NGO)**, seeking to improve the condition and welfare of **children** through global advocacy; citizen mobilization; and programs in **health**, **education**, economic empowerment, and psychosocial support. Save the Children is active in Latin America, Africa, the Middle East, and the United States.

SCALE OF ASSESSMENT. The regular **budget of the United Nations** and **peacekeeping operations** are financed through assessed contributions. The most important principle used in apportioning the expenses of the organization among member states is their capacity to pay as measured by the share of their gross national product in global GNP. Other criteria used include national income, per capita income, and the capacity to obtain foreign currencies. A floor and ceiling have been placed in the UN members' assessed contributions on the assumption that every country should contribute something and that no country should acquire an inordinate financial leverage. Originally, the highest rate was 40 percent (for the United States) which was subsequently reduced to 25 percent and now 22 percent. The lowest rate for poor countries was 0.04 percent and has been brought down to 0.001 percent. The top major contributors are thus assessed two-thirds of the UN budget while half the members of the organization contribute 1 percent. Developing countries benefit from further discounts for peacekeeping operations. The scale of assessment is reevaluated every three years by the General Assembly's **Committee on Contributions** in frequently acrimonious debates. *See also* BUDGET (UNITED NATIONS); FINANCIAL CRISIS.

SCHACHTER, OSCAR (1915–2003). American lawyer and university professor who served in the **United Nations Relief and Rehabilitation Administration (UNRRA)** from 1945 to 1946. He held key senior posts in the Legal Department of the United Nations **Secretariat** from 1946 to 1965 and directed the research of the fledgling **United Nations Institute for Training and Research (UNITAR)** from 1966 until his retirement from UN service in 1975 when he embraced a teaching career at the Columbia Faculty of Law. As a scholar of **international law**, he wrote influential essays on the **use of force**, dispute settlement, international economic and resource law, and **outer space** and helped shape the legal framework that guided United Nations **peacekeeping**.

SCIENCE AND TECHNOLOGY FOR DEVELOPMENT. It has been recognized since the 1960s that the transfer of advances in science and technology to the **developing countries** of the Southern Hemisphere could greatly contribute to their **development.** Already in 1963, the United Nations sponsored an experts' conference on the application of science and technology for the benefit of the less developed countries in Geneva. The same year, the **Economic and Social Council (ECOSOC)** established an Advisory Committee on the Application of Science and Technology to Development (ACAST). For a while, at the insistence of developing countries that pressed for technology transfer in the 1974 Declaration on the **New International Economic Order**, science and technology for development was a major concern to the United Nations and its **specialized agencies.** Another UN conference on science and technology for development was held in Vienna in 1979, and in its wake, the **General Assembly** established an Intergovernmental Committee on Science and Technology for Development opened to all states and an Advisory Committee on Science and Technology for Development, which replaced ACAST with a broader membership including scientists as well as representatives of government policy makers and the private sector. A Center for Science and Technology for Development that was set up within the secretariat and the assembly in 1982 approved the creation of a trust fund to assist in the development and transfer of technology.

Resistance by Northern industrial countries to these developing countries inspired institutional innovations led to their demise in the early 1990s. In 1992, the assembly merged the Intergovernmental Committee on Science and Technology for Development and the Advisory Committee on Science and Technology for Development into a **Commission on Science and Technology for Development (CSTD)**. The secretariat's center on science and technology was dismantled as an autonomous entity and its functions transferred to the **United Nations Conference on Trade and Development (UNCTAD)** and the **United Nations Development Programme (UNDP)**. Voluntary contributions to the trust fund for science and technology were few and far between and remained way below developing countries' expectations.

With the rise of market-based development approaches, the political discourse has shifted from the need for **codes of conduct** for science and technology transfer to a new recognition of and emphasis on the role of the private sector in the transfer of science and technology and the need to protect patents and **intellectual property rights**. At the same time, **Agenda 21**, adopted at the 1992 Earth Summit in Rio de Janeiro has refocused political attention on the transfer of environmentally sound technologies, the preservation of indigenous technologies and knowledge, and the building of endogenous capacity. *See also* FOREIGN DIRECT INVESTMENT (FDI); UNITED NATIONS CONFERENCE ON SCIENCE AND TECHNOLOGY FOR DEVELOPMENT (VIENNA, 1979); UNITED NATIONS CONFERENCE ON THE PEACEFUL USES OF NUCLEAR ENERGY (GENEVA, March 23–April 10, 1987).

SEABED AUTHORITY (INTERNATIONAL) (ISA). International organization established in accordance with the 1982 **United Nations Convention on the Law of the Sea (UNCLOS)** to administer the resources of seabed and ocean floor beyond the limits of national jurisdiction. The organs of the ISA include an assembly, on which all states parties are represented and that acts as the supreme authority of the organization; a council, which consists of 36 members and functions as an executive organ of the ISA; the "Enterprise," which is the business arm of the authority; and a secretariat. ISA is headquartered in Kingston, Jamaica, and cooperates closely with the United Nations in regard to information exchange, budget, administrative and financial matters, and the application of common personnel standards. *See also* COMMON HERITAGE OF MANKIND.

SEABED DEMILITARIZATION TREATY (1971). Like the **Antarctic Treaty** and the **Outer Space Treaty**, the Seabed Treaty is an **arms control** treaty seeking to prevent the introduction of nuclear weapons into an area hitherto free of them. Originally proposed by Malta in 1967, the treaty was negotiated primarily by the United States and the Soviet Union within the framework of the **Conference of the Committee on Disarmament (CCD)**. It was finalized after more than two years of discussions centered around the issues of the definition of territorial waters and verification procedures. Approved by the **General Assembly** in 1970, the treaty entered into force in 1972 and prohibits parties from emplacing nuclear weapons or weapons of mass destruction on the seabed and the ocean floor beyond a 12-mile coastal zone. *See also* CONFERENCE ON DISAR-

MAMENT (CD); DISARMAMENT; UNITED NATIONS CON-
VENTION ON THE LAW OF THE SEA (UNCLOS, 1982);
WEAPONS OF MASS DESTRUCTION (WMDs).

SECOND WORLD ASSEMBLY ON AGING (2002). Convened in
Madrid to provide a forum for the consideration of the opportunities and challenges of rapidly **aging** populations in the 21st century,
the conference adopted an International Plan of Action outlining national and international measures designed to mainstream aging and
the concerns of older persons into development frameworks and
poverty eradication strategies. The blueprint identified three major
priorities: the integration and empowerment of older persons; advancing their health and well-being; and creating an enabling and
supportive environment for the aged through improved living conditions. *See also* SOCIAL INTEGRATION; WORLD ASSEMBLY
ON AGING (1982).

SECRETARIAT (UNITED NATIONS). Headed by the **secretary-
general**, the secretariat administers the programs, policies, and day-
to-day activities entrusted to the secretary-general by the **Security
Council** and the **General Assembly**. A core international civil service staff of some 14,000 serve in offices in New York, Geneva, Vienna, and elsewhere. This figure does not include an additional
18,000 civil servants working for such subsidiary organs as the
United Nations Development Programme (UNDP), the **United
Nations High Commissioner for Refugees (UNHCR)**, and the
United Nations Children's Fund (UNICEF).

Article 100 of the United Nations **Charter** instructs the secretary-
general and the staff not to seek or receive instructions from any government and calls upon member states to recognize and respect "the
exclusively international character" of their position and responsibilities. Practice has not always met these lofty principles, thus leading
to criticisms of bureaucratic inefficiency, cronyism, overlapping and
duplicating functions, waste, and, less frequently, fraud. Efforts to address these problems through administrative cost-cutting measures,
the consolidation of departments, and practices encouraging greater
coherence and integration of UN activities consumed much of the
tenure of Secretary-General **Boutros Boutros-Ghali**. Upon taking

office, his successor, **Kofi Annan**, initiated further administrative and managerial reforms. *See also* PERSONNEL QUESTIONS.

SECRETARY-GENERAL. All UN administrative functions are handled by the **secretariat**, with the secretary-general as its head. The **charter** does not prescribe a term for the secretary-general, but a five-year term has become standard. **Trygve Lie**, the first secretary-general, was succeeded by **Dag Hammarskjöld** (1953–1961), who served until his death. **U Thant**, acting as secretary-general, was elected in 1962 and reelected in 1966 thus serving until 1971. Succeeding secretaries-general were **Kurt Waldheim** (1972–1981), **Javier Perez de Cuellar** (1982–1991), **Boutros Boutros-Ghali** (1992–1996), **Kofi Annan** (1997–2006), and **Ban Ki-Moon** (2007–).

The secretary-general transcends a merely administrative role by his authority to bring situations to the attention of various organs of the United Nations as an impartial party in effecting conciliation, and especially by his power to "perform such . . . functions as are entrusted to him" by other UN organs. Also strengthening the office of the secretary-general is the large **secretariat** staff, which is recruited on a wide geographic basis and is required to work exclusively in the interests of the organization.

SECURITY COUNCIL (SC). Designed as an organ with primary responsibility for preserving peace. Unlike the **General Assembly**, the council was given the power to enforce coercive measures and was organized as a compact executive organ. Also unlike the assembly, the council functions continuously at the seat of the United Nations.

The council has 15 members. Five are permanent: China (until 1971, the Republic of China [Taiwan]), France, Great Britain, the United States, and Russia (until 1991, the USSR). The 10 (originally 6) nonpermanent members are elected for two-year terms by the General Assembly. Equitable geographic distribution is required. Customarily, there are five nonpermanent members from African and Asian states, one from Eastern Europe, two from Latin America, and two from Western Europe and elsewhere. In the council the presidency is occupied for one-month terms in the alphabetical order of the members' names in English. In 1997, a UN commission proposed changes to the council, including adding five new permanent members without **veto** powers, adding four additional nonpermanent members, and placing restrictions on the use of the veto. The proposed changes were regarded by many nations as a groundwork for further negotiations on the eventual restructuring of the council, which are still evolving.

There are two systems of **voting** in the Security Council. On procedural matters, the affirmative vote of any nine members is necessary, but on substantive matters the nine affirmative votes required must include those of the five permanent members. This requirement of Big Five unanimity embodies the so-called veto. In practice, the council has, on most substantive matters, not treated an abstention by a permanent member as a veto. In two situations, however, those of recommending applicants for United Nations **membership**, and of approving proposed amendments to the **charter**, the actual concurrence of all permanent members has been required. The veto has prevented much substantive action by the UN, but it embodies the reality that the resolution of major crises required agreement of the major powers.

Under the charter, the council may take measures on any danger to world peace. It may act upon complaint of a member or a nonmember, on notification by the secretary-general or by the General Assembly, or by its own volition. In general, the council considers matters of two sorts. The first is "disputes" (or situations that may rise to them) that might endanger peace. Here the council, acting under Chapter VI of the United Nations Charter, is limited to making recommendations to the parties after it has exhausted other methods of reaching a solution. In the case of more serious matters, such as "threats to the peace," "breaches of the peace" and "acts of aggression," the council (under Chapter VII of the charter) may take enforcement measures. These may range from full and partial rupture of economic or diplomatic relations to military operations of any scope deemed necessary. By the terms of the charter, the UN was forbidden to intervene in matters "which are essentially . . . domestic," but this limitation was not intended to hinder the Security Council to prevent threats to peace. The charter was intentionally ambiguous regarding domestic issues that could also be construed as threats to the peace and left a potential opening for intervention in domestic issues that threaten to have dangerous international repercussions.

The council also exercised the **trusteeship** functions of the United Nations in "strategic areas" (this function has come to an end with the termination of the United Nations Trusteeship over islands located in the Pacific Ocean). The council recommends to the General Assembly the appointment of the **secretary-general** and the admission of new member states. Together with the General Assembly, the council elects the judges of the **International Court of Justice (ICJ)**.

Throughout the **Cold War** the council was essentially unable to use its vast power. This did not necessarily paralyze the organization, as the General Assembly, to a certain extent, was able to fill the vacuum. With the end of the Cold War, however, the Security Council has reasserted its "primacy" in the maintenance of peace and security, frequently invoking Chapter VII of the charter to justify its interventions. *See also* HIGH-LEVEL PANEL ON THREATS, CHALLENGES, AND CHANGE (HLP); PEACEFUL SETTLEMENT OF DISPUTES; PEACEKEEPING; REFORM, UNITED NATIONS; SANCTIONS; STRATEGIC TRUST TERRITORIES; UNITING FOR PEACE RESOLUTION (1950).

SELF-DEFENSE, RIGHT OF. Long standing principle of interstate relations recognized in **international law**. Article 51 of the United Nations **Charter** encapsulates and amends this state practice by stipulating that "Nothing in the present Charter shall impair the inherent right of individual and collective self-defense if an armed attack occurs against a Member of the United Nations *until* the **Security Council** has taken measures necessary to maintain international peace and security" (author's emphasis).

In the thinking of the drafters of the charter, a state had the authority to take temporary emergency self-defense measures to face a recognizable and imminent threat only until the Security Council was able to act. Once the emergency phase was over, however, the council regained its sole and final authority over the matter. State practice has significantly been different from these charter injunctions, as the case of the second **Persian Gulf War** suggests. *See also* AGGRESSION; CUBAN MISSILE CRISIS (1962); HIGH-LEVEL PANEL ON THREATS, CHALLENGES, AND CHANGE (HLP); PREEMPTION; USE OF FORCE.

SELF-DETERMINATION. The principle whereby people have a right to choose how they will organize and be governed. It is contained in Article 1.2 of the United Nations **Charter**, which states that one of the UN's essential purposes is "respect for the principle of equal rights and self-determination of peoples." It is the keystone of the charter's **"Declaration Regarding Non-Self-Governing Territories."**

In a 1960 landmark resolution, the **Declaration on the Granting of Independence to Colonial Countries and Peoples**, the **General Assembly** proclaimed that the "subjection of peoples to alien subjugation . . . constitutes a denial of fundamental **human rights**." The norm of self-determination hotly contested by Western European colonial powers until the late 1950s has gained increasing acceptability. Political realities have, however, frequently foiled its implementation and led to inconsistent outcomes. *See also* ALGERIAN QUESTION; ARAB-ISRAELI CONFLICT; CHECHNYA CONFLICT; DECOLONIZATION; ITALIAN COLONIES (1949–1951); MANDATE SYSTEM OF THE LEAGUE OF NATIONS; PORTUGUESE COLONIES; SOUTH WEST AFRICA; TRUSTEESHIP SYSTEM; TUNISIAN QUESTION; UNITED MISSION FOR THE REFERENDUM IN WESTERN SAHARA (MINURSO, 1991–present).

SEN, AMARTYA (1933–). Indian economist who has done extensive work on methods and techniques of economic measurement, real income, poverty, inequality, and unemployment in developing countries. His major contribution is a theory of causation of famines that focuses on entitlement relations rather than food supply issues in the elimination of **hunger**. More generally, his work on welfare economics highlights the need to integrate considerations of liberty and rights in the development of more effective **poverty** eradication policies in developing countries and has led to a major redefinition of the concept of **development** as reflected in the notion of **human development** advocated by the **United Nations Development Programme (UNDP)**. Sen won the **Nobel Prize** in economics in 1998 for his contributions to welfare economics.

SEYNES, PHILIPPE DE (1911–2004). French national who headed the Economic and Social Department of the United Nations **Secretariat**

for 20 years from 1955 to 1975. His strong intellectual leadership durably shaped the economic and social work of the United Nations.

SHELTER. Recognized as a right by the **International Covenant on Economic, Social, and Cultural Rights (ICESCR)**, adequate housing has been a long-standing focus of United Nations developmental work carried out by the **United Nations Conference on Human Settlements (Habitat)** under the authority of the **Commission on Human Settlements** of the **Economic and Social Council (ECOSOC)**. The **General Assembly** proclaimed 1987 the International Year of Shelter for the Homeless. Shelter issues, as they relate to development concerns, have been discussed in two United Nations sponsored **global conferences**, the **United Nations Conference on Human Settlements (Habitat I)** in 1976 and the **United Nations Conference on Human Settlements (Habitat II)** in 1996. *See also* BASIC HUMAN NEEDS.

SHIPPING. The bulk of the United Nations work in international shipping has focused on the development of maritime conventions. Since its creation in 1920, the **International Labour Organization (ILO)** has adopted numerous conventions (mandatory for ratifying states) and nonbinding recommendations pertaining to working conditions on board ocean-going ships, addressing such issues as hours of work, minimum wages, occupational safety and health standards, recruitment, and accommodations. The **International Maritime Organization (IMO)** has provided the forum for the development of international conventions seeking to improve the safety of international shipping routes and to prevent pollution from ships.

In its early years of operation, the **United Nations Conference on Trade and Development (UNCTAD)** was particularly concerned with the maritime interests of **developing countries** that were critical of liner conferences, shipping line cartels that provide scheduled vessel service over specific trade routes and collectively discuss and set port-to-port rates. The issue of liner conferences was debated for 10 years, culminating in the adoption in 1974 of a **Code of Conduct** for Liner Conferences, which opened liner conferences to new members from developing countries. The code came into force in 1983.

With the increasing recognition of the importance of free-market principles, shipping issues no longer rank high in UNCTAD's activities, as they now mainly deal with technical assistance for the facilitation of regional shipping cooperation and the promotion of shipping competition.

SIERRA LEONE CONFLICT (1991–2002). Civil war broke out in Sierra Leone in 1991 when rebel forces based in the eastern part of the country and Liberia took up arms against the government. The long drawn-out conflict was rooted in a mix of bad governance, denial of fundamental **human rights**, economic mismanagement, and social exclusion. It was also marked by extreme lawlessness and atrocities and dragged on until 1999, with the conclusion of a UN-brokered peace treaty between the Sierra Leone government and the rebels. The agreement collapsed in 2001, and peace was restored through the intervention of a large UN **peacekeeping** force, the **United Nations Mission in Sierra Leone (UNAMSIL).**

The rebellion was prolonged by the insurgents' control of the country's diamond mining region and illicit sale of rough diamonds on world markets to finance their war effort. Recognizing that diamonds had been fueling the conflict, the **Security Council** imposed a ban on the export of unregistered Sierra Leonean diamonds in 2000 and went further the following year by imposing **sanctions** on neighboring **Liberia** for supporting the insurgents. A coalition of human rights, humanitarian, and religious groups with the support of diamond exporting and importing countries successfully pressured the diamond and jewelry industry into accepting the creation of a certification system to ensure that no rough diamonds from a conflict zone would be allowed in world markets.

A **Special Court for Sierra Leone** has been set up jointly by the United Nations and the government of Sierra Leone in 2003 to try those who bear a major responsibility for war crimes, crimes against humanity, and other serious violations of international humanitarian law. Some 50,000 people died in the conflict, 2 million Sierra Leoneans have been displaced, and 100,000 civilians were deliberately mutilated.

The presence of a strong UN force paved the way toward significant progress in the implementation of the peace process and the consolidation of state and local authority. The transition has been aided by the work of a Truth and Reconciliation Commission (TRC) and the special court (the first trials began in June 2004). Over a million displaced persons have returned to their homes. Significant strides have been made in the rehabilitation of the social infrastructure, and the national economy is gaining momentum.

The country still faces major emergency relief and immediate recovery challenges. Key human rights issues still need to be monitored. The rehabilitation of the economic and social infrastructure of the country, the prevalence of endemic and pervasive poverty, and high levels of unemployment and desperate conditions of resettled people in most parts of the country are additional challenges confronting the government. In 2004, the Security Council began scaling down the size of the UN military force. But the success of this "carefully managed transfer of authority" hinges on internal conditions of stability and recovery and continuing international support. *See also* CHILDREN IN ARMED CONFLICTS; CONVENTION ON THE RIGHTS OF THE CHILD (CRC, 1990); UNITED NATIONS CONFERENCE ON THE ILLICIT TRADE IN SMALL ARMS AND LIGHT WEAPONS (NEW YORK, 9–20 July 2001); UNITED NATIONS MISSION IN SIERRA LEONE (UNAMSIL, October 1999–present); UNITED NATIONS OBSERVER MISSION IN SIERRA LEONE (UNOMSIL, June 1998–October 1999); WAR CRIMES TRIBUNALS.

SINGER, HANS (1910–2005). British development economist. His early work dealt with unemployment but thereafter focused on the "vicious circles of poverty" in **developing countries**, with particular attention to the role of the state and the importance of human capital formation. From 1947 to 1969, he served in various positions in the United Nations and played an important role in the debates over the **Special United Nations Fund for Economic Development (SUNFED)** and the creation of the **World Food Programme (WFP)**, the **United Nations Development Program (UNDP)**, the **African Development Bank (AfDB)**, and the **United Nations Industrial Development Organization (UNIDO)**. He was also instrumental in changing the focus of the **United Nations Children's Fund (UNICEF)** from an emergency fund to an organization concerned with the long-term interests of children. His empirical studies in the early 1950s of the "costs" of **international trade** for developing countries deeply influenced development thinking as it corroborated **Raul Prebisch**'s terms of trade theory.

SMALL ARMS AND LIGHT WEAPONS. The end of the **Cold War** and the accelerated pace of **globalization** have facilitated the legal and illegal transfers of small arms across borders, while an upsurge of intrastate conflicts created a growing demand for them. Some 600 million small arms and light weapons are estimated to be in circulation, one for every 12 people on earth. Most of these weapons are in the hands of legal authorities, but a significant number end up in the hands of irregular troops, criminals, drug traffickers, and terrorists, thus leading to grave breaches of **human rights** and **humanitarian law**, especially in weak states torn by civil wars. The proliferation of these weapons has also obstructed the implementation of **Security Council** arms embargoes, hindered worldwide humanitarian efforts, and exacerbated the phenomenon of child soldiers. In 2001, the **United Nations Conference on the Illicit Trade in Small Arms and Light Weapons** produced a program of action with recommendations at the national, regional, and global level. *See also* CHILDREN IN ARMED CONFLICTS.

SMALL ISLAND DEVELOPING STATES (SIDS). A **group** of some 40 island states (formally known as the **Alliance of Small Island States**) functioning as a lobby and negotiating instrument within the United Nations. These states share a common predicament of geographic and economic vulnerability, including limited natural resources, a fragile land and marine environment, and the threat of possible damage from a rise in sea level caused by **climate change**. See *also* DEVELOPING COUNTRIES; INTERNATIONAL MEETING TO REVIEW THE IMPLEMENTATION OF THE PROGRAMME OF ACTION FOR THE SUSTAINABLE DEVELOPMENT OF SMALL ISLAND DEVELOPING STATES (PORT-LOUIS, MAURITIUS, 10–14 January 2005); UNITED NATIONS CONFERENCE ON THE SUSTAINABLE DEVELOPMENT OF SMALL DEVELOPING STATES (BARBADOS, 1994); UNITED NATIONS CONVENTION ON THE LAW OF THE SEA (UNCLOS, 1982).

SMALLPOX. Highly contagious disease that was endemic in most parts of the world. It is believed that as recently as the 1950s smallpox killed 2 million people each year. The **World Health Organization (WHO)** carried out a worldwide vaccination campaign that succeeded in eradicating the disease by the late 1970s. *See also* HEALTH; MILLENNIUM DECLARATION.

SOCIAL INTEGRATION. Term suggesting that certain groups in society share special vulnerabilities and require special attention from governments and the international community in order to prevent their marginalization. Such groups include **youth**, the elderly, people with disabilities, **migrant workers**, **minorities**, and **indigenous populations**. Their concerns have been addressed primarily by the **Economic and Social Council (ECOSOC)** and its **Commission for Social Development** and the **International Labour Organization (ILO)**. The activities of the United Nations on behalf of these groups have focused on the elaboration of international norms and standards and recommendations for action by governments based on research and data gathering. The **General Assembly** has also drawn attention to the special needs of these groups through the proclamation of special years and decades. *See also* AGING; DISABLED; FAMILY; UNITED NATIONS PERMANENT FORUM FOR INDIGENOUS PEOPLES (UNPFIP); HUMAN RIGHTS; WOMEN; WORLD COMMISSION ON THE SOCIAL DIMENSION OF GLOBALIZATION.

SOCIETY FOR INTERNATIONAL DEVELOPMENT (SID). International nongovernmental network of individuals and organizations founded in 1957 to promote systemic and long-term solutions to social justice and institutional global transformation issues through research and policy analysis. SID-supported research has focused on such subjects as global governance, sustainable livelihoods, and the strengthening of **civil society** in postconflict situations. *See also* NONGOVERNMENTAL ORGANIZATIONS (NGOs).

SOMALIA. Shortly after a 1991 coup that overthrew the central government, civil war among rival factions vying for power broke out within Somalia, prompting a devastating famine that resulted in the loss of some 300,000 lives. A UN-brokered truce was declared, and UN peacekeepers and food supplies arrived. But the truce was observed only sporadically, and late in 1992, troops from the United States and other nations attempted to restore political stability and establish free and open humanitarian aid routes. Widespread looting of food distribution sites persisted, fueled by hostility toward international relief efforts by heavily armed rival militant factions. As efforts to reestablish a central government failed, international troops became enmeshed in tribal conflicts. Clan fighting increased in 1994, and the United States and other nations withdrew their forces.

In spite of several efforts at national reconciliation, the country still has no organized central government. By any standards of human development—per capita income, malnutrition, infant mortality—Somalia remains one of the poorest countries in the world, as it is plagued by chronic droughts and floodings, eroding food security and making large areas inaccessible to humanitarian aid. UN agencies—notably the **World Food Programme (WFP)**, the **United Nations Children's Fund (UNICEF)**, and the **United Nations High Commissioner for Refugees (UNHCR)**—have haltingly helped sustain the lives of the most vulnerable through food distributions, immunization campaigns, and water system rehabilitation projects. *See also* UNITED NATIONS OPERATION IN SOMALIA (UNOSOM I, April 1992–March 1993 and UNOSOM II, March 1993–March 1995).

SOUTH AFRICA. *See* APARTHEID.

SOUTH CENTER. Established by treaty among countries members of the **Group of Seventy-Seven** in 1994, the South Center is a think tank undertaking policy-oriented analytical work on issues of common interest to Southern Hemisphere states such as cooperation among **developing countries**, **development policies**, international economic relations, North-South relations, international **governance**, and the management of **globalization**.

The center's research work is principally designed to identify the converging interests of developing countries, promote their cooperation, and strengthen the basis of their demands in the **North-South dialogue**. *See also* SOUTH COMMISSION; THIRD WORLD NETWORK (TWN).

SOUTH COMMISSION. Established in 1986 at the urging of a conference of the **Nonaligned Movement (NAM)**, this group of eminent persons from **developing countries** was chaired by Julius Nyerere, the former president of Tanzania. Its 1990 report focused on the contributions that developing countries could make in resolving the development and environmental issues they face. Cast against the background of evolving North-South relations, the commission's recommendations focused on the need for greater South-South cooperation, especially in those financial and monetary matters of concern to the **Bretton Woods institutions**. Several of its recommendations enjoined Northern countries to dismantle their protectionist policies and called for the democratization of the United Nations and of the international monetary system. *See also* COMMISSION ON GLOBAL GOVERNANCE; COMMISSION ON INTERNATIONAL DEVELOPMENT (PEARSON COMMISSION); INDEPENDENT COMMISSION ON INTERNATIONAL DEVELOPMENT ISSUES (ICIDI); INDEPENDENT COMMISSIONS; INDEPENDENT WORKING GROUP ON THE FUTURE OF THE UNITED NATIONS; REFORM, UNITED NATIONS; SOUTH CENTER; WORLD COMMISSION ON ENVIRONMENT AND DEVELOPMENT.

SOUTH OSSETIA. *See* GEORGIA CONFLICT.

SOUTHWEST AFRICA. African territory under German colonial rule until the end of World War I when it was placed under South Africa's administration within the framework of the **mandate system of the League of Nations**. After the demise of the League, the **General Assembly** requested South Africa to continue its administration of the territory under the United Nations **Trusteeship system**. South Africa refused to comply on the ground that the mandate had expired with the dissolution of the League and it informed the United Nations that it would accordingly cease to transmit information on the Territory as called for by the Trusteeship system.

In a 1950 advisory opinion, the **International Court of Justice (ICJ)** ruled that the Southwest African mandate should come under United Nations supervision, but the court's advice was ignored by South Africa. The court again became a party to the dispute in 1966 when it dismissed on procedural grounds an action initiated by Ethiopia and Liberia to obtain a binding legal decision on the former mandate. In the court's view, the right to sue on this matter belonged to the League, not to its members. The General Assembly then acted unilaterally, terminating the mandate and proclaiming South Africa's occupation of West South Africa illegal. The assembly also created an 11-member Council for Southwest Africa—subsequently renamed the Council for Namibia to reflect its rechristening of the territory—to administer it until independence.

The Council for Namibia was never allowed by South Africa to serve in that capacity, but it became the focal point of continuing and increasing pressures against South Africa's occupation of Namibia. In 1968, the Security Council determined that the presence of South Africa was illegal and called for its withdrawal, a view that was endorsed by the ICJ in several advisory opinions. At the same time, South Africa faced growing opposition within Namibia with the creation of an opposition organization, the Southwest African People's Organization (SWAPO) in 1960, which began guerrilla operations in 1966. In 1973, the General Assembly recognized SWAPO as the sole "authentic" representative of the Namibian people.

Proposals for a political settlement of the issue providing for elections for a constituent assembly under the supervision of a United Nations peacekeeping operation were circulating in the Security Council as early as 1978. But agreement stalled as the Namibian issue came to be linked to the withdrawal of Cuban troops stationed in neighboring **Angola**, which also served as a sanctuary for SWAPO military units. The thawing of the **Cold War** and intensifying cooperation between the United States and the USSR broke the impasse. South Africa agreed to cease hostilities against Angola and to cooperate with the **secretary-general** to ensure Namibia's independence through UN-supervised elections, while Cuba agreed to withdraw its troops from Angola. *See also* APARTHEID; DECOLONIZATION; SELF-DETERMINATION; UNITED NATIONS TRANSITION ASSISTANCE GROUP (UNTAG, February 1989–April 1999).

SOVEREIGNTY. In international law, the doctrine that states have the exclusive right to govern their internal affairs and external foreign relations. In legal terms, states are equals and cannot be subject to any higher authority without their consent. The "sovereign equality" of states is a major constitutive **principle of the United Nations Charter** as reflected in its provision that the United Nations may not intervene in matters that are essentially within the domestic jurisdiction of its members. The one-state-one-vote mode of decision making in the **General Assembly** is another instance of the principle.

The charter at the same time allows for derogations to the principle of sovereign equality of states. Five members of the **Security Council** are permanent members, with a **veto** power over its decisions. In addition, the domestic jurisdiction clause of the charter can be overridden by the council in the case of enforcement measures applied by the council acting under Chapter VII of the charter. Recent developments in the practice of the Security Council have led a number of observers to argue that the exercise of sovereignty by governments entails a "responsibility to protect" their citizens and that failure to do so may, under certain circumstances, make it incumbent for the international community to intervene by forceful means to redress violations of **human rights**. Still other observers have pointed out that **globalization** and the spread of **information technology** have significantly eroded state sovereignty and are redefining its practical outer limits. *See also* HIGH-LEVEL PANEL ON THREATS, CHALLENGES, AND CHANGE (HLP); HUMANITARIAN INTERVENTION; INTERNATIONAL COMMISSION ON INTERVENTION AND STATE SOVEREIGNTY; SOVEREIGNTY OVER NATURAL RESOURCES.

SOVEREIGNTY OVER NATURAL RESOURCES. Long-standing, divisive issue pitting developed against **developing countries** that was debated repeatedly by the **General Assembly** throughout the 1950s and 1960s. Invoking the Charter principles of "sovereign equality" and "**nonintervention**," developing countries argued that they had a permanent sovereignty, that is, control, over the exploration, development, and disposition of their natural wealth and resources. Through several resolutions of the assembly, developing countries in effect, sought to obtain a collective recognition of their right to regulate the economic activities of foreign capital and, if necessary, to nationalize and freely exploit their natural wealth as part of their development policies. The principle has never been accepted by Northern countries. *See also* NEW INTERNATIONAL ECONOMIC ORDER (NIEO); SOVEREIGNTY; TRANSNATIONAL CORPORATIONS (TNCs).

SPECIAL AND EMERGENCY SESSIONS OF THE GENERAL ASSEMBLY. Special sessions of the **General Assembly** may be called at the request of the **Security Council** or a majority of member states on specific topics requiring further debate (Article 20 of the charter). The assembly has held numerous special sessions on a wide range of subjects including **apartheid**, the question of **Palestine**, the **financing of the United Nations**, **Namibia**, **disarmament**, international economic cooperation, drug control, the **environment**, **population**, **women**, **social integration** and **development**, **human settlements**, and **HIV/AIDS**. A large number of them have taken place in recent years as a means for the assembly to review progress in the agreements reached in UN **global conferences**. These "+5" and "+10" reviews, as they are known, have followed the 1990 **World Summit for Children**, the 1992 **United Nations Conference on Environment and Development**, the 2005 **International Meeting to Review the Implementation of the Programme of Action for the Sustainable Development of Small Island Developing States**, the 1994 **International Conference on Population and Development (ICPD)**, the 1995 **World Summit for Social Development**, the 1995 Beijing **World Conference on Women**, and the 1996 **United Nations Conference on Human Settlements**, among others.

Under the 1950 **Uniting for Peace Resolution**, "emergency special sessions" can be convened within 24 hours by any nine members of the **Security Council** or by a majority of member states. Ten emergency special sessions have addressed situations in which the Security Council was deadlocked: the Middle East (1958 and 1967), the **Hungarian question** (1956), **Suez** (1956), the **Congo** (1960), **Afghanistan** (1980), **Palestine** (1980 and 1982), Namibia (1981), the occupied Arab territories (1982), and illegal Israeli actions in occupied East Jerusalem and the rest of the occupied Palestinian territories (1997, 1998, 1999, 2000, 2001, 2002, 2003, 2004). *See also* AFRICAN ECONOMIC CONDITIONS; ARAB-ISRAELI CONFLICT; NAMIBIAN QUESTION; NEW INTERNATIONAL ECONOMIC ORDER (NIEO).

SPECIAL COMMITTEE ON DECOLONIZATION. Committee set by the General Assembly in 1962 to oversee the implementation of the assembly's **Declaration on the Granting of Independence to Colonial Countries and Peoples**. The committee made up primarily of former colonies was given the broad authority to hear petitions, send missions to the field and make recommendations. It quickly overshadowed the body that examined information transmitted by the administering authorities of nonself-governing territories in accordance with the charter's **Declaration Regarding Non-Self-Governing Territories** (Chapter XI).

When the committee started operations, it listed over 60 territories that had not achieved self-government or independence. Today, only a handful of small islands with tiny populations remain dependencies. The status of Gibraltar, **Western Sahara**, French Caledonia, and **Puerto Rico** are among the last controversial issues on the committee's agenda. *See also* DECOLONIZATION; SELF-DETERMINATION.

SPECIAL COMMITTEE ON THE CHARTER OF THE UNITED NATIONS AND ON THE STRENGTHENING OF THE ROLE OF THE ORGANIZATION. Subsidiary body established by the **General Assembly** in 1975 to examine in the light of suggestions made by member states ways and means to strengthen the role of the United Nations with regard to the maintenance of peace and security, development cooperation, and the promotion of international law. The assembly has regularly renewed the mandate of the committee over the years, but its labors have produced no tangible results. *See also* REFORM, UNITED NATIONS.

SPECIAL COURT FOR SIERRA LEONE. Unlike the **International Criminal Tribunal for the Former Yugoslavia (ICTY)** and the **International Criminal Tribunal for Rwanda (ICTR)**, this court was established by an agreement between the Sierra Leone government and the United Nations. The court tries those accused of crimes against humanity and war crimes that occurred during the **Sierra Leone conflict** including attacks against civilian population, attacks against peacekeepers, and the forced recruitment of children into paramilitary groups. Specifically, the charges include murder, rape, extermination, acts of terror, enslavement, looting and burning, sexual slavery, conscription of children into armed forces, and attacks on United Nations peacekeepers. *See also* CHILDREN IN ARMED CONFLICTS; WAR CRIMES TRIBUNALS.

SPECIAL REPRESENTATIVES OF THE SECRETARY-GENERAL (SRSGs). Senior aides of the **secretary-general** appointed to assist him in the **mediation** or resolution of local or regional disputes and conflicts. The practice was initiated by **Trygve Lie** in 1948 with the appointment of **Ralph Bunche** as the "personal representative of the secretary-general" to the UN mediator for the Middle East, **Count Folke Bernadotte**. It has since vastly expanded with the growing peacekeeping role of the organization in interstate and intrastate conflicts. Variously known as "special envoys," "special coordinators," or "personal representatives," these officials carry out supportive diplomacy and mediation functions for conflict prevention and resolution. They are frequently attached to or head a United Nations **peacekeeping** mission, and coordinate **postconflict peace-building** activities. The secretary-general also relies on similar advisers for thematic, crosscutting issues such as **children and armed conflict**, **gender** and the advancement of **women**, the **Global Compact**, **HIV/AIDS**, **internally displaced persons**, and the **least developed countries**, among others. See also CYPRUS QUESTION (1960–); IRAN-IRAQ WAR (1980–1988).

SPECIAL UNITED NATIONS FUND FOR ECONOMIC DEVELOPMENT (SUNFED). Established in 1957 by the **General Assembly** as a mechanism for the provision of capital investment by developed states in less developed countries. The creation of such a fund had been a long-standing demand of **developing countries**, especially in the wake of the massive injection of financial assistance by the United States for the reconstruction of Europe through the Marshall Plan.

While a few developed countries were willing to contribute to the fund, the main potential donor—the United States—hesitated about making a large contribution toward the target of $250 million set by the assembly before it could begin operations. President **Eisenhower** proposed instead to use the savings accruing from nuclear superpower **disarmament** for capital development purposes, but the idea floundered on the ongoing stalemate in nuclear disarmament negotiations with the Soviet Union. Concern about a possible increasing influence of the Soviet Union in the Third World eventually prompted the Eisenhower administration to change its position and to pledge contributions equaling two-thirds of what other nations gave. On that basis, the assembly decided to proceed with the creation of SUNFED. The fund's resources, however, never reached the funding level target set by the assembly. Its activities remained limited to preinvestment surveys to pave the way for increased private and public investment and assistance in the developing world, assisting in the establishment of training and research institutes, and exploring the feasibility of development projects.

Eventually, in 1965, the fund was merged with the **Expanded Programme of Technical Assistance (EPTA)** to form the **United Nations Development Programme (UNDP)**. Developing countries' pressure for a capital fund under the authority of the General Assembly never slackened, eventually leading to the creation of a **United Nations Capital Development Fund (UNCDF)** in 1966. This new entity, however, never attracted much funding. It has been able to survive until now by focusing its work on market-oriented small projects. *See also* LEWIS, SIR ARTHUR (1915–1991); SINGER, HANS (1910–2005).

SPECIALIZED AGENCIES OF THE UNITED NATIONS. Intergovernmental international organizations constituted through separate treaties and performing a wide variety of functions ranging from highly technical and specific tasks (such as the **International Civil Aviation Organization [ICAO]** or the **International Telecommunications Union [ITU]**) to broad and frequently politically controversial responsibilities (like the **United Nations Educational, Scientific, and Cultural Organization [UNESCO]** and the **International Monetary Fund [IMF]**). These organizations in some cases came into existence before the United Nations, as is the case for the **International Labour Organization (ILO)**, the **Food and Agriculture Organization (FAO)**, and the **Bretton Woods institutions (BWIs)**. They all have their own constitution, governing bodies, budgets, and secretariats and are therefore largely autonomous. Those that entered into cooperation agreements with the **Economic and Social Council (ECOSOC)** (subject to approval by the **General Assembly**) are known as "specialized agencies." Together with the United Nations proper, they constitute "the United Nations system." The ILO, FAO, UNESCO, **World Health Organization (WHO)**, ICAO, **Interna-**

tional Maritime Organization (IMO), International Fund for Agricultural Development (IFAD), ITU, Universal Postal Union (UPU), World Meteorological Organization (WMO), World Intellectual Property Organization (WIPO), United Nations Industrial Development Organization (UNIDO), International Bank for Reconstruction and Development (IBRD), International Monetary Fund (IMF), and United Nations World Tourism Organization (UNWTO) are specialized agencies of the United Nations. In addition to the specialized agencies, the International Atomic Energy Agency (IAEA) and the World Trade Organization (WTO) (successor organization to the General Agreement on Tariffs and Trade [GATT]) operate in a similar manner. In this highly decentralized setting, harmonizing the working relations between the United Nations and the specialized agencies is more a matter of voluntary coordination than oversight and takes place within the framework of the Chief Executive Board (CEB).

STATISTICAL COMMISSION (UNITED NATIONS). A subsidiary body of the Economic and Social Council (ECOSOC) created in 1946. The commission has played a key role in promoting the development of national statistics and in improving their comparability. It has also assisted the council in the coordination of the statistical work of the specialized agencies. See also STONE, SIR RICHARD (1913–1991).

STOCKHOLM CONFERENCE. See UNITED NATIONS CONFERENCE ON THE HUMAN ENVIRONMENT (STOCKHOLM, 1972).

STONE, SIR RICHARD (1913–1991). British economist who received the Nobel Prize in 1984 for his contributions to the development of methods to measure national and international economies. Drawing from his previous work in the United Kingdom, Stone headed immediately after World War II an international group of experts under the auspices of the United Nations for the preparation of standardized forms for national accounts that could be recommended for international use. His models for national accounts achieved wide international application providing a common basis for comparisons between countries of levels of economic activities, economic structures, and inflation analysis. *See also* STATISTICAL COMMISSION (UNITED NATIONS).

STRATEGIC TRUST TERRITORIES. Group of Pacific islands seized from Japan by the United States during World War II that were placed under American administration under the **Trusteeship system**. Because of their military importance and as a safeguard against possible UN interference, the United States insisted that the Trust Territory of the Pacific Islands be designated as a "strategic area" and that all matters relating to the Territory were the province of the **Security Council** rather than the **Trusteeship Council** where there is no **veto**. The islands comprising it have become independent and opted for a status of "free association" with the United States.

STRONG, MAURICE (1929–). Canadian businessman and public official with extensive ties to both the public and private sectors. A staunch advocate of environmental causes, he headed various civil society organizations like the **Earth Council** and the **World Resources Institute (WRI)** and was a member of the **World Commission on Environment and Development**. He was asked by **Secretary-General U Thant** to organize the 1972 **United Nations Conference on the Human Environment**, which in effect placed environmental issues on the agenda of the United Nations. He briefly served as the first director of the **United Nations Environmental Programme (UNEP)** and, subsequently, as secretary-general of the conference, played a key role in the preparations and outcome of the 1992 **United Nations Conference on Environment and Development (UNCED)**, the so-called Earth Summit. As senior advisor to **Kofi Annan**, he was the architect of the 1997 UN **reform** proposals of the secretary-general.

SUBCOMMISSION ON THE PROMOTION AND PROTECTION OF HUMAN RIGHTS. Formerly called the Subcommission on the Protection of Minorities, this body of independent human rights experts is overseen by the **Commission for Human Rights** and has drafted a number of human rights instruments that developed into treaties, including the **International Convention on the Elimination of All Forms of Racial Discrimination** and the United Nations Declaration on the Human Rights of Nonnationals. The sub-commission prepared the first draft of Article 27 of **the International Covenant on Civil and Political Rights (ICCPR)** on the rights of **minorities**.

SUDAN. Since gaining its independence in 1956, the largest country in Africa has been the scene of a series of civil wars pitting the Arab Islamic government against Southern animists or Christian black Africans that has left more than 2 million dead and displaced over 4 million people. Prodded by the United States, the United Kingdom, and Norway, peace talks gained momentum in 2002–2004 with the signing in January 2005 of several accords, including a cease-fire agreement. The accords provide that the south may become autonomous pending the organization of a referendum on the key issue of independence. In addition, they contain clauses spelling out how the revenues from the oil resources of the region would be shared. In March 2005, the Security Council set up the **United Nations Mission in the Sudan (UNMIS)** to support the implementation of the agreements and perform a number of human rights and humanitarian activities.

This major breakthrough has been overshadowed, however, by another equally disturbing ferocious internal conflict which flared up in 2003 in the Western region of Darfur, pitting this time the central government against Muslim rebel groups also seeking power-sharing arrangements with Khartoum. The Sudanese government struck back, recruiting Arab militiamen and coordinating attacks on towns and villages suspected to be sympathetic to the rebels, while rejecting any internationalization of the conflict and erecting regulations that slowed down the delivery of humanitarian relief. The result has been a massive humanitarian catastrophe. Death toll estimates range from 200,000 to 400,000. More than 1.8 million people have been driven from their homes and are totally dependent on relief agencies for food, shelter, clothing and medical treatment. Another 200,000 have fled to neighboring Chad. The international humanitarian effort has undoubtedly saved lives but remains hostage to the willingness of the Sudanese government and local authorities in the field to play by the rules of the humanitarian game.

The **Security Council** has repeatedly condemned the cease-fire violations and the attacks on civilians and humanitarian workers, "vowing" "no impunity" for war crimes in Darfur. While lauding the **African Union (AU)** decision to deploy up to 7,000 troops there with a limited mandate, the council has also threatened on several occasions to impose sanctions against the Sudanese government if it failed to stem the violence. But its determination has been stymied by internal splits and veto threats. The Sudanese government denies any wrongdoing, claiming that the Darfur crisis is an internal matter of no concern to the international community. Some members of the council objected to the imposition of sanctions on Sudan. Another dispute has been whether the perpetrators of atrocities should be brought to trial in the **International Criminal Court (ICC)**, an idea promoted by France with the support of a majority of the members of the council that are also party to the ICC statute but opposed by the United States.

Unable to agree on matters of policy, the council gave a semblance of progress in its handling of the crisis by requesting in October 2004 the **secretary-general** to establish a five-member independent commission to "investigate reports of violations of international humanitarian law and human rights law in Darfur by all parties, to determine . . . whether or not acts of genocide have occurred, and to identify the perpetrators of such violations with a view to ensuring that those responsible are held accountable." The report of the commission issued four months later found that while the Sudanese government had not conducted a policy of genocide, both its forces and allied militias had carried out "indiscriminate attacks, including killing of civilians, torture, enforced disappearances, destruction of villages, rape and other forms of sexual violence, pillaging and forced displacement." The panel also concluded that rebel forces in Darfur were responsible for possible war crimes and recommended that the council refer its dossier on the crimes to the ICC.

On that basis, the Security Council, acting under Chapter VII of the United Nations **Charter**, adopted two separate resolutions in 2005. The first one imposes sanctions on individuals suspected of having committed atrocities or broken cease-fire agreements, bans travel by individuals deemed guilty of these offenses and freezes their assets, and forbids the Sudanese government from conducting offensive military operations in Darfur. The second resolution refers the Darfur situation to the prosecutor of the ICC.

SUEZ CANAL CRISIS (1956–1957). At the same time as the **Hungarian crisis** erupted, a serious crisis developed over control of the Suez Canal, which connects the Mediterranean Sea with the Red Sea. In July 1956, the Egyptian government nationalized the canal. Attempts to reach an agreement with Egypt on a new form of international control for the canal failed. In late October, Israel, accusing Egypt of planning an attack, sent troops to the Sinai Peninsula, and France and Britain dispatched an expeditionary force ostensibly to separate the combatants, while actually seizing control of the canal. The crisis increased in intensity when the Soviet Union signaled its readiness to use force to stop the French-British and Israeli invasions and the United States followed by strengthening its naval presence in the region.

Seized of the matter, the **Security Council** was blocked by French and British vetoes. Acting under the **Uniting for Peace Resolution** and responding to an initiative of Canadian Foreign Minister **Lester Pearson**, the **General Assembly** called for a cease-fire and authorized the **secretary-general** to plan for a United Nations emergency force to keep the peace between the opposing forces until a political settlement could be achieved. Under American pressure, Britain, France, and Israel agreed to a cease-fire on 6 November. The first contingents of the **United Nations Emergency Force (UNEF I)** were sent into Egypt on 15 November to provide a buffer between Egypt and Israel. In March 1957, under the supervision of the United Nations, the Suez Canal was cleared of wreckage and reopened to shipping. It remained under Egyptian control. Lester Pearson won the 1957 **Nobel Peace Prize** for contributing to the creation of UNEF I. *See also* PEACEKEEPING.

SUSTAINABLE DEVELOPMENT. *See* COMMISSION ON SUSTAINABLE DEVELOPMENT (UNITED NATIONS) (CSD); WORLD COMMISSION ON ENVIRONMENT AND DEVELOPMENT.

SWISSPEACE. Policy-oriented think tank founded in 1988 with the goal of promoting independent peace research. This Swiss-based institute focuses its work on conflict analysis and **postconflict peacebuilding** issues with particular attention to the causes of wars and violent conflicts, the development of tools for the early recognition of tensions, and the formulation of conflict mitigation and peace-building strategies. *See also* EARLY WARNING.

– T –

TAJIKISTAN CONFLICT (1992–1997). Former Soviet Republic that became independent and joined the **Commonwealth of Independent States (CIS)** in 1991 following the collapse of the Soviet Union. Civil war erupted in 1992 pitting the government against armed Islamic insurgent forces and lasted until 1994 with a cease-fire brokered by the United Nations, which was subsequently monitored by the **United Nations Mission of Observers in Tajikistan (UNMOT)**. The United Nations role in the resolution of the crisis was primarily one of **mediation** that started in 1992 with the dispatch of special envoys by the **secretary-general**. Their efforts eventually led to the conclusion of a peace and reconciliation agreement between the Tajik parties in 1997.

TAX AGREEMENTS. *See* AD HOC GROUP OF EXPERTS ON INTERNATIONAL COOPERATION IN TAX MATTERS.

TECHNICAL ASSISTANCE. Broad range of activities designed to enhance the human and institutional capabilities of **developing countries** and foster their economic and social development through the transfer, adaptation, and utilization of ideas, knowledge, practices, skills, and technology. Such activities include the financing of experts, consultants and trainees, feasibility studies, engineering and construction services for capital projects, institution-building efforts, research related to development, and the like.

Technical assistance or **"capacity development"** has become a major component of the work of the United Nations, involving expenditures exceeding $7 billion a year spread over 150 countries. Technical assistance involves flows of activities from North to South but there have been efforts to expand them among developing countries themselves. In 1978, the United Nations organized a Conference on Technical Cooperation among Developing Countries (TCDC) that recommended that the UN development system devote a significant

portion of its resources to TCDC. *See also* EXPANDED PRO-
GRAMME OF TECHNICAL ASSISTANCE (EPTA), UNITED NA-
TIONS DEVELOPMENT PROGRAMME (UNDP); UNITED NA-
TIONS VOLUNTEERS (UNV).

TELECOMMUNICATIONS. Term referring to the transmission of
data through radio, telegraphy, television, telephony, and computer
networking. For a long time, the United Nations work in this area focused on strengthening the interconnectivity of national communications infrastructures, the integration of new technologies into
global telecommunications networks, and the adoption of international regulations and treaties governing the sharing of radio frequencies spectrums and satellite orbital positions. This work was
(and remains) primarily carried out by the **International Telecommunications Union (ITU).**

Globalization, expanding **international trade**, and the deregulation of national economies have focused attention on the developmental aspects of telecommunications and underlined the significance of information and communication technologies — from
television and radio to the mobile phone and Internet — in the
achievement of development objectives and the protection of the **environment**. The provision of access to information and technological
know-how and the elimination of a North-South "digital divide" have
become major concerns and were among the main subjects tabled for
discussion at the 2005 **World Summit on the Information Society
(WSIS)** sponsored by the ITU. The vital role of telecommunications
technologies in disaster preparedness and the delivery of **humanitarian assistance** has also been increasingly recognized by **humanitarian agencies** and the **Office for the Coordination of Humanitarian Affairs (OCHA)**. *See also* EARLY WARNING; INFORMATION
TECHNOLOGY (IT).

TEN-NATION COMMITTEE ON DISARMAMENT. Main United
Nations disarmament negotiating forum in 1960–1961. *See also*
CONFERENCE ON DISARMAMENT (CD); DISARMAMENT.

TERMS OF TRADE. The ratio of the price of an export commodity(s)
to the price of an import commodity(s). The terms of trade of a country

are said to improve if that index rises. Improvements in a country's terms of trade is good for that country in the sense that it has to pay less for the products it imports and has to give up less exports for the imports it receives. Conversely, sharp swings or durable declines in a country's terms of trade can seriously disrupt or slow down output growth. Pessimistic assessments of long-term trends in developing countries' terms of trade were central in triggering their demands contained in the 1974 **Declaration on the Establishment of a New International Economic Order**. *See* INTEGRATED PROGRAMME FOR COMMODITIES (IPC); PREBISCH, RAUL (1901–1986).

TERRORISM. The main role of the United Nations and its **specialized agencies** has been to develop an international legal framework binding states to cooperate in the fight against terrorism. Several conventions—on the taking of hostages (1979), the safety of United Nations personnel (1994), the suppression of terrorist bombings (1997), and the suppression of the financing of terrorism (1999)—originate from the **General Assembly**.

The **International Civil Aviation Organization (ICAO)**, the **International Maritime Organization (IMO)**, and the **International Atomic Energy Agency (IAEA)** have also developed international agreements on the suppression of seizure of aircraft (1970), the safety of maritime navigation (1988), the physical protection of nuclear materials (1980), and the marking of plastic explosives for the purpose of detection (1991) among others.

The **Security Council** has occasionally adopted sanctions against states suspected of providing assistance to international terrorism. Acting under Chapter VII of the UN Charter, the council in September 2001 condemned the terrorist attacks of 11 September against the United States and established a counterterrorism committee mandating all states to share information in order to increase their capacity to fight terrorism.

In the context of the UN's efforts to prevent and combat terrorism, the **United Nations Office on Drugs and Crime (UNODC)** has a program of technical and advisory services providing legislative assistance to countries to become parties to, and implement, the UN antiterrorism conventions and protocols and Security Council Resolution 1373.

The 2005 report of the **High-Level Panel on Threats, Challenges, and Change** contains a definition of terrorism that had been thwarted for a long time by political disagreements over cases involving situations of foreign occupation. The panel defines terrorism as "any action that is intended to cause death or serious bodily harm on civilians or noncombatants when the purpose of such an act, by its nature or context, is to intimidate a population, or to compel a government or international organization to do or to abstain from doing any act." *See also* CRIME PREVENTION; WEAPONS OF MASS DESTRUCTION (WMDs).

THANT, U (1909–1974). Burmese educator, journalist, and diplomat, U Thant was the Permanent Representative of Burma to the United Nations at the time of his nomination as the interim **secretary-general** for the unexpired part of the term of **Dag Hammarskjöld**. He was elected for a full term in 1962, won a second mandate, and served as secretary-general until 1971.

His efforts at mediating international conflicts, notably in the case of the Vietnam War, were thwarted by the **Cold War**. Under Egyptian pressure, he made the controversial decision to withdraw the first **United Nations Emergency Force (UNEF I)** from Egypt, which many saw as a prelude to the 1967 Arab-Israeli War.

THIRD WORLD. *See* DEVELOPING COUNTRIES.

THIRD WORLD NETWORK (TWN). Independent international network of organizations and individuals based in Malaysia. TWN conducts research on economic, social, and environmental questions of concern to **developing countries** arising from **globalization** issues; the structure and operation of the **international trade** system; and the **World Trade Organization**'s **(WTO)** Agreement on **Trade-Related Aspects of Intellectual Property Rights (TRIPs).** TWN also seeks to provide a platform for the broad representation of Southern interests and perspectives in international forums, such as the United Nations **global conferences**. *See also* SOUTH CENTER.

THOMAS, ALBERT (1878–1932). French statesman and trade unionist and socialist leader. He worked with Jean Jaurès on the journal *l'Humanité* and was active in socialist politics. In 1910, he was elected to the Chamber of Deputies, and during World War I he held cabinet positions, serving notably as minister of munitions. From 1920 to 1932, he headed the secretariat of the **International Labour Organization (ILO)**, where he exerted a strong organizational and policy leadership that sharply contrasted with the self-effacing style of his successor, Sir Eric Drummond.

TIMOR-LESTE. Portuguese colony until 1974. Plans for the independence of East Timor as it was then called, were thwarted by a civil war between factions in favor of independence and those wanting to join Indonesia. Within days after Portugal relinquished control, Indonesia intervened militarily and annexed the province. Indonesia's 24-year-long occupation was repeatedly condemned by the United Nations and was not officially recognized by any major Western powers. **Cold War** balance of power considerations and economic interests, however, discouraged Western powers from forcefully intervening, thus contributing to widespread violations of **human rights** committed by the Indonesian military in its efforts to crush the nationalist movement. Human rights organizations estimate that some 200,000 East Timorese died during this period.

A change in government in 1998 made it possible for the Indonesian authorities to agree to granting a limited autonomy for East Timor. In 1999, in accord with the Portuguese government, the **secretary-general** was authorized to organize a "popular consultation" to ascertain whether East Timor wished to accept the special autonomy status offered by Indonesia or opt for political independence. To oversee a transitional period pending the outcome of popular vote, the **Security Council** set up the **United Nations Mission in East Timor (UNAMET)**.

Following the vote favoring by a wide margin independence over autonomy, violence broke out at the instigation of militias supported by elements of the Indonesian military. With the consent of the Indonesian government, the Security Council authorized the dispatch of a multinational force under Australian command to restore peace and security, protect UNAMET, and facilitate humanitarian operations. Indonesia eventually withdrew completely from East Timor, clearing the way to the establishment of the **United Nations Transi-**

tional Administration in East Timor (UNTAET), fully responsible for the administration of East Timor until the election of a constituent assembly and the constitution of a government. Following the promulgation of a constitution, the election of a president and the transformation of the Constituent Assembly into a National Parliament, East Timor became independent in May 2002 under the name of Timor. UNTAET was dissolved and the United Nations maintained a minor developmental presence until 2006 when, in the wake of civil disturbances among police and military forces, the Security Council established a new, expanded operation—the United Nations Integrated Mission in Timor-Leste (UNMIT)—to support the government in "consolidating stability, enhancing a culture of democratic governance, and facilitating political dialogue among Timorese stakeholders, in their efforts to bring about a process of national reconciliation and to foster social cohesion."

The struggle for independence has taken a heavy toll on the new nation. Its physical infrastructure has been destroyed. With an average annual income of $520, Timor-Leste is the poorest country in Asia. There is potential for revenues from vast offshore oil and gas fields in the Timor Sea, but the country cannot be expected to be self reliant for many years and requires international assistance. *See also* AHMED, RAFEEUDDIN (1932–); TRANSITIONAL ADMINISTRATION; UNITED NATIONS MISSION OF SUPPORT IN EAST TIMOR (UNMISET, May 2002–May 2005).

TINBERGEN, JAN (1903–1994). Dutch economist noted for his pioneering work on econometric models who won the first **Nobel Prize** for Economics in 1969. The first chairman of the **Committee for Development Policy** (then known as Committee for Development Planning [CDP]), he focused the committee's work on long-term planning and forecasting about key issues for **development** such as **population** growth, **food** and educational needs, industrial production, and **international trade**. *See also* PROJECT LINK.

TRADE AND DEVELOPMENT. Industrialization and economic growth took place in developed countries under conditions of trade protection. But following the world economic crisis of the 1930s, the United States has advocated a worldwide reduction of tariffs, the removal of trade barriers, the prohibition of all nontariff barriers, equal access to the markets of raw materials of the world, and limits on the rights of governments to interfere with private trade. These trade policies, the centerpiece of **liberal internationalism** enshrined in the proposal to establish an **International Trade Organization (ITO)**, were designed to complement the system set in place in 1944 at the **Bretton Woods Conference** with the creation of the **International Bank for Reconstruction and Development (IBRD)** and the **International Monetary Fund (IMF)**.

Developing countries also view external trade as a crucial element of their overall development strategies. From their standpoint, not only should international trade contribute to employment generation and the fulfillment of their **food, health**, and **education** needs, together with **official development assistance**, it should also help them accumulate the capital resources necessary to their economic takeoff. To become an engine of growth and development, international trade could not be totally "free" but should make special provision for practical regulatory measures that would improve developing countries' **terms of trade**, enhance their export capacity, and sustain their balance of payments. These ideas were encapsulated in **Raul Prebisch**'s theory centered on deteriorating "terms of trade" between industrial and developing countries, which posited that as providers of raw materials and agricultural products of declining value, developing countries needed to produce and sell more to purchase fewer and fewer of the North's manufactured products.

Known in development circles as "structuralism," Prebisch's theory won a large political following and inspired the demands of the **Nonaligned Movement (NAM)**, the **Group of Seventy-Seven (G-77)**, and the **Organization of Petroleum Exporting Countries (OPEC)** articulated in the 1974 **Declaration on the Establishment of a New International Economic Order** and an **Integrated Programme for Commodities (IPC)**. These proposals were negotiated primarily within the framework of the **United Nations Conference on Trade and Development (UNCTAD)** throughout the 1960s and 1970s and led to such policy innovations as the creation by the **International Monetary Fund (IMF)** of a Compensatory Financing Facility to assist Third World countries in managing foreign exchange crises triggered by sharp falls in the prices of commodities they export and a **General System of Preferences (GSP)**, allowing Third World exports of manufactures to enter First World markets at lower tariff rates than those applied to exports from other industrialized countries.

All other demands emanating from Prebisch's structuralism—notably the IPC, the establishment of a **Common Fund**, and the issuance of binding **codes of conduct** to regulate the activities of **multinational corporations**—were resisted and/or rejected by Northern countries, which saw them as a blueprint for a redistribution of global economic power through the United Nations. Beginning in the 1980s, the tide swung back to neoliberal economic prescriptions and a large number of Third World countries, weakened by their **debt** overhang, embarked on extensive programs of deregulation, liberalization, and privatization as part of the structural adjustment programs of the IMF.

The increasing **globalization** of the world economy has further accelerated the relative decline of the United Nations as a mechanism of trade-related negotiations and moved to center stage the role of the **World Trade Organization (WTO)**, where developing countries continue to complain about their inability to obtain a fair share of benefits from a liberalized international trade system. While preaching the virtues of free trade, promoting it through the WTO, and demanding that developing countries eliminate their trade barriers, Northern countries have themselves adopted highly restrictive and protectionist policies. Agricultural growth is a strong determinant of overall growth and poverty reduction in poor countries, but agricultural support to farmers in the **European Union (EU)** and the United States creates unfair competition in world markets and deprives developing countries of a significant market share and considerable foreign exchange. Market access for developing countries' agricultural and textile products remains a source of unresolved vexing problems, and some argue that the costs of Northern protectionism for developing countries amount to a loss of $700 billion in their annual export earnings or 12 percent of their combined gross national product (GNP). Southern countries also charge that services, **intellectual property rights**, and investment rules fail to strike an appropriate balance between the need to reward innovation and the ability of governments to promote broader social objectives.

The current value of world merchandise trade amounts to over $7 trillion, nearly one third of which ($2.1 trillion) originates from developing economies. The scope and continuing expansion of the international trading system more than ever makes it a determinant of growth and development. Trade has in fact become intrusive as it affects critical domestic policies in both Southern and Northern countries and is likely to gain further salience in future international negotiations within or outside of the United Nations. *See also* ECONOMIC COMMISSION FOR LATIN AMERICA AND THE CARIBBEAN (ECLAC); ELECTRONIC COMMERCE (E-COMMERCE); INTELLECTUAL PROPERTY RIGHTS (IPRs); NORTH-SOUTH DIALOGUE; TRADE-RELATED ASPECTS OF INTELLECTUAL PROERTY RIGHTS (TRIPs).

TRADE-RELATED ASPECTS OF INTELLECTUAL PROPERTY RIGHTS (TRIPs). Governments give creators of ideas and knowledge "**intellectual property rights**" (IPRs) to prevent others from using their inventions, designs, and other creations. Such IPRs can take a variety of forms including the **copyrighting** of books, paintings, and films; the patenting of inventions; and the registering of trademarks for brand names and product logos. The assumption is that such protection encourages creativity and invention and thus benefits society in the long term. The scope and extent of protection and enforcement of property rights has varied widely throughout the world, and as an increasing number of internationally traded products contain a higher proportion of invention and design, these differences have become a source of rising tensions in international economic relations.

The **World Trade Organization**'s **(WTO)** Agreement on Trade-Related Aspects of Intellectual Property Rights negotiated between 1986 and 1994 within the framework of the **General Agreement on Tariffs and Trade (GATT)** is an attempt to introduce internationally agreed rules for intellectual property rights and for related disputes to be settled more systematically. The basic purpose of the TRIPs Agreement is to ensure that adequate standards of protection exist in all WTO member countries and to bring these rights under common international rules on the basis of most-favored-nation treatment. Although the Agreement allows developed and developing countries different periods of time to delay the application of its principles, the TRIPs have become a contentious North-South international trade issue. *See also* ELECTRONIC COMMERCE (E-COMMERCE); HIV/AIDS; INTERNATIONAL TRADE; TRANSNATIONAL CORPORATIONS (TNCs); WORLD INTELLECTUAL PROPERTY ORGANIZATION (WIPO).

TRAFFICKING IN PERSONS. Wide range of illegal actions including the prostitution of **women** and **children** and the exploitation of **migrant workers** which have been the subject of several international conventions. Efforts to ban these activities and prevent them through international cooperation predate the **League of Nations.** In 1949, the United Nations **General Assembly** adopted the Convention for the Suppression of the Traffic in Persons and of the Exploitation of the Prostitution of Others, which superseded all previous conventions. Since then, these issues have been extensively discussed in numerous UN sponsored **global conferences** devoted to **women, children,** and **population** in the **Commission for Human Rights,** the **Commission on Crime Prevention and Criminal Justice,** and quinquennial United Nations' congresses on **crime prevention** and the treatment of offenders.

The most important legal instruments developed under the aegis of the United Nations are the 1949 Convention for the Suppression of the Traffic in Persons and of the Exploitation of the Prostitution of Others, the **Convention on the Rights of the Child (CRC),** and the **United Nations Convention against Transnational Organized Crime.**

TRANSITIONAL ADMINISTRATION. Probably the most complex **peacekeeping operations** undertaken by the United Nations in the sense that the organization assumes sovereign powers on a temporary basis and is involved in activities directed at building or rebuilding the institutions of the state that extend beyond traditional peacekeeping and peace building.

In his **Agenda for Peace, Secretary-General Boutros Boutros-Ghali** said that this included "reforming or strengthening governmental institutions" (1992). In his Supplement to An Agenda for Peace (1995), the secretary-general referred to "the creation of structures for the institutionalization of peace."

An early instance of such UN operation can be found in the **United Nations Temporary Executive Administration (UNTEA)** where the role of the United Nations was limited to a transfer of power from Dutch to the Indonesian authorities. More recent examples include the **United Nations Transitional Authority in Cambodia (UNTAC)**, the **United Nations Transition Assistance Group (UNTAG)**, the **United Nations Interim Mission in Kosovo (UNMIK)**, the **United Nations Transitional Administration in East Timor (UNTAET)**, and, with a substantially reduced mandate, the **United Nations Assistance Mission in Afghanistan (UNAMA)**. Most of the time, the United Nations has become involved in nation building without clear guidelines or political consensus. *See also* SELF-DETERMINATION; UNITED NATIONS TRANSITIONAL ADMINISTRATION FOR EASTERN SLAVONIA, BARANJA, AND WESTERN SIRMIUM (UNTAES, 19 January 1996–15 January 1998).

TRANSNATIONAL ACTORS. *See* NONSTATE ACTORS.

TRANSNATIONAL CORPORATIONS (TNCs). Also known as multinational corporations (MNCs), these are business companies based in one state with affiliated branches or subsidiaries operating in other states. The role of TNCs in international relations is complex and has been for decades the subject of sharply conflicting interpretations. Some see them as agents of their home national governments. Conversely, others portray national governments as agents of their TNCs. Still others argue that TNCs, with their global transnational infrastructure of facilities, services, communications links, and management, act globally in the sole interests of their stakeholders and owe loyalty to no national state. TNCs are thus viewed as a factor contributing to an erosion of state **sovereignty**.

The role of TNCs in the process and promotion of **development** has also generated a long-standing and still ongoing controversy. For some, TNCs are indispensable engines of development: they assist in the aggregation of investment capital that can fund development; introduce and dispense advanced technology to less developed countries; and generate employment, income, and wealth. Critics, on the other hand, point out that the activities of TNCs often result in increasing the wealth of local elites at the expense of the poor and in widening the gap between rich and poor within and among countries. They may also be complicit in violations of human rights by infringing on workers' rights or as a result of their association with repressive governments or local insurgencies. TNCs may also cause indiscriminate environmental damage and their activities may erode the traditional cultures of **indigenous peoples**.

None of these debates is by any means settled but it is clear that TNCs prosper in a stable international atmosphere based on freedom of **international trade**, of movement, and of capital flows, all governed by market forces with minimal governmental intervention. In that sense, TNCs are both a product as well as one of the driving forces of **globalization** and global **interdependence**. It is also clear that economic globalization has vastly expanded the reach of corporate power and multinational corporations are recognized now as bona fide **nonstate actors** in international relations and conflicts. Many international businesses control enormous economic resources. The largest among them have annual profits exceeding the gross national product of numerous countries and they exert considerable power and influence. Many companies operate across boundaries in ways often exceeding the regulatory capacities of any national system and, in effect, their activities, production methods, employment practices, and investment decisions affect millions of individual workers, communities, and the environment.

The impact of the TNCs investment and presence in **developing countries** has been a recurring source of controversy within the United Nations. Throughout the 1960s and 1970s, developing countries sought—in vain—to regulate their activities through binding legal **codes of conduct**. Since the end of the **Cold War**, political attention has shifted to the development of voluntary schemes of corporate social responsibility such as the 1999 **Global Compact** of **Secretary-General Kofi Annan**. The **International Labour Organization (ILO)** has also drawn attention to the need to develop policies counteracting the rising social and economic inequalities stemming from the process of globalization.

The role of the TNCs in internal wars where rebel groups and governments vie for control of local natural resources such as cobalt, copper, gold, diamonds, timber, and oil exploited by private companies has also mobilized the international community as the sale of these natural resources, which also involves illegal traders, transport companies, and arms smugglers, has fueled civil wars in Africa with devastating human and environmental consequences. During the 1990s, diamonds funded the civil war in **Angola**, prompting the **Security Council** to enforce sanctions on diamonds sales by the National Union for the Total Independence of Angola (UNITA) rebel group. Further conflicts related to **natural resources** have also affected the **Democratic Republic of the Congo**, **Liberia**, **Sierra Leone**, and **Sudan**. Present efforts to curb the activities of TNCs in conflict zones have focused on the development of voluntary guidelines. For instance, the **United Nations Subcommission for the Promotion and Protection of Human Rights** is working on a draft "Norms on the Responsibilities of Transnational Corporations and Other Enterprises with Regard to Human Rights," a set of ethics guidelines on the responsibilities of companies for **human rights** and **labor** rights, and provides guidelines for companies operating in conflict zones.

Data on transnational corporations is given in annual reports of the United Nations, notably the *World Investment Report* published annually by the **United Nations Conference on Trade and Development (UNCTAD)**. *See also* BUSINESS AND THE UNITED NATIONS.

TRANSNATIONAL ORGANIZED CRIME. *See* UNITED NATIONS CONVENTION AGAINST TRANSNATIONAL ORGANIZED CRIME (2003).

TRANSPARENCY INTERNATIONAL (TI). Nongovernmental organization (NGO) devoting its awareness-raising work to combating and preventing corruption. TI also advocates policy reforms and promotes the implementation of multilateral conventions by monitoring compliance by governments, corporations, and banks. *See also* UNITED NATIONS CONVENTION AGAINST CORRUPTION (2003).

TREATY BODIES. Legal term used to refer to committees established to monitor the implementation of United Nations **human rights** treaties and conventions by states that have ratified or acceded to these instruments. Instances of such bodies include the **Human Rights Committee**; the **Committee on Economic, Social, and Cul-**

tural Rights; the **Committee on the Elimination of Racial Discrimination**; the **Committee on the Elimination of Discrimination against Women**; the **Committee against Torture**; and the **Committee on the Rights of the Child**. Similar bodies perform similar functions in regard to the protection of minorities and slavery. States parties to such treaties and conventions submit regular reports to these committees on the legislative and administrative measures they have taken to put into effect the provisions of a particular convention.

TREATY ON THE NONPROLIFERATION OF NUCLEAR WEAPONS. *See* NONPROLIFERATION OF NUCLEAR WEAPONS, TREATY ON THE (NPT, 1968).

TRUMAN, HARRY S. (1884–1972). President of the United States from 1945 to 1953 who, in the wake of **President Franklin Delano Roosevelt**'s death, played a leading role in the creation of the United Nations and in securing U.S. participation in it. His internationalist commitment was grounded on the ideas that the root causes of World War II lay in the American failure to join the **League of Nations** and in the incapacity of the League to prevent **aggression** throughout the 1930s. Like his predecessor in the White House, he conceived the United Nations as an arena in which the United States could exert the leadership that it had turned down in 1919. The **Cold War** did force him to abandon his commitment to the system of **collective security** enshrined in the UN Charter as many of his foreign policy initiatives—notably the Marshall Plan—were taken outside of the UN framework. But he was mindful to enlist and secure the broad support of the United Nations throughout the **Korean War**.

TRUST TERRITORY. A territory placed temporarily under the protection of an established state with the responsibility to promote its inhabitants' **self-determination** and welfare. Under the **League of Nations**, such territories were known as **mandates**. *See also* DECOLONIZATION; STRATEGIC TRUST TERRITORIES; TRUSTEESHIP COUNCIL; TRUSTEESHIP SYSTEM.

TRUSTEESHIP COUNCIL. One of the principal organs of the United Nations intended to administer **Trust Territories** placed under its authority. Composed of an equal number of administering and non-administering governmental representatives, the council was granted limited powers of information gathering, discussion, and recommendation. It had no coercive powers over an administering state but received annual reports based on a comprehensive questionnaire from administering states. It could also receive individual petitions directly and send visiting missions to gain knowledge of conditions in Trust Territories.

By the early 1990s, all eleven Trust Territories (Cameroons [under British and French administration], Ruanda-Urundi [under Belgian administration], Tanganyika [under British administration], Togoland [under British and French administration], Nauru [administered by Australia on behalf of Australia, New Zealand, and the United Kingdom], New Guinea [administered by Australia], the North Pacific Islands [Micronesia, the Marshall Islands, the northern Mariana Islands and Palau under United States administration], Western Samoa [under New Zealand administration], and Somaliland [under Italian administration]) had achieved independence or chosen voluntary association with an existing nation on the basis of UN-administered plebiscites.

The very success of the Trusteeship Council has raised questions about its continuing existence, some arguing that it should be abolished, others that its mandate should be reviewed and altered in the light of the increasing involvement of the United Nations in **transitional administration** situations. *See also* DECOLONIZATION; TRUSTEESHIP SYSTEM.

TRUSTEESHIP SYSTEM. Successor arrangements to the **mandate system of the League of Nations'** that placed a number of colonies under the loose oversight of the United Nations. The system was a compromise reached at the 1945 **United Nations Conference on International Organization** in San Francisco between colonial powers that favored a continuation of the mandate system and newly independent developing countries that called for extending these arrangements to all colonies. The resulting provisions of the **Charter** (Article 77) stipulated that a nonself-governing territory could be brought within the system through the agreement of an administering power and the agreement of the **General Assembly**. No single colonial power ever made use of that stipulation.

Under the terms of the charter, the objectives of the Trusteeship System were to further international peace and security and to promote the political, economic, social, and educational advancement of the inhabitants of a **Trust Territory** toward self-government or independence. Viewed in relation to the "Declaration Regarding Non-Self-Governing Territories" (Chapter XI of the Charter), the Trusteeship System was a mechanism for the peaceful transition from colonial status to independence. It was also the first manifestation of the subsequent broader attack in the United Nations on colonialism and the sweep of **self-determination** in the postwar. *See also* DECLARATION ON THE GRANTING OF INDEPENDENCE TO COLONIAL COUNTRIES AND PEOPLES (1960); DECOLONIZATION; SELF-DETERMINATION.

TRUTH AND RECONCILIATION COMMISSIONS (TRCs). Bodies established to investigate **human rights** violations committed by military, government, or other forces during a civil war or under a previous political regime. They are not courts of law. Instead, their primary purpose is to provide a forum for victims to relate their stories, to assign responsibility for violations to certain individuals and to record who was responsible for extra-judicial killings such as assassinations, "disappearances," massacres, and gross violations of human rights. The expectation is that by making the truth public and part of the nation's common history, such commissions facilitate the process of national reconciliation.

Truth commissions are usually established immediately after a peace settlement has been reached, and their mandate ceases with the submission of a report of their findings. TRCs have been widely used tools in the transition from conflict or oppression to democracy, especially in Central and South America and South Africa. For example, the creation of TCRs was written in the peace settlements brokered by the **United Nations**, ending the civil wars in **Guatemala** and **El Salvador**. *See also* WAR CRIMES TRIBUNALS.

TUNISIAN QUESTION. Nationalist pressure for independence began in 1934, with the formation of the Néo-Destour (New Constitution) Party (NDP) under the leadership of Habib Bourguiba. At the end of World War II, the Néo-Destour joined the French government in attempting to find a peaceful means of satisfying Tunisian demands. Popular resistance continued to increase, and pressures by **developing countries** to have the matter discussed by the **General Assembly** intensified, eventually prompting France to grant internal autonomy to Tunisia. Franco-Tunisian conventions were signed in 1955 providing for responsibility for all matters, except foreign affairs and defense, to be transferred to the Tunisian government. Demands for Tunisian independence both within the country and at the United Nations went on unabated, leading to the opening of further negotiations concluded in 1956 with the signing of an agreement abrogating the 1881 Bardo Treaty instituting a French Protectorate over Tunisia and recognizing Tunisia's full independence. *See also* ALGERIAN QUESTION; DECOLONIZATION.

TURNER, TED (1938–). American media network executive turned philanthropist. The Turner Foundation, which he founded in 1990, gives millions of dollars to environmental causes. In 1997, he donated $1 billion to a new foundation to support the United Nations, the largest single donation by a private individual in history. *See also* TURNER FOUNDATION; UNITED NATIONS FUND FOR INTERNATIONAL PARTNERSHIPS (UNFIP).

TURNER FOUNDATION. Public charity responsible for administering **Ted Turner**'s $1 billion contribution to the United Nations in support of its work in the areas of **women** and **population**, **children**'s **health**, peace and security, prevention and **human rights**, and the **environment**. *See also* UNITED NATIONS FOUNDATION FOR INTERNATIONAL PARTNERSHIPS (UNFIP).

– U –

UNAIDS. *See* JOINT UNITED NATIONS PROGRAMME ON HIV/AIDS (UNAIDS).

UNITED NATIONS ADMINISTRATIVE TRIBUNAL. Independent organ established by the **General Assembly** in 1949 to hear and pass judgment on applications by United Nations staff alleging breaches in the terms of their contractual employment. The jurisdiction of the tribunal applies to the staff of the **secretariat**; the voluntarily funded programs such as the **United Nations Development Programme (UNDP)**, the **United Nations Children's Fund (UNICEF)**, the **United Nations Population Fund (UNFPA)**, and the **International Court of Justice (ICJ)**; and a number of **specialized agencies**. *See also* PERSONNEL QUESTIONS.

UNITED NATIONS ADVANCE MISSION IN CAMBODIA (UNAMIC). Mission set up in October 1991 to help maintain the cease-fire among warring factions in Cambodia and to make preparations for the arrival of the **United Nations Transitional Authority in Cambodia (UNTAC)**. UNAMIC was eventually merged into UNTAC in March 1992.

UNITED NATIONS ANGOLA VERIFICATION MISSION (UNAVEM I, December 1988–June 1991). Established by the **Security Council** at the request of Angola and Cuba to verify the phased withdrawal of Cuban troops from **Angola**. The mission was terminated upon completion of the Cuban troops withdrawal. *See also* UNITED NATIONS ANGOLA VERIFICATION MISSION (UNAVEM II, June 1991–February 1995); UNITED NATIONS ANGOLA VERIFICATION MISSION (UNAVEM III, February 1995–June 1997).

UNITED NATIONS ANGOLA VERIFICATION MISSION (UNAVEM II, June 1991–February 1995). Successor operation to the first **United Nations Angola Verification Mission (UNAVEM I)** initially created to oversee the peace arrangements agreed by the Angolan government and the National Union for the Total Independence of Angola (UNITA) and subsequently to observe presidential and legislative elections held in 1992. The rejection of the elections' outcome by UNITA plunged **Angola** back into civil war. A new peace agreement concluded in 1994 led to the disbanding of UNAVEM II and the creation of **UNAVEM III**.

UNITED NATIONS ANGOLA VERIFICATION MISSION (UNAVEM III, February 1995–June 1997). The third in a series of United Nations operations in **Angola**. Its mandate was to provide

good offices and **mediation** to the Angolan parties, to monitor the cease-fire and the process of national reconciliation, to verify the quartering and demobilization of National Union for the Total Independence of Angola (UNITA) forces, to monitor the neutrality of the Angolan national police and the disarming of civilians, and to facilitate humanitarian activities related to the peace process. The complexity of these tasks, inadequate military and human resources, and continuing mistrust between the Angolan government and UNITA hampered the work of UNAVEM III and contributed to its dissolution in 1997 and the launching of yet another more modest United Nations **peacekeeping** mission. *See also* CONFLICT PREVENTION; UNITED NATIONS ANGOLA VERIFICATION MISSION (UNAVEM I, December 1988–June 1991); UNITED NATIONS ANGOLA VERIFICATION MISSION (UNAVEM II, June 1991–February 1995); UNITED NATIONS OBSERVER MISSION IN ANGOLA (MONUA, June 1997–February 1999).

UNITED NATIONS AOUZOU STRIP OBSERVER GROUP (UNASOG, April–June 1994). Ownership over the Aouzou Strip was contested by Libya and Chad until the two countries referred the matter to the **International Court of Justice (ICJ)**. In its judgment, the court defined the boundaries between Libya and Chad and awarded the Strip to Chad. UNASOG was set up by the **Security Council** to monitor the withdrawal of Libyan forces from the Strip which was completed in June 1994.

UNITED NATIONS ASSISTANCE MISSION IN AFGHANISTAN (UNAMA). Established by the **Security Council** as part of an effort to integrate the humanitarian, human rights, relief, recovery, and reconstruction activities work of UN agencies in **Afghanistan**. Headquartered in Kabul, UNAMA has a staff of over 400 persons headed by a **special representative of the secretary-general**. *See also* TRANSITIONAL ADMINISTRATION.

UNITED NATIONS ASSISTANCE MISSION IN RWANDA (UNAMIR, October 1993–March 1996). After three years of fighting, the mainly Hutu government of **Rwanda** and Tutsi-led insurgents operating from neighboring Uganda reached an agreement in 1993 providing for a provisional government and for elections. The

United Nations Assistance Mission in Rwanda was established by the **Security Council** to monitor the cease-fire agreement until completion of the transition period and assist with mine clearance and the coordination of humanitarian and relief activities.

The mandate of UNMIR was adjusted several times following a wave of genocidal massacres in April 1994. The civil war came to an end when Tutsi insurgents took control of the country three months later and UNAMIR was given the mandate to exercise its good offices to help achieve national reconciliation, facilitate the return and reintegration of refugees, support the provision of humanitarian aid, and protect UN personnel and premises, including the newly created **International Criminal Tribunal for Rwanda**. The mission was terminated in 1996 at the request of Rwanda.

A 1999 independent inquiry initiated by the **secretary-general** singled out the mission's lack of resources, the persistent lack of political commitment by member states to act decisively and "serious mistakes" within the **secretariat** as factors contributing to the failure of UNAMIR to prevent and stop the **genocide**.

UNITED NATIONS ASSOCIATION OF THE UNITED STATES OF AMERICA (UNA-USA). American **nongovernmental organization (NGO)** belonging to the wider network of the **World Federation of United Nations Associations**. UNA-USA traces its origins to an association that sprang out of the League of Nations Association in 1943 to promote acceptance of the **Dumbarton Oaks Proposals**. UNA-USA seeks to educate Americans and build constituencies for the United Nations through high-level policy studies and an extensive grassroots outreach machinery of local chapters and divisions. Since 1999, the **Business Council for the United Nations (BCUN)** joined the UNA-USA as one of its divisions. Prior to the opening of each session of the **General Assembly** and until 2005, UNA-USA published *Global Agenda*, an authoritative broad overview of the major questions on the agenda of the assembly.

UNITED NATIONS BOARD OF AUDITORS. One of the oversight bodies of the United Nations that carries out external audits of the accounts of the United Nations and its funds and programs. The board reports findings and recommendations to the **General Assembly**

through the **Advisory Committee on Administrative and Budgetary Questions (ACABQ)**. *See also* BUDGET (UNITED NATIONS).

UNITED NATIONS CAPITAL DEVELOPMENT FUND (UNCDF). Established in 1966 by the UN **General Assembly** as a substitute for the **Special United Nations Fund for Economic Development (SUNFED)**, the original purpose of the UNCDF was to supplement existing sources of capital assistance for small-scale investment in developing countries. Its mandate was changed in 1973 and UNCDF now focuses on small-scale capital investment projects in the poorest countries.

UNITED NATIONS CENTRE ON HUMAN SETTLEMENTS (UNCHS or HABITAT). An organ within the United Nations **Secretariat** entrusted with the task of promoting socially and environmentally sustainable settlements, development, and adequate **shelter** for all. Habitat's major role is to carry out normative and technical assistance activities in support of the global plan of action adopted at the 1996 **United Nations Conference on Human Settlements (Habitat II)**. *See also* COMMISSION ON HUMAN SETTLEMENTS (UNITED NATIONS).

UNITED NATIONS CHILDREN'S FUND (UNICEF). Originally, a temporary fund created by the **General Assembly** in 1946 to administer residual funds from the **United Nations Relief and Rehabilitation Administration (UNRRA)** "to be utilized for the benefit of **children** and adolescents of countries which were the victims of aggression," UNICEF was given permanent status in 1953.

UNICEF is still the provider of emergency supplies of food, vaccine, and field equipment in crisis situations but has shifted its activities toward longer-range programs such as the reduction of infant mortality through immunization campaigns; girls' **education**; family education in better nutrition; teacher training; protecting children from violence, exploitation, abuse, and discrimination; and policy research.

UNICEF-led efforts have had a major impact. Today, three out of four children are immunized before their first birthday, a major stride forward from the early 1970s when fewer than 10 percent of children were vaccinated. UNICEF was the recipient of the **Nobel Peace Prize** in 1965. *See also* CHILDREN IN ARMED CONFLICTS; COMMITTEE ON THE RIGHTS OF THE CHILD (CRC); CONVENTION ON THE RIGHTS OF THE CHILD (CRC, 1990); SAVE THE CHILDREN; SINGER, HANS (1910–2005); WATER; WORLD SUMMIT FOR CHILDREN (NEW YORK, 1990).

UNITED NATIONS CIVILIAN POLICE MISSION IN HAITI (MIPONUH, December 1997–March 2000). Set up in December 1997 upon expiration of the **United Nations Transition Mission in Haiti (UNTMIH)** to assist in the further modernization and development of the Haitian national police, MIPONUH completed its mandate in December 2000 and was replaced by the **International Civilian Mission Support in Haiti (MICAH)**. *See also* HAITI; INTERNATIONAL CIVILIAN MISSION IN HAITI (MICIVIH, 1993–1999); UNITED NATIONS MISSION IN HAITI (UNMIH, September 1993–June 1996); UNITED NATIONS OBSERVER GROUP FOR THE VERIFICATION OF ELECTIONS IN HAITI (ONUVEH); UNITED NATIONS STABILIZATION MISSION IN HAITI (MINUSTAH, April 2004–present); UNITED NATIONS SUPPORT MISSION IN HAITI (UNSMIH, 1996–1997).

UNITED NATIONS CIVILIAN POLICE SUPPORT GROUP (UNPSG). Authorized on 19 December 1997 for a nine-month period by the **Security Council** to replace the **United Nations Transitional Administration for Eastern Slavonia, Baranja, and Western Sirmium (UNTAES)**. The Group, in cooperation with the **Organization for Security and Cooperation in Europe (OSCE)**, monitored the performance of the Croatian police in the two-way return of displaced persons between Croatia and Serbia. In October, the OSCE took over the group's responsibilities. *See also* REGIONAL ARRANGEMENTS.

UNITED NATIONS COMMISSION FOR INDIA AND PAKISTAN (UNCIP, 1948–1950). Established by the **Security Council** in 1948 to seek a peaceful solution to the **Kashmir dispute** pitting India against Pakistan. The commission also had observation functions that were transferred to the **United Nations Military Observer Group in India and Pakistan (UNMOGIP)** when UNCIP was dissolved in 1950.

UNITED NATIONS COMMISSION ON INTERNATIONAL TRADE LAW (UNCITRAL). Created by the **General Assembly** in 1966 for the purpose of furthering the progressive harmonization and unification of **international trade** law, the commission has developed conventions, models, laws, and rules on the international sale and transport of goods, commercial arbitration and conciliation, construction contracts, electronic commerce, and cross-border insolvency. *See also* FUNCTIONALISM; INTERNATIONAL LAW.

UNITED NATIONS COMMITTEE ON THE PEACEFUL USES OF OUTER SPACE (COPUOS). Created in 1958 by the **General Assembly** shortly after the launching of the first artificial satellite and converted into a permanent body the following year, this committee provides a framework for the voluntary exchange of information relating to **outer space** activities and assists in the study of measures for the promotion of international cooperation in the peaceful uses and exploration of outer space. In the same enabling resolution, the assembly requested the **secretary-general** to maintain a public registry of launchings based on the information supplied by states placing objects into Earth's orbit and beyond. Five international treaties have been elaborated under the auspices of the committee dealing respectively with the exploration and use of outer space, the rescue of astronauts, liability for damage caused by space objects, the registration of objects launched into outer space, and the activities of states on the moon and other celestial bodies *See also* ARMS CONTROL; DISARMAMENT; OUTER SPACE TREATY (1967).

UNITED NATIONS CONFERENCE ON DESERTIFICATION (NAIROBI, 1977). Although several United Nations agencies—notably the **United Nations Educational, Scientific, and Cultural Organization (UNESCO)** and the **Food and Agriculture Organization (FAO)**—had conducted research and gathered considerable information on environmental constraints in arid regions for some time, the issue of **desertification** received only scant attention at the 1972 **United**

Nations Conference on the Human Environment in Stockholm. A catastrophic drought that affected the Sahelian region in Africa in the early 1970s focused attention on the problem and prompted calls for the convening of a global conference to address the problem. The 1977 Nairobi gathering was preceded by an extensive scientific preparatory work and resulted in the adoption of a set of recommendations recognizing that land degradation was a leading cause of **poverty** requiring coordinated efforts at the national and international levels to restore damaged lands, improve **food security** and encourage the transition to sustainable agriculture and land management. One of the achievements of the 1992 **United Nations Conference on Environment and Development** was the adoption of a **United Nations Convention to Combat Desertification (UNCCD)**. *See also* AGENDA 21; DESERTIFICATION; ENVIRONMENTAL SECURITY.

UNITED NATIONS CONFERENCE ON ENVIRONMENT AND DEVELOPMENT (UNCED, RIO DE JANEIRO, 1992). Held in June 1992, exactly 20 years after the **United Nations Conference on the Human Environment**, the United Nations Conference on Environment and Development (the **Earth Summit** as it came to be called), was the climax of an intensive and broad-based two-year process of planning and negotiations. UNCED basically produced a compromise between the **development** agenda of Southern countries and the **environment** agenda of Northern countries, thus giving a stamp of collective legitimacy to the concept of sustainable development articulated by the **World Commission on Environment and Development**, the so-called **Brundtland** Commission.

In concrete terms, UNCED resulted in the adoption of a number of nonbinding texts like **Agenda 21**, the Rio Declaration on Environment and Development, and the Statement of Forest Principles. The conference also led to the adoption of two treaties, the **United Nations Framework Convention on Climate Change (UNFCCC)** and the United Nations **Convention on Biological Diversity (CBD)**. In addition, UNCED established a follow-up mechanism, the **Commission on Sustainable Development (CSD)**, to monitor the implementation of the consensus achieved at the conference together with a modest scheme of financing sustainable development projects, the **Global Environmental Facility**. *See also* INDEPENDENT

COMMISSIONS; WORLD SUMMIT ON SUSTAINABLE DE-VELOPMENT (WSSD) (JOHANNESBURG, 2002).

UNITED NATIONS CONFERENCE ON HUMAN SETTLE-MENTS (HABITAT I, VANCOUVER, 1976). First global meeting to address the linkages between human settlement and the **environment**, most especially the problems arising from rapid **population** growth and deepening rural-urban imbalances. *See also* COMMIS-SION ON HUMAN SETTLEMENTS (UNITED NATIONS); UNITED NATIONS CENTRE ON HUMAN SETTLEMENTS (UNCHS or HABITAT); UNITED NATIONS CONFERENCE ON HUMAN SETTLEMENTS (HABITAT II, ISTANBUL, 1996); UR-BANIZATION.

UNITED NATIONS CONFERENCE ON HUMAN SETTLE-MENTS (HABITAT II, ISTANBUL, 1996). Follow-up conference to the 1976 **United Nations Conference on Human Settlements** and last in a series of global conferences sponsored by the United Na-tions dealing with various aspects of **human security** throughout the 1990s. While Habitat II shared many goals of the Vancouver confer-ence, this "City Summit" broadened the objective of improving liv-ing conditions in human settlements by linking it to issues related to democracy, **human rights**, people's participation, environmental sustainability, decentralization of government, **women**'s empower-ment, and public-private partnerships. Also remarkable was the ex-tensive participation of local governmental authorities in the confer-ence. *See also* URBANIZATION.

UNITED NATIONS CONFERENCE ON INTERNATIONAL OR-GANIZATION. Convened at San Francisco on 25 April 1945 at the invitation of the United States in the name of the "sponsoring Gov-ernments" that had participated in the **Dumbarton Oaks Confer-ence**, the assigned function of the conference was to draft the charter of a new world organization.

For a period of about two months, the conference debated the Dumbarton Oaks proposals as well as proposals and comments sub-mitted by other participating governments. The decision-making process was relatively open, as substantive questions were reviewed in technical committees and commissions before being put to special majority votes in plenary sessions. This allowed the smaller powers to place checks on the peaceful settlement functions of the **Security Council**, to enlarge the power and functions of the **General Assembly**, and to broaden the activities of the United Nations in economic and social affairs. They were, however, unable to change the basic provisions of the Dumbarton Oaks proposals pertaining to the **veto** and the discretionary role of the Security Council in cases of a threat to or breach of the peace, as it was understood that securing the participation of the major powers was a key condition of the effectiveness of the United Nations.

The charter was signed on 26 June 1945 and took effect on 24 October, having been ratified by China, France, the Soviet Union, the United Kingdom, the United States, and a majority of other signatory states.

UNITED NATIONS CONFERENCE ON NEW AND RENEWABLE SOURCES OF ENERGY (NAIROBI, 1981). Convened at a time when it was widely thought that the world faced an imminent **energy** crisis, this international gathering called attention to the need to monitor and assess the use of traditional energy sources such as fuelwood, coal, and fossil fuel and for global steps to develop alternative new and renewable sources of energy. Though still well justified, the assumption that prompted the convening of this conference has faded away while attention shifted to the notion of sustainability as it relates to **development** and **poverty** eradication. *See also* UNITED NATIONS CONFERENCE ON ENVIRONMENT AND DEVELOPMENT (UNCED, RIO DE JANEIRO, 1992); UNITED NATIONS CONFERENCE ON THE HUMAN ENVIRONMENT (STOCKHOLM, 1972); UNITED NATIONS FRAMEWORK CONVENTION ON CLIMATE CHANGE (UNFCCC); WORLD COMMISSION ON ENVIRONMENT AND DEVELOPMENT.

UNITED NATIONS CONFERENCE ON SCIENCE AND TECHNOLOGY FOR DEVELOPMENT (VIENNA, 1979). Global meeting convened at the insistence of **developing countries** that sought to reduce their dependence on Northern industrial countries and strengthen their scientific and technological capacity. The conference yielded few tangible results. Taking place shortly after the adoption of the divisive and controversial **Declaration on the Establishment of a New International Economic Order**, the conference foundered over the polarizing demand of developing countries to regulate **transnational corporations** dominating international technology markets by means of binding **codes of conduct**. Likewise, developing countries' demands for additional financial resources for enlarged international activities in **science and technology** also went unheeded.

UNITED NATIONS CONFERENCE ON THE HUMAN ENVIRONMENT (STOCKHOLM, 1972). First major United Nations conference on the **environment**, which resulted in the adoption of a Declaration on the Human Environment, a set of aspirational policy principles designed to preserve and improve the environment. The linkage between environment and development was established later by the 1992 **United Nations Conference on Environment and Development (UNCED)**. The presence of many **nongovernmental organizations (NGOs)** marked the beginning of a new and more visible role for NGOs in intergovernmental forums. One of the tangible outcomes of the conference was the creation of the **United Nations Environment Programme (UNEP)**.

UNITED NATIONS CONFERENCE ON THE ILLICIT TRADE IN SMALL ARMS AND LIGHT WEAPONS (NEW YORK, 9–20 July 2001). Meeting intended to address the increasing threat to **human security** posed by the illicit trafficking in **small arms and light weapons**. After heated debates, the conference agreed on a program of action urging governments to require gun manufacturers to mark and trace their guns, to establish laws regulating arms brokers, to ensure export controls, to criminalize the illicit production and trade of small weapons, and to destroy surplus stocks. It also called for regulations to shield children from small arms and to end the recruitment of child soldiers. The document was watered down in the face of resistance by several countries on such issues as civilian ownership of weapons and the transfer of weapons to **nonstate actors**. *See also* CHILDREN IN ARMED CONFLICTS.

UNITED NATIONS CONFERENCE ON THE LAW OF THE SEA. *See* UNITED NATIONS CONVENTION ON THE LAW OF THE SEA (UNCLOS, 1982).

UNITED NATIONS CONFERENCE ON THE LEAST DEVEL-OPED COUNTRIES (PARIS, 1981). First in a series of several global conferences convened by the United Nations to draw attention to the special development issues facing the poorest and economically weakest countries among **developing countries**. The conference recommended the adoption of national and international measures aimed at improving their **food security** and production, **rural development**, human resources, and foreign trade. These calls as well as exhortations for substantially increased transfers of resources and preferential financial measures by developed countries have so far yielded mixed and limited results. *See also* LEAST DEVELOPED COUNTRIES (LDCs); TRADE AND DEVELOPMENT.

UNITED NATIONS CONFERENCE ON THE PEACEFUL USES OF NUCLEAR ENERGY (GENEVA, 23 March–10 April 1987). Major conference that brought together delegates from over 100 countries, representatives of numerous United Nations and other international organizations, and individual experts. This global forum generated a wealth of scientific as well as practical information and data on the subject. It also provided a useful setting for the consideration of concerns on the applications of nuclear techniques in such fields as **food** and **agriculture**, **health** and medicine, hydrology, **industry**, and scientific and technological research for development. The conference urged that international peaceful nuclear cooperation should be enhanced and broadened, but it failed to reach agreement on "principles universally acceptable for international cooperation in the peaceful uses of nuclear energy and appropriate ways and means for the promotion of such co-operation" in accordance with mutually acceptable considerations of nonproliferation." *See also* DISARMAMENT; NONPROLIFERATION OF NUCLEAR WEAPONS, TREATY ON THE (NPT, 1968); SCIENCE AND TECHNOLOGY FOR DEVELOPMENT.

UNITED NATIONS CONFERENCE ON STRADDLING FISH STOCKS AND HIGHLY MIGRATORY FISH STOCKS (1995). Increasingly loud complaints by coastal states that the industrial-scale fishing operations of "distant-water" states on the high seas were destroying fish stocks within their national territorial jurisdiction prompted the 1992 **United Nations Conference on Environ-**

ment and Development (UNCED) to recommend that governments negotiate an international agreement to resolve these issues. After two years of negotiations, a United Nations Conference on Straddling Fish Stocks and Highly Migratory Fish Stocks produced in 1995 a legally binding instrument supplementing the 1982 **United Nations Convention on the Law of the Sea (UNCLOS)**. The agreement defines ways and means to conserve fish stocks and prevent international conflicts over fishing on the high seas.

UNITED NATIONS CONFERENCE ON THE SUSTAINABLE DEVELOPMENT OF SMALL DEVELOPING STATES (BARBADOS, 1994). Called forth by the **Earth Summit**, this global conference drew attention to the common issues facing **small island developing states (SIDS)** and recommended national and international policies in support of their efforts in such areas as **climate change** and sea level rise, natural and environmental disasters, waste management, coastal and marine resources, fresh **water**, **energy**, and tourism. The **General Assembly** held a special session in 1999 to take stock of the implementation of this program of action. Another global conference was held in 2005 in Mauritius suggesting that the repeated calls of the SIDs for special assistance by the international community may still go unheeded. *See also* AGENDA 21; INTERNATIONAL MEETING TO REVIEW THE IMPLEMENTATION OF THE PROGRAMME OF ACTION FOR THE SUSTAINABLE DEVELOPMENT OF SMALL ISLAND DEVELOPING STATES (PORT-LOUIS, MAURITIUS, 10–14 January 2005).

UNITED NATIONS CONFERENCE ON TRADE AND DEVELOPMENT (UNCTAD). A subsidiary body of the **General Assembly** created in 1964 at the insistence of **developing countries** in the hope that this new institution would be more responsive to their economic and developmental needs than the **Bretton Woods institutions** and the **General Agreement on Tariffs and Trade (GATT)**, which formed the basis of the postwar **international trade** and financial order.

For over two decades, UNCTAD functioned as a forum for the negotiation of key aspects of the **Declaration on the Establishment of a "New International Economic Order"** and pressed for reforms in the rules of the international trading and financial system. The creation of the **General System of Preferences (GSP)** giving Southern countries' exports preferential treatment in the North and the establishment of borrowing facilities in the **International Monetary Fund (IMF)** to help finance the shortfall of export earnings of the South can be traced back to proposals and discussions originating from UNCTAD. Other divisive North-South issues inconclusively discussed within UNCTAD focused on rules for the control of restrictive business practices, international commodity agreements, the establishment of a Common Fund, and **debt** alleviation measures for low-income developing countries.

Faced with continuing mixed responses by Northern governments ranging from outright opposition to qualified acceptance of its work, UNCTAD underwent a major redefinition of its mandate in the early 1990s and now primarily deals with the developmental implications of private investment. *See also* CODES OF CONDUCT; INTEGRATED PROGRAMME FOR COMMODITIES (IPC); TRADE AND DEVELOPMENT; TRANSNATIONAL CORPORATIONS (TNCs).

UNITED NATIONS CONFIDENCE RESTORATION OPERATION (UNCRO, March 1995–January 1996). Established by the **Security Council** to replace the **United Nations Protection Force (UNPROFOR)** in Croatia and deployed in Serb-controlled Western Slavonia, the Krajina region, Eastern Slavonia, and the Prevlaka peninsula. Its purpose was to monitor and report on the crossing of military personnel and weapons between Croatia and Bosnia Herzegovina and Croatia and Serbia, to facilitate **humanitarian assistance** to Bosnia and Herzegovina through the territory of Croatia, and to monitor the demilitarization of the Prevlaka peninsula. *See also* UNITED NATIONS TRANSITIONAL ADMINISTRATION FOR EASTERN SLAVONIA, BARANJA, AND WESTERN SIRMIUM (UNTAES, 19 January 1996–15 January 1998).

UNITED NATIONS CONVENTION AGAINST CORRUPTION (2003). International legal instrument designed to complement the **United Nations Convention against Transnational Organized Crime**. Negotiated at the prodding and under the auspices of the **General Assembly**, this treaty will require countries to criminalize basic forms of corruption such as bribery and the embezzlement of public funds, trading in influence, and the concealment and "laundering" of the proceeds of corruption. It also binds its parties to render specific forms of mutual legal assistance in the prevention and investigation of corrupt practices; in the gathering and transfer of evidence for use in court; the extradition of offenders; and the tracing, freezing, seizure, and confiscation of the illicitly acquired assets. *See also* COMMISSION ON CRIME PREVENTION AND CRIMINAL JUSTICE (UNITED NATIONS); CRIME PREVENTION; WASHINGTON CONSENSUS.

UNITED NATIONS CONVENTION AGAINST ILLICIT TRAFFIC IN NARCOTIC DRUGS AND PSYCHOTROPIC SUBSTANCES (1988). International agreement designed to prevent the laundering of money obtained from illicit trafficking in narcotic drugs. This convention, which entered into force in 1990 provides additional mechanisms for enforcing two previously adopted treaties, the 1961 Single Convention on Narcotic Drugs and the 1971 Convention on Psychotropic Substances. *See also* COMMISSION ON NARCOTIC DRUGS (UNITED NATIONS); CRIME PREVENTION.

UNITED NATIONS CONVENTION AGAINST TRANSNATIONAL ORGANIZED CRIME (2003). Organized criminal groups have used advances in transportation and communication technologies to develop new opportunities for theft, diversion, smuggling, and other crimes such as the smuggling of migrants and trafficking in human beings, which yield enormous profits. This convention, adopted by the **General Assembly** in 2000 and in force since 2003, commits the states parties to adopting crime control measures including the criminalization of participation in an organized criminal group, money laundering, corruption, and obstruction of justice. The convention also enjoins its states parties to cooperate in matters of extradition, administrative and regulatory controls, and law enforcement measures.

The General Assembly has since adopted three protocols to the convention on the prevention and punishment of women and children trafficking, the smuggling of migrants, and the illicit manufacturing and trafficking in firearms. They are not yet in force. *See also* NON-STATE ACTORS; TRAFFICKING IN PERSONS; UNITED NATIONS CONVENTION AGAINST CORRUPTION (2003).

UNITED NATIONS CONVENTION ON THE LAW OF THE SEA (UNCLOS, 1982). Sovereignty disputes, spreading pollution, and conflicting claims about the resources of the seas were some of the key factors that prompted the convening of the Third United Nations Conference on the Law of the Sea in New York in 1973. The conference's work came to an end nine years later with the adoption in 1982 of a comprehensive treaty regulating all aspects of the resources of the sea and uses of the oceans. Outstanding concerns on the part of some industrial states over the mining of minerals lying on the deep ocean floor outside of nationally regulated ocean areas were resolved in July 1998, thus paving the way for all states to become parties to the Convention on the Law of the Sea. The convention makes provision for mechanisms for the settlement of disputes among the states parties. It also establishes that the resources of the seabed beyond the limits of national jurisdiction constitute the **common heritage of mankind** to be administered by an International Seabed Authority headquartered in Jamaica. *See also* AMERASINGHE, HAMILTON SHIRLEY (1913–1980); FISHING AND FISHERIES; INTERNATIONAL LAW; INTERNATIONAL TRIBUNAL FOR THE LAW OF THE SEA; SEABED AUTHORITY (INTERNATIONAL) (ISA); UNITED NATIONS CONFERENCE ON STRADDLING FISH STOCKS AND HIGHLY MIGRATORY FISH STOCKS (1995).

UNITED NATIONS CONVENTION TO COMBAT DESERTIFI-CATION (UNCCD, 1996). Preparations for the drafting of a convention on **desertification** and land degradation were initiated by the **General Assembly** in 1992 at the request of the **United Nations Conference on Environment and Development (UNCED)**. The UNCCD was adopted in 1994 and entered into force two years later. The convention recognizes the physical, biological, and socioeconomic aspects of desertification; the importance of redirecting technology transfer; and the involvement of local communities in combating desertification and land degradation. It also calls for intensified international cooperation in support of the collection and exchange of information, research, capacity building, and the promotion of an integrated approach in the development of national strategies to combat desertification.

The implementation of the convention is reviewed by annual "conferences of the parties," which have highlighted major unresolved challenges. At the national level, the convention raises politically sensitive problems related to the decentralization of authority, improvements in land tenure systems, and the empowerment of farmers and pastoralists. At the international level, it has elicited little political interest, and financial support by major donor countries and multilateral institutions remains insufficient. *See also* AGENDA 21.

UNITED NATIONS CRIME CONGRESSES. Efforts to create a common framework of guidelines for criminal justice can be traced back to the establishment in 1872 of an International Prison Commission, which later became the International Penal and Penitentiary Commission (IPPC). The IPPC became affiliated with the **League of Nations** and continued to hold conferences in European capitals.

Following the demise of the League, the **General Assembly** dissolved the IPPC in 1950 and transferred to the United Nations the task of holding regular international conferences on crime control matters. Every five years since 1955, the United Nations has organized crime congresses that have resulted in the development of international instruments that have been widely adopted and incorporated into national policies and professional practice. The United Nations Standard Minimum Rules for the Treatment of Prisoners and the Declaration on the Protection of All Persons from Being Subjected to Torture and Other Cruel, Inhuman, or Degrading Treatment or Punishment are instances of common guidelines of criminal justice that are still used today, have shaped national policies, inspired **human rights** organizations, and led to the elaboration of international human rights instruments by the **Commission for Human Rights**. *See also* CONVENTION AGAINST TORTURE AND OTHER CRUEL, INHUMAN, OR DEGRADING TREATMENT OR PUNISHMENT (UNITED NATIONS) (1984); CRIME PREVENTION; GLOBAL CONFERENCES (UNITED NATIONS); HUMAN RIGHTS; UNITED NATIONS CONVENTION AGAINST TRANSNATIONAL ORGANIZED CRIME (2003); UNITED NATIONS INTERREGIONAL CRIME AND JUSTICE RESEARCH INSTITUTE (UNICRI); UNITED NATIONS OFFICE ON DRUGS AND CRIME (UNODC).

UNITED NATIONS DECLARATION ON MINORITIES (1992). Formally known as the Declaration on the Rights of Persons belonging to National or Ethnic, Religious and Linguistic Minorities, this resolution of the **General Assembly** (47/135) sets forth rights making it possible for persons belonging to **minorities** to preserve and develop their group identity, language, religion, and culture. The declaration also confirms the rights of minorities to establish their own associations and to participate in public political life. Established in 1995, a subsidiary of the **United Nations Subcommission for the Promotion and Protection of Human Rights**, the Working Group on Minorities has been entrusted with the task of developing ways and means to implement the declaration. *See also* DECLARATIONS; SELF-DETERMINATION.

UNITED NATIONS DEVELOPMENT FUND FOR WOMEN (UNIFEM). Initially called the Voluntary Fund for the UN Decade for Women, this New York–based organization was created in 1976 at the beginning of the UN Decade for Women (1976–1985) and immediately after the first UN-sponsored conference on women in Mexico. The United Nations Development Fund became a separate entity within the **United Nations Development Programme (UNDP)** in 1985 with the broadened mandate to fund activities designed to encourage the participation of women in the planning and practice of mainstream **development** projects. *See also* GLOBAL CONFERENCES (UNITED NATIONS); WOMEN; WORLD CONFERENCE ON WOMEN (BEIJING, 4–15 September 1995).

UNITED NATIONS DEVELOPMENT PROGRAMME (UNDP). Established in 1965 by the General Assembly through the merger of two predecessor programs (the **Special United Nations Fund for Economic Development [SUNFED]** and the **Expanded Programme for Technical Assistance [EPTA]**), the United Nations Development Programme has evolved into a major multilateral organization for grant-based **technical assistance**.

UNDP supports projects strengthening developing countries' capacity for sustainable human **development** with a focus on **poverty** alleviation, the management of **natural resources**, the protection of the **environment**, and good governance. The bulk of UNDP resources is allocated to countries with a per capita income not exceeding $750. Since 1990, UNDP has published an annual **Human**

Development Report, which has stimulated and reshaped development policies and debates. *See also* SINGER, HANS (1910–2005); UNITED NATIONS CAPITAL DEVELOPMENT FUND (UNCDF); UNITED NATIONS DEVELOPMENT FUND FOR WOMEN (UNIFEM); UNITED NATIONS VOLUNTEERS (UNV).

UNITED NATIONS DISASTER RELIEF ORGANIZATION (UNDRO). Created in 1972, after a series of catastrophic disasters in the 1960s, to strengthen the United Nations collective response to **natural disasters**. The primary task of UNDRO was to coordinate the organization of disaster relief services, notably the distribution of food, clothing, and medical supplies. The office also sought to encourage disaster prevention through the use of improved forecasting and **early warning** systems as well as disaster preparedness through the development of emergency plans and the stockpiling of rescue and relief items. UNDRO was merged into the Department of Humanitarian Affairs, which was set up in 1992 and subsequently renamed the **Office for the Coordination of Humanitarian Affairs (OCHA)**. *See also* SMALL ISLAND DEVELOPING STATES (SIDS); WORLD CONFERENCE ON DISASTER REDUCTION (KOBE, HYOGO, JAPAN, 18–22 January 2005); WORLD CONFERENCE ON NATURAL DISASTER REDUCTION (YOKOHAMA, JAPAN, 1994).

UNITED NATIONS DISENGAGEMENT OBSERVER FORCE (UNDOF, 1974–). Operation set up by the **Security Council** in the aftermath of the 1973 Middle East war to monitor a US-brokered disengagement agreement between Israeli and Syrian forces in the Golan Heights. UNDOF maintains and patrols an area of separation between the two countries within which no military forces other than UNDOF are permitted. So far, UNDOF has successfully accomplished its objective. *See also* OBSERVATION MISSIONS (UNITED NATIONS).

UNITED NATIONS EDUCATIONAL, SCIENTIFIC, AND CULTURAL ORGANIZATION (UNESCO). One of the largest **specialized agencies** of the United Nations created in 1945 to contribute to peace and security "by promoting collaboration among nations through education, science and culture." Within the framework of this broad mandate, a major activity of UNESCO has been to provide technical assistance in **education** for the elimination of **illiteracy**; training in basic vocational skills; the promotion of the natural sciences, social sciences, humanities, and mass communication; and the development and preservation of national **cultural heritages**. UNESCO has also endeavored to encourage international cooperation in research relating to environmental sciences and **natural resources** and fostered interchange among scientists, scholars, and artists by means of subventions to national professional societies and scholarships and fellowships.

Several treaties have been concluded under the auspices of UNESCO, notably an international **Convention Concerning the Protection of the World Cultural and National Heritage** and a Convention against Discrimination in Education. A Convention for the Safeguarding of the Intangible Cultural Heritage is now in the process of being ratified.

The wide-ranging and diffuse mandate of UNESCO has been a major contributing factor in the expansion of the agency's activities. But in turn, the increasing number of activities undertaken by UNESCO has elicited criticism—mainly from the main donor countries and the United States in particular—about the runaway growth of its budget, lack of priorities and accountability, and limited practical impact. Dissatisfaction led to outright opposition as **Third World** countries, with the support of Soviet bloc nations, marshaled majorities voting in support of resolutions that called for the establishment of a **New World Information and Communication Order (NWICO)**, which some feared would legitimize governmental control over the world news media.

The charge of "politicization" and "anti-Western" policies stuck and, in 1983, the United States notified UNESCO that it would withdraw from the organization. Great Britain and Singapore also left in 1985. Faced with a loss of more than 25 percent of its budget, UNESCO has since then sought to streamline and consolidate its programs and much of the militancy of **developing countries** petered out after the end of the **Cold War**. Great Britain rejoined in 1997 and so did the United States in the wake of the September 2001 events. *See also* COPYRIGHT; CULTURAL HERITAGE; WATER.

UNITED NATIONS EMERGENCY FORCE (UNEF I, November 1956–June 1967). Created by the **General Assembly** under the **Uniting For Peace Resolution** to observe and supervise the withdrawal of the armed forces of France, Israel, and the United Kingdom following their attack on Egypt in the wake of the nationalization of the Suez Canal. UNEF also served as a buffer between Egypt and Israel until May 1967, when Egypt requested its withdrawal. Largely the brainchild of Canadian Foreign Minister **Lester Pearson** and **Secretary-General Dag Hammarskjöld**, UNEF I set a major precedent in defining the principles of future UN **peacekeeping** operations, notably the need to secure the consent or acquiescence of the parties concerned, the nonparticipation of the great powers in the force, and their political neutrality and nonfighting functions. *See also* ARAB-ISRAELI CONFLICT; SUEZ CANAL CRISIS (1956–1957); UNITED NATIONS EMERGENCY FORCE (UNEF II, October 1973–July 1979); URQUHART, SIR BRIAN.

UNITED NATIONS EMERGENCY FORCE (UNEF II, October 1973–July 1979). Authorized by the **Security Council** to supervise the cease-fire between Egyptian and Israeli forces and the redeployment of the two countries' armed forces and to control buffer zones between the combatants. The mission was terminated when Egypt and Israel signed a peace treaty in 1979. *See also* ARAB-ISRAELI CONFLICT; UNITED NATIONS EMERGENCY FORCE (UNEF I, November 1956–June 1967).

UNITED NATIONS ENVIRONMENT PROGRAMME (UNEP). An offshoot of the 1972 **United Nations Conference on the Human Environment** in Stockholm, UNEP is the main organizational arm of the UN acting as a catalyst, educator, advocate, and facilitator for the promotion of the use and sustainable **development** of the global **environment**. Headquartered in Nairobi, Kenya, UNEP has six regional offices monitoring environmental issues in Africa, Europe, North America, Asia and the Pacific, Latin America and the Caribbean, and West Asia. UNEP's work includes assessing global, regional, and national environmental conditions and trends; developing international and national environmental instruments; and facilitating the transfer of knowledge and technology for sustainable development.

UNEP supports a growing network of expert "centres of excellence" such as the World Conservation Monitoring Centre (WCMC), the Global Resource Information Database (GRID), the Collaborating Centre on Energy and Environment (UCCEE), the Collaborating Centre on Water and Environment (UCC), and the Water Global Reporting Initiative (GRI). UNEP also hosts several environmental convention secretariats including the Convention on International Trade in Endangered Species of Wild Fauna and Flora, the **Convention on Biological Diversity (CBD)**, the Convention on Migratory Species, and an expanding number of chemicals-related agreements, including the **Basel Convention on the Control of Transboundary Movements of Hazardous Wastes and Their Disposal** and the Stockholm Convention on Persistent Organic Pollutants (POPs).

The effectiveness of the organization has been hampered by turf wars within the UN, declining financial resources, and clashing demands from the North and the South about the priority accorded to the environment vs. development. *See also* ACID RAIN; DESERTIFICATION; EARLY WARNING; EARTHWATCH; ECONOMIC COMMISSION FOR EUROPE (ECE); ENERGY; ENVIRONMENTAL MODIFICATION CONVENTION (ENMOD, 1977); ENVIRONMENTAL SECURITY; FISHING AND FISHERIES; GLOBAL ENVIRONMENTAL MONITORING SYSTEM (GEMS); GLOBAL WARMING; UNITED NATIONS CONFERENCE ON ENVIRONMENT AND DEVELOPMENT (UNCED, RIO DE JANEIRO, 1992).

UNITED NATIONS FORUM ON FORESTS (UNFF). Intergovernmental subsidiary body of the **Economic and Social Council (ECOSOC)** established in 2000 as an arena for dialogue among governments and **nongovernmental organizations (NGOs)** to promote the management, conservation, and sustainable development of forests. The origins of the forum can be traced back to the 1992 **United Nations Conference on Environment and Development (UNCED)**, which, because of North-South conflicting views, could only agree on a nonlegally binding statement on the sustainable development of forests. Forest-related issues continued to be discussed in the **Commission on Sustainable Development (CSD)** until the forum was set up by ECOSOC. Major North-South differences persist, however, on such matters as the international trade in forest products, the environmental impact of deforestation, and financial and technical assistance to developing countries. *See also* FORESTRY.

UNITED NATIONS FRAMEWORK CONVENTION ON CLIMATE CHANGE (UNFCCC). Opened for signature at the 1992 **United Nations Conference on Environment and Development (UNCED)**, this convention came into force in 1994. Its objective is to stabilize greenhouse gas concentrations, and it requires its parties to develop national inventories of greenhouse gas emissions; to formulate national programs to mitigate **climate change**; and to promote technologies and practices that control, reduce, or prevent emissions. The convention's principal policy-making body is the Conference of the Parties, which meets every year. It is supported by the Climate Change Secretariat based in Bonn, Germany. *See also* ENVIRONMENT; INTERNATIONAL COUNCIL FOR SCIENCE (ICSU); KYOTO PROTOCOL; MONTREAL PROTOCOL ON SUBSTANCES THAT DEPLETE THE OZONE LAYER (1987); WORLD CLIMATE RESEARCH PROGRAM (WCRP).

UNITED NATIONS FUND FOR INTERNATIONAL PARTNERSHIPS (UNFIP). Body set up within the United Nations **Secretariat** to screen projects prepared by United Nations entities for funding by the **Turner Foundation**. UNFIP is governed by an advisory board chaired by the **deputy secretary-general**.

UNITED NATIONS GOOD OFFICES MISSION IN AFGHANISTAN AND PAKISTAN (UNGOMAP, October 1988–March 1990). Authorized by the **Security Council** to monitor the timetable and modalities of the withdrawal of Soviet forces from Afghanistan agreed to in the 1988 Geneva accords between Afghanistan, Pakistan, and the Soviet Union. *See also* GOOD OFFICES; PEACEFUL SETTLEMENT OF DISPUTES.

UNITED NATIONS GROUP OF EXPERTS ON GEOGRAPHICAL NAMES. Expert body of the **Economic and Social Council (ECOSOC)** set up to study and propose policies and methods for resolving problems in the standardization of geographical names at the national and international levels. *See also* FUNCTIONALISM.

UNITED NATIONS HIGH COMMISSIONER FOR HUMAN RIGHTS (UNHCHR). Principal United Nations official responsible for the promotion of international cooperation for civil, cultural, economic, political, and social **human rights** protection; the universal ratification and implementation of human rights instruments; and the development of new human rights norms. After years of debates stumbling over misgivings by **developing countries** that the post could be used to scrutinize their political and civil policies, the office was created in 1993 by the **General Assembly** pursuant to a recommendation originating from the Vienna **World Conference on Human Rights** held the same year.

The mandate of the office is broad and vague, and its resources are meager (some 3 percent of the United Nations regular budget). In effect, the commissioner has no other power than to act as a moral authority and voice for human rights victims, relying for that purpose on frequent public statements and appeals on human rights crises and extensive travels throughout the world. During his brief tenure, the first incumbent, **Jose Ayala-Lasso** of Ecuador showed a marked preference for **quiet diplomacy**. In contrast, his successor, the former president of Ireland **Mary Robinson**, was a forceful public advocate of human rights. The third commissioner, **Sergio Viera de Mello**, met with a tragic and untimely death in Iraq while on special humanitarian assignment for the **secretary-general**. The current incumbent is **Louise Arbour** of Canada.

The commissioner submits annual reports on international human rights to the **Commission for Human Rights**. A notable accomplishment of the office so far has been the establishment of human rights field missions inside a number of countries where they monitor human rights developments.

UNITED NATIONS HIGH COMMISSIONER FOR REFUGEES (UNHCR). Successor organization to the wartime **United Nations Relief and Rehabilitation Administration (UNRRA)** and the **International Refugee Organization (IRO)**, the UNHCR was created in 1950 by the **General Assembly**. The new agency started work in 1951, focusing its assistance on the well-being and resettlement of 1.2 million European refugees left homeless by World War II.

As was the case with the **United Nations Children's Fund (UNICEF)**, UNHCR was given the status of a temporary, time-bound agency. Its original mandate was limited to three years, but it was extended every five years as refugee crises kept multiplying around the globe. In December 2003, the General Assembly removed this time cap and decided to extend the UNHCR's mandate indefinitely until the refugee crisis was resolved. Thus, while initially concerned principally with European refugees uprooted by World War II, the UNHCR has progressively expanded the scope of its activities to a global scale. It now has a staff of over 6,000 personnel with offices in over 100 countries helping some 20 million refugees. The UNHCR has also been asked to help **internally displaced persons (IDPs)** who are not covered by international refugee conventions because they have not crossed internationally recognized frontiers. Their number has grown dramatically in the 1990s with the spread of internal conflicts and civil wars, and over the years the UNHCR has participated in more than 30 operations to help them, notably in **Timor-Leste** and **Kosovo**. The UNHCR currently provides assistance to some 4.4 million IDPs. Overall, in its first five decades of operation, the agency has helped an estimated 50 million people.

The basic administrative costs of the UNHCR are covered by the UN regular **budget**, but its programs are entirely financed by voluntary contributions from governments and, to a lesser extent, from intergovernmental organizations, corporations, and individuals. As the number of persons assisted by the UNHCR rose to a high of 27 million in 1994, its budget also expanded from $564 million in 1990 to more than $1 billion annually for most of the 1990s.

The main raison d'etre of the UNHCR is to provide refugees with "international legal protection," that is, to ensure respect for their most basic **human rights**, including their ability to seek **asylum** and to ensure that they are not returned involuntarily to a country where they have reason to fear persecution. In that context, the UNHCR promotes international refugee agreements, monitors government compliance with **international law**, and, in partnership with numerous **nongovernmental organizations (NGOs)**, provides material assistance to refugees. In addition, the UNHCR work has acquired a developmental component. The agency coordinates the provision and delivery of shelter, food, water, sanitation, and medical care and has developed specific projects designed to meet the basic needs of

women, **children**, and the elderly. Under its "quick impact" projects, the UNHCR implements small-scale programs to rebuild schools and clinics; repair roads, bridges, and wells with a view to bridging the gap between emergency assistance to refugees and people returning home; and longer-term **development** aid undertaken by other agencies.

The UNHCR currently carries out major assistance programs in the Balkans; North Caucasus; Palestine; Iraq; Afghanistan; Sri Lanka; the Horn of Africa; Central, West, and Southern Africa; Afghanistan; and Colombia. Every two years, UNHCR publishes *The State of the World's Refugees*. *See also* CONVENTION RELATING TO THE STATUS OF REFUGEES AND STATELESS PERSONS (1951); OGATA, SADAKO (1927–).

UNITED NATIONS INDIA-PAKISTAN OBSERVATION MISSION (UNIPOM). Deployed from September 1965 to March 1966 to observe a cease-fire and supervise the withdrawal of Indian and Pakistani armed personnel along the India-Pakistan border except in the areas where the **United Nations Military Observer Group in India and Pakistan (UNMOGIP)** operated.

UNITED NATIONS INDUSTRIAL DEVELOPMENT ORGANIZATION (UNIDO). Created as an "autonomous organization" by the **General Assembly** in 1966 at the insistence of the **developing countries** to support their drive for industrialization, UNIDO became a **specialized agency** in 1985. Hampered from the beginning by resistance from developed countries, which perceived UNIDO as yet another instrument of pressure on them to assist in the industrialization of developing countries (one of its goals was to support the Third World goal to account for 25 percent of the world industrial output by the year 2000), the agency considerably changed the modalities of its activities in the 1990s. UNIDO now seeks to promote industrial development through research, surveys, training programs, technical aid, and information exchange in cooperation with the public and private sectors and civil society organizations. Its regular budget resources are relatively modest ($130 million in 2001), but its technical cooperation is sizable; the largest portion is targeted at Sub-Saharan Africa and countries in transition.

UNITED NATIONS INFORMATION CENTERS (UNICs). Branch offices of the United Nations Department of Public Information, normally located in the capitals of United Nations member states, that disseminate information about the purposes and activities of the organization. There are currently approximately 60 UNICs throughout the world.

UNITED NATIONS INSTITUTE FOR DISARMAMENT RESEARCH (UNIDIR). Semiautonomous body within the United Nations **Secretariat** carrying out policy **research** on **disarmament** and security issues. An Advisory Board on Disarmament Matters created by the **General Assembly** in 1978 to advise the **secretary-general** on arms limitations also serves as UNIDIR's board of trustees. The secretary-general appoints the members of the board and reports annually on its activities to the General Assembly. The secretary-general also transmits each year a report of the Director of UNIDIR on the work of the institute. UNIDIR currently focuses its research on human security and disarmament in their global and regional contexts.

UNITED NATIONS INSTITUTE FOR TRAINING AND RESEARCH (UNITAR). Autonomous body established in 1965 for the purpose of enhancing the effectiveness of the organization through training and **research**. The institute's work became controversial in the 1970s, as it was seen by some of its main financial government backers as unduly supportive of the developing countries' political and economic demands. Threatened with financial insolvency, the institute was able to survive by drastically changing its original mandate. One of UNITAR's main functions is now to conduct training programs in multilateral diplomacy and international cooperation for diplomats accredited to the United Nations and national officials involved in United Nations affairs.

UNITED NATIONS INTERIM ADMINISTRATION MISSION IN KOSOVO (UNMIK, 10 June 1999–present). Interim civilian administration led by the United Nations created by the **Security Council** in 1999. UNMIK's tasks are to perform basic civilian administrative functions, promote a "substantial" autonomy and self-government in **Kosovo** pending determination of its future status, coordinate humanitarian and **disaster relief** of all international agencies, support the reconstruction of key infrastructure, maintain civil law and order, promote human rights, and assure the safe return of refugees and displaced persons. *See also* TRANSITIONAL ADMINISTRATION.

UNITED NATIONS INTERIM FORCE IN LEBANON (UNIFIL, 19 March 1978–present). Peacekeeping operation authorized by the **Security Council** in 1978 in the wake of Israel's invasion of Lebanon with the broad and difficult mandate of "confirming the withdrawal of Israeli forces, restoring international peace and security, and assisting the Government of Lebanon in ensuring the return of its effective authority in the area." Israel did withdraw from Southern Lebanon, but UNIFIL was unable to prevent infighting between Christian and Muslim groups, to deter Palestinian Liberation Organization (PLO) raids across the border, and to forestall the 1982 Israeli armed incursion into Lebanon. In the wake of the Summer 2006 Israeli intervention in southern Lebanon, the Security Council decided to strengthen UNIFIL and change its mandate. Now, in addition to monitoring the cessation of hostilities, UNIFIL provides support to the Lebanese armed forces as they deploy throughout the south of Lebanon and assists in ensuring humanitarian access to civilian populations and the voluntary and safe return of displaced people.

UNITED NATIONS INTERREGIONAL CRIME AND JUSTICE RESEARCH INSTITUTE (UNICRI). Policy oriented **research** entity conducting studies in support of the work of United Nations intergovernmental bodies dealing with the socioeconomic and legal aspects of **crime prevention**. *See also* COMMISSION ON CRIME PREVENTION AND CRIMINAL JUSTICE (UNITED NATIONS); COMMISSION ON NARCOTIC DRUGS (UNITED NATIONS); UNITED NATIONS OFFICE ON DRUGS AND CRIME (UNODC).

UNITED NATIONS IRAN-IRAQ MILITARY OBSERVER GROUP (UNIIMOG, August 1988–February 1991). Observation operation set up on 9 August 1988 at the end of the stalemated **Iran-Iraq War** to verify and supervise the cease-fire and withdrawal of the two countries' respective forces to their internationally recognized boundaries. It was terminated in 1991 following compliance by Iran and Iraq with the terms of their agreement.

UNITED NATIONS IRAQ-KUWAIT OBSERVATION MISSION (UNIKOM, April 1991–October 2003). Established on 3 April 1991 by the **Security Council** in the wake of the forced withdrawal of Iraqi forces from Kuwait at the end of the first **Persian Gulf War**, the United Nations Iraq-Kuwait Observation Mission was mandated to monitor a demilitarized zone along the boundary between Iraq and Kuwait to deter violations of the boundary. *See also* PERSIAN GULF WAR, SECOND (March–April 2003).

UNITED NATIONS KOREAN RECONSTRUCTION AGENCY (UNKRA). Authorized by the **General Assembly** in December 1950, the function of UNKRA was to help in the rehabilitation of the Korean economy and public services. UNKRA's operations, which entailed costs amounting to some $150 million, were phased out in 1958. *See also* KOREAN WAR (25 June 1950–27 July 1953).

UNITED NATIONS MILITARY OBSERVER GROUP IN INDIA AND PAKISTAN (UNMOGIP, 1949–present). The accession of the state of Jammu and **Kashmir** to India following the 1947 partition of the Indian continent has ever since been a matter of dispute between India and Pakistan. In order to investigate and mediate the dispute, the **Security Council** set up the **United Nations Commission for India and Pakistan (UNCIP)** in January 1948.

Fighting between the two countries came to an end in July 1949 with the signature of an agreement establishing a cease-fire line to be supervised by observers. Deployed in January 1949, UNMOGIP's functions are to continue to supervise the cease-fire in Kashmir following the termination of UNCIP, investigate complaints of cease-fire violations and submit its findings to each party and to the **secretary-general**. However, UNMOGIP proved helpless in preventing the outbreak of hostilities between India and Pakistan in 1965 and 1971 as well as repeated cease-fire violations.

UNITED NATIONS MISSION FOR THE REFERENDUM IN WESTERN SAHARA (MINURSO, 1991–present). Administered by Spain until 1976, Western Sahara was claimed by Algeria,

Mauritania, and Morocco. Their claims were opposed by the Frente Popular para la Liberación de Sagui el-Hamra y de Rio de Oro (Frente POLISARIO) representing the local inhabitants. Morocco decided to "reintegrate" the territory within its borders, Mauritania renounced all claims to Western Sahara in 1979, and fighting broke out between Morocco and the POLISARIO supported by Algeria.

Morocco claimed that it had ties of sovereignty over the territory because the people of Western Sahara historically owed religious allegiance to the Sultan of Morocco. In a 1975 **advisory opinion**, the **International Court of Justice** ruled that it had found no such legal ties as might affect "the principle of **self-determination** through the free and genuine expression of the will of the peoples of the Territory" contained in the 1960 **General Assembly Declaration on the Granting of Independence to Colonial Countries and Peoples**.

A UN-administered cease-fire between independence-oriented guerillas and Morocco has been in effect since 1991, and in accordance with a plan proposed by the **secretary-general**, the **Security Council** set up the United Nations Mission for the Referendum in Western Sahara to monitor a cease-fire and to assist the **special representative of the secretary-general** in the organization of a referendum enabling the people of Western Sahara to choose between independence and integration with Morocco. MINURSO has been able to monitor the cease-fire compliance, oversee the exchange of prisoners of war, and undertake the registering of voters. But diverging views between Morocco and the POLISARIO over the identification of potential voters and the repatriation of refugees have so far stymied efforts to hold the referendum.

UNITED NATIONS MISSION IN BOSNIA AND HERZEGOVINA (UNMIBH, 21 December 1995–21 December 2002). Fighting in Bosnia Herzegovina came to an end in October 1995. Three months later, **Bosnia** and Herzegovina, Croatia, and the Federal Republic of Yugoslavia entered into an agreement whereby they committed themselves to respect the "sovereign equality of one another," settle their disputes by peaceful means, and "refrain from any action against the territorial integrity or political independence of Bosnia and Herzegovina or any other State." The peace agreement provided for the deployment of a multinational force led by the **North Atlantic Treaty Organization (NATO)** to replace the **United Nations Protection Force (UNPROFOR)** in order to maintain public security and gave the mandate to the United Nations to monitor the reform and restructuring of law enforcement institutions.

In that context, the **Security Council** established the United Nations International Police Task Force and a United Nations civilian office in Bosnia Herzegovina, which came to be known as the United Nations Mission in Bosnia and Herzegovina. The tasks of UNMIBH were to assist in reforming and restructuring the local police, assessing the functioning of the existing judicial system, and monitoring the performance of the police

The international police force, which involved some 10,000 individual police officers from some 50 nations, was dissolved in 2002 and its mission handed to a **European Union (EU)** police force.

UNITED NATIONS MISSION IN COTE D'IVOIRE (MINUCI, May 2003–February 2004). Following the death of President Félix Houphouet-Boigny in 1993, Cote d'Ivoire has been beset by increasing political instability and a protracted political power struggle culminating in a military coup in 1999. The United Nations Mission in Cote d'Ivoire was set up by the **Security Council** to bolster national reconciliation efforts. Its functions were to advise the **special representative of the secretary-general** on military matters, to monitor the military situation, and to promote confidence-building measures among the Ivoirian parties involved. It includes a military component complementing the operations undertaken by French and **Economic Community of West African States (ECOWAS)** military forces. *See also* COTE D'IVOIRE (2002–); UNITED NATIONS OPERATION IN COTE D'IVOIRE (UNOCI, 27 February 2004–present).

UNITED NATIONS MISSION IN EAST TIMOR (UNAMET, June–October 1999). Mission authorized by the **Security Council** to oversee the organization of a referendum on the disposition of the territory of **Timor-Leste**. *See also* UNITED NATIONS MISSION OF SUPPORT IN EAST TIMOR (UNMISET, May 2002–May 2005); UNITED NATIONS TRANSITIONAL ADMINISTRATION IN EAST TIMOR (UNTAET, October 1999–May 2002).

UNITED NATIONS MISSION IN ETHIOPIA AND ERITREA (UNMEE, July 2002–present). In June 2000, Ethiopia and Eritrea, with the assistance of Algeria and the **Organization of African Unity (OAU)**, signed a cease-fire agreement that brought to an end two years of fighting over a border dispute. UNMEE's major role has been to monitor the cessation of hostilities, to assist in the observance of security measures agreed upon by the two countries, and to provide technical assistance for humanitarian demining activities. The two countries have yet to agree on the demarcation of their border. The mission's peace operations have been impeded by intermittent restrictions on freedom of movement. In October 2005, Eritrea demanded a reduction in UNMEE forces and, a month later, the Security Council threatened **sanctions** against both parties if the problem was not resolved.

UNITED NATIONS MISSION IN HAITI (UNMIH, September 1993–June 1996). Following the return to power of President Jean-Bertrand Aristide, the **Security Council** authorized the launching of the United Nations Mission in **Haiti** in September 1993 with the responsibility to stabilize the political environment, train a new national police force, and organize free and fair elections to succeed President Aristide. Elections were held in 1995 and UNMIH was replaced by the **United Nations Support Mission in Haiti (UNSMIH)**, whose mandate was primarily limited to the professionalization of the Haitian national police. UNMIH's strength reached 6,000 soldiers and police. *See also* INTERNATIONAL CIVILIAN MISSION IN HAITI (MICIVIH, 1993–1999); INTERNATIONAL CIVILIAN MISSION SUPPORT IN HAITI (MICAH, 1999–2001); UNITED NATIONS OBSERVER GROUP FOR THE VERIFICATION OF ELECTIONS IN HAITI (ONUVEH); UNITED NATIONS STABILIZATION MISSION IN HAITI (MINUSTAH, April 2004–present); UNITED NATIONS TRANSITION MISSION IN HAITI (UNTMIH, August–November 1997).

UNITED NATIONS MISSION IN LIBERIA (UNMIL, August 2003–present). Second **peacekeeping** operation dispatched by the **Security Council** in **Liberia** after the conclusion of a peace agreement among the warring parties in the civil war. By that agreement, the UN force assists an interim government in disarming and demobilizing all armed groups, providing security at vital locations and government buildings, facilitating the delivery of **humanitarian assistance**, protecting civilians facing violence in areas of its immediate deployment, and organizing national elections. *See also* UNITED NATIONS OBSERVER MISSION IN LIBERIA (UNOMIL, September 1993–September 1997).

UNITED NATIONS MISSION IN SIERRA LEONE (UNAMSIL, October 1999–present). Operation authorized by the **Security Council** essentially to strengthen the military component of its predecessor mission, the **United Nations Observer Mission in Sierra Leone (UNOMSIL).** Whereas UNOMSIL never had more than some 200 unarmed military observers, UNAMSIL included initially 6,000 military personnel and was subsequently enlarged to comprise over 15,000 troops in addition to 250 military observers. The role of UNAMSIL is to assist the government in the implementation of disarmament, demobilization, and reintegration measures; to monitor adherence to a cease-fire; to facilitate the delivery of **humanitarian assistance**; to support the work of United Nations civilian officials, **human rights** officers, and civil affairs officers; and to provide support for the preparations of elections. *See also* SANCTIONS; SIERRA LEONE CONFLICT (1991–2002); SPECIAL COURT FOR SIERRA LEONE.

UNITED NATIONS MISSION IN THE CENTRAL AFRICAN REPUBLIC (MINURCA, April 1998–February 2000). Political and civil turmoil within the Central African Republic led in 1997 to the deployment of a multinational force of African states supported by France to restore order and security. In March 1998, the **Security Council** approved the operation, and upon its termination decided to establish MINURCA to continue assisting in the maintenance of law and order, supervise disarmament measures, train a national police, and provide technical support for legislative and presidential elections. Following the withdrawal of the peacekeeping mission, the United Nations remains present in the country through a United Nations Peace-Building Office (BONUCA). Political instability fed by persisting economic and social tensions has not abated.

UNITED NATIONS MISSION IN THE SUDAN (UNMIS, 24 March 2005–present). Peacekeeping operation set up by the **Security Council** under Chapter VII of the charter to support the implementation of the peace accords reached by the Sudanese government and Southern insurgents. The 10,000 military personnel and over 1,000-strong international civilian staff are expected to monitor and verify the implementation of the cease-fire; assist in the disarmament, demobilization, and reintegration of combatants; help in the promotion of the rule of law and the protection of **human rights;** and facilitate the return and resettlement of **refugees.** *See also* SUDAN.

UNITED NATIONS MISSION OF OBSERVERS IN TAJIKISTAN (UNMOT, 1994–2000). In the wake of the breakup of the Soviet Union, Tajikistan became independent in 1991. Soon after, civil war erupted. Acting on recommendations of the **secretary-general**, the **Security Council** set up UNMOT to assist in the monitoring of a cease-fire agreement reached by the parties involved. The council subsequently expanded the mandate of UNMOT to help in the implementation of a peace agreement providing for parliamentary elections and the disarmament of insurgents The UN mission was conducted in cooperation with a peacekeeping force of the **Commonwealth of Independent States (CIS)** and the **Organization for Security and Cooperation in Europe (OSCE).**

UNITED NATIONS MISSION OF SUPPORT IN EAST TIMOR (UNMISET, May 2002–May 2005). In May 2002, East Timor became independent, changing its name to **Timor-Leste** and becoming on 27 September, the 191st UN member state. This mission was established by the **Security Council** as a successor mission to the **United Nations Mission in East Timor (UNAMET)** and the **United Nations Transitional Administration in East Timor (UNTAET)** to ensure peace and stability in independent East Timor. Its mandate was to provide assistance in the development of the country's core administrative and law enforcement structures and contribute to the maintenance of the external and internal security. UNMISET was brought to an end by the council on 20 May 2005 to be followed up by a small political mission, the United Nations Office in Timor-Leste

(UNOTIL), established by the council to consolidate the gains achieved under UNMISET.

UNITED NATIONS MONITORING, VERIFICATION, AND IN-SPECTION COMMISSION (UNMOVIC). Set up by the **Security Council** in 1999 to replace the former **United Nations Special Commission (UNSCOM).** UNMOVIC took over the mandate of UNSCOM to verify **Iraq**'s compliance with its obligation to destroy its weapons of mass destruction. UNMOVIC inspectors were withdrawn from Iraq in the wake of the outbreak of the 2003 **Persian Gulf War**. In accordance with its mandate, UNMOVIC still reports regularly to the Security Council, but sharp disagreements within the council have prevented it from redefining the functions of UNMOVIC and determining its future. *See also* AGGRESSION; BLIX, HANS (1928–); COLLECTIVE SECURITY; OIL FOR FOOD PROGRAM (OFFP, 1997–2003); PERSIAN GULF WAR, FIRST (January–February 1991); SANCTIONS.

UNITED NATIONS NEW AGENDA FOR THE DEVELOPMENT OF AFRICA (UN-NADAF). A compact of mutual commitments by African countries and the international community adopted by the **General Assembly** in 1991 to foster growth and development in Africa in the 1990s. An independent panel of experts commissioned by the United Nations Secretariat concluded in 2002 that the initiative had by and large failed. *See also* AFRICAN ECONOMIC CONDITIONS; LAGOS PLAN OF ACTION; NEW PARTNERSHIP FOR AFRICA'S DEVELOPMENT (NEPAD); UNITED NATIONS PROGRAMME OF ACTION FOR AFRICAN ECONOMIC RECOVERY AND DEVELOPMENT (UN-PAARD, 1986–1990).

UNITED NATIONS OBSERVATION GROUP IN LEBANON (UNOGIL, June–December 1958). Observation force established to monitor the **Lebanese** border with Syria and report to the **Security Council** any infiltration of personnel or supply of armaments across the border from Syria. The group only had a six-month-long existence.

UNITED NATIONS OBSERVER GROUP FOR THE VERIFICATION OF ELECTIONS IN HAITI (ONUVEH). Created by the **General Assembly** at the request of the government of **Haiti** to observe the December 1990–January 1991 elections for the Haitian presidency and constituted by the **secretary general**, ONUVEH certified that the election had taken place in democratic and free conditions. The newly elected president, Jean-Bertrand Aristide, was overthrown by a military coup in September 1991, thus triggering a long series of subsequent UN interventions. *See also* INTERNATIONAL CIVILIAN MISSION IN HAITI (MICIVIH, 1993–1999); INTERNATIONAL CIVILIAN MISSION SUPPORT IN HAITI (MICAH, 1999–2001); UNITED NATIONS CIVILIAN POLICE MISSION IN HAITI (MIPONUH, December 1997–March 2000); UNITED NATIONS MISSION IN HAITI (UNMIH, September 1993–June 1996); UNITED NATIONS STABILIZATION MISSION IN HAITI (MINUSTAH, April 2004–present); UNITED NATIONS SUPPORT MISSION IN HAITI (UNSMIH, 1996–1997); UNITED NATIONS TRANSITION MISSION IN HAITI (UNTMIH, August–November 1997).

UNITED NATIONS OBSERVER GROUP IN CENTRAL AMERICA (ONUCA, 7 November 1989–16 January 1992). First large-scale peacekeeping operation of the United Nations in the Americas, the United Nations Observer Group in Central America was established by the **Security Council** to conduct on-site verification of the compliance by the governments of Costa Rica, El Salvador, Guatemala, Honduras, and Nicaragua with their 1989 security agreement to cease assistance to irregular forces and insurrectionist movements in the region. The tasks entrusted to ONUCA evolved over time and expanded to include a role in the demobilization of Nicaraguan armed groups.

ONUCA successfully supported the peace process in Central America and on recommendation of the secretary-general, the Security Council terminated its mission in 1992. The military observers serving with ONUCA were subsequently transferred to the **United Nations Observer Mission in El Salvador** (ONUSAL). *See also* ARIAS, OSCAR (1941–); CENTRAL AMERICA CONFLICTS; NICARAGUA QUESTION.

UNITED NATIONS OBSERVER MISSION FOR VERIFICATION OF THE ELECTIONS IN NICARAGUA (ONUVEN, 1988). A 15-year-long civil war pitting the left-wing government of

Nicaragua against resistance movements supported by the United States came to an end in 1988. The settlement called for the voluntary demobilization and repatriation of the insurgents and the organization of national elections. At the request of Nicaragua, ONUVEN monitored the electoral process and its preparations. Specifically, its mandate was to receive and report on complaints and any irregularities or interference in the electoral process. The elections were held in February 1990 and were confirmed as free and fair. *See also* CENTRAL AMERICA CONFLICTS; NICARAGUA QUESTION; UNITED NATIONS OBSERVER GROUP IN CENTRAL AMERICA (ONUCA, 7 November 1989–16 January 1992).

UNITED NATIONS OBSERVER MISSION IN ANGOLA (MONUA, June 1997–February 1999). Successor mission to the **United Nations Verification Mission in Angola (UNAVEM III)**, MONUA's mandate was to assist in the consolidation of peace and national reconciliation in **Angola** and help create conditions for the long-term stability, democratic development, and rehabilitation of the country. Its tasks included the monitoring and verification of the integration of National Union for the Total Independence of Angola (UNITA) elements into the state structures, the police, and the armed forces; helping develop the capacity of national institutions in the field of human rights and investigating allegations of **human rights** abuses; and supporting the demobilization and reintegration of UNITA former combatants.

UNITED NATIONS OBSERVER MISSION IN BOUGAINVILLE (UNOMB, 1 January 2004–30 June 2005). Little noticed but brutal war between pro-independence groups and the government of Papua New Guinea that started over the use and control of natural resources. (Bougainville is rich in copper and possibly gold.) The war dragged on throughout the 1980s and 1990s with considerable loss of life (20,000 are believed to have been killed). The secessionist revolt ended in 1997, and a 2001 peace agreement provided for the presence of a United Nations political office in Bougainville to assist in its implementation. UNOMB took over at the beginning of 2004 to help with the peace process in the disarmament of combatants and the organization of elections for an autonomous government in Bougainville. The elections were duly conducted in June 2005, thus bringing to an end the mission of UNOMB.

UNITED NATIONS OBSERVER MISSION IN EL SALVADOR (ONUSAL, July 1991–April 1995).

Established by the **Security Council** to verify the implementation of the December 1992 agreements that put an end to the 10-year civil war between the central government and the Frente Farabundo Marti para la Liberacion Nacional. The agreements involved cease-fire measures, a reform and reduction of the armed forces, the creation of a new police force, reform of the judicial and electoral systems, measures to promote human rights, land tenure, and other economic and social issues.

ONUSAL monitored elections, which were successfully carried out in 1994. Upon completion of its mandate in April 1995, a small group of United Nations civilian personnel stayed behind to verify the implementation of outstanding points of the agreements and to provide **good offices** to the parties. *See also* ARIAS, OSCAR (1941–); NICARAGUA QUESTION; UNITED NATIONS OBSERVER GROUP IN CENTRAL AMERICA (ONUCA, 7 November 1989–16 January 1992).

UNITED NATIONS OBSERVER MISSION IN GEORGIA (UNOMIG, August 1993–present).

Originally established by the **Security Council** in August 1993 to verify compliance with a cease-fire agreement between the government of **Georgia** and the breakaway region of Abkhazia. Resumed fighting led to a change and broadening of the mandate of the mission in 1994 to include observing the operation of a peacekeeping force of the **Commonwealth of Independent States (CIS)** within the framework of a new cease-fire agreement reached by the parties. In spite of the efforts of the **special representative of the secretary-general** and repeated calls of the Security Council to achieve a comprehensive political settlement, little progress has been made in the determination of the political status of Abkhazia within the state of Georgia and the voluntary return of **refugees** and **internally displaced persons**.

UNITED NATIONS OBSERVER MISSION IN LIBERIA (UNOMIL, September 1993–September 1997).

Mission undertaken by the United Nations in support of the efforts of the **Economic Community of West African States (ECOWAS)** to bring an end to a civil war that started in late 1989. Its purpose was to investigate violations of the cease-fire agreement, to monitor compliance with the arms embargo imposed on **Liberia** earlier by the **Security Council**, and to observe the conduct of legislative and presidential elections. UNOMIL was dissolved following the election of a new government, which announced a policy of reconciliation and national unity. UNOMIL's success was short lived, as Liberia plunged again into civil war thwarting United Nations subsequent peace-building efforts. *See also* UNITED NATIONS MISSION IN LIBERIA (UNMIL, August 2003–present).

UNITED NATIONS OBSERVER MISSION IN SIERRA LEONE (UNOMSIL, June 1998–October 1999). When civil war broke out in Sierra Leone in 1991, a special envoy of the **secretary general** sought to mediate a peaceful resolution of the conflict. Parliamentary and presidential elections were held in 1996, but the insurgents did not accept their outcome. A military coup supported by the insurgents overthrew the elected government leading the **Security Council** to impose **sanctions** and an oil embargo and authorizing the **Economic Community of West African States (ECOWAS)** to secure their implementation. Military intervention by ECOWAS in early 1998 resulted in the return to power of the elected government and the lifting of sanctions. UNOMSIL was set by the Security Council to monitor the military and security situation as well as the disarmament and demobilization of combatants and to oversee respect for **humanitarian law**. Fighting nevertheless continued, marred by large-scale atrocities, **human rights** abuses against civilians, and the displacement of some 450,000 people. UNOMSIL was dissolved in 1999 and replaced by a new and significantly larger **peacekeeping** operation—the **United Nations Mission in Sierra Leone (UNAMSIL)**.

UNITED NATIONS OBSERVER MISSION IN UGANDA-RWANDA (UNOMUR, June 1993–September 1994). Mission authorized by the **Security Council** to verify that no military shipments crossed the Uganda-Rwanda border in support of the Tutsi insurgency in **Rwanda**. Meant to be a confidence-building measure and to assist the initial efforts of the **United Nations Assistance Mission in Rwanda (UNAMIR)** to defuse tensions between Hutus and Tutsis in Rwanda, the functions of UNOMUR were overtaken by events and the outbreak of the **genocide** of Tutsis in April 1994.

UNITED NATIONS OFFICE ON DRUGS AND CRIME (UNODC). Located in Vienna, this unit of the secretariat comprises the United Nations Drug Control Program and the Centre for International Crime Prevention. It also includes a Terrorism Prevention Branch and a Global Program against money laundering, corruption, organized crime, and trafficking in human beings. The activities of UNODC include research and studies on new and emerging forms of crime and the compilation of current statistics on illicit drug consumption worldwide as well as the provision of expert training for law enforcement and judicial professionals. The office also assists countries in the elaboration, ratification, and implementation of international criminal law conventions such as the **United Nations Convention against Transnational Organized Crime**, the **United Nations Convention against Corruption**, and the **United Nations Convention against the Illicit Traffic in Narcotic Drugs and Psychotropic Substances**. It also services UN-sponsored quinquennial congresses that have resulted in the adoption of criminal justice standards and norms for incorporation in national legislation and policies in such areas as the independence of the judiciary, the protection of victims, alternatives to imprisonment, and the treatment of prisoners. *See also* COMMISSION ON CRIME PREVENTION AND CRIMINAL JUSTICE (UNITED NATIONS); COMMISSION ON NARCOTIC DRUGS (UNITED NATIONS); NARCOTIC DRUGS; UNITED NATIONS CRIME CONGRESSES; UNITED NATIONS INTERREGIONAL CRIME AND JUSTICE RESEARCH INSTITUTE (UNICRI).

UNITED NATIONS OPERATION IN BURUNDI (ONUB, 21 May 2004–present). Acting under Chapter VII of the United Nations **Charter**, the **Security Council** determined in May 2004 that the situation in **Burundi** constituted a threat to international peace and security and established ONUB to support international and national efforts to restore a lasting peace and national reconciliation in the country. The main functions of the force are to ensure the respect of cease-fire agreements; carry out the disarmament, demobilization, and reintegration of combatants; monitor illegal flows of arms across borders in cooperation with the **United Nations Organization Mission in the Democratic Republic of the Congo (MONUC)**; and facilitate the return of refugees and internally displaced persons.

UNITED NATIONS OPERATION IN COTE D'IVOIRE (UNOCI, 27 February 2004–present). Continuing political and military tensions in late 2003 to early 2004 in **Cote d'Ivoire** prompted the **secretary-general** to recommend a strengthening of the United Nations presence in the country. In response to the secretary-general's proposals, the **Security Council** established the United Nations Operation in Cote d'Ivoire. The mandate of the **United Nations Mission in Cote d'Ivoire (MINUCI)** thus came to an end and its responsibilities were transferred to UNOCI.

The mission has been set within the framework of Chapter VII of the UN Charter and may "use all necessary means to carry out its mandate." Its functions are to maintain law and order and monitor the cessation of hostilities and movements of armed groups; to disarm, demobilize, reintegrate, repatriate, and resettle all combatants; to protect United Nations personnel, institutions, and civilians, especially in regard to the distribution of **humanitarian assistance** and the protection and promotion of **human rights**; and to support the organization of open, free, fair, and transparent elections.

UNITED NATIONS OPERATION IN MOZAMBIQUE (UNOMOZ, December 1992–December 1994). After gaining independence from Portugal in 1975, civil war erupted in **Mozambique** between the government and the Mozambican National Resistance (RENAMO) supported by South Africa. The two parties eventually reached a settlement in 1992 that included the establishment by the **Security Council** of the United Nations Operation in Mozambique to monitor and support the cease-fire, oversee demobilization and reintegration of forces, and organize national elections. The 6,500-troop operation succeeded in these tasks as multiparty elections were held in October 1994. In addition, UNOMOZ helped in the resettlement of 3.7 million people displaced by the war. *See also* PORTUGUESE COLONIES.

UNITED NATIONS OPERATION IN SOMALIA (UNOSOM I, April 1992–March 1993 and UNOSOM II, March 1993–March 1995). Following the disintegration of the central government and against a background of intensifying civil war that threatened more than 4 million people with starvation and disease, the United Nations Operation in **Somalia** was established by the **Security Council** in April 1992 to monitor a cease-fire in Mogadishu and escort the delivery of humanitarian supplies to some 1.5 million people at risk. The mission's mandate and strength were subsequently enlarged to protect humanitarian convoys and distribution centers throughout the country.

Persisting disagreements among Somali factions led the Security Council to welcome the offer of the United States to help secure a safe environment for the delivery of **humanitarian assistance** and authorize, under Chapter VII of the charter, the use of "all necessary means" to do so. Operation Restore Hope, involving the deployment of 37,000 troops from over 20 countries and undertaken under unified United States command, took control of some 40 percent of the country's territory, but incidents of violence continued and the central government remained ineffective.

UNOSOM II was established in March 1993 to take appropriate action, including enforcement measures, to complete, through disarmament and reconciliation, the task begun by the Unified Task Force (UNITAF) in the framework of Operation Restore Hope. Violent incidents against UNOSOM II peacekeepers and the botched United States military attempt to capture the leader of one of the major Somali factions paved the way to President William J. Clinton's decision to withdraw American forces by March 1994. Other participating countries followed suit and UNOSOM II was dissolved in early March 1995.

The major political achievement of the United Nations intervention in Somalia was to help bring about a cease-fire (UNOSOM II strength reached 28,000 military and police personnel and 2,800 civilian staff). The UN presence was also instrumental in improving the humanitarian situation. Yet, continuing conflict among Somali factions has stymied its ambitious plans for rebuilding Somalia's central government structures, and prospects for national reconciliation remain dim. UNOSOM thus remains controversial. The undertaking tarnished the image of the United Nations as an impartial and neutral peacekeeper. U.S. determination to keep the operation short and to withdraw from it also precipitated a durable retreat from earlier widespread enthusiasm for such operations.

UNITED NATIONS OPERATION IN THE CONGO (ONUC, July 1960–June 1964). Rioting, tribal disorders, mutiny by the Congolese army and the secession of Katanga, one of the country's mineral rich provinces, quickly followed the independence of the Congo from Belgium on 30 June in 1960. Belgium intervened militarily to protect its nationals thus prompting the Congolese government to request the assistance of the United Nations. Two weeks later, the **Security Council** set up the United Nations Operation in the Congo (ONUC, by its French acronym) with the initial mandate to ensure the withdrawal of Belgian forces, to assist in the maintenance of law and order, and to provide **technical assistance**.

The function of ONUC was subsequently modified by the **General Assembly** acting under the **Uniting for Peace Resolution** to include maintaining the territorial integrity of the Congo, preventing the occurrence of civil war, and securing the removal of all foreign mercenaries. At peak strength, ONUC reached 20,000 troops and succeeded in securing the withdrawal of Belgian troops. Foreign mercenaries also left. The secession of Katanga was forestalled.

The political costs of the operation were, however, enormous. Early decisions by ONUC in support of the central government made the balance tilt against leftist factions seeking control of the government thereby incurring the wrath of the Soviet Union, and the U.S.-Soviet consensus in the Security Council, which had made the operation possible in the first place, evaporated. The Soviet Union and other countries objected to the involvement of the General Assembly and refused being assessed for the costs of the operation ($400 million in its four-year existence). One of the unexpected outcomes of the crisis was a major constitutional and political crisis from which the UN never fully recovered, compounded by the tragic demise of **Secretary-General Dag Hammarskjöld** in a plane crash in the war zone. *See also* URQUHART, SIR BRIAN (1919–).

UNITED NATIONS ORGANIZATION MISSION IN THE DEMOCRATIC REPUBLIC OF THE CONGO (MONUC, February 2000–present). **Peacekeeping** operation established in 2000 by the **Security Council** in implementation of a 1999 accord between the **Democratic Republic of the Congo (DRC)**, **Angola**, Namibia, **Rwanda**, Uganda, Zimbabwe, and insurgent groups within the DRC.

The original mandate of MONUC was primarily to monitor the implementation of the agreement, to supervise and verify the disengagement and redeployment of the parties' forces, and to facilitate **humanitarian assistance** and **human rights** monitoring. In subsequent years, the Security Council has augmented the military strength of the mission to over 17,000 uniformed personnel and, in 2004, enlarged its objectives to ensure the protection of civilians and humanitarian workers and to use force to deter threats to the internal peace process and to the civilian work of the United Nations, particularly in the northeastern part of the DRC. *See also* UNITED NATIONS OPERATION IN BURUNDI (ONUB).

UNITED NATIONS PEACEKEEPING FORCE IN CYPRUS (UNFICYP, 1964–). Established in 1964 by the **Security Council** to prevent the reoccurrence of fighting between the Greek and Turkish communities and to contribute to the restoration of law and a "return to normal conditions." The functions of UNFICYP were broadened after the 1974 Turkish military intervention to include the supervision of a de facto cease-fire between Turkish and Cypriot communities and to maintain surveillance of a buffer zone established between the areas controlled by their respective forces. Repeated efforts at **mediation** by the UN secretaries-general have so far been inconclusive, and in the absence of a comprehensive political settlement, UNFICYP has been extended by the Security Council for six-month periods.

UNITED NATIONS PERMANENT FORUM FOR INDIGENOUS PEOPLES (UNPFIP). One of the subsidiary expert bodies of the **Economic and Social Council (ECOSOC)**, the forum was established in 2000 with a mandate to advise ECOSOC on issues relating to the economic and social development of **indigenous people** and to promote the integration and coordination of the United Nations system activities on indigenous questions. See also CULTURAL HERITAGE; CULTURE AND DEVELOPMENT.

UNITED NATIONS POPULATION DIVISION. Unit of the **Department of Economic and Social Affairs (DESA)** in the United Nations **Secretariat** producing analytical studies and analyses in support of the work of the United Nations **Commission on Population and Development** and the implementation of the programs of action adopted by the **International Conference on Population and Development (ICPD)** sponsored by the United Nations. Its estimates and projections for all countries are an authoritative source of information about a wide range of demographic subjects and their determinants. The division has recently focused its work on such critical and politically controversial issues as the demographic impact of **HIV/AIDS** and international **migration**. *See also* POPULATION; POPULATION PROGRAMS OF THE UNITED NATIONS; UNITED NATIONS POPULATION FUND (UNFPA).

UNITED NATIONS POPULATION FUND (UNFPA). The world's largest international source of funding for **population** and reproductive health programs, the fund has provided nearly $6 billion in assistance to developing countries since it began operations in 1969 under the name of the United Nations Fund for Population Activities. Its programs support voluntary family planning, the prevention of sexually transmitted diseases including **HIV/AIDS** and the promotion of **women**'s equality. *See also* COMMISSION ON POPULATION AND DEVELOPMENT (UNITED NATIONS); INTERNATIONAL CONFERENCE ON POPULATION AND DEVELOPMENT (ICPD, CAIRO, 1994); POPULATION PROGRAMS OF THE UNITED NATIONS; UNITED NATIONS POPULATION DIVISION.

UNITED NATIONS PREVENTIVE DEPLOYMENT FORCE (UNPREDEP, 1995–1999). Originally part of the **United Nations Protection Force (UNPROFOR)**, in March 1995 the **Security Council** restructured UNPROFOR and established the United Nations Preventive Deployment Force to forestall the possibility that fighting in the Serbian province of **Kosovo** could spill over into Macedonia. The mission of UNPREDEP was to patrol Macedonia's borders and report on developments that might undermine the country's stability. A rare instance of the deployment of a UN peacekeeping mission designed to forestall the outbreak of a conflict, UNPREDEP was terminated on 28 February 1999 when China vetoed a further extension of its mandate. *See also* PREVENTIVE DEPLOYMENT; PREVENTIVE DIPLOMACY.

UNITED NATIONS PROGRAMME OF ACTION FOR AFRICAN ECONOMIC RECOVERY AND DEVELOPMENT (UN-PAARD, 1986–1990). Blueprint of policies recommended by the **General Assembly** at its 1986 13th special session in the wake of the drought that led to famine in large parts of the African continent in 1983–1984. The document highlighted the need for additional international financial assistance to help Africa recover from the catastrophic impact of the famine and to meet given sectoral economic growth targets. By and large, these objectives were not met, prompting the assembly in 1991 to recommend another array of national and international measures. *See also* AFRICAN ECONOMIC CONDITIONS; LAGOS PLAN OF ACTION; UNITED NATIONS NEW AGENDA FOR THE DEVELOPMENT OF AFRICA (UN-NADAF); NEW PARTNERSHIP FOR AFRICA'S DEVELOPMENT (NEPAD).

UNITED NATIONS PROTECTION FORCE (UNPROFOR, 1992–1995). In 1991, Slovenia and Croatia seceded from the Federal Republic of **Yugoslavia**. Croatian Serbs, with the support of the national army, opposed the move and war broke out between Croatia and Yugoslavia. The United Nations Protection Force was initially deployed in Croatia to help create the conditions of a peace settlement. As war spread to **Bosnia** following Bosnia Herzegovina's declaration of independence and the subsequent intervention of Serb and Croatian armies, the **Security Council** imposed economic **sanctions** on Yugoslavia and broadened the mandate of UNPROFOR to ensure the security of Sarajevo and other Bosnian towns declared "safe areas" and the delivery of **humanitarian assistance**. The 1995 Dayton Peace Accord brought to an end the 42-month-long war and the Security Council authorized the deployment of an Implementation Force led by the **North Atlantic Treaty Organization (NATO)** to ensure compliance with the agreement.

One of the most complex, costly, and controversial **peacekeeping** operations undertaken by the United Nations, UNPROFOR was unable to forestall widespread occurrences of "ethnic cleansing" and the outbreak of a major refugee crisis. The failure of the Security Council to address effectively the political and military aspects of the breakup of the Yugoslav Federation tarnished the public image of the United

Nations and led to a critical reassessment of the organization's peace-keeping operations. *See also* BRAHIMI REPORT; UNITED NATIONS CONFIDENCE RESTORATION OPERATION (UNCRO, March 1995–January 1996); UNITED NATIONS MISSION IN BOSNIA AND HERZEGOVINA (UNMIBH, 21 December 1995–21 December 2002); UNITED NATIONS PREVENTIVE DEPLOYMENT FORCE (UNPREDEP, 1995–1999).

UNITED NATIONS RELIEF AND REHABILITATION ADMINISTRATION (UNRRA). Forerunner of the United Nations emergency relief programs, this agency operated from 1943 to 1947 and spent nearly $4 billion in food, clothing, and medicine assistance to European and Asian countries. Its functions were subsequently assumed by the **United Nations Children's Fund (UNICEF)**, the **United Nations High Commissioner for Refugees (UNHCR)**, and the **World Health Organization (WHO)**. *See also* REFUGEES.

UNITED NATIONS RELIEF AND WORKS AGENCY (UNRWA). Established in 1948 following the first **Arab-Israeli conflict** to carry out direct relief and work programs for Palestinian **refugees**. In the absence of a solution to the Palestine refugee problem, the agency has turned into the main provider of basic services in **education**, **health**, relief, and social services to close to 4 million registered Palestinian refugees in the Middle East.

UNITED NATIONS RESEARCH INSTITUTE FOR SOCIAL DEVELOPMENT (UNRISD). In operation since 1963 in Geneva as an autonomous **research** group within the United Nations, UNRISD conducts research on social development issues and policies. It has in recent years placed particular emphasis on work related to the 1995 **World Summit for Social Development** and its follow-up.

UNITED NATIONS SPECIAL COMMISSION (UNSCOM). Among the terms and conditions imposed on **Iraq** by the **Security Council** in 1991 in the wake of the first **Persian Gulf War** was the creation of a system of UN-directed supervision of Iraq's **weapons of mass destruction** and ballistic missiles and production facilities. The mandate of UNSCOM was to carry out on-site inspections of Iraq's biological, chemical, and missile capabilities and to supervise the destruction of such weapons. The commission also assisted the **International Atomic Energy Agency (IAEA)** in similar tasks assigned to it by the Security Council for nuclear weapons. The commission was replaced by the **United Nations Monitoring, Verification, and Inspection Commission (UNMOVIC)** in 1999. *See also* SANCTIONS.

UNITED NATIONS STABILIZATION MISSION IN HAITI (MINUSTAH, April 2004–present). Latest UN mission mounted for **Haiti** since 1993, established in the wake of civil unrest that gripped the country and led to the ouster of President Jean-Baptiste Aristide. In cooperation with the **Organization of American States (OAS)** and the Caribbean Community (CARICOM), MINUSTAH's tasks are to maintain peace and security; foster democratic governance and institutional development; assist Haiti's transitional government in organizing free and fair municipal, parliamentary, and presidential elections as soon as possible; strengthen the rule of law; and support the country's **human rights** institutions and groups. Its work has been hampered by continuing civil violence and widespread insecurity. *See also* INTERNATIONAL CIVILIAN MISSION IN HAITI (MICIVIH, 1993–1999); INTERNATIONAL CIVILIAN MISSION SUPPORT IN HAITI (MICAH, 1999–2001); REGIONAL ARRANGEMENTS; UNITED NATIONS CIVILIAN POLICE MISSION IN HAITI (MIPONUH, December 1997–March 2000); UNITED NATIONS MISSION IN HAITI (UNMIH, September 1993–June 1996); UNITED NATIONS OBSERVER GROUP FOR THE VERIFICATION OF ELECTIONS IN HAITI (ONUVEH); UNITED NATIONS SUPPORT MISSION IN HAITI (UNSMIH, 1996–1997); UNITED NATIONS TRANSITION MISSION IN HAITI (UNTMIH, August–November 1997).

UNITED NATIONS SUBCOMMISSION FOR THE PROMOTION AND PROTECTION OF HUMAN RIGHTS. Main subsidiary body of the **Commission for Human Rights** established in 1947 under the authority of the **Economic and Social Council (ECOSOC)**. This panel of 26 experts undertakes studies, mainly in the light of the **Universal Declaration of Human Rights (UDHR)**, and makes recommendations to the commission on ways to prevent discrimination of any kind relating to **human rights** and fundamental freedoms and the protection of racial, national, religious, and linguistic **minorities**.

UNITED NATIONS SUPPORT MISSION IN HAITI (UNSMIH, 1996–1997). Operation designed to assist the government of **Haiti** to train a more effective national police force. Created by the **Security Council** on 28 June 1996, its mandate expired in July 1997 and was taken over by the **United Nations Transition Mission in Haiti (UNTMIH)**. *See also* INTERNATIONAL CIVILIAN MISSION IN HAITI (MICIVIH, 1993–1999); INTERNATIONAL CIVILIAN MISSION SUPPORT IN HAITI (MICAH, 1999–2001); UNITED NATIONS CIVILIAN POLICE MISSION IN HAITI (MIPONUH, December 1997–March 2000); UNITED NATIONS MISSION IN HAITI (UNMIH, September 1993–June 1996); UNITED NATIONS OBSERVER GROUP FOR THE VERIFICATION OF ELECTIONS IN HAITI (ONUVEH); UNITED NATIONS STABILIZATION MISSION IN HAITI (MINUSTAH, April 2004–present).

UNITED NATIONS SYSTEM STAFF COLLEGE. Created by the **General Assembly** in 2002 to provide knowledge management, learning, and training to the staff of the entire United Nations system. Located on the campus of the International Training Center of the **International Labour Organization (ILO)** in Turin, the college carries out activities designed to enhance the coherence and management competence of the **international civil service** and to strengthen the capacity of UN organizations to carry out their developmental mandates more effectively. *See also* PERSONNEL QUESTIONS.

UNITED NATIONS TEMPORARY EXECUTIVE AUTHORITY (UNTEA). *See* WEST NEW GUINEA (WEST IRAN) QUESTION.

UNITED NATIONS TRANSITION ASSISTANCE GROUP (UNTAG, February 1989–April 1999). A proposal for the independence of **Southwest Africa** under South African control was endorsed by the **Security Council** as early as 1978, and plans were then made by the **secretariat** for a **peacekeeping** force to supervise elections and oversee the transition to independence. South Africa's objections and **Cold War** politics stymied these plans until 1988.

UNTAG was established by the Security Council in February 1989 to ensure the early independence of the territory under the name of Namibia through free and fair elections under the supervision and control of the United Nations. UNTAG was essentially a political operation. Its tasks, in addition to the planning and preparations for elections, involved the dismantling of the South African military structure; the confinement to bases in **Angola** of the forces of the Southwest Africa People's Organization, which had fought for independence since 1966; the repeal of discriminatory legislation; the return of refugees; and the release of political prisoners. Namibia became independent in April 1990 following adoption of a constitution for the country by the newly elected Constituent Assembly. *See also* APARTHEID; DECOLONIZATION; TRANSITIONAL ADMINISTRATION.

UNITED NATIONS TRANSITION MISSION IN HAITI (UNTMIH, August–November 1997). Third in the series of United Nations **peacekeeping** operations in **Haiti** established at the suggestion of the **secretary-general** by the **Security Council** for a single period of four months, ending in November 1997, to assist the Haitian government in the professionalization of the national police. The mission included 250 civilian police and 50 military personnel and took over the functions of its predecessor **United Nations Support Mission in Haiti (UNSMIH)**. *See also* INTERNATIONAL CIVILIAN MISSION IN HAITI (MICIVIH, 1993–1999); INTERNATIONAL CIVILIAN MISSION SUPPORT IN HAITI (MICAH, 1999–2001); UNITED NATIONS CIVILIAN POLICE MISSION IN HAITI (MIPONUH, December 1997–March 2000); UNITED NATIONS MISSION IN HAITI (UNMIH, September 1993–June 1996); UNITED NATIONS OBSERVER GROUP FOR THE VERIFICATION OF ELECTIONS IN HAITI (ONUVEH); UNITED NATIONS STABILIZATION MISSION IN HAITI (MINUSTAH, April 2004–present).

UNITED NATIONS TRANSITIONAL ADMINISTRATION FOR EASTERN SLAVONIA, BARANJA, AND WESTERN SIRMIUM (UNTAES, 19 January 1996–15 January 1998). Serbo-Croat region of the former **Yugoslavia** that was the scene of bitter fighting between Croatian and Serbian forces between 1991 and 1995.

In 1991, rebel Serbs took control of Eastern Slavonia, after which they expelled some 80,000 non-Serbs living in the region. In 1995, Croatian forces recaptured Krajina and Western Slavonia thus provoking another exodus of some 60,000 Serbs into Eastern Slavonia.

In November 1995, the Croatian government and Croatian Serb leaders signed an agreement that sanctioned Croatia's territorial gains and provided for the peaceful reintegration of Eastern Slavonia into Croatia under United Nations supervision. UNTAES was subsequently set up by the **Security Council** to oversee the reintegration of Eastern Slavonia into Croatia. It was also mandated to function as an interim political authority to allow refugees to return safely to their homes, to demilitarize local Serbian forces, to train a police force, to organize free and fair elections, and to promote redevelopment and reconstruction of the region. The UNTAES mandate was only for two years and expired in January 1998. *See also* TRANSITIONAL ADMINISTRATION.

UNITED NATIONS TRANSITIONAL ADMINISTRATION IN EAST TIMOR (UNTAET, October 1999–May 2002). Established in October 1999 by the **Security Council** as an integrated multidimensional operation responsible for the administration of East Timor during its transition to independence as **Timor-Leste**. Its mandate was to provide security and maintain law and order, establish an effective administration, assist in the development of civil and social services, and ensure the delivery of **humanitarian assistance**. It handed over its powers to a newly elected national government in 2002. *See also* TRANSITIONAL ADMINISTRATION; UNITED NATIONS MISSION IN EAST TIMOR (UNAMET, June–October 1999); UNITED NATIONS MISSION OF SUPPORT IN EAST TIMOR (UNMISET, May 2002–May 2005).

UNITED NATIONS TRANSITIONAL AUTHORITY IN CAMBODIA (UNTAC, 1991–1993). The 1991 Paris Peace Agreements on **Cambodia** brokered by the permanent members of the **Security Council**, the members of the Association of South-East Asian Nations, and other interested countries brought to an (inconclusive) end the Cambodian civil war. As called for in the agreement, the United Nations mounted the United Nations Transitional Authority in Cambodia, the largest operation undertaken by the organization since the **United Nations Operation in the Congo (ONUC)**, with 22,000 troops, 3,600 police monitors, and 2,400 civilian administrators and a final cost of $1.6 billion.

UNTAC was given "all powers necessary" to help in the implementation of these agreements. Its mandate was to supervise the cease-fire, regroup, and disarm all armed forces of the Cambodian parties, repatriate and resettle Cambodian **refugees**, and provide transitional governance of the country until the organization of free and fair general elections. Operational as of March 1992, UNTAC faced considerable resistance and was dissolved on schedule on September 1993, leaving behind a mixed record of limited humanitarian and political accomplishments. *See also* TRANSITIONAL ADMINISTRATION.

UNITED NATIONS TRUCE SUPERVISION ORGANIZATION (UNTSO, 1948–present). Established in 1948, originally to supervise the observance of a truce between Israel and its Arab neighbors. UNTSO has since performed various tasks including the observation of the cease-fire in the Suez Canal area in 1956 and the Golan Heights following the 1967 Arab-Israeli war. Lack of a comprehensive peace agreement explains its continuing existence. *See also* ARAB-ISRAELI CONFLICT.

UNITED NATIONS UNIVERSITY (UNU). The largest among the constellation of autonomous United Nations **research** entities, UNU is a network of institutes and programs acting as a think tank for the United Nations system and a builder of capacities, particularly in **developing countries**. Its headquarters is in Tokyo.

UNITED NATIONS VERIFICATION MISSION IN GUATEMALA (MINUGUA, 1997–2005). Created by the **Security Council** on 20 January 1997 to oversee compliance with the peace agreement reached in 1996 in the **Guatemala** civil war. The functions of the observer group entailed primarily the monitoring, separation, **disarmament**, and demobilization of combatants. The mission was designed to complement the policing of **human rights** violations and institution-building activities of a Human Rights Verification Mission in

Guatemala set up in 1994 by the **General Assembly**. *See also* CENTRAL AMERICA CONFLICTS.

UNITED NATIONS VOLUNTEERS (UNV). Patterned along the model of the United States Peace Corps, the United Nations Volunteers was created in 1970 by the UN **General Assembly**. Located in Bonn, Germany, and largely funded by the **United Nations Development Programme (UNDP)**, the program mobilizes young mid-career professionals to work on a wide range of **technical assistance** projects, humanitarian aid programs, community-based participatory development projects among low income groups, and **United Nations peacekeeping** and **postconflict peace-building** activities. Over 5,000 volunteers worked for UNV in 2006.

UNITED NATIONS WORLD TOURISM ORGANIZATION (UNWTO). Originally an umbrella organization for national tourist offices, the World Tourism Organization became an intergovernmental body in 1967. In 2003, it entered into an agreement with the **Economic and Social Council (ECOSOC)**, making it one of the **specialized agencies** of the United Nations. Its main function is to promote the transfer of tourism know-how to **developing countries**.

UNITED NATIONS YEMEN OBSERVATION MISSION (UNYOM, 1963–1964). Established in July 1963 to observe and certify the implementation of a disengagement agreement between Saudi Arabia and Egypt, which had supported opposite sides in Yemen's civil war. Repeated violations of the agreement led to its withdrawal in September 1964.

UNITING FOR PEACE RESOLUTION (1950). Resolution of the **General Assembly** proposed by the United States and six other states in the midst of the **Korean War** authorizing the convening of emergency sessions of the assembly within 24 hours whenever the **Security Council** is deadlocked by a **veto** and "fails to exercise its primary responsibility for the maintenance of international peace and security in any case where there appears to be a threat to the peace, breach of the peace, or act of aggression." Any nine members of the

Security Council or a majority of United Nations members can call for a special emergency session. The resolution was designed to circumvent the veto of the permanent members of the Security Council and was adopted over the objections of the Soviet Union, which argued that it represented an illegal intrusion of the General Assembly into the **charter**-mandated work of the Security Council in the maintenance of peace and security. Its subsequent utilization has been clouded by similar claims of illegality (notably France and the United Kingdom in the 1956 **Suez Canal Crisis**) and policy reversals (the Soviet Union requested a special emergency of the assembly to deal with the Middle East in 1967, and the United States has considerably cooled its earlier enthusiasm).

UNIVERSAL DECLARATION OF HUMAN RIGHTS (UDHR, 1948). First international document addressing the issues of **human rights**, which hitherto had been considered the exclusive responsibility of governments. The 30 articles of the declaration enumerate the civil and political rights of individuals as well as their economic, social, and cultural rights. It was adopted by the **General Assembly** by a vote of 48 to 0 with 8 abstentions (6 Eastern European nations, Saudi Arabia, and South Africa) after a grueling debate that reflected the ideological split between Western countries, which insisted on individual freedoms, and Soviet bloc countries, which insisted on economic and social rights.

As a resolution of the General Assembly, the declaration is not binding and represents only a "common standard of achievement for all peoples and all nations." Nevertheless, it has served as the basis for the drafting of two treaties that are binding on their states parties, the **International Covenant on Civil and Political Rights (ICCPR)** and the **International Covenant on Economic, Social, and Cultural Rights (ICESCR)**. It has also provided the groundwork for many regional human rights documents. In addition, the declaration may serve as a basis for identifying consistent patterns of gross violations that in turn trigger the confidential complaint and investigation procedures provided for in the mandate of the **United Nations Commission for Human Rights**. *See also* TREATY BODIES.

UNIVERSAL POSTAL UNION (UPU). Second oldest international organization after the **International Telecommunications Union (ITU)** headquartered in Bern, Switzerland. The Universal Postal Union is the primary forum for cooperation between national postal services. It sets rules for international mail exchange and provides advisory, mediating, and technical assistance services to its members. *See also* FUNCTIONALISM.

UNIVERSITY FOR PEACE (UP). Established in Costa Rica as a treaty organization with its own charter in an international agreement endorsed by the **General Assembly** in 1980, the University for Peace carries out a program of **education**, training, and **research** for peace focused on **conflict prevention**, **human security**, **human rights**, **environmental security**, and postconflict rehabilitation.

URBANIZATION. One of the most significant postwar demographic developments has been the explosive growth of cities in the developing countries. United Nations estimates suggest that this process, fed by continuing migratory rural-urban flows and the **globalization** of the world economy, will continue unabated and that the size of the urban population in the South, as a percentage of its total population, will increase from 40 to 56 percent between 2000 and 2030.

The emergence of enormous "megacities" has strained the delivery of local social services beyond capacity. It has been accompanied by the growth of slum settlements and shantytowns without clean **water**, sewerage systems, or electricity and higher levels of **poverty** and unemployment. These issues were addressed in the 1977 and 1996 United Nations Conference on Human Settlements and the 1996 **United Nations Conferences on Human Settlements (Habitat I and II)**. *See also* EMPLOYMENT; UNITED NATIONS CENTRE ON HUMAN SETTLEMENTS (UNCHS or HABITAT).

URQUHART, SIR BRIAN (1919–). British national who had a long and distinguished career at the United Nations that spanned over four decades beginning under the tenure of **Trygve Lie** and ending with his retirement from UN service in 1986. He served in various capacities under **Ralph Bunche** and was closely involved in the **peace-**

keeping operations conducted by the United Nations in the Congo and Cyprus. He subsequently rose to the rank of undersecretary-general for special political affairs, working on Middle East issues and Namibia. A prolific writer, Sir Brian has published biographies of **Dag Hammarskjöld** and Ralph Bunche as well several influential studies on UN **reform**. *See also* UNITED NATIONS EMERGENCY FORCE (UNEF I, November 1956–June 1967); UNITED NATIONS OPERATION IN THE CONGO (ONUC, July 1960–June 1964); UNITED NATIONS PEACEKEEPING FORCE IN CYPRUS (UNFICYP, 1964–).

URQUIDI, VICTOR (1919–2004). Mexican economist. As a member of the Mexican delegation at the **Bretton Woods Conference**, he played an influential role in the drafting of the statutes of the **World Bank** and the **International Monetary Fund (IMF)**, helping bring about a greater emphasis on their **development** functions. With other economists in the **Economic Commission for Latin America and the Caribbean (ECLAC)**, where he worked from 1951 to 1960, Urquidi shaped the course of development thinking in the early 1950s focusing on the structural problems facing **developing countries** at the international level and advocating a strong role for the state in the development and implementation of development policies. He also was one of the leading figures contributing to the establishment of regional economic integration institutions in Central America.

USE OF FORCE. The use of force is governed by three major (though elusive) principles contained in the United Nations **Charter**. Members of the organization must refrain from the threat or use of force in their international relations (Article 2.4). They may have recourse to individual or collective **self-defense** in cases of armed attacks until the **Security Council** has taken measures necessary to the maintenance of international peace and security. Only the Security Council may decide on measures involving the use of force (Articles 41 and 42).

Since the charter defines neither war nor **aggression**, these provisions have spawned an unending political debate about the boundaries of the norm prohibiting the use of force. In 1970, the **General Assembly** sought to define force in a Declaration on Principles of

380 • VETO

International Law concerning Friendly Relations and Cooperation among States in Accordance with the Charter of the United Nations. In 1987, the assembly made a further attempt in another lengthy Declaration on the Enhancement of the Effectiveness of the Principle of Refraining from the Threat or Use of Force in International Relations.

In any event, state practice in regard to Article 51 has been inconsistent. In the 1962 **Cuban Missile Crisis**, the Security Council had no control over the U.S. decision to impose a quarantine over Cuba. In 1986, the **International Court of Justice (ICJ)** rejected the U.S. argument that the principle of collective self-defense justified the mining of Nicaraguan harbors and the training of counterinsurgents. Collective self-defense, however, was the legal basis for the UN-authorized **Persian Gulf War** against Iraq after its 1990 invasion of Kuwait. Likewise, in the wake of the 11 September 2001 terrorist attack on the United States, the Security Council passed a resolution expressing "its readiness to take all necessary steps to respond to the terrorist attack . . . , and to combat all forms of terrorism, in accordance with its responsibilities under the Charter of the United Nations." The debate has been rekindled by the application of the doctrine of "**preemption**" in the 2003 second Persian Gulf War, which many see as a thinly veiled form of unilateralism and a rejection of the basic principles of the charter. *See also* HIGH-LEVEL PANEL ON THREATS, CHALLENGES, AND CHANGE (HLP); HUMANITARIAN INTERVENTION; HUMAN RIGHTS; NONUSE OF FORCE.

– V –

VETO. A word not to be found in the United Nations **Charter**, as Article 27.3 simply states that "decisions of the **Security Council** shall be made by an affirmative vote of nine members including the concurring votes of the permanent members." The charter thus stipulates that a decision cannot be taken by the council if a permanent member votes against it (abstentions do not count as opposition).

The veto has been invoked over 250 times to date—5 times by China, 18 times by France, 32 times by the United Kingdom, 120 times by the Soviet Union and its successor state the Russian Federation, and 76 times by the United States. Most of the vetoes have been cast during the **Cold War**, and they have been invoked more rarely since 1990.

Widely decried in the early years of the United Nations and now the focus of considerable attention in all discussions about "United Nations **reform**," the use of the veto has not necessarily paralyzed the United Nations, as many of them were repetitive, overridden, or circumvented by such measures as the **Uniting for Peace Resolution**. It is, however, a pragmatic acknowledgement of the realities of power in international politics and a reminder that it would be impolitic to mobilize the organization on a question that elicits the active opposition of its most powerful members.

VIENNA CONVENTION ON DIPLOMATIC RELATIONS (1961). Comprehensive law-making treaty of universal application adopted by a 1961 United Nations Conference on Diplomatic Privileges and Immunities held in Vienna. Its text was prepared by the **International Law Commission** and codifies customary rules of diplomatic relations between states. A separate 1963 convention defines the legal regime of interstate consular relations. *See also* CONVENTION ON THE PRIVILEGES AND IMMUNITIES OF THE UNITED NATIONS (1946).

VIENNA CONVENTION ON THE LAW OF TREATIES (1969). International agreement prepared under the aegis of the **International Law Commission** essentially codifying preexisting state practice on treaties. The convention entered into force in 1980.

VOTING. Equality of voting rights is a long-standing common rule governing formal decision making in international organizations since they are based on the principle of the sovereign equality of states that comprise them. This system prevailed until the end of World War II, notably in the **League of Nations**, where decisions required the agreement of all members (matters of procedures were decided by simple majority votes).

New voting arrangements were made with the establishment of the United Nations. Article 18 of the **charter** provides that, regardless of size and resources, each member of the **General Assembly** has one vote. Decisions on "important questions" require a two-thirds majority. Decisions on other questions require a simple majority.

These rules have provided the model for most other organs and conferences of the United Nations. There are, however, important notable exceptions to this pattern. Decisions by the **Security Council** require the affirmative vote of at least 9 of its 15 members, including those of the permanent members. The **Economic and Social Council (ECOSOC)** and the **Trusteeship Council** follow the one-member-one-vote rule, but all decisions, substantive or procedural, are taken by a simple majority. In the **Bretton Woods institutions**, voting power is weighted according to capital contributions. Decisions require special majorities and, in some cases, unanimity. A number of **specialized agencies** recognize differences in interest and power among states. Ten of the 28 seats of the governing body of the **International Labour Organization (ILO)** are reserved to states of "chief industrial importance." Eligibility for selection to the council of the **International Maritime Organization (IMO)** is based on a state's share of world shipping and maritime trade.

While the rule of unanimity as a mode of decision making has virtually disappeared in the United Nations system, the principle of equality of voting rights—especially in the General Assembly—has prompted criticisms that numerical majorities of small and poor countries can impose decisions on a minority of states that they alone have the resources and capacity to implement. Various alternatives to majority votes, including schemes of **weighted voting**, have been suggested, but none has proved acceptable to a majority. In practice, most of the decisions of the **General Assembly** are adopted by **consensus** without a formal vote. *See also* BUDGET (UNITED NATIONS); GROUPS AND GROUPINGS; SOVEREIGNTY; VETO.

– W –

WALDHEIM, KURT (1918–). Austrian diplomat who replaced **U Thant** as the fourth **secretary-general** of the United Nations in 1972. He won a second five-year term in 1976 but failed in an unprecedented third-term bid in 1981, as China vetoed his candidacy. Waldheim's tenure was overshadowed by the growing ascendancy of Third World countries in the United Nations, many of them believing that he was more sensitive to Western powers' preferences and that he had sought to sidetrack their drive toward the adoption of a **Declaration on the Establishment of a New International Economic Order**.

Through extensive traveling and attempts at mediating conflicts, Waldheim sought to play a leadership role in international affairs. His efforts came to naught, by and large, as a result of the intransigence of the parties involved, as was the case in the 1971 India-Pakistan dispute, the Middle East war of 1973, the Vietnam invasion of **Cambodia**, South Africa's occupation of **Southwest Africa**, the Vietnam war, the decade-long **Iran-Iraq War**, and the **Cyprus question**. His 1980 **good offices** efforts, at the request of the **Security Council**, failed to resolve the **Iran hostage crisis**.

Kurt Waldheim was elected president of Austria in 1986 despite charges that he had concealed his wartime service in Yugoslavia with the German Army during World War II. The question of his possible involvement in war crimes was not conclusively settled.

WAR CRIMES TRIBUNALS. War crime law has been an evolutionary and tortuous process reflecting an imperfect and still unfolding quest for justice and accountability. Some of the law applicable to war crimes predates World War I, as is the case for the basic rules for land warfare, the treatment of prisoners, and the protection of civilians. The 1919 Versailles Treaty, which ended World War I, called for the prosecution of the German monarch for having started the war, but the Kaiser fled to the Netherlands. At the allies' insistence, Germany put its own war criminals on trial, but many legal experts consider the proceedings and their outcome a sham. Similarly, the atrocities committed by the Turks against the Armenian minority went unpunished.

In August 1945, the Allies agreed to try Axis war criminals and established the **International Military Tribunal for the Prosecution and Punishment of the Major War Criminals** in Nuremberg to try military and civilian Axis leaders accused of plotting aggressive warfare, the extermination of civilian populations, the use of slave labor, the looting of occupied countries, and the maltreatment and murder of prisoner of wars. Of the 22 men tried by the tribunal based in Nuremberg, 19 were convicted. The Allies set up a similar 11-nation **International Military Tribunal for the Far East** in Tokyo to conduct war crimes trials involving 28 Japanese defendants. They faced the same charges and 7 received death sentences.

Critics have questioned the legal and political basis of these trials, pointing to violations of the **sovereignty** principle and the reliance of the prosecution on ex-post facto charges. The fact that the Nuremberg tribunal could be viewed by some as a form of "victor's vengeance" prompted the United Nations **General Assembly** to adopt a resolution in 1947 affirming "the principles of international law recognized by the Charter of the Nuremberg tribunal and the judgement of the Tribunal." In so doing, the assembly brought support to the proposition that proscription of the Nuremberg crimes had been recognized broadly as international customary law. The Nuremberg Principles also endorsed the controversial propositions that individuals as well as states have obligations under **international law** and that the proscriptions of international law prevail over national law.

Subsequently, numerous **human rights** instruments have been adopted under the aegis of the United Nations underscoring the growing concern about war crimes and seeking to respond to the charges directed at the Nuremberg and Tokyo tribunals. They include notably the 1948 **Universal Declaration of Human Rights (UDHR)**, the 1948 **Convention on the Prevention and Punishment of the Crime of Genocide**, the four 1949 conventions strengthening the rights of civilians and prisoners of war during wartime, and the 1984 **Convention against Torture and Other Cruel, Inhuman, or Degrading Treatment or Punishment**.

International outrage over atrocities committed in **Bosnia** and **Rwanda** led the United Nations **Security Council** to set up war crimes tribunals: the **International Criminal Tribunal for the Former Yugoslavia (ICTY)**, in operation since May 1993, and the **International Criminal Tribunal for Rwanda (ICTR)**, created in November 1994. The ICTY officially established rape as a war crime.

The tribunals have been supported by most national governments and human rights organizations. Some of them believe that they can serve as a useful deterrent to atrocities. Others, however, criticize them for a variety of reasons, ranging from bias (as in the case in the ICTY where more Serbs than Croats and Muslims have been prosecuted) to violations of national sovereignty. Unquestionably, international war crimes tribunals have inherent weaknesses: they have no enforcement power and must rely on national governments to seize and transport suspects. Trials have been slow to start and their operation has been plagued by low morale, administrative incompetence, and mishandling of funds. Despite increasing international recognition of the need to prosecute war crimes, the more recent experiences of the **Special Court for Sierra Leone** and **Cambodia** suggest that such offenses still often remain unpunished. In Indonesia, national courts have tried a number of Indonesian officials for war crimes in **Timor-Leste** during 1999, but the proceedings have mostly ended in whitewash acquittals.

In 1998, the UN General Assembly voted in favor of a treaty authorizing a permanent international court for war crimes. The United States, China, and 5 other nations opposed the treaty, and 21 nations abstained, but the treaty formally came into effect in July 2002 after having received the minimum required number of ratifications. In accordance with its statute, the **International Criminal Court (ICC)** may prosecute war crimes, genocide, crimes of **aggression** (when an agreement is reached on its definition), and crimes against humanity committed after its creation. The United States opposes implementation of the treaty out of fear that American officials or military personnel might be arrested abroad on baseless charges.

WASHINGTON CONSENSUS. Short-hand term, often used as synonymous with "**globalization**" reflecting the development policy views and advice prevailing in the **Bretton Woods institutions**, that is, the World Bank and the **International Monetary Fund**. Fiscal discipline, tax reform, interest rate liberalization, trade liberalization, liberalization of inflows of **foreign direct investment**, privatization, and deregulation are the main components of the set of policy reforms that officials of the bank and the IMF believe would promote growth and development in **developing countries**.

These policy prescriptions gained increasing credence and influence in the 1990s and have evolved since into an "Augmented" Washington Consensus focused on good corporate governance, anticorruption measures, flexible labor markets, financial codes and standards, the creation of social safety nets, and targeted poverty reduction. Whether in its earlier or latest meaning, the concept has always been a rallying slogan for antiglobalization protesters, developing-country politicians and officials, and trade negotiators, among others. *See also* LIBERAL INTERNATIONALISM; TRADE AND DEVELOPMENT; UNITED NATIONS CONVENTION AGAINST CORRUPTION (2003).

WATER. Water development underpins **food security**, industrial growth, and the sustainability of the **environment**. Water is also essential for drinking and household uses. Access to safe drinking water and sanitation is critical to maintain **health**, particularly for children. But more than 1 billion people lack enough safe water to meet minimum levels of health and income. Some 20 percent of the world's population is believed to face water shortages, a figure that could rise to 30 percent by 2025 affecting 50 countries.

Water is a scarce resource facing heavy and unsustainable levels of demand. From 1950 to 1995, withdrawals for domestic and industrial uses quadrupled. At this rate, and factoring in **population** growth, and increasing demand for agricultural and industrial purposes, total water withdrawals would increase by 50 percent in 2025 over the 1995 level.

The United Nations concern with problems arising from possible water shortages can be traced back to the 1977 United Nations Water Conference and thereafter to the 1981–1990 International Drinking Water Supply and Sanitation Decade and the 1992 **United Nations Conference on Environment and Development (UNCED)**. The work of the organization is focused primarily on the sustainable development and management of freshwater resources. The **Department of Economic and Social Affairs (DESA)**, the **Food and Agricultural Organization (FAO)**, the **United Nations Development Programme (UNDP)**, the **United Nations Children's Fund (UNICEF)**, the **United Nations Educational, Scientific, and Cultural Organization (UNESCO)**, and the **World Bank** are the main entities active in this field. At the intergovernmental level, water-related issues are dealt with by the **Commission on Sustainable Development (CSD)**. *See also* HIGH-LEVEL PANEL ON THREATS, CHALLENGES, AND CHANGE (HLP).

WEAPONS OF MASS DESTRUCTION (WMDs). The phrase "weapons of mass destruction" was coined in the late 1930s to describe the use of strategic bombing on civilian populations during the Spanish civil war. During the **Cold War**, the term exclusively referred to **nuclear weapons**. Nowadays, it also commonly refers to biological, radiological, and chemical weapons.

In 1996, at the request of the **General Assembly**, the **International Court of Justice (ICJ)** rendered an **advisory opinion** on the legality of the use (or threat of use) of nuclear weapons. In this case, the court ruled that the possession of nuclear weapons was not illegal under **international law**. However, **humanitarian law** applied to the use of nuclear weapons, notably the norms that it is illegal for a combatant to specifically target civilians and that some weapons causing indiscriminating damage are specifically outlawed.

While this legal debate goes on, in effect, WMDs have rarely been used. Yet, their destructiveness is a source of considerable unease, and **disarmament** negotiations have focused on the prevention of their further proliferation. The controversial doctrine of "**preemption**" advocated by President **George W. Bush** to justify the US-led second **Persian Gulf War** in 2003 rests in part on the assumption that the possession or capacity to develop WMDs by "rogue states" poses extreme national security threats that need to be stymied by preventative military strikes. *See also* ANTIPERSONNEL MINES (APMs); ARMS CONTROL; BACTERIOLOGICAL WEAPONS; CHEMICAL WEAPONS; COMPREHENSIVE TEST BAN TREATY (CTBT); CONVENTION ON THE PROHIBITION OF THE DEVELOPMENT, PRODUCTION, AND STOCKPILING OF BACTERIOLOGICAL (BIOLOGICAL) AND TOXIN WEAPONS AND ON THEIR DESTRUCTION (1972); CONVENTION ON THE PROHIBITION OF THE DEVELOPMENT, PRODUCTION, STOCKPILING, AND USE OF CHEMICAL WEAPONS AND ON THEIR DESTRUCTION (1997); DISARMAMENT; INTERNATIONAL ATOMIC ENERGY AGENCY (IAEA); NONPROLIFERATION OF NUCLEAR WEAPONS, TREATY ON THE (NPT, 1968); NONUSE OF FORCE; NUCLEAR WEAPONS FREE ZONES (NWFZs); OUTER SPACE TREATY (1967); PARTIAL TEST BAN TREATY (PTBT, 1963); SEABED DEMILITARIZATION TREATY (1971); SMALL ARMS AND LIGHT WEAPONS.

WEATHER WATCH. Set of programs and arrangements coordinated and monitored by the **World Meteorological Organization (WMO)** combining observing systems, telecommunications facilities and data processing centers operated by its member states for the instantaneous exchange of weather information and weather forecasting. *See also* EARLY WARNING; WORLD CLIMATE RESEACH PROGRAM (WCRP).

WEIGHTED VOTING. The most common kind of **voting** situation in international organizations is one in which each state is entitled to a vote and a majority of votes is necessary and sufficient to pass a resolution. This is the so-called one-nation-one-vote rule as it is practiced in the United Nations **General Assembly** and the **Economic and Social Council (ECOSOC)** in deference to the fiction of the sovereign equality of states. There are voting bodies, however, in which members may control an unequal number of votes, hence the term "weighted voting." For example, in the Council of Ministers of the **European Union (EU)**, the voting strength of the large member states is greater than that of the smaller members. In the UN context, systems of weighted voting are rarely used except in the **World Bank** and the **International Monetary Fund (IMF)** and a few technical **specialized agencies**. The **veto** power enjoyed by the permanent members of the **Security Council** is a form of weighted voting. *See also* SOVEREIGNTY.

WEST NEW GUINEA (WEST IRAN) QUESTION. When Indonesia won independence from the Netherlands in 1949, the Dutch government refused to relinquish West New Guinea due to its distinct Melanesian population. Indonesia maintained its claim to all former territory held by the Dutch, and armed conflict ensued. Under pressure by the United States and through the **mediation** of the United Nations, the Netherlands agreed in 1962 to relinquish the territory. Under the terms of the agreement, the Dutch were to leave the territory and transfer authority to a United Nations Temporary Executive Authority (UNTEA) for a period of six years until a national referendum was held to determine Papuan preference for independence or integration into Indonesia. Indonesia took over the administration from UNTEA almost immediately. A referendum under tight Indonesian control and marred by numerous irregularities paved the way to the formal integration of West New Guinea into Indonesia. *See also* DECOLONIZATION; SELF-DETERMINATION; TRANSITIONAL ADMINISTRATION.

WESTERN SAHARA DISPUTE (1976–present). *See* UNITED NATIONS MISSION FOR THE REFERENDUM IN WESTERN SAHARA (MINURSO, 1991–present).

WILSON, WOODROW (1856–1924). American educator turned politician, Wilson was elected president in 1912 and served for two terms from 1913 to 1921. Portraying American entrance into World War I in 1917 as a crusade to make the world "safe for democracy," he enunciated American war aims in "Fourteen Points" spelling out a number of key principles to govern a postwar international order. These included reliance on international public diplomacy; **disarmament** measures; an adjustment of colonial claims based on the principle and right of **self-determination**; the promotion of democracy worldwide; the removal of all economic barriers, especially in **international trade**; and a system of **collective security** through "a general association of nations . . . affording mutual guarantees of political independence and territorial integrity to great and small states alike." The last principle provided the basis for the establishment of the **League of Nations** as an essential component of the Versailles Treaty of June 1919 which, for some 20 years, helped maintain a fragile peace in Europe. The Versailles Treaty failed to win the advice and consent of the American Senate by seven votes. *See also* LIBERAL INTERNATIONALISM.

WOMEN. Although the **League of Nations** and the **International Labour Organization (ILO)** had done some work in support of women throughout the interwar period, the United Nations **Charter** is the first global treaty calling for equality between women and men. No less than four Articles—1, 55, 68, and 76—of the charter affirm that **human rights** and fundamental freedoms belong to all "without distinction as to race, sex, language or religion." The equality of men and women enshrined in the Preamble to the United Nations Charter is restated in the Preamble and Article 2 of the **Universal Declaration of Human Rights (UDHR)**.

On that basis, the organization initially focused its work on the collection of data documenting the subordination of women in such areas as civil and political rights, access to **education** and **employment** and, subsequently, on the progressive codification of women's rights in **international law** and **humanitarian law**. Over the years, the **General Assembly** has adopted several declarations on the elimination of discrimination and violence against women, the participation of women in promoting peace and cooperation, and the protection of women and **children in armed conflicts**. The assembly has also authorized the initiation of negotiations that have led to the adoption of several conventions setting international standards in support of women's rights. The most important one is the 1979 **Convention on the Elimination of All Forms of Discrimination against Women (1979)** and its Optional Protocol which are often described as an international bill of rights for women.

The United Nations has also provided a political space for the advocacy of women's rights. The UN observed 1975 as International Women's Year and held the first conference on women in Mexico City. Additional UN global conferences have since been held in Copenhagen (1980) and Nairobi (1985). The latest, the **World Conference on Women**, took place in Beijing in 1995. These meetings have centered on the creation of a consensus recognizing women's role and contribution to economic and social development. The declaration emanating from the 1993 **World Conference on Human Rights** in Vienna further secured the legal foundations of equality between the sexes by recognizing that women's rights are human rights and calling for the appointment of a Special Rapporteur on Violence against Women who reports to the United Nations **Commission for Human Rights**.

Within the **secretariat** and since the 1995 Beijing Conference, a special adviser on gender issues advises the **secretary-general**. The adviser also acts as director of the United Nations Division for the Advancement of Women within the **Department of Economic and Social Affairs (DESA)**. The division serves as a coordinating mechanism for the work of the UN on women, conducts research on **gender** issues, and supports the work of the **Commission on the Status of Women (CSW)** and the **Committee on the Elimination of Discrimination against Women (CEDAW)**. Note should be taken of a dynamic and enterprising interagency networking group within DESA with liaison and coordinating functions in promoting the mainstreaming of gender concerns in the legislative mandates emanating from the main policy organs of the United Nations and the work of the secretariat. One of the accomplishments of the group has been to win approval by the **Security Council** of the idea that women and gender concerns should be factored in the planning of peacekeeping operations.

Other UN bodies specifically dealing with women issues include the **International Research and Training Institute for the Advancement of Women (INSTRAW)** and the **United Nations Development Fund for Women (UNIFEM)**. *See also* UNITED NATIONS CONVENTION AGAINST TRANSNATIONAL ORGANIZED CRIME (2003).

WORLD ASSEMBLY ON AGING (1982). Devoted to the problems arising from the **aging** of population worldwide, this United Nations **global conference** convened in Vienna highlighted the fact that this demographic trend would also increasingly and in significant ways affect **developing countries** in the second half of the 20th century. In 1992, the **General Assembly** devoted four plenary meetings to an International Conference on Aging, which reviewed the implementation of the International Plan of Action adopted 10 years earlier in Vienna and resulted in the adoption of a Proclamation on Aging and the designation of 1999 as the International Year of Older Persons. *See also* AGING; SECOND WORLD ASSEMBLY ON AGING (2002).

WORLD BANK (WB). *See* INTERNATIONAL BANK FOR RECONSTRUCTION AND DEVELOPMENT (IBRD).

WORLD BANK GROUP. A group of financially and legally distinct but closely associated institutions under the aegis of the **International Bank for Reconstruction and Development (IBRD)** that includes, in addition to the IBRD, the **International Development Association (IDA)**, the **International Finance Corporation (IFC)**, and the **Multilateral Investment Guarantee Agency (MIGA)**.

WORLD BUSINESS COUNCIL FOR SUSTAINABLE DEVELOPMENT. Privately-funded American organization seeking to enlist corporate support for United Nations **development** activities. The Business Council acts as a link between corporations, nonprofit organizations, and international agencies of the United Nations system. It played a key role in mobilizing U.S. business and government support for and participation in the 2002 United Nations **International Conference on Financing for Development**. It is still actively involved in the conference's follow up activities. The council is also active in promoting entrepreneurship and venture capital development and information technology programs in **developing countries**. It has close ties with the **United Nations Association of the United States of America (UNA-USA)**. *See also* BUSINESS AND THE UNITED NATIONS.

WORLD CLIMATE RESEARCH PROGRAM (WCRP). Established in 1980 under the joint sponsorship of the **World Meteorological Organization (WMO)**, the **United Nations Educational, Scientific, and Cultural Organization (UNESCO)**, and the **International Council for Science (ICSU)** for the scientific study of Earth's climate and the impact of human activities on it. The research undertaken by the WCRP provides much of the basis for responding to issues raised in the **United Nations Framework Convention on Climate Change (UNFCCC)**. *See also* WEATHER WATCH.

WORLD COMMISSION ON ENVIRONMENT AND DEVELOPMENT. Commission comprising politicians, civil servants, and environment and development experts formed at the request of the **General Assembly** to identify long-term strategies to deal more effectively with environmental issues. After more than three years of work and on the basis of extensive scientific advice, the commission, chaired by former Norwegian Prime Minister **Gro Harlem Brundtland**, published its report, *Our Common Future*, in 1987. The report made the case that efforts to deal with environmental issues would remain ineffectual as long as they were not accompanied by concurrent national and international policies addressing **poverty** and inequalities in the world economy. Central to this argument was the concept of "**sustainable development**." Equity, growth and environmental maintenance were simultaneously possible, the report maintained, defining sustainability as "development that meets the needs of the present generation without compromising the ability of future generations to meet their own needs." Extensive changes in national and international policies concerned with **food, employment, energy, water**, and **science and technology** were thus necessary to enable all countries and **developing countries** in particular to achieve their full economic potential while at the same time enhancing their resource base. These issues were taken up at the 1992 **United Nations Conference on Environment and Development**. *See also* COMMISSION ON GLOBAL GOVERNANCE; COMMISSION ON INTERNATIONAL DEVELOPMENT (PEARSON COMMISSION); INDEPENDENT COMMISSION ON INTERNATIONAL DEVELOPMENT ISSUES (ICIDI); INDEPENDENT COMMISSIONS; REFORM, UNITED NATIONS; SOUTH COMMISSION; WORLD COMMISSION ON THE SOCIAL DIMENSION OF GLOBALIZATION.

WORLD COMMISSION ON THE SOCIAL DIMENSION OF GLOBALIZATION. High-level group set up at the initiative of the **International Labour Organization (ILO)** to look into the social implications of **globalization**. The commission's report, *A Fair Globalization: Creating Opportunities for All*, draws attention to the social inequalities arising from the process of globalization, calls for an "urgent rethink" of current policies and institutions of **global governance**, and proposes a series of coordinated measures to improve governance and accountability at the national and international levels. These include fairer international **trade** rules; investment, **finance**, and **migration labor** standards; social protection; and measures to mobilize international resources to meet the goals of the **Millennium Declaration**. *See also* INDEPENDENT COMMISSIONS; SOCIAL INTEGRATION.

WORLD CONFERENCE AGAINST RACISM, RACIAL DISCRIMINATION, XENOPHOBIA AND RELATED INTOLERANCE (DURBAN, SOUTH AFRICA, 2001). Third in a series of UN-sponsored conferences to define strategies to combat racism. Sharp and divisive North-South cleavages resurfaced as **developing countries** pressed for reparations for abuses committed under colonial rule and others used it as a forum against Israel's occupation policies, thus alienating a large number of developed countries. The conference also dealt with contentious issues such as "Islamophobia" and anti-Arab prejudice, slavery, and discrimination against migrant workers. By and large, the conference failed to achieve tangible results. *See also* HUMAN RIGHTS; INTERNATIONAL CONVENTION ON THE ELIMINATION OF ALL FORMS OF RACIAL DISCRIMINATION (1965); MIGRATION (INTERNATIONAL); RACIAL DISCRIMINATION; TREATY BODIES.

WORLD CONFERENCE ON DISASTER REDUCTION (KOBE, HYOGO, JAPAN, 18–22 January 2005). Long-planned event intended to assess progress made in the area of disaster reduction since the 1994 **World Conference on Natural Disaster Reduction**. This conference gained in significance as a result of the catastrophic December 2004 Indian Ocean tsunami that claimed over 200,000 lives. The conference adopted the "Hyogo Framework for Action: 2005–2015," which calls for placing disaster risk at the center of national policies, strengthening the capacity of disaster-prone countries to address risk, and investing heavily in disaster preparedness. It also endorsed a declaration recommending that a "culture of disaster prevention and resilience" must be fostered, recognizing the relationship between **natural disaster** reduction, **sustainable development**, and **poverty** reduction. Delegations also pledged to create a regional tsunami **early warning** system in the Indian Ocean that would draw from the experience of the existing Pacific Ocean tsunami early warning systems and rely on the coordinating mechanism of the **Intergovernmental Oceanographic Commission (IOC)** of the **United Nations Educational, Scientific, and Cultural Organization (UNESCO)**. *See also* OFFICE FOR THE COORDINATION OF HUMANITARIAN AFFAIRS (OCHA); SMALL ISLAND DEVELOPING STATES (SIDS); UNITED NATIONS DISASTER RELIEF ORGANIZATION (UNDRO).

WORLD CONFERENCE ON HUMAN RIGHTS (VIENNA, 1993). Second conference on **human rights** issues organized by the United Nations after a contentious and lengthy preparatory process (the preceding meeting had been held in Teheran in 1968). Called by the **General Assembly** to assess progress made in the field of human rights since the adoption of the **Universal Declaration of Human Rights (UDHR)**, the conference drew an unprecedented degree of participation by government delegates and the international human rights community (some 7,000 participants, including academics, **treaty bodies**, national institutions, and over 800 **nongovernmental organizations [NGOs]**).

How to broaden the United Nations' human rights agenda while deepening it were the key questions addressed by the conference. The Vienna Declaration and Programme of Action finally agreed by the conference and subsequently endorsed by the General Assembly reaffirmed the principles that have guided the development of human rights through the United Nations, recognized the interdependence between democracy, development, and human rights; identified steps to promote and protect the rights of **women, children,** and **indigenous peoples**; and called for the establishment of a **United Nations High Commissioner for Human Rights (UNHCHR)** to strengthen the monitoring capacity of the United Nations system.

At the same time, the conference underlined the continuing tension between state **sovereignty** and international accountability in the promotion and protection of human rights. Many governments still question the legitimacy of international concern in human rights matters. This ambiguity was reflected in the Vienna Declaration as it reaffirms the universality of human rights while recognizing that there are regional specificities that cannot be ignored. The declaration's emphasis on the need for speedy ratification of all still unratified human rights instruments is another reminder of the ambivalent commitment of governments. *See also* WORLD CONFERENCE ON WOMEN (BEIJING, 4–15 September 1995).

WORLD CONFERENCE ON NATURAL DISASTER REDUCTION (YOKOHAMA, JAPAN, 1994). Held on the occasion of the mid-term review of the 1990–1999 International Decade for Natural Disaster Reduction, this conference adopted guidelines for natural disaster prevention, preparedness, and mitigation and a plan of action that served as blueprints for national and international action in the field of disaster reduction. Disaster prevention and preparedness are now recognized as a crucial component of sustainable development, notably in the Johannesburg Plan of Implementation of the 2002

World Summit on Sustainable Development. Continuing increasing human and economic losses due to natural disasters prompted the convening of a second world conference in 2005. *See also* NATURAL DISASTER; OFFICE FOR THE COORDINATION OF HUMANITARIAN AFFAIRS (OCHA); UNITED NATIONS DISASTER RELIEF ORGANIZATION (UNDRO); WORLD CONFERENCE ON DISASTER REDUCTION (KOBE, HYOGO, JAPAN, 18–22 January 2005).

WORLD CONFERENCE ON WOMEN (BEIJING, 4–15 September 1995). Fourth in a series of **global conferences** sponsored by the United Nations that began in 1975 for the purpose of enhancing the social, economic, and political empowerment of **women**. The conference focused on the crosscutting issues of equality, **development**, and peace, reviewing them from a **gender** perspective and emphasizing the links between the advancement of women and the progress of society as a whole. The Platform for Action adopted by the conference reaffirmed the responsibility of governments in protecting the **human rights** of women and girl-children, including their reproductive rights and right to control their sexuality, as an integral part of universal human rights, as had already been asserted by the 1993 **World Conference on Human Rights**. It also set time-specific targets in such areas as **health, education**, decision making and legal reform, with the ultimate goal of eliminating all forms of discrimination against women in private and public life.

WORLD COUNCIL OF CHURCHES (WCC). Transnational **nongovernmental organization (NGO)** in consultative status with the **Economic and Social Council (ECOSOC)**. The WCC brings together more than 340 churches, denominations, and church fellowships in over 100 countries and territories throughout the world, representing some 400 million Christians. The WCC is primarily a religious ecumenical movement concerned in the first place with the cause of church unity worldwide. Nevertheless, through political analysis and documentation, advocacy, and awareness-building campaigns, the WCC has fought against **apartheid** in South Africa, supported efforts to bring an end to the long civil conflict in **Sudan**, and defended **human rights** in Latin America. It is also concerned with international issues related to the prevention and resolution of armed conflicts and wars and has been active in assistance for **natural disasters** and **refugee** problems.

WORLD EMPLOYMENT CONFERENCE (1976). Formally known as the Tripartite Conference on Employment, Income Distribution and Social Progress and the International Division of Labor, the purpose of this conference, organized under the aegis of the **International Labour Organization (ILO)**, was to review the effectiveness of the ILO world **employment** programs in the light of persisting high **poverty** and unemployment levels in **developing countries**. From this vantage point, the conference provided an opportunity to examine the linkages between employment creation and poverty alleviation, on the one hand, and technological innovation, **rural development**, **international trade**, migration, income distribution, and **official development assistance**, on the other. One of its important outcomes was to emphasize the centrality of income redistribution policies in development strategies designed to meet the **basic human needs** of populations.

WORLD FEDERALIST MOVEMENT (WFM). Worldwide network of organizations and individuals advocating a "just world order through a strengthened United Nations." Initially, the WFM promoted a form of international governance close to **world government**. Since the mid-1960s, it has refocused its efforts on UN institutions seeking to make them more effective and democratic. The WFM has thus made proposals to transform the **General Assembly** into a law-making world parliament. In that context, WFM conducts policy-oriented research through its **Institute for Global Policy (IGP)**. WFM is a **nongovernmental organization (NGO)** with consultative status in the **Economic and Social Council (ECOSOC)**.

WORLD FEDERATION OF UNITED NATIONS ASSOCIATIONS (WFUNA). Founded in 1946 as a "peoples' movement for the United Nations," the main objective of this network of national associations is to mobilize popular support for the programs and work of the organization. An important aspect of its advocacy work has been its efforts in support of international **human rights**.

WFUNA has also been active in the field of **disarmament** and **development**, often acting as an informal forum for global consultations and dialogue between East and West and North and South. WFUNA has consultative status with the **Economic and Social Council (ECOSOC)**. *See also* UNITED NATIONS ASSOCIATION OF THE UNITED STATES OF AMERICA (UNA-USA).

WORLD FOOD PROGRAMME (WFP). Established initially on an experimental basis by the **General Assembly** in 1961 as a joint program of the United Nations and the **Food and Agriculture Organization (FAO)**, the World Food Programme was set up to provide emergency food needs arising from malnutrition, to assist in preschool and school feeding, and to distribute food as an aid to economic and social **development**. It was turned into a permanent body in 1965 and has since become a major provider of food supplies in humanitarian emergencies. The program is voluntarily funded, and food aid reached 113 million people in 80 countries in 2004. *See also* HUMANITARIAN ASSISTANCE.

WORLD FOOD SUMMIT (13–17 November 1996). Global conference organized by the **Food and Agriculture Organization (FAO)** in response to continued widespread undernutrition throughout the world and growing concerns about the capacity of agriculture to meet future needs, especially in Africa. At the time, the FAO estimated that in the absence of any corrective policies, there could be 680 million hungry people in the world by the year 2010, more than 250 million of them in sub-Saharan Africa.

The conference met at FAO headquarters in Rome, brought together some 10,000 participants, and resulted in the adoption of the Rome Declaration on World Food Security and the World Food Summit Plan of Action. The Rome Declaration sets forth "commitments" that lay the basis for achieving sustainable **food security** and the Plan of Action spells out a series of objectives and actions for the implementation of these commitments, including the target of reducing by half the number of undernourished people by no later than 2015. These pledges were reaffirmed in a 2002 follow-up high-level meeting. *See also* AGRARIAN REFORM; AGRICULTURAL DEVELOPMENT; HUNGER; MILLENNIUM DECLARATION.

WORLD GOVERNMENT. The view that international peace and security can never be achieved in a world divided into separate sovereign states. In such a system, international politics is driven by an endless struggle for power rooted in human nature, fear, suspicion, and insecurity. Self-help and survival thus become of the essence among states. Just as the state of nature in civil society was abolished by the creation of national governments with a monopoly over the means of coercion, this state of war in international society must be ended by the establishment of a system of government overriding the authority of states and backed by overwhelming power. *See also* WORLD FEDERALIST MOVEMENT (WFM).

WORLD HEALTH ORGANIZATION (WHO). One of the **specialized agencies** of the United Nations created in 1948 to promote the attainment by all peoples of the highest possible level of **health**. The constitution of the WHO defines health not merely as the absence of disease but as a state of complete physical and social well-being.

The WHO has important rule-making powers for sanitary and quarantine regulations, the standardization of medical nomenclature and diagnostic procedures, the definition of safety standards for pharmaceutical substances traded in international commerce, and their advertising and labeling. In addition, the WHO carries out extensive programs of health services and technical assistance and has played a key role in international efforts to control and eradicate malaria and smallpox and in the immunization of children against diphtheria, measles, whooping cough, poliomyelitis, tetanus, and tuberculosis. Through its research and worldwide intelligence network of regional and national offices, the WHO performs epidemiological **early warning**, monitoring and information functions. The WHO cooperates closely with the **Commission on Narcotic Drugs** in the control of narcotics under the 1988 **United Nations Convention against Illicit Traffic in Narcotic Drugs and Psychotropic Substances**.

Since the adoption of the **Alma-Ata Health Declaration** at the 1978 International Conference on Primary Health Care in Alma Ata, a joint initiative of the WHO and the **United Nations Children's Fund (UNICEF)**, the WHO's health programs have been firmly embedded in socioeconomic considerations. The objective of the WHO is now health for all, that is, attaining a level of health for all people that would enable them to lead socially and economically productive lives, which requires a more equitable distribution of health resources and a participatory approach at the local level. The prevailing thinking within the WHO is that health is a **human right**. *See also* FUNCTIONALISM.

WORLD INTELLECTUAL PROPERTY ORGANIZATION (WIPO). Established in 1970, the World Intellectual Property Organization became a **specialized agency** of the United Nations in 1974. Its role is to harmonize national intellectual property legislation and procedures, to provide services to international applications for industrial property rights as well as legal and technical assistance to developing countries, to act as a conduit for the exchange of information, and to facilitate the resolution of intellectual property disputes. *See also* COPYRIGHT; INTELLECTUAL PROPERTY RIGHTS (IPRs); WORLD TRADE ORGANIZATION (WTO).

WORLD MARITIME UNIVERSITY (WMU). Voluntarily funded institution based in Malmo, Sweden, and operating under the auspices of the **International Maritime Organization (IMO)**. Since 1983, this university has been providing mid-career applied education and training at postgraduate level in marine affairs related to the activities of the IMO, such as maritime administration and law, marine resource management, marine safety and environmental protection, and port development and management.

WORLD METEOROLOGICAL ORGANIZATION (WMO). One of the UN **specialized agencies**, which commenced operations in 1951 as the successor to the International Meteorological Organization. Its purposes are to generate weather information for public and commercial use, including international airline and shipping industries, and to encourage research and training in meteorology. *See also* EARLY WARNING; WORLD CLIMATE RESEARCH PROGRAM (WCRP); WORLD WEATHER WATCH.

WORLD RESOURCES INSTITUTE (WRI). Environmental think tank carrying out authoritative policy-oriented research on climate change analysis, market-based policies conducive to the protection of the environment, and the expansion of economic opportunities and socially equitable development. The WRI, in cooperation with the **United Nations Development Programme (UNDP)**, the **United Nations Environment Programme (UNEP)**, and the **International Bank for Reconstruction and Development (IBRD)**, produces biennial reports on global environment and governance issues.

WORLD SUMMIT FOR CHILDREN (NEW YORK, 1990). Major gathering of world leaders organized by the **United Nations Children's Fund (UNICEF)** to draw attention to the problems of **children**. The summit adopted a Declaration on the Survival, Protection and Development of Children identifying goals to be achieved by 2000 for children's health, nutrition, education, and access to safe water and sanitation. The **General Assembly** held a special session on children in 2002 that reaffirmed and broadened those objectives. *See also* GLOBAL CONFERENCES (UNITED NATIONS); GRANT, JAMES (1922–1995).

WORLD SUMMIT FOR SOCIAL DEVELOPMENT (COPENHAGEN, 1995). This UN **global conference** dealt with three core developmental issues: **poverty** eradication, productive **employment**, and **social integration**, particularly for disadvantaged groups. Its main contribution was to refocus attention on the social dimensions of development in development thinking and policies, a consideration that had been neglected in the market-oriented policies that prevailed in the 1980s and early 1990s and led to increasing inequalities within and among states.

A follow-up special session of the **General Assembly** reaffirmed the centrality of social concerns in national and international development strategies, called for new innovative sources of private and public funding for poverty eradication, and set a global target for poverty reduction—halving the proportion of people living in extreme poverty by 2015. *See also* BASIC HUMAN NEEDS; INTERNATIONAL LABOUR ORGANIZATION (ILO); MILLENNIUM DECLARATION; WORLD EMPLOYMENT CONFERENCE (1976).

WORLD SUMMIT ON SUSTAINABLE DEVELOPMENT (WSSD) (JOHANNESBURG, 2002). Convened after two years of intense preparations and protracted negotiations over issues such as finance and **trade**, renewable **energy**, good governance, and **human rights**, this summit assessed the implementation of **Agenda 21** adopted 10 years earlier at the **United Nations Conference on Environment and Development**. WSSD did result in a painstakingly crafted Plan of Implementation that essentially reaffirmed the principles and provisions of Agenda 21. The implementation plan also addresses a number of issues—**energy**, **sanitation**, corporate responsibility and accountability, and **ocean fishing**—which had not been adequately dealt with in Agenda 21. However, it does not contain set targets and time frames, nor does it provide for additional finance to meet the broad objectives of Agenda 21.

WORLD SUMMIT ON THE INFORMATION SOCIETY (WSIS) (GENEVA, 10–12 December 2003/TUNIS, TUNISIA, 16–18 November 2005). Two-phased UN **global conference** organized by the **International Telecommunications Union (ITU)** with the aim of promoting consensus on policies designed to bridge the so-called digital divide separating rich from poor countries and broaden the access of all regions of the world to the benefits provided by **information technology (IT)**. The summit gave renewed visibility to this emerging North-South contentious issue but, by and large, failed to produce well-defined public policy options addressing the development opportunities made possible by IT. Three major problems overshadowed the preparatory process leading to the Tunis Summit: Internet governance, financing strategies, and the implementation mechanisms for an action plan developed in the first phase of the WSIS in 2003 in Geneva. The WSIS outcome documents, the "Tunis Commitment" and the "Tunis Agenda for the Information Society" do provide for the creation of an Internet Governance Forum (IGF), which will serve as a platform for discussion by governments, UN agencies, businesses, and civil society of crosscutting public policy issues related to the development and management of the Internet. The IGF is expected to begin work in 2006, but its establishment leaves untouched the current regime that allows the U.S.-based Internet Corporation for Assigned Names and Numbers (ICANN) to continue as the main governing body of the global computer network. The financing of the development of information technology in developing countries basically remained an unresolved issue. The WCIS outcome documents merely welcome the creation of the Digital Solidarity Fund, a voluntary fund financing mechanism launched in March 2005, and call for higher priority to be given to IT in existing financial agreements, such as those reached at the 2002 **International Conference on Financing for Development**. In regard to implementation, the Tunis Agenda only underlines the necessity of "knowledge-sharing" between all "stakeholders" in "building an inclusive development oriented information society."

WORLD TRADE ORGANIZATION (WTO). Successor to the **General Agreement on Tariffs and Trade (GATT)** that came into being in 1995 and serves as a forum for the negotiation of trade rules and as a trade dispute settlement body. Total trade in 2000 was 22 times the level of 1950. This pattern of growth was achieved through a series of trade liberalization negotiations, or "rounds," held under GATT. The first rounds dealt primarily with tariff reductions but were later concerned with antidumping and nontariff measures. The last round—the 1986–1994 Uruguay Round—led to the creation of WTO.

In 2000, new talks started extending to trade in agriculture and services, which were incorporated into a broader agenda adopted at the fourth WTO Ministerial Conference in Doha, Qatar, in November 2001. Current negotiations cover nonagricultural tariffs, trade and environment, antidumping and subsidies, investment, competition policy, trade facilitation, transparency and government procurement, and **Trade-Related Aspects of Intellectual Property Rights (TRIPs)**. *See also* TRADE AND DEVELOPMENT.

WORLD WEATHER WATCH. The backbone of the **World Meteorological Organization (WMO)** scientific and technical activities, it provides up-to-the minute worldwide weather information through telecommunications links and a network of about 10,000 land observation posts, 7,000 ship stations, and 300 moored and drifting buoys.

WORLDWATCH. Widely respected independent **research** organization based in Washington, D.C., focusing its work on the linkages between environmental and social policy. Worldwatch issues authoritative publications, notably its yearly *State of the World*.

– Y –

YALTA CONFERENCE (1945). Attended by **Franklin D. Roosevelt**, **Winston Churchill**, and Joseph Stalin, the conference helped resolve a number of issues left outstanding at the **Dumbarton Oaks Conference**. Agreement was reached on the establishment of a new court to replace the Permanent Court of International Justice of the **League of Nations**, the manner in which the new organization should deal with **decolonization**, and, above all, the **voting** formula to be used in the **Security Council**. *See also* UNITED NATIONS CONFERENCE ON INTERNATIONAL ORGANIZATION; VETO.

YOUTH. Worldwide, there are 1.1 billion young people between the ages of 15 and 24 representing around 18 percent of the world population. Nearly 9 out of 10 live in developing regions. Overall, young people today are better off than previous generations, but many are still severely hindered by **poverty**, a lack of **education**, **health** risks, unemployment, and the impact of conflict. Nearly a quarter of the young people living in **developing countries** survive on less than one dollar a day, and 133 million remain illiterate. Up to 10 million youth are estimated to be undernourished, and 7,000 are believed to become infected with HIV daily. Compared to adults, the rate of unemployment among youth is usually two to three times higher, as they account for 40 percent of the unemployed. Armed conflicts have also taken a huge toll on young people: 2 million **children** were killed and 6 million more were left disabled as a result of wars during the last decade.

Through research and advocacy, the role of the United Nations has mainly been to draw attention to the specificity and scope of youth problems and to mobilize international and national efforts to help them. The **General Assembly** proclaimed 1985 as International Youth Year and in 1995, the assembly adopted a World Program of Action for Youth calling for a wide array of measures dealing with education, **employment**, extreme poverty, health, **environment**, drugs, and juvenile delinquency.

The focal point within the United Nations system on matters relating to youth issues is the **Department of Economic and Social Affairs (DESA)**. Other concerned UN bodies include the **United Na-**

tions Centre on Human Settlements (Habitat), the **United Nations Office on Drugs and Crime (UNODC)**, the **United Nations Development Programme (UNDP)**, the **United Nations Environment Programme (UNEP)**, the **United Nations Population Fund (UNFPA)**, the Office of the **United Nations High Commissioner for Human Rights (UNHCHR)**, the **United Nations Children's Fund (UNICEF)**, and the **Joint United Nations Programme on HIV/AIDS (UNAIDS)**. Also several **specialized agencies** focus on problems of youth, notably, the **International Labour Organization (ILO)**, the **Food and Agriculture Organization (FAO)**, the **United Nations Educational, Scientific, and Cultural Organization (UNESCO)**, and the **World Health Organization (WHO)**.

YUGOSLAVIA. *See* BOSNIAN CONFLICT (1992–1995); INDEPENDENT INTERNATIONAL COMMISSION ON KOSOVO; INTERNATIONAL CRIMINAL TRIBUNAL FOR THE FORMER YUGOSLAVIA (ICTY); KOSOVO QUESTION; UNITED NATIONS INTERIM ADMINISTRATION MISSION IN KOSOVO (UNMIK, 10 June 1999–present); UNITED NATIONS MISSION IN BOSNIA AND HERZEGOVINA (UNMIBH, 21 December 1995–21 December 2002); UNITED NATIONS PREVENTIVE DEPLOYMENT FORCE (UNPREDEP, 1995–1999); UNITED NATIONS PROTECTION FORCE (UNPROFOR, 1992–1995); UNITED NATIONS TRANSITIONAL ADMINISTRATION FOR EASTERN SLAVONIA, BARANJA, AND WESTERN SIRMIUM (UNTAES, 19 January 1996–15 January 1998).

Appendix A
Charter of the United Nations

PREAMBLE

We the Peoples of the United Nations Determined

to save succeeding generations from the scourge of war, which twice in our lifetime has brought untold sorrow to mankind, and

to reaffirm faith in fundamental human rights, in the dignity and worth of the human person, in the equal rights of men and women and of nations large and small, and

to establish conditions under which justice and respect for the obligations arising from treaties and other sources of international law can be maintained, and

to promote social progress and better standards of life in larger freedom,

And for These Ends

to practice tolerance and live together in peace with one another as good neighbors, and

to unite our strength to maintain international peace and security, and

to ensure by the acceptance of principles and the institution of methods, that armed force shall not be used, save in the common interest, and

to employ international machinery for the promotion of the economic and social advancement of all peoples,

Have Resolved to Combine Our Efforts to Accomplish These Aims

Accordingly, our respective Governments, through representatives assembled in the city of San Francisco, who have exhibited their full powers found to be in good and due form, have agreed to the present Charter of the United Nations and do hereby establish an international organization to be known as the United Nations.

CHAPTER I

Purposes and Principles

Article 1
The Purposes of the United Nations are:

1. To maintain international peace and security, and to that end: to take effective collective measures for the prevention and removal of threats to the peace, and for the suppression of acts of aggression or other breaches of the peace, and to bring about by peaceful means, and in conformity with the principles of justice and international law, adjustment or settlement of international disputes or situations which might lead to a breach of the peace;
2. To develop friendly relations among nations based on respect for the principle of equal rights and self-determination of peoples, and to take other appropriate measures to strengthen universal peace;
3. To achieve international cooperation in solving international problems of an economic, social, cultural, or humanitarian character, and in promoting and encouraging respect for human rights and for fundamental freedoms for all without distinction as to race, sex, language, or religion; and
4. To be a center for harmonizing the actions of nations in the attainment of these common ends.

Article 2
The Organization and its Members, in pursuit of the Purposes stated in Article 1, shall act in accordance with the following Principles.

1. The Organization is based on the principle of the sovereign equality of all its Members.

2. All Members, in order to ensure to all of them the rights and benefits resulting from membership, shall fulfill in good faith the obligations assumed by them in accordance with the present Charter.

3. All Members shall settle their international disputes by peaceful means in such a manner that international peace and security, and justice, are not endangered.

4. All Members shall refrain in their international relations from the threat or use of force against the territorial integrity or political independence of any state, or in any other manner inconsistent with the Purposes of the United Nations.

5. All Members shall give the United Nations every assistance in any action it takes in accordance with the present Charter, and shall refrain from giving assistance to any state against which the United Nations is taking preventive or enforcement action.

6. The Organization shall ensure that states which are not Members of the United Nations act in accordance with these Principles so far as may be necessary for the maintenance of international peace and security.

7. Nothing contained in the present Charter shall authorize the United Nations to intervene in matters which are essentially within the domestic jurisdiction of any state or shall require the Members to submit such matters to settlement under the present Charter; but this principle shall not prejudice the application of enforcement measures under Chapter VII.

CHAPTER II

Membership

Article 3
The original Members of the United Nations shall be the states which, having participated in the United Nations Conference on International Organization at San Francisco, or having previously signed the Declaration by United Nations of January 1, 1942, sign the present Charter and ratify it in accordance with Article 110.

Article 4
1. Membership in the United Nations is open to all other peaceloving states which accept the obligations contained in the present

Charter and, in the judgment of the Organization, are able and willing to carry out these obligations.

2. The admission of any such state to membership in the United Nations will be effected by a decision of the General Assembly upon the recommendation of the Security Council.

Article 5

A member of the United Nations against which preventive or enforcement action has been taken by the Security Council may be suspended from the exercise of the rights and privileges of membership by the General Assembly upon the recommendation of the Security Council. The exercise of these rights and privileges may be restored by the Security Council.

Article 6

A Member of the United Nations which has persistently violated the Principles contained in the present Charter may be expelled from the Organization by the General Assembly upon the recommendation of the Security Council.

CHAPTER III

Organs

Article 7

1. There are established as the principal organs of the United Nations: a General Assembly, a Security Council, an Economic and Social Council, a Trusteeship Council, an International Court of Justice, and a Secretariat.
2. Such subsidiary organs as may be found necessary may be established in accordance with the present Charter.

Article 8

The United Nations shall place no restrictions on the eligibility of men and women to participate in any capacity and under conditions of equality in its principal and subsidiary organs.

CHAPTER IV

The General Assembly

Composition

Article 9

1. The General Assembly shall consist of all the Members of the United Nations.
2. Each member shall have not more than five representatives in the General Assembly.

Functions and Powers

Article 10

The General Assembly may discuss any questions or any matters within the scope of the present Charter or relating to the powers and functions of any organs provided for in the present Charter, and, except as provided in Article 12, may make recommendations to the Members of the United Nations or to the Security Council or to both on any such questions or matters.

Article 11

1. The General Assembly may consider the general principles of co-operation in the maintenance of international peace and security, including the principles governing disarmament and the regulation of armaments, and may make recommendations with regard to such principles to the Members or to the Security Council or to both.
2. The General Assembly may discuss any questions relating to the maintenance of international peace and security brought before it by any Member of the United Nations, or by the Security Council, or by a state which is not a Member of the United Nations in accordance with Article 35, paragraph 2, and, except as provided in Article 12, may make recommendations with regard to any such questions to the state or states concerned or to the Security Council or to both. Any such question on which action is necessary shall be referred to the Security Council by the General Assembly either before or after discussion.

3. The General Assembly may call the attention of the Security Council to situations which are likely to endanger international peace and security.

4. The powers of the General Assembly set forth in this Article shall not limit the general scope of Article 10.

Article 12

1. While the Security Council is exercising in respect of any dispute or situation the functions assigned to it in the present Charter, the General Assembly shall not make any recommendation with regard to that dispute or situation unless the Security Council so requests.

2. The Secretary-General, with the consent of the Security Council, shall notify the General Assembly at each session of any matters relative to the maintenance of international peace and security which are being dealt with by the Security Council and shall similarly notify the General Assembly, or the Members of the United Nations if the General Assembly is not in session, immediately the Security Council ceases to deal with such matters.

Article 13

1. The General Assembly shall initiate studies and make recommendations for the purpose of:
   a. promoting international cooperation in the political field and encouraging the progressive development of international law and its codification;
   b. promoting international cooperation in the economic, social, cultural, educational, and health fields, and assisting in the realization of human rights and fundamental freedoms for all without distinction as to race, sex, language, or religion.

2. The further responsibilities, functions and powers of the General Assembly with respect to matters mentioned in paragraph 1(b) above are set forth in Chapters IX and X.

Article 14

Subject to the provisions of Article 12, the General Assembly may recommend measures for the peaceful adjustment of any situation, regardless of origin, which it deems likely to impair the general welfare or friendly relations among nations, including situations resulting from a violation of the provisions of the present Charter setting forth the Purposes and Principles of the United Nations.

Article 15

1. The General Assembly shall receive and consider annual and special reports from the Security Council; these reports shall include an account of the measures that the Security Council has decided upon or taken to maintain international peace and security.
2. The General Assembly shall receive and consider reports from the other organs of the United Nations.

Article 16

The General Assembly shall perform such functions with respect to the international trusteeship system as are assigned to it under Chapters XII and XIII, including the approval of the trusteeship agreements for areas not designated as strategic.

Article 17

1. The General Assembly shall consider and approve the budget of the Organization.
2. The expenses of the Organization shall be borne by the Members as apportioned by the General Assembly.
3. The General Assembly shall consider and approve any financial and budgetary arrangements with specialized agencies referred to in Article 57 and shall examine the administrative budgets of such specialized agencies with a view to making recommendations to the agencies concerned.

Voting

Article 18

1. Each member of the General Assembly shall have one vote.
2. Decisions of the General Assembly on important questions shall be made by a two-thirds majority of the members present and voting. These questions shall include: recommendations with respect to the maintenance of international peace and security, the election of the non-permanent members of the Security Council, the election

of the members of the Economic and Social Council, the election of members of the Trusteeship Council in accordance with paragraph 1(c) of Article 86, the admission of new Members to the United Nations, the suspension of the rights and privileges of membership, the expulsion of Members, questions relating to the operation of the trusteeship system, and budgetary questions.

3. Decisions on other questions, Composition including the determination of additional categories of questions to be decided by a two-thirds majority, shall be made by a majority of the members present and voting.

Article 19

A Member of the United Nations which is in arrears in the payment of its financial contributions to the Organization shall have no vote in the General Assembly if the amount of its arrears equals or exceeds the amount of the contributions due from it for the preceding two full years. The General Assembly may, nevertheless, permit such a Member to vote if it is satisfied that the failure to pay is due to conditions beyond the control of the Member.

Procedure

Article 20

The General Assembly shall meet in regular annual sessions and in such special sessions as occasion may require. Special sessions shall be convoked by the Secretary-General at the request of the Security Council or of a majority of the Members of the United Nations.

Article 21

The General Assembly shall adopt its own rules of procedure. It shall elect its President for each session.

Article 22

The General Assembly may establish such subsidiary organs as it deems necessary for the performance of its functions.

CHAPTER V

The Security Council

Composition

Article 23

1. The Security Council shall consist of fifteen Members of the United Nations. The Republic of China, France, the Union of Soviet Socialist Republics, the United Kingdom of Great Britain and Northern Ireland, and the United States of America shall be permanent members of the Security Council. The General Assembly shall elect ten other Members of the United Nations to be nonpermanent members of the Security Council, due regard being specially paid, in the first instance to the contribution of Members of the United Nations to the maintenance of international peace and security and to the other purposes of the Organization, and also to equitable geographical distribution.

2. The non-permanent members of the Security Council shall be elected for a term of two years. In the first election of the nonpermanent members after the increase of the membership of the Security Council from eleven to fifteen, two of the four additional members shall be chosen for a term of one year. A retiring member shall not be eligible for immediate re-election.

3. Each member of the Security Council shall have one representative.

Functions and Powers

Article 24

1. In order to ensure prompt and effective action by the United Nations, its Members confer on the Security Council primary responsibility for the maintenance of international peace and security, and agree that in carrying out its duties under this responsibility the Security Council acts on their behalf.

2. In discharging these duties the Security Council shall act in accordance with the Purposes and Principles of the United Nations.

416 • APPENDIX A

The specific powers granted to the Security Council for the discharge of these duties are laid down in Chapters VI, VII, VIII, and XII.

3. The Security Council shall submit annual and, when necessary, special reports to the General Assembly for its consideration.

Article 25
The Members of the United Nations agree to accept and carry out the decisions of the Security Council in accordance with the present Charter.

Article 26
In order to promote the establishment and maintenance of international peace and security with the least diversion for armaments of the world's human and economic resources, the Security Council shall be responsible for formulating, with the assistance of the Military Staff Committee referred to in Article 47, plans to be submitted to the Members of the United Nations for the establishment of a system for the regulation of armaments.

Voting

Article 27
1. Each member of the Security Council shall have one vote.
2. Decisions of the Security Council on procedural matters shall be made by an affirmative vote of nine members.
3. Decisions of the Security Council on all other matters shall be made by an affirmative vote of nine members including the concurring votes of the permanent members; provided that, in decisions under Chapter VI, and under paragraph 3 of Article 52, a party to a dispute shall abstain from voting.

Procedure

Article 28
1. The Security Council shall be so organized as to be able to function continuously. Each member of the Security Council shall for this purpose be represented at all times at the seat of the Organization.

2. The Security Council shall hold periodic meetings at which each of its members may, if it so desires, be represented by a member of the government or by some other specially designated representative.
3. The Security Council may hold meetings at such places other than the seat of the Organization as in its judgment will best facilitate its work.

Article 29

The Security Council may establish such subsidiary organs as it deems necessary for the performance of its functions.

Article 30

The Security Council shall adopt its own rules of procedure, including the method of selecting its President.

Article 31

Any Member of the United Nations which is not a member of the Security Council may participate, without vote, in the discussion of any question brought before the Security Council whenever the latter considers that the interests of that Member are specially affected.

Article 32

Any Member of the United Nations which is not a member of the Security Council or any state which is not a Member of the United Nations, if it is a party to a dispute under consideration by the Security Council, shall be invited to participate, without vote, in the discussion relating to the dispute. The Security Council shall lay down such conditions as it deems just for the participation of a state which is not a Member of the United Nations.

CHAPTER VI

Pacific Settlement of Disputes

Article 33

1. The parties to any dispute, the continuance of which is likely to endanger the maintenance of international peace and security,

shall, first of all, seek a solution by negotiation, enquiry, mediation, conciliation, arbitration, judicial settlement, resort to regional agencies or arrangements, or other peaceful means of their own choice.

2. The Security Council shall, when it deems necessary, call upon the parties to settle their dispute by such means.

Article 34

The Security Council may investigate any dispute, or any situation which might lead to international friction or give rise to a dispute, in order to determine whether the continuance of the dispute or situation is likely to endanger the maintenance of international peace and security.

Article 35

1. Any Member of the United Nations may bring any dispute, or any situation of the nature referred to in Article 34, to the attention of the Security Council or of the General Assembly.

2. A state which is not a Member of the United Nations may bring to the attention of the Security Council or of the General Assembly any dispute to which it is a party if it accepts in advance, for the purposes of the dispute, the obligations of pacific settlement provided in the present Charter.

3. The proceedings of the General Assembly in respect of matters brought to its attention under this Article will be subject to the provisions of Articles 11 and 12.

Article 36

1. The Security Council may, at any stage of a dispute of the nature referred to in Article 33 or of a situation of like nature, recommend appropriate procedures or methods of adjustment.

2. The Security Council should take into consideration any procedures for the settlement of the dispute which have already been adopted by the parties.

3. In making recommendations under this Article the Security Council should also take into consideration that legal disputes should as a general rule be referred by the parties to the International Court of Justice in accordance with the provisions of the Statute of the Court.

Article 37

1. Should the parties to a dispute of the nature referred to in Article 33 fail to settle it by the means indicated in that Article, they shall refer it to the Security Council.
2. If the Security Council deems that the continuance of the dispute is in fact likely to endanger the maintenance of international peace and security, it shall decide whether to take action under Article 36 or to recommend such terms of settlement as it may consider appropriate.

Article 38

Without prejudice to the provisions of Articles 33 to 37, the Security Council may, if all the parties to any dispute so request, make recommendations to the parties with a view to a pacific settlement of the dispute.

CHAPTER VII

Action with Respect to Threats to the Peace, Breaches of the Peace, and Acts of Aggression

Article 39

The Security Council shall determine the existence of any threat to the peace, breach of the peace, or act of aggression and shall make recommendations, or decide what measures shall be taken in accordance with Articles 41 and 42, to maintain or restore international peace and security.

Article 40

In order to prevent an aggravation of the situation, the Security Council may, before making the recommendations or deciding upon the measures provided for in Article 39, call upon the parties concerned to comply with such provisional measures as it deems necessary or desirable. Such provisional measures shall be without prejudice to the rights, claims, or position of the parties concerned. The Security Council shall duly take account of failure to comply with such provisional measures.

Article 41

The Security Council may decide what measures not involving the use of armed force are to be employed to give effect to its decisions, and it may call upon the Members of the United Nations to apply such measures. These may include complete or partial interruption of economic relations and of rail, sea, air, postal, telegraphic, radio, and other means of communication, and the severance of diplomatic relations.

Article 42

Should the Security Council consider that measures provided for in Article 41 would be inadequate or have proved to be inadequate, it may take such action by air, sea, or land forces as may be necessary to maintain or restore international peace and security. Such action may include demonstrations, blockade, and other operations by air, sea, or land forces of Members of the United Nations.

Article 43

1. All Members of the United Nations, in order to contribute to the maintenance of international peace and security, undertake to make available to the Security Council, on its call and in accordance with a special agreement or agreements, armed forces, assistance, and facilities, including rights of passage, necessary for the purpose of maintaining international peace and security.

2. Such agreement or agreements shall govern the numbers and types of forces. their degree of readiness and general location, and the nature of the facilities and assistance to be provided.

3. The agreement or agreements shall be negotiated as soon as possible on the initiative of the Security Council. They shall be concluded between the Security Council and Members or between the Security Council and groups of Members and shall be subject to ratification by the signatory states in accordance with their respective constitutional processes.

Article 44

When the Security Council has decided to use force it shall, before calling upon a Member not represented on it to provide armed forces in fulfillment of the obligations assumed under Article 43, invite that Member, if the Member so desires, to participate in the decisions of the

Security Council concerning the employment of contingents of that Member's armed forces.

Article 45

In order to enable the United Nations to take urgent military measures Members shall hold immediately available national air-force contingents for combined international enforcement action. The strength and degree of readiness of these contingents and plans for their combined action shall be determined, within the limits laid down in the special agreement or agreements referred to in Article 43, by the Security Council with the assistance of the Military Staff Committee.

Article 46

Plans for the application of armed force shall be made by the Security Council with the assistance of the Military Staff Committee.

Article 47

1. There shall be established a Military Staff Committee to advise and assist the Security Council on all questions relating to the Security Council's military requirements for the maintenance of international peace and security, the employment and command of forces placed at its disposal, the regulation of armaments, and possible disarmament.
2. The Military Staff Committee shall consist of the Chiefs of Staff of the permanent members of the Security Council or their representatives. Any Member of the United Nations not permanently represented on the Committee shall be invited by the Committee to be associated with it when the efficient discharge of the Committee's responsibilities requires the participation of that Member in its work.
3. The Military Staff Committee shall be responsible under the Security Council for the strategic direction of any armed forces placed at the disposal of the Security Council. Questions relating to the command of such forces shall be worked out subsequently.
4. The Military Staff Committee, with the authorization of the Security Council and after consultation with appropriate regional agencies, may establish regional subcommittees.

Article 48

1. The action required to carry out the decisions of the Security Council for the maintenance of international peace and security shall be taken by all the Members of the United Nations or by some of them, as the Security Council may determine.
2. Such decisions shall be carried out by the Members of the United Nations directly and through their action in the appropriate international agencies of which they are members.

Article 49

The Members of the United Nations shall join in affording mutual assistance in carrying out the measures decided upon by the Security Council.

Article 50

If preventive or enforcement measures against any state are taken by the Security Council, any other state, whether a Member of the United Nations or not, which finds itself confronted with special economic problems arising from the carrying out of those measures shall have the right to consult the Security Council with regard to a solution of those problems.

Article 51

Nothing in the present Charter shall impair the inherent right of individual or collective self-defense if an armed attack occurs against a Member of the United Nations, until the Security Council has taken measures necessary to maintain international peace and security. Measures taken by Members in the exercise of this right of self-defense shall be immediately reported to the Security Council and shall not in any way affect the authority and responsibility of the Security Council under the present Charter to take at any time such action as it deems necessary in order to maintain or restore international peace and security.

CHAPTER VIII

Regional Arrangements

Article 52

1. Nothing in the present Charter precludes the existence of regional arrangements or agencies for dealing with such matters relating to

the maintenance of international peace and security as are appropriate for regional action, provided that such arrangements or agencies and their activities are consistent with the Purposes and Principles of the United Nations.

2. The Members of the United Nations entering into such arrangements or constituting such agencies shall make every effort to achieve pacific settlement of local disputes through such regional arrangements or by such regional agencies before referring them to the Security Council.

3. The Security Council shall encourage the development of pacific settlement of local disputes through such regional arrangements or by such regional agencies either on the initiative of the states concerned or by reference from the Security Council.

4. This Article in no way impairs the application of Articles 34 and 35.

Article 53

1. The Security Council shall, where appropriate, utilize such regional arrangements or agencies for enforcement action under its authority. But no enforcement action shall be taken under regional arrangements or by regional agencies without the authorization of the Security Council, with the exception of measures against any enemy state, as defined in paragraph 2 of this Article, provided for pursuant to Article 107 or in regional arrangements directed against renewal of aggressive policy on the part of any such state, until such time as the Organization may, on request of the Governments concerned, be charged with the responsibility for preventing further aggression by such a state.

2. The term enemy state as used in paragraph 1 of this Article applies to any state which during the Second World War has been an enemy of any signatory of the present Charter.

Article 54

The Security Council shall at all times be kept fully informed of activities undertaken or in contemplation under regional arrangements or by regional agencies for the maintenance of international peace and security.

CHAPTER IX

International Economic and Social Co-operation

Article 55

With a view to the creation of conditions of stability and well-being which are necessary for peaceful and friendly relations among nations based on respect for the principle of equal rights and self-determination of peoples, the United Nations shall promote:

a. higher standards of living, full employment, and conditions of economic and social progress and development;

b. solutions of international economic, social, health, and related problems; and international cultural and educational co-operation; and

c. universal respect for, and observance of, human rights and fundamental freedoms for all without distinction as to race, sex, language, or religion.

Article 56

All Members pledge themselves to take joint and separate action in co-operation with the Organization for the achievement of the purposes set forth in Article 55.

Article 57

1. The various specialized agencies, established by intergovernmental agreement and having wide international responsibilities, as defined in their basic instruments, in economic, social, cultural, educational, health, and related fields, shall be brought into relationship with the United Nations in accordance with the provisions of Article 63.

2. Such agencies thus brought into relationship with the United Nations are hereinafter referred to as specialized agencies.

Article 58

The Organization shall make recommendations for the coordination of the policies and activities of the specialized agencies.

Article 59

The Organization shall, where appropriate, initiate negotiations among the states concerned for the creation of any new specialized agencies required for the accomplishment of the purposes set forth in Article 55.

Article 60

Responsibility for the discharge of the functions of the Organization set forth in this Chapter shall be vested in the General Assembly and, under the authority of the General Assembly, in the Economic and Social Council, which shall have for this purpose the powers set forth in Chapter X.

CHAPTER X

The Economic and Social Council

Composition

Article 61

1. The Economic and Social Council shall consist of fifty-four Members of the United Nations elected by the General Assembly.
2. Subject to the provisions of paragraph 3, eighteen members of the Economic and Social Council shall be elected each year for a term of three years. A retiring member shall be eligible for immediate re-election.
3. At the first election after the increase in the membership of the Economic and Social Council from twenty-seven to fifty-four members, in addition to the members elected in place of the nine members whose term of office expires at the end of that year, twenty-seven additional members shall be elected. Of these twenty-seven additional members, the term of office of nine members so elected shall expire at the end of one year, and of nine other members at the end of two years, in accordance with arrangements made by the General Assembly.
4. Each member of the Economic and Social Council shall have one representative.

Functions and Powers

Article 62

1. The Economic and Social Council may make or initiate studies and reports with respect to international economic, social, cultural, educational, health, and related matters and may make recommendations with respect to any such matters to the General Assembly, to the Members of the United Nations, and to the specialized agencies concerned.
2. It may make recommendations for the purpose of promoting respect for, and observance of, human rights and fundamental freedoms for all.
3. It may prepare draft conventions for submission to the General Assembly, with respect to matters falling within its competence.
4. It may call, in accordance with the rules prescribed by the United Nations, international conferences on matters falling within its competence.

Article 63

1. The Economic and Social Council may enter into agreements with any of the agencies referred to in Article 57, defining the terms on which the agency concerned shall be brought into relationship with the United Nations. Such agreements shall be subject to approval by the General Assembly.
2. It may coordinate the activities of the specialized agencies through consultation with and recommendations to such agencies and through recommendations to the General Assembly and to the Members of the United Nations.

Article 64

1. The Economic and Social Council may take appropriate steps to obtain regular reports from the specialized agencies. It may make arrangements with the Members of the United Nations and with the specialized agencies to obtain reports on the steps taken to give effect to its own recommendations and to recommendations on matters falling within its competence made by the General Assembly.
2. It may communicate its observations on these reports to the General Assembly.

Article 65

The Economic and Social Council may furnish information to the Security Council and shall assist the Security Council upon its request.

Article 66

1. The Economic and Social Council shall perform such functions as fall within its competence in connection with the carrying out of the recommendations of the General Assembly.
2. It may, with the approval of the General Assembly, perform services at the request of Members of the United Nations and at the request of specialized agencies.
3. It shall perform such other functions as are specified elsewhere in the present Charter or as may be assigned to it by the General Assembly.

Voting

Article 67

1. Each member of the Economic and Social Council shall have one vote.
2. Decisions of the Economic and Social Council shall be made by a majority of the members present and voting.

Procedure

Article 68

The Economic and Social Council shall set up commissions in economic and social fields and for the promotion of human rights, and such other commissions as may be required for the performance of its functions.

Article 69

The Economic and Social Council shall invite any Member of the United Nations to participate, without vote, in its deliberations on any matter of particular concern to that Member.

Article 70

The Economic and Social Council may make arrangements for representatives of the specialized agencies to participate, without vote, in its deliberations and in those of the commissions established by it, and for its representatives to participate in the deliberations of the specialized agencies.

Article 71
The Economic and Social Council may make suitable arrangements for consultation with non-governmental organizations which are concerned with matters within its competence. Such arrangements may be made with international organizations and, where appropriate, with national organizations after consultation with the Member of the United Nations concerned.

Article 72
1. The Economic and Social Council shall adopt its own rules of procedure, including the method of selecting its President.
2. The Economic and Social Council shall meet as required in accordance with its rules, which shall include provision for the convening of meetings on the request of a majority of its members.

CHAPTER XI

Declaration Regarding Non-Self-Governing Territories

Article 73
Members of the United Nations which have or assume responsibilities for the administration of territories whose peoples have not yet attained a full measure of self-government recognize the principle that the interests of the inhabitants of these territories are paramount, and accept as a sacred trust the obligation to promote to the utmost, within the system of international peace and security established by the present Charter, the well-being of the inhabitants of these territories, and, to this end:
   a. to ensure, with due respect for the culture of the peoples concerned, their political, economic, social, and educational advancement, their just treatment, and their protection against abuses;
   b. to develop self-government, to take due account of the political aspirations of the peoples, and to assist them in the progressive development of their free political institutions, according to the particular circumstances of each territory and its peoples and their varying stages of advancement;

c. to further international peace and security;
d. to promote constructive measures of development, to encourage research, and to cooperate with one another and, when and where appropriate, with specialized international bodies with a view to the practical achievement of the social, economic, and scientific purposes set forth in this Article; and
e. to transmit regularly to the Secretary-General for information purposes, subject to such limitation as security and constitutional considerations may require, statistical and other information of a technical nature relating to economic, social, and educational conditions in the territories for which they are respectively responsible other than those territories to which Chapter XII and XIII apply.

Article 74

Members of the United Nations also agree that their policy in respect of the territories to which this Chapter applies, no less than in respect of their metropolitan areas, must be based on the general principle of good-neighborliness, due account being taken of the interests and well-being of the rest of the world, in social, economic, and commercial matters.

CHAPTER XII

International Trusteeship System

Article 75

The United Nations shall establish under its authority an international trusteeship system for the administration and supervision of such territories as may be placed thereunder by subsequent individual agreements. These territories are hereinafter referred to as trust territories.

Article 76

The basic objectives of the trusteeship system, in accordance with the Purposes of the United Nations laid down in Article 1 of the present Charter, shall be:

a. to further international peace and security;
b. to promote the political, economic, social, and educational advancement of the inhabitants of the trust territories, and their

progressive development towards self-government or independence as may be appropriate to the particular circumstances of each territory and its peoples and the freely expressed wishes of the peoples concerned, and as may be provided by the terms of each trusteeship agreement;

c. to encourage respect for human rights and for fundamental freedoms for all without distinction as to race, sex, language, or religion, and to encourage recognition of the interdependence of the peoples of the world; and

d. to ensure equal treatment in social, economic, and commercial matters for all Members of the United Nations and their nationals and also equal treatment for the latter in the administration of justice without prejudice to the attainment of the foregoing objectives and subject to the provisions of Article 80.

Article 77

1. The trusteeship system shall apply to such territories in the following categories as may be placed thereunder by means of trusteeship agreements:
   a. territories now held under mandate;
   b. territories which may be detached from enemy states as a result of the Second World War, and
   c. territories voluntarily placed under the system by states responsible for their administration.
2. It will be a matter for subsequent agreement as to which territories in the foregoing categories will be brought under the trusteeship system and upon what terms.

Article 78

The trusteeship system shall not apply to territories which have become Members of the United Nations, relationship among which shall be based on respect for the principle of sovereign equality.

Article 79

The terms of trusteeship for each territory to be placed under the trusteeship system, including any alteration or amendment, shall be agreed upon by the states directly concerned, including the mandatory power in the case of territories held under mandate by a Member of the United Nations, and shall be approved as provided for in Articles 83 and 85.

Article 80

1. Except as may be agreed upon in individual trusteeship agreements, made under Articles 77, 79, and 81, placing each territory under the trusteeship system, and until such agreements have been concluded, nothing in this Chapter shall be construed in or of itself to alter in any manner the rights whatsoever of any states or any peoples or the terms of existing international instruments to which Members of the United Nations may respectively be parties.

2. Paragraph 1 of this Article shall not be interpreted as giving grounds for delay or postponement of the negotiation and conclusion of agreements for placing mandated and other territories under the trusteeship system as provided for in Article 77.

Article 81

The trusteeship agreement shall in each case include the terms under which the trust territory will be administered and designate the authority which will exercise the administration of the trust territory. Such authority, hereinafter called the administering authority, may be one or more states or the Organization itself.

Article 82

There may be designated, in any trusteeship agreement, a strategic area or areas which may include part or all of the trust territory to which the agreement applies, without prejudice to any special agreement or agreements made under Article 43.

Article 83

1. All functions of the United Nations relating to strategic areas, including the approval of the terms of the trusteeship agreements and of their alteration or amendment, shall be exercised by the Security Council.

2. The basic objectives set forth in Article 76 shall be applicable to the people of each strategic area.

3. The Security Council shall, subject to the provisions of the trusteeship agreements and without prejudice to security considerations, avail itself of the assistance of the Trusteeship Council to perform those functions of the United Nations under the trusteeship system relating to political. economic, social, and educational matters in the strategic areas.

Article 84

It shall be the duty of the administering authority to ensure that the trust territory shall play its part in the maintenance of international peace and security. To this end the administering authority may make use of volunteer forces, facilities, and assistance from the trust territory in carrying out the obligations towards the Security Council undertaken in this regard by the administering authority, as well as for local defense and the maintenance of law and order within the trust territory.

Article 85

1. The functions of the United Nations with regard to trusteeship agreements for all areas not designated as strategic, including the approval of the terms of the trusteeship agreements and of their alteration or amendment, shall be exercised by the General Assembly.
2. The Trusteeship Council, operating under the authority of the General Assembly, shall assist the General Assembly in carrying out these functions.

CHAPTER XIII

The Trusteeship Council

Composition

Article 86

1. The Trusteeship Council shall consist of the following Members of the United Nations:
   a. those Members administering trust territories;
   b. such of those Members mentioned by name in Article 23 as are not administering trust territories; and
   c. as many other Members elected for three-year terms by the General Assembly as may be necessary to ensure that the total number of members of the Trusteeship Council is equally divided between those Members of the United Nations which administer trust territories and those which do not.
2. Each member of the Trusteeship Council shall designate one specially qualified person to represent it therein.

Functions and Powers

Article 87

The General Assembly and, under its authority, the Trusteeship Council, in carrying out their functions, may:

   a. consider reports submitted by the administering authority;

   b. accept petitions and examine them in consultation with the administering authority;

   c. provide for periodic visits to the respective trust territories at times agreed upon with the administering authority; and

   d. take these and other actions in conformity with the terms of the trusteeship agreements.

Article 88

The Trusteeship Council shall formulate a questionnaire on the political, economic, social, and educational advancement of the inhabitants of each trust territory, and the administering authority for each trust territory within the competence of the General Assembly shall make an annual report to the General Assembly upon the basis of such questionnaire.

Voting

Article 89

   1. Each member of the Trusteeship Council shall have one vote.

   2. Decisions of the Trusteeship Council shall be made by a majority of the members present and voting.

Procedure

Article 90

   1. The Trusteeship Council shall adopt its own rules of procedure, including the method of selecting its President.

   2. The Trusteeship Council shall meet as required in accordance with its rules, which shall include provision for the convening of meetings on the request of a majority of its members.

Article 91

The Trusteeship Council shall, when appropriate, avail itself of the assistance of the Economic and Social Council and of the specialized agencies in regard to matters with which they are respectively concerned.

CHAPTER XIV

The International Court of Justice

Article 92
The International Court of Justice shall be the principal judicial organ of the United Nations. It shall function in accordance with the annexed Statute which is based upon the Statute of the Permanent Court of International Justice and forms an integral part of the present Charter.

Article 93
1. All Members of the United Nations are ipso facto parties to the Statute of the International Court of Justice.
2. A state which is not a Member of the United Nations may become a party to the Statute of the International Court of Justice on conditions to be determined in each case by the General Assembly upon the recommendation of the Security Council.

Article 94
1. Each Member of the United Nations undertakes to comply with the decision of the International Court of Justice in any case to which it is a party.
2. If any party to a case fails to perform the obligations incumbent upon it under a judgment rendered by the Court, the other party may have recourse to the Security Council, which may, if it deems necessary, make recommendations or decide upon measures to be taken to give effect to the judgment.

Article 95
Nothing in the present Charter shall prevent Members of the United Nations from entrusting the solution of their differences to other tribunals by virtue of agreements already in existence or which may be concluded in the future.

Article 96

1. The General Assembly or the Security Council may request the International Court of Justice to give an advisory opinion on any legal question.
2. Other organs of the United Nations and specialized agencies, which may at any time be so authorized by the General Assembly, may also request advisory opinions of the Court on legal questions arising within the scope of their activities.

CHAPTER XV

The Secretariat

Article 97

The Secretariat shall comprise a Secretary-General and such staff as the Organization may require. The Secretary-General shall be appointed by the General Assembly upon the recommendation of the Security Council. He shall be the chief administrative officer of the Organization.

Article 98

The Secretary-General shall act in that capacity in all meetings of the General Assembly, of the Security Council, of the Economic and Social Council, and of the Trusteeship Council, and shall perform such other functions as are entrusted to him by these organs. The Secretary-General shall make an annual report to the General Assembly on the work of the Organization.

Article 99

The Secretary-General may bring to the attention of the Security Council any matter which in his opinion may threaten the maintenance of international peace and security.

Article 100

1. In the performance of their duties the Secretary-General and the staff shall not seek or receive instructions from any government or from any other authority external to the Organization. They shall

refrain from any action which might reflect on their position as international officials responsible only to the Organization.

2. Each Member of the United Nations undertakes to respect the exclusively international character of the responsibilities of the Secretary-General and the staff and not to seek to influence them in the discharge of their responsibilities.

Article 101

1. The staff shall be appointed by the Secretary-General under regulations established by the General Assembly.
2. Appropriate staffs shall be permanently assigned to the Economic and Social Council, the Trusteeship Council, and, as required, to other organs of the United Nations. These staffs shall form a part of the Secretariat.
3. The paramount consideration in the employment of the staff and in the determination of the conditions of service shall be the necessity of securing the highest standards of efficiency, competence, and integrity. Due regard shall be paid to the importance of recruiting the staff on as wide a geographical basis as possible.

CHAPTER XVI

Miscellaneous Provisions

Article 102

1. Every treaty and every international agreement entered into by any Member of the United Nations after the present Charter comes into force shall as soon as possible be registered with the Secretariat and published by it.
2. No party to any such treaty or international agreement which has not been registered in accordance with the provisions of paragraph I of this Article may invoke that treaty or agreement before any organ of the United Nations.

Article 103

In the event of a conflict between the obligations of the Members of the United Nations under the present Charter and their obligations under any other international agreement, their obligations under the present Charter shall prevail.

Article 104

The Organization shall enjoy in the territory of each of its Members such legal capacity as may be necessary for the exercise of its functions and the fulfillment of its purposes.

Article 105

1. The Organization shall enjoy in the territory of each of its Members such privileges and immunities as are necessary for the fulfillment of its purposes.
2. Representatives of the Members of the United Nations and officials of the Organization shall similarly enjoy such privileges and immunities as are necessary for the independent exercise of their functions in connection with the Organization.
3. The General Assembly may make recommendations with a view to determining the details of the application of paragraphs 1 and 2 of this Article or may propose conventions to the Members of the United Nations for this purpose.

CHAPTER XVII

Transitional Security Arrangements

Article 106

Pending the coming into force of such special agreements referred to in Article 43 as in the opinion of the Security Council enable it to begin the exercise of its responsibilities under Article 42, the parties to the Four-Nation Declaration, signed at Moscow October 30, 1943, and France, shall, in accordance with the provisions of paragraph 5 of that Declaration, consult with one another and as occasion requires with other Members of the United Nations with a view to such joint action on behalf of the Organization as may be necessary for the purpose of maintaining international peace and security.

Article 107

Nothing in the present Charter shall invalidate or preclude action, in relation to any state which during the Second World War has been an enemy of any signatory to the present Charter, taken or authorized as a result of that war by the Governments having responsibility for such action.

CHAPTER XVIII

Amendments

Article 108
Amendments to the present Charter shall come into force for all Members of the United Nations when they have been adopted by a vote of two thirds of the members of the General Assembly and ratified in accordance with their respective constitutional processes by two thirds of the Members of the United Nations, including all the permanent members of the Security Council.

Article 109
1. A General Conference of the Members of the United Nations for the purpose of reviewing the present Charter may be held at a date and place to be fixed by a two-thirds vote of the members of the General Assembly and by a vote of any seven members of the Security Council. Each Member of the United Nations shall have one vote in the conference.
2. Any alteration of the present Charter recommended by a two-thirds vote of the conference shall take effect when ratified in accordance with their respective constitutional processes by two thirds of the Members of the United Nations including all the permanent members of the Security Council.
3. If such a conference has not been held before the tenth annual session of the General Assembly following the coming into force of the present Charter, the proposal to call such a conference shall be placed on the agenda of that session of the General Assembly, and the conference shall be held if so decided by a majority vote of the members of the General Assembly and by a vote of any seven members of the Security Council.

CHAPTER XIX

Ratification and Signature

Article 110
1. The present Charter shall be ratified by the signatory states in accordance with their respective constitutional processes.

2. The ratifications shall be deposited with the Government of the United States of America, which shall notify all the signatory states of each deposit as well as the Secretary-General of the Organization when he has been appointed.

3. The present Charter shall come into force upon the deposit of ratifications by the Republic of China, France, the Union of Soviet Socialist Republics, the United Kingdom of Great Britain and Northern Ireland, and the United States of America, and by a majority of the other signatory states. A protocol of the ratifications deposited shall thereupon be drawn up by the Government of the United States of America which shall communicate copies thereof to all the signatory states.

4. The states signatory to the present Charter which ratify it after it has come into force will become original Members of the United Nations on the date of the deposit of their respective ratifications.

Article 111

The present Charter, of which the Chinese, French, Russian, English, and Spanish texts are equally authentic, shall remain deposited in the archives of the Government of the United States of America. Duly certified copies thereof shall be transmitted by that Government to the Governments of the other signatory states.

IN FAITH WHEREOF the representatives of the Governments of the United Nations have signed the present Charter.

DONE at the city of San Francisco the twenty-sixth day of June, one thousand nine hundred and forty-five.

Appendix B
Universal Declaration of Human Rights Adopted by the General Assembly on 19 December 1948

Preamble

Whereas recognition of the inherent dignity and of the equal and inalienable rights of all members of the human family is the foundation of freedom, justice and peace in the world,

Whereas disregard and contempt for human rights have resulted in barbarous acts which have outraged the conscience of mankind, and the advent of a world in which human beings shall enjoy freedom of speech and belief and freedom from fear and want has been proclaimed as the highest aspiration of the common people,

Whereas it is essential, if man is not to be compelled to have recourse, as a last resort, to rebellion against tyranny and oppression, that human rights should be protected by the rule of law,

Whereas it is essential to promote the development of friendly relations between nations,

Whereas the peoples of the United Nations have in the Charter reaffirmed their faith in fundamental human rights, in the dignity and worth of the human person and in the equal rights of men and women and have determined to promote social progress and better standards of life in larger freedom,

Whereas Member States have pledged themselves to achieve, in co-operation with the United Nations, the promotion of universal respect for and observance of human rights and fundamental freedoms,

Whereas a common understanding of these rights and freedoms is of the greatest importance for the full realization of this pledge,

Now, Therefore THE GENERAL ASSEMBLY proclaims THIS UNIVERSAL DECLARATION OF HUMAN RIGHTS as a common

standard of achievement for all peoples and all nations, to the end
that every individual and every organ of society, keeping this Declaration constantly in mind, shall strive by teaching and education to
promote respect for these rights and freedoms and by progressive
measures, national and international, to secure their universal and effective recognition and observance, both among the peoples of Member States themselves and among the peoples of territories under their
jurisdiction.

Article 1
All human beings are born free and equal in dignity and rights. They are
endowed with reason and conscience and should act towards one another in a spirit of brotherhood.

Article 2
Everyone is entitled to all the rights and freedoms set forth in this Declaration, without distinction of any kind, such as race, colour, sex,
language, religion, political or other opinion, national or social origin, property, birth or other status. Furthermore, no distinction shall
be made on the basis of the political, jurisdictional or international
status of the country or territory to which a person belongs, whether
it be independent, trust, non-self-governing or under any other limitation of sovereignty.

Article 3
Everyone has the right to life, liberty and security of person.

Article 4
No one shall be held in slavery or servitude; slavery and the slave trade
shall be prohibited in all their forms.

Article 5
No one shall be subjected to torture or to cruel, inhuman or degrading
treatment or punishment.

Article 6
Everyone has the right to recognition everywhere as a person before the
law.

Article 7

All are equal before the law and are entitled without any discrimination to equal protection of the law. All are entitled to equal protection against any discrimination in violation of this Declaration and against any incitement to such discrimination.

Article 8

Everyone has the right to an effective remedy by the competent national tribunals for acts violating the fundamental rights granted him by the constitution or by law.

Article 9

No one shall be subjected to arbitrary arrest, detention or exile.

Article 10

Everyone is entitled in full equality to a fair and public hearing by an independent and impartial tribunal, in the determination of his rights and obligations and of any criminal charge against him.

Article 11

1. Everyone charged with a penal offence has the right to be presumed innocent until proved guilty according to law in a public trial at which he has had all the guarantees necessary for his defence.
2. No one shall be held guilty of any penal offence on account of any act or omission which did not constitute a penal offence, under national or international law, at the time when it was committed. Nor shall a heavier penalty be imposed than the one that was applicable at the time the penal offence was committed.

Article 12

No one shall be subjected to arbitrary interference with his privacy, family, home or correspondence, nor to attacks upon his honour and reputation. Everyone has the right to the protection of the law against such interference or attacks.

Article 13

1. Everyone has the right to freedom of movement and residence within the borders of each state.

2. Everyone has the right to leave any country, including his own, and to return to his country.

Article 14

1. Everyone has the right to seek and to enjoy in other countries asylum from persecution.
2. This right may not be invoked in the case of prosecutions genuinely arising from non-political crimes or from acts contrary to the purposes and principles of the United Nations.

Article 15

1. Everyone has the right to a nationality.
2. No one shall be arbitrarily deprived of his nationality nor denied the right to change his nationality.

Article 16

1. Men and women of full age, without any limitation due to race, nationality or religion, have the right to marry and to found a family. They are entitled to equal rights as to marriage, during marriage and at its dissolution.
2. Marriage shall be entered into only with the free and full consent of the intending spouses.
3. The family is the natural and fundamental group unit of society and is entitled to protection by society and the State.

Article 17

1. Everyone has the right to own property alone as well as in association with others.
2. No one shall be arbitrarily deprived of his property.

Article 18

Everyone has the right to freedom of thought, conscience and religion; this right includes freedom to change his religion or belief, and freedom, either alone or in community with others and in public or private, to manifest his religion or belief in teaching, practice, worship and observance.

Article 19

Everyone has the right to freedom of opinion and expression; this right includes freedom to hold opinions without interference and to seek, receive and impart information and ideas through any media and regardless of frontiers.

Article 20

1. Everyone has the right to freedom of peaceful assembly and association.
2. No one may be compelled to belong to an association.

Article 21

1. Everyone has the right to take part in the government of his country, directly or through freely chosen representatives.
2. Everyone has the right of equal access to public service in his country.
3. The will of the people shall be the basis of the authority of government; this will shall be expressed in periodic and genuine elections which shall be by universal and equal suffrage and shall be held by secret vote or by equivalent free voting procedures.

Article 22

Everyone, as a member of society, has the right to social security and is entitled to realization, through national effort and international cooperation and in accordance with the organization and resources of each State, of the economic, social and cultural rights indispensable for his dignity and the free development of his personality.

Article 23

1. Everyone has the right to work, to free choice of employment, to just and favourable conditions of work and to protection against unemployment.
2. Everyone, without any discrimination, has the right to equal pay for equal work.
3. Everyone who works has the right to just and favourable remuneration ensuring for himself and his family an existence worthy

of human dignity, and supplemented, if necessary, by other means of social protection.

4. Everyone has the right to form and to join trade unions for the protection of his interests.

Article 24

Everyone has the right to rest and leisure, including reasonable limitation of working hours and periodic holidays with pay.

Article 25

1. Everyone has the right to a standard of living adequate for the health and well-being of himself and of his family, including food, clothing, housing and medical care and necessary social services, and the right to security in the event of unemployment, sickness, disability, widowhood, old age or other lack of livelihood in circumstances beyond his control.

2. Motherhood and childhood are entitled to special care and assistance. All children, whether born in or out of wedlock, shall enjoy the same social protection.

Article 26

1. Everyone has the right to education. Education shall be free, at least in the elementary and fundamental stages. Elementary education shall be compulsory. Technical and professional education shall be made generally available and higher education shall be equally accessible to all on the basis of merit.

2. Education shall be directed to the full development of the human personality and to the strengthening of respect for human rights and fundamental freedoms. It shall promote understanding, tolerance and friendship among all nations, racial or religious groups, and shall further the activities of the United Nations for the maintenance of peace.

3. Parents have a prior right to choose the kind of education that shall be given to their children.

Article 27

1. Everyone has the right freely to participate in the cultural life of the community, to enjoy the arts and to share in scientific advancement and its benefits.

2. Everyone has the right to the protection of the moral and material interests resulting from any scientific, literary or artistic production of which he is the author.

Article 28

Everyone is entitled to a social and international order in which the rights and freedoms set forth in this Declaration can be fully realized.

Article 29

1. Everyone has duties to the community in which alone the free and full development of his personality is possible.
2. In the exercise of his rights and freedoms, everyone shall be subject only to such limitations as are determined by law solely for the purpose of securing due recognition and respect for the rights and freedoms of others and of meeting the just requirements of morality, public order and the general welfare in a democratic society.
3. These rights and freedoms may in no case be exercised contrary to the purposes and principles of the United Nations.

Article 30

Nothing in this Declaration may be interpreted as implying for any State, group or person any right to engage in any activity or to perform any act aimed at the destruction of any of the rights and freedoms set forth herein.

Appendix C
Membership of the United Nations

Year	Number	Member States
1945	Original 51	Argentina, Australia, Belgium, Bolivia, Brazil, Belarus, Canada, Chile, China, Colombia, Costa Rica, Cuba, Czechoslovakia, Denmark, Dominican Republic, Ecuador, Egypt, El Salvador, Ethiopia, France, Greece, Guatemala, Haiti, Honduras, India, Iran, Iraq, Lebanon, Liberia, Luxembourg, Mexico, Netherlands, New Zealand, Nicaragua, Norway, Panama, Paraguay, Peru, Philippines, Poland, Russian Federation, Saudi Arabia, South Africa, Syrian Arab Republic, Turkey, Ukraine, United Kingdom of Great Britain and Northern Ireland, United States of America, Uruguay, Bolivarian Republic of Venezuela, Yugoslavia*
1946	55	Afghanistan, Iceland, Sweden, Thailand
1947	57	Pakistan, Yemen
1948	58	Myanmar
1949	59	Israel
1950	60	Indonesia
1955	76	Albania, Austria, Bulgaria, Cambodia, Finland, Hungary, Ireland, Italy, Jordan, Lao People's Democratic Republic, Libyan Arab Jamahiriya, Nepal, Portugal, Romania, Spain, Sri Lanka
1956	80	Japan, Morocco, Sudan, Tunisia
1957	82	Ghana, Malaysia
1958	82	Guinea
1960	99	Benin, Burkina Faso, Cameroon, Central African Republic, Chad, Congo, Côte d'Ivoire, Cyprus, Democratic Republic of the Congo, Gabon, Madagascar, Mali, Niger, Nigeria, Senegal, Somalia, Togo
1961	104	Mauritania, Mongolia, Sierra Leone, United Republic of Tanzania

Year	Number	Member States
1962	110	Algeria, Burundi, Jamaica, Rwanda, Trinidad and Tobago, Uganda
1963	112	Kenya, Kuwait
1964	115	Malawi, Malta, Zambia
1965	117	Gambia, Maldives, Singapore
1966	122	Barbados, Botswana, Guyana, Lesotho
1967	123	Democratic Yemen
1968	126	Equatorial Guinea, Mauritius, Swaziland
1970	127	Fiji
1971	132	Bahrain, Bhutan, Oman, Qatar, United Arab Emirates
1973	135	Bahamas, Federal Republic of Germany, German Democratic Republic**
1974	138	Bangladesh, Grenada, Guinea-Bissau
1975	144	Cape Verde, Comoros, Mozambique, Papua New Guinea, Sao Tome and Principe, Suriname
1976	147	Angola, Samoa, Seychelles
1977	149	Djibouti, Viet Nam
1978	151	Dominica, Solomon Islands
1979	152	Saint Lucia
1980	154	Saint Vincent and the Grenadines, Zimbabwe
1981	157	Antigua and Barbuda, Belize, Vanuatu
1983	158	Saint Kitts and Nevis
1984	159	Brunei Darussalam
1990	159**	Liechtenstein, Namibia
1991	166	Democratic People's Republic of Korea, Estonia, Federated States of Micronesia, Latvia, Lithuania, Marshall Islands, Republic of Korea
1992	179	Armenia, Azerbaijan, Bosnia and Herzegovina* Croatia,* Georgia, Kazakhstan, Kyrgyzstan, Moldova, San Marino, Slovenia,* Tajikistan, Turkmenistan, Uzbekistan
1993	184	Andorra, Czech Republic, Eritrea, Monaco, Slovak Republic, The former Yugoslav Republic of Macedonia*
1994	185	Palau
1999	188	Kiribati, Nauru, Tonga
2000	189	Tuvalu, Serbia and Montenegro*
2002	191	Switzerland, Timor-Leste

*The Socialist Federal Republic of Yugoslavia was an original member of the United Nations until its dissolution following the establishment of Bosnia and Herzegovina, the Republic of Croatia, the Republic of Slovenia, the former Yugoslav Republic of Macedonia, and the Federal Republic of Yugoslavia. The General Assembly admitted Bosnia and Herzegovina on 22 May 1992 and Croatia and Slovenia on 22 May 1992. On 8 April 1993, the Assembly admitted as a member of the United Nations the state "The Former Yugoslav Republic of Macedonia" pending settlement of differences over its proper name.

The Federal Republic of Yugoslavia was admitted as a Member of the United Nations by the General Assembly on 1 November 2000.

Since 4 February 2003, the state of the Federal Republic of Yugoslavia is known as Serbia and Montenegro.

**The Federal Republic of Germany and the German Democratic Republic became members of the United Nations on 18 September 1973. Since 1990, the two German States merged to form one sovereign state.

Source: "Basics facts about the UN," DPI, 2000.

Appendix D
Assessed Contributions* to the UN Regular Budget of the 15 Largest Assessed Contributors for 2003–2004 (Percentage of Total Assessed Contributions and Change in Ranked Position)

UN Regular Budget for 2004: US$ 1,483
UN Regular Budget for 2003: US$ 1,409

Country	Total Assessment 2004	Percentage of Assessment 2004	Total Assessment 2003	Percentage of Assessment 2003	Percent Change from Previous Year	Change in Ranked Position (Previous Rank in Parentheses)
US	363	24.477%	341	24.202%	0.276%	1 (1)
Japan	280	18.881%	263	18.666%	0.215%	2 (2)
Germany	124	8.361%	132	9.368%	-1.007%	3 (3)
United Kingdom	88	5.934%	75	5.323%	0.611%	4 (5)
France	87	5.866%	87	6.175%	-0.308%	5 (4)
Italy	70	4.720%	68	4.826%	-0.106%	6 (6)
Canada	40	2.697%	35	2.484%	0.213%	7 (7)
Spain	36	2.428%	34	2.413%	0.014%	8 (8)
China	29	1.955%	21	1.490%	0.465%	9 (13)
Mexico	27	1.821%	-	-	-	10 (-)
Republic of Korea	26	1.753%	25	1.774%	-0.021%	11 (10)
Netherlands	24	1.618%	23	1.632%	-0.014%	12 (11)
Australia	23	1.551%	22	1.561%	-0.010%	13 (12)
Brazil	22	1.483%	32	2.271%	-0.788%	14 (9)
Switzerland	17	1.146%	17	1.207%	-0.060%	15 (14)

* Sums in $US millions, rounded to the nearest million.
Source: UN Documents, www.globalpolicy.org/finance/tables/reg-budget/assessedlarge04.htm

453

Appendix E
Nomenclature of the United Nations System

The United Nations system

PRINCIPAL ORGANS

Trusteeship Council | Security Council | General Assembly | Economic and Social Council | International Court of Justice | Secretariat

Subsidiary Bodies
Military Staff Committee
Standing Committee and ad hoc bodies
International Criminal Tribunal for the Former Yugoslavia
International Criminal Tribunal for Rwanda
UN Monitoring, Verification and Inspection Commission (Iraq)
United Nations Compensation Commission
Peacekeeping Operations and Missions

Subsidiary Bodies
Main committees
Other sessional committees
Standing committees and ad hoc bodies
Other subsidiary organs

Programmes and Funds
UNCTAD United Nations Conference on Trade and Development
ITC International Trade Centre (UNCTAD/WTO)
UNDCP United Nations Drug Control Programme[1]
UNEP United Nations Environment Programme
UNICEF United Nations Children's Fund

UNDP United Nations Development Programme
UNIFEM United Nations Development Fund for Women
UNV United Nations Volunteers
UNCDF United Nations Capital Development Fund
UNFPA United Nations Population Fund

UNHCR Office of the United Nations High Commissioner for Refugees
WFP World Food Programme
UNRWA[2] United Nations Relief and Works Agency for Palestine Refugees in the Near East
UN-HABITAT United Nations Human Settlements Programme (UNHSP)

Research and Training Institutes
UNICRI United Nations Interregional Crime and Justice Research Institute
UNITAR United Nations Institute for Training and Research

UNRISD United Nations Research Institute for Social Development
UNIDIR[2] United Nations Institute for Disarmament Research

INSTRAW International Research and Training Institute for the Advancement of Women

Other UN Entities
OHCHR Office of the United Nations High Commissioner for Human Rights
UNOPS United Nations Office for Project Services
UNU United Nations University
UNSSC United Nations System Staff College
UNAIDS Joint United Nations Programme on HIV/AIDS

Functional Commissions
Commissions on:
Human Rights
Narcotic Drugs
Crime Prevention and Criminal Justice
Science and Technology for Development
Sustainable Development
Status of Women
Population and Development
Commission for Social Development
Statistical Commission

Regional Commissions
Economic Commission for Africa (ECA)
Economic Commission for Europe (ECE)
Economic Commission for Latin America and the Caribbean (ECLAC)
Economic and Social Commission for Asia and the Pacific (ESCAP)
Economic and Social Commission for Western Asia (ESCWA)

Other Bodies
Permanent Forum on Indigenous Issues (PFII)
United Nations Forum on Forests
Sessional and standing committees
Expert, ad hoc and related bodies

Related Organizations
WTO[3] World Trade Organization
IAEA[4] International Atomic Energy Agency
CTBTO Prep.Com[5] PrepCom for the Nuclear-Test-Ban-Treaty Organization
OPCW[5] Organization for the Prohibition of Chemical Weapons

Specialized Agencies[6]
ILO International Labour Organization
FAO Food and Agriculture Organization of the United Nations
UNESCO United Nations Educational, Scientific and Cultural Organization
WHO World Health Organization

WORLD BANK GROUP
IBRD International Bank for Reconstruction and Development
IDA International Development Association
IFC International Finance Corporation
MIGA Multilateral Investment Guarantee Agency
ICSID International Centre for Settlement of Investment Disputes

IMF International Monetary Fund
ICAO International Civil Aviation Organization
IMO International Maritime Organization
ITU International Telecommunication Union
UPU Universal Postal Union
WMO World Meteorological Organization
WIPO World Intellectual Property Organization
IFAD International Fund for Agricultural Development
UNIDO United Nations Industrial Development Organization
WTO[5] World Tourism Organization

Departments and Offices
OSG Office of the Secretary-General
OIOS Office of Internal Oversight Services
OLA Office of Legal Affairs
DPA Department of Political Affairs
DDA Department for Disarmament Affairs
DPKO Department of Peacekeeping Operations
OCHA Office for the Coordination of Humanitarian Affairs
DESA Department of Economic and Social Affairs
DGACM Department for General Assembly and Conference Management
DPI Department of Public Information
DM Department of Management
OHRLLS Office of the High Representative for the Least Developed Countries, Landlocked Developing Countries and Small Island Developing States
UNSECOORD Office of the United Nations Security Coordinator
UNODC United Nations Office on Drugs and Crime
UNOG UN Office at Geneva
UNOV UN Office at Vienna
UNON UN Office at Nairobi

Notes: Solid lines from a Principal Organ indicate a direct reporting relationship; dashes indicate a non-subsidiary relationship. [1] The UN Drug Control Programme is part of the UN Office on Drugs and Crime. [2] UNRWA and UNIDIR report only to the GA. [3] The World Trade Organization and World Tourism Organization use the same acronym. [4] IAEA reports to the Security Council and the General Assembly (GA). [5] The CTBTO Prep.Com and OPCW report to the GA. [6] Specialized agencies are autonomous organizations working with the UN and each other through the coordinating machinery of the ECOSOC at the intergovernmental level, and through the Chief Executives Board for coordination (CEB) at the inter-secretariat level.

Published by the UN Department of Public Information
DPI/2342—March 2004

Appendix F
Timelines

PEACEKEEPING: ONGOING AND PRINCIPAL OPERATIONS

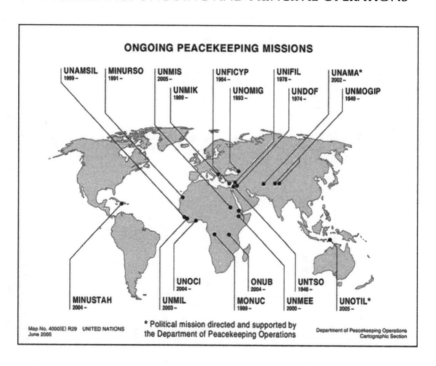

Date	Mission	Peak Authorized Strength Total Expenditures	Purpose
1947–1952	United Nations Special Committee on the Balkans (UNSCOB)	40	Monitor violations of Greek border
1948–	UN Truce Supervision Organization (UNTSO)	570 $27.69m*	Monitor Arab-Israeli ceasefire
1949–	UN Military Observer Group in India and Pakistan (UNMOGIP)	102 $7.25m*	Monitor India-Pakistan cease-fire in Kashmir
1956–1967	UN Emergency Force I (UNEF I)	6,073 $214.2m	Supervise withdrawal of foreign troops from Suez Canal and act as a buffer between Egypt and Israel
1958	UN Observation Group in Lebanon (UNOGIL)	591 $3.7m	Prevent troops and clandestine aid from Syria into Lebanon
1960–1964	UN Operation in the Congo (ONUC)	19,828 $400.1m	Maintain public order, prevent foreign intervention and preserve territorial integrity of Congo
1962–1963	UN Security Force in West New Guinea (UNSF)	1,500 $32.4m	Monitor cease-fire during transition from Dutch to Indonesian rule
1963–1964	UN Yemen Observation Mission (UNYOM)	189 $1.8m	Supervise disengagement of Saudi Arabia and Egypt from Yemen's civil war
1964–	UN Peacekeeping Force in Cyprus (UNFICYP)	6,400 $51.99m**	Prevent foreign intervention and internal conflict of Greek and Turkish Cypriots
1965–1966	Mission of the Representative of the SG in the Dominican Republic (DOMREP)	2 $275,831	Monitor cease-fire between rival factions
1965–1966	UN India-Pakistan Observation Mission (UNIPOM)	96 $1.7m	Monitor cease-fire
1973–1979	UN Second Emergency Force (UNEF II)	6,973 $446.5m	Supervise cease-fire, troop disengagement and act as buffer zone between Egypt and Israel

Dates	Mission	Personnel	Cost	Purpose
1974–	UN Disengagement Observer Force (UNDOF)	1,450	$43.03m **	Maintain cease-fire and patrol Syria-Israel border in Golan Heights
1978–	UN Interim Force in Lebanon (UNIFIL)	7,000	$97.8m **	Supervise Israeli troop withdrawal and help restore Lebanese government authority
1988–1990	UN Good Offices Mission in Afghanistan and Pakistan (UNGOMAP)	50	$14.0m	Supervise Soviet withdrawal and monitor Geneva agreement on Afghanistan
1988–1991	UN Iran-Iraq Military Observer Group (UNIIMOG)	400	$117.9m	Supervise Iran-Iraq cease-fire
1988–1991	UN Angola Verification Mission I (UNAVEM I)	70	$16.4m	Verify withdrawal of Cuban troops from Angola
1989–1990	UN Transition Assistance Group (UNTAG)	4,493	$383.3m	Assist Namibia's transition to independence and supervise elections
1989–1992	UN Observer Group in Central America (ONUCA)	1,038	$88.5m	Monitor compliance by Costa Rica, El Salvador, Guatemala, Honduras, and Nicaragua on cease-fire in Nicaragua and disarmament of irregular forces in the area
1989–1990	UN Observer Group for the Verification of Elections in Nicaragua (ONUVEN)	120		Monitor elections in Nicaragua
1990–1991	UN Observer Group for the Verification of Elections in Haiti (ONUVEH)	193	$6.5m	Observe elections in Haiti
1991–2003	UN Iraq-Kuwait Observation Mission (UNIKOM)	1,400	$600.0m	Enforce demilitarized zone between Iraq and Kuwait after first Persian Gulf War
1991–1995	UN Angola Verification Mission II (UNAVEM II)	475	$175.8m	Enforce cease-fire in Angolan civil war
1991–1995	UN Observer Mission in El Salvador (ONUSAL)	1,330	$107.7m	Enforce cease-fire in civil war and monitor human rights

(continued)

Date	Mission	Peak Authorized Strength Total Expenditures	Purpose
1991–	UN Mission for the Referendum in Western Sahara (MINURSO)	375 $44.04m **	Monitor cease-fire and organize referendum on independence or union with Morocco
1991–1992	UN Advance Mission in Cambodia (UNAMIC)	1,090	Prepare way for UN Transitional Authority in Cambodia (UNTAC)
1992–1995	UN Protection Force (UNPROFOR)	44,034 $4.6b	Encourage cease-fire in Croatia and Bosnia-Herzegovina, protect civilian areas and relief programs
1992–1993	UN Transitional Authority in Cambodia (UNTAC)	19,200 $2b	Supervise demobilization of Cambodian factions, ensure interim governmental functions, and plan and conduct elections
1992–1993	UN Operation in Somalia I (UNOSOM I)	4,269 $42.9m	Monitor and enforce cease-fire between Somali factions and protect relief shipments
1992–1994	UN Operation in Mozambique (UNOMOZ)	10,133 $492.6m	Monitor cease-fire in civil war, disarm combatants, train national army, organize elections, and provide humanitarian assistance
1993–1995	UN Operation in Somalia II (UNOSOM II)	28,000 $1.6b	Stabilize Somalia through peacemaking operations and assist humanitarian efforts
1993–1994	UN Observer Mission in Uganda-Rwanda (UNOMUR)	81 $2.3m	Observe cease-fire between Rwanda and rebels based in Uganda
1993–	UN Observer Mission in Georgia (UNOMIG)	406 $33.59m**	Verify cease-fire between Georgia and Abkhaz separatists and observe CIS peacekeeping force

Date	Mission		Purpose
1993–1997	UN Observer Mission in Liberia (UNOMIL)	568 $104m	Monitor cease-fire and elections
1993–1996	UN Mission in Haiti (UNMIH)	1,740 $315m	Assist in strengthening of government institutions and monitor elections
1993–1996	UN Assistance Mission in Rwanda (UNAMIR)	5,640 $453.9m	Monitor cease-fire and after genocide prevent massacres of civilians, assist refugees, and provide humanitarian relief
1994	UN Aouzou Strip Observer Group (UNASOG)	15 $64,471	Monitor Libya's withdrawal from disputed territory awarded by International Court of Justice to Chad
1994–2000	UN Mission of Observers in Tajikistan (UNMOT)	120 $64m	Monitor cease-fire in civil war
1995–1997	UN Angola Verification Mission III (UNAVEM III)	4,220 $134.9m	Monitor cease-fire and disarmament
1995–1996	UN Confidence Restoration Operation in Croatia (UNCRO)	6,581 Expenses included in UNPROFOR	Attempt to achieve cease-fire
1995–1999	UN Preventive Deployment Force (UNPREDEP)	1,110 $166m	Replace UNPROFOR in Macedonia and monitor border with Albania
1995–2002	UN Mission in Bosnia–Herzegovina (UNMIBH)	2,057 $145m annually	Monitor law enforcement, human rights, and demining, and provide relief in Bosnia–Herzegovina
1996–1998	UN Transitional Administration in Eastern Slavonia, Baranja and Western Sirmium (UNTAES)	2,847 $435.2m	Facilitate integration of region in Croatia
1996–2002	UN Mission of Observers in Prevlaka (UNMOP)	37 $145m annually	Monitor demilitarization of Prevlaka Peninsula

(continued)

Date	Mission	Peak Authorized Strength Total Expenditures	Purpose
1996–1997	UN Support Mission in Haiti (UNSMIH)	1,700 $56.1m	Modernize Haiti police and army
1997	UN Verification Mission in Guatemala (MINUGUA)	188 $4.57m	Monitor cease-fire in civil war
1997–1999	UN Observer Mission in Angola (MONUA)	3,568 $293.7m	Follow on to UNAVEM III. Monitor cease-fire and disarmament
1997	UN Transition Mission in Haiti (UNTMIH)	300 $20.6m	Help political stabilization of Haiti
1997–2000	UN Civilian Mission in Haiti (MIPONUH)	525 $20.4m	Modernize Haiti's police forces
1998	UN Civilian Police Support Group (UNPSG)	398 $30.48m	Monitor Croatian Police
1998–2000	UN Mission in the Central African Republic (MINURCA)	1,624 $101.3m	Maintain security and stability in the country
1998–1999	UN Observer Mission in Sierra Leone (UNOMSIL)	352 $42.6m	Monitor disarmament and demobilization of armed factions in civil war
1999–	UN Interim Administration in Kosovo (UNMIK)	7,000 278 m	Exert all administrative and regulatory authority in the province
1999–	UN Mission in Sierra Leone (UNAMSIL)	17,500 $301.87m **	Help stabilize political situation and disarm combatants
1999–2002	UN Transitional Administration in East Timor (UNTAET)	13,390 $477m **	Exert administrative functions leading to full independence
1999–	UN Organization Mission in the Democratic Republic of the Congo (MONUC)	10,934 $746.10m **	Monitor cease-fire and promote political settlement
2000–	UN Mission in Ethiopia and Eritrea (UNMEE)	4,200 $216.03m **	Supervise cease-fire between the two countries

2002–	UN Mission of Support in East Timor (UNMISET)	6,000 $85.33m **	Two-year mission to assist in development of government structures, maintaining law enforcement and public security, and assisting in developing police service.
2003–	UN Mission in Liberia (UNMIL)	16,115 $864.82m **	Oversee cease-fire and train police
2003–2004	UN Mission in Cote d'Ivoire (MINUCI)	76 $29.9m	Facilitate the implementation of peace process
2004–	UN Operation in Cote d'Ivoire (UNOCI)	7,873 $384.35m **	Assist the Government of National Reconciliation with the implementation of cease-fire agreement
2004–	UN Stabilization Mission in Haiti (MINUSTAH)	10,020 $379.05m **	Maintain law and order, organize elections, strengthen the rule of law, and support human rights institutions and groups.
2004–	UN Operation in Burundi (ONUB)	7,020 $333.17m**	Oversee implementation of cease-fire
2005–	UN Mission in Sudan (UNMIS)	10,000 $315.99***	Verify and support implementation of peace agreements and perform humanitarian and human rights functions.

Source: UN Peacekeeping website: http://www.un.org/Depts/dpko/dpko/timeline/index.html
$m: Millions.
$b: Billions.
*Expenditures for 2004.
**Expenditures proposed for 1 July 2004–30 June 2005.
***Expenditures for the period 1 July–31 October 2005.

DISARMAMENT, ARMS CONTROL, AND TERRORISM

(Date of adoption/date of entry in force [for treaties only])

1925	Protocol for the Prohibition of the Use in War of Asphyxiating, Poisonous or Other Gases, and of Bacteriological Methods of Warfare
1959/1961	Antarctic Treaty
1963/1969	Convention on Offences and Certain Other Acts on Board of Aircraft ("Tokyo Convention"—safety of aviation)
1963/1963	Treaty Banning Nuclear Weapons Tests in the Atmosphere, in Outer Space and Under Water
1967/1967	Treaty on Principles Governing the Activities of States in the Exploration and Use of Outer Space, Including the Moon and Other Celestial Bodies
1967**	Treaty for the Prohibition of Nuclear Weapons in Latin America and the Caribbean (Treaty of Tlatelolco)
1967/1968	Agreement on the Rescue of Astronauts, the Return of Astronauts, and the Return of Objects Launched into Outer Space
1970/1970	Convention for the Suppression of Unlawful Seizure of Aircraft ("Hague Convention")
1970	Declaration on Principles of International Law Concerning Friendly Relations and Co-operation among States in Accordance with the Charter of the United Nations (G.A. Resolution 2625)
1968/1970	Treaty on the Non-Proliferation of Nuclear Weapons (NPT**)
1971/1972	Convention on International Liability for Damage Caused by Space Objects
1971/1972	Treaty on the Prohibition of the Emplacement of Nuclear Weapons and Other Weapons of Mass Destruction on the Seabed and the Ocean Floor and in the Subsoil Thereof (Seabed Treaty)
1971/1973	Convention for the Suppression of Unlawful Acts against the Safety of Civil Aviation ("Montreal Convention")
1973/1977	Convention on the Prevention and Punishment of Crimes against Internationally Protected Persons
1975/1976	Convention on Registration of Objects Launched into Outer Space
1972/1975	Convention on the Prohibition of the Development, Production, and Stockpiling of Bacteriological (Biological) and Toxin Weapons and on Their Destruction (BWC)
1977/1978	Convention on the Prohibition of Military or Any Other Hostile Use of Environmental Modification Techniques (ENMOD)
1979/1983	International Convention against the Taking of Hostages
1979/1984	Agreement Governing the Activities of States on the Moon and Other Celestial Bodies
1980	Transparency in Armaments: UN Instrument for Reporting Military Expenditures

1981/1983	Convention on Prohibitions or Restrictions on the Use of Certain Conventional Weapons Which May Be Deemed Injurious or to Have Indiscriminate Effects
1980/1983	Protocol on Prohibitions or Restrictions on the Use of Mines, Booby-Traps and Other Devices
1980/1987	Convention on the Physical Protection of Nuclear Material
1985/1986	South Pacific Nuclear Free Zone Treaty (Treaty of Rarotonga)
1988/1989	Protocol for the Suppression of Unlawful Acts of Violence at Airports Serving International Civil Aviation, supplementary to the Montreal Convention
1991***	Transparency in Armaments: UN Register of Conventional Arms
1988/1992	Protocol for the Suppression of Unlawful Acts against the Safety of Fixed Platforms Located on the Continental Shelf
1988/1992	Convention for the Suppression of Unlawful Acts against the Safety of Maritime Navigation
1991/1998	Convention on the Marking of Plastic Explosives for the Purpose of Detection
1992/2002	Treaty on Open Skies
1993/1997	Convention on the Prohibition of the Development, Production, Stockpiling, and Use of Chemical Weapons and on Their Destruction (CWC)
1995/1997	Treaty on the Southeast Asia Nuclear Weapons Free Zone (Bangkok Treaty)
1996*	Comprehensive Nuclear Test Ban Treaty (CTBT)
1996*	African Nuclear Weapons Free Zone Treaty (Pelindaba Treaty)
1997/1998	Inter-American Convention against the Illicit Manufacturing of and Trafficking in Firearms, Ammunition, Explosives, and Other Related Materials
1997/1999	Convention on the Prohibition of the Use, Stockpiling, Production, and Transfer of Antipersonnel Mines and on Their Destruction
1997/2001	UN International Convention for the Suppression of Terrorist Bombings
1999/2002	International Convention for the Suppression of the Financing of Terrorism
1999/2002	Inter-American Convention on Transparency in Conventional Weapons Acquisitions
2001/2005	Protocol against the Illicit Manufacturing of and the Trafficking in Firearms, Their Parts and Components and Ammunition, Supplementing the United Nations Convention against Transnational Organized Crime.
1999/2002	International Convention for the Suppression of the Financing of Terrorism
2000/2003	UN Convention against Transnational Organized Crime (Firearms Protocol)
2005*	International Convention for the Suppression of Acts of Nuclear Terrorism.

* Not yet in force.
**Entered for each government individually.
***Adopted by the General Assembly in resolution 46/36 of 6 December 1991.

ENVIRONMENT

(Date of adoption/date of entry in force [for treaties only])

1971/1972	Treaty on the Prohibition of the Emplacement of Nuclear Weapons and Other Weapons of Mass Destruction on the Seabed and the Ocean Floor and in the Subsoil Thereof (Seabed Treaty)
1972	Stockholm Declaration of UN Conference on Human Environment
1973/1975	Convention on International Trade in Endangered Species of Wild Fauna and Flora (CITES)
1976	Declaration and Plan of Action Habitat Conference
1977	Declaration and Plan of Action of UN Conference on Desertification
1979/1983	Convention on Long Range Transboundary Air Pollution
1981	World Health Assembly Global Strategy for Health for All
1982/1994	United Nations Convention on the Law of the Seas
1985/1988	Vienna Convention for the Protection of the Ozone Layer
1987/1989	Montreal Protocol on Substances that Deplete the Ozone Layer
1989/1992	Basel Convention on the Control of Transboundary Movements of Hazardous Wastes and Their Disposal
1991/1997	Convention on Environmental Impact Assessment in a Transboundary Context
1992/1993	Convention on Biological Diversity
1992/1996	Convention on the Protection and Use of Transboundary Watercourses and International Lakes
1992/1992	Convention on the Transboundary Effects of Industrial Accidents
1992	Earth Summit: Agenda 21 (UN Conference on Environment and Development)
1992/1994	UN Framework Convention on Climate Change
1994/1996	UN Convention to Combat Desertification
1994/1996	Lusaka Agreement on Cooperative Enforcement Operations Directed at Illegal Trade in Wild Fauna and Flora
1997*	Convention on the Law of the Non-navigational Uses of International Watercourses
1998/2004	Rotterdam Convention on the Prior Informed Consent Procedure for Certain Hazardous Chemicals and Pesticides in International Trade
1998/2001	Convention on Access to Information, Public Participation in Decision-Making and Access to Justice in Environmental Matters
1999/2005	Protocol on Water and Health
1995/2001	United Nations Agreement for the Implementation of the Provisions of the United Nations Convention on the Law of the Sea of 10 December 1982 Relating to the Conservation

	and Management of Straddling Fish Stocks and Highly Migratory Fish Stocks
2002	International Code of Conduct on the Distribution of Pesticides
2000/2003	Cartagena Protocol on Biosafety to the Convention on Biological Diversity
2001/2004	Stockholm Convention on Persistent Organic Pollutants
1997/2005	Kyoto Protocol (to the UN Framework Convention on Climate Change)
2003/2005	WHO Framework Convention on Tobacco Control

*Not yet in force.

HUMAN RIGHTS

(Date of adoption/date of entry in force [for treaties only])

1926/1927	Slavery Convention
1948	Universal Declaration of Human Rights
1949/1950	Geneva Conventions on the Laws of War
1950	Principles of International Law Recognized in the Charter of the Nuremberg Tribunal and in the Judgment of the Tribunal
1949/1951	Convention for the Suppression of the Traffic in Persons and of the Exploitation of the Prostitution of Others
1948/1951	Convention on the Prevention and Punishment of the Crime of Genocide
1953/1953	Protocol Amending the Slavery Convention
1951/1954	Convention Relating to the Status of Refugees
1952/1954	Convention on the Political Rights of Women
1955	Standard Minimum Rules for the Treatment of Prisoners
1954/1956	Convention for the Protection of Cultural Property in the Event of Armed Conflict
1957/1957	Supplementary Convention on the Abolition of Slavery
1957/1959	Abolition of Forced Labour Convention (ILO Convention No. 105)
1954/1960	Convention Relating to the Status of Stateless Persons
1961	Declaration on the Granting of Independence to Colonial Countries and Peoples (G.A. Resolution 1514 [XV])
1962	Permanent Sovereignty over Natural Resources (G.A. Resolution 1803 [XVII])
1960/1962	Convention against Discrimination in Education
1967	Declaration on Territorial Asylum (G.A. Resolution 2312 [XXII])
1966/1967	Protocol Relating to the Status of Refugees
1968	Proclamation of Teheran, Final Act of the International Conference on Human Rights

1966/1969	International Convention on the Elimination of All Forms of Racial Discrimination
1969	Declaration on Social Progress and Development (G.A. Resolution 2542 [XXIV])
1970/1971	International Convention for the Suppression of Unlawful Seizure of Aircraft
1974	Universal Declaration on the Eradication of Hunger and Malnutrition Adopted by the World Food Conference
1974	Declaration on the Protection of Women and Children in Emergency and Armed Conflict (G.A. Resolution 3318 [XXIX])
1961/1975	Convention on the Reduction of Statelessness
1975	Declaration on the Rights of Disabled Persons (G.A. Resolution 3447 [XXX])
1966/1976	International Covenant on Civil and Political Rights
1966/1976	International Covenant on Economic, Social and Cultural Rights
1966/1976	Optional Protocol to the International Covenant on Civil and Political Rights
1977	Code of Conduct for Law Enforcement Officials (G.A. Resolution 34/169)
1981	Declaration on the Elimination of All Forms of Intolerance and of Discrimination Based on Religion or Belief (G.A. Resolution 36/55)
1979/1981	Convention on the Elimination of All Forms of Discrimination against Women
1981/1983	Convention Concerning Occupational Safety and Health and the Working Environment (ILO No. 155)
1979/1983	International Convention against the Taking of Hostages
1984	Declaration on the Right of Peoples to Peace (G.A. Resolution 39/11)
1985	Declaration on the Human Rights of Individuals Who Are Not Nationals of the Country in Which They Live
1985	Basic Principles on the Independence of the Judiciary (Seventh UN Congress on the Prevention of Crime and the Treatment of Offenders)
1986	UN General Assembly Declaration on the Right to Development
1984/1987	Convention against Torture and Other Cruel, Inhuman or Degrading Treatment or Punishment
1989/1990	Convention on the Rights of the Child
1989/1991	Second Optional Protocol to the International Covenant on Civil and Political Rights Aiming at the Abolition of the Death Penalty
1989/1991	Convention Concerning Indigenous and Tribal Peoples in Independent Countries (ILO No. 169)
1992	Declaration on the Protection of All Persons from Enforced Disappearances (G.A. Resolution 47/133)

1993	Vienna Declaration, World Conference on Human Rights
1993	Declaration on the Elimination of Violence against Women (G.A. Resolution 48/104)
1993	Declaration on the Rights of Persons Belonging to National or Ethnic, Religious or Linguistic Minorities (G.A. Resolution 47/135)
1994	Draft Declaration on the Rights of Indigenous Peoples (UN Document E/CN.4/Sub.2/1994/2/Add.1 [1994])
1998	Guiding Principles on Internal Displacement
1997	UNESCO's Universal Declaration on the Human Genome and Human Rights
1994/1999	Convention on the Safety of United Nations and Associated Personnel
1999/2000	Convention Concerning the Prohibition and Immediate Action for the Elimination of the Worst Forms of Child Labour (ILO No. 182)
1999/2000	Optional Protocol to the Convention on the Elimination of All Forms of Discrimination against Women
2001	World Conference against Racism, Racial Discrimination, Xenophobia and Related Intolerance, Declaration and Program of Action
2000/2003	Convention against Transnational Organized Crime
2000/2003	Protocol to Prevent, Suppress and Punish Trafficking in Persons, Especially Women and Children, Supplementing the UN Convention against Transnational Organized Crime
2000*	Protocol against the Smuggling of Migrants supplementing the United Nations Convention against Transnational Organized Crime
2002*	Optional Protocol to the Convention against Torture
2000/2002	Optional Protocol to the Convention on the Rights of the Child on the Involvement of Children in Armed Conflicts
2000/2002	Optional Protocol to the Convention on the Rights of the Child on the Sale of Children, Child Prostitution and Child Pornography
2002	Rome Statute of the International Criminal Court
1990/2003	International Convention on the Protection of the Rights of All Migrant Workers and Members of their Families
2003*	United Nations Convention against Corruption

* Not yet in force.

INTERNATIONAL LAW

(Date of adoption/date of entry in force [for treaties only])

1961/1975	Convention on the Reduction of Statelessness
1997*	Convention on the Law of the Non-Navigational Uses of International Watercourses
1961/1964	Vienna Convention on Diplomatic Relations
1969/1980	Vienna Convention on the Law of Treaties
1963/1967	Vienna Convention on Consular Relations
1978/1996	Vienna Convention on Succession of States in Respect to Treaties

*Not yet in force

Bibliography

CONTENTS

I.	Introduction	472
II.	Information Sources	475
	A. Collections, Handbooks, Chronologies, and Dictionaries: Background Information	475
	B. Bibliographies	479
	C. Periodicals	479
	1. United Nations Periodicals	480
	2. Newsletters and Bulletins of the Specialized Agencies	481
	D. United Nations Publications	481
III.	Books and Articles	482
	A. Origins, Establishment, and Evolution of the United Nations System	482
	B. The Changing International Setting: The Cold War, Decolonization, Self-Determination, the Post–Cold War, Globalization, and Terrorism	485
	C. National Policies toward the United Nations	490
	D. The Legal, Institutional, and Financial Framework	493
	E. The UN Political Process (Actors and Decision Making)	495
	1. Civil Society	495
	2. The Private Sector	497
	3. Decision Making	498
	4. Memoirs and Autobiographies	500
	F. Peace and Security	503
	1. Dispute Settlement, Mediation, Prevention, and Conflict Resolution	503
	2. Collective Security	507
	3. Peacekeeping and Peacebuilding	512
	4. Humanitarianism	525
	5. Disarmament and Arms Control	529

G. Sustaining Social and Economic Development 534
1. Approaches to Development 534
2. Global Conferences 536
3. Functionalism: The Specialized Agencies, the Bretton Woods Institutions, and the World Trade Organization 538
4. Capacity Development 543
5. Sustainable Development; Money, Finance, and Trade; Science and Technology 544
H. Promoting Human Rights 550
I. International Law 560
J. Reforming the UN 563
K. Prospects for the Future: The UN and Global Governance 566

I. INTRODUCTION

There is no dearth of information sources, documentary material, and books on the United Nations and its specialized agencies. In fact, both the general reader and students of international relations may promptly be overwhelmed by the sheer quantity of the material available. The rapidly expanding web of Internet material has only further compounded the challenge. By necessity, any bibliography on the United Nations must be selective. The following is only a modest sample of material selected with a view to introducing the general and more specialized reader to the basic work and functioning of the United Nations and avoid aimless wandering. The focus is on material issued by the United Nations and books published in the English language.

The United Nations itself issues thousands of documents and publications. A good introduction to UN documentation is Peter I. Hajnal, *Directory of United Nations Documentary and Archival Sources* (Hanover, NH: Academic Council on the United Nations System / Millwood, NY: Kraus International Law / New York: United Nations, 1991). The Dag Hammarskjöld Library at United Nations headquarters in New York and the UN Library in Geneva contain the most complete collection of UN documents and publications. Both libraries are open only to staff members and personnel of the Permanent Missions to the United Nations. However, the catalog of the UN Library in New York facilitates research on UN documents since 1979, speech citations since 1983, voting records for the Security Council since 1946, and voting records for the General Assembly since 1983. It is available online at http://unbisnet.un.org/.

Since 1946, the Dag Hammarskjöld Library has been distributing United Nations documents and publications to users around the world through its depository library system. There are currently more than 400 depository libraries in over 140 countries maintaining United Nations material, which can be consulted free of charge by the general public. For details, see www.un.org/depts/dhl/deplib/deplibssytem.htm.

It should be noted that some of the recurring publications of the United Nations provide an indispensable source of data and information for researcher and informed public alike. The *Annual Report of the Secretary General on the Work of the Organization* and the *Yearbook of the United Nations* are good starting points that may be complemented, depending on the interests of the reader, by such publications as the *Global Environment Outlook* (UNEP), *The Human Development Report* (UNDP), *The State of the World's Children* (UNICEF), *The State of the World Population* (UNFPA), *The State of the World's Refugees* (UNHCR), *The World Development Report* (World Bank), *The World Health Report* (WHO), and *The World Investment Report* (UNCTAD). A more extensive listing of these publications can be found below.

The United Nations also publishes a number of useful periodicals, such as the *CEPAL Review, Natural Resources Forum*, and *Population Bulletin of the United Nations*. Likewise, the specialized agencies produce many newsletters and bulletins covering their work and the problems they are concerned with. UN press releases are not official documents and are not always error proof. They nevertheless provide valuable insights and leads about topical recent or current debates and actions taken. Their full text is available since October 1995 on www.un.org/News/Press/full.htm.

Internet users will find considerable information on the UN website. The home page of the United Nations (www.un.org/english) is a portal to international information about the UN and international issues. The *United Nations Documentation: Research Guide* (www.un.org/Depts/dhl/resguide) is an excellent overall guide prepared by the staff of the Dag Hammarskjöld Library. *Basic Research Tools* (www.un.org/Depts/dhl/resguide/basic.htm) identifies a few key print sources before electronic sources begin. The *UN System Pathfinder* (www.un.org/Depts/dhl/pathfind/frame/start.htm) is more comprehensive in its coverage of reference-type materials and includes key publications of historical value. Just released UN online information, major reports, publications, and documents can be found on www.un.org/Depts/dhl/unpulse/. The United Nations Document Centre provides access to selected documents: www.un.org/documents/.

The websites of other United Nations bodies, including the specialized agencies, contain extensive documentation for recent years and sometimes for the entire history of the organization.

Archival records are preserved in the Archives and Records Centre (ARC) at the United Nations headquarters. Archivists respond to enquiries from scholars and other external users, identifying records appropriate to their research interests, providing access according to existing security classification regulations, and arranging reproduction service. On-site visits to the ARC Centre can be made by appointment and preregistration. Researcher application forms may be found on www.un.org/Depts/archives.

The Web provides extensive information about the organization from non-UN sources. The following, among many others, are especially useful: the Academic Council on the UN System (ACUNS); ASIL Electronic Resources for International Law, Princeton University; the UN Scholar's Work Station at Yale University; the University of Minnesota Human Rights Library; and the United Nations Association of the United States of America.

The secondary literature on the United Nations (books and periodicals) is immense, especially in the English language, the exclusive focus of this bibliography. As can be expected, the dominant paradigms about the nature and work of the United Nations and the problems it faces all originate from North American scholarship. This may explain the fact that works concerned with international peace and security and human rights tend to outnumber those dealing with economic and social development. An effort was made in this bibliography to redress this imbalance by listing works by European and non-Western scholars, whenever they were available in English.

Good introductions to international organizations and politics or particular topics and themes, eminently accessible and rich in information, may be found in the Scarecrow Dictionary series, which covers a wide range of United Nations institutions and international relations subjects. The noninitiated may opt for the memoirs and autobiographies of former United Nations officials and other "insiders," which are unavoidably biased but always rich in insights and revealing stories. In this respect, Sir Brain Urquhart's books are particularly enlightening. Linda Fasulo's *An Insider's Guide to the UN* is a recent useful addition to the genre. More scholarly oriented readers may consult the valuable works of Thomas Weiss et al., *The United Nations and Changing World Politics*, and Lawrence Ziring et al., *The United Nations: International Organization and World Politics*.

For the convenience of the reader, the books listed below have been arranged in broad categories beginning with the origins and establishment of the United Nations. In this respect, attention is drawn to the 1958 seminal work of Ruth Russell retracing in painstaking detail the making of the UN Charter and its genesis in U.S. government agencies. The following sections of the bibliography deal with the changing international environment of the United Nations and its impact on the activities and work of the organization, changing national policies toward the UN, and the UN multilateral deliberative processes. The 1980 study of Johann Kaufman remains a classic and indispensable reference to an understanding of UN decision making. A recent and excellent overview e UN political processes can be found in Courtney Smith, *Politics and Process at the United Nations: The Global Dance*, published in 2005.

The contributions of the United Nations to the maintenance of peace and security, economic and social development, human rights, and international law are treated in the subsequent sections of the bibliography. None of the works written in the early 1960s by Inis Claude on the use of force by the United Nations has lost any of its relevance. They can be usefully supplemented by more recent analyses of David Malone on the activities of the Security Council before and after the Cold War. Larry Minear has probably written the most thoughtful—conceptually and operationally—study of the Humanitarian Enterprise. Orchestrated by Richard Jolly, Louis Emmerij, and Thomas Weiss, the various volumes published under the broad aegis of the UN Intellectual History Project are indispensable to the understanding of the development work of the United Nations. Paul Gordon Lauren's book on the evolution of international human rights stands out in the immense and ever expanding literature on human rights. The 2004 work of Ramesh Thakur et al. on the impact of international commissions yields valuable insights into the numerous factors explaining the piecemeal process of United Nations reform.

II. INFORMATION SOURCES

A. Collections, Handbooks, Chronologies, and Dictionaries: Background Information

Adamec, Ludwig W. *Historical Dictionary of Afghan Wars, Revolutions and Insurgencies*. Lanham, Md.: Scarecrow Press, 2005.

Alger, Chadwick F. *The United Nations System: A Reference Handbook*. Santa Barbara, Calif.: ABC CLIO, 2005.

Allen, Tim. *A Dictionary of Humanitarianism*. New York: Routledge, 2005.

Anderson, Sean K., and Stephen Sloan. *Historical Dictionary of Terrorism*, 2nd ed. Lanham, Md.: Scarecrow Press, 2002.

Annual Review of United Nations Affairs. Dobbs Ferry, N.Y.: Oceana, 1949–. Together with its supplement, *Chronology and Fact Book of the United Nations*. Dobbs Ferry, N.Y.: Oceana, 1941–1992.

Arnold, Guy. *Historical Dictionary of the Non-Aligned Movements and Third World*. Lanham, Md.: Scarecrow Press, 2006.

———. *Historical Dictionary of Civil Wars in Africa*. Lanham, Md.: Scarecrow Press, 1999.

———. *Historical Dictionary of Aid and Development Organizations*. Lanham, Md.: Scarecrow Press, 1996.

Baratta, Joseph. P. *United Nations System*. New Brunswick, N.J.: Transaction Publishers, 1995.

Basic Facts About the United Nations, 1972-. New York: United Nations.

Boczek, Boleslaw Adam. *International Law: A Dictionary*. Lanham, Md.: Scarecrow Press, 2005.

———. *Historical Dictionary of International Tribunals*. Lanham, Md.: Scarecrow Press, 1994.

Boucher-Saulnier, Francoise. *The Practical Guide to Humanitarian Law*. Lanham, Md.: Rowman & Littlefield, 2002.

Burns, Richard Dean (ed). *Encyclopedia of Arms Control and Disarmament*. New York: Scribner's, 1993.

Chronology and Fact Book of the United Nations. 8th ed. Dobbs Ferry, N.Y.: Oceana, 1992.

Clements, Frank A. *Historical Dictionary of Arab and Islamic Organizations*. Lanham, Md.: Scarecrow Press, 2001.

Davis, Simon, and Joseph Smith. *The A to Z of the Cold War*. Lanham, Md.: Scarecrow Press, 2005.

Edwards, Paul M. *The A to Z of the Korean War*. Lanham, Md.: Scarecrow Press, 2005.

———. *The Korean War: A Historical Dictionary*. Lanham, Md.: Scarecrow Press, 2003.

Encyclopedia of the United Nations and International Agreements. 3rd ed. 4 vols. New York: Routledge, 2003.

Everyone's United Nations: A Complete Handbook of the Activities and Evolution of the UN. New York: United Nations, 1979–.

Facts on File: A Weekly Digest with Cumulative Index. New York: Pearson's Index, Facts on File, Inc. 1940– .

Ganguly, Rajat. *A Dictionary of Ethnic Conflict*. New York: Routledge, 2005.

Gibson, John S. *Dictionary of International Human Rights Law*. Lanham, Md.: Scarecrow Press, 1996.

Gorman, Robert F. *Great Debates at the United Nations: An Encyclopedia of Fifty Key Issues, 1845–2000*. Westport, Conn.: Greenwood Press, 2001.

———. *Historical Dictionary of Refugee and Disaster Relief Organizations*. 2nd ed. Lanham, Md.: Scarecrow Press, 2000.

———. *Historical Dictionary of Human Rights and Humanitarian Organizations*. Lanham, Md.: Scarecrow Press, 1997.

A Global Agenda: Issues before the . . . General Assembly of the United Nations: An Annual Publication of the United Nations Association of the United States of America. Lanham, Md.: University Press of America, 1991–2005.

Go-Between (Newsletter published by the Nongovernmental Liaison Service six times per year).

Gorman, Robert F. *Historical Dictionary of Human Rights and Humanitarian Organizations*. 2nd ed. Lanham, Md.: Scarecrow Press, 2000.

Grant, John P., and J. Craig Barker, eds. *Parry & Grant Encyclopedic Dictionary of International Law*. 3rd ed. Dobbs Ferry, N.Y.: Oceana Publications, 2003.

Greenfield, Stanley R., ed. *Who's Who in the United Nations*. 2nd ed. Detroit, Mich.: Omni graphics, 1992.

Humphreys, Norman K. *Historical Dictionary of the International Monetary Fund*. Landham, Md: Scarecrow Press, 1999.

Image and Reality: Questions and Answers about the United Nations. New York: United Nations (irregular).

Issues before the . . . General Assembly of the United Nations. Annual. New York: United Nations Association of the United States of America, 1976–1991.

Larsen, Jeffrey A., and James M. Smith. *Historical Dictionary of Arms Control and Disarmament*. Lanham, Md.: Scarecrow Press, 2005.

Lawson, Edward. *Encyclopedia of Human Rights*. Washington, D.C.: Taylor & Francis, 1996.

Lee, Kelley. *Historical Dictionary of the World Health Organization*. Lanham, Md.: Scarecrow Press, 1998.

McDougall, Derek. *Historical Dictionary of International Organizations in Asia and the Pacific*. Lanham, Md.: Scarecrow Press, 2001.

Mays, Terry M. *Historical Dictionary of Multinational Peacekeeping*. 2nd ed. Lanham, Md.: Scarecrow Press, 2003.

Moore, John A., and Jerry Pubantz. *Encyclopedia of the United Nations*. New York: Facts on File, 2002.

Newell, Clayton R. *Historical Dictionary of the Persian Gulf War 1990–1991*. Lanham, Md.: Scarecrow Press, 1998.

Osmanczyk, Edmund Jan (Anthony Mango, ed.). *Encyclopedia of the United Nations and International Agreements*. 3rd ed. New York: Routledge, 2003.

Patil, Anjali. *The UN Veto in World Affairs, 1945–1990: A Complete Record and Case Histories of the Security Council's Veto*. Sarasota, Fla.: UNIFO / London: Mansell, 1992.

Rimanelli, Marco. *Historical Dictionary of the North Atlantic Treaty Organization*. Lanham, Md.: Scarecrow Press, 2006.

Roy, Joaquin, and Aimee Kanner. *Historical Dictionary of the European Union*. Lanham, Md.: Scarecrow Press, 2006.

Salda, Anne. *Historical Dictionary of the World Bank*. 2nd ed. Lanham, Md.: Scarecrow Press, 2006.

Schechter, Michael. *Historical Dictionary of International Organizations*. Lanham, Md. Scarecrow Press, 1998.

Sharp, Walter Gary Sr., ed. *United Nations Peace Operations: A Collection of Primary Documents and Readings Governing the Conduct of Multilateral Peace Operations*. New York: American Heritage Custom Publishing Group, 1995.

Siekmann, Robert C. R. *Basic Documents on United Nations and Related Peacekeeping Forces: With an Appendix on UN Military Observer Missions*. 2nd ed. Dordrecht, Netherlands: Martinus Nijhoff, 1989.

Smith, Joseph, and Simon Davis. *Historical Dictionary of the Cold War*. Lanham, Md.: Scarecrow Press, 2000.

Spaudling, Seth, and Lin Lin. *Historical Dictionary of the United Nations Educational, Scientific and Cultural Organization (UNESCO)*. Lanham, Md.: Scarecrow Press, 1997.

Talbot, Ross B. *Historical Dictionary of the International Food Agencies: FAO, WFP, WFC, IFAD*. Lanham, Md.: Scarecrow Press, 1994.

The United Nations and Its Predecessors. 2 vols. Oxford: Oxford University Press, 1997.

The UN at Fifty: Statements by World Leaders, New York, 22–24 October 1995. New York: United Nations, 1996.

United Nations Handbook. Wellington, New Zealand: Ministry of External Relations and Trade, 1976–.

Urwin, Derek W. *Historical Dictionary of European Organizations*. Lanham, Md.: Scarecrow Press, 1994.

Van Ginneken, Anique H. M. *Historical Dictionary of the League of Nations*. Lanham, Md.: Scarecrow Press, 2006.

Volger, Helmut, ed. *A Concise Encyclopedia of the United Nations*. The Hague, The Netherlands: Kluwer Law International, 2002.

Wellens, Karel C. *Resolutions and Statements of the United Nations Security Council (1946–2000): A Thematic Guide*. New York: Kluwer Law International, 2001.

Wilson, Larman C., and David W. Dent. *Historical Dictionary of Inter-American Organizations*. Lanham, Md.: Scarecrow Press, 1997.

Who's Who in the United Nations and Related Agencies. 2nd ed. Detroit, Mich.: Omnigraphic, Inc. 1992.

Worldmark Encyclopedia of the Nations, the United Nations. 7th ed. New York: John Wiley & Sons, 1988.

Wunderlich, Uwe, and Meera Warrier. *A Dictionary of Globalization*. New York: Routledge, 2005.

Yearbook of the United Nations. New York: United Nations, 1947–.

Yearbook of the United Nations, 50th Anniversary Edition. New York: United Nations, 1997.

B. Bibliographies

Atherton, Alexine L. *International Organizations: A Guide to Information Sources*. Detroit, Mich.: Gale Research Company, 1976.

Baratta, Joseph P. *United Nations System*. Oxford: Clio, 1995.

———. *Strengthening the United Nations: A Bibliography on U.N. Reform and World Federalism*. New York: Greenwood Press, 1987.

Cole, H. S. D. *The New International Economic Order: A Selective Bibliography*. New York: United Nations, 1980.

Croddy, Eric. *Chemical and Biological Warfare: Annotated Bibliography*. Lanham, Md.: Scarecrow Press, 1997.

Fermann, Gunnar. *Bibliography on International Peacekeeping*. Dordrecht, Netherlands: Martinus Nijhoff, 1992.

Haas, Michael. *International Organization: An Interdisciplinary Bibliography*. Stanford, Calif.: Hoover Institution Press, 1971.

Legault, Albert. *Peacekeeping Operations: A Bibliography*. Paris: International Information Center on Peacekeeping Operations, 1967.

Peace by Pieces: United Nations Agencies and Their Roles: A Reader and Selective Bibliography. Lanham, Md.: Scarecrow, 1991.

Shope, Virgina C. *Peacekeeping: A Selected Bibliography*. Carlisle Barracks, Pa: U.S. Army War College Library, 1994.

Walters, Gregory J. *Human Rights in Theory and Practice: A Selected and Annotated Bibliography*. Lanham, Md.: Scarecrow Press, 1995.

C. Periodicals (Published in the United States Unless Otherwise Noted)

Alternatives
American Journal of International Law
Arms Control Today
Bulletin of Peace Proposals (Oslo)
Civil Wars
Environment Politics
Environmental Policy and Law
Ethics and International Affairs
European Human Rights Law Review
European Journal of International Relations
Foreign Affairs
ForeignPolicy
Global Governance

Human Rights and Human Welfare
Harvard Human Rights Journal
Human Rights Quarterly
International Affairs (London)
International and Comparative Law Quarterly
International Conciliation (1907–1972)
International Journal (Toronto)
International Journal of Children's Rights
International Journal on World Peace
International Organization (London)
International Peacekeeping
International Relations (London)
International Review of the Red Cross
International Security
Journal of Conflict Resolution
Journal of International Affairs
Journal of Peace Research (Oslo)
Journal of World Intellectual Property
Millennium
Population and Development Review
Review of International Political Economy (UK)
Review of International Studies
Science, Technology & Development
Security Studies
Seton Hall Journal of Diplomacy and International Relations
Terrorism and Political Violence
The International Journal of Human Rights
The Journal of Humanitarian Assistance
The Journal of Strategic Studies
Third World Quarterly
Transnational Organized Crime
World Politics

1. United Nations Periodicals

CEPAL Review
Development Policy Journal (UNDP)
Journal of Development Planning (1969–1992)
Natural Resources Forum
Population Bulletin of the United Nations

United Nations Chronicle (May 1964–present). Monthly, then quarterly. Was preceded by *United Nations Bulletin* (August 1946–June 1954). Weekly, then monthly and *United Nations Review* (July 1954–April 1964).

2. Newsletters and Bulletins of the Specialized Agencies

The IAEA Bulletin (IAEA)
ICAO Journal (ICAO)
Bulletin of the World Health Organization (WHO)
Ceres (FAO)
Choices (UNDP)
Disarmament News (UNIDIR)
Dispatches (UNFPA)
ITU News (ITU)
International Labour Review (ILO)
News (UNRISD)
The New Courier (UNESCO)
Refugees Magazine (UNHCR)
UNICRI Journal (UNICRI)
Union Postale. Bern, Switzerland: Universal Postal Union, 1987–.
WIPO Magazine (WIPO)
The World of Work (ILO)

D. United Nations Publications

Annual Report of the Secretary General on the Work of the Organization
Economic and Social Survey of Asia and the Pacific (ESCAP)
Economic Survey of Africa (ECA)
Economic Survey of Europe (ECE)
Economic Survey of Latin America and the Caribbean (ECLAC)
Economic Survey of Western Asia (ESCWA)
Demographic Yearbook (United Nations)
Global Employment Trends (ILO)
Global Environment Outlook (UNEP)
Human Development Report (UNDP)
Industrial Development Report (UNIDO)
International Instruments of the United Nations: A Compilation of Agreements, Charters, Declarations, Principles, Proclamations, Protocols, Treaties
The Least Developed Countries (UNCTAD)
Repertoire of the Practice of the Security Council

Repertory of Practice of United Nations Organs
Rural Poverty Report (IFAD)
The State of Food and Agriculture (FAO)
The State of the World's Children (UNICEF)
The State of the World Population (UNFPA)
The State of the World's Refugees (UNHCR)
The State of World Rural Poverty (IFAD)
Statistical Yearbook (United Nations)
Statistical Yearbook (UNESCO)
Trade and Development Report (UNCTAD)
United Nations Juridical Yearbook
World Development Report (World Bank)
World Drug Report (UNODCP)
World Economic and Social Survey (DESA)
World Employment Report (ILO)
World Employment Yearbook (ILO)
World Health Report (WHO)
World Investment Report (UNCTAD)
World Public Sector Report (DESA)
World Telecommunications Development Report (ITU)
Yearbook of the International Court of Justice
Yearbook of the International Law Commission
Yearbook of Labour Statistics (ILO)
Yearbook of Tourism Statistics (WTO)

III. BOOKS AND ARTICLES

A. Origins, Establishment, and Evolution of the United Nations System

Archer, Clive. *International Organization*. 3rd ed. London, 2001.

Armstrong, David, Lorna Lloyd, and John Redmond. *International Organization in World Politics*. New York: Palgrave, 2005.

Armstrong, James D. *From Versailles to Maastricht: International Organization in the Twentieth Century*. New York: St. Martin's Press, 1996.

Barnett, Michael, and Martha Finnemore. *Rules for the World: International Organizations in Global Politics*. Ithaca: N.Y. Cornell University Press, 2004.

Bowles, Newton R. *The Diplomacy of Hope: The United Nations since the Cold War*. New York: I. B. Taurus, 2004.

Burton, M. E. *The Assembly of the League of Nations*. Chicago: University of Chicago Press, 1943.

Carr, Edward Hallett. *The Twenty Years' Crisis 1919–1939*. New York: Harper & Row Publishers, 1964.

Claude, Inis Jr. *Swords into Plowshares. The Problems and Progress of International Organizations*. 4th ed. New York: Random House, 1971.

———. *The Changing United Nations*. New York: Random House, 1968.

Diehl, Paul F., ed. *The Politics of Global Governance: International Organizations in an Interdependent World*. Boulder, Colo.: Lynne Rienner, 2005.

Documents of the United Nations Conference on International Organization. New York: United Nations Information Organization, 1945–1946.

Eagleton, Clyde. *International Government*. New York: Ronald Press, 1948.

Falk, Richard A., Samuel S. Kim, and Saul H. Mendlovitz, eds. *The United Nations and a Just World Order*. Boulder, Colo.: Westview Press, 1991.

Franck, Thomas M. *Nation Against Nation: What Happened to the UN Dream and What the US Can Do about It*. New York: Oxford University Press, 1985.

Gareis, Sven Bernhard, and Johannes Varwick. *The United Nations*. New York: Palgrave, 2005.

Glassner, Martin Ira, ed. *The United Nations at Work*. Westport, Conn.: Praeger, 1998.

Goodrich, Leland, Edvard Hambro, and Anne Patricia Simon. *Charter of the United Nations*. New York: Columbia University Press, 1969.

Goodrich, Leland, and Edvard Hambro. *Charter of the United Nations: Commentary and Documents*. Boston: World Peace Foundation, 1949.

Gordenker, Leon. *Thinking about the United Nations System*. Hanover, N.H.: Academic Council on the United Nations, 1990.

Hening, Ruth, ed. *The League of Nations*. New York: Barnes and Noble, 1973.

Hilderbrand, Robert C. *Dumbarton Oaks: The Origins of the United Nations and the Search for Postwar Security*. Chapel Hill: University of North Carolina Press, 1997.

Hoopes, Townsend, and Douglas Brinkley. *FDR and the Creation of the UN*. New Haven, Conn.: Yale University Press, 1997.

Hull, Cordell. *The Memoirs of Cordell Hull*. 2 vols. New York: Macmillan, 1948.

Kennedy, Paul. *The Parliament of Man: The Past, Present, and Future of the United Nations*. New York: Random House, 2006.

Latanne, John H. *Development of the League of Nations Idea: Documents and Correspondence of Theodore Marburg*. New York: Macmillan, 1932.

Luard, Evan. *A History of the United Nations: The Years of Western Domination*. London: Macmillan, 1982.

Macmillan, Margaret. *Paris 1919*. New York: Random House, 2003.

Mangone, Gerard J. *A Short History of International Organization*. New York: McGraw-Hill, 1954.

May, Ernest R., and Angeliki E. Laiou, eds. *The Dumbarton Oaks Conversations and the United Nations 1944–1994*. Washington, D.C.: Dumbarton Oaks Research Library and Collection. Distributed by Harvard University Press, 1998.

Meisler, Stanley. *United Nations: The First Fifty Years*. New York: Atlantic Monthly Press, 1997.

Mingst, Karen A., M. P. Karns, and G. A. Lopez, eds. *United Nations in the Post-Cold War Era*. Boulder Colo.: Westview Press, 1999.

Northedge, F. S. *The League of Nations: Its Life and Times, 1920–1946*. New York: Holmes and Meier, 1986.

Report to the President on the Results of the San Francisco Conference. Department of State Publication 2349, Conference Series 71. Washington, D.C.: US Government Printing Office, 1945.

Righter, Rosemary. *Utopia Lost: The United Nations and World Order*. New York: Twentieth Century Fund, 1995.

Roberts, Adam, and Benedict Kingsbury, eds. *United Nations, Divided World: The UN's Roles in International Relations*. Oxford: Oxford University Press, 1993.

Rochester, J. Martin. *Waiting for the Millennium: The United Nations and the Future of World Order*. Columbia: University of South Carolina Press, 1993.

Rosenau, James N. *The United Nations in a Turbulent World*. Boulder, Colo.: Lynne Rienner, 1992.

Russell, Ruth (assisted by Jeanette E. Muther). *A History of the United Nations Charter*. Washington, D.C.: Brookings Institution, 1958.

Ryan, Stephen. *The United Nations and International Politics* (Studies in Contemporary History). New York: St. Martin's Press, 2000.

Schlesinger, Stephen. *Act of Creation: The Founding of the United Nations*. Boulder, Colo.: Westview Press, 2003.

Simma, Bruno, ed. *The Charter of the United Nations: A Commentary*. 2nd ed. New York: Oxford University Press, 2002.

Sweetser, Arthur. *The League of Nations at Work*. New York: Longmans, 1930.

Taylor, Paul, and A. J. R. Groom, eds. *The United Nations at the Millennium: the Principle Organs*. London: Continuum, 2000.

Walters, F. P. *A History of the League of Nations*. Oxford: Oxford University Press, 1952.

Weiss, Thomas G., D. P. Forsythe, and R. A. Coate. *United Nations: Changing World Politics*. 4th ed. Boulder, Colo.: Westview Press, 2004.

White, Nigel. *The United Nations System: Toward International Justice*. Boulder, Colo.: Lynne Rienner, 2002.

Wilcox, Francis O., and Carl M. Marcy. *Proposals for Changes in the United Nations*. Washington, D.C.: Brookings Institution, 1955.

Yoder, Amos. *The Evolution of the United Nations System.* New York: Crane Russak, 1989.

Zimmern, Alfred P. *The League of Nations and the Rule of Law, 1918–1935.* New York: Macmillan, 1936.

Ziring, Lawrence, Robert Riggs, and Jack Plano. *The United Nations: International Organization and World Politics.* Fort Worth, TX: Harcourt College Publishers, 2000.

Zweifel, Thomas D. *International Organizations and Democracy: Accountability, Politics, and Power.* Boulder, Colo.: Lynne Rienner, 2005.

B. The Changing International Setting: The Cold War, Decolonization, Self-Determination, the Post–Cold War, Globalization, and Terrorism

Ahion, Philippe, and Jeffrey Williamson. *Growth, Inequality, and Globalization.* New York: Cambridge University Press, 1999.

Alexander, Yonah, and Milton Hoening, eds. *Super Terrorism: Biological, Chemical, and Nuclear.* Ardsley, N.Y.: Transnational Publishers, 2001.

Allen, Mark D. *Global Lies? Propaganda, the UN and World Order.* New York: Palgrave MacMillan, 2003.

Appadurai, Arjun. *Modernity at Large: Cultural Dimensions of Globalization.* Minneapolis: University of Minnesota Press, 1996.

Art, Robert J., and Patrick M. Cronin, eds. *The United States and Coercive Diplomacy.* Washington, D.C.: United States Institute of Peace Press, 2003.

Bacevich, Andrew J. *American Empire: The Realities and Consequences of U.S. Diplomacy.* Cambridge, Mass.: Harvard University Press, 2002.

Barnet, Richard, and John Cavanagh. *Global Dreams: Imperial Corporations and the New World Order.* New York: Simon & Schuster, 1994.

Bartmann, Barry, Henry Srebrnik, and Tozun Bahcheli, eds. *De Facto States: The Quest for Sovereignty.* Portland, Ore.: Frank Cass Publishers, 2003.

Bassiouni, M. Cherif. *International Terrorism: A Compilation of U.N. Documents (1972–2001).* Ardsley, N.Y.: Transnational Publishers, 2002.

——. *International Terrorism: Multilateral Conventions (1937–2001).* Ardsley, N.Y.: Transnational Publishers, 2001.

Berger, Peter L., and Samuel P. Huntington eds. *Many Globalizations: Cultural Diversity in the Contemporary World.* New York: Oxford University Press, 2002.

Bhagwati, Jagdish N. *In Defense of Globalization.* New York: Oxford University Press, 2004.

Blakesley, Christopher. *Terrorism, Drugs, International Law, and the Protection of Human Liberty.* Ardsley, N.Y.: Transnational Publishers, 1992.

Braillard, Philippe, and Mohammad Reza Djalili. *The Third World and International Relations*. Boulder, Colo.: Lynne Rienner, 1986.

Braman, Sandra, and Annabelle Sreberny-Mohammadi: *Globalization, Communication and Transnational Civil Society*. Hampton Press, N.J.: 1996.

Brecher, Michael. *The Struggle for Kashmir*. New York: Oxford University Press, 1953.

Brown, Michael, ed. *Grave New World: Security Challenges in the Twenty-First Century*. Washington, D.C.: Georgetown University Press, 2003.

Brysk, Allison, ed. *Globalization and Human Rights*. Berkeley: University of California Press, 2002.

Bull, Hedley. *The Anarchical Society*. 2nd edition. New York: Columbia University Press, 1995.

Byers, Michael, and Georg Nolte. *United States Hegemony and the Foundations of International Law*. New York: Cambridge University Press, 2003.

Chakraborty, Bimal. *The United Nations and the Third World: Shifting Paradigms*. New Delhi: Tata McGraw-Hill, 1977.

Chem-Langhëë, Bongfen. *The Paradoxes of Self-Determination in the Cameroons under United Kingdom Administration: The Search for Identity, Well-Being and Continuity*. Lanham, Md.: University Press of America, 2004.

Chomsky, Noam. *Hegemony or Survival: America's Quest for Global Dominance*. New York: Metropolitan Books, 2003.

Combs, Cindy C. *Terrorism in the Twenty-First Century*. Englewood Cliffs, N.J.: Prentice Hall, 1997.

Coulter, John. W. *The Pacific Dependencies of the United States*. New York: Macmillan, 1957.

Cowen, Tyler. *Destruction: How Globalization is Changing the World's Cultures*. Princeton, N.J.: Princeton University Press, 2002.

Cox, Kevin R., ed. *Spaces of Globalization: Reasserting the Power of the Local*. New York: Guilford, 1997.

Crabb, C. V. D. *The Elephants and the Grass: A Study of Non-Alignment*. New York: Praeger, 1965.

Danspeckgruber, Wolfgang, ed. *The Self-Determination of Peoples: Community, Nation, and State in an Interdependent World*. Boulder, Colo.: Lynne Rienner Publishers, 2002.

Danspeckgruber, Wolfgang, with Sir Arthur Watts. *Self-Determination and Self-Administration: A Sourcebook*. Boulder, Colo.: Lynne Rienner, 1997.

Davids, Douglas J. *Narco Terrorism: A Unified Strategy to Fight a Growing Terrorist Menace*. Ardsley, N.Y.: Transnational Publishers, 2002.

——, ed. Eden, Paul, and Therese O'Donnell, eds. *September 11, 2001: A Turning Point in International and Domestic Law?* Ardsley, N.Y.: Transnational Publishers, 2004.

Emerson, Rupert. *From Empire to Nation*. Cambridge, Mass.: Harvard University Press, 1960.

Falk, Pamela. S., ed. *The Political Status of Puerto Rico*. Lexington, Mass.: Lexington Books, 1986.

Fedorowich, Kent, and Martin Thomas, eds. *International Diplomacy and Colonial Retreat*. Portland, Ore.: Frank Cass, 2000.

Foot, Rosemary, Neil S. MacFarlane, and Michael Mastanduno, eds. *US Hegemony and International Organizations*. Oxford: Oxford University Press, 2003.

Gaddis, John Lewis. *The United States and the End of the Cold War: Implications, Reconsiderations, Provocations*. New York: Oxford University Press, 2003.

———. *We Know Now: Rethinking Cold War History*. New York: Clarendon Press, 1997.

Gelber, Yoav. *Palestine 1948: War, Escape, and the Emergence of the Palestine Refugee Problem*. Portland, Ore.: Sussex Academic Press, 2001.

Gilpin, Robert. *The Challenge of Global Capitalism: The World Economy in the 21st Century*. Princeton, N.J.: Princeton University Press, 2002.

Ginat, Joseph, and Edward J. Perkins, eds. *Palestinian Refugees: Old Problems—New Solutions*. Norman: University of Oklahoma Press, 2002.

Grimal, Henri. *Decolonization: The British, French, Dutch, and Belgian Empires, 1919–1963*. Boulder, Colo.: Westview Press, 1978.

Gurr, Ted Robert. *Minorities at Risk: A Global View of Ethnopolitical Conflicts*. Washington, D.C.: United States Institute of Peace Press, 1993.

Haynes, Jeff. *Religion, Globalization, and Political Culture in the Third World*. New York: St. Martin's Press, 1999.

Held, David, Anthony McGrew, David Goldblatt, and Jonathan Perraton. *Global Transformations: Politics, Economics and Culture*. Stanford, Calif.: Stanford University Press, 1999.

Held, David, and Anthony McGrew, eds. *The Global Transformations Reader: An Introduction to the Globalization Debate*. Cambridge, Mass.: Polity Press, 2003.

Holland, R. F. *European Decolonization, 1918–1981*. New York: St. Martin's Press, 1985.

Hoogvelt, Ankie. *Globalization and the Postcolonial World: The New Political Economy of Development*. Baltimore, Md.: The Johns Hopkins University Press, 1997.

Huntington, Samuel P. *The Clash of Civilizations and the Remaking of the World Order*. New York: Simon & Schuster, 1996.

———. *The Third Wave: Democratization in the Late Twentieth Century*. Norman: University of Oklahoma Press, 1991.

Hutchinson, John, and Anthony D. Smith, eds. *Ethnicity*. Oxford: Oxford University Press, 1996.

——. *Nationalism*. Oxford: Oxford University Press, 1994.

Ikenberry, G. John, ed. *America Unrivaled: The Future of the Balance of Power*. Ithaca, N.Y.: Cornell University Press, 2002.

International Bar Association. *International Terrorism: Legal Challenges and Responses: A Report by the International Bar Association's Task Force on International Terrorism*. Ardsley, N.Y.: Transnational Publishers, 2003.

International Instruments Related to the Prevention and Suppression of International Terrorism. New York: United Nations Office of Legal Affairs, 2001.

Jackson, Robert H. *Quasi-states: Sovereignty, International Relations and the Third World*. Cambridge: Cambridge University Press, 1990.

Jaipal, Rikhi. *Non-Alignment: Origins, Growth, and Potential for World Peace*. New Delhi: Allied Publishers, 1983.

Kaul, Inge, Pedro Conceição, Katell Le Goulven, and Ronald U. Mendoza, eds. *Providing Global Public Goods: Managing Globalization*. New York: Oxford University Press, 2003.

Kay, David. *The New Nations in the United Nations 1960–1967*. New York: Columbia University Press, 1970.

Kennedy, Paul. *Preparing for the Twenty-First Century*. New York: Random House, 1993.

——. *The Rise and Fall of the Great Powers: Economic Change and Military Conflict from 1500 to 2000*. New York: Random House, 1988.

Keohane, Robert O., and Joseph S. Nye. *Power and Interdependence*. 2nd ed. New York: Scott, Foresman, 1989.

Khan, Rahmatullan. *Kashmir and the United Nations*. Delhi, India: Vikas, 1969.

Kim, Samuel S. *The Quest for a Just World Order*. Boulder, Colo.: Westview Press, 1984.

Klare, Michael T., and Daniel C. Thomas. *World Security: Challenges for a New Century*. New York: St. Martin's Press, 1998.

Korbel, Josef. *Danger in Kashmir*. Princeton, N.J.: Princeton University Press, 1954.

Kupchan, Charles A. *The End of the American Era: U.S. Foreign Policy and the Geopolitics of the Twenty-First Century*. New York: Knopf, 2002.

Kuznick, Peter J., and James Gilbert, eds. *Rethinking Cold War Culture*. Washington, D.C.: Smithsonian Institution Press, 2001.

Lafeber, Walter. *America, Russia, and the Cold War, 1945–1996*. New York: McGraw-Hill, 2001.

Lemon, Anthony, ed. *The Geography of Change in South Africa*. Chichester, England: Wiley, 1995.

Lowell L. Bryan, and Diana Farrell. *Market Unbound: Unleashing Global Capitalism.* New York: John Wiley, 1996.

Martin, L. W., ed. *Neutralism and Nonalignment: The New States in the World.* New York: Praeger, 1962.

Mearsheimer, John J. *The Tragedy of Great Power Politics.* New York: W.W. Norton, 2001.

Michie, Jonathan, ed. *The Handbook of Globalization.* Northampton, Mass.: Edward Elgar Publishing, 2003.

Mittelman, James, ed. *Globalization Syndrome.* Princeton, N.J.: Princeton University Press, 2000.

Mlinar, Zdravko. *Globalization and Territorial Identities.* Avebury, Vt.: 1992.

Monge, Jose Trias. *Puerto Rico: The Trials of the Oldest Colony in the World.* New Haven, Conn.: Yale University Press, 1997.

Morgenthau, Hans J. *Politics among Nations. The Struggle for Power and Peace.* 6th ed. Revised by Kenneth W. Thompson. New York: McGraw-Hill, Inc., 1985.

Morris, Benny. *The Birth of the Palestinian Refugee Problem 1947–1949.* Cambridge: Cambridge University Press, 1989.

Nanda, Ved P., ed. *Law in the War on International Terrorism.* Ardsley, N.Y.: Transnational Publishers, 2005.

Nandi, Proshanta K., and Shahid M. Shahidullah. *Globalization and the Evolving World Society.* Boston: Brill, 1998.

Pomerance, Michla. *Self-Determination in Law and Practice: The New Doctrine of the United Nations.* The Hague, The Netherlands: Martinius Nijhoff, 1982.

Prestowitz, Clyde V. *Rogue Nation: American Unilateralism and the Failure of Good Intentions.* New York: Basic Books, 2003.

Rajan, M. S., *Nonalignment and Nonaligned Movement: Retrospect and Prospect.* Delhi, India: Vikas Publishing, 1990.

Rivlin, Benjamin. *The United Nations and the Italian Colonies.* New York: Carnegie Endowment for International Peace, 1950.

Robertson, Justin, and Maurice A. East, eds. *Diplomacy and Developing Nations: Post–Cold War Foreign Policy-Making Structures and Processes.* New York: Routledge, 2005.

Rodrik, Dani. *Has Globalization Gone Too Far?* Washington, D.C.: Institute for International Economics, 1997.

Rosenau, James N. *Distant Proximities: Dynamics beyond Globalization.* Princeton, N.J.: Princeton University Press, 2003.

Sady, Emil J. *The United Nations and Dependent Peoples.* Washington, D.C.: Brookings Institution, 1956.

Sassen, Saskia. *Losing Control? Sovereignty in an Age of Globalization.* New York: Columbia University Press, 1996.

Schaeffer, Robert K. *Understanding Globalization: The Social Consequences of Political, Economic and Environmental Change*. Lanham, Md.: Rowman & Littlefield, 1997.

Schneider, Gerald, Katherine Barnieri, and Nils Petter Gledisch. *Globalization and Armed Conflict*. London: Rowman & Littlefield, 2003.

Seligson, Mitchell A., and John T. Passe-Smith. *Development and Underdevelopment: The Political Economy of Global Inequality*. Boulder, Colo.: Lynne Rienner, 1998.

Sellers, Mortimer, ed. *The New World Order: Sovereignty, Human Rights, and the Self-Determination of Peoples*. Oxford, 1996.

Spiro, David E. *The Hidden Hand of American Hegemony: Petrodollar Recycling and International Markets*. Ithaca, N.Y.: Cornell University Press, 1999.

Stiglitz, Joseph E. *Globalization and Its Discontents*. New York: W.W. Norton, 2002.

Sylvan A. Donald, and Michael Keren, eds. *International Intervention*. Portland, Ore.: Frank Cass Publishers, 2002.

Taylor, Alastair M. *Indonesian Independence and the United Nations*. Ithaca, NY.: Cornell University Press, 1960.

Toussaint, Charmian E. *The Trusteeship System of the United Nations*. New York: Praeger, 1956.

Urquhart, Brian. *Decolonization and World Peace*. Austin: University of Texas Press, 1989.

Vaubel, Roland, and Thomas D. Willett. *The Political Economy of International Organizations: A Public Choice Approach*. Boulder, Colo.: Westview Press, 1991.

Wainhouse, David W. *Remnants of Empires: The United Nations and the End of Colonialism*. New York: Harper & Row, 1967.

Ward, Barbara. *The Rich Nations and the Poor Nations*. New York: W.W. Norton, 1962.

Wenger, Andreas, and Doron Zimmermann. *International Relations: From the Cold War to the Globalized World*. Boulder, Colo.: Lynne Rienner, 2003.

Willetts, Peter. *The Non-Aligned Movement: The Origins of the Third World Alliance*. London: Pinter, 1978.

C. National Policies toward the United Nations

Alger, Chadwick F., Gene Lyons, and John Trent. *The United Nations System: The Policies of Member States*. Tokyo: United Nations University Press, 1995.

Bergesen, Helge, Hans Henrik Holm, and Robert D. McKinlay, eds. *The Recalcitrant Rich: A Comparative Analysis of the Northern Responses to the Demands for a New International Economic Order*. New York: St. Martin's Press, 1982.

Chakraborty, Bimal. *The United Nations and the Third World: Shifting Paradigms*. New Delhi: Tata McGraw-Hill, 1977.

Cooper, Andrew F. *Tests of Global Governance: Canadian Diplomacy and United Nations Conferences*. Tokyo: United Nations University Press, 2004.

Deller, Nicole, Arjun Makhijani, and John Burroughs. *Rule of Power or Rule of Law? An Assessment of U.S. Policies and Actions regarding Security-Related Treaties*. New York: Apex Press, 2003.

Dulles, John Foster. "The General Assembly." *Foreign Affairs* (October 1945): 165–75.

Ferguson, Niall. *Colossus: The Price of America's Empire*. New York: Penguin Press, 2004.

Ferguson, Tyrone. *The Third World and Decision-Making in the International Monetary Fund: The Quest for Full and Effective Participation*. London: Pinter Publishers, 1988.

Foot, Rosemary, S. Neil MacFarlane, and Michael Mastanduno, eds. *U.S. Hegemony and International Organizations*. New York: Oxford University Press, 2003.

Gati, Tobi Trister, ed. *The US, the UN and the Management of Global Change*, New York: New York University Press, 1983.

Grant, Cedric, "Equity in International Relations: A Third World Perspective." Special issue on "Ethics, the Environment and the Changing International Order, *International Affairs* 71, no. 3 (July 1995): 567–87.

Gregg, Robert W. *About Face? The United States and the United Nations*. Boulder, Colo.: Lynne Rienner, 1993.

Hasan, Sarwar. *Pakistan and the United Nations*. New York: Manhattan Publishing Company, 1960.

Jonah, James O. C. *Differing State Perspectives on the United Nations in the Post–Cold War Era*. John W. Holmes Memorial Lecture. Reports and Papers No. 4. Providence, R.I.: Academic Council on the United Nations System, 1993.

Johnson, Chalmers. *The Sorrows of Empire: Militarism, Secrecy, and the End of the Republic*. New York: Metropolitan Books, 2004.

Karns, Margaret P., and Karen A. Mingst, eds. *The United States and Multilateral Institutions: Patterns of Changing Instrumentality and Influence*. Boston: Unwin Hyman, 1990.

Harrod, Jeffrey, and Nico Schrijver, eds. *The UN Under Attack*. Brookfield, Vt.: Gower, 1988.

Kaufman, Natalie Hevener. *Human Rights Treaties and the Senate: A History of Opposition*. Chapel Hill: University of North Carolina Press, 1990.

Kay, David. *The New Nations in the United Nations 1960–1967*. New York: Columbia University Press, 1970.

Kennedy, David, and John Riggs, eds. *U.S. Policy and the Global Environment*. Queenstown, Md.: Aspen Institute, 2000.

Krause, Keith, and W. A. Knight. *State, Society, and the UN System*. Tokyo: United Nations University Press, 1995.

Liang-Fenton, Debra. *Implementing U.S. Human Rights Policy: Agendas, Policies, Practices*. Washington, D.C.: United States Institute of Peace Press, 2004.

Luck, Edward. *Mixed Messages: American Politics and International Organization, 1919–1999*. Washington, D.C.: Brookings Institution, 1999.

MacKinnon, Michael. *The Evolution of US Peacekeeping Policy under Clinton: A Fairweather Friend?* Portland, Ore.: Frank Cass, 1999.

Malone, David M., and Yuen Foong Khong, eds. *Unilateralism and U.S. Foreign Policy: International Perspectives*. Boulder, Colo.: Lynne Rienner, 2003.

Mann, Michael. *Incoherent Empire*. New York: Verso, 2003.

Morrell, James B. *The Law of the Sea: An Historical Analysis of the 1982 Treaty and Its Rejection by the United States*. Jefferson, N.C.: McFarland, 1991.

Ogata, Sadako. "The United Nations and Japanese Diplomacy." *Japan Review of International Affairs* 4, no. 2 (Fall/Winter 1990): 141–65,

Patrick, Stewart, and Shepard Forman, eds. *Multilateralism and U.S. Foreign Policy: Ambivalent Engagement*. Boulder, CO.: Lynne Rienner, 2001.

Pavlic, Breda, and Cees J. Hamelink. *The New International Economic Order: Links between Economics and Communication*. Paris: UNESCO, 1985.

Perito, Robert M. *Where Is the Lone Ranger When We Need Him? America's Search for a Postconflict Stability Force*. Washington, D.C.: United States Institute of Peace Press, 2004.

Pew Center for the People & the Press. *Views of a Changing World*. Washington, D.C.: The Pew Center for the People & the Press, 2003.

Pillar, Paul R. *Terrorism and U.S. Foreign Policy*. Washington, DC.: Brookings Institution, 2001.

Raevsky, A. and I. N. Voroblev. *Russian Approaches to Peacekeeping Operations*. New York: United Nations, 1994.

Riggs, Robert E. *Politics in the United Nations*. Urbana: University of Illinois Press, 1958. Reprinted by Greenwood Press, 1984.

Sauvant, Karl P. *The Group of 77: Evolution, Structure, Organization*. New York: Oceana Publications, 1981.

Shah, Manubhai. *Developing Countries and UNCTAD*. Bombay, India: Vora, 1968.

Sharma, Prem Mohan. *Politics of Peace and UN General Assembly*. New Delhi, India: Abhinav Publications, 1978.

Stromberg, Roland N. *Collective Security and American Foreign Policy: From the League of Nations to NATO*. New York: Praeger, 1963.

Todd, Emmanuel. *After the Empire: The Breakdown of the American Order*. New York: Columbia University Press, 2003.

United Nations Institute for Training and Research. *A New International Economic Order: Selected Documents 1945–1973*. 2 vols. New York: UNITAR, 1976.

Vogt, M. A., and E. E. Ekoko, eds. *Nigeria in International Peace-Keeping, 1960–1992*. Oxford: Malthouse, 1993.

Zammit-Cutajar, Michael, ed. *UNCTAD and the North-South Dialogue: The First Twenty-Five Years*. London: Pergamon, 1985.

D. The Legal, Institutional, and Financial Framework

Ameri, Houshang. *Fraud, Waste and Abuse: Aspects of U.N. Management and Personnel Policies*. Lanham, Md.: University Press of America, 2003.

Bailey, Sidney D., and Sam Daws. *The Procedure of the UN Security Council*. Oxford: Clarendon Press, 1998.

Beigbeder, Yves. *The Internal Management of United Nations Organizations: The Long Quest For Reform*. New York: St. Martin's Press, 1997.

Conforti, B. *The Law and Practice of the United Nations*. The Hague, The Netherlands: Kluwer, 2000.

Gordenker, Leon. *The UN Secretary-General and Secretariat*. New York: Routledge, 2005.

Haas, Peter M., Robert O. Keohane, and Marc A. Levy, eds. *Institutions for the Earth: Sources of Effective International Environmental Institutions*. Cambridge, Mass.: MIT Press, 1993.

Hall, H. Duncan. *Mandates, Dependencies, and Trusteeship*. Washington, D.C.: Carnegie Endowment for International Peace, 1948.

Haviland, Henry Field. *The Political Role of the General Assembly*. New York: Carnegie Endowment for International Peace, 1951.

Herndl, K. *Reflections on the Role, Functions and Procedures of the Security Council in the United Nations*. Dordrecht, Netherlands: Martinus Nijhoff, 1991.

Hill, Martin. *The United Nations System: Coordinating Its Economic and Social Work*. Cambridge: Cambridge University Press, 1978.

Kazimi, M. R. *Financing the U.N. Peace-Keeping Operations*. Delhi, India: Capital Publishing House, 1988.

Knipping, Franz, and Ralph Dietl. *The United Nations System and Its Predecessors*. Vol. 2. New York: Oxford University Press, 1997.

Mangoldt, Hans von, and Volker Ritttberger, eds. *The United Nations and Its Predecessors*. Vol. 1. New York: Oxford University Press, 1979.

Malone, David. "Eyes on the Prize: The Quest for Nonpermanent Seats on the UN Security Council." *Global Governance* 6, no.1 (2000): 3–24.

Marks, Edward. *Complex Emergencies: Bureaucratic Arrangements in the UN Secretariat*. Washington, D.C.: National Defense University Press, 1996.

Meron, Theodor. *The United Nations Secretariat: The Rules and Practice*. Lexington, Mass: D.C. Heath, 1977.

Mills, Susan R. *The Financing of United Nations Peacekeeping Operations*. Occasional Paper No. 3. New York: International Peace Academy, 1989.

Mouritzen, Hans. *The International Civil Service: A Study of Bureaucracy: International Organizations*. Aldershot, England: Dartmouth, 1990.

Murray, James N. Jr. *The United Nations Trusteeship System*. Urbana: University of Illinois Press, 1957.

Padelford, Norman J. *The Financing of Future Peace and Security Operations Under the United Nations*. Washington, D.C.: Brookings Institution, 1962.

Pitt, David, and Thomas G. Weiss, eds. *The Nature of United Nations Bureaucracies*. Boulder, Colo.: Westview Press, 1986.

Ranshofen-Wertheimer, Egon F. *The International Secretariat: A Great Experiment in International Administration*. New York: Carnegie Endowment for International Peace, 1945.

Russett, Bruce, ed. *The Once and Future Security Council*. New York: St. Martin's Press, 1997.

Simma, Bruno. *The Charter of the United Nations: A Commentary*. Oxford: Oxford University Press, 1994.

Singer, David. *Financing International Organization: The United Nations Budget Process*. The Hague, The Netherlands: Martinus Nijhoff, 1961.

Sloan, Blaine. *United Nations General Assembly Resolutions in Our Changing World*. Ardsley, N.Y.: Transnational Publishers, 1991.

Stoessinger, John G. and Associates. *Financing the United Nations System*. Washington, D.C.: Brookings Institution, 1964.

Taylor, Paul, and A. J. R. Groom, eds. *The United Nations at the Millennium: Principal Organs*. London: Continuum, 2000.

Tewary, Indira Narayan. *The Peacekeeping Power of the United Nations General Assembly*. New Delhi, India: S. Chand, 1974.

Weiss, Thomas G. *International Bureaucracy: An Analysis of the Operation of Functional and Global International Secretariats*. Lexington, Mass.: D.C. Heath, 1975.

Wellens, K., ed. *Resolutions and Statements of the United Nations Security Council (1946–1992): A Thematic Guide*. 2nd ed. Dordrecht, The Netherlends: Martinus Nijhoff, 1993.

Whitman, J., and D. Pocock, eds. *After Rwanda: The Coordination of United Nations Humanitarian Assistance*. New York: St. Martin's Press, 1996.

Wightman, David. *Toward Economic Cooperation in Asia: The United Nations Economic and Social Commission for Asia and the Pacific*. New Haven, Conn.: Yale University Press, 1963.

Wright, Quincy. *Mandates under the League of Nations*. Chicago: University of Chicago Press, 1930.

E. The UN Political Process (Actors and Decision Making)

1. Civil Society

Aall, Pamela, Col. Daniel Miltenberger, and Thomas G. Weiss. *Guide to IGOs, NGOs, and the Military in Peace and Relief Operations*. Washington, D.C.: United States Institute of Peace Press, 2000.

Alger, Chadwick. "The Emerging Roles of NGOs in the UN System: From Article 71 to a People's Millennium Assembly." *Global Governance* 8, no.1 (2002): 93–118.

Alger, Chadwick F. "Strengthening Relations Between NGOs and the UN System: Towards a Research Agenda." *Global Society: Journal of Interdisciplinary International Relations* 13, no.4 (1999): 393–410.

Bohlen, Jim. *Making Waves: The Origins and Future of Greenpeace*. New York: Black Rose, 2001.

Cameron, Maxwell A., Robert J. Lawson, Brian W. Tomlin, eds. *To Walk Without Fear: The Global Movement to Ban Landmines*. New York: Oxford University Press, 1999.

Carey, Henry F., and Oliver P. Richmond. *Mitigating Conflict: The Role of NGOs*. Portland, Ore.: Frank Cass, 2003.

Centre for Civil Society and Centre for the Study of Global Governance. *Global Civil Society 2001*. New York: Oxford University Press, 2001.

Edwards, Michael, and John Gaventa, eds. *Global Citizen Action*. Boulder, Colo.: Lynne Rienner, 2001.

Fisher, Julie. *Nongovernments: NGOs and the Political Development of the Third World*. West Hartford, Conn.: Kumarian Press, 1997.

——. *The Road from Rio: Sustainable Development and the Nongovernmental Movement in the Third World*. Westport, Conn.: Praeger, 1993.

Fitzduff, Mari, and Cheyanne Church. *NGOs at the Table: Strategies for Influencing Policy in Areas of Conflict*. New York: Rowman & Littlefield, 2004.

Foster, John. *Futures Beyond Threats: The UN, Civil Society and Global Governance*. Ottawa: North-South Institute, 2002.

Higgott, R., and A. Bieler, eds. *Non-State Actors and Authority in the Global System*. London: Routledge, 1999.

Howell, Jude, and Jenny Pearce. *Civil Society and Development: A Critical Exploration*. Boulder, Colo.: Lynne Rienner, 2002.

Jordan, L., and P. van Tuijl. *Political Responsibility in NGO Advocacy: Exploring the Emerging Structure of Global Democracy*. The Hague, The Netherlands: NOVIB, 1998.

Keck, M., and K. Sikkink. *Activists Beyond Borders: Transnational Advocacy Networks in International Politics*. Ithaca, N.Y.: Cornell University Press, 1998.

Kendig, K. *Civil Society, Global Governance and the United Nations*. Tokyo: United Nations University Press, 1999.

Knut, R. *Globalization and Civil Society: NGO Influence in International Decision-Making*. Geneva: UNRISD, 1997.

Korey, William. *NGOs and the Universal Declaration on Human Rights*. New York: St. Martin's Press, 1998.

Lewis, David, and Tina Wallace. *New Roles and Relevance: Development NGOs and the Challenge of Change*. Bloomfield, Conn.: Kumarian Press, 2000.

Maresca, Louis, and Stuart Maslen, eds. *The Banning of Anti-Personnel Mines: The Legal Contribution of the International Committee of the Red Cross, 1955–1999*. Cambridge: Cambridge University Press, 2001.

Marsiaj, Caroline E. Schwitter. *Role of International NGOs in the Global Governance of Human Rights: Challenging the Democratic Deficit*. Zurich, Switzerland: Schulthess, 2004.

Martens, Kerstin. "Non-governmental Organizations as Corporatist Mediator? An Analysis of NGOs in the UNESCO System." *Global Society: Journal of Interdisciplinary International Relations* 15, no. 4 (2001): 387–405.

Nurser, John S. *For All Peoples and All Nations. The Ecumenical Church and Human Rights*. Washington, D.C.: Georgetown University Press, 2005.

O'Brien, R., et al. *Challenging Global Governance: Social Movements and Multilateral Economic Institutions*. Cambridge: Cambridge University Press, 1998.

Panel of Eminent Persons on UN-Civil Society Relations. *We, the Peoples: Civil Society, the UN and Global Governance*. UN Document A/58/817. www.un.org/reform/panel.htm.

Paul, J. *NGO Access at the United Nations*. New York: Global Policy Forum, 1999.

Pei-Heng, Chiang. *Non-governmental Organizations at the United Nations: Identity, Role, and Function*. New York: Praeger, 1981.

Phillips, Robert L., and C. L. Duane. *Humanitarian Intervention: Just War vs. Pacifism*. Lanham, Md.: Rowman & Littlefield, 1996.

Richmond, Oliver P. *Subcontracting Peace. The Challenges of NGO Peacebuilding*. Williston, Vt.: Ashgate, 2005.

Rotblat, Joseph. *Scientists in the Quest for Peace: A History of the Pugwash Conferences on Science and World Affairs*. Cambridge, Mass.: MIT Press, 1972.

Sikkink, Kathryn. *Activists Beyond Borders: Advocacy Networks in International Politics*. Ithaca, N.Y.: Cornell University Press, 1998.

Smith, Jackie, Charles Chatfield, and Ron Pagnucco, eds. *Transnational Social Movements and Global Politics: Solidarity Beyond the State*. Syracuse, N.Y.: Syracuse University Press, 1997.

Taylor, Rupert. *Creating a Better World: Interpreting Global Civil Society*. Bloomfield, Conn.: Kumarian Press, 2004.

Tolley, Howard. *The International Commission of Jurists: Global Advocates for Human Rights*. Philadelphia: University of Pennsylvania Press, 1994.

Tongeren Paul van, Malin Brenk, Marte Hellema, and Julliette Verhoeven, eds. *People Building Peace: Successful Stories of Civil Society*. Boulder, Colo.: Lynne Rienner, 2005.

United Nations. *Arrangements and Practices for the Interaction of NGOs in All Activities of the UN System: Report of the Secretary General*. New York: UN Document A/53/150, 1998.

Weiss, Thomas G., and L.Gordenker, eds. *NGOs, the UN, and Global Governance*. Boulder, Colo.: Lynne Rienner, 1996.

Willetts, Peter. "From 'Consultative Arrangements' to 'Partnership': The Changing Status of NGOs in Diplomacy at the UN." *Global Governance* 6, no. 2 (2000): 191–213.

——. *The Conscience of the World: The Influence of Non-Governmental Organizations in the UN System*. Washington, D.C.: Brookings Institution, 1998.

Willets, Peter, ed. *Pressure Groups in the Global System: The Transnational Relations of Issue-Oriented Non-Governmental Organizations*. London: Pinter, 1982.

2. The Private Sector

Bailes, Alyson J. K., and Isabel Frommelt. *Business and Security: Public-Private Sector Relationships in a New Security Environment*. New York: Oxford University Press, 2004.

Bomann-Larsen, Lene, and Oddny Wiggen, eds. *Responsibility in World Business: Managing Harmful Side-effects of Corporate Activity*. Tokyo: United Nations University Press, 2004.

Dell, Sidney. *The United Nations and International Business*. Durham, N.C.: Duke University Press, 1990.

Desmond, Livio, and Frank Popoff. *Eco-Efficiency: The Business Link to Sustainable Development*. Cambridge, Mass.: MIT Press, 1997.

Garvey, Niamh, and Peter Newell. *Corporate Accountability to the Poor? Assessing the Effectiveness of Community-Based Strategies*. Brighton, England: Institute of Development Studies, 2004.

Herman, Barry, Federica Pietracci, and Khrishnan Sharma, eds. *Financing for Development: Proposals from Business and Civil Society*. Tokyo: United Nations University Press, 2001.

Kenkins, Rhys, Ruth Pearson, and Gill Seyfang, eds. *Corporate Responsibility and Labour Rights: Codes of Conduct in the Global Economy*. Sterling, Va.: Earthscan Publications, 2002.

Joseph, Sarah. *Corporations and Transnational Human Rights*. Portland, Ore.: Hart, 2004.

McIntosh, Malcolm, Sandra Waddock, and Georg Kell, eds. *Learning to Talk: Corporate Citizenship and the Development of the UN Global Compact*. Sheffield, England: Greenleaf, 2004.

Nelson, Jane. *Building Partnerships: Cooperation Between the United Nations System and the Private Sector*. New York: United Nations, 2002.

Pearson, Charles, ed. *Multinational Corporations, Environment, and the Third World: Business Matters*. Durham, N.C. Duke University Press, 1987.

Schmidheiny, Stephen, and Federico Zorraquin. *Financing Change: The Financial Community, Eco-Efficiency, and Sustainable Development*. Cambridge, Mass.: MIT Press, 1998.

Tesner, Sandrine, with Georg Kell. *The United Nations and Business: A Partnership Rediscovered*. New York: St. Martin's Press, 2000.

3. Decision Making

Alker, Hayward R., and B. M. Russett. *World Politics in the General Assembly*. New Haven, Conn.: Yale University Press, 1965.

Ameri, Houshang. *Politics and Process in the Specialized Agencies of the United Nations*. Aldershot, England: Gower Publishing, 1982.

Bailey, Sidney D. *Voting in the Security Council*. Bloomington: Indiana University Press, 1969.

Bailey, Sidney D., and Sam Daws. *The Procedure of the UN Security Council*. 3rd ed. Oxford: Oxford University Press, 1998.

Barrett, Scott. *Environment and Statecraft: The Strategy of Environmental Treaty-Making*. New York: Oxford University Press, 2003.

Chasek, Pamela. *Earth Negotiations. Analyzing Thirty Years of Environmental Diplomacy*. Tokyo: United Nations University Press, 2001.

Childers, Erskine, ed. *Challenges to the United Nations: Building a Safer World*. New York: St. Martin's Press, 1995.

Cox, Robert W., and H. K. Jacobson, eds. *The Anatomy of Influence: Decision-Making in International Organization*. New Haven, Conn.: Yale University Press, 1973.

Cooper, Andrew F., J. English, and R. Thakur, eds. *Enhancing Global Governance: Towards a New Diplomacy?* Tokyo: United Nations University Press, 2002.

Deng, Francis M., and I. William Zartman. *Conflict Resolution in Africa*. Washington, D.C.: Brookings Institution, 1991.

Hagras, Kamal. *United Nations Conference on Trade and Development: A Case Study in UN Diplomacy*. New York: Praeger, 1965.

Jacobson, Harold K. *Networks of Interdependence: International Organizations and the Global Political System*. 2nd ed. New York: Alfred A. Knopf, 1984.

Jones, Charles A. *The North-South Dialogue: A Brief History*. New York: St. Martin's, 1983.

Kaufman, Johan. *Conference Diplomacy: An Introductory Analysis*. 2nd rev. ed. Dordrecht, The Netherlands: Martinus Nijhoff, 1988.

———. *United Nations Decision-Making*. Rockville, Md.: Sijthoff and Noordthoff, 1980.

Lall, Arthur S. *Multilateral Negotiation and Mediation*. New York: Pergamon Press, 1985.

McHenry, Donald. "The Contact Group and Initial Negotiations (1978–1981)." In *The Namibian Peace Process: Implications and Lessons for the Future*, ed. Herbert Weill and Matthew Braham. Freiburg, Germany: Arnold Bergstraesser Institut, 1994.

Malone, David. *Decision-Making in the UN Security Council: The Case of Haiti, 1990–1997*. Oxford: Clarendon Press; New York: Oxford University Press, 1998.

Marin-Bosch. *Votes in the UN General Assembly*. The Hague, The Netherlands: Kluwer, 1998.

Merrills, J. G. *International Dispute Settlement*. 2nd ed. Cambridge: Cambridge University Press, 1991.

Prantl, Jochen, and Jean Krasno. *Informal Ad Hoc Groupings of States and the Workings of the United Nations*. International Relations Studies and the United Nations Occasional Paper No. 3. Waterloo, Ontario: Academic Council on the United Nations System, 2002.

Rothstein, Robert L. *Global Dialogue: UNCTAD and the Quest for a New International Economic Order*. Princeton, N.J.: Princeton University Press, 1979.

Smith, Courtney B. *Politics and Process at the United Nations: The Global Dance*. Boulder, Colo.: Lynne Rienner, 2005.

Spector, Bertram I., Gunnar Sjostedt, and I. William Zartman, eds. *Negotiating International Regimes: Lessons Learned from the United Nations Conference on Environment and Development (UNCED)*. Boston: Graham & Trotman, 1994.

Szasz, Paul C. *Alternative Voting Systems in International Organizations and the Binding Triad Proposal to Improve U.N. General Assembly Decision-Making*. Wayne, N.J.: Center for U.N. Reform, 2001.

Tolba, Mostafa K., with Iwona Rummel-Bulska. *Global Environmental Diplomacy: Negotiating Environmental Agreements with the World, 1973–1992*. Cambridge, Mass.: MIT Press, 1998.

United Nations Non-Governmental Liaison Service. *Intergovernmental Negotiations and Decision Making at the United Nations: A Guide*. New York: United Nations, 2003.

Weiss, Thomas G. *Multilateral Development Diplomacy in UNCTAD: The Lessons of Group Negotiations, 1964–1984*. New York: St. Martin's Press, 1986.

Williams, Marc. *Third World Cooperation: The Group of 77 in UNCTAD*. New York: St. Martin's Press, 1991.

4. Memoirs and Autobiographies

Acheson, Dean. *Present at the Creation: My Years in the State Department*. New York: Norton, 1969.

Akashi, Yasushi, "The Limits of UN Diplomacy and the Future of Conflict Mediation," *Survival: The IISS Quarterly* 37, no. 4 (Winter 1995–1996): 83–98.

Albright, Madeleine, with Bill Woodward. *Madam Secretary*. New York: Miramax Books, 2003.

Anstee, Margaret. *Never Learned to Type: A Woman at the United Nations*. Chichester, England: Wiley, 2003.

———. *Orphan of the Cold War: The Inside Story of the Collapse of the Angolan Peace Process, 1992–93*. New York: St. Martin's, 1996.

Bingham, June. *U Thant: The Search for Peace*. New York: Alfred A. Knopf, 1966.

Blix, Hans. *Disarming Iraq*. New York: Pantheon, 2004.

Boutros-Ghali, Boutros. *Unvanquished: A U.S.-U.N. Saga*. New York: Random House, 1999.

Boyle, Kevin, ed. *A Voice for Human Rights: Mary Robinson*. Philadelphia: University of Pennsylvania Press, 2005.

Burgess, Stephen F. *The United Nations under Boutros Boutros-Ghali, 1992–1997*. Lanham, Md.: Scarecrow Press, 2001.

Cordovez, Diego, and Selig S. Harrison. *Out of Afghanistan: The Inside Story of the Soviet Withdrawal*. New York: Oxford University Press, 1995.

Dayal, Rajeshwar. *Mission for Hammarskjöld: The Congo Crises*. London: Oxford University Press, 1976.

Eichelberger, Clark, M. *Organizing for Peace: A Personal History of the Founding of the United Nations*. New York: Harper & Row, 1977.

Fasulo, Linda M. *An Insider's Guide to the UN*. New Haven, Conn.: Yale University Press, 2004.

———. *Representing America: Experiences of U.S. Diplomats at the U.N*. New York: Praeger, 1984.

Finger, Seymour Maxwell. *American Ambassadors at the UN: People, Politics, and Bureaucracy in Making Foreign Policy*. New York: Holmes & Meier, 1988.

Finger, Seymour Maxwell, and Arnold A. Saltzman. *Bending with the Winds: Kurt Waldheim and the United Nations*. New York: Praeger, 1990.

Firestone, Bernard J. *The United Nations under U Thant, 1961–1971*. Lanham, Md.: Scarecrow Press, 2001.

Foote, Walter, ed. *The Servants of Peace: A Selection of the Speeches and Statements of Dag Hammarskjöld*. London: Bodley Head, 1962.

Gaglione, Anthony. *The United Nations under Trygve Lie, 1945–1953*. Lanham, Md.: Scarecrow Press, 2001.

Goulding, Marrack. *Peacemonger*. London: John Murray, 2002.

Hammarskjöld, Dag. *Markings*. New York: Alfred A. Knopf, 1964.

Hazzard, Shirley. *Countenance of Truth: The United Nations and the Waldheim Case*. New York: Viking, 1990.

Heller, Peter B. *The United Nations under Dag Hammarskjöld, 1953–1961*. Lanham, Md.: Scarecrow Press, 2001.

Hill, Charles, ed. *The Papers of the United Nations Secretary-General Boutros Boutros-Ghali*. New Haven, Conn.: Yale University Press, 2003.

Koh, Tommy T. *Quest for World Order: Perspectives of a Pragmatic Idealist*. Singapore: Eastern Universities Press, 1998.

Lankevich, George J. *The United Nations under Javier Perez de Cuellar, 1972–1981*. Lanham, Md.: Scarecrow Press, 2001.

Lash, Joseph P. *Dag Hammarskjöld: Custodian of the Brushfire Peace*. New York: Doubleday, 1961.

Lie, Trygve. *In the Cause of Peace*. New York: Macmillan, 1954.

Miller, Richard Irwin. *Dag Hammarskjöld and Crisis Diplomacy*. New York: Oceana Publications, 1961.

Moynihan, Daniel. *A Dangerous Place*. Boston: Little, Brown, 1969.

Nassif, Ramses. *U Thant in New York, 1961–1971: A Portrait of the Third UN Secretary-General*. London: Hurst & Company, 1988.

Ogata, Sadako. *Turbulent Decade: Confronting the Refugee Crises of the 1990s*. New York: Norton, 2005.

Ould-Abdalah, Ahmedou. *Burundi on the Brink, 1993–95. A UN Special Envoy Reflects on Preventive Diplomacy*. Washington, D.C.: United States Institute of Peace Press, 2000.

Pearson, Geoffrey A. H. *Seize the Day: Lester B. Pearson and Crisis Diplomacy*. Ottawa: Carleton University Press, 1994.

Perez de Cuellar, Javier. *Pilgrimage for Peace: A Secretary-General's Memoir*. New York: St. Martin's Press, 1997.

Picco, Giandomenico. *Man Without a Gun: One Diplomat's Secret Struggle to Free the Hostages, Fight Terrorism, and End a War*. New York: Random House, 1999.

Picco, Giandomenico, et al. *Crossing the Divide: Dialogue of Civilizations*. South Orange, N.J.: Seton Hall University, 2001.

Richardot, Jean. *Journeys for a Better World: A Personal Adventure in War and Peace: An Inside Story of the United Nations by One of Its First Senior Officials*. Lanham, Md.: University Press of America, 1993.

Rikhye, Indar Jit. *The Art of Keeping the Peace: Trumpets and Tumults: The Memoirs of a Peacekeeper*. New Delhi, India: Manohar Publishers, 2002.

——. *Military Adviser to the Secretary-General: U.N. Peacekeeping and the Congo Crisis*. New York: St. Martin's Press and International Peace Academy, 1993.

——. *Theory and Practice of Peacekeeping*. New York: St. Martin's Press, 1984.

——. *The Sinai Blunder*. London: Cass, 1980.

Rivlin, Benjamin. *Ralph Bunche, the Man and His Times*. New York: Holmes and Meier, 1990.

Romulo, Carlos P. *Forty Years: A Third World Soldier at the UN*. London: Greenwood, 1986.

Ryan, James Daniel. *The United Nations under Kurt Waldheim, 1972–1981*. Lanham, Md.: Scarecrow Press, 2001.

Sadik, Nafis. *Making a Difference: Twenty-five Years of UNFPA Experience*. London: Banson, 1994.

——. *Population Policies and Programmes: Lessons Learned from Two Decades of Experience*. New York: New York University Press, 1991.

Sokalsky, Henryk J. *An Ounce of Prevention: Macedonia and the UN Experience in Preventive Diplomacy*. Washington, D.C.: United States Institute of Peace Press, 2003.

Thant, U. *View from the UN*. Garden City, New York: Doubleday, 1978.

Urquhart, Brian. *A Life in Peace and War*. New York: Harper & Row Publishers, 1987.

———. *Hammarskjöld*. New York: Alfred A. Knopf, 1972.

Waldheim, Kurt. *In the Eye of the Storm: A Memoir*. London: Weidenfeld & Nicholson, 1985.

———. *Building the Future: The Search for Peace in the Interdependent World*. New York: Free Press, 1980.

Zacher, Mark W. *Dag Hammarskjöld's United Nations*. New York: Columbia University Press, 1970.

F. Peace and Security

1. Dispute Settlement, Mediation, Prevention, and Conflict Resolution

Agwani, Mohammed Shafi, ed. *The Lebanese Crisis, 1958: A Documentary Study*. New York: Asia Publishing House, 1965.

Alwan, Mohamed. *Algeria Before the United Nations*. New York: R. Speller, 1959.

Annan, Kofi. "Prevention of Armed Conflict: Report of the Secretary General." UN Document A/55/985-S/2001/574.

Arnson, Cynthia, ed. *Comparative Peace Processes in Latin America*. Washington, D.C.: Woodrow Wilson Center Press, 1999.

Bailey, Sidney D. *How Wars End: The United Nations and the Termination of Armed Conflicts, 1946–1964*. 2 vols. New York: Oxford University Press, 1982.

Ballentine, Karen, and Heiko Nitzschke, eds. *Profiting from Peace: Managing the Resource Dimension of Civil War*. Boulder, Colo.: Lynne Rienner, 2005.

Bardehle, Peter. "The Role of the United Nations in the Settlement of the Iran-Iraq War, 1980-88." *Conflict Quarterly* 12 (Spring 1992): 36–50.

Boisson de Chazournes, Laurence, Cesare Romano, and Ruth MacKenzie, eds. *International Organizations and International Dispute Settlement: Trends and Prospects*. Ardsley, N.Y.: Transnational Publishers, 2002.

Boudreau, Thomas E. *Sheathing the Sword: The U.N. Secretary-General and the Prevention of Inter-Nation Conflict*. Westport, Conn.: Greenwood Press, 1991.

Boutros-Ghali, Boutros. *An Agenda for Peace*. New York: United Nations, 1995.

Boyd, Andrew. *Fifteen Men on a Powder Keg: A History of the United Nations Security Council*. New York: Stein & Day, 1971.

Bradner, Heidi, and Anatol Lieven. *Chechnya: Tombstone of Russian Power*. New Haven, Conn.: Yale University Press, 1999.

Brus, Marcel, Sam Muller, and Serv Wiemers, eds. *The United Nations Decade of International Law: Reflections on International Dispute Settlement*. Dordrecht, The Netherlands: Martinus Nijhoff, 1991.

Burton, John H., and Margaret E. McGuiness, eds. *Words Over Wars: Mediation and Arbitration to Prevent Deadly Conflict*. Lanham, Md.: Rowman & Littlefield, 2002.

Carnegie Commission on Preventing Deadly Conflict. *Preventing Deadly Conflict: Final Report with Executive Summary*. New York: Carnegie Corporation of New York, 1997.

Carment, David, and Albrecht Schnabel, eds. *Conflict Prevention: Path to Peace or Grand Illusion?* Tokyo: United Nations University Press, 2003.

Chayes, Antonia Handler, and Abram Chayes. *Planning for Intervention: International Cooperation in Conflict Management*. Cambridge, Mass.: Kluwer Law International, 1999.

Crocker, Chester A., Fen Osler Hampson, and Pamela Aall. *Taming Intractable Conflicts: Mediation in the Hardest Cases*. Washington, D.C.: United States Institute of Peace Press, 2004.

———, eds. *Turbulent Peace. The Challenges of Managing International Conflict*. Washington, D.C.: United States Institute of Peace Press, 2001.

———. *Herding Cats: The Management of Complex International Conflicts: The Theory and Practice of Mediation*. Boulder, Colo.: Lynne Rienner, 1996.

Davies, John L., and Ted Robert Gurr, *Preventive Measures, Building Risk Assessment and Crisis Early Warning Systems*. Lanham, Md.: Rowman & Littlefield, 1998.

Deng Francis M., and I. William Zartman. *Conflict Resolution in Africa*. Washington, D.C.: Brookings Institution, 1991.

Deval, Thomas, and Carlotta Gall. *Chechnya: Calamity in the Caucasus*. New York: New York University Press, 2000.

Djalili, Mohammad-Reza, Frederic Grare, and Shirin Akiner, eds. *Tajikistan: The Trials of Independence*. New York: St. Martin's Press, 1997.

Dore, Isaak I. *The International Mandate System and Namibia*. Boulder, Colo.: Westview Press, 1985.

Dunlop, John B. *Russia Confronts Chechnya: Roots of a Separatist Conflict*. Cambridge: Cambridge University Press, 1998.

Evangelista, Matthew. *The Chechen Wars: Will Russia Go the Way of the Soviet Union?* Washington, D.C.: Brookings Institution Press, 2002.

Gordenker, Leon. *The UN Secretary-General and the Maintenance of Peace*. New York: Columbia University Press, 1967.

Hamburg, David. *No More Killing Fields: Preventing Deadly Conflict*. Oxford: Rowman & Littlefield, 2002.

Hampson, Fen Osler. *Nurturing Peace: Why Peace Settlements Succeed or Fail*. Washington, D.C.: United States Institute of Peace Press, 1996.

Hampson, Fen Osler, and David M. Malone, eds. *From Reaction to Conflict Prevention: Opportunities for the UN System*. Boulder, Colo: Lynne Rienner, 2002.

Jentleson, Bruce W., ed. *Opportunities Missed, Opportunities Seized: Preventive Diplomacy in the Post–Cold War World.* Oxford: Rowman & Littlefield, 2000.

Jordan, Robert S., ed. *Dag Hammarskjöld Revisited: UN Secretary-General as a Force in World Politics.* Durham, N.C.: Carolina Academic Press, 1983.

Kakar, M. Hasan. *Afghanistan: The Soviet Invasion and the Afghan Response, 1979–1982.* Berkeley: University of California Press, 1995.

Kotz, Audie. *Norms in International Relations: The Struggle Against Apartheid.* Ithaca, N.Y.: Cornell University Press, 1995.

Lall, Arthur S. *Multilateral Negotiation and Mediation.* New York: Pergamon Press, 1985.

——. *The UN in the Middle East Crisis, 1967.* New York: Columbia University Press, 1968.

Larus, Joel, ed. *From Collective Security to Preventive Diplomacy: Readings in International Organization and the Maintenance of Peace.* New York: John Wiley, 1965.

Lund, Michael S. *Preventing Violent Conflict: A Strategy for Preventive Diplomacy.* Washington, D.C.: United States Institute of Peace Press, 1996.

Martin, Ian. *Self-Determination in East Timor: The United Nations, the Ballot, and International Intervention.* Boulder, Colo.: Lynne Rienner Publisher, 2001.

Maundi Mohammed O., I. William Zartman, Gilbert M. Khadiagala, and Kwaku Nuamah. *Getting In: Mediators' Entry into the Settlement of African Conflicts.* Herndon, Va.: United States Institute of Peace Press, 2005.

Palley, Claire. *An International Relations Debacle: The UN Secretary-General's Mission of Good Offices in Cyprus, 1999–2004.* Oxford: Hart Publishing, 2005.

Parson, Anthony. *From Cold War to Hot Peace: UN Interventions 1947–1995.* London: Michael Joseph, 1995.

Peck, Connie. *Sustainable Peace: The Role of the UN and Regional Organizations in Preventing Conflict.* New York: Rowman & Littlefield, 1998.

——. *The United Nations as a Dispute Settlement System: Improving Mechanisms for the Prevention and Resolution of Conflicts.* The Hague, The Netherlands: Kluwer Law International, 1996.

Peck, Connie, and David A. Hamburg. *Sustainable Peace: The Role of the UN and Regional Organizations in Preventing Conflict.* Lanham, Md.: Rowman & Littlefield, 1998.

Ramcharan, B. G. *International Law and the Practice of Early Warning: The Emerging Global Watch.* Dordrecht, The Netherlands: Martinus Nijhoff, 1991.

Richmond, Oliver P. *Mediating in Cyprus: The Cypriot Communities and the United Nations.* Portland, Ore.: Frank Cass, 1998.

Rfouh, Faisal O. M. *Quest for Peace: United Nations and Palestine*. New Delhi, India: National Book Organization, 1986.

Romano, Cesare, Laurence Boisson de Charzournes, and Ruth MacKenzie (Eds.). *International Organizations and International Dispute Settlement: Trends and Prospects*. New York: Transnational Publishers, 2002.

Rovine, Arthur W. *The First Fifty Years: The Secretary-General in World Politics, 1920–1970*. Leyden: A. W. Sijthoff, 1970.

Rubin, Barnett. *Blood on the Doorstep: The Politics of Preventive Action*. New York: The Century Foundation Press, 2002.

Rubin, Barnett R. *Cases and Strategies for Preventive Action*. New York: Council on Foreign Relations, 2001.

Rupesinghe, Kumar, and Michiko Kuroda. *Early Warning and Conflict Resolution*. New York: St. Martin's Press, 1992.

Sassen, Saskia. *Preventing Deadly Conflict*. New York: Carnegie Corporation of New York, 1997.

Schmeidl, Susanne, and Howard Adelman, eds. *Early Warning and Early Response*. New York: Columbia University Press, 1998.

Schnabel, Albrecht, and David Carment, eds. *Conflict Prevention from Rhetoric to Reality*. Vol. 1, *Organizations and Institutions*. Lanham, Md.: Lexington Books, 2004.

———. *Conflict Prevention from Rhetoric to Reality*. Vol. 2, *Opportunities and Innovations*. Lanham, Md.: Lexington Books, 2005.

Sparks, Donald L., and December Green. *Namibia: The Nation After Independence*. Boulder, Colo.: Westview Press, 1992.

Sriram, Chandra Lekha, and Karin Wermester, eds. *From Promise to Practice: Strengthening UN Capacities for the Prevention of Violent Conflict*. Boulder, Colo.: Lynne Rienner, 2003.

Stedman, Stephen John. *Peacemaking in Civil War: International Mediation in Zimbabwe*. London: Lynne Rienner, 2001.

Sutterlin, James S. *The United Nations and the Maintenance of International Security: A Challenge to be Met*. 2nd ed. Westport, Conn: Praeger Publishers, 2003.

Williams Garland H. *Engineering Peace: The Military Role in Postconflict Reconstruction*. Washington, D.C.: United States Institute of Peace Press, 2004.

Willliams, Abiodun. *Preventing War: The United Nations and Macedonia*. Oxford: Rowman & Littlefield, 2000.

Woodward, Peter. *The Horn of Africa: State Politics and International Relations*. New York: I.B. Tauris, 1996.

World Bank. *The Transition from War to Peace: An Overview*. Washington, D.C.: The World Bank, 1999.

Zartman, William I. *Cowardly Lions: Missed Opportunities for Preventing Deadly Conflict and State Collapse*. Boulder, Colo.: Lynne Rienner, 2005.

———. *Ripe for Resolution: Conflict and Intervention in Africa*. New York: Oxford University Press, 1989.

2. Collective Security

Amate, C. O. C. *Inside the OAU: Pan-Africanism in Practice*. New York: St. Martin's Press, 1986.

Arnson, Cynthia J., ed. *Comparative Peace Processes in Latin America*. Washington, D.C.: Woodrow Wilson Center Press; Stanford, Calif.: Stanford University Press, 1999.

Baba, Noor Ahmad. *Organization of the Islamic Conference: Theory and Practice of Pan-Islamic Cooperation*. New Delhi, India: 1995.

Bailey, Sydney D. *The UN Security Council and Human Rights*. New York: St Martin's, 1994.

———. *Veto in the Security Council*. New York: Carnegie Endowment for International Peace, 1968.

Becker, Charles M., and Jan H. Hofmeyr. *The Impact of Sanctions on South Africa* Washington, D.C.: Investor Responsibility Research Center, 1990.

Bedjaoui, Mohammed. *The New World Order and the Security Council*. Dordrecht, The Netherlands: Martinus Nijhoff, 1994.

Berdal, Mats, and Monica Serrano, eds. *Transnational Organized Crime and International Security, Business as Usual?* Boulder, Colo.: Lynne Rienner, 2002.

Bethlehem, D. L., ed. *The Kuwait Crisis: Sanctions and their Economic Consequences*. Cambridge: Grotius Publications, 1991.

Bloomfield, Lincoln P., et al. *Collective Security in a Changing World*. Occasional Paper No. 10. Providence, R.I.: Watson Institute, 1993.

Bothe, Michael, Natalino Ronzitti, and Allan Rosas eds. *The OSCE in the Maintenance of Peace and Security*. The Hague, The Netherlands: Kluwer Law International, 1997.

Boyd, Andrew. *Fifteen Men on a Powder Keg: A History of the United Nations Security Council*. New York: Stein & Day, 1971.

Boulden, Jane, and Thomas G. Weiss, eds. *Terrorism and the UN: Before and After September 11*. Bloomington: Indiana University Press, 2004.

Brabant, Koenraad Van, ed. S*anctions: The Current Debate: A Summary of Selected Readings*. London: The Humanitarian Policy Group and the Relief and Rehabilitation Network at the Overseas Development Institute, March 1999.

Brown, Michael E., and Richard N. Rosecrance, eds. *The Costs of Conflict: Prevention and Cure in the Global Arena*. Lanham, Md.: Rowman & Littlefield, 1999.

Brune, Lester H. *America and the Iraqi Crisis, 1990–1992: Origins and Aftermath*. Claremont, Calif.: Regina Books, 1993.

Butler, Richard. *The Greatest Threat: Iraq, Weapons of Mass Destruction and the Crisis of Global Security*. New York: Public Affairs, 2000.

Carter, Barry E. *International Economic Sanctions: Improving the Haphazard U.S. Legal Regime*. Cambridge: Cambridge University Press, 1988.

Carter Center of Emory University. *Final Report of the Meeting on the Viability of International Economic Sanctions*. Working Paper Series. Atlanta: Atlanta, Ga.: Carter Center, 1996.

Center for Economic and Social Rights. *UN Sanctioned Suffering in Iraq*. New York: CESR, 1996.

Claude, Inis. *The OAS, the UN, and the US*. New York: Carnegie Endowment for International Peace, 1964.

———. *The United Nations and the Use of Force*. New York: Carnegie Endowment for International Peace, 1961.

Conion, Paul. *United Nations Sanctions Management: A Case Study of the Iraq Sanctions Committee 1990–1994*. Ardsley, N.Y.: Transnational Publishers, 2000.

Cordesman, Anthony H. *The Lessons and Non-Lessons of the Air and Missile Campaign in Kosovo*. Westport, Conn.: Praeger, 2001.

Cortright, David, and George A. Lopez. *Sanctions and the Search for Security: Challenges to UN Action*. Boulder, Colo.: Lynne Rienner, 2002.

———. *The Sanctions Decade: Assessing UN Strategies in the 1990s*. Boulder, Colo.: Lynne Rienner, 2000.

———. *Economic Sanctions: Panacea or Peacebuilding in a Post–Cold War World?* Boulder, Colo.: Westview, 1995.

Damrosch, Lori Fisler, ed. *Enforcing Restraint: Collective Intervention in International Conflicts*. New York: Council on Foreign Relations Press, 1993.

Daniel, Donald C. F., and B. C. Hayes, with Chantal de Jonge Oudraat. *Coercive Inducement and the Containment of International Crises*. Washington, D.C.: United States Institute of Peace Press, 1998.

Daoudi, M. S., and M. S. Danjani. *Economic Sanctions: Ideals and Experience*. London: Routledge & Kegan Paul, 1983.

Davidson, Nicol, ed. *Paths to Peace: The UN Security Council and its Presidency*. New York: Pergamon, 1981.

Dekker, Ige F. *The Gulf War of 1980–1988: The Iran-Iraq War in International Legal Perspective*. Boston: Martinus Nijhoff, 1992.

Dinstein, Yoram. *War, Aggression and Self Defense*. The Hague, The Netherlands: Grotius, 1988.

Doxey, Margaret P. *United Nations Sanctions: Current Policy Issues*. Halifax, Nova Scotia: Dalhousie University, Center for Policy Studies, 1999.

———. *International Sanctions in Contemporary Perspective*. New York: St. Martin's Press, 1987.

Dupuy, René-Jean, ed. *The Development of the Role of the Security Council: Peace-Keeping and Peace-Building*. Dordrecht, The Netherlands: Martinus Nijhoff, 1993.

El-Ayouty, Yassin. *The Organization of African Unity after Thirty Years*. Westport, Conn.: Praeger, 1994.

Ferencz, Ben. *Global Survival: Security through the General Assembly*. Dobbs Ferry, N.Y.: Oceana, 1994.

Finkelstein, Marina S., and L. S. Finkelstein, eds. *Collective Security*. San Francisco: Chandler, 1966.

Finnemore, Martha. *When States Intervene: Changing Belief About the Use of Force*. Ithaca, N.Y.: Cornell University Press, 2003.

Gibbons, Elizabeth D. *Sanctions in Haiti: Human Rights and Democracy under Assault*. Washington, D.C.: The CSIS Press, 1999.

Gleijeses, Piero. *The Dominican Crisis*. Baltimore, Md.: Johns Hopkins University Press, 1978.

Gow, James, ed. *Iraq, the Gulf Conflict, and the World Community*. New York: Macmillan, 1992.

Gowlland-Debbas, Vera. "The Functions of the United Nations Security Council in the International Legal System." In *The Role of Law in International Politics: Essays in International Relations and International Law*, ed. Michael Byers. Oxford: Oxford University Press, 2000.

Grant, John P. *The Lockerbie Trial: A Documentary History*. Dobbs Ferry, N.Y.: Oceana Publications, 2004.

——. *The UN Comprehensive Terrorism Conventions*. Edinburgh, Scotland: Dunedin Academic Press, 2003.

Gray, Christine, *International Law and the Use of Force*. Oxford: Oxford University Press, 2000.

Hilaire, Max. *United Nations Law and the Security Council*. Williston, Vt.: Ashgate Publishing Company, 2005.

Ismael, Tareq Y., and William W. Haddad, eds. *Iraq: The Human Cost of History*. Ann Arbor, Mich.: Pluto Press, 2003.

Hume, Cameron R. *The United Nations, Iran, and Iraq: How Peacemaking Changed*. Bloomington: Indiana University Press, 1994.

Johnstone, Ian. *Aftermath of the Gulf War: An Assessment of UN Action*. Boulder, Colo.: Lynne Rienner, 1994.

Khor, Martin, and Chin Oy Sim. *Security Council Reform and Democratization: An Overview*. Geneva: International NGO Network on Global Governance and Democratization of International Relations, 1994.

King, R. P. *United Nations and the Iran-Iraq War*. New York: Ford Foundation, 1987.

Krasno, Jean, and James Sutterlin. *The United Nations and Iraq: Defanging the Viper*. Westport, Conn.: Greenwood Press/Praeger, 2002.

Krieger, Heike. *The Kosovo Conflict and International Law: An Analytical Documentation, 1974–1999*. New York: Cambridge University Press, 2001.

Ku, Charlotte, and Harold K. Jacobson. *Democratic Accountability and the Use of Force in International Law*. Cambridge: Cambridge University Press, 2003.

Lawyers Committee for Human Rights. *Improvising History: A Critical Evaluation of the United Nations Observer Mission in El Salvador*. New York: Lawyers Committee for Human Rights, 1995.

Leighton-Brown, David, ed. *The Utility of International Economic Sanctions*. New York: St. Martin's Press, 1987.

Lepgold, Joseph, and Thomas Weiss, eds. *Collective Conflict Management and Changing World Politics*. Albany: State University of New York Press, 1997.

Leurdijk, Dick, and Dick A. Zandee. *Kosovo: From Crisis to Crisis*. New York: Ashgate, 2001.

Lillich, Richard, ed. *The United Nations Compensation Commission*. Ardsley, N.Y.: Transnational Publishers, 1995.

Lorenz, Joseph P. *Peace, Power, and the United Nations: A Security System for the Twenty-First Century*. Boulder, Colo.: Westview, 1985.

McWhinney, Edward. *The September 11 Terrorist Attack and the Invasion of Iraq in Contemporary Law: Opinions on the Emerging World Order System*. Boston: Martinus Nijhoff Publishers, 2004.

Malone, David, ed. *The UN Security Council: From the Cold War to the 21st Century*. Boulder, Colo.: Lynne Rienner, 2004.

Maundi, Mohammed O., I. William Zartman, Gilbert M. Khadiagala, and Kwaku Nuamah. *Getting In: Mediators' Entry into the Settlement of African Conflicts*. Herndon, Va.: United States Institute of Peace Press, 2005.

Minear, Larry, David Cortright, Julia Wagler, George A. Lopez, and Thomas G. Weiss. *Toward More Humane and Effective Sanctions Management: Enhancing the Capacity of the United Nations System*. Occasional Paper No. 31. Providence, R.I.: Watson Institute, 1998.

Naidu, Mumulla Venkat Rao. *Collective Security and the United Nations: A Definition of the UN Security System*. Delhi, India: Macmillan, 1974.

Naldi, Gino J. *The Organization of African Unity: An Analysis of its Role*. New York: Mansell, 1989.

———, ed. *Documents of the Organization of African Unity*. New York: Mansell, 1992.

Niblock, Tim. *"Pariah States" and Sanctions in the Middle East: Iraq, Libya, Sudan*. Boulder, Colo.: Lynne Rienner, 2004.

Norris, John. *Collision Course. NATO, Russia, and Kosovo*. New York: Praeger, 2005.

O'Connell, Mary Ellen, Michael Bothe, and Natalino Ronzitti, eds. *Redefining Sovereignty: The Use of Force after the End of the Cold War*. Ardsley, N.Y.: Transnational Publishers, 2004.

O'Neill, William G. *Kosovo*. Boulder, Colo.: Lynne Rienner, 2002.

Pax Christi International. *Economic Sanctions and International Relations*. Brussels: Pax Christi, 1993.

Pieth, Mark, ed. *Financing Terrorism*. Dordrecht, The Netherlands: Kluwer Academic Publishers, 2003.

Price, Richard M., and Mark W. Zacher, eds. *The United Nations and Global Security*. New York: Palgrave, 2004.

Pugh, Michael, and Waheguru Pal Singh, Sidhu, eds. *The United Nations and Regional Security: Europe and Beyond*. Boulder, Colo.: Lynne Rienner, 2003.

Rajaee, Farhang, ed. *The Iran-Iraq War: The Politics of Aggression*. Gainesville: University Press of Florida, 1993.

Renner, Michael. *Remaking U.N. Peacekeeping: U.S. Policy and Real Reform*. Washington, D.C.: National Commission for Economic Conversion and Disarmament, 1995.

Rifaat, A. M. *International Aggression*. Stockholm: Almqvist & Wiksell and International Atlantic / Highlands, N.J.: Humanities Press, 1979.

Rubin, Barnett R. *The Fragmentation of Afghanistan: State Formation and Collapse in the International System*. New Haven, Conn.: Yale University Press, 2002.

Russett, Bruce, ed. *The Once and Future Security Council*. New York: St. Martin's, 1997.

Saksena, K. P. *The United Nations and Collective Security: A Historical Analysis*. Delhi, India: D.K. Publishing House, 1974.

Sarooshi, Danesh. *The United Nations and the Development of Collective Security: The Delegation by the UN Security Council of its Chapter VII Powers*. Oxford: Clarendon, 1999.

Slater, Jerome. *Intervention and Negotiation: The United States and the Dominican Revolution*. New York: Harper and Row, 1970.

Spillmann, Kurt R., and Joachim Krause. *Kosovo: Lessons Learned for International Cooperative Security*. New York: Peter Lang, 2000.

Stoessinger, John G. *The United Nations and the Superpowers*. New York: Random House, 1973.

Stremlau, John. *Sharpening International Sanctions: Towards a Stronger Role for the United Nations*. Washington, D.C.: Carnegie Commission on Preventing Deadly Conflict, 1996.

Sutherland, James. *The United Nations and the Maintenance of International Security. A Challenge to Be Met*. Westport, Conn.: Praeger, 1995.

Thomas, A. V. *The OAS*. Cambridge: Cambridge University Press, 1963.

Trevan, Tim. *Saddam's Secrets: The Hunt for Hidden Weapons*. London: Harper Collins, 1999.

Van Brabant, Koenraad. *Can Sanctions Be Smarter? The Current Debate: Report of a Conference Held in London, 16–17 December 1998*. London: The

Humanitarian Policy Group and the Relief and Rehabilitation Network at the Overseas Development Institute, May 1999.

——— , ed. *Sanctions: The Current Debate: A Summary of Selected Readings*. London: The Humanitarian Policy Group and the Relief and Rehabilitation Network at the Overseas Development Institute, March 1999.

Wallensteen, Peter, Carina Staibano, and Mikael Eriksson, eds. *Making Targeted Sanctions Effective: Guidelines for the Implementation of UN Policy Options*. Uppsala, Sweden: Uppsala University, 2003.

Weiss, Thomas G., ed. *Beyond UN Subcontracting*. New York: St. Martin's Press, 1998.

——— . *Collective Security in a Changing World*. Boulder, Colo: Lynne Rienner, 1993.

Weiss, Thomas G., David Cortright, George A. Lopez, and Larry Minear. *Political Gain and Civilian Pain: Humanitarian Impacts of Economic Sanctions*. Lanham, Md.: Rowman & Littlefield, 1997.

White, Nigel D. *The United Nations and the Maintenance of International Peace and Security*. New York: Manchester University Press, 1990.

Whitman, Jim, and Ian Bartholomew. *The Chapter VII Committee—A Policy Proposal: Military Means for Political Ends—Effective Control of UN Military Enforcement*. Global Security Programme. Cambridge: Cambridge University, 1993.

Williams, Phil, and Ernesto V. Savona, eds. *United Nations and Transnational Organized Crime*. Portland, Ore.: Frank Cass, 1996.

Woods, Ngaire, ed. *Explaining International Relations Since 1945*. Oxford: Oxford University Press, 1996.

Yetiv, Steve A. *The Persian Gulf Crisis*. Westport, CT.: Greenwood Press, 1997.

Zacher, Mark William. *International Conflicts and Collective Security, 1946–1977: The United Nations, Organization of American States, Organization of African Unity, and Arab League*. New York: Praeger, 1979.

3. Peacekeeping and Peacebuilding

Abi-Saab, Georges. *The United Nations Operations in the Congo 1960–1964*. Oxford: Oxford University Press, 1978.

Adebajo, Adekeye. *Building Peace in West Africa: Liberia, Sierra Leone, and Guinea-Bissau*. Boulder, Colo.: Lynne Rienner, 2002.

——— . *Liberia's Civil War: Nigeria, ECOMOG, and Regional Security in West Africa*. Boulder, Colo.: Lynne Rienner, 2002.

Allan, James H. *Peacekeeping: Outspoken Observations by a Field Officer*. Westport, Conn.: Praeger, 1996.

Allard, Kenneth. *Somalia Operations: Lessons Learned*. Washington, D.C.: National Defense University Press, 1995.

Allsebrook, Mary. *Prototypes of Peacemaking: The First Forty Years of the United Nations*. Chicago: St. James Press, 1986.

Anderson, Mary, and Lara Olson. *Confronting War: Critical Lessons for Peace Practitioners*. Cambridge, Mass.: The Collaborative For Development Action, Inc. 2003.

Azimi, Nassrine, ed. *United Nations Transitional Authority in Cambodia: Debriefing and Lessons*. The Hague, The Netherlands: Kluwer Law International, 1996.

Ballentine, Karen, and Jake Sherman, eds. *The Political Economy of Armed Conflict: Beyond Greed and Grievance*. Boulder, Colo.: Lynne Rienner, 2003.

Barnett, Michael. *Eyewitness to a Genocide: The United Nations and Rwanda*. Ithaca, N.Y.: Cornell University Press, 2002.

Benton, Barnara, ed. *Soldiers for Peace: Fifty Years of United Nations Peacekeeping*. New York: Facts on File, 1996.

Berdal, Mats, and Richard Caplan, guest eds. "The Politics of International Administration." Special Issue, *Global Governance* 10, no. 1 (Jan–Mar. 2004).

Berdal, Mats, and David M. Malone, eds. *Greed and Grievance: Economic Agendas in Civil Wars*. Boulder, Colo.: Lynne Rienner, 2000.

Berman, Eric G., and Katie E. Pearson. *African Peacekeepers: Partners or Proxies?* Clementsport, Nova Scotia: Canadian Peacekeeping Press, 1998.

Berridge, Geoff R. *Return to the UN: UN Diplomacy in Regional Conflicts*. Basingstoke, England: Macmillan, 1991.

———. "The Angola/Namibia Settlement: Diplomacy and the Angola/Namibia Accords." *International Affairs* 65, no. 3 (Summer 1989): 463–579.

Bhatia, Michael V. *War and Intervention: A Global Survey of Peace Operations*. Bloomfield, Conn.: Kumarian Press, 2003.

Bieber, Florian, and Zidas Daskalovski. *Understanding the War in Kosovo*. Portland, Ore.: Frank Cass, 2003.

Biermann, Wolfgang. *The Evolution of UN Peace-keeping Operations in the Post–Cold War Era*. Copenhagen: Center for Peace and Conflict Research, 1995.

Boulden, Jane. *The United Nations and Mandate Enforcement: Congo, Somalia, and Bosnia*. Kingston, Ontario: Centre for International Relations, Queens University, 1999.

Bowden, Mark. *Black Hawk Down*. New York: Atlantic Monthly Press, 1999.

Bowett, Derek William. *United Nations Forces: A Legal Study*. New York: Praeger, 1964.

Bowles, Newton R. *The Diplomacy of Hope: The United Nations Since the Cold War*. Ottawa: United Nations Association in Canada and World Federation of United Nations Associations, 2001.

Boyce, James K. *Investing in Peace: Aid and Conditionality After Civil Wars*. Oxford: Oxford University Press, 2002.

——, ed. *Economic Policy for Building Peace*. Boulder, Colo.: Lynne Rienner, 1996.

Boyd, James M. *United Nations Peace-Keeping Operations: A Military and Political Appraisal*. New York: Praeger, 1971.

——. *Cyprus: Episode in Peacekeeping*. New York: Columbia University Press, 1966.

Brahimi, Lakhdar. *Report of the Panel on United Nations Peace Operations*. UN Document A/55/305, August 21, 2000.

Brecher, Michael. *The Struggle for Kashmir*. New York: Oxford University Press, 1953.

Briscoe, Neil. *Britain and UN Peacekeeping 1948–1967*. New York: Palgrave MacMillan, 2003.

Brittain, Victoria. *Death of Dignity: Angola's Civil War*. Chicago: Pluto Press, 1998.

Brown, Michael E., ed. *The International Dimensions of Internal Conflict*. Cambridge, Mass.: MIT Press, 1996.

Burns, Arthur Lee, and Nina Heathcote. *Peacekeeping by UN Forces, From Suez to Congo*. New York: Praeger, 1963.

Caplan, Richard. *International Governance of War-Torn Territories: Rule and Reconstruction*. New York: Oxford University Press, 2005.

——. *A New Trusteeship? The International Administration of War-Torn Territories*. Oxford: Oxford University Press, 2002.

Carpenter, Ted Galen, ed. *Delusions of Grandeur: The United Nations and Global Intervention*. Washington, D.C.: Cato Institute, 1997.

Cassidy, Robert M. *Peacekeeping in the Abyss: British and American Peacekeeping Doctrine After the Cold War*. Westport, Conn.: Greenwood Publishing, 2003.

Chaudhri, Mohammed A. *United Nations Peace Mechanisms and Rules*. Karachi, Pakistan: Council for Pakistan Studies, 1973.

Chesterman, Simon. *You, the People: Transitional Administration, State-Building, and the United Nations*. Oxford: Oxford University Press, 2004.

——. *East Timor in Transition: From Conflict Prevention to State-Building*. New York: International Peace Academy, 2001.

Chesterman, Simon, ed. *Civilians in War*. Boulder, Colo.: Lynne Rienner, 2001.

Chesterman, Simon, Michael Ignatieff, and Ramesh Thakur, eds. *Making States Work: State Failure and the Crisis of Governance*. Tokyo: United Nations University, 2004.

Chopra, Jarat. *Peace-Maintenance; the Evolution of International Political Authority*. New York: Routledge, 1999.

——. *United Nations Authority in Cambodia*. Providence, R.I.: Brown University, 1994.

Chopra, Jarat, Age Eknes, and Toralv Nordbo. *Fighting for Hope in Somalia*. Oslo: Norwegian Institute of International Affairs, 1995.

Chopra, V. D., and M. Rasgotra., eds. *Genesis of Regional Conflicts: Kashmir, Afghanistan, West Asia, Chechnya*. New Delhi, India: Gyan, 1995.

Clarke, Walter M., and Jeffrey M. Herbst, eds. *Learning from Somalia: The Lessons of Armed Intervention*. Boulder, Colo.: Westview Press, 1997.

Cohn, Ilene. *Child Soldiers : The Role of Children in Armed Conflict*. New York: Oxford University Press, 1994.

Coleman, Christopher C. *The Salvadoran Peace Process: A Preliminary Inquiry*. Oslo: Norwegian Institute of International Affairs, 1993.

Colletta, Nat J., and Michele L. Cullen. *Violent Conflict and the Transformation of Social Capital: Lessons from Cambodia, Rwanda, Guatemala, and Somalia*. Washington, D.C.: The World Bank, 2000.

Cooper, Neil, and Michael Pugh, with Jonathan Goodhand. *War Economies in a Regional Context: The Challenge of Transformation*. Boulder, Colo.: Lynne Rienner, 2004.

Cordesman, Anthony H. *The Lessons and Non-lessons of the Air and Missile Campaign in Kosovo*. Westport, Conn.: Praeger, 2001.

Corwin, Phillip. *Dubious Mandate: A Memoir of the UN in Bosnia, Summer 1995*. Durham, N.C.: Duke University Press, 1999.

Coulon, Jocelyn. *Soldiers of Diplomacy: The United Nations, Peacekeeping, and the New World Order*. Toronto: University of Toronto Press, 1998.

Cousens, Elizabeth M., and Chetan Kumar, with Karin Wermester, eds. *Peacebuilding as Politics: Cultivating Peace in Fragile Societies*. Boulder, Colo.: Lynne Rienner, 2000.

Cox, Arthur M. *Prospects for Peacekeeping*. Washington, D.C.: The Brookings Institution, 1967.

Cox, David, Alastair M. Taylor, and J. L. Granatstein. *Peacekeeping: International Challenge and Canadian Response*. Toronto: Canadian Institute of International Affairs, 1968.

Crocker, Chester A., Fen Osler Hampson, and Pamela Aall, eds. *Turbulent Peace: The Challenges of Managing International Conflict*. Washington, D.C.: United States Institute of Peace Press, 1992.

Damrosch, Lori Fisler, ed. *Enforcing Restraint: Collective Intervention in Internal Conflicts*. New York: Council on Foreign Relations Press, 1993.

Daniel, Donald C. F., and Bradd C. Hayes, eds. *Beyond Traditional Peacekeeping*. New York: St. Martin's Press, 1995.

Daniel, Donald C. F., Bradd C. Hayes, and Chantal Jonge Oudraat. *Coercive Inducement and the Containment of International Crises*. Washington, D.C.: United States Institute of Peace Press, 1999.

Dawson, Pauline. *The Peacekeepers of Kashmir: The UN Military Observer Group in India and Pakistan*. London: St. Martin's Press, 1994.

Deng, Francis M., Sadikiel Kimaro, Terrence Lyons, Donald Rothchild, and I. William Zartman. *Sovereignty as Responsibility: Conflict Management in Africa*. Washington, D.C.: The Brookings Institution, 1996.

Des Forges, Alison. *Leave None to Tell the Story: Genocide in Rwanda*. New York: Human Rights Watch, 1999.

Diehl, Paul F. *International Peacekeeping*. Baltimore, Md.: Johns Hopkins University Press, 1993.

Dimitrijevic, Nebojsa. *The Crisis in the Former Yugoslavia and the U.N. Peace-Keeping*. Geneva: Institut Universitaire de Hautes Etudes Internationales, 1994.

Dobbing, James, Keith Crane, Seth G. Jones, Andrew Rathmell, Brett Steele, and Richard Teltschik. *The UN's Role in Nation Building: From the Congo to Iraq*. Lanham, Md., Rowman & Littlefield, 2005.

Donini, Antonio. *The Policies of Mercy: UN Coordination in Afghanistan, Mozambique, and Rwanda*. Providence, R.I.: Thomas J. Watson Jr. Institute for International Studies, 1996.

Doyle, Michael W. *UN Peacekeeping in Cambodia: UNTAC's Civil Mandate*. Boulder, Colo.: Lynne Rienner, 1995.

Durch, William J., ed. *UN Peacekeeping, American Politics, and the Uncivil Wars of the 1990s*. New York: St. Martin's Press, 1996.

——. *The Evolution of UN Peacekeeping: Case Studies and Comparative Analysis*. New York: St. Martin's Press, 1993.

Durch, William J., and Barry M. Blechman. *Keeping the Peace: The United Nations in the Emerging World Order*. Washington, D.C.: Henry L. Stimson Center, 1992.

Dwan, Renata. *International Policing in Peace Operations: The Role of Regional Organizations*. Oxford: Oxford University Press, 2003.

Ehrlich, Thomas. *Cyprus, 1958–1967*. Oxford: Oxford University Press, 1974.

Elganzoury, Abdelazim A. *Evolution of the Peacekeeping Powers of the General Assembly of the United Nations*. Cairo, Egypt: General Egyptian Book Organization, 1978.

Eltringham, Nigel. *Accounting for Horror: Post-Genocide Debates in Rwanda*. Sterling, Va.: Pluto Press, 2004.

Evered, Timothy C. *United Nations Electoral Assistance and the Evolving Right to Democratic Governance*. Livingston, N.J.: The Center for U.N. Reform Education, 1996.

Fabian, Larry L. *Soldiers Without Enemies: Preparing the United Nations for Peacekeeping*. Washington, D.C.: Brookings Institution, 1971.

Findlay, Trevor. *Fighting for Peace: The Use of Force in Peace Operations*. New York: Oxford University Press, 2002.

——. *Cambodia: The Legacy and Lessons of UNTAC*. Oxford: Oxford University Press, 1995.

Flores, Acuna T. *The United Nations Mission in El Salvador: A Humanitarian Law Perspective*. The Hague, Netherlands: Kluwer Law Internaitonal, 1995.

Forman, Shepard, and Stewart Patrick, eds. *Good Intentions: Pledges of Aid for Postconflict Recovery*. Boulder, Colo.: Lynne Rienner, 2000.

Franck, Thomas M., and John Carey, eds. *The Legal Aspects of the United Nations Action in the Congo: Background Papers and Proceedings of the Second Hammarskjöld Forum*. Dobbs Ferry, N.Y.: Oceana, 1963.

Frye, William R., ed. *A United Nations Peace Force*. New York: Oceana, 1957.

Gall, Carlotta, and Thomas de Waal. *Chechnya: Calamity in the Caucasus*. New York: New York University Press, 1998.

Gerson, Allan, and Nat J. Colletta. *Privatizing Peace: From Conflict to Security*. Ardsley, N.Y.: Transnational Publishers, 2002.

Gibbs, David N. *The Political Economy of Third World Intervention: Mines, Money, and U.S. Policy in the Congo Crisis*. Chicago: University of Chicago Press, 1991.

Ginifer, Jeremy, ed. *Beyond the Emergency: Development Within UN Peace Missions*. Portland, Ore.: Frank Cass, 1997.

Girardet, Edward R., ed. *Somalia, Rwanda, and Beyond: The Role of the International Media in Wars and Humanitarian Crises*. Dublin: Crosslines Communications / New York: Italian Academy for Advanced Studies at Columbia University, 1995.

Gordon, King. *The United Nations in the Congo: A Quest for Peace*. New York: Carnegie Endowment for International Peace, 1962.

Gordon, Stuart, and Francis Toase, eds. *Aspects of Peacekeeping*. Portland, Ore.: Frank Cass, 2001.

Grote, Rainer. "The United Nations and the Establishment of a New Model of Governance for Central America: The Case of Guatemala." In *Max Planck Yearbook of United Nations Law*. Vol. 2, ed. Jochen A. Frowein and Rudiger Wulfrum, 239–86. The Hague, The Netherlands: Kluwer Law International, 1998.

Hampson, Fen Osler. *Nurturing Peace: Why Peace Settlements Succeed or Fail*. Washington, D.C.: United States Institute of Peace Press, 1996.

Hannum, Hurst. *Autonomy, Sovereignty and Self-Determination*. Philadelphia: University of Pennsylvania Press, 1996.

Harbottle, Michael N. *The Blue Berets: The Story of the United Nations Peacekeeping Forces*. Harrisburg, Pa.: Stackpole, 1971.

Hare, Paul. *Angola's Last Best Hope*. Washington, D.C.: U.S. Institute of Peace Press, 1998.

Hearn, Roger. *UN Peacekeeping in Action: The Namibian Experience*. Commack, N.Y.: Nova Science Publishers, 1999.

Heininger, Janet E. *Peacekeeping in Transition: The United Nations in Cambodia*. New York: The Twentieth Century Fund Press, 1994.

Hempstone, Smith. *Rebels, Mercenaries and Dissidents: The Katanga Story*. New York: Praeger, 1962.

Higgins, Rosalyn. *The New United Nations: Appearance and Reality*. Hull, England: University of Hull Press, 1993.

——. *United Nations Peacekeeping, Documents and Commentary*. 4 vols. London: Oxford University Press, 1960-81.

Hillen, John. *Blue Helmets: The Strategy of U.N. Military Operations*. Washington, D.C.: Brassey's, 1998.

Hirsch, John L. *Sierra Leone: Diamonds and the Struggle for Democracy*. Boulder, Colo.: Lynne Rienner, 2001.

Hirsch, John L. and Robert B. Oakley. *Somalia and Operation Restore Hope*. Washington, D.C.: United States Institute of Peace Press, 1995.

Hodges, Tiny. *Angola: Anatomy of an Oil State*, 2nd ed. Bloomington: Indiana University Press, 2004.

Holm, Tor Tanke, and Espen Barth Eide, eds. *Peacebuilding and Police Reform*. Portland, Ore.: Frank Cass, 2000.

Hoskyns, Catherine. *The Congo Since Independence: January 30–December 1961*. London: Oxford University Press, 1965.

House, Arthur. *The U.N. in the Congo: The Political and Civilian Efforts*. Washington, D.C.: University Press of America. 1978.

Huband, Mark. *The Liberian Civil War*. Portland, Ore.: Frank Cass, 1998.

Human Rights Watch. *Sudan, Oil, and Human Rights*. New York: Human Rights Watch, 2003.

Hyde, Emmanuel A. *The United Nations Policy of Non-Intervention in Internal Affairs of the Congo: A Study in the Problem of Peace-Keeping with International Force*. Philadelphia: University of Pennsylvania, 1966.

Ignatieff, Michael. *Empire Lite: Nation Building in Bosnia, Kosovo, Afghanistan*. London: Minerva, 2003.

International Peace Academy. *Transforming War Economies: Challenges for Peacemaking and Peacebuilding*. Report of the 725th Wilton Park Conference, in association with the International Peace Academy. Wiston House, Sussex, 27–29 October 2003. New York: International Peace Academy, 2003.

Ishiyama, John T., and M. Breuning. *Ethnopolitics in the "New Europe."* Boulder, Colo.: Lynne Rienner, 1998.

Ishizuka, Katsumi. *Ireland and International Peacekeeping*. Portland, Ore.: Frank Cass, 2003.

Jacobson, Harold K., "ONUC's Civilian Operations: State-Preserving and State-Building." *World Politics* 17, no. 1 (Oct., 1964): 75-107.

James, Alan. *Peacekeeping in International Politics*. London: Macmillan and International Institute for Strategic Studies, 1990.

——. *The Politics of Peace-keeping*. New York: Praeger, 1969.

Jeong, Ho-Won. *Peacebuilding in Postconflict Societies: Strategy and Process*. Boulder, Colo.: Lynne Rienner, 2005.

Jett, Dennis. *Why Peacekeeping Fails*. New York: St. Martin's Press, 1999.

Johnstone, Ian. *Rights and Reconciliation: UN Strategies in El Salvador*. Boulder, Colo.: Lynne Rienner, 1995.

Jonas, Susanne. *Of Centaurs and Doves: Guatemala's Peace Process*. Boulder, Colo.: Westview Press, 2000.

Jones, Bruce D. *Peacemaking in Rwanda: The Dynamics of Failure*. Boulder, Colo.: Lynne Rienner, 2001.

Junne, Gerd, and Willemijn Verkoren, eds. *Post Conflict Development*. Boulder, Colo.: Lynne Rienner, 2005.

Keating, Tom, and W. Andy Knight, eds. *Building Sustainable Peace*. Edmonton: University of Alberta Press/Tokyo: United Nations University, 2004.

Khan, Shaharyar. *The Shallow Graves of Rwanda*. New York: I.B. Tauris Publishers, 2000.

Krasno, Jean, Don Daniel, and Bradd Hayes, eds. *Leveraging for Success in United Nations Peace Operations*. Westport, Conn.: Praeger, 2003.

Kumar, Krishna, ed. *Women and Civil War: Impact, Organizations, and Action*. Boulder, Colo.: Lynne Rienner Publisher, 2001.

Joseph, Joseph S. *Cyprus: Ethnic Conflict and International Concern*. New York: Peter Lang, 1985.

Junne, Gerd, and Willemijn Verkoren, eds. *Postconflict Development: Meeting New Challenges*. Boulder, Colo.: Lynne Rienner, 2005.

Khan, Rahmatullan. *Kashmir and the United Nations*. Delhi, India: Vikas, 1969.

Lauterpacht, Elihu. *The Suez Canal Settlement: A Selection of Documents 1956–1959*. London: Stevens & Sons, 1960.

Lawyers Committee for Human Rights. *The United Nations Observer Mission in El Salvador*. New York: Lawyers Committee for Human Rights, 1995.

Lefever, Ernest W. *Uncertain Mandate: Politics of the UN Congo Operation*. Baltimore, Md.: Johns Hopkins University Press, 1967.

———. *Crisis in the Congo: A United Nations Force in Action*. Washington, D.C.: Brookings Institution, 1965.

Lehmann, Ingrid A. *Peacekeeping and Public Information: Caught in the Crossfire*. Portland, Ore.: Frank Cass, 1999.

Lepgold, Joseph, and Thomas G. Weiss, eds. *Collective Conflict Management and Changing World Politics*. Albany: State University of New York Press, 1997.

Lind, Jeremy, and Kathryn Sturman, eds. *Scarcity and Surfeit: The Ecology of Africa's Conflicts*. Nairobi, Kenya: Africa Center for Technology Studies / Pretoria, South Africa: Institute for Security Studies, 2002.

Liu, F. T. *United Nations Peacekeeping and the Non-Use of Force*. Boulder, Colo.: Lynne Rienner, 1992.

Lyons, Terrence, and Ahmed I. Samatar. *Somalia: State Collapse, Multilateral Intervention, and Strategies for Political Reconstruction*. Washington, D.C.: The Brookings Institution, 1995.

Lynch, Dov. *Engaging Eurasia's Separatist States*. Washington, D.C.: United States Institute of Peace Press, 2004.

MacFarlane, Neil S., Larry Minear, and Stephen Shenfield. *Armed Conflict in Georgia: A Case Study in Humanitarian Action and Peacekeeping*. Providence, R.I.: Watson Institute for International Studies, 1996.

Mackinlay, John. *The Peacekeepers: An Assessment of Peacekeeping Operations at the Arab-Israeli Interface*. London: Unwin Hyman, 1989.

Mackinley, John, and Peter Cross, eds. *Regional Peacekeepers: The Paradox of Russian Peacekeeping*. Tokyo: United Nations University Press, 2003.

Maguire, Robert, et al. *Haiti Held Hostage: International Responses to the Quest for Nationhood 1986 to 1996*. Occasional Paper No. 23. Providence, R.I.: Watson Institute for International Studies, 1996.

Malan, Mark. *Sierra Leone: Building the Road to Recovery*. Pretoria, South Africa: Institute for Security Studies, 2003.

Malan, Mark, Angela McIntyre, and Phenyo Rakate. *Peacekeeping in Sierra Leone: UNAMSIL Hits the Home Straight*. Pretoria, South Africa: Institute for Security Studies, 2002.

Maley, William, Charles Sampford, and Ramesh Thakur, eds. *From Civil Strife to Civil Society: Civil and Military Responsibilities in Disrupted States*. Tokyo: United Nations University Press, 2003.

Mares, David R. *Drug Wars and Coffee Houses. The Political Economy of the International Drug Trade*. Washington, D.C.: CQ Press, 2005.

Martelli, George. *Experiment in World Government: An Account of the United Nations in the Congo 1960–1964*. London: Johnson Publications, 1966.

Marten, Kimberly Zisk. *Enforcing the Peace: Learning from the Imperial Past*. New York: Columbia University Press, 2004.

Martin, Ian. *Self-Determination in East Timor: The United Nations, the Ballot, and the International Intervention*. Boulder, Colo.: Lynne Rienner, 2001.

Mayall, James, ed. *The New Interventionism, 1991–1993: United Nations Experience in Cambodia, Former Yugoslavia, and Somalia*. Cambridge: Cambridge University Press, 1996.

Mays, Terry M. *Africa's First Peacekeeping Operation: The OAU in Chad, 1981–1982*. Westport, Conn: Praeger Publishers, 2002.

McDermott, Anthony, and Kjell Skjelsbaek, eds. *A Thankless Task: The Role of UNIFIL in Southern Lebanon*. Oslo: Norwegian Institute of International Affairs, 1988.

Mezerik, A. G., ed. *The United Nations Emergency Force (UNEF), 1956–1957; Creation, Evolution, End of Mission*. New York: International Review Service, 1969.

Miller, Linda. *World Order and Local Disorder: The UN and Internal Conflict*. Princeton, N.J.: Princeton University Press, 1967.

Montgomery, Tommie Sue. *Revolution in El Salvador: From Civil Strife to Civil Peace*, 2nd ed. Boulder, Colo.: Westview Press, 1992.

———, ed. *Peacemaking and Democratization in the Western Hemisphere*. Boulder, Colo.: Lynne Rienner, 2000.

Murphy, John F. *The United Nations and the Control of International Violence for the New Century*. Totowa, N.J.: Allanheld, Osmun, 1982.

Nest, Michael, with Francois Grignon and Emizet F. Kisangani, eds. *The Democratic Republic of the Congo: Economic Dimensions of War and Peace*. Boulder, Colo.: Lynne Rienner, 2006.

Nevins, Joseph. *A Not-So-Distant Horror: Mass Violence in East Timor*. Ithaca, N.Y.: Cornell University Press, 2005.

Newman, Edward, and Roland Rich, eds. *The UN Role in Promoting Democracy: Between Ideals and Reality*. Tokyo: United Nations University, 2004.

Newman, Edward, and Albrecht Schnabel. *Recovering from Civil Conflict: Reconciliation, Peace and Development*. Portland, Ore.: Frank Cass, 2002.

Oakley, Robert B., M. J. Dziedzic, and E. M. Goldberg, eds. *Policing the New World Disorder: Peace Operations and Public Security*. Washington, D.C.: National Defense University Press, 1998.

O'Brien, Conor Cruise. *To Katanga and Back: A U.N. Case History*. New York: Simon and Schuster, 1962.

Olsson, Louise, and Torrun L. Truggestad, eds. *Women and International Peacekeeping*. Portland, Ore.: Frank Cass, 2001.

Otunnu, Olara A., and Doyle, Michael W., eds. *Peacekeeping and Peacemaking for the New Century*. Lanham, Md.: Rowman & Littlefield, 1998.

Parakatil, Francis. *India and United Nations Peacekeeping*. New Delhi, India: S. Chand, 1975.

Paris, Roland. *At War's End: Building Peace After Civil Conflict*. New York: Cambridge University Press, 2004.

Peck, Connie. *Sustainable Peace*. New York: Rowman & Littlefield, 1998.

Pelcovits, Nathan A. *The Long Armistice: UN Peacekeeping and the Arab-Israeli Conflict, 1948–1960*. Boulder, Colo.: Westview Press, 1993.

Petterson, Scott. *Me Against My Brother, At War in Somalia, Sudan, and Rwanda: A Journalist Report from the Battlefields of Africa*. New York: Routledge, 2000.

Pugh, Michael, and Waheguru Pal Singh Sidhu, eds. *The United Nations and Regional Security: Europe and Beyond*. Boulder, Colo.: Lynne Rienner, 2003.

Ratner, Steven R. *The New UN Peacekeeping: Building Peace in Lands of Conflict After the Cold War*. New York: St. Martin's Press, 1996.

Renner, Michael. *Ending Violent Conflict*. Washington, D.C.: Worldwatch Institute, 1999.

Report of the Independent Inquiry into the Actions of the United Nations during the 1994 Genocide in Rwanda. UN Document, S/1999/1257 of December 16, 1999.

Reychler, Luc, and Thania Paffenholz, eds. *Peacebuilding: A Field Guide*. Boulder, Colo.: Lynne Rienner, 2001.

Richmond Oliver P., and James Ker-Lindsay, eds. *The Work of the UN in Cyprus: Promoting Peace and Development*. New York: Palgrave, 2001.

Richardson, Henry J., "Constitutive Questions on the Negotiations for Namibian Independence." *American Journal of International Law* 78, no.1 (January 1984): 76–120.

Rigby, Andrew. *Justice and Reconciliation: After the Violence*. Boulder, Colo.: Lynne Rienner, 2001.

Rikhye, Indar Jit. *The Theory and Practice of Peacekeeping*. London: C. Hurst and Company for the International Peace Academy, 1984.

———. *The Thin Blue Line: International Peace-keeping and its Future*. New Haven, Conn.: Yale University Press, 1974.

Rikhye, Indar Jit, and Kjell Skjelsbaek, eds. *The United Nations and Peacekeeping: Results, Limitations and Prospects—The Lessons of 40 Years Experience*. New York: St. Martin's Press, 1991.

Rose, Michael. *Fighting for Peace: Lessons from Bosnia*. London: Warner, 1999.

Rosner, Gabriella E. *The United Nations Emergency Force*. New York: Columbia University Press, 1964.

Rossanet, Bertrand de. *Peacemaking and Peacekeeping in Yugoslavia*. The Hague, The Netherlands: Kluwer Law International, 1996.

Russell, Ruth B. *United Nations Experience with Military Forces: Political and Legal Aspects*. Washington, D.C.: Brookings Institution, 1964.

Saltford, John. *The United Nations and the Indonesian Takeover of West Papua, 1962–1969: The Anatomy of Betrayal*. London: Routledge Curzon, 2002.

Sanderson, J. M. "Global Flux and the Dilemma of the Use of Force in United Nations Peace-keeping." *Strategic Analysis* 18, no. 3 (June 1995): 349–74.

Schmidl, Erwin A., ed. *Peace Operations Between War and Peace*. Portland, Ore.: Frank Cass, 2000.

Schnabel, Albrecht, and Hans-Georg Ehrhart, eds. *Security Sector Reform and Post-Conflict Peacebuilding*. Tokyo: United Nations University Press, 2005.

Schrijver, Nico. "Introducing Second Generation Peace-keeping: The Case of Namibia." *African Journal of International and Comparative Law* 6, no. 1 (March 1994): 1–13.

Sesay, Mohamed Gibril, and Charlie Hughes. *Go Beyond First Aid: Democracy Assistance and the Challenges of Institution Building in Post-Conflict Sierra Leone*. The Hague: Netherlands Institute of International Relations, 2005.

Shelley, Toby. *Endgame in the Western Sahara: What Future for Africa's Last Colony?* London: Zed Books, 2004.

Skjelbaek, Kjell. *Peacekeeping and Peacemaking: The Role of the United Nations in the Cyprus Conflict.* Oslo: Norwegian Institute of International Affairs, 1980.

Skogmo, Bjorn. *UNIFIL: International Peacekeeping in Lebanon, 1978–1988.* Boulder, Colo.: Lynne Rienner, 1989.

Simmonds, K. R. *Legal Problems Arising From the United Nations Military Operations in the Congo.* The Hague, The Netherlands: Martinus Nijhoff, 1968.

Smith, Hugh, ed. *International Peacekeeping: Building on the Cambodian Experience.* Canberra: Australian Defence Studies Center, Australian Defence Force Academy, 1994.

Smith, Michael G. *Peacekeeping in East Timor.* Boulder, Colo.: Lynne Rienner, 2003.

Soto, Alvaro de, and Graciana del Castillo. "Implementation of Comprehensive Peace Accords: Staying the Course in El Salvador." *Global Governance* 1, no. 2 (May–August 1995): 189–203.

——. "Obstacles to Peacebuilding." *Foreign Policy* 94 (Spring 1994): 69–83.

Stahler-Sholk, Richard. "El-Salvador's Negotiated Transition: From Low-Intensity Conflict to Low-Intensity Democracy." *Journal of Interamerican Studies and World Affairs* 36 (Winter 1994): 1–59.

Stedman, Stephen John, Donald Rothchild, and Elizabeth M. Cousens, eds. *Ending Civil Wars: The Implementation of Peace Agreements.* Boulder, Colo.: Lynne Rienner, 2002.

Stegenga, James Alan. *The United Nations Force in Cyprus.* Columbus: Ohio State University Press, 1968.

Strohmeyer, Hansjorg. "Collapse and Reconstruction of a Judicial System: The United Nations Missions in Kosovo and East Timor. *American Journal of International Law* 95, no.1 (Jan., 2001): 46–63.

Struelens, Michel. *The United Nations in the Congo or O.N.U.C. and International Politics.* Brussels: Max Arnold, 1976.

Synge, Richard. *Mozambique: UN Peacekeeping in Action, 1992–94.* Washington, D.C.: United States Institute of Peace Press, 1997.

Swift, Richard N. *The United Nations Special Committee on Peacekeeping Operations: Status and Prospects.* New York: New York University, 1970.

Taylor, Alastair M. *Indonesian Independence and the United Nations.* London: Stevens & Sons, 1960.

Thakur, Ramesh C. *International Peacekeeping in Lebanon: United Nations Authority and Multinational Force.* Boulder, Colo.: Westview Press, 1987.

Thakur, Ramesh C., and Carlyle A. Thayer, eds. *A Crisis of Expectations: UN Peacekeeping in the 1990s.* Boulder, Colo.: Westview Press, 1995.

Tomuschat, Christian, ed. *Kosovo and the International Community: a Legal Assessment*. Norwell, Mass.: Kluwer Law International, 2002.

Tvedten, Inge. *Angola: Struggle for Peace and Reconstruction*. Boulder, Colo.: Westview Press, 1997.

United Nations. *Women, Peace and Security*. New York: United Nations, 2002.

——. *The Blue Helmets*. New York: United Nations, 1996.

——. *The United Nations and Cambodia, 1991–1995*. New York: United Nations, 1995.

——. *The United Nations and El Salvador, 1990–1995*. New York: United Nations. 1995.

——. *The United Nations and Rwanda, 1993–1996*. New York: United Nations, 1996.

——. *The United Nations and Somalia*. New York: United Nations, 1996.

——. *The Fall of Srebrenica*. Report of the Secretary-General, UN Document A/54/549, November 15, 1999.

Wainhouse, David W. *International Peacekeeping at the Crossroads: National Support, Experience and Prospects*. Baltimore, Md.: Johns Hopkins University Press, 1973.

——. *National Support of International Peacekeeping and Peace Observation Operations*. 2 vols. Baltimore, Md.: Johns Hopkins University Press, 1970.

——. *International Peace Observation: A History and Forecast*. Baltimore, Md.: Johns Hopkins University Press, 1966.

Walker, Thomas W., and Ariel C. Armony, eds. *Repression, Resistance, and Democratic Transition in Central America*. Wilmington, Del.: Scholarly Resources, 2000.

Weil, Herbert, and Matthew Braham. *The Namibian Peace Process: Implications and Lessons for the Future*. Freiburg, Germany: Arnold Bergstraesser Insitut, 1994.

Weiss, Thomas G. *The United Nations and Civil Wars*. Boulder, Colo.: Lynne Rienner, 1995.

Weiss, Thomas G., and Jarat Chopra. *United Nations Peacekeeping: An ACUNS Teaching Text*. Hanover, N.H.: Academic Council on the United Nations System, 1992.

Weller, M. *Regional Peace-keeping and International Enforcement: The Liberian Crisis*. New York: Cambridge University Press, 1994.

Wesley, Michael. *Casualties of the New World Order: The Causes of Failures of UN Missions in Civil Wars*. New York: St. Martin's Press, 1997.

Whitman, Jim. *Peacekeeping and the UN Agencies*. Portland, Ore.: Frank Cass, 1999.

Woodhouse, Tom, and Oliver Ramsbotham, eds. *Peacekeeping and Conflict Resolution*. Portland, Ore.: Frank Cass, 2000.

Woodward, Susan L. *Balkan Tragedy: Chaos and Dissolution After the Cold War*. Washington, D.C.: Brookings Institution, 1995.

Yost, David S. *NATO Transformed: The Alliance's New Roles in International Security*. Washington, D.C.: United States Institute of Peace Press, 1999.

Zacarias, Agostinho. *The United Nations and International Peacekeeping*. New York: St. Martin's Press, 1996.

Zeidan, Abdel-Latif M. *The United Nations Emergency Force, 1956–1967*. Stockholm: Almqvist and Wisksell International, 1976.

4. Humanitarianism

Abiew, Frances Kofi. *The Evolution of the Doctrine and Practice of Humanitarian Intervention*. The Hague, The Netherlands: Kluwer Law International, 1999.

Augelli, Enrico, and Craig N. Murphy. "Lessons of Somalia for Future Multilateral Humanitarian Assistance Operations." *Global Governance* 1, no. 3 (Sept/Dec. 1995): 339–65.

Belgrad, Eric A., and Notza Nachmias, eds. *The Politics of International Humanitarian Aid Operations*. Westport, Conn.: Praeger, 1997.

Bergman, Carol, ed. *Another Day in Paradise: International Humanitarian Workers Tell Their Stories*. Maryknoll, N.Y.: Orbis Books, 2004.

Bhatia, Michael V. *War and Intervention: Issues for Contemporary Peace Operations*. Bloomfield, Conn.: Kumarian Press, 2003.

Black, Maggie. *Children First: The Story of UNICEF, Past and Present*. New York: Oxford University Press, 1996.

Braunmühl, Claudia von, and Manfred Kulessa. *The Impact of UN Sanctions on Humanitarian Assistance Activities*. A Report on a Study Commissioned by the United Nations Department of Humanitarian Affairs. Berlin: Gesellschaft für Communication Management Interkultur Training, December 1995.

Cahill, M. Kevin, ed. *A Framework for Survival: Health, Human Rights and Humanitarian Assistance in Conflicts and Disaster*. New York: Routledge, 1999.

Chandler, David. *From Kosovo to Kabul: Human Rights and Humanitarian Intervention*. Ann Arbor, Mich.: Pluto Press, 2002.

Chesterman, Simon. *Civilians in War*. Boulder, Colo.: Lynne Rienner, 2001.

——. *Just War or Just Peace? Humanitarian Intervention and International Law*. Oxford: Oxford University Press, 2001.

Claude, Inis. *National Minorities: An International Problem*. Cambridge, Mass.: Harvard University Press, 1955.

Danieli, Yael, ed. *Sharing the Front Line and the Back Hills: Peacekeepers, Humanitarian Aid Workers, and the Media in the Midst of Crisis*. Amityville, N.Y.: Baywood, 2001.

Danish Institute of International Affairs. *Humanitarian Intervention: Legal and Political Aspects*. Copenhagen: Danish Institute of International Affairs, 1999.

Davies, Michael C., Wolfgang Dietrich, and Bettina Scholdan. *International Intervention in the Post–Cold War World: Moral Responsibility and Power Politics*. New York: M.E. Sharpe, 2003.

Deng, Francis, and Larry Minear. *Challenges of Famine Relief: Emergency Operations in the Sudan*. Washington, D.C.: The Brookings Institution, 1992.

Dijkzeul, Dennis, ed. *Between Force and Mercy: Military Action and Humanitarian Aid*. Berlin: Berliner Wissenschafts-Verlag, 2004.

Forsythe, David P. *Humanitarian Politics: The International Committee of the Red Cross*. Baltimore, Md.: Johns Hopkins University Press, 1977.

Harriss, John. *The Politics of Humanitarian Intervention*. New York: Pinter, 1995.

Helton, Arthur C. *The Price of Indifference: Refugees and Humanitarian Action in the New Century*. New York: Oxford University Press, 2002.

Hoffmann, Stanley. *The Ethics and Politics of Humanitarian Intervention*. Notre Dame, Ind.: University of Notre Dame Press, 1996.

Holborn, Louise W. *The International Refugee Organization*. London: Oxford University, 1956.

——— . *Refugees—A Problem of Our Times: The Work of the United Nations High Commissioner for Refugees, 1951–1972*. 2 vols. Metuchen, N.J.: Scarecrow Press, 1975.

Hoffman, Peter J., and Thomas G. Weiss. *Sword & Salve: Confronting New Wars and Humanitarian Crises*. New York: Rowman & Littlefield, 2005.

Holmes, Wendy (for the International Rescue Committee). *Protecting the Future: HIV Prevention, Care and Support Among Displaced and War-Affected Populations*. Bloomfield, Conn.: Kumarian Press, 2003.

Holzgrefe, J. L., and Robert O. Keohane, eds. *Humanitarian Intervention: Ethical, Legal and Political Dilemmas*. Cambridge: Cambridge University Press, 2003.

Hubert, Don. *The Landmine Ban: A Case Study in Humanitarian Advocacy*. Occasional Paper No. 42. Providence, R.I.: Watson Institute for International Studies, 2000.

International Commission on Intervention and State Sovereignty. *The Responsibility to Protect: Report of the International Commission on Intervention and State Sovereignty*. Ottawa: International Development Research Center, 2001.

Kennedy, David. *Dark Sides of Virtue: Reassessing International Humanitarianism*. Princeton, N.J: Princeton University Press, 2004.

Knudsen, Tonny Bremss. *Humanitarian Intervention: Contemporary Manifestations of an Explosive Doctrine*. London: Routledge, 2004.

Kurspahic, Kemal. *Prime Time Crime: Balkan Media in War and Peace*. Washington, D.C.: United States Institute of Peace Press, 2003.

Loescher, Gil. *Beyond Charity: International Cooperation and the Global Refugee Crisis*. New York: Oxford University Press, 1993.

McWhinney, Edward. *The United Nations and a New World Order for the Millennium: Self-Determination, State Succession, and Humanitarian Intervention*. Boston: Kluwer Law International, 2000.

Machel, Graca. *The Impact of Armed Conflict on Children: A Critical Review of Progress Made and Obstacles Encountered in Increasing Protection for War-affected Children*. New York: Palgrave, 2001.

Mertus, Julie A. *War's Offensive on Women: The Humanitarian Challenge in Bosnia, Kosovo, and Afghanistan*. Bloomfield, Conn.: Kumarian Press, 2000.

Minear, Larry. *The Humanitarian Enterprise. Dilemmas and Discoveries*. Bloomfield, Conn.: Kumarian Press, 2002.

Minear, Larry, and Philippe Guillot. *Soldiers to the Rescue: Humanitarian Lessons from Rwanda*. Paris: Development Centre, Organization for Economic Co-operation and Development, 1996.

Minear, Larry, Colin Scott, and Thomas G. Weiss. *News Media, Civil War, and Humanitarian Action*. Boulder, Colo.: Lynne Rienner, 1996.

Minear, Larry, and Thomas G. Weiss. *Humanitarian Politics*. New York: Foreign Policy Association, 1995.

——. *Mercy under Fire: War and the Global Humanitarian Community*. Boulder, Colo.: Westview Press, 1995.

Moore, Jonathan. *Hard Choices: Moral Dilemmas in Humanitarian Intervention*. Lanham, Md.: Rowman & Littlefield, 1998.

Murphy, Sean D. *Humanitarian Intervention: The United Nations in an Evolving World Order*. Philadelphia: University of Pennsylvania Press, 1996.

Nafziger, E. Wayne, Frances Stewart, and Raimo Vayrynen, eds. *War Hunger and Displacement: The Origins of Humanitarian Emergencies*. Volume 1: Analysis. Volume 2: Case Studies. New York: Oxford University Press, 2000.

Obiaga, Ndubisi. *The Politics of Humanitarian Organizations Interventions*. Lanham, Md.: University Press of America, 2004.

Orford, Anne. *Reading Humanitarian Intervention: Human Rights and the Use of Force in International Law*. Cambridge: Cambridge University Press, 2003.

Phillips, Robert L., and Duane L. Cady. *Humanitarian Intervention: Just War vs. Pacifism*. Lanham, Md.: Rowman & Littlefield, 1996.

Pugh, Michael Charles. *The Challenge of Peacebuilding: The Disaster Relief Model*. Plymouth, England: University of Plymouth, 1995.

Ramsbotham, Oliver, and T. Woodhouse. *Humanitarian Intervention in Contemporary Conflict*. Cambridge: Polity, 1996.

Rieff, David. *A Bed for the Night. Humanitarianism in Crisis*. New York: Simon and Schuster, 2002.

Roberts, Adam. *Humanitarian Action in War: Aid, Protection, and Impartiality in a Policy Vacuum*. Oxford: Oxford University Press, 1996.

Rotberg, Robert I., and Thomas G. Weiss, eds. *From Massacres to Genocide: The Media, Public Policy, and Humanitarian Crises*. Washington, D.C.: The Brookings Institution, 2003.

Schiff, Benjamin N. *Refugees Unto the Third Generation: UN Aid to Palestinians*. Syracuse, N.Y.: Syracuse University Press, 1995.

Schnabel, Albrecht, and Ramesh Thakur, eds. *Kosovo and the Challenge of Humanitarian Intervention: Selective Indignation, Collective Action and International Citizenship*. Tokyo: United Nations University Press, 2000.

Smillie, Ian, ed. *Patronage or Partnership: Local Capacity Building in Humanitarian Crises*. Bloomfield, Conn.: Kumarian Press, 2001.

Smillie, Ian, and Larry Minear. *The Charity of Nations: Humanitarian Action in a Calculating World*. Bloomfield, Conn.: Kumarian Press, 2004.

Strobel, Warren P. *Late-Breaking Foreign Policy: The News Media's Influence on Peace Operations*. Washington, D.C.: United States Institute of Peace Press, 1997.

Tesson, Fernando R. *Humanitarian Intervention: An Inquiry into Law and Morality*. 2nd ed. Ardsley, N.Y.: Transnational Publishers, 1997.

Thomas, Raju G. C. *Yugoslavia Unraveled: Sovereignty, Self-Determination, Intervention*. Lanham, Md.: Lexington Books, 2003.

United Nations High Commissioner for Refugees. *The State of the World's Refugees 2000*. New York: Oxford University Press, 2001.

Walter, Jonathan, ed. *World Disasters Report 2001: Focus on Recovery*. Bloomfield, Conn.: Kumarian Press, 2001.

――― . *World Disasters Report 2002: Focus on Reducing Risk*. Bloomfield, Conn.: Kumarian Press, 2002.

――― . *World Disasters Report 2003: Focus on Ethics and Aid*. Bloomfield, Conn.: Kumarian Press, 2003.

――― . *World Disasters Report 2004: Focus on Community Resilience*. Bloomfield Conn.: Kumarian Press, 2005.

Weiss, Thomas G. *Military-Civilian Interactions: Intervening in Humanitarian Crises*. New York: Rowman & Littlefield, 1999.

Weiss, Thomas G., and Cindy Collins. *Humanitarian Challenges and Intervention: World Politics and the Dilemmas of Help*. Boulder, Colo.: Westview Press, 1996.

Weiss, Thomas G., and Larry Minear. *Humanitarian Action in Times of War: A Handbook for Practitioners*. Boulder, Colo.: Lynne Rienner, 1993.

Welsh, Jennifer M. *Humanitarian Intervention and International Relations*. New York: Oxford University Press, 2004.

Willett, S., ed. *Participatory Monitoring of Humanitarian Mine Action: Giving Voice to Citizens of Nicaragua, Mozambique and Cambodia*. New York: United Nations, 2003.

Yamashita, Hikaru. *Humanitarian Space and International Politics: The Creation of Safe Areas*. Burlington, Vt.: Ashgate, 2004.

Zarjevski, Yefime. *A Future Preserved: International Assistance to Refugees*. New York: Pergamon Press, 1988.

5. Disarmament and Arms Control

Al-Duaij, Nada. *Environmental Law of Armed Conflict*. Ardsley, N.Y.: Transnational Publishers, 2003.

Alexander, Yonah, and Milton M. Hoenig, eds. *Super Terrorism: Biological, Chemical, and Nuclear*. Ardsley, N.Y.: Transnational Publishers, 2001.

Alves, Pericles G., and Daiana B. Cipollone, eds. *Curbing Illicit Trafficking in Small Arms and Sensitive Technologies: An Action-Oriented Agenda*. New York: United Nations, 1998.

Andemicael, Berhanykun, and John Mathiason. *Eliminating Weapons of Mass Destruction: Prospects for Effective International Verification*. New York: Palgrave Macmillan, 2005.

Badash, Lawrence. *Scientists and the Development of Nuclear Weapons: From Fission to the Limited Partial Test Ban Treaty, 1939–1963*. Atlantic Highlands, N.J.: Humanities Press, 1995.

Benson, William. *Light Weapons Controls and Security Assistance: A Review of Current Practice*. London: International Alert and Saferworld, 1998.

Bernauer, T. *The Chemistry of Regime Formation: Explaining International Cooperation for a Comprehensive Ban on Chemical Weapons*. Brookfield, Vt.: Dartmouth Publishing Company, 1993.

Bloomfield, Lincoln P., and Harlan Cleveland, eds. *Disarmament and the U.N.: Strategy for the United States*. Princeton, N.J.: Aspen Institute for Humanistic Studies, 1978.

Bothe, Michael, A. Rosas, and N. Ronzitti. *The New Chemical Weapons Convention: Implementation and Prospectus*. Boston: Kluwer Law International, 1999.

Bourantonis, Dimitris. *The United Nations and the Quest for Nuclear Disarmament*. Brookfield, Vt.: Dartmouth Publishing Company, 1993.

Boutwell, Jeffrey, and Michael T. Klare, eds. *Lethal Commerce: The Global Trade in Small Arms and Light Weapons*. Lanham, Md.: Rowman & Littlefield, 1999.

Calogero, Francesco, M. Goldberger, and S. P. Kapitza, eds. *Verification: Monitoring Disarmament*, Boulder, Colo.: Westview, 1991.

Chari, P. R., and Arpit Rajain, eds. *Biological Weapons: Issues and Threats*. Singapore: Marshall Cavendish Academic, 2004.

Chatterji, Manas, H. Jager, and A. Rima, eds. *The Economics of International Security: Essays in Honor of Jan Tinbergen*. New York: St. Martin's Press, 1994.

Cirincione, Joseph, ed. *Repairing the Regime: Preventing the Spread of Weapons of Mass Destruction*. New York: Routledge, 2000.

Cornish, Paul. *Controlling the Arms Trade: The West versus the Rest*. London: Bowerdean Publishing, 1996.

Cukier, Wendy, and Victor W. Sidel. *The Global Gun Epidemic: From Saturday Night Specials to AK-47s*. Westport, Conn.: Praeger, 2005.

Dando, Malcolm M., Cyril Klement, Marian Negut, and Graham S. Pearson, eds. *Maximizing the Security and Development Benefits from the Biological and Toxin Weapons*. The Hague, The Netherlands: Kluwer Law International, 2003.

De Andreis, M., and Francesco Calogero. *The Soviet Nuclear Weapon Legacy*. SIPRI Research Report No. 10. Oxford: Oxford University Press, 1995.

Dekker, Guido den. *The Law of Arms Control: International Supervision and Enforcement*. Boston, Mass.: Martinus Nijhoff Publishers, 2001.

Dhanapala, Jayantha, with Randy Rydell. *Multilateral Diplomacy and the NPT: An Insider's Account*. Geneva: United Nations, 2005.

Dhanapala, Jayantha, et al. *Small Arms Control: Old Weapons, New Issues*. Geneva: United Nations Institute for Disarmament Research, 1999.

Dhanapala, J., ed. *The United Nations, Disarmament and Security: Evolution and Prospects*. New York: United Nations, 1991.

Epstein, William. *The United Nations and Disarmament: Achievements on the Way to a Nuclear-Free World: Information Guide for Photo Exhibition*. New York: United Nations, 1998.

———. *The United Nations and Nuclear Disarmament: Achievements in the Way to a Nuclear-free World*. New York: United Nations, 1997.

———. *The Prevention of Nuclear War: A United Nations Perspective*. Cambridge, Mass.: Oelgeschlager, Gunn & Hain, Publishers, 1984.

Geissler, Erhard, ed. *Strengthening the Biological Weapons Convention by Confidence-Building Measures*. New York: Oxford University Press, 1990.

Graham, Thomas Jr., et. al. *Cooperation in the Maintenance of Peace and Security and Disarmament*. New York: United Nations, 1994.

Guillemin, Jeanne. *Biological Weapons: From the Invention of State-Sponsored Programs to Contemporary Bioterrorism*. New York: Columbia University Press, 2005.

Guruswamy, Lakshman D. and Suzette R. Grillot, eds. *Arms Control and the Environment*. Ardsley, N.Y.: Transnational Publishers, 2001.

Gyarmati, Istvan, et al. *Missile Development and Its Impact on Global Security*. New York: United Nations Department for Disarmament Affairs, 1999.

Herring, Eric, ed. *Preventing the Use of Weapons of Mass Destruction*. Portland, Ore.: Frank Cass, 2000.

Hewlett, Richard G., and Jack M. Holl. *Atoms for Peace and War, 1953–1961: Eisenhower and the Atomic Energy Commission*. Berkeley: University of California Press, 1989.

Hill, Stephen. *United Nations Disarmament in Intra-State Conflict*. Southampton Studies in Intl. Policy. New York: Palgrave Macmillan, 2003.

Historical Survey of the Activities of the League of Nations 1920–1937. UN Document A/AC 50/2, 1951.

Hoffmann, Walter, ed. *A New World Order: Can It Bring Security to the World's People? Essays on Restructuring the United Nations*. Washington, D.C.: World Federalist Association, 1991.

Hogg, Ian V., and John S.Weeks. *Military Small Arms of the 20th Century*. 7th ed. Iola: Wis.: Krause Publications, 2000.

Hubert, Don. *The Landmine Ban: A Case Study in Humanitarian Advocacy*. Occasional Paper No. 42. Providence, R.I.: Watson Institute for International Studies, 2000.

Human Rights Watch. *Landmine Monitor 2000: Toward a Mine-Free World*. New York: Human Rights Watch, 2000.

Jorgensen-Dahl, Arnfinn, and Willy Ostreng, eds. *The Antarctic Treaty System in World Politics*. New York: St. Martin's Press, 1991.

Klare, Michael T. *Resource Wars: The New Landscape of Global Conflict*. New York: Metropolitan Books, 2001.

Krause, Keith, ed. *Culture and Security: Multilateralism, Arms Control and Security Building*. Portland, Ore.: Frank Cass, 1999.

Krause, Keith, and Peter Bachelor. *Small Arms Survey, 2002*. Oxford: Oxford University Press, 2002.

Lederberg, Joshua, ed. *Biological Weapons: Limiting the Threat*. Cambridge, Mass.: MIT Press, 1999.

Littlewood, Jez. *The Biological Weapons Convention: A Failed Revolution*. Williston, Vt.: Ashgate Publishing Company, 2005.

Maslen, Stuart. *Commentaries on Arms Control Treaties*. Vol. 1, *The Convention on the Prohibition of the Use, Stockpiling, Production, and Transfer of Antipersonnel Mines and on Their Destruction*. Oxford Commentaries on International Law. Oxford: Oxford University Press, 2003.

Menon, P. K. *United Nations Efforts to Outlaw the Arms Race in Outer Space.* New York: Paragon Books, 1988.

Menos, Dennis. *The Superpowers and Nuclear Arms Control: Rhetoric and Reality.* New York: Praeger, 1990.

Meyrowitz, Elliott. *Prohibition of Nuclear Weapons: The Relevance of International Law.* Dobbs Ferry, N.Y.: Transnational Publishers, 1990.

Myrdal, Alva. *The Game of Disarmament: How the United States and Russia Run the Arms Race.* New York: Pantheon, 1982.

Nanda, Ved P., and David Kreiger. *Nuclear Weapons and the World Court.* Ardsley, N.Y.: Transnational Publishers, 1998.

NGO Committee on Disarmament. *Disarmament: The Future of Disarmament.* New York: United Nations, 1998.

Panofsky, W. K. H. *Arms Control and SALT II.* Seattle: University of Washington Press, 1979.

Perkovich, George, et al. *Universal Compliance: A Strategy for Nuclear Security.* Washington, D.C.: Carnegie Endowment for International Peace, 2005.

Pilat, Joseph F., Robert E. Pendley, and Charles E. Ebinger. *Atoms for Peace: An Analysis After Thirty Years.* Boulder, Colo.: Westview Press, 1985.

Prawitz, Jan, and James F. Leonard. *A Zone Free of Mass Destruction in the Middle East.* New York: United Nations, 1996.

Quester, George H. *International Safeguards for Eliminating Weapons of Mass Destruction.* Washington, D.C.: Henry L. Stimson Center, 1996.

Rana, Swadesh. *Small Arms and Intra-State Conflicts.* UNIDIR Research Paper. New York: United Nations, 1995.

Rhinelander, John B., and Lawrence Scheunman, eds. *At the Nuclear Crossroads: Choices About Nuclear Weapons and Extension of the Non-Proliferation Treaty.* Lanham, Md.: University Press of America, 1995.

Roberts, Brad, "From Nonproliferation to Antiproliferation." *International Security* 18, no.1 (Summer 1993): 139–73.

Rotblat, Joseph, Jack Steinberger, Bhalchandra Udgaonkar, and Frank Blackaby, eds. *A Nuclear Weapon–Free World: Desirable? Feasible?* Boulder, Colo.: Westview, 1993.

Rotfeld, Adam Daniel, et al. *Arms Control and Disarmament: A New Conceptual Approach.* New York: United Nations Department for Disarmament Affairs, 2000.

Russell, Bertrand. *The Atomic Bomb and the Prevention of War.* Chicago: Bulletin of Atomic Scientists, 1946.

Schroeder, Emily, and Lauren Newhouse. *Gender and Small Arms: Moving into the Mainstream.* Pretoria, South Africa: Institute for Security Studies, 2004.

Sims, Nicholas A. *The Evolution of Biological Disarmament.* New York: Oxford University Press, 2001.

Sokolski, Henry, and Jim Ludes, eds. *Twenty-First Century Weapons Prolifera-tion*. Portland, Ore.: Frank Cass, 2001.

Spanier, John, and Joseph L. Nogee. *The Politics of Disarmament: A Study in Soviet-American Gamesmanship*. New York: Praeger, 1962.

Spiers, Edward M. *Chemical and Biological Weapons: A Survey of Prolifera-tion*. New York: St. Martin's Press, 1994.

Stockholm International Peace Research Institute. *SIPRI Yearbook: Arma-ments, Disarmaments and International Security*. Oxford: Oxford University Press, 1997.

Sur, Serge, ed. *Verification of Disarmament or Limitation of Armaments: In-struments, Negotiations, Proposals*. New York: United Nations, 1992.

——. (ed.). *Disarmament Agreements and Negotiations: The Economic Di-mension*. New York: UN Institute for Disarmament Research, 1991.

Thakur, Ramesh, and Ere Haru, eds. *The Chemical Weapons Convention: Im-plementation, Challenges and Opportunities*. Tokyo: United Nations Uni-versity Press, 2006.

Thakur, Ramesh C. *Nuclear Weapons–Free Zones*. New York: St. Martin's Press, 1998.

Tulliu, S., and Schmalberger, T. *Coming to Terms with Security: A Lexicon for Arms Control, Disarmament and Confidence-Building*. New York: United Nations, 2001.

United Nations. *The United Nations and Nuclear Non-Proliferation*. New York: United Nations, 1995.

——. *United Nations Conference on Disarmament Issues: Disarmament in the Last Half Century and Its Future Prospects*. New York: United Nations, 1995

——. *U.N. Disarmament Studies*. New York: Taylor & Francis, 1989.

——. *The United Nations and Disarmament, 1945–1984*. New York: United Nations, 1985.

——. *Economic and Social Consequences of the Arms Race and Military Ex-penditures*. New York: United Nations, 1972, 1978, and 1983.

——. *The Relationship Between Disarmament and Development*. Report of the Secretary-General (the Thorsson Report). New York: United Nations, 1982.

——. *Disarmament and Development*. New York: United Nations, 1973.

——. *Disarmament 1945–1970*. New York: United Nations, 1970.

United Nations Development Program. *UNDP Small Arms Reduction Pro-gram: A Primer* New York: UNDP, 2001.

Vidas, Davor, and Olav S. Stoke, eds. *Governing the Antarctic: The Effective-ness and Legitimacy of the Antarctic Treaty System*. Cambridge: Cambridge University Press, 1997.

Willett, Susan. *Costs of Disarmament—Rethinking the Price Tag: A Methodological Inquiry into the Costs and Benefits of Arms Control.* New York: United Nations, 2002.

Wittner, Lawrence. *The Struggle Against the Bomb.* Vol. 2, *Resisting the Bomb 1954–1970.* Stanford, Calif.: Stanford University Press, 1997.

Wu, Leneice N. *The Baruch Plan: U.S. Diplomacy Enters the Nuclear Age.* Washington, D.C.: U.S. Govt. Printing Office, 1972.

G. Sustaining Social and Economic Development

1. Approaches to Development

An Agenda for Development. New York: United Nations, 1997.

Agenda 21: The UN Programme of Action from Rio. New York: United Nations, 1992.

Berthelot, Yves, ed. *Unity and Diversity in Development Ideas: Perspectives from the Regional Commissions.* Bloomington: Indiana University Press, 2004.

Bhagwati, Jagdish N., ed. *The New International Economic Order: The North-South Debate.* Cambridge, Mass.: MIT Press, 1977.

Brinkherhoff, Jennifer M. *Partnership for International Development: Rhetoric or Results?* Boulder, Colo.: Lynne Rienner, 2002.

Chenery, Hollis, et al. *Redistribution with Growth: Policies to Improve Income Distribution in Developing Countries in the Context of Economic Growth.* London: Oxford University Press, 1974.

Cornia, Giovanni A., Richard Jolly, and Frances Stewart, eds. *Adjustment with a Human Face.* Oxford: Clarendon Press, 1987.

Dell, Sidney. *International Development Policies: Perspectives for Industrial Countries.* Durham, N.C.: Duke University Press, 1991.

Dell, Sidney, ed. *Policies for Development: Essays in Honor of Gamani Corea.* Basingstoke, England: Macmillan Press, 1988.

Devaki, Jain. *Women, Development, and the UN: A Sixty-Year Quest for Equality.* Bloomington: Indiana University Press, 2005.

Donini, Antonio, Norah Niland, Karin Wermester, eds. *Nation-Building Unraveled? Aid, Peace, and Justice in Afghanistan.* Bloomfield, Conn.: Kumarian Press, 2004.

Emmerij, Louis, ed. *Economic and Social Development into the Twenty-First Century.* Baltimore, Md.: Johns Hopkins University Press, 1997.

Emmerij, Louis, Richard Jolly, and Thomas G. Weiss. *Ahead of the Curve? UN Ideas and Global Challenges.* Bloomington: Indiana University Press, 2001.

Fomerand, Jacques. *Mirror, Tool, or Linchpin for Change? The UN and Development.* International Relations Studies and the United Nations Occasional

Papers No. 2. Waterloo, Ontario: Academic Council on the United Nations System, 2003.

Ghai, Dharam, et al. *The Basic Needs Approach to Development: Some Issues Regarding Concepts and Methodology*. Geneva: ILO, 1977.

Helleiner, Eric. *States and the Reemergence of Global Finance: From Bretton Woods to the 1990s*. Ithaca, N.Y.: Cornell University Press, 1994.

International Labour Organisation. *Employment, Growth and Basic Needs: A One-World Approach*. Geneva: ILO, 1976.

Jolly, Richard, Louis Emmerij, and Frederic Lapeyre. *UN Contributions to Development Thinking and Practice*. Bloomington: Indiana University Press, 2004.

Krasner, Stephen. *Structural Conflict*. Berkeley: University of California Press, 1985.

Legum, Colin, ed. *The First U.N. Development Decade and its Lessons for the 1970s*. New York: Praeger, 1970.

Mehrotra, Santosh, and Richard Jolly, eds. *Development With a Human Face. Experiences in Social Achievement and Economic Growth*. New York: Oxford University Press, 1998.

Murphy, Craig. *Emergence of the NIEO Ideology*. Boulder, Colo.: Westview Press, 1984.

Nussbaum, Martha C. *Women and Human Development: The Capabilities Approach*. New York: Cambridge University Press, 1993.

Rogers, Halsey, Nicholas H. Stern, and Ian Goldin. *The Role and Effectiveness of Development Assistance: Lessons from World Bank Experience*. A Research Paper from the Development Economics Vice Presidency of the World Bank. Washington, D.C.: The World Bank, 2002.

Rothstein, Robert L. *Global Bargaining: UNCTAD and the Quest for a New International Economic Order*. Princeton, N.J.: Princeton University Press, 1979.

Sen, Amartya. *Development as Freedom*. New York: Knopf, 1999.

——. *Poverty and Famines: An Essay on Entitlement and Deprivation*. Oxford: Clarendon Press, 1981.

——. *Resources, Values, and Development*. Cambridge, Mass.: Harvard University Press, 1984.

Snyder, Margaret. *Transforming Development: Women, Poverty and Politics*. London: Intermediate Technology Publications, 1995.

Streeten, Paul, et al. *First Things First: Meeting Basic Needs in the Developing Countries*. New York: Oxford University Press, 1981.

Thomas, Caroline. *Global Governance, Development and Human Security: The Challenge of Poverty and Inequality*. Ann Arbor, Mich.: Pluto Press, 2000.

Toye, John. "The Origins and Interpretation of the Prebisch-Singer Thesis." *History of Political Economy* 35, no. 3 (Fall 2003): 437–67.

Toye, John, and Richard Toye. *The UN and Global Political Economy: Trade, Finance and Development*. Bloomington: Indiana University Press, 2004.

Transparency International. *Global Corruption Report 2004*. Ann Arbor, Mich.: Pluto Press, 2004.

United Nations. *Measures for the Economic Development of Under-Developed Countries*. Report by a Group of Experts Appointed by the Secretary-General of the United Nations. New York: United Nations, 1951.

——. *The United Nations and the Advancement of Women, 1945–1996*. New York: DPI, 1996.

——. *A Better World for All*. Washington D.C.: IMF/OECD/UN/Word Bank, 2000.

United Nations Conference on Trade and Development. *Beyond Conventional Wisdom in Development Policy: An Intellectual History of UNCTAD 1964–2004*. New York: United Nations, 2004.

Uvin, Peter. *Aiding Violence: The Development Enterprise in Rwanda*. Bloomfield, Conn.: Kumarian Press, 1998.

Ward, Michael. *Quantifying the World: UN Ideas and Statistics*. Bloomington: Indiana University Press, 2004.

Weiss, Thomas, Tatiana Carayannis, Louis Emmerij, and Richard Jolly. *UN Voices: The Struggle for Development and Justice*. Bloomington: Indiana University Press, 2005.

World Bank. *Can Africa Claim the Twenty-First Century?* Washington, D.C: World Bank, 2000.

——. *The Quality of Growth*. Washington, D.C.: The World Bank, 2000.

——. *Accelerated Development in Sub-Saharan Africa: An Agenda for Action*. Washington, D.C.: World Bank, 1981.

2. Global Conferences

Adam, Rogers. *The Earth Summit: A Planetary Reckoning*. Los Angeles: Global View Press, 1993.

Alston, Philip, ed. *The Best Interests of the Child*. Oxford: Clarendon Press, 1994.

Berstein, Robert, ed. *The Compromise of Liberal Environmentalism*. New York: Columbia University Press, 2001.

Campiglio, Luigi. *The Environment After Rio: International Law and Economics*. London: Graham & Trotman, 1994.

Cassen, Robert, ed. *Population and Development: Old Debates, New Conclusions*. Washington, D.C.: Overseas Development Council, 1994.

Finkle, Jason L., and Barbara B. Crane. "The Politics of Bucharest: Population, Development, and the New International Economic Order." *Population and Development Review* 1, no. 1 (1973): 87–114.

Fomerand, Jacques. "UN Conferences: Media Events or Genuine Diplomacy?" *Global Governance* 2 (1996): 361–75.

Galey, Margaret. *United Nations Conference of the UN Decade for Women*. Report of Congressional Staff Advisers for the US Delegation. Washington, D.C.: GPO, 1980.

Gardner, Richard. *Negotiating Survival: Four Priorities After Rio*. New York: Council on Foreign Relations, 1992.

Grubb, Michael, et al. *The "Earth Summit" Agreements: A Guide and Assessment: An Analysis of the Rio '92 UN Conference on Environment and Development*. London: Earthcan, 1993.

Hanson, Elizabeth. *The United Nations Conference on Science and Technology for Development*. Hanover, N.H.: American Universities Field Staff, 1990.

Holdgate, M. W., M. Kassas, and G. White, eds. *The World Environment 1972–1983: A Report by the United Nations Environment Programme, Natural Resources and the Environment*. Dublin: Tycooly, 1982.

Johnson, Stanley. *The Politics of Population: the International Conference on Population and Development*, Cairo, 1994. London: Earthscan, 1995.

Martin, Edwin M. *Conference Diplomacy: A Case Study of the World Food Conference*. Washington, D.C: Institute for the Study of Diplomacy of Georgetown University, 1979.

Middleton, Neil, Phil O'Keefe, and Sam Mayo. *The Tears of the Crocodile: From Rio to Reality in the Developing World*. London: Pluto Press, 1993.

Mintzer, Irving M., and J. Amber Leonard. *Negotiating Climate Change: The Inside Story of the Rio Convention*. New York: Cambridge University Press, 1994.

Morehouse, Ward, ed. *Third World Panacea or Global Boondoggle? The UN Conference on Science and Technology for Development Revisited*. Lund, Sweden: Research Policy Institute University of Lund, 1984.

Rosegrant, Mark W., Ximing Cai, and Sarah A. Cline. *Global Water Outlook to 2025: Averting an Impending Crisis*. Washington, D.C.: International Water Management Institute and International Foods Policy Research Institute. 2005.

Rowland, Wade. *The Plot to Save the World: The Life and Times of the Stockholm Conference on the Human Environment*. Toronto: Clarke Irwin, 1973.

Sachs, Wolfgang, ed. *Global Ecology: A New Arena of Political Conflict*. London: Zed Books, 1993.

Schechter, Michael G. *United Nations Global Conferences*. New York: Routledge, 2005.

———. ed. *United Nations Sponsored World Conferences: Focus on Impact and Follow Up*. Tokyo, United Nations University Press, 2001.

Singer, H. W., and Richard Jolly, eds. "Fifty Years of the UN and Economic and Social Development." Special issue, *IDS Bulletin* 26, no.4 (October 1995).

Stone, Peter. *Did We Save the Earth at Stockholm?* London: Earth Island, 1973.

Tolba Mostafa K., and A. El-Kholy. *The World Environment 1972–1992: Two Decades of Challenge*. London: Chapman and Hall, 1992.

United Nations. *The World Conferences: Developing Priorities for the Twenty-first Century*. New York: United Nations, 1997.

———. *World Conference on Human Rights: The Vienna Declaration and Program of Action*. New York: United Nations, 1995.

———. *Declaration on Social Development and Programme of Action of the World Summit for Social Development*. New York: United Nations, 1995.

———. *Human Settlements: The Environmental Challenge*. New York: United Nations, 1974.

Walls, James. *Land, Man and Sand: Desertification and Its Solutions*. New York: Macmillan Publishers, 1980.

Ward, Barbara, and Rene Dubos. *Only One Earth: The Care and Maintenance of a Small Planet*. Harmondsworth, England: Penguin, 1972.

Weiss, Thomas G., and Robert S. Jordan. *The World Food Conference and Global Problem-Solving*. New York: Praeger, 1976.

Wilkowski, Jean M. *Conference Diplomacy II: The UN Conference on Science and Technlogy for Development, Vienna, 1979*. Washington, D.C.: Institute for the Study of Diplomacy, Georgetown University, 1982.

World Commission on Environment and Development (Brundtland Commission). *Our Common Future*. Oxford: Oxford University Press, 1987.

3. Functionalism: The Specialized Agencies, the Bretton Woods Institutions, and the World Trade Organization

Abbot, John. *Politics and Poverty: A Critique of the Food and Agriculture Organization of the United Nations*. London: Routledge, 1992.

Andenas, Mads, and Federico Ortino, eds. *WTO Law and Process*. London: British Institute of International and Comparative Law, 2005.

Anderson, Sarah, ed. *Views from the South: The Effects of Globalization and the WTO on the Third World*. Oakland, Calif.: Food First, 2000.

Ayres, Robert. *Banking on the Poor: The World Bank and World Poverty*. Cambridge, Mass.: MIT Press, 1983.

Bazin, Herve. *The Eradication of Smallpox*. San Diego, Calif.: Academic Press, 2000.

Berkov, Robert. *The World Health Organization: A Study in Decentralized International Administration*. Geneva: Librairie Droz, 1957.

Birdsall, Nancy, and John Williamson, with Brian Deese. *Delivering on Debt Relief: From IMF Gold to a New Aid Architecture*. Washington, D.C.: Center for Global Development: Institute for International Economics, 2002.

Buergenthal, Thomas. *Law-Making in the International Civil Aviation Organization*. Syracuse, N.Y.: Syracuse University Press, 1969.

Buira, Ariel, ed. *Challenges to the World Bank and IMF*. London: Anthem Press, 2003.

Chossudowsky, Michel. *The Globalisation of Poverty: Impacts of IMF and World Bank Reforms*. London: Zed Books, 1998.

Codding, George A., Jr. *The Universal Postal Union*. New York: New York University Press, 1964.

Codding George A. Jr., and Anthony M. Rutkowski. *The International Telecommunications Union in a Changing World*. Dedham, Mass.: Artech House, 1982.

Cox, Robert W., and Harold K. Jacobson. *The Anatomy of Influence: Decision Making in International Organization*. New Haven, Conn.: Yale University Press, 1973.

Culpeper, Roy. *The Multilateral Banks: Titans or Behemoths?* Boulder, Colo.: Lynne Rienner Publishers, 1997.

Danaher, Kevin, ed. *50 Years Is Enough: The Case Against the World Bank and the International Monetary Fund*. Boston, Mass: South End Press, 1994.

Dell, Sidney. *The Inter-American Development Bank: A Study in Development Financing*. New York: Praeger, 1972.

De Vries, Margaret G. *The International Monetary Fund, 1945–1965: The Twenty Years of International Monetary Cooperation*. Washington, D.C.: International Monetary Fund, 1969.

——. *The International Monetary Fund, 1966–1971: The System Under Stress*. Washington, D.C.: IMF, 1976.

——. *The International Monetary Fund, 1972–1978*. Washington, D.C.: IMF, 1985.

Diebold, William Jr. *The End of the ITO*, Princeton, N.J.: Princeton University Press, 1952.

Eichengreen, Barry. *Globalizing Capital: A History of the International Monetary Fund*. Princeton, N.J.: Princeton University Press, 1996.

Forsythe, David P., ed. *The United Nations in the World Political Economy*. New York: St. Martin's Press, 1989.

Gareau, Frederick H. *The United Nations and Other International Institutions: A Critical Analysis*. Chicago: Burnham, 2002.

Goldstein, Paul. *International Copyright: Principles, Law, and Practice*. New York: Oxford University Press, 2001.

Ghebali,Victor-Yves, Roberto Ago, and Nicolas Valticos. *International Labour Organization*. Boston, Mass.: Nijhoff Publishers, 1989.

Griesgraber, Jo Marie, and Bernhard G. Gunter, eds. *The World Bank: Lending on a Global Scale*. Chicago: Pluto Press, 1996.

Grynberg, Roman. *WTO at the Margins: The Experience of South Pacific Countries*. York, England: Commonwealth Secretariat, 2003.

Guha-Khasnobis, Basudeb, ed. *The WTO, Developing Countries and the Doha Development Agenda*. New York: Macmillan, 2004.

Haas, Ernst B. *Beyond the Nation-State: Functionalism and International Organization*. Stanford, Calif.: Stanford University Press, 1964.

Haq, Mahbub ul, ed. *The UN and the Bretton Woods Institutions: New Challenges for the Twenty-First Century*. New York: St. Martin's Press, 1995.

Haq Mahbub ul, Richard Jolly, Paul Streeten, and Khadija Haq, eds. *The UN and the Bretton Woods Institutions*. London: Macmillan, 1995.

Hoekman, Bernard M. *The Political Economy of the World Trading System: From GATT to WTO*. Oxford: Oxford University Press, 1995.

Hoggart, Richard. *An Idea and Its Servants: UNESCO from Within*. New York: Oxford University Press, 1978.

Honeywell, Martin, ed. *The Poverty Brokers: The IMF and Latin America*. London: Latin America Bureau, 1983.

Hudec, Robert E. *The New WTO Dispute Settlement: An Overview of the First Three Years*. Geneva: Graduate Institute of International Studies, 1998.

———. *Enforcing International Trade Law: The Evolution of the Modern GATT Legal System*. Salem, N.H.: Butterworth Legal Publishers, 1993.

———. *Developing Countries in the GATT Legal System*. Brookfield, Vt.: Gower for the Trade Policy Research Centre, 1987.

———. *The GATT Legal System and World Trade Diplomacy*. New York: Praeger, 1975.

Imbert, Mark F. *The U.S.A., I.L.O., UNESCO, and IAEA: Politicization and Withdrawal in the Specialized Agencies*. London: Macmillan in association with the Center for International Policy Studies, University of Southampton, 1989.

International Civil Aviation Organization. *Memorandum on ICAO: The Story of the International Civil Aviation Organization*. Montreal: ICAO, 1951.

International Labour Office. *Fundamental Rights at Work and International Labour Standards*. Geneva: International Labour Organization, 2003.

Jenks, Clarence Wilfred. *Human Rights and International Labour Standards*. London: Stevens, 1960.

Kapur, Devesch, John Prior Lewis, Richard C. Webb, eds. *The World Bank: Its First Half Century*. Vol. 1, *History*; vol.2, *Perspectives*. Washington, D.C.: The Brookings Institution, 1997.

Kenen, Peter B. *The International Financial Architecture: What's New? What's Missing?* Washington, D.C.: Institute for International Economics, 2001.

Kenen, Peter B., ed. *Managing the World Economy: Fifty Years After Bretton Woods*. Washington, D.C.: Institute for International Economics, 1994.

Korner, Peter, Gero Maas, et al. *The IMF and the Debt Crisis: A Guide to the Third World's Dilemmas*. London: Zed Press, 1986.

Lambert, Youry. *The United Nations Industrial Development Organization: UNIDO and Problems of International Economic Cooperation*. Westport, Conn.: Praeger, 1993.

McQuillan, Lawrence J., and Peter C. Montgomery. *The International Monetary Fund, Financial Medic to the World? A Primer on Mission, Operations, and Public Policy Issues*. Stanford, Calif.: Hoover Institution Press, 1999.

McWhinney, Edward. *From GATT to the WTO: The Multilateral System Trading System in the New Millennium*. Boston, Mass.: Kluwer Law International, 2000.

Macrory, Patrick F., Arthur E. Appleton, Micahel G. Plummer, eds. *The World Trade Organization*. New York: Springer, 2005.

Mankabady, Samir. *The International Maritime Organization: Accidents at Sea*. London: Routledge Kegan & Paul, 1987.

Mangoldt, Hans von. *The United Nations and Its Predecessors*. 2 vols. Oxford: Oxford University Press, 1997.

Mason, S., and R. E. Asher. *The World Bank Since Bretton Woods*. Washington, D.C.: The Brookings Institution, 1973.

Matsushita, Mitsuo, Thomas Schoenbaum, and Petros Mavroidis. *The World Trade Organization: Law Practice, and Policy*. Oxford: Oxford University Press, 2003.

Mitrany, David. *A Working Peace System*. Chicago: Quadrangle, 1966.

Palmeter, David, and Petros C. Mavroidis. *Dispute Settlement in the World Trade Organization: Practice and Procedure*. Cambridge: Cambridge University Press, 2004.

Payer, Cheryl. *The Debt Trap: The IMF and the Third World*. New York: Monthly Review Press, 1975.

Peet, Richard. *Unholy Trinity: The IMF, World Bank, and the World Trade Organization*. New York: Zed Books, 2003.

Petersman, H. G. *Financial Assistance to Developing Countries: The Changing Role of the World Bank and the International Monetary Fund*. Geneva: Institut Universitaire de Hautes Etudes Internationales, 1988.

Sampson, Anthony. *The WTO and Sustainable Development*. Tokyo: United Nations University, 2005.

Savage, James. *The Politics of International Telecommunication Regulation*. Boulder, Colo.: Westview Press, 1989.

Scheinman, Lawrence. *The International Atomic Energy Agency and World Nuclear Order*. Washington, D.C.: Resources for the Future, 1987.

Schild, Georg. *Bretton Woods and Dumbarton Oaks: American Economic and Political Postwar Planning in the Summer of 1944*. New York: St. Martin's Press, 1995.

Sell, Susan. *Private Power, Public Law: The Globalization of Intellectual Property Rights*. Cambridge: Cambridge University Press, 2003.

Sewell, James P. *UNESCO and World Politics*. Princeton, N.J.: Princeton University Press, 1975.

Shihata, Ibrahim F. I., Franziska Tschofen, and Antonio R. Parra, eds. *The World Bank in a Changing World: Selected Essays*. Dordrecht, The Netherlands: Martinus Nijhoff Publishers, 1991.

Shotwell, James T. *The Origins of the ILO: History, Documents*. 2 vols. New York: Columbia University Press, 1934.

Simmonds, K. R. *The International Maritime Organization*. London: Simmonds & Hill Publishing, 1994.

Srinivasan, T. N. *Developing Countries and the Multilateral Trading System: From GATT to the Uruguay Round and the Future*. Boulder, Colo.: Westview Press, 1998.

Stewart, Terence P. *After Doha: The Changing Attitudes and Ideas of the New WTO Round*. Ardsley, N.Y.: Transnational Publishers, 2002.

Stewart, Terence P., Amy S. Dwyer, Patrick J. McDonough, Marta M. Prado, and Amy A. Karpel. *Rules in a Rules-Based WTO: Key to Growth: The Challenges Ahead*. Ardsley, N.Y.: Transnational Publishers, 2002.

Stone, Randall W. *Lending Credibility: The International Monetary Fund and the Post-Communist Transition*. Princeton, N.J.: Princeton University Press, 2002.

United Nations Industrial Development Organization. *United Nations Industrial Organization: 30 years of Industrial Development, 1966–1996*. ICS in association with UNIDO, 1995.

Upton, Barbara. *The Multilateral Development Banks. Improving U.S. Leadership*. Westport, Conn.: Praeger, 2000.

Vreeland, James. *The IMF and Economic Development*. New York: Cambridge University Press, 2003.

Wells, Robert N. Jr., ed. *Peace by Piece—United Nations Agencies and Their Roles: A Reader and Selective Bibliography*. Metuchen, N.J.: Scarecrow Press, 1991.

West, Gerald T., and Ethel I. Tarazona. *MIGA and Foreign Direct Investment: Evaluating Developmental Impacts*. Washington, D.C: World Bank, 1998.

Wilcox, Clair. *A Charter for World Trade*. New York: Macmillan, 1949.

Williams, Douglas. *The Specialized Agencies and the United Nations: A System in Crisis*. New York: St. Martin's Press, 1987.

Williamson, John, ed. *IMF Conditionality*. Cambridge, Mass.: MIT Press, 1983.

Young, Zoe. *A New Green Order? The World Bank and the Politics of the Global Environment Facility*. Ann Arbor, Mich.: Pluto Press, 2002.

Zacker, Mark W. *The United Nations and Global Commerce*. New York: United Nations, 1999.

4. Capacity Development

Abel, Elie, et al. *Many Voices, One World*. The McBride Report. Paris: UNESCO: 1980.

Bergesen, Helge O., and Leiv Lunde. *Dynosaurs or Dynamos: The United Nations and the World Bank at the Turn of the Century*. London: Earthscan, 1999.

Bergesen, Helge O., Hans Henrik Holm, and Robert D. McKinlay, eds. *The Recalcitrant Rich: A Comparative Analysis of the Northern Responses to the Demands for a New International Economic Order*. New York: St. Martin's Press, 1982.

Bissell, Richard E. *The United Nations Development Program: Failing the World's Poor*. Washington, D.C.: Heritage Foundation, 1985.

Browne, Stephen, ed. *Developing Capacity through Technical Cooperation: Country Experience*. London: Earthscan, 2002.

Commission on International Development. *Partners in Development: Report*. New York: Praeger, 1969.

Fox, Annette Baker. "President Truman's Fourth Point and the United Nations," *International Conciliation* 452 (June 1949): 465–85.

Fukuda-Parr, Sakiko, Carlos Lopes, and Khalil Mlik, eds. *Capacity for Development: New Solutions to Old Problems*, London: Earthscan, 2002.

Jackson, R. G. A. *A Study of the Capacity of the United Nations Development System*. Geneva: UNESCO, 1969.

Kirdar, Uner. *The Structure of United Nations Economic Aid to Underdeveloped Countries*. The Hague: Nijhoff, 1966.

Klingebiel, Stephan. *Effectiveness and Reform of the United Nations Development Program (UNDP)*. Portland, Ore.: Frank Cass, 1999.

Mack, Robert. T. *Raising the World's Standards of Living: The Coordination and Effectiveness of Point Four, United Nations Technical Assistance, and Related Programs*. New York: Citadel Press, 1953.

Murphy, Craig. *The UN Development Programme: A Better Way?* New York: Cambridge University Press, 2006.

Nashat, Mahyar. *National Interest and Bureaucracy Versus Development Aid: A Study of United Nations Expanded Programme of Technical Assistance to the Third World*. Geneva: Tribune Editions, 1978.

Porter, Doug, Bryan Allen, and Gaye Thompon. *Development in Practice: Paved with Good Intentions*. New York: Routledge, 1991.

Santiso, Carlos. "Promoting Democratic Governance and Preventing the Recurrence of Conflict: The Role of the United Nations Development Programme in Post-Conflict Peace-Building." *Journal of Latin American Studies* 34, no. 3 (2002): 555–86.

Sharp, Walter R. *Field Administration in the United Nations System: The Conduct of International Economic and Social Programs*. Westport, Conn.: Greenwood, 1978.

United Nations Conference on Trade and Development. *Meeting the Development Challenge: Technical Cooperation Programmes of UNCTAD.* New York: United Nations, 1995.

——. *Technological Capacity-Building and Technology Partnerships: Field Findings, Country Experiences and Programmes.* New York: United Nations, 1995.

United Nations Development Program. *Progress against Poverty in Africa.* New York: UNDP, 2002.

United Nations Volunteers. *Volunteers against Conflict.* Tokyo: United Nations University Press, 1996.

5. Sustainable Development; Money, Finance, and Trade; Science and Technology

Acquaah, Kwamena. *International Regulation and Transnational Corporations: The New Reality.* New York: Praeger, 1986.

Addison, Tony, Henrik Hansen, and Finn Tarp, eds. *Debt Relief for Poor Countries.* New York: Macmillan, 2004.

Addison, Tony, and Alan Roe, eds. *Fiscal Policy for Development.* New York: Macmillan, 2004.

Amin, Samir. *Capitalism in the Age of Globalization: The Management of Contemporary Society.* London, Zed Books, 1997.

Amrita, Narlikar. *International Trade and Developing Countries: Coalitions in GATT and WTO.* London: Routledge, 2003.

Ansari, Javed A. *The Political Economy of International Economic Relations.* Boulder, Colo.: Lynne Rienner, 1986.

Bernstein, Steven. *The Compromise of Liberal Environmentalism.* New York: Columbia University Press, 2001.

Bloch, Henry Simon. *The Challenge of the World Trade Conference.* New York: Columbia University Press, 1965.

Bodansky, Daniel. *The History of the Global Climate Change Regime.* Seattle: University of Washington, 1998.

Brown, Christopher. *The Political and Social Economy of Commodity Control.* New York: Praeger, 1980.

Carl, Beverly M. *Trade and the Developing World in the 21st Century.* Ardsley, N.Y.: Transnational Publishers, 2001.

Carraro, Carlo, ed. *Governing the Global Environment.* Cheltenham: Edward Elgar Publishing, 2003.

Castro, Josue. *Geography of Hunger.* Boston: Little, Brown, 1952.

Cayuela, Jose. *ECLAC: 40 Years (1948–1988).* Santiago, Chile: Economic Commission for Latin America and the Caribbean, 1988.

Cole, H. S. D. *Global Models and the New International Economic Order*. London, 1975.

Conca, Ken, and Geoffrey D. Dabelko. *Green Planet Blues: Environmental Politics from Stockholm to Kyoto*. 2nd ed. Boulder, Colo.: Westview Press, 1998.

Cornia, Andrea, ed. *Inequality, Growth, and Poverty in an Era of Liberalization and Globalization*. New York: Oxford University Press, 2004.

Delvin, Robert. *Debt and Crisis in Latin America*. Princeton, N.J.: Princeton University Press, 1989.

Devaki, Jain. *Women, Development, and the UN: A Sixty-Year Quest for Equality and Justice*. Bloomington: Indiana University Press, 2005.

Dixon, Robert K. *The U.N. Framework Convention on Climate Change Activities Implemented Jointly (AIJ) Pilot: Experiences and Lessons Learned*. Dordrecht, The Netherlands: Kluwer, 1999.

Eichengreen, Barry. *Globalizing Capital: A History of the International Monetary System*. Princeton, N.J.: Princeton University Press, 1996.

Elson, Diane, with Hande Kekkik. *Progress of the World's Women 2002*. Vol. 2, *Gender, Equality and the Millennium Development Goals*. New York: UNIFEM, 2003.

Esty, Dan. *Greening the GATT: Trade, Environment, and the Future*. Washington, D.C.: Institute for International Economics, 1994.

Evans, David. *International Commodity Policy:UNCTAD and NIEO in Search of a Rationale*. Brighton, England: Institute of Development Studies, 1978.

Faure, Michael, Joyeeta Gupta, and Andries Nentjes, eds. *Climate Change and the Kyoto Protocol*. Cheltenham, England: Edward Elgar Publishing, 2003.

French, Hilary F. *Partnership for the Planet: An Environmental Agenda for the United Nations*. Washington, D.C.: Worldwatch Institute, 1995.

Friedeberg, Alfred S. *The UNCTAD of 1964*. Rotterdam, The Netherlands: Univesitare Pers, 1970.

Gardner, Richard N. *Negotiating Survival: Four Priorities After Rio*. New York: Council on Foreign Relations Press, 1992.

——— . *Sterling-Dollar Diplomacy: The Origins and Prospects of Our International Economic Order*. New York: McGraw Hill, 1969.

George, Susan. *The Debt Boomerang: How Third World Debt Harms Us All*. Boulder, Colo.: Westview Press, 1991.

——— . *A Fate Worse Than Debt: The World Financial Crisis and the Poor*. New York: Grove Press, 1990.

Gilhooly, Denis, ed. *Creating an Enabling Environment: Proceedings of the Berlin Global Forum of the United Nations ITC Task Force*. New York: United Nations, 2005.

Gosovic, Branislav. *UNCTAD Conflict and Compromise: The Third World's Quest for an Equitable World Economic Order Through the United Nations*. Leyden, The Netherlands: A.W. Sijthoff, 1972.

Griffin, Keith. *World Hunger and the World Economy*. Basingstoke, England: Macmillan, 1987.

Grubb, Michael, et al. *The "Earth Summit" Agreements: A Guide and Assessment: An Analysis of the Rio 92 UN Conference on Environment and Development*. London: Earthscan, 1993.

Gruhn, Isebill. *Regionalism Reconsidered: The Economic Commission for Africa*. Boulder, Colo.: Westview Press, 1979.

Haas, Peter M., Robert Keohane, and Marc A. Levy. *Institutions for the Earth: Sources of Effective International Environmental Protection*. Cambridge, Mass.: MIT Press, 1990.

Haq, Mahbub ul, Inge Kaul, and Isabelle Grunberg, eds. *The Tobin Tax, Coping with Financial Volatility*. New York: Oxford, 1996.

Helmore, Kristin. *Sustainable Livelihoods: Building on the Wealth of the Poor*. Bloomfield, Conn.: Kumarian Press, 2001.

Hempel, Lamont C. *Environmental Governance: The Global Challenge*. Washington, D.C.: Island Press, 1996.

Hong, Burton, ed. *Intellectual Property and Biological Resources: Perspectives on Contemporary Issues*. Singapore: Academic Publishing, 2004.

Husain, I., and Diwant, I. *Dealing with the Debt Crisis. A World Bank Symposium*. Washington, D.C.: The World Bank, 1989.

International Organization for Migration. *World Migration 2005: Costs and Benefits of International Migration*. Geneva: International Organization for Migration, 2005.

James, Jeffrey. *Globalization, Information Technology and Development*. New York: St. Martin's Press, 1999.

Jin, Zhouying. *Global Technological Change*. Bristol, England: Intellect Books, 2005.

Johnson, Stanley P. *World Population and the United Nations: Challenge and Response*. Cambridge: Cambridge University Press, 1987.

Khan, Azizur Rahman, and Rehman Sobhan, eds. *Trade, Planning and Rural Development: Essays in Honour of Nurul Islam*. Basingtoke, England: Macmillan, 1990.

Kiely, Ray, and Phil Marfleet. *Globalisation and the Third World*. New York: Routledge, 1998.

Koop, C. Everett, Clarence E. Pearson, M. Roy Schwartz, eds. *Critical Issues in Global Health*. San Francisco, Calif.: Jossey-Bass, 2002.

Koul, Autar K. *The Legal Framework of UNCTAD in World Trade*. Leyden, The Netherlands: A.W. Sijthoff, 1977.

Krueger, Anne O. *Perspectives on Trade and Development*. Chicago: University of Chicago Press, 1990.

Kuik, Onno, Paul Peters, and Nico Schrijver, eds. *Joint Implementation to Curb Climate Change: Legal and Economic Aspects*. Boston, Mass.: Kluwer Academic Publishers, 1994.

Kummer, Katarina. *International Management of Hazardous Wastes: The Basel Convention and Related Legal Rules*. New York: Oxford University Press, 2000.

Kunich, John C. *Ark of the Broken Covenant: Protecting the World's Biodiversity Hotspots*. Westport, Conn.: Greenwood Publishing, 2003.

Kyambalesa, Henry. *The Quest for Technological Development: Constraints, Caveats and Initiatives*. Lanham, Md.: University Press of America, 2001.

Lee, Henry, ed. *Shaping National Responses to Climate Change: A Post-Rio Guide*. Washington, D.C.: Island Press, 1995.

Le Prestre, Philippe G., ed. *Governing Global Biodiversity: The Evolution and Implementation of the Convention on Biological Diversity*. Burlington, Vt.: Ashgate, 2002.

Levy, Jean Pierre and Gunnar G. Schram. *United Nations Conference on Straddling Fish Stocks and Highly Migratory Fish Stocks*. Boston, Mass.: Martinus Nijhoff, 1996.

Lewis, Mark. *The Growth of Nations: Culture, Competitiveness, and the Problem of Globalization*. Bristol, England: Bristol Academic Press, 1996.

McConnell, Fiona. *The Biodiversity Convention: A Negotiating History: A Personal Account of Negotiating the United Nations Convention on Biological Diversity, and After*. London: Kluwer Law International, 1996.

MacDonald, Scott B., Margie Lindsay, and David L. Crum, eds. *The Global Debt Crisis: Forecasting for the Future*. London: Pinter Publishers, 1990.

Maitra, Priyatosh. *The Globalization of Capitalism in Third World Countries*. Westport, Conn.: Praeger, 1996.

Mansell, Robin, and Uta When, eds. *Knowledge Societies: Information Technology for Sustainable Development*. New York: Oxford University Press, 1998.

Massey, Douglas S., and J. Edward Taylor. *International Migration: Prospects and Policies in a Global Market*. New York: Oxford University Press, 2004.

Meller, Patricio, ed. *The Latin American Development Debate: Neostructuralism, Neomonetarism, and Adjustment Processes*. Boulder, Colo.: Westview Press, 1991.

Mizayaki, Nobuyuki, Zafar Aseel, and Kouichi Ohwada, eds. *Mankind and the Ocean*. Tokyo: United Nations University Press, 2005.

Onimode, Bade. *The IMF, the World Bank and the African Debt: Social and Political Impact*. London: Zed Books, 1989.

Onwuka, Ralph I., and O. Aluko. *The Future of Africa and the New International Economic Order*. New York: St. Martin's, 1986.

Payoyo, Peter Baurista, ed. *Ocean Governance: Sustainable Development of the Seas*. Tokyo: United Nations University, 1994.

Patterson, Neil, et al. *Foreign Direct Investment: Trends, Data Availability, Concepts, and Recording Practices*. Washington, D.C.: International Monetary Fund, 2004.

Porter, Garfeth, Janet Welsh Brown, and Pamela S. Chasek. *Global Environ-ment Politics*. 3rd ed. Boulder, Colo.: Westview Press, 1999.

Robinson, Nicholas A. *Strategies Toward Sustainable Development: Imple-menting Agenda 21*. Dobbs Ferry, N.Y.: Oceana Publications, 2004.

Rosendal, Kristin G. *The Convention on Biological Diversity and Developing Countries*. Boston: Kluwer Academic, 2000.

Sachs. Jeffrey D. *The End of Poverty: Economic Possibilities for Our Time*. New York: Penguin Press, 2005.

Salomon, Jean-Jacques, Francisco R. Sagasti, and Celine Sachs-Jeantet, eds. *The Uncertain Quest: Science, Technology, and Development*. Tokyo: United Nations University Press, 1994.

Sampath, Padmashree Gehl. *Regulating Bioprospecting: Institutions for Drug Research, Access and Benefit Sharing*. Tokyo: United Nations University Press, 2005.

Satterthwaite, David, ed. *The Millennium Development Goals and Local Processes: Hitting the Target or Missing the Point?* London: International In-stitute for Environment and Development, 2003.

Schrijver, Nico. *Sovereignty Over Natural Resources: Balancing Rights and Duties*. New York: Cambridge University Press, 1997.

Sitarz, Daniel, ed. *Agenda 21: The Earth Summit Strategy to Save Our Planet*. Boulder, Colo.: Earthpress, 1994.

Sobhan, Rehman. *Agrarian Reform and Social Transformation*. Atlantic High-lands, N.J: Zed Books, 1993.

Soroos, Marvin S. *The Endangered Atmosphere: Preserving a Global Com-mons*. Columbia: University of South Carolina Press, 1997.

Stevis, Dimitris, and Valerie J. Assetto, eds. *The International Political Econ-omy of the Environment: Critical Perspectives*. Boulder, Colo.: Lynne Rien-ner, 2001.

Symonds, R., and M. Carder. *The UN and the Population Question*. London: Chatto and Windus for Sussex University Press, 1973.

Suskind, Lawrence E. *Environmental Diplomacy: Negotiating More Effective Global Agreements*. New York: Oxford University Press, 1994.

Taylor, Paul, and A. J. R. Groom, eds. *Global Issues in the United Nations Framework*. London: Macmillan, 1989.

Teeple, Gary. *Globalization and the Decline of Social Reform*. Atlantic High-lands, N.J: Humanities Press, 1995.

Tewari, Kned, and M. Ramaiah, eds. *The Urban Challenge: A Collection of Lectures by Dr. Arcot Ramachandran*. Bangalore, India, 2005.

Thomas, Caroline, and Peter Wilkin: *Globalization and the South*. New York: St. Martin's Press, 1997.

Toye, John, and Richard Toye. *Trade, Finance, and Development*. Blooming-ton: Indiana University Press, 2004.

United Nations. *1999 World Survey on the Role of Women in Development: Globalization, Gender and Work.* New York: United Nations, 1999.

———. *1994 World Survey on the Role of Women in Development.* New York: United Nations, 1995.

———. *History of UNCTAD: 1964–1984.* New York: United Nations, 1985.

———. *The Millennium Development Goals Report.* New York: United Nations, 2005.

———. *Multinational Corporations in World Development.* New York: United Nations, 1973.

———. *The United Nations and the Advancement of Women.* New York: United Nations, 1996.

———. *Women 2000.* New York: United Nations, 2000.

———. *The World's Women 2000: Trends and Statistics.* New York: United Nations Statistical Division, 2000.

United Nations Center for Human Settlements. *Cities in a Globalizing World. Global Report on Human Settlements 2001.* London and Sterling, VA.: Earthscan, 2001.

United Nations Department of Economic and Social Affairs. *The Costs of Poverty and Vulnerability.* New York: United Nations, 2001.

United Nations Development Programme. *Progress Against Poverty in Africa.* New York: United Nations, 2002.

Uvin, Peter. *Aiding Violence: The Development Enterprise in Rwanda.* West Hartford, Conn.: Kumarian Press, 1998.

Vosti, Stephen A., and Thomas Reardon. *Sustainability, Growth and Poverty Alleviation.* Baltimore, Md.: Johns Hopkins University Press, 1997.

Waldo, Douglas, and C. Alan Parks."Caught in the Crossfire: Third World Economic Development and First World Environmentalism." *Journal of Third World Studies* 17, no. 2 (Fall 2000): 41–52.

Warnock, John W. *The Politics of Hunger: The Global Food System.* New York: Methuen, 1987.

Weaver, James H., Michael T. Rock, and Kenneth Kusterer. *Achieving Broad-Based Sustainable Development.* West Hartford, Conn.: Kumarian Press, 1996.

Weiss, Edith Brown, and John H. Jackson, eds. *Reconciling Environment and Trade.* Ardsley, N.Y.: Transnational Publishers, 2001.

Wilcox, Clair. *A Charter for World Trade.* New York: Macmillan, 1949.

Wood, Robert. *From Marshall Plan to Debt Crisis.* Berkeley: University of California Press, 1986.

World Commission on Environment and Development. *Our Common Future* (Brundtland Commission Report). Oxford: Oxford University Press, 1987.

Yamin, Farhana. "Biodiversity, Ethics and International Law." *International Affairs* (London) 71, no. 3 (1995): 529–46.

Young, Oran R., ed. *The Effectiveness of International Environment Regimes: Causal Connections and Behavioral Mechanisms*. Cambridge, Mass.: MIT Press, 1999.

H. Promoting Human Rights

Advisory Council on International Affairs. *United Nations and Human Rights*. The Hague, The Netherlands: Advisory Council on International Affairs, 2004.

Alston, Philip. *Labour Rights as Human Rights*. New York: Oxford University Press, 2005.

———. *Promoting Human Rights Through Bills of Rights: Comparative Perspectives*. New York: Oxford University Press, 2000.

———, ed. *Non-State Actors and Human Rights*. New York: Oxford University Press, 2005.

Alston, Philip, and Mary Robinson, eds. *Human Rights and Development. Towards Mutual Reinforcement*. New York: Oxford University Press, 2005.

Alston, Philip, and Frederic Megret, eds. *The United Nations and Human Rights: A Critical Appraisal*. 2nd ed. Oxford: Oxford University Press, 2004.

Alston, Philip, Stephen Parkes, and John Seymour, eds. *Children's Rights and the Law*. Oxford: Clarendon, 1992.

Amerasingue, Chittharanjan F. *Jurisdiction of International Tribunals*. The Hague, The Netherlands: Kluwer Law International, 2003.

Anaya, S. James, ed. *International Law and Indigenous Peoples*. Aldershot, England: Ashgate Publishing, 2003.

Andreopoulos, George J., and Richard Pierre Claude. *Human Rights Education for the Twenty-First Century*. Philadelphia: University of Pennsylvania Press, 1997.

Arbour, Madame Justice Louise. *War Crimes and the Culture of Peace*. Toronto: University of Toronto Press, 2003.

Arnold, Roberta. *The ICC as a New Instrument for Repressing Terrorism*. Ardsley, N.Y.: Transnational Publishers, 2004.

Askin, Kelly D., and Dorean M. Koening, eds. *Women and International Human Rights Law*. Ardsley, N.Y.: Transnational Publishers, 2000.

Aspen Institute. *Honoring Human Rights Under International Mandates: Lessons from Bosnia, Kosovo and East Timor*. Washington, D.C.: The Aspen Institute, 2003.

Baderin, Mashood A. *International Human Rights and Islamic Law*. Oxford: Oxford University Press, 2003.

Bales, Kevin. *Understanding Global Slavery. A Reader*. Berkeley: University of California Press, 2005.

Ball, Howard. *Prosecuting War Crimes and Genocide: The Twentieth-Century Experience*. Lawrence: University Press of Kansas Press, 1999.

Bas, Gary Jonathan. *Stay the Hand of Vengeance: The Politics of War Crimes Tribunals*. Princeton, N.J.: Princeton University Press, 2000.

Bassiouni, M. Cherif, ed. *The Statute of the International Criminal Court and Related Instruments: Legislative History 1994–2000*. Ardsley, N.Y.: Transnational Publishers, 2004.

——. *Post-Conflict Justice*. Ardsley, N.Y.: Transnational Publishers, 2002.

——. *The Protection of Human Rights in the Administration of Criminal Justice: A Compendium of United Nations Norms and Standards*. Ardsley, N.Y.: Transnational Publishers, 1994.

Bassiouni, M. Cherif, and Eduardo Vetere, eds. *Organized Crime: A Compilation of U.N. Documents, 1975–1998*. Ardsley, N.Y.: Transnational Publishers, 1998.

Bayefsky, Anne F. *How to Complain to the UN Human Rights Treaty System*. Ardsley, N.Y.: Transnational Publishers, 2003.

——. *The UN Human Rights Treaty System: Universality at the Crossroads*. Ardsley, N.Y.: Transnational Publishers, 2001.

Beigbeder, Yves. *Judging War Criminals: The Politics of International Justice*. New York: St. Martin's Press, 1999.

Benedek, Wolfgang, Alice Yotopoulos-Marangopoulos, eds. *Anti-Terrorist Measures and Human Rights*. Boston, Mass.: Martinus Nijhoff, 2004.

Bennett, Belinda, ed. *Health, Rights and Globalization*. Williston, Vt.: Ashgate Publishing Company, 2005.

Blair, Cherie Booth. *Impact of the International Criminal Court in Strengthening Worldwide Respect for Human Rights*. Geneva: Graduate Institute of International Studies, 2004.

Blake, Nicholas, and Raza Husain. *Immigration, Asylum and Human Rights*. Oxford: Oxford University Press, 2003.

Blau, Judith, and Alberto Moncada. *Human Rights: Beyond the Liberal Vision*. Blue Ridge Summit, Pa.: Rowman & Littlefield, 2005.

Booth, Ken. *The Kosovo Tragedy: Human Rights Dimensions*. Portland, Ore.: Frank Cass, 2001.

Boyle, Francis Anthony. *Palestine, Palestinians and International Law*. Atlanta, Ga.: Clarity Press, 2003.

Broomhall, Bruce. *International Justice and the International Criminal Court: Between Sovereignty and the Rule of Law*. New York: Oxford University Press, 2003.

Brysk, Alison, and Gershon Shafir, eds. *People out of Place: Globalization, Human Rights, and the Citizenship Gap*. New York: Routledge, 2004.

Campbell, Tom, Jeffrey Goldworthy, and Adrienne Stone, eds. *Protecting Human Rights: Instruments and Institutions*. Oxford: Oxford University Press, 2003.

Carey, John, William V. Dunlap, and R. John Pritchard, eds. *International Humanitarian Law: Origins, Challenges, Prospects.* 3 vols. Ardsley, N.Y.: Transnational Publishers, 2003–2004.
Carlson, Scott, and Gregory Gisvold, with Andrew Solomon. *Practical Guide to the International Covenant on Civil and Political Rights.* Ardsley, N.Y.: Transnational Publishers, 2003.
Chalk, Frank, and Kurt Jonassohn. *The History and Sociology of Genocide, Analyses and Case Studies.* New Haven, Conn.: Yale University Press, 1990.
Chandler, David. *Voices from S-21: Terror and History in Pol Pot's Secret Prison.* Berkeley: University of California Press, 1999.
Chuter, David. *War Crimes: Confronting Atrocity in the Modern World.* Boulder, Colo.: Lynne Rienner, 2003.
Clark, Ann Marie. *Diplomacy of Conscience: Amnesty International and Changing Human Rights Norms.* Princeton, N.J.: Princeton University Press, 2001.
Clark, Roger, and Madeleine Sann, eds. *The Prosecution of International Crimes: A Critical Study of the International Tribunal for the Former Yugoslavia.* Somerset, N.J.: Transaction Publishing, 2003.
Clark, Roger. *The United Nations Crime Prevention and Criminal Justice Program: Formation of Standards and Efforts at the Implementation.* Philadelphia: University of Pennsylvania Press, 1994.
Cohen, Cynthia Price, with Lori Kujawski. *The Jurisprudence on the Rights of the Child.* Ardsley, N.Y.: Transnational Publishers, 2004.
Cohen, Cynthia Price, ed. *Human Rights of Indigenous Peoples.* Ardsley, N.Y.: Transnational Publishers, 1998.
Cohn, Ilene. *Child Soldiers: The Role of Children in Armed Conflict.* London: Clarendon Press, 1996.
Coicaud, Jean-Marc, Michael W. Doyle, and Anne-Marie Gardner, eds. *The Globalization of Human Rights.* Tokyo: United Nations University Press, 2003.
Conte, Alex, Scott Davidson, and Richard Burcill. *Defining Civil and Political Rights: The Jurisprudence of the United Nations Human Rights Committee.* Burlington, Vt.: Ashgate, 2004.
Danieli, Yael, Elsa Stamatopolou, and Clarence J. Dias, eds. *The Universal Declaration of Human Rights: Fifty Years and Beyond.* Amityville, N.Y: Baywood, 1999.
Dobkowski, Michel N., and Isidor Wallimann. *The Coming Age of Scarcity: Preventing Mass Death and Genocide in the Twenty-First Century.* Syracuse, N.Y.: Syracuse University Press, 1998.
Dommem, Caroline. *Trading Rights: Human Rights and the WTO.* London: Zed Books, 2004.

Donnelly, Jack. *International Human Rights*. 2nd ed. Boulder, Colo.: Westview, 1998.

———. *Universal Human Rights in Theory and Practice*. Ithaca, N.Y.: Cornell University Press, 1989.

Drinan, Robert F. *The Mobilization of Shame: A World View of Human Rights*. New Haven, Conn.: Yale University Press, 2001.

Dunne, Tim, and Nicholas J. Wheeler, eds. *Human Rights in Global Politics*. Cambridge: Cambridge University Press, 1999.

Ensalaco, Mark, and Linda C. Majaka, eds. *Children's Human Rights: Progress and Challenges for Children Worldwide*. Blue Ridge Summit, Pa.: Rowman & Littlefield, 2005.

Falk, Richard. *Human Rights Horizons*. New York: Routledge, 2000.

Fatsah, Ouguergouz. *The African Charter on Human Rights and Peoples' Rights: A Comprehensuive Agenda for Human Dignity and Sustainable Democracy in Africa*. The Hague, The Netherlands: Kluwer Law International, 2003.

Fawthrop, Tom, and Helen Jarvis. *Getting Away with Genocide. Elusive Justice and the Khmer Rouge Tribunal*. Ann Arbor, Mich.: Pluto Press, 2004.

Feller, Erika, Volker Turk, and Frances Nicholson. *Refugee Protection in International Law: UNHCR's Global Consultations on International Protection*. Cambridge: Cambridge University Press, 2003.

Ferris, Elizabeth G., ed. *Refugees and World Politics*. New York: Praeger, 1985.

Fitzpatrick, Joan M., ed. *Human Rights Protection for Refugees, Asylum-Seekers, and Internally Displaced persons: A Guide to International Mechanisms and Procedures*. Ardsley, N.Y.: Transnational Publishers, 2001.

Flint, Julie, and Alex de Waal. *Darfur: A Short History of a Long War*. New York: Palgrave, 2005.

Forsythe, David P. *The Internationalization of Human Rights*. Lexington, Mass.: D.C. Heath, 1991.

———. *Human Rights and World Politics*. Rev. 2nd ed. Lincoln: University of Nebraska Press, 1989.

———, ed. *Human Rights and Development: International Views*. New York: St. Martin's, 1989.

Franck, Thomas, M. "Are Human Rights Universal?" *Foreign Affairs*, January/February 2001, 191–204.

Frynas, Jedrzej George, and Scott Pegg. *Transnational Corporations and Human Rights*. New York: Palgrave Macmillan, 2003.

Galvis, Constanza Ardila. *The Heart of the War in Columbia*. Bloomfield, Conn.: Kumarian Press, 2000.

Glendon, Mary Ann. *A World Made New: Eleanor Roosevelt and the Universal Declaration of Human Rights*. New York: Random House, 2001.

Goldewijk, Berma Klein, Alalid Contreras Baspineiro, and Paulo Cesar Carbonari, eds. *Dignity and Human Rights: The Implementation of Economic, Social, and Cultural Rights*. Ardsley, N.Y.: Transnational Publishers, 2002.

Gordenker, Leon, Roger Coate, Christer Jonsson, and Peter Soderholm. *International Cooperation in Response to AIDS*, New York: Pinter, 1995.

Gutman, Roy, and David Rieff, eds. *Crimes of War: What the Public Should Know*. New York: Norton, 1999.

Hagan, John. *Justice in the Balkans: Prosecuting War Crimes in the Hague Tribunal*. Chicago: University of Chicago Press, 2003.

Hancock, Jan. *Environmental Human Rights: Power, Ethics and Law*. Aldershot, England: Ashgate Publishing, 2003.

Hannum, Hurst, ed. *Guide to International Human Rights Practice*. 4th ed. Ardsley, N.Y.: Transnational Publishers, 2004.

Harris, David J., ed. *The International Covenant on Civil and Political Rights and United Kingdom Law*. Oxford: Oford University Press, 1995.

Helton, Arthur C. *The Price of Indifference. Refugees and Humanitarian Action in the New Century*. New York: Oxford University Press, 2002.

Henkin, Louis, ed. *The International Bill of Rights: The Covenant on Civil and Political Rights*. New York: Columbia University Press, 1981.

Hess, Carla, and Robert Post. *Human Rights in Political Transitions: Gettysburg to Bosnia*. New York: Zone Books, 1999.

Holmstrom, Leif, ed. *Concluding Observations of the UN Committee on Economic, Social and Cultural Rights: Eight to Twenty-Seventh Sessions (1993–2001)*. The Hague, The Netherlands: Kluwer Law International, 2003.

Honwana, Alcinda. *Child Soldiers in Africa: The Ethnography of Political Violence*. Philadelphia: University of Pennsylvania Press, 2005.

Horowitz, Shale, and Albrecht Schnabel, eds. *Human Rights and Societies in Transition. Causes, Consequences, Responses*. Tokyo: United Nations University Press, 2004.

Howard, Bradley Reed. *Indigenous Peoples and the State: The Struggle for Native Rights*. DeKalb: Northern Illinois University Press, 2003.

Human Rights Watch. *Sudan, Oil and Human Rights*. New York: Human Rights Watch, 2003.

———. *The Lost Agenda: Human Rights and UN Field Operations*. New York: Human Rights Watch, 1973.

Ingadottir, Thordis. *The International Criminal Court: Recommendations on Policy and Practice: Financing, Victims, Judges, and Immunities*. Ardsley, N.Y.: Transnational Publishers, 2003.

Ignatieff, Michael. *Human Rights as Politics and Idolatry*. Princeton, N.J.: Princeton University Press, 2003.

International Women's Tribune Centre. *Rights of Women; a Guide to the Most Important United Nations Treaties on Women's Human Rights*. 2nd ed. New York: International Women's Tribune Centre, 1998.

Isakovic, Zlatko. *Democracy, Human Rights and Ethnic Conflicts in the Process of Globalisation*. Copenhagen Peace Research Institute Working Paper, No. 3, 2002. Paper presented at the Canadian Peace Research and Education Association (CPREA) Conference, Kingston, Ontario, May 31–June 3, 2001.

Ishay, Micheline R. *The History of Human Rights: From Ancient Times to the Globalization Era*. Berkeley: University of California Press, 2004.

Jones, Adam, ed. *Genocide, War Crimes and the West: History and Complicity*. London: Zed Books, 2004.

Jones, John R.W. D., and Steven Powles. *International Criminal Practice*, 3rd ed. Ardsley, N.Y.: Transnational Publishers, 2003.

Joseph, Sarah, Jenny Schultz, and Melissa Castan. *The International Covenant on Civil and Political Rights: Cases, Materials, and Commentary*. 2nd ed. New York: Oxford University Press, 2004.

Kent, George. *Freedom From Want: The Human Right to Adequate Food*. Washington, D.C.: Georgetown University Press, 2005.

Kerr, Joanna, ed. *Ours by Right: Women's Rights as Human Rights*. London: Zed Books, 1993.

Kerr, Rachel. *The International Criminal Tribunal for the Former Yugoslavia: An Exercise in Law, Politics, and Diplomacy*. New York: Oxford University Press, 2004.

Klang, Mathias, and Andrew Murray, eds. *Human Rights in the Digital Age*. Oxford: Glasshouse Publishing, 2005.

Kneebone, Susan, ed. *The Refugee's Convention 50 Years On: Globalisation and International Law*. Aldershot, England: Avebury Technical, 2003.

Knop, Karen, ed. *Gender and Human Rights*. Oxford: Oxford University Press, 2004.

Kuper, Jenny. *International Law Concerning Child Civilians in Armed Conflict*. Oxford: Oxford University Press, 1997.

Kuper, Leo. *The Prevention of Genocide*. New Haven, Conn.: Yale University Press, 1985.

Lam, Maivan Clech. *At the Edge of the State: Indigenous Peoples and Self-Determination*. Ardsley, N.Y.: Transnational Publishers, 2000.

Landman, Todd. *Protecting Human Rights: A Comparative Study*. Washington, D.C.: Georgetown University Press, 2005.

Lauren, Paul Gordon. *The Evolution of International Human Rights: Visions Seen*. 2nd ed. Philadelphia: University of Pennsylvania Press, 2003.

Lee, Roy S., ed. *The International Criminal Court: Elements of Crimes and Rules of Procedure and Evidence*. Ardsley, N.Y.: Transnational Publishers, 2001.

Lemon, Anthony, ed. *The Geography of Change in South Africa*. Chichester, England: Wiley, 1995.

Loescher, Lori. *The UNHCR and World Politics. A Perilous Path*. New York: Oxford University Press, 2001.

Lood, Patrick J. *The Effectiveness of Human Rights Institutions.* Westport, Conn.: Praeger, 1998.

Louka, Elli. *Biodiversity and Human Rights: The International Rules for the Protection of Diversity.* Ardsley, N.Y.: Transnational Publishers, 2002.

Lyons, Gene, and James Mayall. *International Human Rights in the 21st Century: Protecting the Rights of Groups.* London: Rowman & Littlefield, 2003.

Macedo, Stephen, ed. *Universal Jurisdiction: National Courts and the Prosecution of Serious Crimes Under International Law.* Philadelphia: University of Pennsylvania Press, 2003.

Mahmood, Mamdani. *When Victims Become Killers: Colonialism, Nativism, and the Genocide in Rwanda.* Princeton, N.J.: Princeton University Press, 2001.

Mahony, Liam, and Luis Enrique Eguren. *Unarmed Bodyguards: International Accompaniment for the Protection of Human Rights.* Bloomfield, Conn.: Kumarian Press, 1997.

Maogoto, Jackson Nyamuya. *War Crimes and Realpolitik: International Justice from World War I to the 21st Century.* Boulder, Colo.: Lynne Rienner, 2004.

——. *State Sovereignty and International Criminal Law: Versailles to Rome.* Ardsley, N.Y.: Transnational Publishers, 2003.

Marks, Stephen P. *Right to Development: A Primer.* New Delhi, India: Sage, 2004.

Meijer, Martha, ed. *Dealing with Human Rights: Asian and Western Views on the Value of Human Rights.* Bloomfield, Conn.: Kumarian Press, 2001.

Meron, Theodor. *War Crimes Law Comes of Age, Essays.* Oxford, Clarendon Press, 1998.

——. *Human Rights and Humanitarian Norms as Customary Law.* Oxford: Clarendon Press, 1989.

——, ed. *Human Rights in International Law: Legal and Policy Issues.* New York: Oxford University Press, 1985.

Mertus, Julie A. *United Nations and Human Rights.* New York: Routledge, 2005.

——. *War's Offensive on Women: The Humanitarian Challenge in Bosnia, Kosovo, and Afghanistan.* Bloomfield, Conn.: Kumarian Press, 2000.

Messine, Anthony A., and Gallya Lahav, eds. *The Migration Reader: Exploring Politics and Policies.* Boulder, Colo.: Lynne Rienner, 2005.

Miller, Carol. *Lobbying the League: Women's International Organizations and the League of Nations.* Oxford: University of Oxford, 1992.

Moghalu, Kingsley. *Rwanda's Genocide: The Politics of Global Justice.* New York: Palgrave, 2005.

Monaghan, Karen, Max du Plessis, and Tajinder Malhi. *Race, Religion and Ethnicity Discrimination: Using International Human Rights Law.* London: Justice, 2003.

Morris, Virginia, and Michael P. Scharf. *An Insider's Guide to the International Criminal Tribunal for the Former Yugoslavia: Documentary History and Analysis*. Ardsley, N.Y.: Transnational Publishers, 1995.

———. *The International Criminal Tribunal for Rwanda*. 2 vols. Ardsley, N.Y.: Transnational Publishers, 1998.

Morsink, Johannes. *The Universal Declaration of Human Rights: Origins, Drafting, and Intent*. Philadelphia: University of Pennsylvania Press, 2000.

Mugwanya, George William. *Human Rights in Africa: Enhancing Human Rights Through the African Regional Human Rights System*. Ardsley, N.Y.: Transnational Publishers, 2003.

Neier, Aryeh. *War Crimes: Genocide, Terror and the Struggle for Justice*. New York: Times Books, 1998.

Newman, Edward, and Joanne Van Selm. *Refugees and Forced Displacement: International Security, Human Vulnerability, and the State*. Washington, D.C.: The Brookings Institution, 2003.

Nicholson, Frances, and Patrick Twomey, eds. *Refugee Rights and Realities*. Cambridge, Mass.: Cambridge University Press, 1999.

Norman, Richard. *Ethics, Killing and War*. New York: Cambridge University Press, 1995.

Nyamuya Maogoto, Jackson. *War Crimes and Realpolitik: International Justice from World War I to the 21st Century*. Boulder, Colo.: Lynne Rienner Publishers, 2004.

Owen, Nicholas, ed. *Human Rights, Human Wrongs: Oxford Amnesty Lectures 2001*. Oxford: Oxford University Press, 2003.

Pasqualucci, Jo M. *The Practice and Procedure of the Inter-American Court of Human Rights*. Cambridge: Cambridge University Press, 2003.

Peleet, Julie. *Landscape of Hope and Despair: Palestinian Refugee Camps*. Philadelphia: University of Pennsylvania Press, 2005.

Peterson, V. Spike, and Anne Sisson Runyan. *Global Gender Issues*. 2nd ed. Boulder, Colo.: Westview Press, 1999.

Pietila, Hilkka, and Jeanne Vickers. *Making Women Matter: the Role of the United Nations*. London: Zed Books, 1990.

Pollis, Adamantia, and Peter Schwab, eds. *Human Rights: New Perspectives, New Realities*. Boulder, Colo.: Lynne Rienner Publisher, 2000.

Poole, Hilary. *Human Rights: The Essential Reference*. Phoenix, Ariz.: Oryx Press, 1999.

Power, Samantha, and Graham Allison. *Realizing Human Rights, Moving from Inspiration to Impact*. New York: St. Martin's Press, 2000.

Price-Cohen, Cynthia., ed. *Human Rights of Indigenous Peoples*. Ardsley, N.Y.: Transnational, 1998.

Pritchard, Sarah, ed. *Indigenous Peoples, the United Nations and Human Rights*. London: Zed Books, 1998.

Quinn, Gerard, and Theresia Degener. *Human Rights and Disability: The Current Use and Future Potential of United Nations Human Rights Instruments in the Context of Disability*. New York: United Nations, 2002.

Raic, David. *Statehood and the Law of Self-Determination*. The Hague, The Netherlands: Kluwer Law International, 2003.

Ratner, Steven R., and Jason S. Abrams. *Accountability for Human Rights Atrocities in International Law: Beyond the Nuremberg Legacy*. 2nd ed. New York: Oxford University Press, 2001.

Rehn, Elisabeth, and Ellen Johnson Sirleaf. *Progress of the World's Women 2002*. Vol. 1, *Women, War, Peace: The Independent Assessment on the Impact of Armed Conflict on Women and Women's Role in Peace Building*. New York: UNIFEM, 2003.

Reydams, Luc. *Universal Jurisdicton: International and Municipal Legal Perspectives*. Oxford: Oxford University Press, 2003.

Rigby, Andrew. *Justice and Reconciliation: After the Violence*. Boulder, Colo.: Lynne Rienner Publishers, 2001.

Risse, Thomas, Stephen Ropp, and Kathryn Sikkink, eds. *The Power of Human Rights: International Norms and Domestic Change*. Cambridge, Mass.: Cambridge University Press, 1999.

Roach, Steven C. *The International Criminal Court, Ethics, and Global Justice*. Lanham, Md.: Rowman & Littlefield, 2006.

Robertson, Geoffrey. *Crimes Against Humanity: The Struggle for Global Justice*. New York: New Press, 2000.

Romano, Cesare P. R., Andre Nollkaemper, and Jann K. Kleffner, eds. *Internationalized Criminal Courts: Sierra Leone, East Timor, Kosovo, and Cambodia*. New York: Oxford University Press, 2004.

Sadat, Leila. *The International Criminal Court and the Transformation of International Law: Justice for the New Millennium*. Ardsley, N.Y.: Transnational Publishers, 2002.

Sands, Philippe, ed. *From Nuremberg to the Hague: The Future of International Criminal Justice*. Cambridge: Cambridge University Press, 2003.

Saulle, Maria Rita. *The Rights of the Child: International Instruments*. Ardsley, N.Y.: Transnational Publishers, 1995.

Schabas, William A. *An Introduction to the International Criminal Court*. Cambridge: Cambridge University Press, 2001.

——. *Genocide in International Law: The Crime of Crimes*. Cambridge: Cambridge University Press, 2000.

Scharf, Michael. *Balkan Justice: The Story Behind the First International War Crimes Trial Since Nuremberg*. Durham, N.C.: Carolina Academic Press, 1997.

Shelton, Dinah. *Remedies in International Human Rights Law*. New York: Oxford University Press, 2001.

Shelton, Dinah, ed. *International Crimes, Peace and Human Rights: The Role of the International Criminal Court*. Ardsley, N.Y.: Transnational Publishers, 2000.

Smith, Kate. *The End of Genocide*. Westport, Conn.: Praeger, 2005.

Smith, Rhona K. M. *Textbook in International Human Rights*. Oxford: Oxford University Press, 2003.

Smith, Rhona K. M., and Christien Van Den Anker. *The Essentials of Human Rights*. New York: Oxford University Press, 2005.

Sohn, Louis B. *Rights in Conflict: The United Nations and South Africa*. Ardsley, N.Y.: Transnational Publishers, 1994.

Sriram, Chandra Lekha. *Confronting Past Human Rights Violations: Justice vs. Peace in Times of Transition*. New York: Frank Cass, 2004.

Steady, Filomina Chioma, and Remie Toure, eds. *Women and the United Nations*. Rochester, Vt.: Schenkman Books, 1995.

Steiner, Henry J., and Philip Alston. *International Human Rights in Context, Law, Politics, Morals*. 2nd ed. New York: Oxford University Press, 2000.

Steiner, Niklaus, Gil Loescher, and Mark Gibney. *Problems of Protection: The UNHCR, Refugees and Human Rights in the 21st Century*. New York: Routledge, Inc, 2003.

Stover, Eric. *The Witnesses: War Crimes and the Promise of Justice in The Hague*. Philadelphia: University of Pennsylvania Press, 2005.

Symonides, Janusz, ed. *Human Rights: International Protection, Monitoring, Enforcement*. Aldershot, England: Ashgate Publishing, 2003.

Teeple, Gary. *The Riddle of Human Rights*. Amherst, N.Y.: Humanity Books, 2004.

Thakur, Ramesh, and Peter Malcontent, eds. *From Sovereign Impunity to International Accountability*. Tokyo: United Nations University Press, 2004.

Thomas, Daniel C. *The Helsinki Effect: International Norms, Human Rights, and the Demise of Communism*. Princeton, N.J.: Princeton University Press, 2001.

Tolley, Howard. *The U.N. Commission for Human Rights*. Boulder, Colo.: Westview Press, 1987.

Tomuschat, Christian. *Human Rights: Between Idealism and Realism*. Oxford: Oxford University Press, 2003.

Ulrich, George, and Krabbe Louise Boserup, eds. *Human Rights in Development: Reparations: Redressing Past Wrongs*. The Hague, The Netherlands: Kluwer Law International, 2003.

UNIFEM. *Not a Minute More: Ending Violence Against Women*. New York: UNIFEM, 2003.

United Nations. *The United Nations and Apartheid, 1948–1994*. New York: United Nations, 1995.

——. *The United Nations and Human Rights, 1945–1995*. New York: United Nations, 1995.

Uvin, Peter. *Human Rights and Development*. Bloomfield, Conn.: Kumarian Press, 2004.

Valentino, Benjamin A. *Final Solutions: Mass Killing and Genocide in the Twentieth Century*. Ithaca, N.Y.: Cornell University Press, 2004.

Vincent, John. *Human Rights and International Relations*. Cambridge: Cambridge University Press, 1986.

Wagner, Teresa, and Leslie Carbone, eds. *Fifty Years after the Declaration: the United Nations' Record on Human Rights*. Lanham, Md.: University Press of America / Washington, D.C.: Family Research Council, 2001.

Walden, Raphael, ed. *Racism and Human Rights*. Boston, Mass.: Martinus Nijhoff, 2004.

Waltzer, Michael. *Just and Unjust Wars: A Moral Argument with Historical Illustrations*. 3rd ed. New York: Basic Books, 2000.

Watson, J. Shand. *Theory and Reality in the International Protection of Human Rights*. Ardsley, N.Y.: Transnational Publishers, 1999.

Weston, Burns H., ed. *Child Labor and Human Rights: Making Children Matter*. Boulder, Colo.: Lynne Rienner, 2005.

Weston, Burns H., and Stephen P. Marks, eds. *The Future of International Human Rights*. Ardsley, N.Y.: Transnational Publishers, 1999.

Wheeler, Ron. "The United Nations Commission for Human Rights, 1982–1997: A Study of Targeted Resolutions." *Canadian Journal of Political Science* 99, no. 32 (1999): 75–102.

Williams, Lucy, Asbjorn Kjonstad, and Peter Robson, eds. *Law and Poverty: Poverty Reduction and the Role of the Legal System*. London: Zed Books, 2003.

Williams, Phil, and Dimitri Vlassis, eds. *Combating Transnational Crime*. Portland, Ore.: Frank Cass, 2001.

Williams, Phil, and Ernesto U. Savona, eds. *The United Nations and Transnational Organized Crime*. Portland, Ore.: Frank Cass, 1996.

Winslow, Anne, ed. *Women, Politics, and the United Nations*. Westport, Conn.: Greenwood Press, 1995.

Woods, Jeanne M., Hope Lewis, and Ibrahim Gassama, eds. *Economic, Social and Cultural Rights: International and Comparative Perspectives*. Ardsley, N.Y.: Transnational Publishers, 2004.

Young, Kirsten. *The Law and Process of the U.N. Human Rights Committee*. Ardsley, N.Y.: Transnational Publishers, 2002.

Zoelle, Diana Grace. *Globalizing Concern for Women's Human Rights*. New York: St. Martin's Press, 2000.

I. International Law

Akinsanya, Adeoye A. *The Law of the Sea: Unilateralism or Multilateralism?* Lagos: University of Lagos Press, 1980.

Alvarez, Jose E. *International Organizations as Law-Makers*. New York: Oxford University Press, 2005.

Amr, Mohamed Sameh M. *The Role of the International Court of Justice As the Principal Judicial Organ of the United Nations*. The Hague, The Netherlands: Kluwer Law International, 2003.

Anaya, A. *Indigenous People in International Law*. Oxford: Oxford University Press, 1996.

Baslar, Kemal. *The Concept of the Common Heritage of Mankind in International Law*. The Hague, The Netherlands. Martinus Nijhoff Publishers, 1998.

Bekker, Pieter H. F. *World Court Decisions at the Turn of the Millennium, 1997–2001*. The Hague, The Netherlands: Martinus Nijhoff, 2002.

Boczek, Boleslaw A. *International Law: A Dictionary*. Lanham, Md.: Scarecrow, 2004.

Boyle, Alan, and David Freestone. *International Law and Sustainable Development: Past Achievements and Future Challenges*. New York: Oxford University Press, 1999.

Crawford, James. *The International Law Commission's Articles on State Responsibility: Introduction Text and Commentaries*. Cambridge: Cambridge University Press, 2002.

Damrosch, Lori Fisler, ed. *The International Court of Justice at a Crossroads*. Ardsley, N.Y.: Transnational Publishers, 1987.

El Baradei, Mohamed. *Crowded Agendas, Crowded Rooms: Institutional Arrangements at UNCLOS III: Some Lessons in Global Negotiations*. New York: UNITAR, 1981.

Elias, Taslim Olawale. *The International Court of Justice and Some Contemporary Problems: Essays on International Law*. The Hague, The Netherlands: Martinus Nijhoff, 1983.

Fromuth, Peter J., ed. *A Successor Vision: The United Nations of Tomorrow*. Lanham, MD.: University Press of America, 1988.

Goswami, Subir. *Politics in Law Making: A Study of the International Law Commission of the UN*. New Delhi, India: Ashish, 1986.

Jones, Dorothy V. *Toward a Just World Order: The Critical Years in the Search for International Justice*. Chicago: University of Chicago Press, 2002.

Joyner, Christopher, ed. *The United Nations and International Law*. Cambridge: Cambridge University Press, 1997.

Lauterpacht, Sir Hersch. *The Development of International Law by the International Court*. Cambridge: Grotius, 1938.

Luck, Edward C., and Michael W. Doyle, eds. *International Law and Organization: Closing the Compliance Gap*. Lanham, Md. : Rowman & Littlefield, 2004.

McWhinney, Edward. *Judicial Settlement of International Disputes: Jurisdiction, Justiciability, and Judicial Law-Making on the Contemporary Interna-*

tional Court. Dordrecht, The Netherlands: Martinus Nijhoff Publishers, 1991.

Maugham, F. H. *UNO and War Crimes.* London: J. Murray, 1951.

Morell, James B. *The Law of the Sea: A Historical Analysis of the 1982 Treaty and Its Rejection by the United States.* Jefferson, N.C.: McFraland, 1992.

Morris, Viriginia, and Michael P. Scharf. *An Insider's Guide to the International Criminal Tribunal for the Former Yugoslavia: A Documentary History and Analysis.* Irvington-on-Hudson, N.Y.: Transnational Publishers, 1995.

Morton, Jeffrey S. *The International Law Commission of the United Nations.* Columbia: University of South Carolina Press, 2000.

Muller, A. S., J. M. Thuranzsky, and D. Raic. *The International Court of Justice: Its Future Role After Fifty Years.* The Hague, The Netherlands: Kluwer, 1996.

Nordquist, Myron H., Satya N. Nandan, Shabtai Rosenne, and Michael W. Lodge, eds. *United Nations Convention on the Law of the Sea 1982: A Commentary, Articles 133 to 199.* The Hague, The Netherlands: Kluwer Law International, 2003.

Oda, Shigeru. *Fifty Years of the Law of the Sea: With a Special Section on the International Courts of Justice.* The Hague, The Netherlands: Kluwer Law International, 2003.

Patel, Bimal N., ed. *The World Court Reference Guide: Judgments, Advisory Opinions and Orders of the Permanent Court of International Justice and the International Court of Justice, 1922–2000.* New York: Kluwer Law International, 2002.

Raa, P. and R. Khan, eds. *The International Tribunal for the Law of the Sea: Law and Practice.* The Hague, The Netherlands: Kluwer Law International, 2001.

Ragazzi, Maurizio, ed. *International Responsibility Today: Essays in Memory of Oscar Schachter.* Boston, Mass.: Martinus Nijhoff, 2005.

Robb, Cairo. *International Environmental Law Reports.* Vol. 5, *Decisions of the International Court of Justice.* Cambridge: Cambridge University Press, 2003.

Rosenne, Shabtai. *The World Court: What It Is and How It Works.* The Hague, The Netherlands: Martinus Nijhoff, 1995.

Sander, Clyde. *Ordering the Oceans: The Making of the Law of the Sea.* Toronto: University of Toronto Press, 1987.

Schachter, Oscar, and Christopher Joyner. *United Nations Legal Order.* Cambridge: Grotius, 1993.

Sebenius, James K. *Negotiating the Law of the Sea.* Cambridge, Mass.: Harvard University Press, 1984.

Sewall, Sarah B., and Carl Kaysen, eds. *The United States and the International Criminal Court.* Lanham, Md.: Rowman & Littlefield, 2000.

Singh, Nagendra. *The Role and Record of the International Court of Justice.* Dordrecht, The Netherlands: Martinus Nijhoff, 1989.

Taylor, Prue. *An Ecological Approach to International Law: Responding to Challenges of Climate Change.* New York: Routledge, 1998.

United Nations. *The International Law Commission Fifty Years After.* New York: United Nations, 2000.

United Nations Office of Legal Affairs. *Work of the International Law Commission,* Vols. 1 and 2. New York: United Nations, 2004.

Wang, James C. F. *Handbook on Ocean Politics and Law.* Westport, Conn.: Greenwood Press, 1992.

Watts, Arthur. *The International Law Commission.* New York: Oxford University Press, 1999.

Wouters, Patricia. *Codification and Progressive Development of International Water Law: The Work of the International Law Commission of the United Nations.* The Hague, The Netherlands: Kluwer Law International, 2003.

J. Reforming the UN

Annan, Kofi. *In Larger Freedom: Toward Development, Security and Human Rights for All.* Report of the Secretary-General. UN document A/59/2005 of 21 March, 2005.

——. *Renewing the United Nations: A Programme for Reform.* Report of the Secretary-General. UN document A/51/590, 14 July 1997.

——. *Strengthening of the United Nations: An Agenda for Further Change.* Report of the Secretary-General. UN document A/57/387, 9 September 2002.

Arnold, Tim. *Reforming the UN: Its Economic Role.* London: Royal Institute of International Affairs, 1995.

Bardonnet, Daniel, ed. *The Adaptation of Structures and Methods at the United Nations: Workshop, The Hague, 4–6 November 1985.* Boston: Martinus Nijhoff, 1986.

Beigbdeber, Yves. *Internal Management of United Nations Organizations: The Long Quest for Reform.* Basingstoke, England: Macmillan, 1997.

Bertrand, Maurice. *The Third Generation World Organization.* Dordrecht, The Netherlands: Martinus Nijhoff Publishers, 1989.

Bertrand, Maurice, and Daniel Warner, eds. *A New Charter for a Worldwide Organisation?* Dordrecht, The Netherlands: Martinus Nijhoff, 1996.

Browne, Marjorie Ann. *United Nations Reform: Issues for Congress.* Washington, D.C.: Library of Congress, Congressional Research Service, 1988.

Childers, Erskine. *Renewing the United Nations System.* Uppsala, Sweden: Dag Hammarskjöld Foundation, 1994.

Childers, Erskine, and Brian Urquhart. *Towards a More Effective United Nations*. Uppsala, Sweden: Dag Hammarskjöld Foundation, 1990.

Commission on Global Governance. *Our Global Neighborhood*. Oxford: Oxford University Press, 1995.

———. *Issues in Global Governance: Papers Written for the Commission on Global Governance*. London: Kluwer Law International, 1995.

Commission on International Development. *Partners in Development: Report*. New York: Praeger, 1969.

Evans, Gareth. *Cooperating for Peace: The Global Agenda for the 1990s and Beyond*. St. Leonard, Australia.: Allen and Unwin, 1993.

Fassbender, Bardo. *UN Council Reform and the Right of Veto: A Constitutional Perspective*. The Hague, The Netherlands: Kluwer Law International, 1998.

Fomerand, Jacques. *Strengthening the United Nations Economic and Social Programs: A Documentary Essay*. Reports and papers, 1990–1992. Hanover, N.H.: Academic Council on the United Nations System, 1990.

Franda, Marcus. *The United Nations in the Twenty-First Century: Management and Reform Processes in a Troubled Organization*. Lanham, M.D.: Rowman & Littlefield, 2005.

Fromuth, Peter J., ed. *A Successor Vision: The United Nations of Tomorrow*. New York: United Nations Association, 1988.

Group of Experts on the Structure of the United Nations System. *A New United Nations Structure for Global Economic Cooperation*. E/AC.62.9. New York: United Nations, 1975.

Heinbecker, Paul, and Patricia Goff, eds. *Irrelevant or Indispensable? The United Nations in the 21st Century*. Waterloo, Ontario: Wilfrid Laurier University Press, 2005.

Hoffmann, Walter. *United Nations Security Council Reform and Restructuring*. Livingston, N.J.: Center for UN Reform Education, 1994.

Imber, Mark. *Environment, Security and UN Reform*. New York: St. Martin's Press, 1994.

Independent Advisory Group on UN. *Financing an Effective United Nations*. New York: Ford Foundation, 1993.

Independent Commission on Disarmament and Security Issues. *Common Security: A Blueprint for Survival*. New York: Simon & Schuster, 1982.

Independent Commission on International Development Issues. *North-South: A Programme for Survival*. Cambridge, Mass.: MIT Press, 1980.

———. *Common Crisis: North-South Cooperation for World Recovery*. Cambridge, Mass.: MIT Press, 1983.

Independent International Commission on Kosovo. *Kosovo Report: Conflict, International Response, Lessons Learned*. New York: Oxford University Press, 2001.

Independent Working Group on the Future of the United Nations. *The United Nations in Its Second Half-Century.* New York: UN Studies at Yale and the Ford Foundation, 1995.

Jackson, Robert G. A. *A Study of the Capacity of the United Nations Development System.* 2 vols. Geneva: United Nations, 1969.

Joint Inspection Unit. *Concluding Report on the Implementation of General Assembly Resolution 32/197 Concerning the Restructuring of the Economic and Social Sectors of the United Nations System.* Geneva: JIU, 1989. JIU/REP/89/7.

Kanninen, Tapio. *Leadership and Reform: The Secretary-General and the UN Financial Crisis of the Late 1980s.* The Hague, The Netherlands: Kluwer Law International, 1995.

Kennedy, Paul, and Bruce Russett, "Reforming the United Nations." *Foreign Affairs* 74, no. 5 (1995): 56–71.

Luck, Edward C. *Reforming the United Nations: Lessons from a History in Progress.* New Haven, Conn.: Academic Council on the United Nations System, 2003.

Martin, Andrew, and John B. S. Edwards. *The Changing Charter: A Study in the Reform of the United Nations.* London: Syvan Press, 1955.

Muller, Joachim. *Reforming the United Nations: The Quiet Revolution.* The Hague, The Netherlands: Kluwer Law International, 2001.

Nordic Council. *The Nordic Countries and the Future of the United Nations.* Final Report from the Conference of the Nordic Council Held in Helsinki from 10–12 January 1995. Stockholm, Sweden: Nordic Council, 1995.

——— . *The United Nations: Issues and Options: Five Studies on the Role of the UN in the Economic and Social Fields.* Commissioned by the Nordic UN Project. Stockholm, Sweden: Nordic UN Project, 1991.

Nordic Project. *The United Nations in Development: Reform Issues in the Economic and Social Fields.* Stockholm, Sweden: The Nordic Project, 1991.

Ogata, Shirujo, and Paul Volcker. *Financing an Effective United Nations: A Report of the Independent Advisory Group on UN Financing.* New York: Ford Foundation, 1993.

Renninger, John. *Survey and Analysis of Evaluations of the United Nations Intergovernmental Structure and Functions in the Economic and Social Fields.* Special Commission on the In-Depth Study of the United Nations Intergovernmental Structure and Functions in the Economic and Social Fields. Informal Paper, No. 15. New York: United Nations Institute for Training and Research, 1987.

——— . *ECOSOC: Options for Reform.* Policy and Efficacy Studies, No.4. New York: United Nations Institute for Training and Research, 1981.

Report of the Open-Ended High-Level Working Group on the Strengthening of the United Nations System. UN document A/51/24, 18 July, 1997.

Saksena, K. P. *Reforming the United Nations: The Challenge of Relevance.* Newbury Park, Calif.: Sage Publications, 1993.

Schwartzberg, Joseph E. *Revitalizing the United Nations: Reform Through Weighted Voting.* New York: Institute for Global Policy, 2004.

South Centre. *For a Strong and Democratic United Nations: A South Perspective on UN Reform.* Geneva: South Centre, 1996.

———. *Reforming the United Nations: A View from the South.* Geneva: South Centre, 1995.

Taylor, Paul, Sam Daws, and Ute Adameczick. *Documents on Reform of the United Nations.* Brookfield, Vt.: Dartmouth, 1996.

Thakur, Ramesh, Andrew Cooper, and John English, eds. *International Commissions and the Power of Ideas.* Tokyo: United Nations University Press, 2004.

Toward Common Goals: Independent Commission on the Future of the United Nations Conference Report. Ottawa: Centre for Research on International Organizations at the University of Ottawa, Group of 78, United Nations Association in Canada and the World Federalists of Canada, 1993.

United Nations. *Report of the Group of High-Level Intergovernmental Experts to Review the Efficiency of the Administrative and Financial Functioning of the United Nations.* Official Records. 41st Session, Supplement No. 49. New York: United Nations, 1986.

———. *Report of the Open-Ended High-Level Working Group on the Strengthening of the United Nations System.* Official Records 50th Session, Supplement No. 24; A/50/24. New York: UN, 1996.

United Nations Group of Experts on the Structure of the United Nations System. *A New United Nations Structure for Global Economic Co-operation.* New York: United Nations, 1975.

United States Commission on Improving the Effectiveness of the United Nations. *Defining Purpose: The U.N. and the Health of Nations..* Washington, D.C.: U.S. Government Printing Office, 1993.

Wilcox, Francis, and Carl M. Marcy. *Proposals for Changes in the United Nations.* Washington DC.: Brookings Institution, 1995.

K. Prospects for the Future: The UN and Global Governance

Alger, Chadwick F., ed. *The Future of the United Nations System: Potential for the Twenty-First Century.* Tokyo: United Nations University, 1998.

Annan, Kofi. *"We the Peoples": The Role of the United Nations in the 21st Century.* New York: United Nations, 2000.

———. "The Quiet Revolution." *Global Governance* 4, no. 2 (1998): 123–38.

――― . *Renewing the United Nations: A Programme for Reform*. New York: UN DPI SG/SM/6284 or GA/9282, 16 July 1997 and attachments.

Augelli, Enrico, and Craig Murphy. *America's Quest for Supremacy and the Third World*. London: Pinter, 1988.

Baudot, Jacques, ed. *Building a World Community: Globalization and the Common Good*. Copenhagen: Royal Danish Ministry of Foreign Affairs, 2000.

Biermann, Frank, and Steffen Bauer, eds. *A World Environment Organization: Solution or Threat for Effective International Environmental Governance*. Williston, Vt.: Ashgate Publishing Company, 2005.

Cavanagh, John, and Jerry Mander, eds. *Alternatives to Economic Globalization: A Better World Is Possible*. 2nd ed.. San Francisco, Calif.: Berrett-Koehler Publishers, 2004.

Childers, Erskine, ed. *Challenges to the United Nations: Building a Safer World*. New York: St. Martin's Press, 1995.

Cox, Robert W., with Timothy Sinclair. *Approaches to World Order*. Cambridge: Cambridge University Press, 1996.

Cusimano, Maryann K., ed. *Beyond Sovereignty: Issues for a Global Agenda*. Belmont, Calif.: Wadsworth/Thompson Learning, 2000.

Deng, Francis, et al. *Sovereignty as Responsibility*. Washington, D.C.: Brookings, 1995.

Desai, Meghnad, and Paul Redfern, eds. *Global Governance, Ethics and Economics of the World Order*. London: Pinter, 1995.

English, John, Ramesh Thakur, and Andrew F. Cooper, eds. *Reforming from the Top. A Leaders' 20 Summit*. Tokyo: United Nations University Press, 2005.

Falk, Richard. *Law in an Emerging Global Village: A Post-Westphalian Perspective*. Ardsley, N.Y.: Transnational Publishers, 1998.

――― . *On Humane Governance*. University Park: Pennsylvania State University Press, 1995.

Finkelstein, Lawrence S. "What Is Global Governance?" *Global Governance* 1, no. 3 (1995): 367–72.

Fukuyama, Francis. *The End of History and the Last Man*. New York: Avon, 1993.

Greider, William. *One World, Ready or Not: The Manic Logic of Global Capitalism*. New York: Simon & Schuster, 1997.

Harriss, Errol E., and James A. Yunker, eds. *Toward Genuine Global Governance: Critical Reflection to our Global Neighbourhood*. Westport, Conn.: Praeger, 1999.

Herod, Andrew, Gearoid O. Tuathail, and Susan M. Roberts: *An Unruly World? Globalization, Governance, and Geography*. New York, Routledge, 1998.

Hewson, Martin, and Timothy J. Sinclair, eds. *Approaches to Global Governance Theory*. Albany, N.Y.: State University of New York Press, 1999.

High-Level Panel on Threats, Challenges and Change. *A More Secure World: Our Shared Responsibility.* United Nations Document A/59/565 of 2 December 2004.

Holton, R. J. *Globalization and the Nation-State.* New York, Macmillan Press, 1998.

Hyden, Goran, Dele Oluwu, and Hastings Oketh Ogendo. *African Perspectives on Governance.* Trenton, N.J.: Africa World Press, 2000.

Idris, Kamil, and Michael Bartolo. *The Better United Nations for a New Millennium.* New York: Columbia University Press, 1999.

International Commission on Intervention and State Sovereignty. *The Responsibility to Protect.* Ottawa: International Development Research Centre, 2001.

Keohane, Robert O. *Power and Governance in a Partially Globalized World.* New York: Routledge, 2002.

Knight, Andy W. *A Changing United Nations: Multilateral Evolution and the Quest for Global Governance.* London: Macmillan, 2000.

Knight, Andy W. ed. *Adapting the United Nations to a Post Modern Era: Lessons Learned.* New York: St. Martins Press, 2001.

Kooiman, Jan, ed. *Modern Governance: New Government-Society Interactions.* London: Sage, 1993.

Korten, David. *Getting to the Twenty-first Century: Voluntary Action and the Global Agenda.* West Hartford, Conn.: Kumarian, 1990.

Krasner, Steven, D. *Sovereignty, Organized Hypocrisy.* Princeton, N.J.: Princeton University Press, 1999.

Krasno, Jean, ed. *The United Nations. Confronting the Challenges of a Global Society.* Boulder, Colo.: Lynne Rienner, 2004.

Lorenz, Joseph P. *Peace, Power and the United Nations: A Security System for the Twenty-First Century.* Boulder, Colo.: Westview Press, 1999.

Mendlovitz, Saul H., and Burns H. Weston, eds. *Preferred Futures for the United Nations.* Ardsley, N.Y.: Transnational Publishers, 1995.

Mittelman, James H. *Globalization: Critical Reflections.* Boulder, Colo.: Lynne Rienner, 1996.

Muldoon, James P. *The Architecture of Global Governance: An Introduction to the Study of International Organization.* Boulder, Colo.: Westview Press, 2004.

Nye, Joseph, and John Donahue, eds. *Governance in a Globalizing World.* Washington, D.C.: The Brookings Institution, 2000.

Paolini, Albert J., Anthony P. Jarvis, and Christian Reus-Smit, eds. *Between Sovereignty and Global Governance: The United Nations, the State, and Civil Society.* New York: St. Martin's Press, 1988.

Rittberger, Volker. *Global Governance and the United Nations System.* Tokyo: United Nations University Press, 2001.

Rosenau, James N., and Ernst-Otto Czempiel, eds. *Governance Without Government: Order and Change in World Politics*. Cambridge: Cambridge University Press, 1992.

Segesvary, Victor. *From Illusion to Delusion: Globalization and the Contradictions of Late Modernity*. San Francisco, Calif.: International Scholars Publications, 1999.

Simai, Mihali. *The Age of Global Transformations: The Human Dimension*. Budapest, Hungary: Akademiai Kioda, 2001.

——. *The Future of Global Governance: Managing Risk and Change in the Interntional System*. Washington, D.C.: U.S. Institute of Peace Press, 1994.

United Nations Non-Governmental Liaison Service. *The United Nations, NGOs, and Global Governance: Challenges for the Twenty-First Century*. Geneva: NGLS, 1996.

United Nations Research Institute for Social Development (UNRISD). *States in Disarray*. Geneva: United Nations, 1995.

Urquhart, Brian, and Erskine Childers. *A World in Need of Leadership: Tomorrow's United Nations*. Uppsala, Sweden: Dag Hammarskjöld Foundation, 1990.

Vayrynen, Raimo V., ed. *Globalization and Global Governance*. Lanham, Md.: Rowman & Littlefield, 1999.

Wapner, Paul. *Environmental Activism and World Civic Politics*. Albany, N.Y.: State University of New York Press, 1996.

Young, Oran R. *Global Governance: Drawing Insights from the Environmental Experience*. Cambridge, Mass.: MIT Press, 1998.

Young, Oran R. *International Governance: Protecting the Environment in a Stateless Society*. Ithaca, N.Y.: Cornell University Press, 1994.

Yunker, James A. *Rethinking World Government*. Lanham, Md.: University Press of America, 2005.

Zolo, Danilo. *Cosmopolis: Prospects for World Government*. Cambridge: Polity Press, 1997.

About the Author

Jacques Fomerand studied law and graduated in political science at the University of Aix-en-Provence, France, and earned a PhD in political science at the City University of New York. He joined the United Nations Secretariat in 1977, where he followed economic, social, and coordination questions in the Office of the Undersecretary-General of the Department of Economic and Social Affairs. From 1992 to June 2003, when he retired from United Nations service, he was director of the United Nations University Office in North America. Jacques Fomerand is now associate professor in the Department of Government at John Jay College of the City University of New York. He also has held teaching appointments at the Institut d'Etudes Politiques of Aix-en Provence, France, Columbia University, Occidental College, Seton Hall University, and Long Island University. He has widely published on matters related to the functioning of the United Nations and North-South relations.